Handbook of the Syllable

Brill's Handbooks
in Linguistics

Series Editors

Brian D. Joseph

The Ohio State University, Columbus, USA (*Managing Editor*)

Artemis Alexiadou, University of Stuttgart, Stuttgart, Germany
Harald Baayen, University of Alberta, Edmonton, Canada
Pier Marco Bertinetto, Scuola Normale Superiore, Pisa, Italy
Kirk Hazen, West Virginia University, Morgantown, USA
Maria Polinsky, Harvard University, Cambridge, USA

VOLUME 1

CONTENTS

THE SYLLABLE IN PERFORMANCE:
SPEECH PRODUCTION AND ARTICULATION

THE SYLLABLE IN PERFORMANCE: SPEECH PERCEPTION
AND EXPERIMENTAL MANIPULATION

This book is printed on acid-free paper.

Library of Congress Cataloging-in-Publication Data

Handbook of the syllable / edited by Charles E. Cairns and Eric Raimy.
    p. cm. — (Brill's handbooks in linguistics ; v. 1)
Includes index.
ISBN 978-90-04-18740-5 (alk. paper)
1. Grammar, Comparative and general—Syllable. 2. Syllabication. 3. Phonetics.
I. Cairns, Charles E. II. Raimy, Eric. III. Title. IV. Series.

P236.H36 2011
414'.8—dc22

                                                                    2010040412

ISSN 1879-629X
ISBN 978 90 04 18740 5

PRINTED BY DRUKKERIJ WILCO B.V. - AMERSFOORT, THE NETHERLANDS

Handbook of the Syllable

Edited by

Charles E. Cairns and Eric Raimy

BRILL

LEIDEN • BOSTON

2011

THE SYLLABLE IN PERFORMANCE:
ORTHOGRAPHY

THE SYLLABLE IN PERFORMANCE:
DIACHRONY

ACKNOWLEDGEMENTS

The contributors have made this volume possible, and the editors hereby express sincere gratitude for their efforts. The editors also wish to thank the authors of the individual chapters for their help with Chapter 1, Introduction; in particular, Paul Kiparsky has kindly offered extensive comments which have greatly improved this chapter. The usual disclaimers apply.

Stuart Davis and Karen Baertsch, the authors of Chapter 3, wish to acknowledge Chiara Frigeni for discussion on the Sardinian data, Christopher Green and Boubacar Diakite for discussion on the Bamana data and Bill Anderson for discussion on the Winnebago (Hocank) data. They thank the editors of the volume and an anonymous reviewer for helpful comments on an earlier draft of this paper. They also acknowledge the valuable comments they received on the oral version of this paper presented at the CUNY Conference on the Syllable in January 2008. They also affirm that all errors in this chapter are their own responsibility.

The author of Chapter 4, San Duanmu, thanks the audience at the CUNY Syllable Conference for their comments on his talk and Chuck Cairns, François Dell and some anonymous reviewers for their comments on earlier drafts.

Chapter 5 has benefited from useful input from many quarters. Its author, Jason Haugen, would especially like to thank Diana Archangeli, Gabriela Caballero, Larry Hagberg, Mike Hammond, Heidi Harley, Cathy Hicks Kennard, Bob Kennedy, Terry Langendoen, Nathan Sanders and Pat Shaw for valuable conversations over aspects of this work. He also thanks Chuck Cairns, Stuart Davis and Robert Vago for providing very helpful feedback on earlier drafts. Portions of this work were supported by NSF grant #BCS-0446333. Many thanks to Maria Florcz Lcyva and Santos Leyva for sharing their knowledge of the Hiaki language with Haugen's research team—Heidi Harley, Mercedes Tubino Blanco and Haugen. All Hiaki data not otherwise attributed come from their field notes. As ever, any remaining errors of fact or interpretation rest on the shoulders of the author alone.

The names of the authors of Chapter 6 are listed alphabetically. Catherine Ringen's research was supported in part by an Arts and

Humanities Grant from the University of Iowa. Robert Vago's research was supported in part by a PSC-CUNY Research Award. Parts of this work were presented at the annual meeting of the Linguistic Society of America, San Francisco, CA (2002), Ninth International Phonology Meeting: Structure and Melody, Vienna, Austria (2002), 11th Manchester Phonology Meeting, Manchester, England (2003), CUNY/NYU/SUNY Linguistics Mini-Conference, New York (2003), Research Institute for Linguistics of the Hungarian Academy of Sciences, Budapest, Hungary (2004), Tel-Aviv University (2006) and CUNY Conference on the Syllable, CUNY Graduate Center, New York (2008). The authors have benefited from comments and discussion of issues addressed in this paper with Jill Beckman, Juliette Blevins, Charles Cairns, Abigail Cohn, Megan Cowhurst, Emily Curtis, Stuart Davis, Wolfgang Dressler, Bruce Hayes, Eugene Helimski, Elizabeth Hume, Larry Hyman, Sharon Inkelas, Junko Itô, Ellen Kaisse, Paul Kiparsky, Astrid Kraehenmann, Rina Kreitman, Marc van Oostendorp, Douglas Pulleyblank, Jerzy Rubach, Péter Siptár and Donca Steriade, none of whom may necessarily agree with their analyses and conclusions.

François Dell, the author of Chapter 7, wishes to thank Dianne Bradley for calling his attention to the article by Sundberg and Bauer-Huppmann (2007), Takeki Kamiyama for helping him with the Japanese example in section 5, and Shigeko Shinohara for lending him Anonymous (1977) and a CD with recordings of some of the songs gathered there. He also thanks John Frampton, John Goldsmith and John Halle for their comments. The shortcomings in this article are his sole responsibility.

The work described in Chapter 8 has been supported by NIH grant DCO2125 and NSF grant BCS-0643054 to the author, by NIH grants DC00075 to Dr. Kenneth Stevens and DC02978 to Dr. Stevens and the author, Stefanie Shattuck-Hufnagel, and by MIT's Undergraduate Research Opportunity Program, which funded Alicia Patterson to categorize the 10,000+ errors in the MITSEC. It has benefited greatly from ongoing discussion with the author's mentors, Merrill Garrett, Dennis Klatt and Ken Stevens, with her collaborators Pat Keating, Alice Turk, Nanette Veilleux and with Victoria Fromkin, who rediscovered the speech error studies carried out by Merringer and Freud in the early 1900s, and showed us how to apply them to modern linguistic and psycholinguistic questions.

The work reported in Chapter 9 was supported by a TALENT stipend (S 29-1) from the Netherlands Organization for Scientific Research (NWO) and by MTKD-CT-2005-029639 from the European Commission. Joana Cholin is grateful to Ansgar Hantsch, Alissa Melinger and Margaret Guillon-Dowens, for helpful comments on earlier versions of this manuscript. The experiments and theoretical advances reported in this chapter have been previously reported (Cholin, Levelt and Schiller 2006, Cholin, Dell and Levelt in press).

The authors of Chapter 10 appreciate the intellectual contributions, keen insight, technical assistance, and valuable advice provided by students and colleagues from both the Neurolinguistics Lab and the Developmental Neurolinguistics Lab at the Graduate Center, CUNY.

Marie-Hélène Côté and Viktor Kharlamov, the authors of Chapter 11 would like to thank Tatyana Kharlamova for her assistance with data collection and Laura Sabourin and Joe Roy for their help with the statistical analyses. This research has been supported by a standard research grant to the first author from the Social Sciences and Humanities Research Council of Canada (#410-2006-1778).

Andries Coetzee, the author of Chapter 12, wants to express his appreciation to Susan Lin, Kevin McGowan and Ania Musial for their help in the design and execution of the experiments that went into this chapter. This chapter also befitted greatly from discussions with several people, and their input is acknowledged: Pam Beddor, Iris Berent, Lisa Davidson, Susie Levi, Kevin McGowan, Susan Lin, Ania Musial, San Duanmu and Sam Epstein, amongst others. Thank you also to the members of Phondi (Phonetics/Phonology Discussion group at the University of Michigan) and the audience at the CUNY Syllable Conference for feedback on the work. This research was made possible by a grant from the Rackham Graduate School at the University of Michigan.

The authors of Chapter 13 would like to thank Dr Ali Idrissi for the design of Arabic stimuli, Ashraf Hassan-Haj for designing an instruction sheet in Arabic and running the experiment with native Arabic participants.

Preparation of Chapter 14 was supported by the Award R01 DC007665 as administered by the National Institute of Deafness and Communication Disorders. Grantees undertaking such projects are encouraged to express freely their professional judgment. Therefore, these chapters do not necessarily reflect the position or policies of the

National Institutes of Health and no official endorsement should be inferred.

The research discussed in Chapter 15 was supported by NIDCD Award R01 DC003277. Iris Berent, Tracy Lennert and Paul Smolensky, its authors, would like to thank Alan Prince, Matt Goldrick and Colin Wilson for their useful discussion.

Ranjan Sen, the author of Chapter 17, should like to thank John Coleman, John Penney and Aditi Lahiri for their assistance with this chapter, as well as Donca Steriade and Stefanie Shattuck-Hufnagel for helpful discussion at the CUNY Conference on the Syllable, January 17–19, 2008, and an anonymous reviewer for useful comments. This work was supported by the Arts and Humanities Research Council.

CHAPTER ONE

INTRODUCTION

Charles Cairns and Eric Raimy

1 *Scope and Background*

This handbook approaches the study of the syllable with theoretical, empirical and methodological heterogeneity as its guiding principle. A perusal of the history of the syllable in phonetics and phonology suggests that this attitude is particularly appropriate for our chosen field of discourse. As Haugen remarked more than fifty years ago (1956, 231), the syllable has always been "something of a stepchild in linguistic description." When Haugen wrote, scholars in many branches and phases of phonetic and phonological sciences had, for almost a century, found it convenient to refer to the syllable, while nobody had done much about defining it; matters are hardly better now than they were then. Definitions abound, to be sure, but the most rigorous are not applicable to all the areas where the syllable is frequently invoked.

Since it was introduced into scientific discourse in the second half of the nineteenth century, there have always been those who deny the existence of the syllable as a directly measurable entity, usually because of the difficulty in identifying boundaries; Hefner (1950, 73), referring to Jespersen (1933), said that such reasoning is like denying the existence of adjacent hills because we cannot determine for sure how much of the valley between them belongs to one and how much to the other. The identification of peaks can also be problematic; the English words *very* and *brother* arguably have one 'chest pulse' (as described below) but by most accounts two syllables, Russian *rta* has two sonority peaks but one syllable, etc.

The syllable had been under scientific scrutiny for more than a century when Kenstowicz (1994, 250) wrote that one reason the syllable continued to be such an elusive entity is that "it lacks any uniform or direct phonetic correlates: it is not a sound, but an abstract unit of prosodic organization through which a language expresses much of its phonology." Of course, this is true of segments as well as of prosodic entities, but the point is well taken.

The first problem in defining the syllable is to agree on the level(s) at which it resides. Some early scholars championed the syllable as a physiological unit (e.g. Stetson's "chest pulse" theory), and others have defined the syllable in acoustic/auditory terms (e.g. Whitney 1865 and Sievers 1881, who characterized the syllable as a domain for organizing sonority). Our historical excursus below, as well as the chapters later in this handbook, show that there is and always has been an overabundance of definitions and models of the syllable in the various branches of phonetics and psycholinguistics. In addition, Saussure's now century-old introduction of the *langue/parole* distinction to the phonetic sciences heralded theoretical phonology, spawning a bewildering array of formal idealizations of the syllable; the next five chapters present a contemporary sample.

There are a number of reasons why it has been difficult to pin down the syllable with either precision or unanimity. One is that it is, by general agreement, a basic unit of linguistic rhythm, an area that has been notoriously resistant to scientific investigation. Humans, like all animals, organize our activities around a variety of tempos with different and sometimes competing beats and rhythmic units. This is evident especially in the language sciences. Lack of agreement on which of the cadences at play in speech and language should serve as the basis for defining the syllable may be one reason for the diversity of views over its nature.

A more general reason for its elusiveness is that the syllable, however conceptualized, has always had different significance to different people, depending in part on which area of language science is under investigation; this is abundantly clear from chapters seven through seventeen of this handbook. The problem is that there exists no single definition of the syllable that is suitable to all these areas. It should now be clear why the eclecticism of this handbook is apposite.

The eclectic approach followed here is antithetical to any suggestion that phonetics, phonology and experimental psycholinguistics are distinct fields with nothing of particular importance to say to one another. In fact, the study of the syllable appears to be a fruitful area for showing that boundaries that appear to separate these three areas of scholarship are counterproductive and should not be maintained.[1]

The chapters that follow are focused more on the phenomena that phoneticians and phonologists had thought would be explained by reference to the syllable than on the theories that have been offered as the explanations; the authors' primary interest is in evaluating and developing theories of the syllable empirically (by confronting them with both new data and new kinds of data) rather than conceptually. Because a study of phenomena is of no interest unless conducted to illuminate or challenge some theoretical perspective, each chapter in this handbook takes theoretical questions seriously. But the organizing theme of the volume as a whole is the range of phenomena to be accounted for by some notion of the syllable, not of the theories that have been put forth to explain those phenomena. An inevitable and, we believe, salutary result of this strategy is a theoretically and methodologically diverse handbook.

The preceding paragraph should raise a caveat in the mind of the critical reader: delineating the fields of *explananda* at the expense of focusing on any of the proposed *explanans* (Hempel and Oppenheim 1948) may be an inherently conservatizing endeavor. Facts do not come to us pre-labeled for what theory is best for accounting for them. There is no more guarantee that the generalizations described in this volume all should be accounted for by a common theory now than there ever has been in the history of the study of the syllable; in fact, it would be astonishing if such were the case. Bearing this in mind, this handbook is meant to provoke thought and discussion about the syllable. There are no claims herein that any particular perspective on the syllable is the most appropriate for all the phenomena widely believed to be within its penumbra.

Our preference for what-questions over why-questions is partly determined by the historical juncture that phonology finds itself in now. The variety of approaches to the syllable illustrated in the following chapters and witnessed in the last century and a half shows that

---

[1] Of course, the fact that the boundaries are obscure does not imply that these are not different fields of study; Jespersen's remark alluded to above applies here *mutatis mutandis.*

there is, and always has been, a diversity of credible and coherent, yet incompatible theories of the syllable. An optimist might say that all these theories represent different aspects of the same entity that we are trying to understand, an entity that shifts its shape when called upon to perform different tasks. A not quite so rosy view would be that this variability in the form of the syllable is a result of scholars' attempts to force the syllable into different—and perhaps not always appropriate—descriptive and explanatory roles. We submit that this effervescence is in fact a sign that it is now timely to stand back and reflect upon the phenomena we are trying to understand in the first place. Just what explanatory and descriptive goals have we been imposing on the syllable? Have they been reasonable? Can we settle on some that might lead to convergence in our view of this entity?

To clarify the goals of the current handbook it is useful to contrast them with those of van der Hulst and Ritter's (1999) monumental and immensely valuable *The Syllable: Views and Facts*. The latter is an exhaustive collection of those (constraint-based) views of syllable structure that are motivated to account for phonotactic and other phenomena relevant to the syllable; the facts adduced in their volume consist of in-depth fragments of the phonological grammars of some twenty languages, illustrating various aspects of syllabic analyses. The current handbook departs from van der Hulst and Ritter's volume in fundamental ways: the laudable (and successfully attained) goal of *The Syllable: Views and Facts* is to focus attention on phonological aspects of the syllable from within a well-defined range of theoretical perspectives; the goal of this handbook is to examine a broad array of phenomena and generalizations that fall within the penumbra of what researchers in various phonological, phonetic and psycholinguistic sciences commonly refer to with the term 'syllable.' Questions around the nature and roles of the syllable are all empirical ones, as are those concerning the compatibility of the various roles assigned to the syllable by researchers in a number of disciplines. Thus, the explananda and attendant methodologies of concern to this handbook are drawn from an eclectic array of topics within the language and speech sciences, while the explananda that motivate the chapters in van der Hulst and Ritter are exclusively within the domain of phonological theory. Indeed, many of the insights discussed in this handbook are drawn from phonetic and psycholinguistic laboratories, as well as studies of orthography and diachronic linguistics.

The remainder of this chapter is divided into two parts, in the first of which (section 2) we give a short overview of the history of the syllable in the language sciences, especially through the advent of generative phonology. There are two reasons for emphasizing pre-generative approaches to the syllable; one is to counter an arrogant tendency to neglect the insights of the founders of our field, whose methods and results continue to inform us. The other is to make it clear that, although we have made progress in phonetics and phonology, there is a tendency to keep reinventing the wheel. The last part of this introductory chapter (section 3) gives a brief overview of the chapters in this book.

2   History of the Syllable

It is productive to view the history of the syllable in the context of the development of our understanding of the basic principles underlying human speech. This field of study became well established by the late eighteenth century, when, under the influence of the enlightenment, scientific principles were systematically applied to human speech and language. Understandably, the first decades of this research were devoted to studying the basic principles involved in the production of individual speech sounds. The first serious proposals concerning the rhythmic organization of speech occurred in the context of a significant deepening of our understanding of phonetics and phonology in the second half of the nineteenth century, as discussed in more detail below. That is when the syllable, variously conceived, became a central entity in phonetics and phonology.

We divide the history of the syllable into three phases. The first starts with the early scientific work on the mechanisms of speech, which laid the groundwork for work on the syllable, and runs up through initial proposals about the syllable, roughly the early twentieth century. The second period was the early twentieth century until the advent of generative grammar. The third period of the syllable in phonology was the early generative approaches; we focus only on essential and early generative views of the syllable for two reasons. One is that there already exist excellent summaries of the syllable in modern phonology: Bell and Hooper (1978), for example, is a penetrating discussion of the syllable as understood about thirty years ago. Selkirk (1982) is another classic landmark that is referenced in contemporary work on the syllable. Blevins's chapter in Goldsmith (1995) is also a broad and in-depth description of the state of the art fifteen years ago. Zec (2007) is another contemporary survey; van der Hulst and Ritter (1999), as mentioned above, contains a thorough presentation of phonological approaches to phonotactic and syllabic structure in phonology. Féry and van de Vijver (2003) is an entire volume devoted to the syllable in optimality theory. Finally, chapter six in Kenstowicz (1994) provides an excellent overview of generative approaches to the syllable within the main stream of American phonology. The last reason for truncating our discussion of recent history is that the subsequent chapters in this handbook themselves provide a broad survey of contemporary views on the syllable.

2.1   *The Early History of the Syllable*

One of the most prominent late eighteenth century scientists of human speech was Wolfgang Ritter von Kempelen, who built a speaking machine and published an accompanying volume (Kempelen 1791) describing the basic mechanisms of speech production, based on his research into human speech production.[2] Kempelen's machine was what Riskin (2003a) refers to as a philosophical experiment. He was following in the tradition of Vaucanson, who in 1738 built a number of automata as "attempts to discern which aspects of living creatures could be reproduced in machinery, and to what degree, and what such reproductions might reveal about their natural subjects" (Riskin 2003a, 601); among Vaucanson's inventions was an automated flute player, developed in part in order to test his theory of the biomechanics and acoustics of flute playing. Riskin (2003a, b) describes a number of other eighteenth century attempts to reveal nature's design of biological mechanisms by means of mechanical simulation, illustrating an erosion of Cartesian dualism in favor of "an emergent materialism and...a growing confidence...that experimentation could reveal nature's actual design" (Riskin 2003a, 603).

More pertinent to our interest in the syllable, Kempelen's machine, like Vaucanson's earlier flute playing android, had no mechanism

---

[2] Dudley and Tarnoczy (1950) describes Kempelen's machine in considerable detail.

intended to simulate rhythmic structure.[3] That is, Kempelen's and Vaucanson's automata, like others built during that period, had no analogue to the syllable, musical beat, or any other element alluding to tempo, cadence, or rhythmicity. Kempelen's device (and those of his nineteenth century successors) produced connected speech by brute force: the hand of the operator continuously varied the shapes of the machine's resonating cavities. A scientific approach to the mechanisms humans employ to produce rhythm had to wait several decades.

The early nineteenth century saw significant progress in understanding the nature of speech sounds. For example, the notion of phonological features as defining characteristics of speech sounds was introduced by Erasmus Darwin (1803), grandfather of Charles Darwin, who made a simpler version of Kempelen's machine. Darwin "proposed a system of 13 unary features by which to describe any and all speech sounds including, notably, the voiceless lateral of Welsh ([ɬ])" Ohala (2004, 135).

Alexander Melville Bell, motivated both by a desire to teach the deaf to speak as well as by scientific curiosity, furthered Darwin's work with his production in 1867 of *Visible Speech*, an ingenious alphabet wherein the symbols graphically represent the activities of the articulatory organs involved in speech production. Each speech sound was in fact defined in terms of a set of features. Bell's major contribution was to view these features as the atomic parts of individual sounds, not simply their accidental characteristics. As Halle (1978) and Halle and Stevens (1962) remind us, Alexander Melville Bell's insight was eclipsed by the establishment of the International Phonetic Alphabet (IPA) later in the century, and was not revived until the development of the Prague school, where feature theory was independently rediscovered. The IPA, of course, represents each individual speech sound as an entity unto itself, not consisting of smaller units.

This opposition between feature theory and the IPA defined a major dialectic in phonetics and phonology. Another was the opposition between a focus on segments versus on rhythmic structure. Alexander Graham Bell, the son of the developer of *Visible Speech*, first urged attention to syllables (Bell 1911). Motivated, like his father, in

---

[3] See Riskin (2003a, 615): "For example, to mark out measures [Vaucanson] had a flutist play a tune while another person beat time with a sharp stylus onto [a] rotating cylinder."

large part by attempts to build an oral-based teaching program for the deaf, he wanted to go beyond his father's work to try to capture more dynamic characteristics of speech. His efforts helped make the syllable important in deaf education in the nineteenth century; according to Stetson (1945, 27), Marichelle (1897), another proponent along with Bell of the oral approach to deaf education, similarly analyzed the syllable as the fundamental unit of speech in an early acoustic study of speech.

Even though Alexander Melville Bell's student Henry Sweet (and Paul Édouard Passy) developed the IPA as a monument to the individual segment, the notion of the syllable as an overarching, organizing entity of some kind was never far from the surface in the literature of that period. For example, it is a theme in Sweet's *A Handbook of Phonetics* (1877), and, as Stetson (1945) enthusiastically reminds us, Sievers, in his *Grundzüge der Lautphysiologie* (1881), analyzed the consonants and vowels as functions of the syllable, which he considered the fundamental unit of speech. As a harbinger of contemporary practice, Viëtor (1885, 1898) introduced the syllable as a way of accounting for geminate consonants and other distributional properties of speech sounds. For example, in describing the distribution of vowels and consonants in German, he wrote:[4]

> A syllable is 'open,' when it terminates in a vowel; it is 'closed,' when the last sound... is a consonant. In German syllabication, simple consonants between vowels are allotted to the second syllable, the former syllable thus remaining 'open.'... Double consonants, and two different consonants, are divided between the two syllables, and thus the first syllable becomes 'closed' (1885, 59).

Viëtor was presaging modern theory when characterizing the syllable as the domain for the distribution of segments.[5] Clearly, the syllable had evolved rapidly into an important descriptive construct by the early twentieth century, giving rise to an interesting and enduring dichotomy: should we view segments—or, better, sequences of segments—as fundamental and syllable structure as secondary, or is

---

[4] Do Viëtor's syllables exhaustively parse the string of phonemes? He does not tell us where the syllable boundary would fall in the case of three intervocalic consonants; would it fall to the left or right of the [s] in [glitsriç], a possible pronunciation of *glitzerig* 'glittering')? Discussion of structure internal to the syllable does not appear until Trubetzkoy's *Grundzüge* (see below).

[5] But see below for doubts cast upon the utility of the syllable for this purpose.

the syllable basic and segments to be defined solely in terms of their function within the syllable? In addition to this question, the most productive tension of the time was between viewing sounds as indivisible units with features as accidental characteristics, versus defining features as the atomic units and individual sounds merely accidental constellations of features.

2.2   The History of the Syllable in the Twentieth Century

Two important developments in the history of the syllable took place in the early twentieth century. On the phonological level was the Prague school's development of the Saussurean idea of defining linguistic units in terms of oppositions; this is the historical track that led to the rediscovery, after Alexander Melville Bell, of features as the atomic elements of segments. The second major development was Stetson's argument that the syllable is defined in terms of pulses of increased subglottal air pressure produced by chest contractions. This idea dominated phonetic discussions of the syllable until the 1960s; although it was refuted then, many of the arguments put forth in its favor remain potent in contemporary literature. Furthermore, some notion of the syllable continuously lurked in the background of all phonological work. For example, American structuralist phonologists made frequent reference to some undefined concept of the syllable as a locus for describing the distribution and categorization of phonemes. Sounds were routinely defined as either 'syllabic' or 'nonsyllabic' in works that contained no definition or description of the syllable.

The remainder of this section is organized according to major contributions to the syllable in the early twentieth century. We deal first with the Prague school, concentrating on Trubetzkoy and Jakobson, although there were other important figures whom we must neglect for reasons of space.[6] Stetson is discussed next, followed by paragraphs devoted to American structuralists.

2.2.1   The Prague School
The Prague school's heyday was from 1926 until the advent of World War II. Although this school had many roots (cf. Anderson 1985, Vachek 1966), Saussure's *Course de linguistique générale* (1916) had

---

[6] Among the neglected are A. Sommerfelt (1931) and A. W. de Groot (1941).

a major impact. In addition to his distinction between *langue* and *parole*, Saussure's most seminal contribution to Prague phonology was his argument that linguistic units are defined exclusively in terms of the oppositions they enter into. This is the idea that led to the Prague school's reinvention of Bell's definition of features as the atomic elements of phonetics (Halle 1978, Halle and Stevens 1962).

Saussure's description of the syllable as explosion–implosion and his emphasis on the syllable as a basic unit of phonological organization were ignored by the Prague school phonologists. However, it became necessary for Trubetzkoy to reinvent the syllable when considering the locus of potentially distinctive supra-segmental features like stress and tone. The fact that the phonetic correlates of stress and tone usually reside in vowels led Trubetzkoy to posit in 1929 that these are vocalic properties. However, he reversed this position ten years later in the *Grundzüge*, where he recognized the syllable—in particular, the syllabic nucleus—as the locus of distinctive prosodic oppositions.

Trubetzkoy (1939) was the first to propose that syllables have internal structure, a proposal that was reinvented by Pike and Pike (1947) and continues to loom large in current debate about the syllable. Trubetzkoy's theory of internal structure was exemplified with a questionable analysis of some Hopi facts (cf. Anderson 1985, 103ff), so it was as inchoate as it was groundbreaking. In addition to saying that syllable structure is a locus for describing stress and pitch, Trubetzkoy, by means of his more articulated theory of internal syllabic structure, enriched Viëtor's notion of the syllable as a domain for describing phoneme sequences.

The syllable played an important role throughout the history of the Prague school. It was a central component of Jakobson's (1941) explanation for aspects of language acquisition and aphasia. As later explained by Jakobson and Halle (1956, 37), this theory said that "ordinarily child language begins, and the aphasic dissolution of language preceding its complete loss ends," with a stage where the only utterance is /pa/. Acoustically, this sequence offers the optimal "contrast between two successive units—the optimal consonant and the optimal vowel. Thus the elementary phonemic frame, the syllable, is established."

The Prague school also distinguished between the syllable as a phonological (*langue*) entity and as a phonetic (*parole*) entity. Stetson's theory of chest pulses, to which we now turn, was assumed to be the phonetic correlate of the syllable.

2.2.2   Stetson's Theory of the Syllable

Following the historical thread laid by Sweet and Sievers, Stetson was a notable proponent of the syllable as the basic unit for the organization of speech. He is best known for his 1928 volume *Motor Phonetics: A study of speech movements in action* (republished posthumously in 1951), wherein he proposed that the phonetic basis for the syllable is a series of pulses of the muscles controlling respiration. In fact, as Twaddell (1953, 424) pointed out in his review of the 1951 edition of *Motor Phonetics*, "Stetson uses the term [syllable] as substantially equivalent to 'chest pulse'."

Stetson's *Bases of Phonology* (1945), less cited than his *Motor Phonetics*, contrasted his theory with both the Prague school and the American phonologists. As the title suggests, this volume was in direct opposition to Trubetzkoy's *Grundzüge*. He complained about Trubetzkoy's insistence that phonemes, viewed as individual segments, are timeless (*zeitlos*) in that they may be issued like the *dits* and *dots* of Morse Code, or like symbols on a ticker tape, where each unit is unaffected by the producing process (although possibly influenced by proximal symbols). Instead, as Sweet, Sievers and Saussure had all insisted, phonological patterning is defined by the dynamic articulation of actual speech, namely, rhythmic behavior that uses the chest pulse as the basic beat.

Stetson upbraided American structuralists like Bloch and Hockett for limiting linguistics to a classificatory science. He reserved particular scorn for their exclusive focus on individual sounds: "speech sounds are not a series of separate noises produced now this way, now that, and adjacent like the beads on a string; they are rather phases of the chest pulse, the syllable," part of the process of the speech production mechanism based on the respiratory apparatus (1945, 6). Some of those beads are consonants that begin a syllable and release it, in that they allow the air stream to escape from the thoracic cavity, which is undergoing contraction by the chest pulse. Others of those beads are arresting consonants because they check the air stream impelled by the closing chest pulse. Vowels, of course, are the beads corresponding to articulatory gestures that allow maximal escape of the air stream during the peak of the chest pulse.

Stetson compared the behavior of the thoracic cavity during speech production with that of a bellows; in order to produce a pulsating, syllable-like effect from a bellows, the hands that control the bellows must make small, rhythmically repeated strokes. This is unlike an organ, where the wind chest maintains a constant pressure and the rhythm is produced by varying the constrictions in the pipes through which the air escapes. Rather, the intercostal muscles produce a separate pulse for each syllable, like the hands on the bellows; thoracic air pressure falls between pulses, but not to ambient pressure levels, because the abdominal muscles maintain pressure throughout a breath group: "The breath group [is]... due to an abdominal movement with its culminations which mark the stresses of the constituent feet. One of these stresses constitutes the main stress of the breath group, while the syllable pulses are produced by the intercostal muscles of the rib cage." In fact, foreshadowing contemporary discussions of the syllable, Stetson (1945, 59) maintained an entire prosodic hierarchy, all controlled by the respiratory mechanism: the lowest level of the hierarchy was the *syllable*, which was controlled by the action of the intercostal muscles; the *foot*, a product of the abdominal-diaphragmatic contraction; and the *breath group*, which also involves abdominal-diaphragmatic muscles; and the *phrase*, the stretch between inhalations.

Ladefoged (1967) showed that the laboratory data Stetson adduced in support of his proposals were equivocal. Ladefoged's data suggest that the organ analogy applies better than does the bellows one. Many empirical problems were becoming known with Stetson's proposals by the 1960s. Lieberman, Griffiths, Mead, and Knudson (1967) reported that they could not replicate Stetson's findings. Hayes (1995) refers to Peterson (1958), who described a patient on a respirator who had no control over the intercostal nor the diaphragmatic muscles, yet could produce speech that "closely resembles normal conversational speech in all aspects," presumably including syllabic organization. (See also Krakow 1999 for a summary of this controversy.)

2.2.3   The American Structuralists

Bloomfield and post-Bloomfieldian American structuralists like Bloch, Trager, Pike and Hockett all referred to some notion of the syllable with varying degrees of explicitness. Bloomfield (1933, 1935), along with Trager and Bloch (1942), assumed the distinction between consonants and vowels (syllabics), yet never defined the syllable. In fact, Bloomfield (1935, 120–1) describes sonority sequencing in terms of syllabicity, yet does not use the term "syllable" anywhere in the book, as many have remarked also about Chomsky and Halle's *The Sound Pattern of English*.

Hockett (1955) offers an immediate constituent theory of syllables, which is based primarily on the linguist's procedures in arriving at a syllabic analysis. Unfortunately, as Chomsky's (1957) review points out, Hockett's definition of the syllable and his description of the procedures for arriving at a syllabic parse are not entirely clear.

Kenneth and Eunice Pike were the first to develop a highly articulated theory of the syllable with a rich internal structure. Borrowing some of Stetson's terminology, Pike and Pike (1947, 78) say that "the structure of... syllables does not consist of a series of sounds equally related, like beads on a string, but is rather like an overlapping series of layers of bricks. The different layers in the syllable tend to have different phonetic, distributional and grammatical characteristics." They, and Pike (1947, 1967), argued for a theory of syllable structure along the lines of Trubetzkoy's, with a possibly branching nucleus; their empirical base consisted of distributional constraints, loci for pitch and stress, as well as phonological alternations.

Although the American structuralists ended up agreeing with Stetson that there is more to phonological patterning than the beads-on-a-string analogy would imply, none agreed with him that phonemes are secondary and syllables primary. As among the adherents to the Prague school, the structuralists viewed syllables as supra-segmental structures imposed on preexisting strings of phonemes.

2.2.4 *The Syllable in Generative Grammar*

Chomsky and Halle (1968), the *Sound Pattern of English* (SPE), notoriously failed to give serious consideration to the syllable; as we have seen, SPE shares this lacuna with Bloomfield's *Language*. Of course, as was commonly the case with the American structuralists, there is frequent reference to the feature "syllabic," but no definition of the syllable. SPE was an exclusively linear approach which was surprisingly successful without incorporating prosodic structure in the phonological representations. This success attenuates the effectiveness of empirical arguments about whether syllables are necessary in phonology. Instead, arguments about the nature of syllables are usually based on theoretical elegance, predictions made from formal representations, and behavioral data. Subsequent work in phonology takes up the omission of discussion of prosodic features where SPE simply stated "our investigations of these features have not progressed to a point where a discussion in print would be useful" (329).

Anderson (1969, 141) was the first to pose the critical question concerning the utility of the syllable in generative grammar: "Are there in general phonological rules which can be stated more appropriately in terms of the syllable...than in terms simply of [the] segment"? This was in response to Kohler (1966), who had denied the syllable in part because of the hoary boundary question. A number of phonologists answered this question in the affirmative and the tack initially taken was to explore rules for placing syllable boundaries in phonological representations consisting essentially of strings of phonemes. Hooper (1972), for example, showed that SPE's "weak cluster," invoked to explain such phenomena as antepenultimate stress in words like *algebra*, really required syllable boundaries. Hooper (1972, 1976), as well as Hoard (1971), posited rules that insert syllable boundaries to handle a wide range of generalizations from several languages; Venneman (1972, 1978) and Murray and Venneman (1983) also show the utility of invoking syllable boundary insertion rules to account for historical generalizations in Germanic diachronic phonology (in interesting contrast to the conclusions drawn in connection with Romance in chapter seventeen of this handbook). Clearly, any discussion of hierarchical structure internal to the syllable was perforce absent from their discussions.

Kahn (1976) was the first American dissertation to closely examine the syllable in generative grammar. He pursued two lines of argument, one based on native speaker intuitions about the syllable and the other on the utility of the syllable in expressing generalizations in generative grammar (Kahn was apparently unaware of Anderson 1969). Lightner (1972), Lass (1971) and Halle (1971) had pointed out that consonants and word boundaries frequently behave as a natural class in the formulation of phonological rules; Kahn suggested that a syllable-based approach obviates this problem. Kahn pointed out that the rules for positing syllable boundaries proposed by previous scholars frequently provide bizarre syllable divisions. Kahn argued instead for a set of rules that exhaustively anchor segments to a (flat) syllable structure on an autonomous autosegmental tier; Kahn's theory was thus the first to employ autosegmental phonology in a theory of syllable structure.

Fudge (1969, 1987) provided the first, fully developed theory of the syllable as a structured entity within a generative framework. Following the Prague school, he said that the syllable has two functions, to serve as the locus for distinctive prosodic features and to account for phonotactic constraints, the main topic of his paper. Fudge emphasized that there is an important distinction between phonological and phonetic syllables, citing the French *mute e* as defining the nucleus of an underlying syllable which is deleted phonetically. Fudge defined constituents within the syllable by means of labeled nodes; a specified class of phonemes was allowed within each constituent. His syllables have the familiar *onset* and *rhyme*, and the rhyme is further broken into the *nucleus* and *coda*. Each of these constituents in turn contained labeled positions; this notion was also promoted by Cairns and Feinstein (1982). Phonotactic constraints that could not be accounted for by labeled nodes with defined classes for each were handled by collocational restrictions that applied to segments within a constituent. For example, Fudge had a constraint that says if the second position of an English onset consists of /l/, the first position in the onset cannot be a coronal. Interconstituent sequencing generalizations were handled by a distinct set of constraints by both Fudge and Cairns and Feinstein.

One important way of distinguishing among syllable theories is whether they posit flat syllables or internal syllable hierarchy. Clements and Keyser (1983) offered a minimal extension of Kahn and handled a broader range of phenomena (e.g. length, complex segments, syllable weight, and compensatory lengthening). Clements and Keyser differed from Kahn mostly in espousing a tripartite syllable structure, with onset, peak and coda all three depending from the syllable node. This was in deliberate opposition to Fudge's (1969, 272–273) claim justifying a more elaborate structure containing the constituent rhyme, which consists of peak and coda. Fudge had justified this constituent with the observation that "certain peaks do not co-occur with certain codas… while there is no such constraint between onset and peak." Clements and Keyser disputed this claim (1983, 20), arguing that "co-occurrence restrictions holding between the nucleus and preceding elements of the syllable appear to be just as common as co-occurrence restrictions holding between the nucleus and following elements." Fudge (1987) answered Clements and Keyser's arguments with the observation that, on the one hand, his 1969 theory can handle onset-peak co-occurrence restrictions, and, on the other hand, both within English and across languages, peak-coda restrictions are far more common, thus the two kinds of constraints are qualitatively different. Furthermore, Fudge (1987) argued that word games typically support a coda-rhyme structure, as does a frequency analysis of speech errors.

2.2.5 *Which Comes First, the Syllable or the (Sequence of) Segments?*
The question of which comes first, the syllable or the (sequence of)
segments, remains as much a perennial issue in the era of generative
phonology as it has since Sievers. Clements and Keyser (1983, 27), said
that "syllable trees are not built up in the course of phonological derivations but are already present, fully formed, in the lexical representations that constitute the input to the phonological component." Along
similar lines, Cheng (1966), Fudge (1969, 1987) and Anderson (1987),
as well as others, proposed mechanisms for generating syllables independent of the rest of the grammar, along with devices for inserting
phonemes into syllabic positions. Nasukawa (2007) and van der Hulst
(2005, 2007), for example, maintain that syllabic structures are lexically stored, and phonemes are filled in by rule or convention; the latter characterizes syllables as "the phonological mobile". These theories
all have in common that they do not construct syllables on preexisting strings of segments, but rather derive segmental strings from syllables. This view is widely held; for example, it is explicit throughout
van der Hulst and Ritter (1999) and underlies much of the literature
on the syllable in generative phonology referred to in the preceding
paragraphs. This is connected to the common belief that the syllable
is necessary for phonotactics.

   But whether the syllable is necessary for phonotactics and if it is fea-
sible to derive segment sequences from syllable structure are empirical
questions. One problem is that syllabification is not always exhaustive; many languages are known to have sequences of unsyllabified
consonants (Bagemihl 1991, Czaykowska-Higgins and Willett 1997,
Vaux and Wolfe 2009), so the syllable cannot be the domain for all
statements regarding the positions in which specific segments are
allowed.

   More to the point, Blevins (2003), building on Steriade (1999),
shows numerous compelling examples where phonological sequencing
generalizations and cross-linguistic universal patterns refer to properties of the phonological string and not to syllable structure. Of course,
as Blevins points out, there are many cases "where phonotactic constraints and syllable structure appear to converge." She suggests that
"...this is because syllabifications are derivative of phonotactics, not
vice versa" (2003, 393).

   Generalizations concerning permissible order of elements cannot
rely on syllable structure exclusively, because it would in any case be
necessary to specify the order among syllables. Consider the English

loan from Tamil *catamaran*; hypothetical **matacaran*, **tamacaran*, would serve as equally plausible loans into English, yet they differ from the existing word only by syllable order. The possibility of using foot structure to order syllables only moves this question higher in the prosodic hierarchy and requires more prosodic information to be stored in the lexicon. So, even the most syllable-centric view of phonology cannot confine all ordering generalizations to intra-syllabic status.

Observe finally that resyllabification is rampant throughout phonology and phonetics; the effervescence of the syllable makes it a poor candidate for the bearer of lexical precedence relations, suggesting that syllables are derived phenomena.

2.2.6 *What Elements Constitute Syllables?*
Clements and Keyser (1983, 8) proposed "a third tier in syllable representation which mediates between the syllable tier and the segmental tier and which we call the CV-tier." This view was quickly abandoned, and since Hyman (1985) there have been two competing models of phonological representations in the literature: segmental theories (based either on an x-slot tier or a CV-tier) and moraic theories. This distinction is well represented in the following chapters. Mora theory was defended by Hayes (1989) who posited lexical moras (in addition to moras inserted by rule or convention), but not lexical syllable structure. He observed that the existence of lexical syllables would suggest the existence of unattested lexically contrastive placements of syllable boundaries.

Sloan (1991) defends a theory of syllabification based on the x-slot tier. Sloan provided a detailed analysis of templatic and syllabic phonology in Southern Sierra Miwok which, she argued, was inconsistent with a moraic theory. In an often overlooked appendix, she exposed inconsistencies in a central argument in favor of moraic models of the syllable; space precludes a full exposition of her argument in this chapter.

2.3 *Conclusion of the History of the Syllable*

This quick romp through the history of the syllable has perforce neglected some important and influential schools of thought. For example, no mention has been made of *government phonology*, initiated by Kaye, Lowenstamm and Vergnaud (1990), which is amply covered in van der Hulst and Ritter (1999). Nor have we mentioned

Hyman's suggestion that some languages (e.g. Gokana) may lack sylla-bles altogether, nor the claim that W. Arrernte may be a language with only VC syllables; exploration of these claims would take us deeper into theoretical phonology than appropriate for this volume.

The history of the syllable in phonology and phonetics has, from the early days of the attempt to understand the basic mechanisms of human speech, been characterized by productive interactions between opposing views in a number of areas. The opposition between viewing features and segments as atomic elements continues to be prominent in the field: for example, government phonology differs from most other generative schools in denying that segments are defined in terms of constituent features. Similarly, the tension between positing the syllable as basic and segment strings as derived versus the other way around continues to flourish. As Riskin (2003a, 612) says of the ten-sions underlying the development of artificial life since the eighteenth century, the history of the syllable sketched above has not "been the simple unfolding of a suprahistorical dialectic; on the contrary, the dialectic represents a historical moment, one in which we are still liv-ing." The theoretical and methodological diversity that has character-ized the history of the syllable in phonology and phonetics continues today, as is amply demonstrated in the remainder of this handbook.

3   Overview of the Present Handbook

The sixteen chapters that follow represent the breadth and, we would like to think, depth of empirical domains commonly thought of as falling under the rubric of the syllable. The remaining chapters are divided into two broad categories, the role of the syllable in the gram-mar (five chapters, section 3.1) and in performance (eleven chapters, section 3.2). A brief overview of each chapter is offered in the remain-der of this introduction.

3.1   The Syllable in Grammar

The next five chapters investigate grammatical phenomena that throw light on the nature of the syllable in phonology. These are compen-satory lengthening (chapter two), typological generalizations (chap-ter three), phonotactics (chapters four and five), and the behavior of geminates (chapter six). (1) presents the main three formal models of the syllable that are assumed in this part of the handbook.

(1)   a.

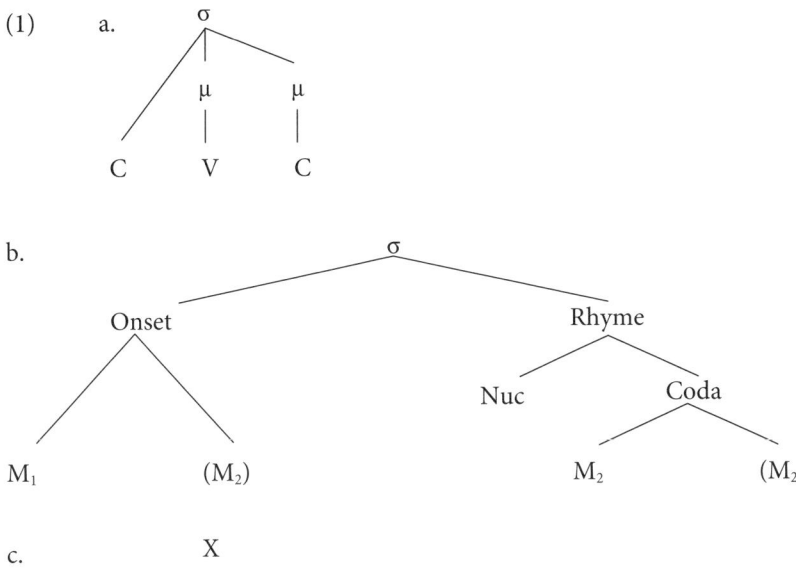

Chapter two, "Compensatory Lengthening," by Paul Kiparsky, analyzes compensatory lengthening (CL), introducing data new to the field (Finnish dialects) as well as a reanalysis of data that other scholars had analyzed before (Samothraki Greek). The moraic model, (1a), invokes faithfulness constraints as an analysis of CL because of its reliance on mora preservation. Kiparsky's chapter explores three problems posed by CL. One is that in languages where moras are predictable (and therefore, by "richness of the base," cannot be reliably encoded in the long term memory of stems), CL nevertheless consistently takes place. Kiparsky shows that these phenomena constitute an argument for stratal OT, where constraints at the stem level supply the moras to which the constraints at the word level may be faithful.

The second problem is that in some languages (e.g. Samothraki Greek) apparently weightless elements, namely /r/ in the onset, trigger CL which was a problem in the original Hayes (1989) analysis of CL. Here again, Stratal OT offers a solution; the /r/'s in question are analyzed as part of the nucleus at the stem level. They are therefore mora-bearing at the word level, where CL takes place.

Kiparsky also introduces a novel solution to another problem that is troublesome for standard views of OT, namely chain shifts. All Finnish dialects have productive consonant gradation, whereby in certain environments /tt/ becomes [t] and /t/ becomes [d]. Rejecting other approaches within OT, he argues in favor of a theory of Super-Optimality, a proposal for a class of constraints that evaluate Input-Output pairs; this amounts to a limited bidirectionality on constraint evaluation. Note that Kiparsky's theory of the syllable is the same as in most versions of OT; Kiparsky's innovation lies in his adaptation of Stratal OT and Super-Optimality, not in a new theory of syllable structure.

The syllabic model in (1b) is reminiscent of the labeled nodes of Fudge (1969, 1987, 1989) and Cairns and Feinstein (1982). Stuart Davis and Karen Baertsch, in chapter three ("On the Relationship Between Codas and Onset Clusters") explore evidence indicating that codas and the second member of complex onsets are the same category, which they label M_2. In addition to "pan-syllabic constraints" (such as those that rule out English words like "*klull" by means of a ban on repeating the same constituent within the same syllable) and the putative implicational universal that predicts codas in languages that allow complex onsets (either a language allows M_2 or it doesn't), they give three detailed examples showing the utility of their approach. The first is the fact that Campidanian Sardinian, in its diachronic development from Latin, lost both the second member of the onset and the coda, suggesting a close connection between the two syllabic positions. Second, they show that Colloquial Bamana, which they assume to be derived from Standard Bamana, simultaneously acquired both the second position of the onset and the coda. Finally, their syllabic model provides insight into Dorsey's Law in Winnebago that other models do not capture as efficiently. Comparing this and the preceding chapter might lead one to the anarchic belief that the phonologist's conception of the syllable is dependent on the descriptive task at hand; moras are useful for CL, and labeled nodes are useful for the sorts of generalizations addressed by Davis and Baertsch.

The diagram in (1c), originally proposed by Kiparsky (1981), is based on yet a third range of phenomena, namely distributional generalizations in English and other languages. Syllables can be represented as metrical structures, where 'W' and 'S' stand for 'weak' and 'strong,' respectively, and the 'x' refers to a mark on the lowest line of a metrical tier. This theory is described by San Duanmu in chapter four, "The CVX Theory of Syllable Structure." Duanmu's theory claims that a word has the general structure CMCESCECM, where CM is one or more affix or affix-like consonants, CE is one extra consonant, and

S is one or more syllables whose maximal structure is CVX (CVV or CVC). Morphological arguments are adduced as part of the justification for CM and CE. Again, a new descriptive goal, a new syllabic structure.

Chapter five, "The Syllable as Delimitation of the Base for Reduplication" by Jason Haugen, argues for the necessity of assuming the syllable as an element of linguistic theory to account for reduplication phenomena in Yaqui, Yapese, Mayo, and other languages. This argument is orthogonal to internal syllable structure. Haugen demonstrates an interesting opacity: in cases where stem final vowels delete due to certain affixes, yielding word-medial consonant clusters, it is the underlying syllable that reduplicates, not the surface syllable. This analysis is compatible with any model of the syllable that defines both the left and right edges of the syllable.

Catherine Ringen and Robert Vago extend the debate between the x-tier versus moraic approaches in chapter six, "Geminates, Heavy or Long?", using the behavior of geminates as evidence for syllable structure. They argue for a universal structure for geminates that contains double units on the timing tier and no prosodic properties such as the mora. These authors say that the mora analysis of geminates makes false predictions about the appearance of stress in, for example, Selkup and Ngalakgan, languages where stress is attracted by weight but not by geminates. A range of phonological phenomena from several languages, including distribution, the action of phonological processes such as metathesis and epenthesis, all suggest that geminates should be viewed as occupying two slots on the X-tier, as opposed to viewing them as inherently mora-bearing.

3.2 *The Syllable in Performance*

Research into the role of the syllable in speech planning, metrics, speech perception, language change, and other more "performance" oriented aspects of language suggests some very intriguing results. For example, a range of experimental work suggests that the form and even existence of syllables as revealed in the laboratory is partly dependent on the tasks required of the subjects. Work in other areas, such as metrics, song and historical linguistics, also suggest that syllables are like chameleons—their shape may shift, and in fact they may even be invisible at times, in order to facilitate extra-linguistic demands, and do so in different ways for different demands. Perhaps some of the differences among theories of the grammatical syllable reflect the variety of kinds of syllables that may appear at different points in the grammar and performance.

The following chapters are divided into five categories: one chapter is about song and metrics, three are concerned with speech production and articulation, five focus on speech perception and experimental manipulation of speech, one examines what we can learn about syllable structure from a study of syllabaries, and the last chapter inquires about role of the syllable in accounting for diachronic facts.

François Dell, in chapter seven, "Singing in Tashlhiyt Berber, a Language that Allows Vowelless Syllables," explores the alignment of speech to music. It is traditionally assumed that syllables, as opposed to any other linguistic units, are aligned with musical notes. Dell shows that this assumption is valid for Tashlhiyt Berber, despite the fact that syllables with consonantal nuclei are not good bearers of musical notes. In order to accommodate the needs of song, certain adjustments are made: a syllable may be drawn out over two notes, or a schwa may be inserted in contexts where none occur in normal speech. These adjustments are irrelevant phonologically and metrically.

Chapter eight, the first of the three chapters devoted to the syllable in speech production and articulation, argues for a marginal role for the syllable. Stefanie Shattuck-Hufnagel argues in "The Syllable in Speech Production and Planning" that the empirical justification for assuming a central role for the syllable in early stages of speech production is pretty slim. The evidence from speech errors supporting syllable as planning units that undergo serial ordering is not as strong as generally believed. Instead, the word may provide a more appropriate domain both for position similarity constraints on sublexical interaction errors, as well as for position preference for errors in onset position. The ambiguity of other kinds of traditionally invoked evidence for the syllable also casts some doubt on the centrality of the syllable to speech planning. The most likely role for syllable-sized units in production is as one of a number of types of stored abstract motor-control plans that are retrieved in the later stages of sound-level production planning and subsequently adjusted to fit their prosodic contexts.

The second chapter about the role of the syllable in speech production and articulation, chapter nine, Joana Cholin's "Do Syllables Exist? Psycholinguistic Evidence for the Retrieval of Syllabic Units in Speech Production," draws a similar conclusion about the relevance of the syllable in phonetic and phonological planning of speech production, basing her arguments on a very different line of investigation. Her reaction-time experiments indicate the relevance of frequency effects of syllables, supporting the assumption that abstract motor programs for syllables are stored in long term memory and retrieved during production. Cholin also found that Dutch and English speakers exhibited different patterns of frequency effects. In English (where syllable boundaries are not very transparent), frequency effects were found when the frequency manipulation was on the first syllable and when it was on the second syllable. In contrast, in Dutch (where syllable boundaries are more transparent), a frequency effect was only observed when the frequency manipulation was on the first syllable. Dutch speakers may be able to start articulation as soon as the first syllable is retrieved, while English speakers must plan a larger prosodic unit to begin speaking. Taken together, these results suggest that syllables are stored motor units, regardless of the transparency of the language's syllables.

Chapter ten is the third chapter about the syllable in speech production. "Segmental and Syllabic Processing in Healthy Younger and Older Adults: an Electrophysiological Study," by Yael Neumann, Loraine K. Obler, Valerie Shafer and Hilary Gomes, reported ERP data to compare segmental vs. syllabic processing. Their chapter reinforces both the previous authors and earlier studies that show a distinct stage of syllabic processing in preparing a word for speech production, the efficiency of which varies relative to segmental processing across the life span.

The next set of chapters deals with speech perception and experimental manipulation of the syllable. Chapter eleven, "The Impact of Experimental Tasks on Syllabification" by Marie-Hélène Côté and Viktor Kharlamov, shows the variability of subjects' judgments of the edges of syllables as a function of the tasks asked of them. They presented subjects with a single set of stimuli and asked them to perform five distinct experimental tasks: whole word repetition with pause insertion, last syllable repetition, first syllable repetition, written slash-insertion task and a written well-formedness evaluation questionnaire. On-line syllabification is influenced by a number of disparate factors, the relative weight of which vary as a function of experimental task. This chapter furthers the suspicion that the syllable is a chameleon-like entity that can change form (within limits) to facilitate the task at hand.

Andries W. Coetzee continues the use of behavioral data to investigate the nature of the syllable in chapter twelve, "Syllables in Speech Processing: Evidence from Perceptual Epenthesis." Coetzee points out that the syllable is an abstract entity that does not have invariant cues in the acoustic signal; therefore, he investigates the possibility of finding experimental evidence for the syllable. By presenting subjects with stimuli that do not conform to language specific rules of allophonic distribution, we can see the syllable structure imposed by the subjects on the acoustic stream. Focusing on the distribution of unaspirated voiceless stops following /s/ in English, he argues that the mapping from acoustic signal to linguistic precept makes crucial reference to the syllable.

The next chapter also assumes a central role for the concept of the syllable. Chapter thirteen, "Anglophone Perceptions of Arabic Syllable Structure," by Azra Ali, Michael Ingleby and David Peebles, investigates McGurk fusion rates in Anglophones and Arabophones. These fusion rates are known to vary as a function of onset vs. coda position: they are significantly lower in onset than in coda position. Languages lacking coda consonants should show uniform fusion rates for all consonants. Therefore, the McGurk effect can be used to test theories of syllabification of Arabic which conflict on whether or not coda consonants are allowed. These authors suggest that there are linguistically valid grounds for preferring a theory of Arabic syllable structure that does not contain codas; furthermore, Arabophones show uniform fusion rates, whereas the fusion rates for Anglophones varies as a function of onset vs. coda position. This clever and unexpected experimental angle for investigating syllable structure argues not only for a central role of the syllable in speech perception, but in fact for internal syllabic structure that reflects differences of mental models among members of different linguistic cultures.

The authors of chapter fourteen "Syllable Structure and Sonority: the Case of Russian Speaking Children with Specific Language Impairment," Darya Kavitskaya and Maria Babyonyshev, investigate phonological difficulties experienced by Russian children who have specific language impairment. Using pseudo-word repetition tasks, they showed the existence of a continuum of complexity of syllable structure: CV is the easiest and CCVCC is the hardest. The effect of complex codas is more pronounced than the effect of complex onsets. Their study illuminates the role that sonority plays in determining syllable complexity: in performing repetition tasks, children tend to drop the more sonorant consonant in a complex onset. Only liquids delete in obstruent liquid clusters, whereas either the first or second consonant deletes in obstruent-obstruent onsets. The authors propose the significant conclusion that their findings lend preliminary support to the view that the syllable is not epiphenomenal, but rather a crucial part of the grammar.

Chapter fifteen, "Syllable Markedness and Misperception: It's a Two-way Street" by Iris Berent, Tracy Lennertz and Paul Smolensky, also demonstrates the centrality both of the syllable and of sonority in speech perception. In their experimental tasks, subjects had much more difficulty with onsets of falling sonority than with onsets of rising sonority. The consistent misperception of onsets of falling sonority, either obstruents or nasal-initial clusters, is consistent with the hypothesis that people are equipped with broad preferences that favor sonority rises to falls, preferences that generalize to onsets unattested in their lexicon.

Amalia Gnanadesikan points out in chapter sixteen, "Syllables and Syllabaries: What Writing Systems Tell us About Syllable Structure," that becoming literate requires becoming consciously aware of some of the linguistic structures in one's language. Most early writing systems are syllabaries (or logosyllabaries), so the syllable must be available to both explicit and tacit knowledge. Despite discrepancies between the sign inventory of most syllabaries and the phonological syllables actually within the relevant languages, she demonstrates that syllabaries do in fact provide evidence of syllabic units. They also show other properties of syllables, including onset-over-coda preference, extrasyllabicity of /s/, moras, and the onset/rhyme distinction. It appears, then, that syllabaries may encode detailed structural properties of syllables, more than is revealed in any of the other performance oriented tasks discussed elsewhere in this handbook. Recall that moras, for example, do not figure as elements in the syllabic models offered by Davis and Baertsch and by Duanmu; her generalizations also speak to the psychological reality of nonexhaustive parsing, sonority, the relative markedness of codas, and internal structure within onsets and rimes.

As we have seen, there is considerable dispute in the literature as to whether the syllable is crucial to an account of phonotactics, or whether an analysis of linear segmental sequences suffices. Ranjan Sen, in chapter seventeen, "Diachronic Phonotactic Development in Latin: the Work of Syllable Structure or Linear Sequence?" evaluates the pro- vs. con- arguments with reference to the diachronic development of Latin. The two accounts make different predictions regarding word-internal sequences, so the development of the rich set of clusters in Proto-Indo-European into classical Latin provides a promising empirical testing ground. Although syllable structure arguably played an indirect role, as did morphology, linear sequence alone—with no reference to syllable structure—directly accounts for the most significant phonotactic developments from PIE to Latin. Between linear sequence and morpheme structure constraints, there is not much work for syllable structure to do regarding phonotactic development.

This and the following chapters illustrate that some notion of the syllable has had and continues to have an irresistible appeal to researchers in a number of phonetic and linguistic sciences, wispy and tenuous though it may be. We find there to be ample evidence to support the existence of the syllable but this conclusion does not really address the concerns about the syllable. The real question about the syllable is not whether it exists or not but what does the syllable do. Each of the contributions to this handbook develops answers to this particular question and answers which tell us what the syllable is not doing are as useful as answers which tell us what role the syllable plays in grammar.

References

Anderson, John. 1969. Syllabic or non-syllabic phonology. *Journal of Linguistics* 5: 136–142.

——. 1987. The limits of linearity. In *Explorations in Dependency Phonology*, edited by John Anderson and Jacques Durand, 169–190. Dordrecht: Foris.

Anderson, Stephen R. 1985. *Phonology in the Twentieth Century*. Chicago: University of Chicago Press.

Bagemihl, Bruce. 1991. Syllable structure in Bella Coola. *Linguistic Inquiry* 22: 589–646.

Bell, Alan and Joan Hooper. 1978. *Syllables and Segments*, Amsterdam and New York: North-Holland Publishing Co.

Bell, Alexander Graham. 1911. *The Mechanics of Speech*. New York: Funk and Wagnalls.

Bell, Alexander Melville. 1867. *Visible Speech: The Science of Universal Alphabetics*. London: Simkin, Marshall.

Blevins, Juliette. 1995. The syllable in phonological theory. In *The handbook of phonological theory*, edited by John Goldsmith, 206–244. Cambridge, MA: Blackwell.

——. 2003. The independent nature of phonotactic constraints: an alternative to syllable-based approaches. In *The syllable in optimality theory*, edited by Caroline Féry and Ruben van de Vijver, 375–403. Cambridge: Cambridge University Press.

Bloch, Bernard and George Trager. 1942. *Outline of Linguistic Analysis*. Baltimore: Linguistic Society of America.

Bloomfield, Leonard. 1933. *Language*. New York: Holt.

——. 1935. The stressed vowels of American English. *Language* 11: 97–116.

Cairns, Charles and Mark Feinstein. 1982. Markedness and the theory of syllable structure. *Linguistic Inquiry* 13: 193–225.

Cheng, Robert L. 1966. Mandarin phonological structure. *Journal of Linguistics* 2: 135–158.

Chomsky, Noam. 1957. Review of "A manual of phonology," by Charles F. Hockett. *International Journal of American Linguistics* 23: 223–242.

Chomsky, Noam and Morris Halle. 1968. *The Sound Pattern of English*. New York: Harper and Row.

Clements, George N. and Samuel J. Keyser. 1983. *CV phonology: A generative theory of the syllable*. Cambridge, MA: MIT Press.

Czaykowska-Higgins, Ewa and Marie Louise Willet. 1997. Simple syllables in Nxaʿamxcin. *International Journal of American Linguistics* 63: 385–411.

Darwin, Erasmus. 1803. *The temple of nature*. London: J. Johnson.

Dudley, Homer and T. H. Tarnoczy. 1950. The speaking machine of Wolfgang von Kempelen. *Journal of the Acoustical Society of America* 22: 151–166.

Féry, Caroline, and Ruben van de Vijver. 2003. *The syllable in optimality theory*. Cambridge: Cambridge University Press.

Fromkin, Victoria. 1971. The non-anomalous nature of anomalous utterances. *Language*. 47: 27–52.

Fudge, Erik. 1969. Syllables. *Journal of Linguistics* 5: 253–87.

——. 1987. Branching structure within the syllable. *Journal of Linguistics* 23: 359–377.

——. 1989. Syllable structure: A reply to Davis. *Journal of Linguistics* 25: 219–220.

Goldsmith, John, ed. 1995. *The Handbook of Phonological Theory*. Cambridge, Mass.: Blackwell.

Groot, Albert W. de 1941. Voyelle, consonne et syllabe. *Archives néerlandaises de phonétique expérimental*, XVII.

Halle, Morris. 1971. Word boundaries as environments in rules. *Linguistic Inquiry* 2: 540–541.

——. 1978. Knowledge unlearned and untaught: What speakers know about the sounds of their language. In *Linguistic theory and psychological reality*, edited by Morris Halle, Joan Bresnan and G.A.Miller, 294–303. Cambridge, MA: MIT Press. Reprinted in Morris Halle. 2002. *From Memory to Speech and Back: Papers on Phonetics and Phonology*. Berlin: Mouton de Gruyter, 95–104.

Halle, Morris and Kenneth Stevens. 1962. Speech recognition: A model and a program for research. *IRE Transactions of the PGIT IT-8*. pp. 155–159. Reprinted in Morris Halle. 2002. *From Memory to Speech and Back: Papers on Phonetics and Phonology*. Berlin: Mouton de Gruyter, 25–36.

Haugen, Einar. 1956. The syllable in linguistic description. In *For Roman Jakobson* edited by Morris Halle, Horace Lunt, Hugh MacLean, and Cornelis van Schooneveld, 213–221. The Hague: Mouton.

Hayes, Bruce. 1989. Compensatory lengthening in moraic phonology. *Linguistic Inquiry* 20: 253–306.

——. 1995. *Metrical stress theory: Principles and case studies*. Chicago: University of Chicago Press.

Hefner, Roe-Merrill. S. 1950. *General phonetics*. Madison: University of Wisconsin Press.

Hempel, Carl G. and Paul Oppenheim. 1948. Studies in the Logic of Explanation. *Philosophy of Science* 15: 135–75. Reproduced in Carl G. Hempel. 1965. *Aspects of Scientific Explanation*. New York: Free Press.

Hoard, James E. 1971. Aspiration, tenseness, and syllabification in English. *Language* 47: 133–140.

Hockett, Charles. 1942. A system of descriptive phonology. *Language*. 18: 3–21.

——. 1955. *A Manual of Phonology*. Indiana University Publications in Anthropology and Linguistics 11.

Hooper, Joan Bybee. 1972. The syllable in phonological theory. *Language* 48: 525–540.

——. 1976. *An introduction to natural generative phonology*. New York: Academic Press.

Hulst, Harry van der. 2005. The molecular structure of phonological segments. In *Headhood, Elements, Specification and Contrastivity*, edited by Phillip Carr, Jacques Durand and Colin Ewen, 193–234. Amsterdam: John Benjamins Publishing Company.

——. 2007. A dependency-based perspective on linearization in phonology. Presented at the CUNY Phonology Forum Conference on Precedence in Phonology. http://www.cunyphonologyforum.net/forum.php

Hulst, Harry van der and Nancy A. Ritter, eds. 1999. *The Syllable: Views and Facts*. Berlin & New York: Walter de Gruyter.

Hyman, Larry M. 1985. *A theory of phonological weight*. Dordrecht: Foris.

Jakobson, Roman. 1941. *Kindersprache, Aphasie und allgemeine Lautgesetze*. Uppsala: Uppsala Universitets Aarskrift.

Jakobson, Roman and Morris Halle. 1956. *Fundamentals of Language*. 'S-Gravenhage: Mouton & Co.

Jesperson, Otto. 1933. *Essentials of English Grammar*. London: Allen & Unwin.

Kahn, Daniel. 1976. Syllable-based generalizations in English phonology. PhD diss., MIT.

Kaye, Jonathan, Jean Lowenstamm and Jean-Roger Vergnaud. 1990. Constituent structure and government in phonology. *Phonology* 7: 193–231.

Kempelen, Wolfgang von. 1791. *Mechanismus der menschlichen Sprache nebst der Beschreibung seiner sprechenden Maschine*. Wien: J. B. Degen.

Kenstowicz, Michael. 1994. *Phonology in Generative Grammar*. Oxford: Blackwell.

Kiparsky, Paul. 1981. Remarks on the metrical structure of the syllable. In *Phonologica 1980*, edited by Wolfgang V. Dressler, Oskar E. Pfeiffer and John E. Rennison, 245–256. Innsbruck: Institute für Sprachwissenschaft der Universität Innsbruck.

Kohler, Klaus. 1966. Is the syllable a phonological universal? *Journal of Linguistics* 2: 207–208.

Krakow, Rena A. 1999. Physiological organization of syllables: a review. *Journal of Phonetics* 27: 23–54.

Ladefoged, Peter. 1967. *Three areas of experimental phonetics.* Oxford: Oxford University Press.

Lass, Roger. 1971. Boundaries as obstruents. *Journal of Linguistics* 7: 15–30.

Lieberman, Phillip, John D. Griffiths, Jere Mead and Ronald Knudson. 1967. Absence of syllabic "chest pulses." *Journal of the Acoustical Society of America* 41: 1614.

Lightner, Theorore. 1972. *Problems in the Theory of Phonology, Vol. 1.* Edmunton: Linguistic Research Inc.

Marichelle, Hector. 1897. *La parole d'apres le trace du phonographe.* Paris.

Murray, Robert W. and Theo Venneman. 1983. Sound change and syllable structure in Germanic Phonology. *Language* 59: 514–528.

Nasukawa, Kuniya. 2007. Relational properties in phonology: Precedence and dependency. Presented at the CUNY Phonology Forum Conference on Precedence in Phonology. http://www.cunyphonologyforum.net/forum.php

Ohala, John. 2004. Phonetics and Phonology then, and then, and now. In *On Speech and Language: Studies for Sieb G. Nooteboom*, edited by Hugo Quené and Vincent van Heuven, 133–140. Utrecht: Netherlands Graduate School of Linguistics.

Peterson, Gordon E. 1958. Some observations on speech. *Quarterly Journal of Speech* 44: 402–412.

Pike, Kenneth L. 1947. On the phonemic status of English diphthongs. *Language* 23: 151–159.

——. 1967. *Language in relation to a unified theory of the structure of human behavior.* The Hague: Mouton.

Pike, Kenneth L. and Eunice Pike. 1947. Immediate constituents of Mazateco syllables. *International Journal of American Linguistics* 13: 78–91.

Riskin, Jessica. 2003a. The defecating duck, or, the ambiguous origins of artificial life. *Critical Inquiry* 29: 599–633.

——. 2003b. Eighteenth-century wetware. *Representations* 83: 97–125.

Saussure, Ferdinand de. 1916. *Cours de linguistique générale.* Paris: Payot.

Selkirk, Elisabeth. 1982. The syllable. In *The structure of phonological representations*, part 2, edited by Harry van der Hulst and Norval Smith, 337–383. Dordrecht: Foris.

Sloan, Kelly Dawn. 1991. Syllables and Templates: Evidence from Southern Sierra Miwok. PhD diss., MIT.

Sommerfelt, Alf. 1931. Sur l'importance générale de la syllable. Travaux du cercle linguistique de Prague IV.

Steriade, Donca. 1999. Alternatives to syllable-based accounts of consonantal phonotactics. In *Proceedings of LP '98: Item order in language and speech*, vol. 1, edited by Osamu Fujimura, Brian D. Joseph and Bohumil Palek, 205–245. Prague: Charles University in Prague – The Karolinum Press.

Stetson, Raymond Herbert. 1928, 1951. *Motor Phonetics: A study of speech movements in action.* (2nd edition, 1951), Amsterdam: North Holland Publishing Company.

——. 1945. *Bases of Phonology.* Oberlin, Ohio: Oberlin College.

Sweet, Henry. 1877. *A handbook of phonetics.* Oxford: Clarendon Press.

Trager, George L. and Bernard Bloch. 1941. The syllabic phonemes of English. *Language* 17: 223–246.

Trubetzkoy, Nikolai S. 1929. Zur allgemeinen Theorie der phonologischen Vokalsys-teme, *Travaux du Cercle linguistique du Prague* I: 39–67. Reprinted in J. Vachek. 1964. *A Prague School Reader in Linguistics*, 108–142. Bloomington: Indiana University Press.

——. 1939. *Grundzüge der Phonologie*. Travaux du cercle linguistique de Prague VII. Reprinted, Göttingen: Vandenhoeck und Ruprecht, 1967. Translated by Christiane A.M. Baltaxe as *Principles of phonology*. Berkeley and Los Angeles: University of California Press.

Twaddell, William Freeman. 1953. Stetson's model and the 'supra-segmental pho-nemes.' *Language* 29: 415–453.

Vachek, Josef. 1966. *The Linguistic School of Prague*. Bloomington: Indiana University Press.

Vaux, Bert and Andrew Wolfe. 2009. The appendix. In *Contemporary views on archi-tecture and representations in phonology*, edited by Eric Raimy and Charles E. Cairns, 101–144. Cambridge, MA.: MIT Press.

Vennemann, Theo. 1972. On the theory of syllabic phonology. *Linguistische Berichte* 18: 1–18.

——. 1978. Universal syllabic phonology. *Theoretical Linguistics*. 5: 175–215.

Viëtor, Wilhelm. 1885. *German pronunciation*. Heilbronn: Henninger Bros.

——. 1898. *Elemente der Phonetik*. 4. Auflage. Leipzig.

Whitney, William Dwight. 1865. The relation of vowel and consonant. *Journal of the American Oriental Society* 8. Reprinted in William Dwight Whitney, *Oriental and linguistic studies: Second series*. New York: Charles Scribner's Sons, 1874.

Zec, Draga. 2007. The syllable. In *The Cambridge handbook of phonology*, edited by Paul de Lacy, 161–194. New York: Cambridge University Press.

THE SYLLABLE IN GRAMMAR

CHAPTER TWO

COMPENSATORY LENGTHENING

Paul Kiparsky

1 *A Challenge for OT*

1.1 *Compensatory Lengthening as Weight Conservation*

Compensatory lengthening occurs when the featural content of a nucleus or moraic coda is deleted, or becomes reaffiliated with a non-moraic position—typically an onset—and the vacated mora, instead of being lost, is retained with new content (Hayes 1989).

Compensatory lengthening is most often triggered by the deletion of a weight-bearing coda consonant. In ancient Greek, when an *-s-* in coda position is lost, its mora survives as a lengthening of a neigh-boring segment—the preceding vowel in the majority of dialects, the following consonant in Lesbian and Thessalian: /es-mi/ *ēmi, emmi* 'I am' (cf. /es-ti/ *esti* 'is').

(1) a. Attic

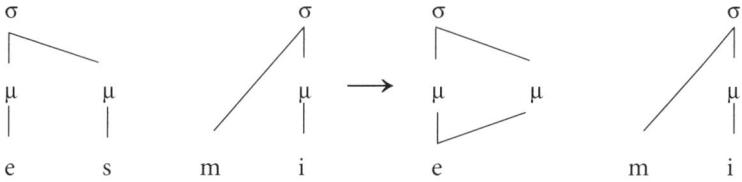

b. Lesbian and Thessalian

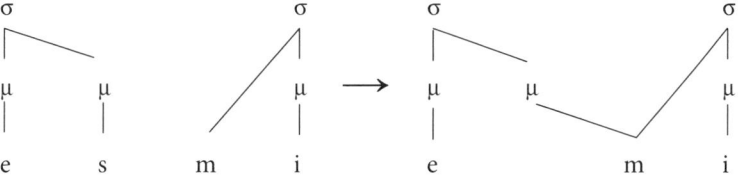

When the original features associated with the mora are completely
replaced by those of a neighboring segment, as in (1), compensatory
lengthening is hardly distinguishable from total assimilation. But there
are types of compensatory lengthening where the weight-bearing element is not lost but rather resyllabified, and these cannot be considered assimilations, but must be understood as weight conservation
effects. In one such type, a nucleus loses its weight by becoming an
onset, while retaining its segmental features, and its former mora is
then manifested as vowel lengthening. For example, in Pāli prevocalic
o can be desyllabified to a glide or approximant *v*. Being an onset, it
becomes weightless. But its mora is preserved as a lengthening of the
following vowel: /so ahaŋ/ *svāhaŋ* 'that I', /so ajja/ *svājja* 'today' (Rhys
Davids and Stede 1921–5, 655).

(2)
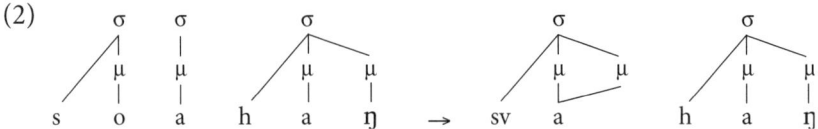

Similarly, when moraic codas are resyllabified as onsets, the preceding
nucleus can be compensatorily lengthened. Hayes (1989) illustrates it
with the vowel lengthening that occurs in (East) Ionic Greek when
post consonantal *w* is lost in the next syllable, and the preceding consonant is forced into the onset: e.g. *arwā̃* → *ārā̃*, *ksénwos* → *ksênos*
(versus Attic *arā̃*, *ksénos*). In the most remarkable scenario of all, the
resyllabification is not triggered by deletion. In Luganda, nasals are
reassigned from coda to onset (perhaps as prenasalization), leaving
behind its mora in the form of a lengthening of the vocalic nucleus,
e.g. /muntu/ → *mun.tu* → *muu.ntu* (Clements 1986).

(3)
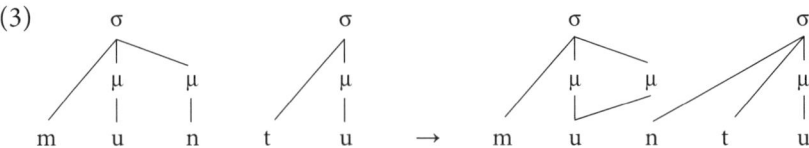

Compensatory lengthening is both a type of sound change, and a type
of synchronic phonological process. The compensatory lengthening
processes cited in (1)–(3) originate as sound changes, but they must
also be part of the synchronic grammars of the respective languages,

since they result in systematic predictable phonological alternations. Because the trigger of synchronic compensatory lengthening is not visible on the surface, it raises the specter of phonological opacity.

In addition, the Luganda case poses an even bigger puzzle. The analysis presupposes an unconditioned resyllabification of medial nasal clusters from *Vn.CV* to *V.nCV*. How can a single constraint system impose two different syllabifications on one and the same consonant cluster? In principle, Stratal OT makes available a simple analysis of Luganda compensatory lengthening because it allows different strata to have different syllabification patterns. Of course these should not have to be posited just for the sake of the compensatory lengthening data but should have independent motivation. In fact, while the *-n* in Luganda words like *muuntu* is obviously an onset in the output, Larry Hyman (p.c.) cites synchronic evidence from Meinhof's Law that it is syllabified as a coda at the stem level.[1] If the cross-stratal resyllabification required by the autosegmental approach to compensatory lengthening is indeed independently motivated, then Luganda supports Stratal OT over parallel OT.[2]

In this chapter I develop this line of argument in detail on the basis of two instances of compensatory lengthening which are even harder than Luganda. One, from Finnish, is new to the theoretical literature. The other, from Samothraki Greek, has received several recent analyses, all vitiated by the neglect of crucial parts of the data. Both cases are of undoubted synchronic productivity. It turns out that they are resistant not only to parallel OT, but also to Hayes' rule-based autosegmental approach. I propose to show that Stratal OT deals with them handsomely, in a way that salvages the key insight behind the autosegmental theory of compensatory lengthening.

The core theoretical issues raised by compensatory lengthening have to do with: its *actuation*, its *realization* in the lengthened item and in particular the locality relation between the target of lengthening and its trigger, the *distinctiveness* of the resulting weight, and the possibility of apparent *non-moraic triggers*.

---

[1] The gist of Hyman's argument is this: Meinhof's Law takes underlying /n+l/ to *nn* (e.g. /n+lim+a/ *nnima* 'I cultivate'. A vowel preceding this cluster has to be short (and will be shortened if long). This suggests that an input N+CV sequence is initially syllabified as N.CV.

[2] Specifically, classic parallel OT cannot derive Luganda compensatory lengthening at all, and OT-CC (nominally parallel but actually transderivational with quasi-derivations) can derive it only in a stipulative way (Shaw 2007).

1.2 Four Problems

1.2.1 The Actuation Problem

When is weight preserved? For example, why does *w*-deletion entrain vowel lengthening in Ionic but not in Attic (as in (1a) vs. (1b))? Determining when a potential process takes effect is one of the hardest problems in the study of language change, as well as in synchronic phonology. It remains as mysterious for compensatory lengthening as for any other historical or synchronic phonological process. I have no general solution to offer for the actuation problem, but I shall try to show that even here Stratal OT offers some insights, and a small step towards a solution.

1.2.2 The Realization Problem

How is weight preservation manifested? The idea that compensatory lengthening replaces the melodic content of a vacated mora implies that the mora itself should remain on the original syllable, unless something else happens to displace it. The prediction is correct on the whole. But *how* it is realized on that syllable does not seem to be predictable at all. For example, the Greek compensatory lengthening in (1) is manifested as consonant gemination in Lesbian and Thessalian and as vowel lengthening in all other dialects of Greek.

More seriously, there are cases where the preserved weight shows up at some distance from its original site, calling into question the no-crossing constraint on the autosegmental association between features and feature-bearing timing units. The Finnish case examined below is of this type. Hayes was able to deal with some cases of length displacement by "parasitic delinking" rules. As he recognized, this is a purely descriptive move that does not explain *why* the mora migrates. Even worse, we shall see that there are cases of weight displacement which unavoidably violate the no-crossing constraint.

The same problems arise in OT phonology as well, but with the promise of a solution. Compensatory lengthening is triggered by the interaction of markedness constraints that cause a mora (or other weight-bearing unit) to be relinked, and a prosodic faithfulness constraint (such as MAX-μ) that preserves the mora itself. The mora should remain in its original place *unless something forces it to move*. What might that be? I will argue that it is the avoidance of quantitative merger. In other words, weight displacement is a contrast preservation effect, and I propose to formalize it with a version of *super-optimality* as defined in Bidirectional OT, a theory designed to account for recoverability in form/meaning relations (Jäger 2002). I will show that this solution to the realization problem is available in Stratal OT, but not in classic OT or in transderivational OT (classic OT plus transderivational constraints such as sympathy or O/O constraints).

1.2.3 *The Distinctiveness Problem*

How does weight become distinctive, or, in diachronic terms, how does it become phonologized? Specifically, how can compensatory lengthening convert *redundant* weight (such as the predictable moras of short nuclei or the "weight by position" of codas) into *distinctive* vowel or consonant length? Why would the loss of a predictably moraic vowel lead to distinctive vowel length? Why would a syllable become distinctively heavy upon the loss or resyllabification of a predictably heavy coda consonant? The reason this is problematic for OT is that, in the OT reconstruction of Hayes' autosegmental/metrical analysis, the preservation of a mora (or other weight-bearing unit) is triggered by a faithfulness constraint. But faithfulness is a relation between input and output representations (whether expressed by Correspondence constraints or by Containment). Therefore, the mora to which faithfulness triggers compensatory lengthening must be present in the input. But if it is predictable, then its presence in the input cannot be guaranteed, because OT's fundamental postulates of Freedom of Analysis and Richness of the Base requires that any input whatever from GEN is mapped by the language's constraint system into a well-formed output expression of the language. Predictable properties (such as coda weight) may therefore be left unspecified, or specified arbitrarily, in lexical representations. Indeed, it is the possibility of arbitrary input specification that formally reconstructs non-distinctiveness or predictability in OT. However, when a predictable mora of a coda or nucleus is not present in the input, there can be no faithfulness to it, and therefore it shouldn't trigger compensatory lengthening in cases like (1) and (2).

Stratal OT's architecture provides an immediate answer. As in classic OT, predictable structure, including syllable weight and other prosodic information, may be freely specified in lexical representations, in conformity with the principle of the Richness of the Base. However, on the first pass through the stem-level constraint system, the predictable properties will be specified as the language's constraint system dictates, regardless of their lexical representation. From then on they

are indistinguishable from distinctive properties that come fully specified from lexical representations. In particular, the word phonology
receives as input a fully specified representation conforming to the
stem phonology, and that the postlexical phonology in turn receives
as input a fully specified representation conforming to the word level
phonology. The reason compensatory lengthening can translate the
predictable weight of vowels and coda consonants into distinctive
length, then, is that it can operate on representations in which the
moraic value of those elements are already assigned by the constraint
system of a higher stratum.

1.2.4   *The Trigger Problem*

How can apparently weightless elements trigger compensatory lengthening? Why does compensatory lengthening sometimes appear even
when a prevocalic onset consonant is lost, even though onsets are non-
moraic? The trigger problem can be seen as an extreme case of the
distinctiveness problem. Onsets not only *need* not be assigned weight,
because of Richness of the Base, but they *cannot* be assigned weight,
for onsets are universally weightless. And yet there is at least one very
well documented instance where the loss of an onset consonant regularly entrains lengthening of the following nucleus. In the Samothraki
dialect of modern Greek, *r* is deleted in onsets, with compensatory
lengthening word-initially and after a consonant (Katsanis 1996).

(4) /róɣos/   [óoɣus]   'spider *sp.*'
     /ráxi/   [áax̌]   'ridge'
     /ráfi/   [áaf]   'shelf'
     /brostá/   [buustá]   'in front of'
     /vródo/   [vóodu]   'thunder'
     /epítropo/   [pítuupu]   'bishop's representative'

In section 3.1 I show that this is a live synchronic alternation in Samothraki Greek, and propose an analysis according to which the *r* consonants which cause lengthening are initially syllabified as part of the
nucleus and then deleted with compensatory lengthening. The idea of
an "initial syllabification" followed by deletion makes critical use of
Stratal OT's level-ordering and cannot be expressed in other versions
of OT.

2 Compensatory Lengthening in Finnish

2.1 Consonant Gradation as a Trigger of Compensatory Lengthening

2.1.1 A Lenition Chain Shift

Consonant Gradation lenites geminate and singleton stops in the onset of a heavy syllable, and some lenited singletons are deleted in dialectally varying contexts.[3]

(5) a. /mato-t/   →   *madot*   'worms'
     b. /matto-t/   →   *matot*   'carpets'

All dialects of Finnish have essentially the same overall chain shift pattern, conditioned by the same context. A top-level descriptive formulation is:

(6) Consonant Gradation

   After a sonorant in the onset of a heavy syllable
   a. geminate stops are degeminated,
   b. singleton stops are lenited.

The contextual condition "after a sonorant" excludes initial stops and stops in obstruent clusters. We may assume that initial stops are exempted by a dominant positional faithfulness constraint. The failure of obstruents in clusters to undergo lenition follows partly from independent constraints on output syllable structure (e.g. *sd, *sj), though additional constraints (subject to some dialect variation) are required for some cases.[4] Assuming then that the restrictions on the left context are imposed by dominant constraints, we can formulate the constraints that drive Consonant Gradation itself as follows:

---

[3] "In the onset of a heavy syllable" is a nonstandard formulation of the triggering context. It is proposed and defended at length in Kiparsky (2003a), and I will adopt it here without further justification; the characterization of the context is in any case not essential to the present argument.

[4] For example, the absence of Consonant Gradation in a word like /putke-t/ *putket* (*putjet*) 'tubes' does not reflect any hard constraint on -*tj*- clusters, which occur in words like *ketju* 'chain', *budjetti* 'budget'.

(7) a. DEGEMINATION: $^*T_\mu\mu\mu$ (no moraic stop in the onset of a heavy
                                     syllable)
    b. LENITION: $^*T\mu\mu$ (no stop in the onset of a heavy syllable)

Degemination never feeds lenition: see (5b) /matto-t/ → *matot* (not
**madot*) 'carpets'. The two parts of Consonant Gradation form a *chain
shift*: the contrast is not merged but transposed. Chain shifts are a
prima facie descriptive challenge for OT because they involve opacity
by definition; in this case, the problem is to prevent Lenition from
applying to the output of Degemination. At the level of explanation,
chain shifts raise cross-theoretical questions for all of phonology,
synchronic and diachronic. Before proceeding to the compensatory
lengthening data, I will propose an idea for dealing with chain shifts
in OT. The same idea will turn out to solve the core of the realization
problem for compensatory lengthening.

2.1.2 Chain Shifts and Super-Optimality

There are two main ways to deal with phonological chain shifts in
OT. An older approach uses gradient faithfulness constraints (Kirchner 1997). A recently more popular one uses anti-neutralization constraints, which forbid the merger of contrasts (Flemming 2003, Padgett
2003, Kawahara 2003, Kiparsky 2008). Here I propose a new version of
the latter approach, based on Bidirectional Optimization as proposed
for the syntax-semantics interface by Blutner 2000 and Jäger 2000 (see
Blutner, de Hoop, and Hendriks 2006 for an overview). Jäger defines
an Input-Output pair (I, O) as *super-optimal* if there is no more harmonic super-optimal input-output pair with either I or O.

(8) The Input-Output pair (I, O) is *super-optimal* iff

      a. there is no super-optimal (I, O′) ≻ (I, O), and
      b. there is no super-optimal (I′, O) ≻ (I, O)

Although the definition has an air of circularity, Jäger (2002) shows
that as long as the relation ≻ ("more harmonic than") is well-founded,
there is a unique super-optimal candidate for a given I/O pair.

   The semantics/pragmatics literature does not address the question
how (if at all) super-optimality should figure in grammatical systems
with multiple ranked violable constraints. In phonology, we cannot get
very far without addressing this question. A natural idea is to intro-
duce a rankable violable constraint (9).

(9) S(uper)-Opt(imize)

An Input-Output pair (I, O) is super-optimal

The effect of this constraint is to impose a limited bidirectionality on constraint evaluation. Tableau (10) illustrates how this works for Finnish.

(10)

Finnish			S-Opt	$*T_{\mu\mu\mu}$	$*T\mu\mu$	Max-μ	Id(voi)
A	1.	/ottin/ [odin]	*B1			*	
	2. ☞	/ottin/ [otin]			*	*	
	3.	/ottin/ [ottin]	*A2	*	*		
B	1. ☞	/otin/ [odin]					*
	2.	/otin/ [otin]	*B1		*		

Writing "a better match for" as an abbreviation for "a more harmonic super-optimal input-output pair with the same input (or output) as", we have:

(11) a. A1 is not super-optimal, for B1 is a better match for [odin].
      b. A2 is super-optimal, for there is no better match for /ottin/ or for [otin].
      c. A3 is not super-optimal, for A2 is a better match for /ottin/.
      d. B1 is super-optimal, for there is no better match for /otin/ or for [odin].
      e. B2 is not super-optimal, for B1 is a better match for /otin/.

We get this outcome *only* when /d/ is excluded from the input (this is critical for (11a, d). Classic OT has no such conditions (Richness of the Base). In Stratal OT, this is true only for lexical inputs on the first stratum. (A corollary is that the shape of the lexicon is determined exclusively by the stem-level phonology, not by word-level and postlexical phonology). Because in Stratal OT the character of the input at stratum *n* is fixed by the constraint system of stratum *n-1*, the existence or absence of a given input can be checked by reference to the relevant constraint system. For example, if the stem-level phonology prohibits /d/, then stem-level inputs to word-level phonology necessarily lack /d/ On the other hand, if /d/ were included in the input and S-O were highly ranked, then the requirement to maintain distinctions would block every link of the potential chain shift.

In some dialects of Western Finnish, Consonant Gradation is accompanied by displaced compensatory lengthening. We shall see that super-optimality helps explain the displacement effect. First we need a closer look at the triggering process of Consonant Gradation, specifically at how it does or does not affect syllable structure.

2.1.3 Consonant Gradation Across Dialects

The context of Consonant Gradation is for present purposes the same in all dialects, and so is the degemination part of the process, viz. *tt, pp, kk* → *t, p, k*. The main variation occurs in the lenition of singleton stops, especially /k/. The constraint *Tμμ can be satisfied either by lenition to a fricative or approximant, or, where these are not allowed, by deletion. On this point the dialects divide into three groups:[5] a) *Eastern dialects*, /k/ is deleted under gradation.[6] b) *Western dialects*, /k/ is gradated to an approximant, typically *v* next to rounded vowels and *j* next to unrounded front vowels. Deletion occurs before *a*, sometimes before other vowels (details below). Importantly, a deleted intervocalic consonant leaves hiatus or even a glottal stop behind in this dialect (except when the vowels are identical, in which case they optionally fuse into a single long vowel). c) *Standard Finnish*, along with the *Southwestern* dialects around Turku, has the same three reflexes, but in a different distribution. /k/ gradates to *v* between high rounded vowels, to *j* after a liquid before *e*, and elsewhere deletes with hiatus (there is again optional fusion when the vowels are identical). Schematically:

(12)	/kurke-n/	/mäke-n/	/rako-t/
a. Eastern	*ku.ren*	*mäen, mäin*	*raot, raut*
b. Western	*kur.jen*	*mä.jen*	*ra.vot*
c. Southwestern, Standard	*kur.jen*	*mä.en*	*ra.ot*
	'crane' (Gen.)	'hill' (Gen.)	'cracks' (Nom.)

---

[5] Data from Kettunen (1940, maps 40, 45, 54) and Rapola (1966, 47–89).

[6] Except after a nasal (where it either assimilates to it completely, or remains unchanged as *k*), and in a few other contexts.

The map in figure 1 (from Kettunen 1940) shows this major East/West isogloss for /kurke-n/ *kurjen : kuren* 'crane's'.

The crucial generalization of interest to us is that when deletion of a gradated consonant results in a sequence of unlike vowels, the syllable boundary is retained in Western dialects and erased in Eastern dialects.

The three reflexes are historically derived from *k* via *γ*, which got assimilatorily palatalized to *j*, labialized to *v*, and was otherwise deleted, depending on the vowel context. On top of this, the Western dialects have a layer of dissimilatory deletions which apply to *j* and *v*, giving the reflexes of lenited /k/ in this region an extraordinary diversity. The front glide *j* tends to delete before *i* (an OCP effect). In some places it also deleted before *ä* (perhaps by analogy to the corresponding back vowel *a*, with which it alternates in vowel harmony). Only before *e* is *j* stable everywhere. A number of dialects also delete *v* before rounded vowels, perhaps also an OCP-driven deletion. There is also some variation in the realization of lenited /t/ which we can afford to ignore here.

For ease of reference, here is a summary of the basis outcomes for each place of articulation across dialects. (A few supplementary details will be added in the next section.)

(13) a. Lenition of *t*

     i. After vowels (including diphthongs)

         /t/ → *r* (most Southwestern dialects)

         /t/ → *l*, *ð* (stigmatized older pronunciations in parts of Southwestern Finland)

         /t/ → *d* (standard Finnish only)

         /t/ → Ø, sometimes with transitional *j*, *v*, *h* under conditions that depend on the vocalic context and on the dialect (elsewhere).

     ii. After liquids and nasals (*l*, *r*, *n*), lenited *t* undergoes complete assimilation in all dialects. (NB: Only homorganic nasals occur before stops.)

   b. Lenition of *p*

     i. After vowels (including diphthongs) and liquids: /p/ → *v* in all dialects.

     ii. After *m*: complete assimilation in all dialects.

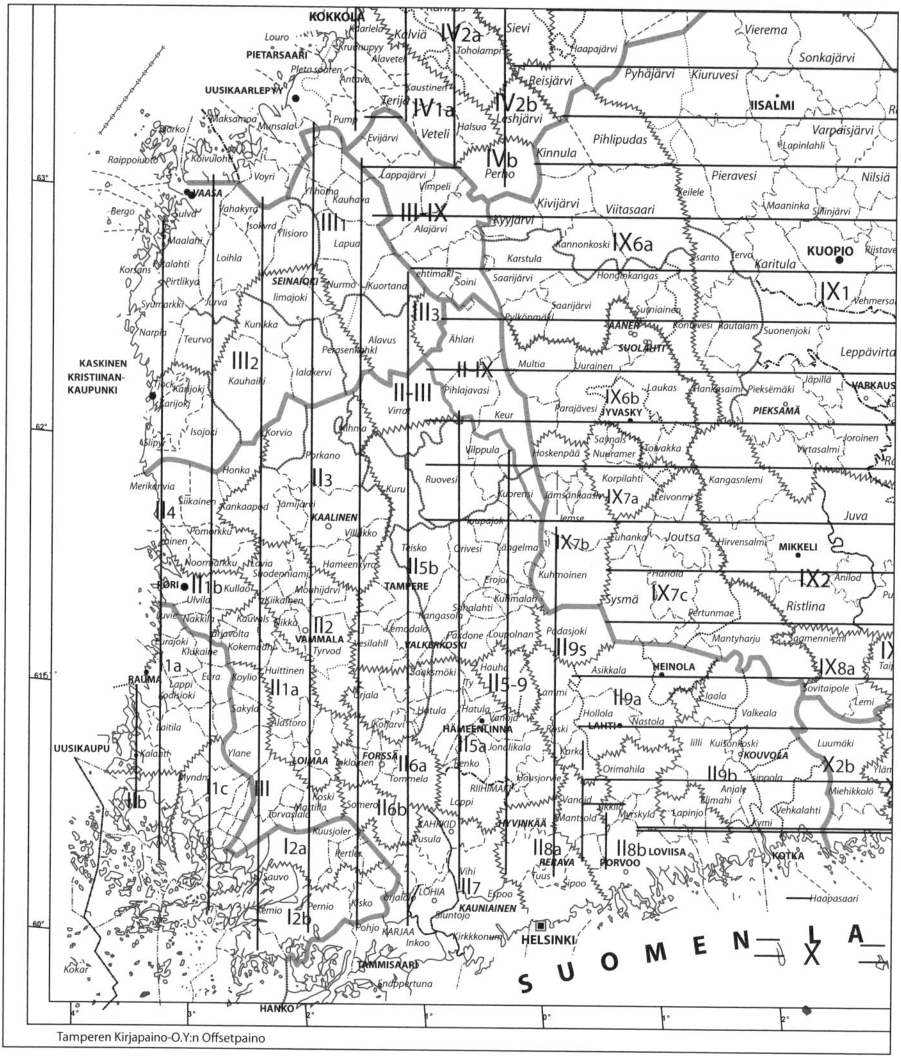

PAUL KIPARSKY

Tamperen Kirjapaino-O.Y:n Offsetpaino

Kettunen Map 54 Legend

kurjen
(Western, Southwestern, Standard)

kuren
(Eastern)

c. Lenition of *k*
  i. After vowels and liquids
  /k/ → *v*, Ø before rounded vowels, /k/ → *j*, Ø before front vowels, /k/ → Ø before *a* (Southwestern dialects, with much fine-grained local variation, and Standard Finnish).
  As above, but /k/ → Ø invariably accompanied by compensatory lengthening of the following vowel (a subset of Southwestern dialects).
  /k/ → Ø across the board, without compensatory lengthening (elsewhere).
  ii. After *ŋ*: complete assimilation in all dialects.

With the basic Consonant Gradation process in place, let us turn to the compensatory lengthening that accompanies it.

2.1.4 *Western Finnish Compensatory Lengthening*

Compensatory lengthening occurs *only* in those Western Finnish dialects where the output of Consonant Gradation is in general not resyllabified. In these dialects it applies across the board wherever the phonological conditions are present. The generalization for these dialects is that *whenever a stop is deleted in the weak grade, and the preceding coda is resyllabified as a result, the vowel of the following syllable becomes long.*

(14) Gradation of -*k*- in env. C__ in Western Finnish

  a. *k* → Ø + V̄ before *a*
   /jalka-t/ → *ja.laat* 'feet, legs'
  b. *k* → *j* or Ø + V̄ before *i, ä*, depending on the dialect
   nälkä-n/ → *näl.jän* ~ *nä.lään* 'hunger' (Gen.)
   /kulke-i-t/ → *kul.jit* ~ *ku.liit* 'you went'
   /arka-ista-a/ → *ar.jis.taa* ~ *ariistaa* 'to be shy'
  c. *k* → *v* or Ø + V̄ before *o, u, ö, y*, depending on the dialect
   /pelko-tta-n/ → *pel.vo.tan* ~ *pe.loo.tan* 'I frighten'
   /halko-t/ → *hal.vot* ~ *ha.loot* 'logs'
   /hylky-t/ → *hyl.vyt* ~ *hy.lyyt* 'wrecks'
  d. *k* → *j* before *e* (no deletion, no lengthening)
   /kurke-t/ → *kur.jet* 'cranes'
   /kulke-n/ → *kul.jen* 'I go'
   /lohke-ttu/ → *loh.jet.tu* 'split' (pp.)

That the vowel lengthening is truly compensatory is established by the following facts. It takes place only when deletion triggers resyllabification of a coda ($CVC_i.C_jVC$ → $CV.C_iVVC$). Gradation by itself never triggers lengthening. When it deletes an intervocalic consonant, no mora is lost, and therefore no lengthening occurs:

(15) /mäke-t/ → mä.et (~ mä.jet)   'hills'   (*mä.eet, *mä.jeet)
     /teko-t/ → te.ot (~ te.vot)   'deeds'   (*te.oot, *te.voot)

When it results in a lenited consonant (*j, v,* or a nasal), it never triggers lengthening:

(16) /kurke-t/ → kur.jet   'cranes'   (*kur.jeet)
     /vehkeke/ → veh.jeK   'device'   (*veh.jeeK)
     /henke-n/ → hengen [-ŋ.ŋ-]   'breath, life' (*hen.geen)
     (Gen.)

Underlying /j/ or /v/ (there is no underlying /ɣ/) do not delete, therefore trigger no lengthening.

(17) /karja/ → kar.ja   'cattle'   (*ka.raa, *ka.ra)
     /velje-n/ → vel.jen   'brother's'   (*ve.leen, *ve.len)
     /veräjä/ → ve.rä.jä   'gate'   (*veräjää, *verää)
     /arvo-n/ → ar.von (Gen.)   'value'   (*a.roon, *a.ron)

Even where the deletion of the gradated consonant is optional, the resyllabification and compensatory lengthening attendant on it are obligatory. Lengthening takes place *always* and *only* when the preceding coda is resyllabified as an onset. So, whenever a post consonantal consonant is optionally deleted in the compensatory lengthening dialects, there are exactly two outputs, never four.[7]

(18) /kulke-i-n/ → kul.jin ~ ku.liin   'I went'   (*ku.lin, *ku.ljiin)
     /halko-t/ → hal.vot ~ ha.loot   'logs'   (*ha.lot, *hal.voot)

Finally, even though it is fed by Consonant Gradation, which is opaque and has a number of lexical and morphological exceptions, compensatory lengthening itself is purely phonologically conditioned. It applies across all morphological categories—nouns and verbs, inflectional and derivational. It is a productive, exceptionless process, not directly triggered by Consonant Gradation, but responding to such resyllabification as Consonant Gradation may cause.

---

[7] Standard Finnish, which has no compensatory lengthening, has *kuljin* and *halot.*

2.1.5 *Interaction with Other Quantitative Constraints*

Diphthongs don't undergo compensatory lengthening. That is due to a general restriction against long nuclei in Finnish word-level phonology, where Consonant Gradation takes effect.

(19) /nahka-i-ksi/ > *nahkoiksi ~ nahoiksi* (*nahooiksi*) 'skins' (Translative).

The relevant constraint is justified in full in Kiparsky (2003a).

In a wedge-like area that intrudes from Eastern Finland into the West (polka-dotted in Kettunen's map reproduced in Figure 2 below), consonants are automatically lengthened between a stressed short vowel (in particular, a word-initial short vowel) and a long vowel, e.g. /kala-an/ → *kallaan* (Iness.) 'into the fish'. This lengthening is prosodically motivated by the moraic trochee foot structure of Finnish. CV́.CVV(C) is too long to be one moraic trochee, and too short to be two moraic trochees. Lengthening allows such a sequence to be parsed into two normal moraic trochees $(CV́C)_\phi(CVV)_\phi$. In the dialects where the consonant lengthening applies, it applies across the board, both before original long vowels, and before those long vowels that come from the compensatory lengthening process discussed above. As the map shows, the distribution of *jallaan* 'foot' (Gen.) from /jalka-n/ in the wedge area exactly matches that of *kallaan* from /kala-an/ 'fish' (Iness.). The former is derived by Consonant Gradation and deletion with compensatory vowel lengthening followed by consonant lengthening (/jalka-n/ > *jal.ɣan* > *ja.laan* > *jal.laan*), the latter directly from the underlying form by consonant lengthening (/kala-an/ > *kal.laan*). Together with the regional variation in the scope of *j-* and *v-* deletion described above, this yields three outputs in forms with post consonantal /k/:

(20) a. /nälkä-n/ → *näl.jän, nä.lään, näl.lään* 'hunger' (Gen.)
b. /kulj-i-n/ → *kul.jin, ku.liin, kul.liin* 'I went'
c. /pelko-n/ → *pel.von, pe.loon, pel.loon* 'fear' (Gen.)
d. /alku-n/ → *al.vun, a.luun, al.luun* 'beginning' (Gen.)
e. /hylky-n/ → *hyl.jyn, hy.lyyn, hyl.lyyn* 'wreck' (Gen.)
f. /tahko-n/ → *tah.von, ta.hoon, tah.hoon* 'whetstone' (Gen.)
g. /poika-n/ → *poi.jan, po.jaan, poi.jaan* 'boy' (Gen.)

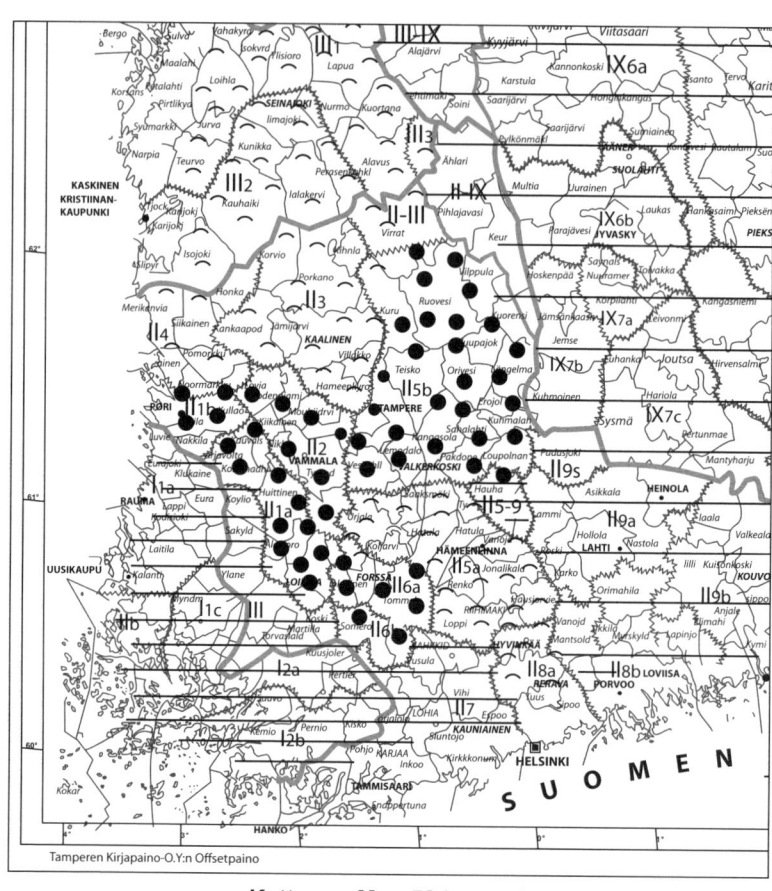

Kettunen Map 52 Legend

jallān   jalan   jalān

To repeat, the gemination in compensatorily lengthened forms such as (20b) *kul.liin* is phonologically conditioned and has the same distribution as gemination in basic *CV.CVV* sequences.

2.2   Coping with Compensatory Lengthening

2.2.1   Problem 1: Compensatory Lengthening Self-Destructively Feeds Consonant Lengthening

Feeding order's reputation of being problem-free for parallel OT is not quite deserved. In the preceding section I justified the following synchronic derivations for the lengthening dialects:

(21) Input   /alku-n/   /talo-on/
      Gradation with C.L.   aluun   —
      Gemination   alluun   talloon

This is an instance of "self-destructive feeding" (Bakovic 2007). A theory that is committed to a one-step derivation, such as parallel OT, must telescope compensatory vowel lengthening and the prosodically driven consonant gemination into a single mapping, /alku-n/ → *alluun*. This loses sight of the motivation of both lengthening processes. The vowel lengthening becomes gratuitous. It can no longer be understood as compensatory. Since the geminated consonant in *alluun* already preserves the mora, what is the point of lengthening the vowel of the second syllable? The wrong mapping /alku-n/ → **allun* should beat /alku-n/ → *alluun* on moraic faithfulness. The wrong mapping can also not be motivated prosodically, for **allun* is at least as good as *alluun*. In short, it seems that the actual output is not optimal on any constraint ranking that can be justified for Finnish phonology. I.e. it is harmonically bounded.

Nor is it clear that OT-CC (McCarthy 2007) can do any better. This theory reconstructs derivations in a parallel guise, as chains leading by successive gradual harmonic improvements to an optimal output. Each link in such a chain must improve on the previous one *within a single constraint system*. The two-step derivation in (21) does not satisfy this requirement. The compensatory lengthening of the second syllable's vowel serves weight conservation but makes the foot structure *worse*, while the consonant gemination improves foot structure but scores *worse* on weight conservation (because it adds a mora). This is synchronically a kind of "Duke of York" derivation, a type questioned by McCarthy (2003) but actually cross-linguistically very well motivated.[8]

2.2.2   Problem 2: Line-Crossing

Quite apart from this interaction with consonant lengthening, Western Finnish compensatory lengthening represents one of the few types of cases that Hayes' (1989) theory can't handle, even descriptively. Simple delinking and reaffiliation predicts the wrong forms *aalun* or *allun*, just as in the Greek example (1).

(22)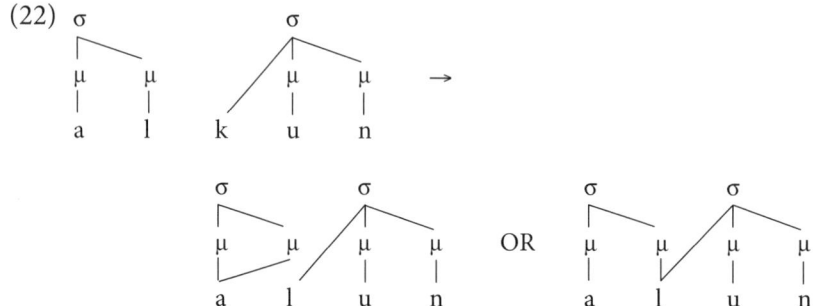

Operations such as "double flop" and "parasitic delinking" (Hayes 1989) won't get the desired derivation /alku-n/ → *aluun*, for *l* and the mora to which it is affiliated must cross paths to reach their new affiliations, in violation of the line-crossing prohibition.

(23)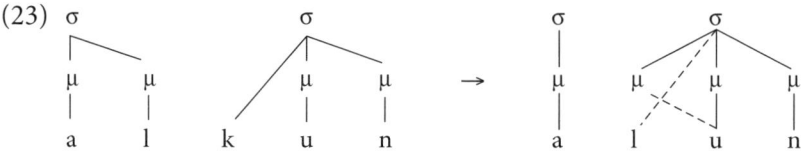

In OT (classic or OT-CC) the line-crossing violation is not necessarily a problem anymore, because the constraint that forbids it can be assumed to be violable like any other constraint. A would-be OT

---

[8] The grand old Duke of York,
He had ten thousand men;
He marched them up to the top of the hill,
And he marched them down again.
Traditional nursery rhyme.

solution still has the onus of identifying the constraint that forces the line-crossing violation and of motivating its high ranking. I will put forward a constraint with that effect in the next section, and show that it only works in Stratal OT.

2.2.3 *Problem 3: Faithfulness to Positional Weight*

A major hurdle for the treatment of compensatory lengthening in classic OT and OT-CC is that it requires *faithfulness to positional weight*. Unlike quantity and syllabicity, positional weight is apparently never distinctive. This implies that it is not subject to Faithfulness, an idea articulated in different ways in Bermúdez-Otero (2001), Campos-Astorkiza (2004), and McCarthy (2007). In other words, although vowel lengthening, consonant gemination, glide formation, and vowel contraction are all subject to Faithfulness constraints, there are no MAX-μ constraints and no DEP-μ constraints. But it is precisely the moraic status of coda consonants that really needs to be subject to Faithfulness constraints for Finnish compensatory lengthening to happen. And in any case, even if the moraic status of coda consonants *were* subject to MAX-μ and DEP-μ constraints, Richness of the Base entails that predictably moraic codas cannot be guaranteed to be underlyingly specified as moraic; therefore their loss or resyllabification does not necessarily affect syllable weight. So we are left with the question why resyllabification of codas leads obligatorily to compensatory lengthening in these dialects.

In OT-CC there are even deeper reasons why moras can't be protected by Faithfulness (McCarthy 2007, 72–77). McCarthy proposes that "IdentONS and other syllable-sensitive positional faithfulness constraints can never *affect* syllabification" (2007, 75) and that "moras can be freely added or removed at no cost in Faithfulness, but changes in quantity and syllabicity violate Ident constraints" (2007, 77).[9]

2.2.4 *Problem 4: The Missing Link*

Western Finnish compensatory lengthening is difficult for OT-CC for another reason as well. An OT-CC derivation (a *candidate chain*)

---

[9] The distinction between merely adding/deleting moras and changing quantity is actually tricky to draw formally, since quantity is represented precisely by moras, but let us assume for the sake of the discussion that it is achieved somehow. Shaw (2007) tackles compensatory lengthening in OT-CC, although I believe his approach does not generalize to the Finnish case.

monotonically accumulates unfaithful mappings by minimal steps
(localized unfaithful mappings). It is not clear how such a chain could
be formed between the input /alku-n/ and the output *aluun*.

(24)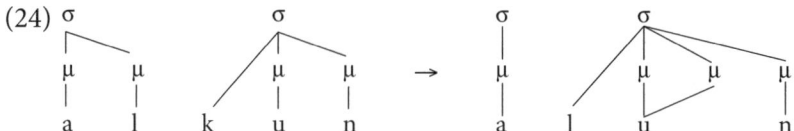

Even if there were moraic/syllabic Faithfulness, and the presence of
underlying moras were ensured, the Western Finnish compensatory
lengthening would still be impossible under the OT-CC regime. The
two available options are: a chain that has an intermediate link that
does not exist in the language, such as *hal.yon* (there is no *ɣ in Finnish), and a chain that has an intermediate link that is well-formed in
the language, such as *ha.lon*. The former chain is ruled out because any
such link introduces a new infraction of an undominated markedness
constraint (such as *ɣ) that dominates Max-C, and therefore cannot
be the best violation, as required. The latter chain is ruled out because
any intermediate link that is well-formed in the language will "col-
lide" with *actual* forms derived from inputs of the same shape, which
do *not* undergo deletion and compensatory lengthening. For example,
if /halko-t/ → *hal.vot* → *ha.loot* 'logs', then why not also /arvo-t/ →
ar.vot → **a.root* 'values'? And if /halko-t/ → *ha.lot* → *ha.loot*, then
why not also /talo-t/ → *ta.lot* → **ta.loot* 'houses'?

"Grandfathering" effects à la Comparative Markedness (McCarthy
2003) provide a solution within transderivational OT, at least at the
technical level. The idea is that "old" (underived) sequences of the form
"*v* + short vowel" would be frozen by Faithfulness, whereas "new"
instances of such sequences with *v* from /k/ *would* undergo lengthening. After lengthening, the triggering consonant would be deleted,
wiping out the context of the lengthening.

Even if Comparative Markedness can get the compensatory lengthening itself, it does not have the resources to account for its opacity
in the gemination dialects, so transderivational OT would still require
OT-CC. But OT-CC's gradualness requirement is at odds with the
leapfrogging derivations that Comparative Markedness provides. So
OT-CC has displaced Comparative Markedness for what appear to be
good reasons, and it cannot simply be added back in. This is not to say

that no combination of OT-CC and Comparative Markedness would be coherent, but it remains to be seen whether one can be found.

2.3 A Stratal OT Solution

2.3.1 Why Positional Weight Counts
Stratal OT dictates that syllabification takes place at the first pass through the constraint system. At the word level, moras assigned at the stem-level are indistinguishable from underlying moras (if there are any). Word-level Faithfulness effects apply to both alike. This is why compensatory lengthening can translate predictable weight into distinctive length through prosodic Faithfulness.

Let us first see how Consonant Gradation triggers resyllabification by ONSET, and consequent compensatory lengthening by MAX-μ. We show the word-level derivation, whose input in this case is just the syllabified underlying form.

(25)

Western Finnish		*Tμμ	MAX-μ	ONSET	MAX-C
Input (from stem level): /hal.kon/					
a.	hal.kon	*			
b.	ha.lon		*		*
c.	hal.on			*	*
d.	ha.loon				*

2.3.2 Super-Optimality Again
Tableau (25) shows why an output with compensatory lengthening is preferred to an output without compensatory lengthening, but it does not show why compensatory lengthening is realized on the vowel of the second syllable rather than somewhere else, i.e. why the output is *haloon* rather than **haalon* or **hallon*. This is what we referred to as the realization problem. From the perspective of locality, the outcome in Finnish is especially surprising. Why should the length of the first syllable's resyllabified coda migrate to the *second* syllable of the word?

The obvious answer is that any lengthening in the first syllable would produce wholesale mergers of important quantitative distinctions of Finnish. Lengthening of an unstressed syllable does not produce any merger, since there are no unstressed long nuclei, and in particular no unstressed long vowels, at this level of representation (Kiparsky 2003).

We already have the technology to formalize this idea. SUPER-OPTI-MALITY, if highly ranked, correctly predicts the locus of compensatory lengthening in Finnish. The derivations which take /hal.kon/ to *haa.lon, *hal.lon, *hal.kon and *ha.lon are not super-optimal because each of these output has a better input match, respectively /haa.lon/, /hal.lon/, /halk.kon/, ha.lon/. These outputs are therefore ruled out. The derivations /hal.kon/ → hal.kon and /hal.kon/ → ha.lon also fail to qualify for another reason, namely that the input has a better output match. This latter reason also rules out /hal.kon/ → *hal.γon, whose output violates *γ. But /hal.kon/ → ha.loon is super-optimal because ha.loon has no better input match, /ha.loon/ not being a possible stem-level output (for, as already stated, the stem level has no unstressed long vowels) and /hal.kon/ has no better output match. The following tableau represents these considerations explicitly.

(26)

Western Finnish		S-Opt	*Tμμ	*γ	Max-μ	Onset	Max-C
Input (from stem level): /hal.kon/							
a.	hal.kon	*	*				
b.	ha.lon	*			*		*
c.	hal.on	*				*	*
d.	haa.lon	*					*
e.	hal.lon	*					
f. ☞	ha.loon						*
g.	hal.von	*					
h.	hal.γon	*		*			

Two further points are of interest here. First, the lengthening of the first syllable is blocked globally, not just when it would result in a merger of actual lexical items. For example, *haalon and *hallon are not actual words of Finnish (as far as I know), but compensatory lengthening in /hal.kon/ → haloon is still displaced to the second syllable. This confirms the choice of SUPER-OPTIMALITY (or some other anti-neutralization constraint defined over classes of representations), over a constraint which penalizes homonymy between individual lexical items.

Secondly, unlike compensatory lengthening, the gemination process in (20) neutralizes length contrasts with impunity. For example, /olka-n/ → *olaan* → *ollaan* 'shoulder' (Gen.) merges with *ollaan* 'be' (3.P.Passive). This indicates that it operates at a level where it outranks SUPER-OPTIMALITY. This is presumably the postlexical phonology. By providing independent evidence that the shortening of the first syllable by Consonant Gradation with compensatory lengthening and the subsequent relengthening of the first syllable are separate processes, it confirms the Duke of York character of the derivation.

2.3.3   *Eastern Finnish*

The remaining question is why there is no compensatory lengthening in Eastern Finnish. Since compensatory lengthening is the result of high-ranking prosodic faithfulness, its absence would be expected in dialects that rank prosodic faithfulness low. That Eastern Finnish dialects do rank prosodic faithfulness low is suggested by the fact that these dialects regularly contract any hiatus created by consonant gradation, e.g. /teko-t/ → *teot, teut*, or *te.vot* 'deeds', /raaka-t/ → *raat, roat*, rather than *te.ot, raa.at* as found in various places in Southwestern Finland. The Western dialects optimize syllable structure even at the price of losing a mora or a syllable, while the Eastern dialects preserve syllables and moras even at the expense of hiatus. Compensatory lengthening introduces a type of syllable otherwise absent at this level of representation, namely unstressed long vowels. The absence of compensatory lengthening in Eastern dialects fits well with the other evidence for their more aggressive syllable structure constraints.

2.3.4   *Conclusion*

A Stratal OT constraint system imposes syllable structure on inputs at the stem level. At the word level, moras assigned at the stem-level have the same status as underlying moras with respect to Faithfulness constraints. In this way, predictable weight can be manifested as distinctive length. Seen in this light, compensatory lengthening is an instance of the much more widespread phenomenon of *derived contrast*, and, in diachronic phonology, *secondary split*.

3   Samothraki Greek

3.1   An Unusual Case of Compensatory Lengthening

3.1.1   Loss of Onsets as the Trigger

The Greek dialect spoken on the island of Samothraki off the coast of
Trace regularly deletes prevocalic *r* in onsets (Heisenberg 1934, Newton 1972a, b, Katsanis 1996). Intervocalic *r* is simply lost, and a resulting sequence of identical vowels is contracted into a long vowel (here
transcribed as a geminate vowel, in accord with the cited sources).[10]

(27)   /γáðaros/   [γáðaus]   'donkey'
       /γaðaro-ráxi/   [γaðáax̌]   'Donkey Ridge'
       /píre/   [píi]   'took's
       /saradapodarúsa/   [saadapudaúsa]   'millipede'
       /éγðera/   [éγðaa]   'flayed (1.Sg.)'

Elsewhere, the deletion of onset *r* results in compensatory lengthening
of the nucleus.

(28)   /róγos/   [óoγus]   'spider *sp.*'
       /ráxi/   [áax̌]   'ridge'
       /iγrí/   [ɣ̌ɨɨ]   'wet' (Pl.)
       /brostá/   [buustá]   'in front of'
       /vródo/   [vóodu]   'thunder'
       /epítropo/   [pítuupu]   'bishop's representative'

Before a consonant and word-finally, *r* is retained.

(29)   /samári/   [samár]   'packsaddle'
       /babúri/   [babúr]   'bee-fly' (Bombylius *sp.*)
       /γrjá/   [γɨrɣ̌á]   'old woman'
       /kryás/   [kɨrɣ̌ás]   'meat'
       /aγrjá/   [aγɨrɣ̌á]   'wild' (plant *sp.*)
       /ávrjo/   [ávɨrɣ̌ü]   'tomorrow'

---

[10] In Samothraki examples, *y* denotes a front glide/approximant. In the Finnish
examples cited above, it denotes a front rounded vowel, and *j* a front glide/approxim-
ant, in accord with the orthography.

3.1.2 *Compensatory Lengthening is Synchronically Active*

Samothraki fully participates in the Northern Greek chain shift of nonlow unstressed vowels.

(30) a. Unstressed *i, u* are deleted (subject to syllabic constraints)
　　 b. Unstressed *e, o* are raised to *i, u*

(31) /mérmig-as/　[mérmigas]　/mermíg-i/　[mirmíǵ]　'ant'
　　 /kórak-as/　　[kóok-as]　　/korák-i/　　[kuáḱ]　　'raven'
　　 /vun-ós/　　　[vnós]　　　　/vun-já/　　[vuñá]　　'mountain(s)'
　　 /míl-i/　　　　[miĺ]　　　　　/-mil-os/　　[-mlus]　　'mill'
　　 　　　　　　　　　　　　　　　　　　　　(in *Palió-mlus*)
　　 /pétr-a/　　　[pétaa]　　　　/-petres/　　[-pitiis]　'rocks'
　　 　　　　　　　　　　　　　　　　　　　　(in *Tsakmakó-pitiis*)

The deletion of unstressed high vowels is blocked by some syllable structure constraints, but it nevertheless expands the repertoire of consonant clusters to some extent. Among initial clusters that arise only by vowel deletion are those with falling sonority, and initial geminates:

(32) /mikr-ó/　　[mkóo]　　'little'
　　 /mikr-í/　　　[mkíi]　　'little' (Pl.)
　　 /kukí/　　　　[kḱí]　　'fava bean'
　　 /ðikásu/　　　[ðkás]　　'your own'

The vowel shift bleeds *r*-deletion,

(33) /rizári/　　[rzár]　　'plant *sp.*' (*Rubia tinctorum*)
　　 /riáki/　　　[rɣák]　　'spring'

and results in productive synchronic *r/Ø* alternations.

(34) /mér-os/　　　*méus*　　/mér-ia/　　　*méŕɣa*　　'place(s)'
　　 /bábur-as/　　*bábuas*　/babúr-i/　　　*babúr*　　'bee-fly'
　　 /ɣliɣór-is/　　*ɣliɣórs*　/ɣliɣor-úðis/　*ɣliɣuúðs*　(names)
　　 /liutér-is/　　*liutérs*　/liuter-úðis/　*liutiúðs*　(names)
　　 /láskar-is/　　*láskars*　/laskar-úðias/　*laskaúðas*　(names)
　　 /sotér-is/　　　*sutírs*　/soter-élias/　*sutiélýas*　(names)

Another piece of evidence that *r*-deletion is synchronically alive is that *r* is restored when the prevocalic context is lost through other changes. This can be seen in a comparison of Heisenberg's data from the 1920s with the modern dialect recorded in Katsanis (1996). It seems that prevocalic *i* as seen in the older form of the dialect underwent glide formation to *y*, eliminating the context for deletion of *r* and causing it to reappear.

(35) a. /ávrio/   *áviü*   'tomorrow'   (older)
         /ávrjo/   *ávi̯rýu*   'tomorrow'   (more recent)
      b. /θirío/   *θiíu*   'beast'   (older)
         /θirjó/   *θirýó*   'beast'   (more recent)
      c. /rufó/   *iifó*   'belch'   (older)
         /rfó/   *rfó*   'belch'   (more recent)

3.1.3 Previous Proposals

In a brief section on Samothraki compensatory lengthening, Hayes (1989) suggested that the process actually was insertion of a prothetic vowel followed by loss of intervocalic *r*, viz. $rV \to VrV \to VV$. Hayes' epenthesis analysis however predicts that $Cr\acute{V}$ should merge with original $CVr\acute{V}$, which is not the case. In fact, there is an accentual contrast between them:

(36) a. $r\acute{V} \to \acute{V}V$ (never $V\acute{V}$)
         e.g. *θrími̯* → *θíim* → *θíiða*
      b. but $Vr\acute{V}$ usually → $V\acute{V}$
         e.g. *xará* → *xaá*

This results in a new accentual contrast $\acute{V}V : V\acute{V}$, similar to the ancient Greek acute:circumflex opposition, though obviously quite unrelated to it historically. The same accentual contrast can result when *r*-deletion is fed by *i*-, *u*- deletion:

(37) a. /ɣurúni/   → *ɣrúń   → *ɣúuń*   'pig'
         /ɣorúni/   → *ɣurúń   → *ɣuúń*   'bee-fly'
      b. /kirízo/   → *kríizu   → *kíizu*
         /kerízo/   → *kirízu   → *kiízu*

Exceptions to the accent generalization do occur, but in one direction only, and seem to be due to a lexical diffusion process $V\acute{V} > \acute{V}V$, often manifested in coexisting variant forms.

(38) *katsará* → *katsaá* ~ *katsáa*   'curly'
      karávi → *kaáv* ~ *káav*   'boat'
      katurúsan → *katuúsan* ~ *katúusan*   'they pissed'

One might suppose that *rV* sequences underwent metathesis, followed by loss of the coda *r*: *rV* → *Vr* → *VV*. The difficulty then is how to keep the metathesized *Vr* from /rV/ distinct from original *Vr*, which is retained. Modern Samothraki freely allows coda *-r*.

(39) *tsaflárs*   (place name)
      fanárýa   'beacons' (place name)
      samár   'packsaddle'

Kavitskaya (2002, 99) suggests that *r* was reinterpreted as vowel length due to its acoustic similarity to vowels. This is probably not quite right because the deletion of *r* (at least as far as it is phonologically active) applies just to *onsets*, while it is coda *r* that would normally be more similar to a vowel than onset *r*. Moreover, Kavitskaya's proposal for Samothraki is in a sense too easy. It involves giving up either the well-supported generalization that compensatory lengthening is weight-preserving, or the equally well-supported generalization that onsets are weightless.

Topintzi (2006) draws attention to the incompatibility of Samothraki compensatory lengthening with OT, and argues that it requires resurrecting segment-based theories of compensatory lengthening. She suggests that *r* is placeless, hence disallowed as an onset. To drive compensatory lengthening she proposes a constraint PosCorr which requires that an input segment must have an output correspondent either segmentally, by means of a *root node*, or prosodically by means of moras. This would be an unfortunate move because segment-based theories predict a range of unattested types of compensatory lengthening, and leave no room for the standard explanation of the type of compensatory lengthening that is triggered by desyllabifica-tion, as in the Pali example in (2), the Luganda example in (3), and the Kihehe and Kimatuumbi cases of *iV-* → *yVV-* well-known from Odden (1996).

Nevertheless I think that Kavitskaya's and Topintzi's proposals each contain an insight which I will adopt. Kavitskaya's idea that *r* is in some sense vowel-like, and Topintzi's idea that it is disallowed as an onset can be combined in a natural way in the moraic theory of syl-lable structure.

3.2   A Stratal OT Account

3.2.1   The Preference for Low-Sonority Onsets

I propose to base the explanation of Samothraki compensatory length-ening on the well-established fact that high-sonority segments do not make good onsets. There are quite a few languages which have /r/ but exclude it from word-initial position, sometimes even syllable-initial positions (de Lacy 2000, Smith 2003, Flack 2007). The Korean native vocabulary has no syllable-initial liquids. Languages with no initial liq-uids include Sestu Campidanian Sardinian (Bolognesi 1998), Basque (Hualde and de Urbina 2003, 29), Piro (Matteson 1965), Mbabaram (Dixon 1991), Golin (Bunn and Bunn 1970), Guugu Yimidhirr (Havi-land 1979), Pitta-Pitta (Blake and Breen 1971), Kuman (Blevins 1994), Telefol (Healey and Healey 1977), Chalcatongo Mixtec (Macaulay 1996), West Greenlandic (Fortescue 1984), Nganasan (Helimski 1998a, 482), Selkup (Helimski 1998b), Northern Bangla (Kamrupa, Bhattacharya 1999) and Japanese (Old Japanese, and modern Japanese Yamato and mimetic stems, Itô and Mester 1993). Most languages of the Dravidian, Tungus, Turkic (Kornfilt 1997, 492), and Yeniseyan families belong. Even some older Indo-European languages lack initial r- (Hittite and Classical Greek).[11]

The ban on sonorous onsets often starts from the top of the sonority hierarchy, so that it also encompasses the still more sonorous glides. Languages that lack initial liquids often lack initial glides. There are however languages which ban onset r- in positions that ostensibly allow glides. Smith (2003) argues that in languages that allow syllable-initial glides but not liquids, the glides are part of the nucleus, i.e. moraic rather than true onsets. There is indeed independent evidence for nuclear/moraic onglides in at least some of these languages, including Toda (Emeneau 1984) and Korean (Sohn 1987). Nuclear/moraic onglides are also found in Spanish (Harris 1983, Harris and Kaisse 1999), French (Kaye and Lowenstamm 1984), Slovak (Rubach 1998), English (Davis and Hammond 1995) and Mizo (Vijayakrishnan MS.). For example, in Spanish and Mizo, sequences of the form *iV* always count as heavy syllables for the purpose of stress assignment and phonotactics.

---

[11] The initial r- of Greek is voiceless/aspirated, which is why it is written with the rough breathing, and transliterated as rh-.

For concreteness, let us assume the definition of sonority in terms of major class features along the lines of Zec (1994) and Clements (1990):

(40)

	Obstruents	Nasals	Liquids	Rhotics	Vowels
non-consonantal	–	–	–	–	+
approximant	–	–	–	+	+
vocalic	–	–	+	+	+
sonorant	–	+	+	+	+

Prince and Smolensky (2004) work out a theory of syllabification which accesses the sonority hierarchy from both ends–from the top through a constraint family which prohibits segments from syllable margins, and from the bottom by a constraint family which prohibits segments from peaks. The former applies in the core cases to the most sonorous segments and in more general versions to successively less sonorous segments, and the latter applies in the core case to the least sonorous segments and in more general versions to successively more sonorous cases.

I will adopt a slightly different approach here. In addition to the familiar minimum sonority licensing constraints on syllables and moras proposed by Zec and others,

(41) Minimum sonority licensing constraints:

    a. $\mu/\sigma \supset$ [- cons, +low]   a mora/syll. must be licensed by a
    b. $\mu/\sigma \supset$ [- cons]   ... by a, i, u
    c. $\mu/\sigma \supset$ [+son, +approx] ... by a, i, u, r
    d. $\mu/\sigma \supset$ [+son, -nasal]   ... by a, i, u, r, l
    e. $\mu/\sigma \supset$ [+son]   ... by a, i, u, r, l, nasals
    f. ...

let us assume a complementary set of maximum sonority licensing constraints on sonorous segments.

(42) Maximum sonority licensing constraints:

$$\begin{array}{lll}
\text{a.} & [\text{-cons, +low}] \supset \mu/\sigma & a \text{ must by licensed by a mora/syll.} \\
\text{b.} & [\text{-cons}] \supset \mu/\sigma & a, i, u \ldots \\
\text{c.} & [\text{+son, +approx}] \supset \mu/\sigma & a, i, u, r \ldots \\
\text{d.} & [\text{+son,-nasal}] \supset \mu/\sigma & a, i, u, r, l \ldots \\
\text{e.} & [\text{+son}] \supset \mu/\sigma & a, i, u, r, l, \text{ nasals} \ldots \\
\text{f.} & \ldots &
\end{array}$$

We can now get the syllable typology by interspersing the standard syllable structure constraints with the sonority constraints in the constraint hierarchy. A simple example: in Spanish, *ye* is a complex nucleus, and in English it is a CV sequence. In terms of our proposal, this means that the Spanish ranking is (42b) $\gg$ ONSET, while the English ranking is ONSET $\gg$ (42b):

(43)

			(42b)	Onset
1a	☞	ia		*
1b		ya	*	

			Onset	(42b)
2a		ia	*	
2b	☞	ya		*

A prediction made by this approach (but not by the classic OT syllable theory) is that, although there are languages where every segment wants to be moraic/syllabic (Berber, famously), there are no languages where every segment wants to be non-moraic/non-syllabic. E.g. no language syllabifies /pit/ as [pyVt], with an epenthetic vowel to get the segments into the margin.

How is the prohibition of onset *r* enforced? Just as satisfaction of the constraints in (41) is achieved by many different processes, including sonorization of coda segments, vocalic epenthesis, and resyllabification, so the constraints in (42) are also implemented by many different processes:

(44) How to avoid sonorous onsets

    a. Vocalization/prothesis: *ya* → *iya*
    b. Deletion: *ya* → *a*
       Proto-Nyulnyulan *wamba* 'man' (Nyikina, Yawuru, Warrwa *wamba*) > Bardi *amba*.[12]
    c. Fortition: *ya* → *ja*
       Indic **y-* > *j-*
    d. Anti-gemination: *aya* ↛ *ayya* even when otherwise VCV → VCCV
       Germanic **iyya* > *iddja*, **uwwa* > *uggwa*
    e. Incorporation into nucleus: diphthongal *ia*
       Italian, Spanish

The same processes are in principle available for *r*, and indeed all are attested.

(45) How to avoid initial *r-*

    a. Prothesis: *ra* → *ara*
       Latin *rana* 'frog' > Campidanian *ará:na*, similarly Basque
    b. Deletion: *ra* > *a*
       North Bangla (Kamrup) *ram* → *am*
    c. Fortition: *ra* → *na* (Korean)
    d. Anti-gemination
       In Sanskrit, *r* is the only consonant which does not occur geminated. In sandhi, *rr* is degeminated with compensatory lengthening: *VrrV* → *v̄rV*[13]
    e. Incorporation into nucleus: diphthongal *ra*

Since glides can be incorporated into the syllabic nucleus as moraic elements, as in Spanish and Mizo, we expect that the same could happen to *r-*. The result would be a nucleus of the form *ra*, technically a rising diphthong. My proposal is that this rather surprising development is just what happened in Samothraki.

---

[12] "Most vowel initial words in Bardi result from a fairly recent phonological change whereby word initial glides w and v were deleted." (McGregor 2004).

[13] Likewise, in Germanic *r* is the only C which does not undergo West Germanic C-gemination: /sitjan/ → [sit.tan], but /nerjan/ = [ner.jan] (↛ *[ner.ran]).

3.2.2 *Samothraki*

According to the proposed scenario, then, the fate of Samothraki *r* was as follows. At some point, glides were lost in the language.[14] In Samothraki, the constraint on onsets was then further tightened by one notch: not only *i*, *u*, but also *r* had to be moraic. Formally, (42c) comes to be ranked high, prohibiting onset glides and onset *r*. To conform to this sonority constraint, initial preconsonantal *r*- (as in *rzári*) became moraic, either syllabic or semisyllabic.[15] The semisyllabic structure was needed anyway for initial geminates, as in /kukí/ [kkí], since there is really no other way of characterizing geminates than to make them moraic. In prevocalic position, there are no syllabic or semisyllabic segments, so this parse is not available. Consequently the only remaining option for prevocalic /r/ is to incorporate it into the nucleus. At a subsequent stage it is then deleted with compensatory lengthening.

(46)

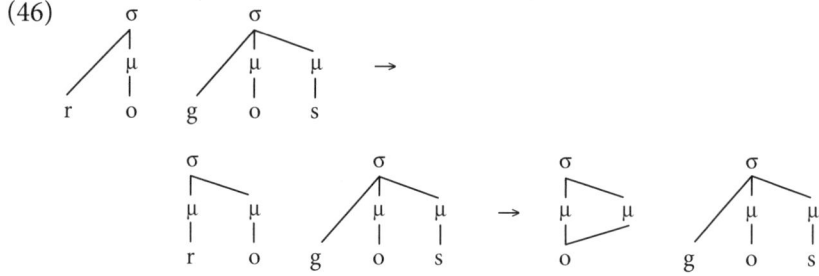

As a synchronic account, this requires two distinct syllabifications of the same input, as in Luganda. Therefore it cannot be implemented in classic or transderivational parallel OT.

  As a historical account, this analysis can be supported by a parallel development in ancient Greek involving the vocalization of laryngeals. The reflexes of *R̥h*- as Greek *RV̄*, with *V̄* having the vowel color of the original laryngeal, are well known, but phonologically rather puzzling. (Here *R* stands for *r* and *l*).

---

[14] Modern [ý], phonetically an approximant, patterns phonologically as a fricative, functioning as the front counterpart to the velar spirant [ɣ], with which it alternates regularly.

[15] On the analysis in Kiparsky (2003b), semisyllables are moras adjoined to a syllable. The details are not important for now; what matters is only that they should be moraic.

(47) Greek -$\underset{\circ}{R}h$- > $R\bar{V}$ via vocalization of laryngeals.

    a. *$\underset{\circ}{R}h_3$ > $R\bar{o}$: *$st\underset{\circ}{r}h_3$-tó- > strōtós   'spread'
    b. *$\underset{\circ}{R}h_2$ > $R\bar{a}$: *$k\underset{\circ}{r}h_2$-tó- > krātós   'mixed' 'bearable'
    c. *$\underset{\circ}{R}h_1$ > $R\bar{e}$: *$p\underset{\circ}{l}h_3$-t^hú- > plēt^{h}ús   'fullness'

In the original syllabification (reconstructed, but uncontroversial), -$\underset{\circ}{R}h$- is a heavy syllable. The idea is that when the laryngeals became syllabic, the weight was retained. The mora associated with the formerly syllabic liquid is reassociated with the melody of former laryngeal, now a vowel.

    Returning to modern Greek: even if this is what happened historically, is there reason to think that it is a synchronic live system? I believe the answer is yes. One piece of evidence is the parallel evolution of /l/, the next element on the sonority scale, in older Samothraki. The data in (48) (recorded around WW I and published in Heisenberg 1934) show that at that time onset /l/ was subject to exactly the same deletion process as /r/,

(48) /fustanéla/   [fustanéa]   '(man's) skirt'
      /katálave/   [katáavi]   'noticed (3.Sg.)'
      /petrovolúse/   [pituuvuúsi]   'threw rocks (3.Sg.)'
      /xalási/   [xaás]   'destroyed (Perf.Inf.)'

and with compensatory lengthening under the same conditions as /r/.

(49) /klépsi/   [kéeps]   'steal (subj.)'
      /san kléftis/   [sa géefts]   'like a thief'
      /eklisía/   [akiišá]   'church'
      /alla aftós/   [aaftós]   'but he'
      /ɣlítose/   [ɣíitusi]   'escaped (3.Sg.)'

Remarkably enough, *l* has been restored in the modern Samothraki dialect (Katsanis 1996).

(50)   Heisenberg 1934   Katsanis 1996
      /xalási/   [xaás]   [xalás]   'destroyed'
      /vrikólakas/   [viikóakas]   [viikólakas]   (place name)
      /nikólas/   [ńkóas]   [ńkólas]   (personal name)

Such restoration would hardly be possible if the speakers did not identify their long vowels with the liquid-glide sequences, known to them partly from alternations internal to the dialect (such as those cited in (34)) and partly no doubt from the corresponding words in the standard language.

If the cross-stratal resyllabification required by the autosegmental approach to compensatory lengthening is indeed independently motivated, then Luganda supports Stratal OT over parallel OT.[16]

4   Conclusion

The Finnish and Samothraki Greek instances of compensatory lengthening examined here appear to be intractable in both classic parallel OT and in transderivational OT, as well as in older rule-based autosegmental approaches. I have argued that Stratal OT deals with them in a way that rescues the essential idea behind the autosegmental theory of compensatory lengthening. The theoretical issues addressed concern the *actuation* of compensatory lengthening, its *realization* and specifically the locality relation between the target of lengthening and its trigger, the *distinctiveness* of the resulting weight, and the possibility of apparent *non-moraic triggers*.

---

[16] Classic parallel OT cannot derive Luganda compensatory lengthening at all, and OT-CC (nominally parallel but with quasi-derivations) can derive it only in a stipulative way (Shaw 2007).

References

Bakovic, Eric. 2007. A Revised Typology of Opaque Generalizations. *Phonology* 24: 217–259.

Bermúdez-Otero, Ricardo. 2001. Underlyingly Nonmoraic Coda Consonants, Faithfulness, and Sympathy. Unpublished ms., http://www.bermudez-otero.com/DEP-mora.pdf

Bhattacharya, Tanmoy. 1999. Bangla. Unpublished ms. http://citeseerx.ist.psu.edu/viewdoc/download?doi=10.1.1.38.7437.pdf

Blake, Barry and J. Gavin Breen. 1971. *The Pitta-Pitta Dialects*. Melbourne: Monash University Press.

Blevins, Juliette. 1994. A Place for Lateral in the Feature Geometry. *Journal of Linguistics* 30: 301–348.

Blutner, Reinhard. 2000. Some Aspects of Optimality in Natural Language Interpretation. *Journal of Semantics* 17, 189–216.

Blutner, Reinhard, Helen de Hoop and Petra Hendriks. 2006. *Optimal Communication*. CSLI Publications, Stanford.

Bolognesi, Roberto. 1998. *The Phonology of Campidanian Sardinian: A Unitary Account of a Self-Organizing Structure*. Amsterdam: HIL.

Bunn, Gordon and Ruth Bunn. 1970. Golin Phonology. *Pacific Linguistics* A 23: 1–7. Canberra, Australian National University.

Campos-Astorkiza, Rebeka. 2004. Faith in Moras: A New Approach to Prosodic Faithfulness. *Proceedings of 34th North East Linguistics Society*. Amherst, MA: GLSA.

Clements, George. N. 1986. Compensatory Lengthening and Consonant Gemination in LuGanda. In *Studies in Compensatory Lengthening*, edited by Leo Wetzels and Engin Sezer, 37–78. Dordrecht: Foris.

——. 1990. The Role of the Sonority Cycle in Core Syllabification. In *Papers in Laboratory Phonology 1: Between the Grammar and Physics of Speech*, edited by John Kingston and Mary Beckman, 283–333. NY: Cambridge University Press.

Davis, Stuart and Michael Hammond. 1995. On the Status of Onglides in American English. *Phonology* 12: 159–182.

de Lacy, Paul. 2000. Markedness in Prominent Positions. In *Proceedings of the 1st HUMIT Student Conference in Language Research (HUMIT 2000)*, edited by Ora Matushansky, Albert Costa, Javier Martin-Gonzalez, Lance Nathan, and Adam Szczegielniak, 53–66. MIT Working Papers in Linguistics 40. Cambridge, MA: MITWPL.

Dixon, Robert M. W. 1991. Mbabaram. In *Handbook of Australian Languages*, vol. 4, edited by Robert M. W. Dixon and Barry J. Blake. Melbourne: Oxford University Press.

Emeneau, Murray B. 1984. *Toda Grammar and Texts*. Philadelphia: American Philosophical Society.

Flack, Kathryn. 2007. The Sources of Phonological Markedness. PhD diss., University of Massachusetts, Amherst.

Flemming, Edward. 2006. The Role of Distinctiveness Constraints in Phonology. Unpublished ms., MIT.

Fortescue, Michael. 1984. *West Greenlandic*. London: Croom Helm.

Harris, James W. 1983. *Syllable Structure and Stress in Spanish: a Nonlinear Analysis*. Linguistic Inquiry Monograph Eight. Cambridge, MA: MIT Press.

Harris, James W. and Ellen M. Kaisse. 1999. Palatal Vowels, Glides and Obstruents in Argentinean Spanish. *Phonology* 16: 117–190.

Haviland, John. 1979. Guugu Yimidhirr. In *Handbook of Australian Languages*, vol. 1, edited by Robert M. W. Dixon and Barry J. Blake, 26–180. Amsterdam: John Benjamins.

68 PAUL KIPARSKY

Hayes, Bruce. 1989. Compensatory Lengthening in Moraic Phonology. *Linguistic Inquiry* 20: 253–306.

Healey, Alan. 1964/1977. *Telefol Phonology.* Canberra: Australian National University.

Healey, Phyllis M. and Alan Healey. 1977. *Telefol Dictionary.* Pacific Linguistics C, 46. Canberra: Australian National University.

Heisenberg, August. 1934. *Neugriechische Dialekttexte.* Leipzig.

Helimski, Eugene. 1998a. Nganasan. In *The Uralic Languages,* edited by Daniel Abondolo, 480–515. London and New York: Routledge.

——. 1998b. Selkup. In *The Uralic Languages,* edited by Daniel Abondolo, 548–579. London and New York: Routledge.

Hualde, José Ignacio and Jon Ortiz de Urbina. 2003. *A Grammar of Basque.* Berlin/New York: Mouton de Gruyter.

Itô, Junko and Armin Mester. 2003. *Japanese Morphophonemics: Markedness and Word Structure.* Linguistic Inquiry Monograph 41. Cambridge, Mass.: MIT Press.

Jäger, Gerhard. 2002. Some Notes on the Formal Properties of Bidirectional Optimality Theory. *Journal of Logic, Language, and Information* 11: 427–451.

Katsanis, Nikolaos. 1996. *To glossikon idioma tis Samothrakis.* [The Dialect of Samothraki]. Thessaloniki.

Kavitskaya, Darya. 2002. *Compensatory Lengthening: Phonetics, Phonology, Diachrony.* London: Routledge.

Kawahara, Shigeto. 2003. Root-Controlled Fusion in Zoque: Root-Faith and Neutralization Avoidance. [Rutgers Optimality Archive #599, http://roa.rutgers.edu].

Kaye, Jonathan and Jean Lowenstamm. 1984. De la syllabicité. In *Forme sonore du langage,* edited by François Dell, Daniel Hirst and Jean-Roger Vergnaud, 123–159. Paris: Hermann.

Kettunen, Lauri. 1940. Suomen Murteet III. A. Murrekartasto. Helsinki.

Kiparsky, Paul. 2003a. Finnish Noun Inflection. In *Generative Approaches to Finnic and Saami Linguistics,* edited by Diane Nelson and Satu Manninen, 109–164. Stanford: CSLI.

——. 2003b. Syllables and Moras in Arabic. In *The Syllable in Optimality Theory,* edited by Caroline Féry and Ruben van de Vijver, 147–182. Cambridge: Cambridge University Press.

——. 2008. Fenno-Swedish Quantity: Contrast in Stratal OT. In *Rules, Constraints, and Phonological Phenomena,* edited by Bert Vaux and Andrew Nevins, 185–219. Oxford: Oxford University Press.

Kirchner, Robert. 1997. Contrastiveness and Faithfulness. *Phonology* 14: 83–111.

Kornfilt, Jaklin. 1997. *Turkish.* London and New York: Routledge.

Macaulay, Monica. 1996. *A Grammar of Chalcatongo Mixtec.* Berkeley: University of California Press.

Matteson, Esther. 1965. *The Piro (Arawakan) Language.* UCPL 42. Berkeley and Los Angeles: University of California Press.

McCarthy, John. 2003. Comparative Markedness. *Theoretical Linguistics* 29: 1–51.

——. 2007. *Hidden Generalizations.* London: Equinox.

McGregor, William. 2004. *The Languages of the Kimberley,* Western Australia.

Newton, Brian. 1972a. *The Generative Interpretation of Dialect.* Cambridge: Cambridge University Press.

——. 1972b. Loss of /r/ in a Modern Greek Dialect. *Language* 48: 566–572.

Odden, David. 1996. *The Phonology and Morphology of Kimatuumbi.* Oxford: Oxford University Press.

Padgett, Jaye. 2003. Contrast and Post-velar Fronting in Russian. *Natural Language and Linguistic Theory* 21: 39–87.

Prince, Alan and Paul Smolensky. 2004. *Optimality theory: Constraint Interaction in Generative Grammar.* Oxford: Blackwell Publishing.

Rapola, Martti. 1966. *Suomen kielen äännehistorian luennot* [Lectures on the Historical Phonology of Finnish]. Helsinki: Suomalais-Ugrilainen Seura.

Rhys Davids, Thomas W. and William Stede, eds. 1921–5. *The Pali Text Society's Pali-English Dictionary*. Chipstead: Pali Text Society.

Rubach, Jerzy. 1998. *The Lexical Phonology of Slovak*. Oxford: Oxford University Press.

Shaw, Jason. 2007. Compensatory Lengthening via Mora Preservation in OT-CC: Theory and Predictions. [Rutgers Optimality Archive #916, http://roa.rutgers.edu]

Smith, Jennifer. 2003. Onset Sonority Constraints and Subsyllabic Structure. [Rutgers Optimality Archive #608, http://roa.rutgers.edu].

Topintzi, Nina. 2006. A (not so) Paradoxical Instance of Compensatory Lengthening: Samothraki Greek and Theoretical Implications. *Journal of Greek Linguistics* 7: 71–119.

Vijayakrishnan, K.G. 1995. Syllable Phonotactics as Prosodic Alignment. In *Linguistic Structure and Language Dynamics in South Asia*, edited by Anvita Abbi, R. S. Gupta and Ayesha Kidwai, 97–115. Delhi: Motilal Banarsidass Publishers Private Limited.

Zec, Draga. 1994. *Sonority Constraints on Prosodic Structure*. New York: Garland.

CHAPTER THREE

ON THE RELATIONSHIP BETWEEN CODAS AND ONSET CLUSTERS

Stuart Davis and Karen Baertsch

1 Introduction

A standard view in syllable theory is that there are no dependency relations between onsets and codas. To cite an example from Zec (2007, 164), "If a language requires onsets, it does not ban or require codas, and vice versa." Similarly, Clements (1990, 303), who defines the domain of sonority sequencing as the demisyllable states that, "the sonority profile of the first part of the syllable [i.e. the beginning of the syllable to the vocalic peak] is independent of the sonority profile of the second" [i.e. from the vocalic peak to the end of the syllable]. This chapter takes issue with this view in one very particular way. This chapter assumes that there is a close relationship between a second member of an onset cluster and a coda consonant, and that this relationship should be accounted for in a formal theory of syllable structure. This chapter presents such a theory, the split margin approach to the syllable in section 2 of the chapter. Sections 3–5 show how the split margin approach to the syllable can offer new insight and explanation into a variety of typological and language specific phenomena. Specifically, section 3 shows how the split margin approach to the syllable can formally account for an implicational universal put forward by Kaye and Lowenstamm (1981), henceforth KL, that the presence of a complex onset in a language implies the presence of a coda (i.e. there are no languages having CCV syllables but lacking CVC syllables). The reverse does not hold; that is, if a language allows codas, it may or may not allow onset clusters. Section 4 examines two cases of the parallel development of onset clusters and codas. The first case concerns diachronic changes in Campidanian Sardinian (also discussed in Davis and Baertsch 2005) while the second case concerns the simultaneous development of onset clusters and codas in colloquial Bamana (also known as Bambara, spoken in Mali and elsewhere in West Africa). In both these languages the parallel changes found in onset clusters and the coda are viewed as independent developments in other approaches to the syllable; we contend that the parallel changes in onset clusters and codas are intimately connected. Section 5 shows how the split margin approach to the syllable offers a deeper explanation for the occurrence of Dorsey's Law epenthesis (i.e. the insertion of a vowel in obstruent-sonorant consonant sequences) in Winnebago. While phonetic explanations have been offered for Dorsey's Law epenthesis in Winnebago (e.g. Fleischhacker 2001, Blevins 2004), these explanations are not deep in the sense that they do not explain why obstruent-sonorant sequences are targeted for epenthesis in Winnebago (as opposed to English where the same sequences do not undergo epenthesis) nor do they connect the phenomenon to other aspects of Winnebago syllable structure. Section 6 concludes the chapter.

2 *The Split Margin Approach to the Syllable*

In the split margin approach to the syllable, as proposed in Baertsch (2002) and further developed by Baertsch and Davis (2003) and Davis and Baertsch (2005), the margin elements of the syllable (i.e. the consonants) are divided into two positions labeled M_1 and M_2. As shown in (1), the M_1 position is reserved for a syllable-initial onset consonant (be it a singleton onset or the first member of an onset cluster). What is novel about the split margin approach in (1) is the M_2 position, which marks both the second member of an onset and the coda consonant in the same way, thus suggesting that there should be a similarity of patterning of the two M_2 positions.[1]

---

[1] Two issues that will not be discussed in this chapter are the analysis of coda clusters and the status of a word-final coda consonant, which, in some languages, has freer phonotactics than a word-internal coda consonant. (See Piggott 1999 for discussion.)

(1) Syllable-internal structure under the split margin approach to the syllable
(M = Margin, P = Peak)

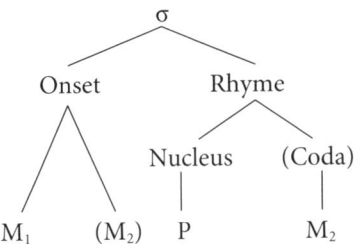

Indeed, there are a number of phonological phenomena from typology, acquisition and phonotactics discussed by Baertsch and Davis (2003) that point to a similarity in patterning between a coda consonant and the second member of an onset such that they should be marked in a similar way. Most importantly, various researchers have observed that both the coda (e.g., Gouskova 2004) and the second member of an onset (e.g., Green 2003) are positions that favor consonants of high sonority while the syllable initial consonant (i.e. the M_1 position in (1)), as noted by such researchers as Clements (1990), favors a consonant with low sonority.

The split margin approach to the syllable expands on Prince and Smolensky's (2004) Margin Hierarchy that gives preference to consonants of low sonority in all margin positions within the syllable. While Prince and Smolensky's Margin Hierarchy captures very well the low sonority preference of a syllable initial consonant it says little about the preference for high sonority in other margin positions. Under the split margin approach to the syllable, as discussed by Baertsch (2002), Prince and Smolensky's (2004) Margin Hierarchy expressed as optimality-theoretic constraints is augmented so as to distinguish between structural positions that prefer low sonority (a syllable initial consonant, the M_1 position) from those preferring high sonority (codas and the second member of an onset cluster, the M_2 position). Prince and Smolensky's Margin Hierarchy is retained in this approach as the M_1 hierarchy, given in (2), which accounts for the low sonority preference of a syllable initial consonant.

(2) The M_1 hierarchy

($*M_1$/[-HI] >> $*M_1$/[+HI]) >> $*M_1$/r >> $*M_1$/l >> $*M_1$/NASAL >> $*M_1$/OBSTRUENT

The M_2 hierarchy given in (3) accounts for the high sonority preference of a singleton coda consonant and the second segment of an onset cluster.[2]

(3) The M_2 hierarchy[3]

$*M_2/\text{Obstruent}$ >> $*M_2/\text{Nasal}$ >> $*M_2/\text{l}$ >> $*M_2/\text{r}$ >> $(*M_2/[+\text{hi}]$ >> $*M_2/[-\text{hi}])$

This theoretical approach affords us a number of advantages. The M_1 hierarchy in (2) encodes the preference for low sonority segments in single onset position and in its interaction with faithfulness constraints allows for a 'maximum sonority level for singleton onsets' beyond which segments will simply not be parsed as onsets. In some cases, this maximum level may be very high (only non-high vowels are absolutely banned from onset position in English) or lower on the sonority scale (as in Yakut, where rhotic consonants along with any segments more sonorous than rhotics are banned; Baertsch 2002). The M_2 hierarchy in (3) encodes the preference for high sonority segments as a single coda and in its interaction with faithfulness constraints can allow for a 'minimal sonority level for singleton codas' (Zec 1995) below which the segment cannot be parsed as a coda. Languages in which only sonorant consonants can appear in coda position include

---

[2] It should be understood that there is a perceptual basis for the high sonority preference of both the coda consonant and the second member of an onset. Since a coda is at the end of the syllable (not followed by a vowel), a sonorant consonant would be more perceptually salient than an obstruent given that the saliency of an obstruent is often in its release into a following vowel. On the other hand, the preference for a sonorant consonant as second member of an onset (over an obstruent) relates to the fact that the release features of a syllable initial obstruent is more readily perceptible when released into a sonorant rather than another obstruent. See Wright (2004) for discussion on the role of perceptual cues in preferred segmental sequencing. Our interest in this chapter, though, is on the formal analysis of the patterning.

[3] Note that we have placed the vocalic portions of the margin hierarchies in (2) and (3) in parentheses. This chapter only focuses on true consonants. The patterning of [+high] elements (i.e. high vowels/glides) as either part of the peak or syllable margin is beyond the scope of the present chapter (but see Smith 2003); their patterning would involve the interaction of constraints from Prince and Smolensky's Peak Hierarchy with the Margin Hierarchies in (2) and (3). As a further point of clarity regarding (2) and (3), if there is a single consonant in a syllable onset it is governed by the M_1 hierarchy and not by the M_2 hierarchy even if it is of high sonority.

Ponapean (Goodman 1997) and Colloquial Bamana (to be discussed in section 4).[4]

Further, there are acquisitional and phonotactic phenomena that link the second member of an onset and a coda that can be neatly accounted for under the split margin approach to the syllable. An interesting acquisitional case discussed in more detail by Baertsch (2002) and Davis and Baertsch (2003) comes from Fikkert's (1994) study of Jarmo, a child acquiring Dutch as his first language. At around 24 months of age, Jarmo has liquids as second members of onsets and as singleton codas, but does not have liquids as single onset consonants. From one perspective such a pattern is difficult to grasp as specifically noted by Fikkert and de Hoop (2009, 350), since one would normally assume that the presence of a liquid as a second member of an onset cluster implies its presence as a singleton onset. However, such an implication does not follow under the split margin approach to the syllable. Jarmo's system can be accounted for in the split margin approach under an analysis where the constraints $*M_2/l$ and $*M_2/r$ are ranked low (below relevant faithfulness constraints) so that [l] and [r] can occur in M_2 position, but where the constraints $*M_1/l$ and $*M_1/r$ are ranked high (above relevant faithfulness constraints), thus preventing these two sounds from surfacing in M_1 position as a single onset.

The phonotactic evidence for a connection between onset clusters and codas comes from observations by Clements and Keyser (1983), Davis (1988), Cairns (1988) and others noting a link in languages like English, Dutch, and German that disallows sequences like *plil, *flilf, and *snan (vs. lilt, nun, pop), probably best stated as what Cairns (1988) terms as 'pan-syllabic constraints' that prevent identical consonants from flanking both sides of a vowel only if there is a (marked) onset cluster. As Cairns (1988, 231) specifically notes, "this would suggest that the /l/ in C_r [rhymal consonant] is marked the same way as in A_o [second member of an onset] and distinct from C_o [initial

---

[4] To be clear, there can be restrictions on codas that are not sonority-based. For example, Zec (1995) notes that there are some languages that restrict codas to segments possessing certain features. She observes that Kiowa coda consonants are limited to labial or coronal segments that are [-continuant]. In Lardil (Hale 1973), surfacing codas must be coronal. Zec refers to such constraints as 'edge constraints.' We also note that languages such as Japanese may require coda consonants to share place features with a following onset (Itô 1988). While we do not discuss these different types of coda restrictions here, a detailed discussion of the various types of coda restrictions can be found in Davis (to appear).

member of an onset] to account for *klull*. The split margin approach in (1) does mark these positions in the same way and such pan-syllabic phonotactic restrictions then can be understood as reflecting an OCP type constraint on the M_2 position.

The following section develops the split margin approach to the syllable further by considering the typological connection between onsets clusters and codas postulated by KL, namely, that the presence of a complex onset in a language implies the presence of a coda.

3   On the Implicational Universal that Complex Onsets Imply the Presence of Codas

One of the most intriguing connections mentioned in the literature regarding a relationship between a second member of an onset and a coda is the implicational universal posited by KL (p. 291) who claim that "the existence of syllables with branching onsets implies the existence of syllables with branching rhymes." Since KL are clear in their article that by branching rhyme they mean branching into a coda (as opposed to branching within a nucleus), we can restate their generalization as 'the presence of a complex onset in a language implies the presence of a coda in that language'. An interesting consequence of this posited implicational universal for syllable typology is that maximal syllable types would be as in (4a–c) while (4d) would be ruled out. This is contrary to Blevins's (1995, 2006) typological survey of the syllable.

(4)   Maximal syllable types under Kaye and Lowenstamm's implicational universal

    a. CV   b. CVC   c. CCVC   d. *CCV

KL do not base their implicational generalization on a typological survey of syllable types across different languages, but on the formal property of syllable markedness. Specifically, they note that syllable rhymes are less marked than syllable onsets since the rhyme is the required component of the syllable. They assume that there is a formal constraint on the syllable that the onset cannot be more marked than the rhyme; consequently if a language allows for a marked onset (i.e. branching or complex onset) then it must allow for a marked (branching) rhyme. That is, just as the presence of an onset implies the presence of a rhyme, the presence of branching in the onset implies the presence of branching in the rhyme. While the empirical basis for KL's implicational universal has never been fully explored, and there are apparent counterexamples (e.g., the West African language Fongbe, in Lefebvre and Brousseau 2002), the relative infrequency of languages whose maximal syllable is CCV suggests that KL's implicational universal is at least a real typological tendency.[5] This section shows that this typological tendency has a formal explanation under the split margin approach to the syllable. We will then briefly discuss whether there are true counterexamples. First, though, in order to demonstrate how the split margin approach predicts that there should not be languages with onset clusters but lacking codas (i.e. no language whose maximal syllable is CCV), we have to detail how onset clusters are formally accounted for under the split margin approach.

In the split margin approach to the syllable, onset clusters are accounted for in an optimality-theoretic grammar by the local conjunction of the M_1 constraints (in 2) with the M_2 constraints (in 3), repeated below as (5) and (6) where the vocalic elements are excluded from the hierarchy.

(5) The M_1 hierarchy

   $^*M_1/r >> {}^*M_1/l >> {}^*M_1/$NASAL $>> {}^*M_1/$OBSTRUENT

(6) The M_2 hierarchy

   $^*M_2/$OBSTRUENT $>> {}^*M_2/$NASAL $>> {}^*M_2/l >> {}^*M_2/r

The conjoined constraints are intrinsically ranked with respect to each other (reflecting the ranking of the component M_1 and M_2 hierarchies).

---

[5] In our discussion of onset clusters throughout this chapter we do not consider syllable-initial sibilant-plus-stop clusters (and other apparent syllable-initial obstruent-obstruent clusters) that occur in some languages to be proper onset clusters. We consider them as 'adjunct clusters'. While these clusters can occur word-initially in many languages, they frequently display behavior that distinguishes them phonologically from other syllable-initial clusters and are often best analyzed with the sibilant (or other initial obstruent) being adjoined at a higher level of prosody, or, perhaps, in the case of /st/ clusters as single segments. (See Davis 1990 and Selkirk 1982 for analyses regarding s-clusters in Italian and English, respectively.) While we have not yet presented a formal analysis of such 'adjunct clusters' in our work on the split margin approach to the syllable, one potential interesting analysis of such clusters is that they involve the adjacent occurrence of M_1 consonants. We leave this for future research.

Given this, a cluster of an obstruent followed by a rhotic will be the favored onset cluster. This is because $*M_1/Obs$ is the lowest ranking M_1 constraint and $*M_2/r$ is the lowest ranking (relevant) M_2 constraint. As a consequence, the conjunction $[_\sigma*M_1/Obs\&*M_2/R$ would be the lowest ranking of the conjoined $*M_1\&*M_2$ constraints (where $[_\sigma$ indicates the domain of the local conjunction as the beginning of the syllable, i.e. the syllable onset). Consider the Spanish data in (7). As these data show, Spanish allows for obstruent-sonorant onset clusters but not obstruent-obstruent ones. An underlying obstruent-obstruent cluster that could potentially surface in syllable-initial position (7c), actually surfaces with a prothetic vowel (a violation of the constraint DEP), but the underlying obstruent-sonorant sequences of (7a–b) are allowed to surface as complex onsets.

(7) Exemplification from Spanish

    a. /blanka/   [blaŋ.ka]   'white'
    b. /pronto/   [pron.to]   'soon'
    c. /sposa/   [εs.po.sa]   'wife'

The patterning of (7) reflects the constraint ranking in (8) with the relevant tableaux shown in (9) and (10). Observe that in the constraint ranking in (8) the conjoined constraints are intrinsically ranked. For example, $[_\sigma*M_1/Obs\&*M_2/Obs$ must be higher ranked than $[_\sigma*M_1/Obs\&*M_2/l$ because as seen in the M_2 hierarchy in (6) $*M_2/Obs$ outranks $*M_2/l$. The Spanish analysis in (8)–(10) demonstrates how the split margin approach neatly accounts for onset clusters, especially the preference for obstruent-sonorant onset clusters.

(8) Constraint ranking for Spanish

    $[_\sigma*M_1/Obs\&*M_2/Obs >> Dep >> [_\sigma*M_1/Obs\&*M_2/l >> [_\sigma*M_1/Obs\&*M_2/r$

(9) /bla/ [bla]

/bla/	$[_\sigma*M_1/Obs\&$ $*M_2/Obs$	Dep	$[_\sigma*M_1/Obs\&$ $*M_2/l$	$[_\sigma*M_1/Obs\ \&$ $*M_2/r$
☞ a. bla			*	
b. εb.la		*!		

(10) /spo/ [ɛs.po]

/spo/	[$_\sigma$*M$_1$/Obs& *M$_2$/Obs	Dep	[$_\sigma$*M$_1$/Obs& *M$_2$/l	[$_\sigma$*M$_1$/Obs & *M$_2$/r
a. spo	*!			
☞ b. ɛs.po		*		

This approach to the analysis of complex onsets provides a natural explanation for KL's implicational universal that the presence of a complex onset in a language implies the presence of codas in that language. Given the logic of constraint conjunction, a conjoined constraint must dominate the individual conjuncts for it to be active in a language. If the conjoined constraint [$_\sigma$*M$_1$/Obs&*M$_2$/r is ranked low enough (below the relevant faithfulness constraints) so as to allow for onset clusters (as in Spanish) then it must follow that rhotics be allowed as single codas given that a conjoined constraint outranks each of the single conjuncts. This is shown in (11).

(11)

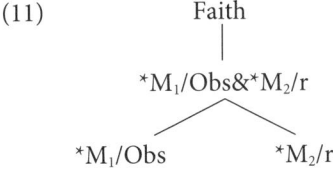

The consequence of this ranking is that if a language allows for an onset cluster, it also allows for the presence of a coda, thus giving a formal explanation for KL's proposed implicational universal that the presence of a complex onset implies the presence of a coda. If we then consider syllable typology, we would expect to find languages whose maximal syllable is CV (constraint ranking 12a), CVC (12b), and CCVC (12c) (where for convenience we use *M$_2$/Son collapsing *M$_2$/l and *M$_2$/r).

(12) Accounting for syllable typology

   a. ranking for a CV language
      [$_\sigma$*M$_1$/Obs&*M$_2$/Son >> *M$_2$/Son >> Faith
   b. ranking for a CVC language
      [$_\sigma$*M$_1$/Obs&*M$_2$/Son >> Faith >> *M$_2$/Son

   c. ranking for a CCVC language
      FAITH >> [$_\sigma$*M$_1$/OBS&*M$_2$/SON >> *M$_2$/SON

However, a language that has a maximal syllable CCV (without having CVC syllables) is problematic given the role of constraint conjunction as shown by the hypothetical ranking in (13).

(13) Hypothetical ranking of a CCV language

    *M$_2$/SON >> FAITH >> [$_\sigma$*M$_1$/OBS&*M$_2$/SON

The main problem with (13) is that a potential candidate with a surface obstruent-sonorant onset cluster CCV would incur a violation of both the low ranked conjoined constraint and the high-ranked *M$_2$/SON (ranked above Faith). The violation of *M$_2$/SON would be fatal. A candidate that would violate Faith (e.g., a candidate CV that has one of the consonants deleted from /CCV/ violating the faithfulness constraint MAX) would be preferred since it would not have any violation of high-ranked *M$_2$/SON. Thus, under the split margin approach to the syllable, there is a formal explanation couched within optimality theory for KL's implicational universal that the presence of a complex onset in a language implies the presence of a coda in that language.

An interesting question then becomes whether or not KL's posited implicational universal phrased here as 'the presence of a complex onset in a language implies the presence of a coda in that language' can be maintained on empirical grounds. We suggest that it can, despite apparent counterexamples such as the West African language Fongbe (Lefebvre and Brousseau 2002). First, as mentioned in footnote 5, we are really only considering obstruent-sonorant onset clusters. Are there languages that allow for obstruent-sonorant onset clusters but do not have codas (which would be unaccounted for given the discussion of (12) and (13) above)? Such languages are not commonly found in the literature, though a number of West African languages (such as Fongbe) are indeed reported to have obstruent-sonorant onsets without having codas. Second, in dealing with languages that only allow for syllable initial clusters of consonant-plus-glide there is always the issue of the analysis of the glide as being part of the onset or part of the nucleus. Thus, this chapter does not consider such languages. Third, a number of languages cited as having a maximal CCV syllable in the literature do also allow for codas. For example, Blevins (2006) cites Cheke Holo as being a language whose maximal syllable in CCV but then notes that codas occur in loanwords. Similarly, the African languages discussed in Morrill (1997) as having CCV as a maximal syllable all take on a coda consonant under certain types of suffixation. Finally, if we consider Fongbe, a language that has obstruent-sonorant onset clusters without having codas (Lefebvre and Brousseau 2002, Bhatt, Ndayiragije, and Nikiema 2008), it is interesting to note that Haitian Creole, which some researchers consider to reflect the grammar of its primary African substrate language Fongbe (Lefebvre 1998), maintains coda consonants. This is somewhat mysterious given the lack of coda consonants in Fongbe. We suggest that while languages with a maximal CCV syllables do exist, such as Fongbe, they are 'coda-friendly'. Formally, this means that they are covert CCVC languages having the ranking shown in (12c). Their lack of coda consonants has more to do with the absence of potential codas in input sequences. When confronted with potential codas in loanwords or situations of language contact, these are not repaired. This is a matter for future research.[6]

4   *The Parallel Development of Onset Clusters and Coda*

In this section we provide more evidence for the split margin approach to the syllable by considering cases where there is parallel development of onset clusters and codas. To be clear, given the discussion of the preceding section, there are languages that have codas that do not have onset clusters, specifically languages with the ranking shown in (12b). Obviously, such languages do not show parallel patterning between onset clusters and codas. Where we expect parallel patterning is in the following situations. One, when a language at one stage has both onset clusters and codas and begins to restrict its coda in certain ways, then onset clusters should also become restricted.[7] Two, if a CV language

---

[6] In a poster paper presented at the CUNY Conference on the Syllable, Bhatt, Ndayiragije, and Nikiema (2008) specifically note the oddity of a language like Fongbe that appears to have obstruent-sonorant onset clusters but without having codas. Their solution, working in the framework of government phonology, is to posit an empty nucleus between the obstruent and the sonorant so that the obstruent-sonorant sequence is not really an onset cluster. In our analysis of Fongbe, we do consider such sequences to be onset clusters; Fongbe is a covert CCVC language with the constraint ranking of (12c).

[7] Note that we do not make a prediction about the reverse scenario. If a CCVC language starts to restrict or eliminate its onset clusters it may or may not restrict or

develops onset clusters then it should also allow codas. In this section we will detail one example of each of these two cases. In 4.1, based on Davis and Baertsch (2005), we consider Campidanian Sardinian, a daughter of Latin in which, diachronically, codas and onset clusters become more restrictive than in Latin in a parallel way. In 4.2 we will consider the simultaneous development of complex onsets and codas in colloquial Bamana (Bambara) from standard Bamana, a language whose maximal syllable is CV. In both Campidanian Sardinian and colloquial Bamana, constraints have acted upon the coda and the second member of an onset in a parallel way reflecting a link between these two positions.

4.1   *Campidanian Sardinian*

Campidanian Sardinian (CS) (Bolognesi 1998, Alber 2001, Smith 2003, Frigeni 2003, 2005) descends from Latin, a CCVC language (ignoring the issue of s-clusters and certain cases of complex codas) in which basically any consonant (regardless of sonority value) could be a single coda. Latin codas can be accounted for by the constraint ranking in (14) where the entire M_2 hierarchy is dominated by Faith.

(14)   Ranking of the M_2 Hierarchy in Latin

     FAITH >> *M_2/OBSTRUENT >> *M_2/NASAL >> *M_2/l >> *M_2/r

Latin allows for onset clusters consisting of an obstruent followed by a sonorant. This means that the relevant conjoined constraints are also ranked below Faith as in (15).

(15)   Ranking permitting obstruent-sonorant onset clusters in Latin

     FAITH >> [$_\sigma$*M_1/OBS&*M_2/l >> [$_\sigma$*M_1/OBS&*M_2/r >> ... >> *M_2/l >> *M_2/r

CS, on the other hand, has a syllable structure that is more restricted than in Latin both with respect to the nature of the coda and the onset clusters. Moreover, the language distinguishes initial syllables which

---

eliminate its coda. This is because given the ranking for CCVC languages as in (12c), onset clusters can become restricted by the demotion of Faith below *M_1&*M_2 but above the simple *M_2 constraints.

allow onset clusters from non-initial syllables which lack them for the most part. (See Alber 2001 on the importance of the initial syllable in CS.) We focus on the initial syllable. In CS, the only (unassimilated) singleton coda allowed is the rhotic. Coda laterals from Latin have rhotic reflexes in CS as exemplified in (16) where Latin forms are indicated in capital letters. (The lateral can occur syllable-initially in CS, a position governed by the M_1 hierarchy.)

(16) ALBUS > arba 'white'
      ORKU > orku 'ogre'

We can account for this by the ranking in (17) whereby the relevant faithfulness constraint, ID[Manner], is ranked below $*M_2/l$. ID[Manner] is violated if a lateral liquid changes to a rhotic liquid or vice-versa. The relevant tableau is shown in (18) where we assume (given richness of the base) an input lateral.

(17) Ranking for CS: $*M_2/l \gg$ ID[Manner] $\gg *M_2/r$

(18) /alba/ [ar.ba] 'white'

/alba/	$*M_2/l$	ID[Manner]	$*M_2/r$
a. al.ba	*!		
☞ b. ar.ba		*	*

In comparison to the ranking in Latin (19), the CS ranking in (17) ranks the Faith constraint, ID[Manner], below $*M_2/l$ disallowing lateral codas but still above $*M_2/r$ thus permitting rhotic codas.

(19) Ranking for Latin: ID[Manner] $\gg *M_2/l \gg *M_2/r$

What is interesting in CS and what previous researchers have noted but have viewed as an independent change is the loss of the lateral when it is the second member of an onset cluster as in (20a). Rhotics in clusters remained (20b).

(20) Onset clusters

	Latin	Sardinian	Gloss
a.	PLUS	prus	'more'
	CLAVE	krai	'key'
	LONGUS	longu	'long')
b.	PRIMU	primu	'first'
	CRAS	krazi	'tomorrow'

The change follows naturally from the ranking in (17) under the split margin approach, as we see in the tableau in (21).

(21) /plus/ [prus] 'more'

/plus/	*M$_2$/l	ID[Manner]	*M$_2$/r
a. plus	*!		
☞ b. prus		*	*

We show the fuller ranking with the relevant conjoined constraints in (22) along with a more detailed tableaux in (23). What (22) shows is that the domination of ID[Manner] by *M$_2$/l also entails its domination by *M$_1$/Obs&*M$_2$/l. Thus, it is expected that if Latin /l/ has become [r] in coda position in Sardinian then it should do the same as the second member of a complex onset. And given the ranking in (22), Latin obstruent-rhotic onset clusters remain unchanged in CS, in (24). Thus, our analysis under the split margin approach formally connects the historical change in the coda (16) with the change in onset clusters (20a).

(22) Fuller ranking for CS
[$_\sigma$*M$_1$/OBS&*M$_2$/l] >> [$_\sigma$*M$_1$/OBS&*M$_2$/r] >> *M$_2$/l >> ID[MANNER] >> *M$_2$/r

(23) /plus/ [prus] 'more'

/plus/	[$_\sigma$*M$_1$/OBS &*M$_2$/l	[$_\sigma$*M$_1$/OBS &*M$_2$/r	*M$_2$/l	ID[MANNER]	*M$_2$/r
a. plus	*!		*		
☞ b. prus		*		*	*

(24) /primu/ [primu] 'first'

/primu/	$[_\sigma$*M_1/Obs &*M_2/l	$[_\sigma$*M_1/Obs &*M_2/r	*M_2/l	ID[Manner]	*M_2/r
☞ a. primu		*			*
b. plimu	*!		*	*	

Note that the exact ranking of $[_\sigma$*M_1/Obs&*M_2/r in (22) is not critical just as long as it is above *M_2/r and below $[_\sigma$*M_1/Obs&*M_2/l. It is the ranking *M_2/l >> ID[Manner] >> *M_2/r that triggers the change in the onset cluster containing an input lateral as in (23), just as it triggers the change in a potential lateral coda as in (18). There are other interesting details of CS codas mentioned by Davis and Baertsch (2005) that we do not discuss here.[8] Nonetheless, as reflected in our analysis presented in (17)–(24), CS provides a clear illustration of the diachronic link between onset clusters and codas such that a restriction that has developed on codas (i.e. the restriction against laterals) is mirrored in the second position of onset clusters because both are M_2 positions. The parallel nature of the restriction is neatly captured in the split margin approach.

4.2   *Bamana*

In the previous subsection we detailed how a language becomes more restricted in its syllable structure with respect to both codas and second members of onsets in a parallel way, reflecting the M_2 position of the syllable. In this section we will consider the opposite case where a language becomes less restrictive in its syllable structure with respect

---

[8] CS codas are more complicated than what is discussed here in that, in addition to the sonority constraint that only allows the highly sonorous rhotic as a single (unassimilated) coda, CS has also witnessed the rise of the Coda Condition (in the sense of Itô 1988 where a coda shares place features with a following onset) in comparison to Latin. Specifically, with the exception of a singleton coda [r], as in *arba* 'white' in (16), CS obeys the Coda Condition. This means that CS codas may include an obstruent only if it is the first part of a geminate (ignoring certain problems regarding the syllabification of s-clusters) or if it is homorganic to a following onset. While we do not analyze this here, one would need to reference the Coda Condition as a constraint in addition to the *M_2 constraints. CS thus offers an interesting interplay of coda (M_2) constraints that reference high sonority (Zec 1995) and the classic Coda Condition (Itô 1988).

to these two positions. We will exemplify this with a consideration of the comparison of standard Bamana (Bambara) with colloquial Bamana. We assume here that the former is the more conservative variety while the latter develops from it.

Consider the comparison of Standard Bamana, which is a CV language (ignoring a possible coda nasal which some consider as syllabic), with Colloquial Bamana in (25). Through vowel syncope, Colloquial Bamana has developed onset clusters and codas. (The data and discussion here are based on Diakite 2006, the author being a native speaker linguist.)

(25) Standard vs. Colloquial Bamana

Standard	Colloquial	gloss
[buu.ru]	[bru]	'bread'
[mo.ri.ba]	[mor.ba]	Name
[ma.ri.fa]	[mar.fa]	'gun'
[ba.ra.ma]	[bra.ma] or [bar.ma]	'pot'
[fa.ra.ti]	[fra.ti] or [far.ti]	'carelessness'
[ka.bi.la]	[ka.bla]	'tribute'
[me.le.ku.ya]	[mel.ku.ya]	'literature'

As the comparison between the Standard and Colloquial Bamana data reveal, the colloquial language has a syncope process that preferably deletes a non-final high vowel, though a non-high vowel can be deleted if there are no target high vowels. The effect of this is to make syllable structure less restrictive in Colloquial Bamana than in Standard Bamana, which is basically a CV language. Through syncope, Colloquial Bamana has developed both complex onsets and codas, so that CVC and CCV syllables are allowed in addition to CV syllables. What is noteworthy is that syncope in Bamana either creates a complex onset in which the second member is a sonorant (e.g., [bra.ma] 'pot', [ka.bla] 'tribute']) or a coda in which the single coda consonant is a sonorant (e.g., [mar.fa] 'gun', [mel.ku.ya] 'literature'). In other words, the result of syncope leaves a sonorant in M_2 position; it never results in an obstruent in that position. Consider, for example the words given in (26) taken from Diakite (2006, 6).

(26) Standard

Standard	Colloquial	gloss
[sa.fu.nɛ]	[sa.fnɛ] *[sfa.nɛ] *[saf.nɛ]	'soap'
[ka.la.bã.ci]	[kla.bã.ci] [kal.bã.ci] *[ka.lab.ci]	'hypocrite'

The examples in (26) make clear that the result of syncope does not leave an obstruent in M_2 position. Given this, we can account for the difference between Standard and Colloquial Bamana by a difference in the ranking of the $*M_2$ constraints. Under the assumption that Standard Bamana is a CV language, all the $*M_2$ constraints would be high ranking. Colloquial Bamana, on the other hand, witnesses the demotion of $*M_2$/sonorant (collapsing $*M_2$/r, $*M_2$/l, and $*M_2$/nasal) below a constraint (or series of constraints) that favor syncopated outputs (which we will call Syncope here and leave the details of it for further research, though Syncope favors the deletion of a word-internal high vowel all else being equal—see Green et al. 2009 for a preliminary study). Standard Bamana would have the constraint ranking in (27) with a relevant tableau in (28). Here we focus on the analysis of codas.

(27) Ranking for Standard Bamana

   $*M_2$/Obs >> $*M_2$/Son >> Syncope >> $*M_1$/Son >> $*M_1$/Obs

(28) /moriba/ [mo.ri.ba] Name

/moriba/	$*M_2$/Obs	$*M_2$/Son	Syncope	$*M_1$/Son	$*M_1$/Obs
☞ a. mo.ri.ba			*	**	*
b. mor.ba		*!		*	*

The winning candidate in (28a) violates Syncope in that it does not undergo syncope. The losing candidate in (28b) respects Syncope, but this results in a violation of the higher ranked $*M_2$/Son constraint since it has [r] in coda position. The winning candidate has no codas thus respecting the higher ranked $*M_2$ constraints. Turning to Colloquial Bamana, we can analyze it by the demotion of the $*M_2$/Sonorant constraint below Syncope. The ranking for Colloquial Bamana is given in (29) with the relevant tableau in (30). (Note that the ranking in (29) between $*M_2$/Son and $*M_1$/Son is not crucial, just as long as $*M_2$/Son is ranked below Syncope.)

(29) Ranking for Colloquial Bamana

   $*M_2$/Obs >> Syncope >> $*M_2$/Son >> $*M_1$/Son >> $*M_1$/Obs

(30) /moriba/ [mor.ba] Name

/moriba/	*M$_2$/Obs	Syncope	*M$_2$/Son	*M$_1$/Son	*M$_1$/Obs
a. mo.ri.ba		*!		**	*
☞ b. mor.ba			*	*	*

The winning candidate in (30b) has a sonorant in its coda. The demotion of *M$_2$/Son below Syncope in Colloquial Bamana allows for a sonorant in coda position.

We now consider the fuller ranking with the relevant conjoined constraints in (31) accounting for the nature of the complex onset. In Standard Bamana complex onsets are not allowed. What (31) shows is that the domination of Syncope by *M$_2$/Son also entails its domination by [$_\sigma$*M$_1$/Obs&*M$_2$/Son. Thus, just as possible forms with a coda consonant cannot surface in Standard Bamana neither can a possible form with a complex onset. This is shown by the tableau in (32).

(31) Ranking for Standard Bamana with conjoined constraints for complex onsets

[$_\sigma$*M$_1$/Obs&*M$_2$/Son >> *M$_2$/Son >> Syncope >> *M$_1$/Son >> *M$_1$/Obs

(32) /kabila/ [ka.bi.la] 'tribute'

/kabila/	[$_\sigma$*M$_1$/Obs & *M$_2$/Son	*M$_2$/Son	Syncope	*M$_1$/Son	*M$_1$/Obs
☞ a. ka.bi.la			*	*	**
b. ka.bla	*!	*			**

Candidate (32b) violates the *M$_2$/Son constraint because [l] is the second member of a complex onset. Candidate (32a) is thus the winner since it does not violate *M$_2$/Son even though it violates Syncope, but that is not a fatal violation since it is lower ranked than *M$_2$/Son. (Note that a possible candidate like [kab.la] for (32) would be ruled out by *M$_2$/Obs which is necessarily higher ranked than *M$_2$/Son given the *M$_2$ hierarchy in (6).)

For Colloquial Bamana, not only has the $^*M_2$/SONORANT constraint been demoted below SYNCOPE as shown by the ranking in (29), but there is the further demotion of the conjoined constraint $[_\sigma^*M_1$/OBS&$^*M_2$/SON below SYNCOPE as shown by the fuller ranking in (33). This accounts for the output with a complex onset as seen by the tableau in (34).

(33)   Ranking for Colloquial Bamana with conjoined constraints for complex onsets

SYNCOPE >> $[_\sigma^*M_1$/OBS&$^*M_2$/SON >> $^*M_2$/SON >> $^*M_1$/SON >> $^*M_1$/OBS

(34)   /kabila/ [ka.bla] 'tribute'

/kabila/	SYNCOPE	$[_\sigma^*M_1$/OBS & $^*M_2$/SON	$^*M_2$/SON	$^*M_1$/SON	$^*M_1$/OBS
a. ka.bi.la	*!			*	**
☞ b. ka.bla		*	*		**

(Note that a possible candidate like [kab.la] for (34) would still be ruled out by $^*M_2$/OBS since that would be higher ranked than the conjoined constraint $[_\sigma^*M_1$/OBS&$^*M_2$/SON though this would not be an intrinsic ranking.) Our detailed analysis of the different varieties of Bamana accounts for the parallel emergence of both onset clusters and codas in Colloquial Bamana.[9] Along with the Campidanian Sardinian case discussed in 4.1 it provides strong evidence for the link between onset clusters and codas that is insightfully captured by the split margin approach.

---

[9] There are restrictions on Bamana syncope that are not discussed here but are explored more fully in Green and Diakite (2008), such as a possible metrical restriction. One interesting observation on Colloquial Bamana syncope is that multiple deletions are disfavored in a single word. That is, typically, only one deletion can occur in a word, even in longer words where there may be more than one potential target. Since syncope always results in the occurrence of an M_2 segment, this suggests that in Colloquial Bamana there can only be at most one M_2 segment in any given word. We leave the analysis of this for future research.

5 *On Dorsey's Law in Winnebago*

This section considers the application of the split margin approach to the syllable to Dorsey's Law in Winnebago (also called Hocank). Our contention is that the split margin approach to the syllable offers a deeper explanation as to why Dorsey's Law occurs in Winnebago in comparison to phonetic explanations. Dorsey's Law in Winnebago inserts an epenthetic vowel to break up a potential obstruent-sonorant onset, as we see in (35). The inserted vowel has the same quality of the vowel that immediately follows the sonorant consonant. (The Winnebago data are from Miner 1979, 1992, 1993 and Hale and White Eagle 1980.)

(35) Dorsey's Law in Winnebago (Hocank)

a.	/hipres/	[hi.pe.res]	'know'
b.	/krepnã/	[ke.re.pã.nã]	'unit of ten'
c.	/sgaa/	[sgaa]	'white'
d.	/kšee/	[kšee]	'revenge'
e.	/haracab-ra/	[ha.ra.cab.ra]	'the taste'
f.	/ha-k-ru-gas/	[ha.ku.ru.gas]	'I tear my own'
g.	/pšoopšoc/	[pšoo.pšoc]	'fine'

Alderete (1995) observes the apparent oddity of Dorsey's law since it acts to break up potential obstruent-sonorant onset clusters which are the most preferred clusters cross-linguistically. As we see in (35c), (35d) and (35g), two adjacent obstruents are not split up; they can occur word-initially or syllable-initially as long as one is a strident. We would consider such obstruent-obstruent sequences as adjunct clusters as mentioned in footnote 5. Note that while obstruent-sonorant sequences do not surface morpheme-internally or over a prefix boundary (the /k/ in (35f) is a reflexive prefix), Winnebago does allow a sequence of an obstruent followed by a sonorant in separate syllables over a suffixal boundary as in (35e) where /-ra/ is a suffix (or enclitic) marking definiteness.

A phonetic explanation for Dorsey's Law epenthesis has been proposed by researchers such as Blevins (2004) and Fleischhacker (2002). For example, Blevins suggests that the audible release of the obstruent before the sonorant is misperceived as a vowel. The vowel is perceived to be colored by the post-sonorant vowel because of anticipatory articulation of vowel gestures and is then phonologized since the inserted vowel counts for stress placement and can be stressed. (See Hale and White Eagle 1980, Halle and Vergnaud 1987, and Strycharczuk 2009 among others for formal analyses of the interaction of Dorsey's Law with stress.) The difficulty we see with this phonetic explanation is that it does not explain why the "misperception" occurs in Winnebago but not in English (or other languages) where the same underlying sequences occur as onset clusters with no vowel epenthesis. Thus we note Alderete's (1995) query—Why would Dorsey's Law break up potential obstruent-sonorant onset clusters when they are cross-linguistically the most preferred complex onsets?

Alderete's (1995, 48) answer is that a syllable contact constraint is active in Winnebago such that there cannot be a sonority rise of greater than one sonority interval over a syllable boundary. Consequently, in Alderete's analysis Dorsey's Law occurs so as to break up bad syllable contact (i.e. rising sonority over a syllable boundary). The difficulty with this analysis is that it seems to predict that word-initial clusters like the one shown in (35b) should not be broken up because syllable contact is not at issue word-initially. Alderete's (1995, 49) analysis suggests that words that begin with such a cluster actually begin with a "silent vowel" so that the syllable contact constraint would apply to them. However, there is no independent evidence for the silent vowel (e.g., it does not interact with stress as the epenthetic vowel does and has no reflex diachronically).

Our proposed explanation for the Dorsey's Law facts in Winnebago is that Dorsey's Law occurs due to language internal pressure for obstruent-sonorant sequences not to surface. The salient observation about Winnebago that is overlooked in the phonetic discussions on Dorsey's Law is that the language disallows sonorant consonants in coda position (Miner 1993). While this observation may seem unconnected to Dorsey's Law, under the split margin approach to the syllable, it is crucially connected. Given the M_2 hierarchy as in (6), if a language does not allow sonorant consonants in coda position, then the entire M_2 hierarchy (abbreviated as $*M_2$ in (36)) dominates Faith (DEP being the faithfulness constraint violated by the winning candidates in Winnebago), though most of the M_1 hierarchy (abbreviated as $*M_1$) is dominated by Faith. Thus, CVC reduplication as in (36) results in the epenthesis shown in candidate (b), motivated not by a syllable contact restriction but by the dispreference of Winnebago to parse a rhotic in coda position.

(36) Winnebago /R+šara/ [šarašara] 'bold in spots'

/ šar+šara /	$*M_2$	Dep	$*M_1$
a. šar.ša.ra	$*M_2$/[r]!		$*M_1$/Obs, $*M_1$/Obs, $*M_1$/[r]
☞ b. ša.ra.ša.ra		*	$*M_1$/Obs, $*M_1$/Obs, $*M_1$/[r], $*M_1$/[r]

Given the high ranked nature of the M_2 hierarchy in Winnebago, it follows that complex onsets (which include an M_2 position) are disallowed as well. Under the split margin approach to the syllable, a language will not allow onset clusters unless at least a portion of the M_2 hierarchy is dominated by Faith (Dep in 37). Given that the M_2 hierarchy outranks Dep as seen in (36), complex onsets cannot surface as shown in (37).

(37) Winnebago /krepnã/ [ke.re.pã.nã] 'unit of ten'

/krepnã/	$*M_2$	Dep	$*M_1$
a. krep.nã	**!		**
b. kre.pã.nã	*!	*	***
☞ c. ke.re.pã.nã		**	****

This analysis thus far provides a principled account of the epenthesis in Winnebago without resorting to structures for which there is no overt evidence. However, the analysis of stem-final consonants in Winnebago remains an outstanding issue. Recall the word meaning 'the taste' in (35e) repeated below in (38). Here we see that Dorsey's Law does not apply over a final stem boundary and the obstruent-sonorant sequence surfaces.

(38) Lack of Dorsey's Law over a stem-final boundary

    /haracab-ra/   [ha.ra.cab.ra] *[ha.ra.ca.ba.ra]   'the taste'

We suggest that stem-final codas that are not word final may, in fact, surface as an M_2 element compelled by a high ranked alignment constraint requiring a stem-final element to be syllable final, i.e. ALIGNR (stem, syllable), namely that the right edge of the stem aligns with the right edge of the syllable. The /b/ in (38) is in stem-final position. This alignment constraint prevents Dorsey's Law from applying to (38) as shown in (39).

(39) /haracab-ra/—[haracab-ra] 'the taste'

/haracab-ra/	ALIGNR(stem, syllable)	*M_2	DEP	*M_1
☞ a. ha.ra.cab.ra		*M_2/Obs		****
b. ha.ra.ca.bra	*!	*M_2/r		****
c. ha.ra.ca.ba.ra	*!		*	*****

We thus understand Dorsey's Law epenthesis as providing evidence for the relation between onset clusters and codas and for the split margin approach to the syllable more generally. Our analysis does not deny the phonetic accounts of Dorsey's Law epenthesis into obstruent-sonorant sequences put forward by such researchers as Blevins (2004) and Fleischhacker (2002), rather it offers a deeper explanation for why obstruent-sonorant sequences are targeted to be broken up in the first place. There is internal systemic pressure from within the phonology of Winnebago for the sonorant not to surface as a second member of the onset since Winnebago does not permit sonorants to surface in coda position. We consider this to constitute a deeper formal explanation for Dorsey's Law in Winnebago.[10]

6   Conclusion

This chapter has offered a detailed exploration of the relationship between codas and onset clusters. Various aspects of this relationship

---

[10] Fleischhacker (2002) and Flemming (2008) offer perceptual accounts of Dorsey's Law epenthesis. They note that epenthesis is more likely to occur to split up an underlying obstruent-sonorant sequence than to split up an underlying obstruent-obstruent sequence. Under Flemming's account, in particular, this has to do with the perceptual similarity of obstruent-sonorant (OS) sequences with obstruent-V-sonorant (OVS) sequences. (Epenthesis is less likely to occur in an obstruent-obstruent sequence because the resulting obstruent-vowel-obstruent sequence would not be that perceptually similar to the underlying obstruent-obstruent sequence.) However, the perceptual similarity account does not tell us why obstruent-sonorant clusters are targeted for repair in Winnebago, nor does it account for the phonological nature of the process (e.g., the process in Winnebago does not apply over a suffix boundary; also, the epenthetic vowel interacts with metrical structure), nor does it reference the nature of Winnebago syllable structure more generally.

have been noted by previous researchers such as Cairns (1988), who comments that pan-syllabic constraints suggest that the coda and the second member of an onset should be marked in the same way, or KL who propose an implicational universal that the presence of an onset cluster implies the presence of the coda, or research on sonority showing that the coda and second member of an onset are positions that prefer consonants of high sonority. While these observations have been made, previous researchers have not offered a formal account to explain these observations nor have they explored the implications of the relationship between the coda and onset clusters. This chapter, building on our previous work (e.g., Baertsch 2002, Baertsch and Davis 2003, Davis and Baertsch 2005), fills this gap by detailing the split margin approach to the syllable and showing how it accounts for the onset cluster/coda relationship. Section 2 shows how the formal relationship between a second member on an onset and a coda (both M_2 positions under the split margin approach to the syllable) allowed us to offer an understanding of some phonotactic and acquisitional phenomena. Sections 3–5 show how the split margin approach to the syllable offers insight and formal explanation to a variety of phenomena, laying a path for the direction of future research. Section 3 details a formal explanation under the split margin view of the syllable for KL's implicational universal that onset clusters in a language imply the presence of codas in that language. Apparent CCV languages such as Fongbe are claimed to be covert CCVC languages. This is a provocative claim that requires further research. Section 4 shows specific cases of parallel development affecting codas and onset clusters. Especially in the case of Campidanian Sardinian in section 4.1 previous research has considered the imposition of similar restrictions on codas and onset clusters to be independent of one another, but we argue that they are intimately connected. This also lays the groundwork for future research. What is the connection between changes that take place (or do not take place) in the coda and in onset clusters and what does the split margin approach to the syllable specifically predict? Section 5 offers a novel explanation and understanding for the occurrence of Dorsey's Law epenthesis in Winnebago. The major criticism of phonetic discussion of the occurrence of Dorsey's Law in Winnebago is that it does not take into account the nature of Winnebago syllable structure more generally. Once it is taken into account through the perspective of the split margin approach to the syllable, we can understand formally why obstruent-sonorant sequences are targeted to be broken up in Winnebago. While there are many empirical issues that are raised by our discussion, we nonetheless conclude that the split margin approach to the syllable developed here offers a novel perspective and understanding about the relationship between consonants within the syllable.

96   STUART DAVIS & KAREN BAERTSCH

References

Alber, Birgit. 2001. Maximizing first positions. *Linguistics in Potsdam* 12 (HILP 5): 1–19.
Alderete, John. 1995. Winnebago accent and Dorsey's Law. *University of Massachusetts Occasional Papers* 18: 21–51.
Baertsch, Karen. 2002. An optimality theoretic approach to syllable structure: The Split Margin Hierarchy. PhD diss., Indiana University.
Baertsch, Karen and Stuart Davis. 2003. The split margin approach to syllable structure. *ZAS Papers in Linguistics* 32: 1–14.
Bhatt, Parth, Juvénal Ndayiragije, and Emmanuel Nikiema. 2008. Are branching syllabic constituents really necessary? Presented at the CUNY Phonology Forum Conference on the Syllable. http://www.cunyphonologyforum.net/syllconf.php
Blevins, Juliette. 1995. The syllable in phonological theory. In *The handbook of phonological theory*, edited by John Goldsmith, 206–244. Cambridge, MA: Blackwell.
——. 2004. *Evolutionary phonology: The emergence of sound patterns.* Cambridge: Cambridge University Press.
——. 2006. Syllable: typology. In *Encyclopedia of language and linguistics*, 2nd ed., vol. 12, edited by Keith Brown, 333–337. Elsevier.
Bolognesi, Roberto. 1998. *The Phonology of Campidanian Sardinian: A Unitary Account of a Self-Organizing Structure.* Amsterdam: HIL.
Cairns, Charles. 1988. Phonotactics, markedness and lexical representation. *Phonology* 5: 209–236.
Clements, George. N. 1990. The role of the sonority cycle in core syllabification. In *Papers in laboratory phonology 1: Between the grammar and physics of speech*, edited by John Kingston and Mary Beckman, 283–333. NY: Cambridge University Press.
Clements, George N. and Samuel J. Keyser. 1983. *CV phonology: A generative theory of the syllable.* Cambridge, MA: MIT Press.
Davis, Stuart. 1988. *Topics in syllable geometry.* New York: Garland Press.
——. 1990. The onset as a constituent of the syllable: Evidence from Italian. *Chicago Linguistic Society* 26, 2: 71–79.
——. To appear. Quantity. In *Handbook of phonological theory*, 2nd edition, edited by John Goldsmith, Jason Riggle, and Alan Yu. Oxford: Blackwell.
Davis, Stuart and Karen Baertsch. 2005. The diachronic link between onset clusters and codas. *Berkeley Linguistics Society* 31: 397–408.
Diakite, Boubacar. 2006. The synchronic link between onset clusters and codas in Bambara. Unpublished Ms., Indiana University, Bloomington.
Fikkert, Paula. 1994. *On the acquisition of prosodic structure.* The Hague: Holland Academic Graphics.
Fikkert, Paula, and Helen de Hoop. 2009. Language acquisition in optimality theory. *Linguistics* 47: 311–357.
Fleischhacker, Heidi. 2001. Cluster-dependent epenthesis asymmetries. In *UCLA Working Papers in Linguistics 7, Papers in Phonology 5*, 71–116. Los Angeles: UCLA Linguistics Department.
Flemming, Edward. 2008. Asymmetries between assimilation and epenthesis. Presented at the 82nd annual meeting of the Linguistic Society of America, January 3–6, in Chicago.
Frigeni, Chiara. 2003. Metathesis and assimilation in liquids from Latin to Campidanian Sardinian: A similarity account. Presented at Going Romance 2003, University of Nijmegen, Nijmegen, Netherlands, November 20–22.
——. 2005. Parasitic /r/ in southern Sardinian. Presented at Montreal Ottawa Toronto Phonology Workshop 2005, McGill University.
Goodman, Beverly. 1997. Ponapean weight and [± consonantal]. Presented at the 28th annual meeting of the North East Linguistics Society meeting, University of Toronto.

Gouskova, Maria. 2004 Relational hierarchies in optimality theory: The case of syllable contact. *Phonology* 21: 201–50.

Green, Christopher, and Boubacar Diakite. 2008. Emergent syllable complexity in Colloquial Bamana. *Journal of West African Languages* 35: 45–56.

Green, Christopher, Stuart Davis, Boubacar Diakite and Karen Baertsch. 2009. Syncope and the drive towards minimization in Colloquial Bamana. In *IUWPL8: African linguistics across the discipline* edited by Jonathan C. Anderson, Christopher R. Green, and Samuel G. Obeng, 109–131. Bloomington, IN: IULC Publications.

Green, Tonio. 2003. Extrasyllabic consonants and onset well-formedness. In *The syllable in optimality theory*, edited by Caroline Féry and Ruben van de Vijver, 238–53. Cambridge: Cambridge University Press.

Hale, Ken. 1973. Deep-surface canonical disparities in relation to analysis and change: An Australian example. *Current Trends in Linguistics* 11: 401–458.

Hale, Ken and Josie White Eagle. 1980. A preliminary metrical account of Winnebago Accent. *International Journal of American Linguistics* 46: 117–132.

Halle, Morris and Jean-Roger Vergnaud. 1987. *An essay on stress*. Cambridge, MA: MIT Press.

Itô, Junko. 1988. *Syllable theory in prosodic phonology*. New York: Garland.

Kaye, Jonathan and Jean Lowenstamm. 1981. Syllable structure and markedness theory: Theory of markedness in generative grammar. In *Proceedings of the 1979 GLOW Conference*, edited by Adriana Belletti, Luciana Brandi and Luigi Rizzi, 287–315. Pisa, Italy: Scuola normale superiore di Pisa.

Lefebvre, Claire. 1998. *Creole genesis and the acquisition of grammar: The case of Haitian Creole*. Cambridge: Cambridge University Press.

Lefebvre, Claire and Anne-Marie Brousseau. 2002. *A grammar of Fongbe*. Berlin: Mouton de Gruyter.

Miner, Kenneth. 1979. Dorsey's Law in Winnebago-Chiwere and Winnebago accent. *International Journal of American Linguistics* 45: 25–33.

——. 1992. Winnebago accent: The rest of the data. In *Indiana University Linguistics Club 25th anniversary volume*, 28–53. Bloomington, IN: Indiana University Linguistics Club.

——. 1993. On some theoretical implications of Winnebago phonology. *Kansas Working Papers in Linguistics* 18: 111–30.

Morrill, Charles. 1997. Language, culture, and society in the Central African Republic: The emergence and development of Sango. PhD diss., Indiana University.

Piggott, Glyne. 1999. At the right edge of words. *The Linguistic Review* 16: 143–85.

Prince, Alan and Paul Smolensky. 2004. *Optimality theory: Constraint interaction in generative grammar*. Oxford: Blackwell Publishing.

Selkirk, Elisabeth. 1982. The syllable. In *The structure of phonological representations*, part 2, edited by Harry van der Hulst and Norval Smith, 337–383. Dordrecht: Foris.

Smith, Jennifer. 2003. Onset sonority constraints and subsyllabic structure. [Rutgers Optimality Archive #608, http://roa.rutgers.edu].

Strycharczuk, Patrycja. 2009. The interaction of Dorsey's Law and stress: A non-foot based approach. Presented at the CUNY Phonology Forum Conference on the Foot. http://www.cunyphonologyforum.net/footconf.php

Wright, Richard. 2004. A review of perceptual cues and cue robustness. In *Phonetically based phonology*, edited by Bruce Hayes, Robert Kirchner and Donca Steriade, 34–57. Cambridge: Cambridge University Press.

Zec, Draga. 1995. Sonority constraints on syllable structure. *Phonology* 12: 85–129.

——. 2007. The syllable. In *The Cambridge handbook of phonology*, edited by Paul de Lacy, 161–194. New York: Cambridge University Press.

CHAPTER FOUR

THE CVX THEORY OF SYLLABLE STRUCTURE

San Duanmu

1 *Introduction*

This chapter has two goals. The first is to offer an outline of the CVX theory of syllable structure (Duanmu 2009). The second is to address some common questions about the theory.

The CVX theory proposes that in all languages the maximal syllable size is CVX, which can be CVV, such as [hau] *how* and [biː] *bee*, or CVC, such as [bɛt] *bet*. At first sight, the proposal seems counter-intuitive, because many English words seem much larger than CVX. For example, *smile* [smail] is CCVVC, *texts* [tɛksts] CVCCCC, and *sprints* [sprɪnts] CCCVCCC. How does the CVX theory analyze such words?

Before we look at the details, it is worth noting that the CVX theory is mainly a description of facts that every theory must reckon with. Let me illustrate it in terms of rhyme size. It is well known that in English and German, non-final rhymes rarely exceed VX (Giegerich 1985, Borowsky 1986, 1989, Hall 2001, 2002). For example, in the CELEX lexicon of English (Baayen et al. 1995), there are 7,401 monomorphemic words, which contain 4,546 nonfinal syllables. Among them, there are just fifty-eight VVC rhymes (1.3%) and thirteen VCC rhymes (0.3%). Thus, it is an important fact that over 98% of nonfinal rhymes are no larger than VX.

Rhymes that exceed VX are mostly found in word-final position. Among the 7,401 monomorphemic English words, 41.4% of them have a final cluster that exceeds VX. Clearly, the high percentage of large word-final clusters is due to extra consonants at the end of a word. What is the explanation for such extra consonants? A popular view is that the English rhyme is large enough to include the extra consonants. The 'large-rhyme' theory has two problems. First, why are non-final rhymes limited to VX? Second, why are word-final consonants so restricted? For example, final consonants beyond VXC are limited to [t, d, s, z, θ]. Why is it so? As far as I am aware, there is no explanation in the large-rhyme theory.

An alternative explanation, which I argue for, is that word-final consonants can be explained by morphology and there is no need to explain
them in terms of large rhymes. Specifically, the CVX theory proposes
that, the first extra C beyond VX is allowed only if a language has
vowel-initial suffixes, where the vowel can take that C as its onset (e.g.
help + ing → [hɛl][pɪŋ] *helping*). In addition, consonants beyond VXC
are allowed only if the language has consonant suffixes and only if the
additional consonants resemble such suffixes. In the case of English,
[t, d, s, z, θ] are all (or resemble) consonant suffixes. In all the languages I have examined, all extra word-final consonants can be related
to the morphology of the language and there is no need to account
for them in terms of large rhymes.

I have offered an outline of the CVX theory. Let us now consider
two common reactions. The first is that the CVX theory is too radical, unlike all the familiar ones, nearly all of which assume a typology
of maximal syllables and nearly all of which assume larger sizes for
English than CVX. However, as I have mentioned, the CVX theory is
basically a synthesis of known facts. What is surprising, to me, is that
such facts have been overlooked for so long. Part of the reason for the
oversight may be that languages often look different, which may have
encouraged typology- or parameter-based approaches.

The second common reservation is that the CVX theory makes so
many assumptions that it is hard to falsify. As we shall see below,
in order to account for some apparent exceptions, I shall indeed get
into various technical details, such as feature theory, complex sounds,
and affricates. However, such technical details often have been or have
to be assumed independently. In addition, apparent exceptions often
constitute a very small fraction of all cases. For example, nonfinal
rhymes that exceed VX are no more than 2%, even if all the exceptions are real, and final consonants not accountable by morphology
are very rare. Regardless of how such exceptions are accounted for,
they should not obscure the fact that the basic generalizations of the
CVX theory are a better reflection of quantitative data than other
theories.

In fact, the CVX theory makes strong predictions that are very easy
to falsify. For example, if in any language nonfinal rhymes in monomorphemic words freely exceed VX, then the CVX theory is wrong. Similarly, if extra consonants beyond VX are allowed in word-final position
in a language that has no suffixes, then the CVX theory is wrong. Such
putative languages remain to be shown. In the absence of them, the sur-

prise is not how flexible the CVX theory is, but how restricted it is. For example, why are so many conceivable words never found in English, such as [aipny] and [ispmy], where the nonfinal rhyme exceeds VX?

Let us now consider the CVX theory in detail. First, consider the full structure of CVX, which is shown in (1).

(1) The maximal syllable: CVX

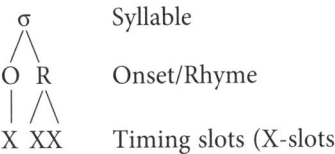

σ   Syllable

O R   Onset/Rhyme

X XX   Timing slots (X-slots)

For familiarity, I call the first slot C or the onset, the second slot V or the nucleus, and the third slot X or the coda. I also assume that VX forms a constituent called the rhyme, although this assumption is not crucial for what the maximal syllable size is (see Davis 1988, who questions the rhyme). Some examples are shown in (2), where I follow a standard assumption that a lax vowel fills one timing slot but a tense vowel can fill two. (However, I shall argue in section 6 that a tense vowel can fill one timing slot when it is in a VC rhyme. For example, the American English [ɒ] fills two timing slots in *law* [lɒ:] but one in *almost* [ɒlmost].)

(2) Sample syllables

Transcription	C	V	X	
[bæt]	[b	æ	t]	*bat*
[bai]	[b	a	i]	*buy*
[wi:]	[u	i	i]	*we*
[jæm]	[i	æ	m]	*yam*
[æn]	[	æ	n]	*Ann*
[ðə]	[ð	ə	]	*the*
[ə]	[	ə	]	*a*
[n̩:]	[	n	n]	'fish' (Shanghai Chinese)
[sz̩:]	[s	z	z]	'four' (Standard Chinese)

Several comments are in order here. First, the C slot can be filled by a consonant, as in *bat*, or a high vowel (transcribed as a glide), as in *we* and *yam*. Second, the V slot can be filled by a syllabic consonant, as in [n̩:] 'fish' in Shanghai Chinese and [sz̩:] 'four' in Standard Chinese. Third, a syllable can be smaller than CVX, because the onset can be missing, as in *Ann*, so can the coda, as in *the*, or both the onset and the coda, as in *a*; however, I shall not focus on such syllables here. Finally, [ii], [nn], and [zz] are not repetitions of the same sound but a sound doubly linked to two timing slots, represented in (3). A doubly linked sound has one articulatory configuration that lasts for two units of time.

(3)   CVX   VX   CVX
       \\/   \\/ |\\/
       b i   n   s z
       [bi:]   [n:]   [sz:]

There are many words that exceed CVX, such as *smile, texts, sprints*. The analysis of such words involves additional issues, detailed in the sections below. In particular, I argue that not every C is syllabified, although every C should be accounted for. For example, I argue that a consonant affix can be kept, even if it is not in a syllable. Similarly, I argue that an extra word-final (or stem-final) C can be kept only if a language has V-initial suffixes, so that the extra C can potentially serve as the onset of the following V. I also argue that if the articulatory gestures of two sounds can overlap, then they can form a 'complex sound'. For example, the gesture of [p] (Labial) and that of [l] (Coronal) are independent and can overlap. Therefore, [pl] can form a complex sound and fit into the onset slot.

The proposal has been demonstrated with the full lexicons of several languages (Duanmu 2009), in particular English and German (for their large final consonant clusters) and Jiarong (for its large initial consonant clusters). Owing to lack of space, this chapter will focus on English data only.

2   *Not Every Consonant is Syllabified*

It is well known that an unsyllabified C is often either deleted or given an epenthetic vowel to form a syllable with. This can be seen in Chinese loans of English names, exemplified in (4).

(4) Extra C in loan words: deletion and vowel epenthesis

	Deletion of [d]	Epenthetic [u]	Epenthetic [ɤ]
English:	[aiɚlənd]	[dʒi:p]	[rænd]
Chinese:	[ai ɚ lan]	[dʒi pʰu]	[lan dɤ]
	'Ireland'	'Jeep'	'Rand'

Syllables in Standard Chinese cannot end in [d] or [p]. In the loan for *Ireland*, there is an extra [d], which is deleted. In the loan for *Jeep*, there is an extra [p], for which a vowel [u] is added. In the loan for *Rand*, there is an extra [d], for which a vowel [ɤ] is added. Whether an extra C is deleted or given an epenthetic V may depend on the length of the source word (e.g. V-epenthesis for monosyllables and deletion for long words), but either way the effect is to eliminate extra Cs.

Many linguists in Government Phonology believe that every C is followed by V, and every V is preceded by C, so that every syllable is CV. The CV-only approach postulates many empty Cs and Vs, and I shall review it in a later section.

Many other linguists, such as Jones (1950), Abercrombie (1967), Haugen (1956a, b), Fudge (1969), Hoard (1971), Kahn (1976), Clements and Keyser (1983), Cairns (1988), Hammond (1999), Hall (2002), and Blevins (2004), do not assume empty Vs but still believe that every consonant must be syllabified (i.e. belonging to a syllable). In this 'all-in' analysis, English allows very large syllables, such as CVCCCC in *texts* [tɛksts], CCVVCC in *smiles* [smailz], and CCCVCCC in *sprints* [sprɪnts].

However, there are two problems in the all-in analysis. First, it is well known that word-medial syllables are generally quite simple, although extra consonants can occur at word edges. This is the case, for example, in Greek (Steriade 1982), English (Borowsky 1986, 1989), German (Giegerich 1985, 1989), Bella Coola (Bagemihl 1991), Spokane Salish (Bates and Carlson 1992), Polish (Bethin 1992), Georgian (Butskhrikidze 2002), and Jiarong (Lin 1993). The all-in analysis essentially assumes that the given language allows extra-large syllables. If so, why are they not found in word-medial positions? Second, there is no explanation why all consonants must be in a syllable. One might think that it is not possible to pronounce a consonant without a syllable, but English does have consonant interjections, such as *shh* [ʃ], *pff* [pf], and *psst* [ps], and English speakers have no trouble pronouncing [s] or [f] alone. If such utterances are not syllables, then consonants can be pronounced without being in a syllable, and there is no need for the all-in analysis. If such utterances are syllables, there is another problem: a word like *text* need not be one syllable but can be three [tɛk][s][t], because [s] and [t] can be syllables themselves. Unless these problems have good answers (of which I am not aware), we should reject the all-in analysis.

If some consonants are not syllabified, why can they still be kept, instead of being deleted or given an epenthetic vowel? I shall argue that being in a syllable is not the only reason for keeping a consonant. Other reasons include the morphology of a language, to be discussed next.

3   *Morphological Factor: Consonant Affixes*

Most word-final consonant clusters in English involve [t, d, s, z, θ]. If we exclude these sounds, the final syllable will be smaller. For example, *tenths* [tɛnθs] is CVCCC, but if we exclude [θ, s], the syllable is CVC. Similarly, *texts* [tɛksts] is CVCCCC, but if we exclude [s, t, s], the syllable is again CVC. The question is: what is the reason to exclude word-final [t, d, s, z, θ]?

Phonetically, [t, d, s, z, θ] are made with the articulator Coronal. One might suggest, therefore, that Coronal sounds can be absorbed into a syllable as a special case. On the other hand, [t, d, s, z, θ] also occur as suffixes in English; indeed they are the only consonant suffixes in English (plus a marginal [n], as in *blow-blown*, although the suffix could be *-en*, thanks to a reviewer for this point). Therefore, it is possible that final [t, d, s, z, θ] are there not because they are in a syllable but because they can serve as suffixes. The point has been made by Goldsmith (1990, 127), who proposes that consonant morphemes are 'licensed' to occur even if they are not in a syllable. I shall call it the affix rule and state it in (5).

(5)   The affix rule: Affix or affix-like sounds can be pronounced, even if they cannot fit into a syllable.

The affix rule is intuitively natural. In the CELEX lexicon of English (Baayen et al 1995), among the 54,447 basic words (lemmas), 41,911 (or 77%) end in C. This means that in most words the final syllable is already full (needs no more C). If consonant suffixes could not be added when the preceding syllable is full, then they would rarely surface and we would not be able to tell whether there is a suffix or not. Also, since the affix rule already accounts for word-final [t, d, s, z, θ], it is redundant to assume that they must also be part of a syllable.

In English, not all final [t, d, s, z, θ] are suffixes. For example, the final [s] and [t] in *text* [tɛkst] are not suffixes. Such sounds are covered by the term 'affix-like' in the affix rule. The idea has been proposed before by Fujimura (1979) and Pierrehumbert (1994), who use the notion 'perceived suffixes' to refer to final [t, d, s, z, θ] that are not suffixes, such as [s] in [æks] *ax*.

The lack of distinction between real affixes and affix-like sounds suggests that phonetic judgment is independent of semantics. I shall call it 'the independence of phonetic judgment', stated in (6).

(6) The independence of phonetic judgment:
     Judgment on phonetic well-formedness is independent of meaning.

For example, if the sequence [æks] sounds good in *backs*, it should sound good in *ax*, even though [s] is a suffix in the former but not in the latter. Similarly, if the sequence [ɛkst] sounds good in *indexed*, it should sound good in *text*, even though [t] is a suffix in the former but not in the latter. It is relevant to note, too, that the acceptability of a new word also depends on the frequency of its phonotactic components (Frisch et al. 2000), in addition to whether the components are found in existing words.

   In summary, the all-in analysis is more complicated in that it cannot explain why non-final syllables are smaller. In addition, the all-in analysis is redundant, because word-final [t, d, s, z, θ] can be explained by morphology and there is no need to assume that they have to be in a syllable. A complete search of the English lexicon shows no counter example (Duanmu 2009).

4   Morphological Factor: Potential V and Anti-allomorphy

If we exclude word-final [t, d, s, z, θ], the largest final sequence in English is VXC, which can be either VVC, as in [baik] *bike*, or VCC, as in [hɛlp] *help*. There are three analyses of VXC, shown in (7), where square brackets indicate syllable boundaries.

(7) Analyses of final VXC

[...VXC]	Large rhyme
[...VX]<C>	Extrasyllabic <C>
[...VX][C(V)]	Onset (of a potential V)

In the first analysis the entire VXC is in a large rhyme (e.g. Kahn 1976, Kiparsky 1981, Giegerich 1992, Harris 1994, Blevins 1995, and Hall 2001). The problem is that nonfinal rhymes are limited to VX (Giegerich 1985, Borowsky 1989), instead of VXC. To say that the maximal rhyme is VX non-finally and VXC finally, as Hall (2001) does, is a restatement of the fact, not an explanation. In addition, should there be VXC rhymes, one would expect them to be more prominent than VX rhymes (e.g. more likely to attract stress), but there is no such evidence. For example, there is no quantitative evidence that a final VXC (such as [ɪnt]) is more likely to attract stress than a final VV (such as [ai]). The difference between final VC and VCC is less obvious: if one C is extrametrical, then we may have a weight difference between V and VC, but if CC can be extrametrical, then both rimes are V.

In the second analysis a word-final C is extrasyllabic (e.g. McCarthy 1979, Hayes 1982, Borowsky 1989, Giegerich 1989, Goldsmith 1990, and Gussmann 2002), and there is a consistent maximal rhyme VX for both final and nonfinal syllables. The question though is why the final C should be excluded from syllabification and why it is allowed to stay.

In the third analysis the final C is the onset of a following V. There are two views of what the V is. In the first, the V can be completely abstract (Burzio 1994). In the second, the V can be real—it is provided by a V-initial suffix (Giegerich 1985, Borowsky 1986). Since a word does not always have a suffix, I refer to the V as a 'potential V'. For example, the [p] in *help* is an extra C when the word occurs alone but it is the onset of the following V in *helper* and *helping*. The question for this analysis is why the final C is kept when there is no following V, such as the [p] in *help, helpful,* and *helpless*. Here I appeal to a requirement known as paradigm uniformity or anti-allomorphy (Burzio 1996), according to which one aims to keep a morpheme in the same shape regardless of the environment. In (8) I state the conditions that support the final C, which are illustrated in (9).

(8)   Conditions for an extra word-edge C

      a. Potential V: A word-final C can serve as the onset of a potential V, which may come with a V-initial suffix. Similarly, a word-initial C can serve as the coda of a potential V, which may come with a V-final prefix.

      b. Anti-allomorphy: Keep a morpheme in the same shape regardless of the environment.

(9)   Final C   Supported by potential V   Supported by anti-allomorphy

    [hɛl]p   [hɛl][pɪŋ], [hɛl][pɚ]   [hɛl]p, [hɛl]p[fʊl], [hɛl]p[lɪs]

    help   *helping, helper*   *help, helpful, helpless*

    [rɪs]k   [rɪs][kɪŋ], [rɪs][ki]   [rɪs]k, [rɪs]k[fri]

    risk   *risking, risky*   *risk, risk-free*

Without the anti-allomorphy requirement, unsyllabified consonants would be deleted and many lexical contrasts would be lost. For example, if we delete the unsyllabified [p], *help, helpful,* and *helpless* would be pronounced as [hɛl], [hɛl][fʊl], and [hɛl][lɪs] respectively, confusing with *hell, hellful,* and *hellless.*

Charles Cairns (personal communication) points out that, while the final [p] in *help* can be attributed to a potential V (e.g. from a V-initial suffix *-ing* or *-er*), the [p] in the noun *kelp* cannot be accounted for this way, because it does not take such suffixes. There are two answers to the problem. First, there are V-initial suffixes for nouns, such as *-y.* Second, such words can be explained by (6): because phonetic judgment is independent of meaning, if final [-lp] does not sound bad for words like *help,* then it does not sound bad for *kelp* either.

One might point out that in a word like *file,* the [l] is velarized (a 'dark' [l]), which is an indication that it is in the rhyme; therefore, the syllabification should be [fail]. In the CVX analysis, [ail] is not a possible rhyme; instead, there are two other reasons why [l] is dark. First, while [l] is dark in the rhyme (for all speakers) and clear in the onset (for some speakers), it is unclear whether [l] is dark or clear when it is unsyllabified. Second, it is possible that *file* has two syllables [fai][ł], where [ł] is syllabic, in the rhyme, and hence dark.

The potential-V analysis also predicts that, if a language has CV prefixes, an extra C may occur as a 'potential coda' in word-initial position. This is schematically shown in (10).

(10) Initial C supported by potential V and anti-allomorphy

Root	Supported by potential V	Supported by anti-allomorphy
CCVC	[CV-C][CVC]	C[CVC]

An example of (10) can be seen in (11), from the Tibeto-Burman language Jiarong, where [tɕʰ] is an affricate (Lin 1993, 36).

(11)
Root	Supported by potential V	Supported by anti-allomorphy
ntɕʰok	[kɐ-n][tɕʰok]	
'dip'	'dip'	
ʒba	[tə-ʒ][ba]	ʒ[ba-n][tɕʰok]
'face'	'face'	'face dip (dimple)'

The root for 'dip' is CCVC. When it follows a CV prefix (or a vowel-final word), the root-initial [n] can serve as the coda of the preceding V.

Similarly, the root for 'face' is CCV. When there is a CV prefix, the root-initial C can serve as the coda of the preceding V. When there is no prefix, as in 'face dip (dimple)', the root-initial C is supported by anti-allomorphy.

The potential-V analysis makes specific predictions for whether and where an extra C may occur in a given language. In a language that has V-initial suffixes, an extra C may occur in root-final position. In a language that has V-final prefixes, an extra C may occur in root-initial position. If the predictions are correct, we have already explained the extra C and there is no reason to assume that it has to be in a syllable, too.

5   Gestural Overlap and Complex Sounds

English has many onsets that are made of a CC cluster, such as [pr] in *pray*, [pl] in *play*, [br] in *bring*, [kw] in *quick*, [mj] in *mute*, and so on. Similar onsets are found in Chinese, too, such as [kwan] 'wide', [twan] 'group', [njan] 'year', [nwan] 'warm', [ljan] 'connect', and so on. We cannot exclude the first C by appealing to the affix rule or a potential V. For example, Chinese has no prefixes. Therefore, the first C in a CC cluster cannot be excluded by the affix rule or explained in terms of a potential V.

It is tempting to suggest that we extend the maximal syllable from CVX to CCVX. However, I shall argue that there is a crucial property of CC onsets that has been overlooked: all CC onsets are possible complex sounds in that their articulatory gestures can overlap. Because overlapping gestures can be made simultaneously, a complex sound takes just one timing slot, as a single sound does. Let me explain it in detail.

I assume that a speech sound (consonant or vowel) is made of one or more articulatory gestures or 'features' (e.g. Ladefoged and Halle 1988, Browman and Goldstein 1989, Halle 2003). For example, [k] is made of the gesture [+stop] by the tongue body (the Dorsal articulator) and [p] is made of the gesture [+stop] by the lips (the Labial articulator) (ignoring laryngeal features). In addition, I assume that speech sounds are made in sequence over time. For example, in [it] *eat* [i] is made before [t] whereas in [ti] *tea* [t] is made before [i]. Moreover, I assume that different gestures can overlap in time, creating a complex sound. The notion of gestural overlap is not controversial. Some well-known examples are shown in (12), where I use [⌐] to indicate gestural overlap (a complex sound).

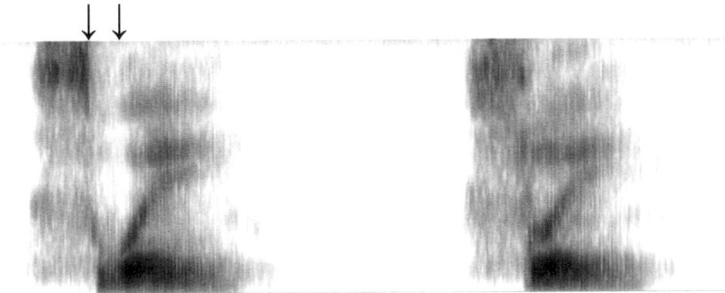

Figure 1   Spectrograms of the English word sway [swei] on the left and the Chinese word [s̄wei] 'year' on the right. The independent duration of [w] (between arrows) is visible in the English word but not in the Chinese word

(12) Gestural sequence vs. gestural overlap (complex sound)

Type	Sound	Example	Language
Sequence	[kp]	[bækpæk] *backpack*	English
Overlap	[k͡p]	[k͡pu] 'die'	Eggon
Sequence	[sw]	[swei] *sway*	English
Overlap	[s̄w]	[s̄wei] 'year'	Chinese

In *backpack*, [k] and [p] are pronounced in sequence as two sounds. In [k͡pu] 'die', a word in the African language Eggon (Ladefoged and Maddieson 1996, 334), [k] and [p] are pronounced nearly simultaneously (although the release of [k] may slightly precede that of [p]). Similarly, Chao (1934) notes that [sw] is pronounced in sequence in the English word [swei] *sway*, where the lip rounding of [w] starts after [s], but simultaneously in the Chinese word [s̄wei] 'year', where the lip rounding of [w] starts at the beginning of [s]. Chao's observation can be demonstrated by the spectrogram in Figure 1.

The notion of complex sounds has been proposed before in a rather loose way; it usually refers to two sounds that share one timing slot. Some examples are shown in (13).

(13) Some previous proposals of complex sounds

Author	Proposal	Example
Selkirk (1982)	[sC]	[sp, st, sk, ...]
Sagey (1986)	'contour features'	[st, ts, nt, tn, ...]
Borowsky (1989)	NC	[mp, nt, ns, ...]

Selkirk (1982, 347) proposes that [s] can pair with any obstruent C to form a single sound, a view shared by Lamontagne (1993). Sagey (1986) proposes that opposite gestures can occur in sequence within a sound, such as [−stop, +stop] in [st] and [+stop, −stop] in [ts]; she calls such sequential gestures 'contour features'. Borowsky (1989) proposes that NC clusters with the same place of articulation can count as one sound, a view shared by Hall (2001). Clearly, such views of complex sounds radically increase the inventory of possible sounds in the world's languages.

Unlike previous proposals, I assume a more restricted version of complex sounds. In my analysis, two sounds cannot form a complex sound if they have conflicting gestures (or 'contour features'), such as [−nasal] and [+nasal], or [+round] and [−round]. The reason is that conflicting gestures cannot overlap (i.e. they cannot be made simultaneously) but must be made in sequence, and therefore it would require more than one timing unit to do so. By adopting a stricter version of complex sounds, we also set a higher standard for the CVX theory.

Reported cases that require contour features include (a) pre- and post-nasalized stops, (b) contour tones, and (c) affricates. I have argued in Duanmu (1994) that case (b) does not involve contour features. Affricates will be discussed shortly. Herbert (1975, 1986) and Duanmu (1990) have argued that case (a) does not involve contour features either. Specifically, Herbert argued that a true pre- or post-nasalized stop should satisfy three conditions: (i) it is not a cluster, (ii) there is a four-way contrast in the language (e.g. [p, b, m, mb]), and (iii) it is not due to the 'shielding effect'. For example, consider the often-cited example of [bmb] and [mbm] in Kaingang, which are not contrastive but predictable from the nasality of the surrounding vowels: [bmb] is used only when the surrounding vowels are both oral, and [mbm] is used only when the surrounding vowels are both nasal. This is what Herbert calls the shielding effect, where a brief [b] shields an oral V from a nasal, and a brief [m] shields a nasal V from [b]. Therefore, [bmb] is phonemically [m] and [mbm] is phonemically [b]. In Duanmu (1990) I argued that none of the languages in the UPSID database that is reported to have pre- or post-nasalized stops passes Herbert's conditions.

A pair of conflicting gestures, such as [+round, −round] by the articulator Labial, [+nasal, −nasal] by the articulator Velum, and [+anterior, −anterior] by the articulator Coronal, have been called 'contour features'. They can be ruled out by the No Contour Principle, first proposed by Duanmu (1994) and given in (14).

(14) No Contour Principle:

An articulator cannot make opposite values of the same feature (F) within a sound (i.e. within one timing slot).

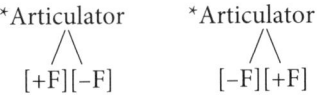

The principle assumes that each gesture takes up a unit of time, and to perform opposite gestures we need two units of time, or the duration of two sounds. It also assumes that all gestures within a sound are simultaneous. For example, [k͡p] is the same as [p͡k].

Although the No Contour Principle allows fewer possible complex sounds than previous analyses do, it also allows many that are not thought to be complex sounds before. For example, onset clusters [pl, pr, kl, kr] can form complex sounds [p͡l, p͡r, k͡l, k͡r]. In addition, the No Contour Principle can distinguish certain clusters that are thought to have the same properties. For example, consider [fr] and [θr], shown in (15) and (16), where [+anterior] means that the Coronal articulator (tongue tip) is front and [−anterior] means that it is back.

(15) [f]   Labial—[+fricative]
      [r]   Coronal—[−fricative, −anterior]
      [f͡r]   Labial—[+fricative], Coronal—[−fricative]

(16) [θ]   Coronal—[+fricative, +anterior]
      [r]   Coronal—[−fricative, −anterior]
      *[θ͡r]   Coronal—[+fricative, −fricative, +anterior, −anterior]

In [f͡r], there are no conflicting gestures; therefore, it is a possible complex sound. In [θ͡r], there are conflicting gestures [+anterior, −anterior]; therefore, it is not a possible complex sound. The CVX theory predicts that [fr] and [θr] will have different distributions, which is correct, to be discussed below.

It is worth noting that, in the theory of underspecification (e.g. Steriade 1987, Archangeli 1988, and Keating 1988), non-contrastive features or articulators are not specified. For example, [f] is unspecified for Coronal and [r] is unspecified for Labial. In addition, while [−voice] is specified for [f] (in contrast to [+voice] in [v]), [voice] is not contrastive for [r] and so [r] is unspecified for [voice]. Therefore, in [f͡r] there are no conflicting gestures [−voice, +voice], but [−voice] only.

In previous analyses, onset clusters are governed by sonority (e.g. Jespersen 1904, Selkirk 1982, Steriade 1982, Kenstowicz 1994, Zec 1994 and others), which I rephrase in (17) and illustrate with English examples in (18).

(17) The sonority analysis of onset clusters:
     The sonority in an onset cluster must show a sufficient rise.

(18) Examples of the sonority analysis of onset clusters

Cluster	Prediction
pr	good: enough sonority rise
fr	good: enough sonority rise
θr	good: enough sonority rise
sr	good: enough sonority rise
*fn	bad: not enough sonority rise

In the CVX theory, an onset cluster is possible only if it can form a complex sound. Some examples are shown in (19).

(19) The complex-sound analysis of onset clusters:

   a. Possible onset clusters (those that can form complex sounds): pr, fr, pl, kr,…
   b. Impossible onset clusters (those that cannot form complex sounds): θr, ʃr, ʃm, ʃn, sr, sl, sm, sn, st, sp, sk, sf,…

In the sonority analysis, [θr] and [sr] are both good, because they have the same sonority rise as [fr]. In contrast, [θr] and [sr] are bad in the complex-sound analysis, even though [fr] is good. The reason is that [f] and [r] do not have conflicting gestures, whereas [θ] and [r] do.

The sonority analysis and the complex-sound analysis make different predictions. The sonority analysis predicts that clusters like [θr, ʃr] are possible word-medial onsets, because they have a proper sonority rise. In addition, clusters like [ʃm, ʃn, sr, sl, sm, sn, st, sp, sk, sf] are possible word-medial onsets, because in the sonority analysis [s] (and [ʃ]) is exempt from the sonority requirement. In contrast, the complex-sound analysis predicts that such clusters are not possible onsets and will not be found word medially. As shown in Duanmu (2009), evidence from an exhaustive search of the English lexicon supports the complex-sound analysis. The result supports the view that sonority plays a much smaller role in phonology than previously thought, a view independently expressed by Harris (2006). Word initially, an extra C can be supported by a 'potential V', because English has V-final prefixes.

Charles Cairns (personal communication) points out that in *asparagus* and *astronomy*, the [p] and [t] are not aspirated, which seems to indicate that [sp] and [str] are medial onsets, which contradict my claim that [sp] and [str] are not possible medial onsets. There are two possible answers to this problem. First, aspiration may not be a reliable indicator of syllable boundary, a point made by Wells (1990). For example, in *gastronomy*, the [t] is unaspirated, yet it would be better to place the syllable boundary between [s] and [t], because [æ] cannot end a regular English word and the syllable [gæ] would violate the Law of Finals (Vennemann 1988). Similarly, in *gestation*, the [t] is unaspirated, yet it would be better to place the syllable boundary after [s], because [ɛ] never ends an English word. Second, there could be a perceived word boundary in words like *asparagus*. For example, *asparagus* is thought to be 'a sparrowgrass' by some English speakers.

Besides onset clusters, there are three other cases where a complex sound can be formed. The first case is affricates, which are formed by a stop plus a fricative, such as [t] + [s] → [t͡s]. The formation of an affricate is not controversial, but the analysis is not obvious. For example, if [t] is [+stop] and [s] is [–stop], [t͡s] would have conflicting gestures [+stop, –stop]. Therefore, [t͡s] should not be a well-formed complex sound. One solution is not to treat affricates as [+stop, –stop], but as [+stop, +strident], where [strident] refers to strong frication (e.g. Steriade 1989, Clements 1999). This analysis has two problems. First, it is hard to interpret the feature [strident] as an articulatory gesture. Second, there are still feature conflicts between a stop, which is [+stop, –strident], and a fricative, which is [–stop, +strident]. We must explain why when a stop and a fricative form an affricate, the features [–stop] and [–strident] are lost.

A better solution is to represent stops and fricatives with independent gestures, instead of opposite ones (Lombardi 1990), so that their gestures are compatible. Specifically, I propose that [+fricative] is a gesture that closes the edges (left and right sides) of an articulator, whereas [+stop] is a gesture that closes the middle of an articulator. In this analysis, [t͡s] is a well-formed complex sound, although it is rarely used as an onset in English (but see *Tswana*, *scherzo*, and *Alzheimer*). Similarly, [p͡s] and [k͡s] are possible complex sounds, although they are more common in German than in English. The notion of affricates can explain some words that appear to be problems. For example, the first syllable in [dɛks][trəʊz] *dextrose* seems to be CVCC, which exceeds CVX. In the present analysis, the syllabification is [dɛk͡s][t͡rəʊ]z, where no syllable exceeds CVX. A question for the proposal is that, if [ps] or [ks] can be single sounds, why do they not occur as onsets in English? The answer, I suggest, is that not all useable phonological forms are used or used with equal frequency. In fact, most useable forms are not used in English, a phenomenon that is called the 'spotty-data problem' in Duanmu (2009).

Another case of complex sounds involve VNC, where NC has the same place of articulation. Such a cluster often becomes ṼC, where Ṽ is a complex sound. The feature analysis of *tent* [tɛnt] → [tɛ̃t] is given in (20), where only relevant features are shown.

(20) Analysis of *tent* [tɛnt] → [tɛ̃t]

	[ɛ	n	t]	→	[ɛ̃	t]
Coronal		(+stop)	+stop			+stop
Dorsal	-back				-back	
Velum		+nasal	-nasal		+nasal	-nasal

I assume that [nt] share the feature Coronal-[+stop], indicated under [t]. When [ɛnt] merge into [ɛ̃t], all features are preserved, and there are no conflicting features in the complex sound [ɛ̃]. It is worth noting that the change of VNC → ṼC is optional in word-final position but required in word-medial position.

Borowsky (1986) observes that non-final rhymes in English are mostly VX. However, there are some exceptions, most of them involving VNC rhymes. For example, the first syllable in *symptom* [sɪmp.təm] seems to be VNC, which exceeds VX. In the present analysis, VNC can be ṼC and *symptom* is [sĩptəm], where no rhyme exceeds VX. The present analysis agrees with independent judgments that VNC is indeed often realized as ṼC. For example, a number of linguists have given similar transcriptions, such as *simple* [sĩpɬ], *sinker* [sĩkə], *symptom* [sĩptəm], and *council* [kãũsɬ] (e.g. Malécot 1960, Bailey 1978, Fujimura 1979, and Cohn 1993).

Yet another case of complex sounds involves V+[r], where V is typically a back vowel. If we represent [r] as Coronal-[−anterior], then [Vr] can form a complex sound. The analysis of [or] is shown in (21).

(21) Analysis of [or] as a complex sound

	[o	r]	→	[o͡r]
Coronal		-anterior		-anterior
Dorsal	+back			+back
Labial	+round			+round

In this analysis, the syllabification of *ordnance* could be [o͡rd] [nən]s, where the first syllable is VX. Similarly, *arctic* could be [a͡rk][tɪk], where the first syllable is again VX.

6 *[V:C] Rhymes*

Another kind of rhyme that occurs in non-final positions is [V:C], where [V:] is a tense vowel, such as [ɒːl] in *also* [ɒːlso] in American English. The [V:C] rhyme is often treated as VXC, because a tense vowel can take two timing slots phonologically. For example, the rhyme of a stressed monosyllable must be either [VC] (as in *bit* [bɪt] and *bet* [bɛt]) or [V:] (as in *bee* [biː] and *law* [lɒː]), but not just [V] (e.g. *[bɪ] or *[bɛ]). This shows that a tense vowel is equivalent to a lax vowel plus a consonant.

If we treat a [V:C] rhyme as VXC, we face two problems. First, there is a general lack of medial VCC rhymes. Second, there is a general lack of medial VVC rhymes, where VV is a diphthong. Therefore, [V:C] does not represent a general case, but a special one.

It has been proposed that while tense vowels can be long, they need not in all environments (Pike 1947, Jones 1950, Abercrombie 1967, Giegerich 1985, and Alcantara 1998). In particular, a tense V can be long when there is no following C in the syllable but short when there is. If so, [V:C] is in fact VC, where V is tense and short but still distinct from a lax vowel. For example, *also* is [ɒlso] in American English, where [ɒ] is short compared with [ɒː] in *author*. Under this proposal, apparent [V:C] rhyme are still VX. It is worth noting that non-final [V:C] rhymes are not common; therefore, regardless of how they should be accounted for, they do not change the fact that most nonfinal rhymes are limited to VX.

In some languages, such as Cantonese and Thai, there is a contrast between [CVC] and [CV:C] syllables. For example, Cantonese has a contrast between [sam] 'heart' and [saːm] 'shirt'. If the contrast lies in vowel length, [CV:C] has four timing slots and poses a challenge to the CVX theory. There are several possible solutions though. First, what appears to be a monosyllabic word can in fact be more than one syllable. For example, while [sam] is CVX, [sa:m] could be [sa:]<m>, where <m> is either extra-syllabic or a separate syllable. Second, a long vowel is shortened in Cantonese (Wang 1999) and Thai (Leben 1971) when the syllable is not final, and it remains to be seen what the representation of non-final syllables should be. Third, there is often a quality difference between reported long and short vowels, and it is sometimes possible to represent their difference without appealing to vowel length. For example, Huang (1970) represents Cantonese [sam] 'heart' as [sʌm] and [sa:m] 'shirt' as [sam]. For lack of space, I leave it open what the correct analysis should be of languages like Cantonese and Thai.

7   Multiple Solutions to the CVX Requirement

In the CVX theory, the only restriction on syllable size is that it does not exceed CVX. Therefore, for a given string of sounds, it is possible to satisfy the requirement in more than one way. Two examples are shown in (22).

(22)   Multiple solutions to the CVX requirement

Word	Sounds	Syllabification options
pumpkin	[pʌmpkən]	[pʌ͡p][kən], [pʌm][p͡kən], [pʌŋ][kən]
arctic	[arktɪk]	[a͡rk][tɪk], [ar][tɪk]
prints	[prɪnts]	[p͡rɪn]ts, [p͡rɪn]t͡s, [p͡rɪt]s, [p͡rɪt͡s]

The options in (22) are not exhaustive. For example, the second syllable of *pumpkin* can be a syllabic [n], which is not shown. All the options satisfy the CVX requirement. The availability of such options could explain possible variations among speakers.

8   Can [lp] be an Onset or [pl] be a Coda?

I proposed above that [pl] can form a complex sound [p͡l]. Several questions can be raised. First, if [p] + [l] can form a complex sound, so should [l] + [p]. Why then is there no word such as *lpum*? The answer is that all articulatory features in a complex sound are simultaneous, so that [p͡l] and [l͡p] are identical. Therefore, *lpum* would be the same as *plum.* It should be noted that [pl] (as in *play*) and [lp] (as in *help*) are not identical in English, because [lp] in *help* is not [l͡p] but a sequence of two sounds.

One might also observe that *help* is not realized as [hɛl͡p], where [p] is pronounced simultaneously as [l] (same as [p͡l] in *plum*). Instead, *help* is pronounced as [hɛlp], where [p] is pronounced after [l]. If [l] and [p] can form a complex sound, why is [hɛl͡p] not used? The answer is that there is no need to incorporate [p] into the preceding syllable, because [p] is already supported by 'anti-allomorphy' (see above). Besides, the sequence [lp] is more similar to that in *hel.per*, and hence is a better way to satisfy anti-allomorphy.

Next, one might ask why there are no such words as *tikl* or *tepl* in English, where [k͡l] and [p͡l] are complex sounds in the coda. A possible answer is that, as is common in the world's languages, there are more restrictions on codas than on onsets. For example, in Standard Chinese, almost any consonant can be the onset, but the coda is limited to [n] and [ŋ]. Similarly, English may simply disfavor complex sounds in the coda. In addition, a final [l] can be syllabic in English, and *tikl* and *tepl* would be disyllabic. Indeed, there are such words in English, such as *tickle* and *nipple*. This point was made by Lamontagne (1993).

Finally, one might ask why there is no medial coda [k͡l] or [p͡l] in English, which could result from a hypothetical word *neplsa* or *tiklny*. There are again two possible answers. First, English may disfavor complex codas. Second, because [l] can be syllabic, *neplsa* or *tiklny* can be trisyllabic, which would usually be spelled as *neppelsa* or *tickelny*. Unlike *neplsa* and *tiklny*, which do not seem to be possible English words, *neppelsa* and *tickelny* seem a lot more natural as potential English words.

9 The CV-only Analysis

Lowenstamm (1996) and Scheer (2004), working in Government Phonology, propose that even CVX is too large. Instead, there is only one syllable size for all languages, which is CV. Let us call it the 'CV-only' analysis. Two examples are shown in (23), where Ø is an empty C or V.

(23) The CV-only analysis

mix	[mɪ][kØ][sØ]
spiked	[sØ][pa][Øi][kØ][tØ]

The CV-only analysis has three problems. First, it makes extensive use of empty sounds that have no phonetic content. In contrast, the CVX theory assumes no such empty sounds.

Second, the CV-only analysis must explain why only some word-edge Cs can occur with an empty V but others cannot. For example, while initial [sØ] is good in English, [fØ] is not (e.g. *stop* is good but **ftop* is not). Similarly, it must explain why extra word-final Cs are mostly [s, z, t, d, θ] in English (e.g. *text* is good but **texp* is not). The CV-only analysis must say, as other theories do, that [s] is special initially and [s, z, t, d, θ] are special word finally. But once we agree that these sounds are special, it is unnecessary to assume that they must also occur with an empty V, or be syllabified at all. This criticism also applies to the analysis of coda consonants by Harris and Gussmann (1998).

A third problem with the CV-only theory is that it opens up alternative solutions that are hard to choose from. For example, assuming exhaustive syllabification, there are at least three conceivable analyses of *spiked*, shown in (24).

(24) Conceivable analyses that are hard to distinguish

CVX-only	[sØØ][pai][kØt]
CV-only	[sØ][pa][Øi][kØ][tØ]
VC-only	[Øs][Øp][aØ][ik][Øt]

The CVX-only analysis (a version of the CV-only analysis, not to be confused with the CVX theory) uses a larger syllable size but fewer syllables and fewer empty elements. The CV-only and VC-only analyses use the same syllable size, the same number of empty elements, and the same number of syllables. All the solutions can represent any word without any problem. It is not obvious how one should choose among the alternatives.

10   Other Languages

Although I have focused on English, there are reasons to believe that the CVX theory has a general nature. First, English has long been thought to have very large syllables. If they turn out to be no larger than CVX, one would like to reexamine other languages that are thought to have very large syllables. Second, there is evidence for the CVX theory from major language families. In the Indo-European family, I have discussed English and German in Duanmu (2009), and others have discussed Polish (Bethin 1992), Georgian (Butskhrikidze 2002), and Hindi (Kumar 2005). In the Sino-Tibetan family, I have discussed Chinese and Jiarong in Duanmu (2009). In the Amerindian group, there is supporting evidence from Bella Coola (Bagemihl 1991) and Spokane Salish (Bates and Carlson 1992). Finally, African languages are known to have simple syllable structures. It is, of course, impossible to discuss all languages in a single study. However, it is worth noting that many of the languages just mentioned are known to have very complex consonant clusters. The fact that a simple syllable structure is possible in analyzing these languages, either by me or by other authors, makes it much less likely that we have missed out on important cases.

Robert Vago (personal communication) suggests that Hungarian might be a problem for the CVX theory, owing to its medial consonant clusters. It is useful to use Hungarian as an example to illustrate the kind of apparent problems and their solutions. According to Olaszy (2007), the largest medial consonant cluster in Hungarian is CCCCC. There are five examples, shown in (25), following the original transcription.

(25) Medial CCCCC clusters (underlined) in Hungarian

akordstruktúra	[akor<u>tStr</u>uktu:ra]	'accord structure'
angsztrőm	[a<u>nkstr</u>O:m]	'angstrom'
marketingstratégia	[mArketi<u>nkStr</u>atE:gia]	'marketing strategy'
platformstratégia	[platfo<u>rmStr</u>atE:gia]	'platform strategy'
sportstratégia	[Spo<u>rtStr</u>atE:gia]	'sports strategy'

Of the five words, four are compounds, where the CCCCC cluster is not truly medial. The remaining example [ankstrO:m] can be syllabified as [ãk͡s][t͡rOm], where [ã], [k͡s], and [t͡r] are well-formed complex sounds. Therefore, all the words are compatible with the CVX theory. I have checked through all medial clusters in Hungarian and none of them constitute a problem.

Dell and Elmedlaoui (2002, 254) report that Berber syllables are usually limited to CVC, but VCC rhymes can arise when the CC is a geminate. Two trisyllabic examples are shown in (26), where I have changed [š] to [ʃ].

(26) VCC rhymes in Berber

/m-qiddʃ-a/ →	[m.qidd.ʃa]	'mischieveous girl'
/t-nʃʃr-i/ →	[t.nəʃʃ.ri]	'you (fem sing) spread'

Two remarks can be made here. First, we may need to examine the phonetic properties of the geminate CC coda and see if they are shortened or if they contrast with a single C in this environment. Second, the VCC rhymes are stem final and so may be subject to the anti-allomorphy requirement. In particular, if there is no suffix, or if the suffix is a consonant, the stems are possibly syllabified as [qid.dʃ] and [nəʃ. ʃr], where no syllable exceeds CVX. In the suffixed forms, the syllabification could be [m.qid<d>.ʃa] and [t.nəʃ<ʃ>.ri], where < > indicate an unsyllabified consonant. The free consonant is kept (rather than deleted) because of the anti-allomorphy requirement. This is similar to the case in English. For example, in *helpful*, the [p] is unsyllabified, but it is kept by anti-allomorphy, because *help* is otherwise a good word, where the [p] is supported by a potential V (see section 4).

11   The Metrical Basis of CVX

If the maximal syllable is indeed CVX, we would like to know why. Without an answer, CVX may still seem to be an arbitrary size.

McCarthy (1979) and Kiparsky (1979, 1981) propose that a syllable structure is in fact a metrical structure. For example, a CCCVCC syllable is represented in (27). Following the metrical theory of Liberman and Prince (1977), S is a strong node and W is a weak node, and the taller the x-column, the stronger a position is.

(27) Metrical representation of a CCCVCC syllable (Kiparsky 1981, 250)

```
                                    x
                       x            x
            x          x            x            x
[[[    W    S    ]     S    ][    S    [    S    W    ]]]
       C    C          C          V          C    C
```

Kiparsky argues that if we interpret W has having less sonority and S as having more, the metrical representation yields an ideal sonority contour, whereby sonority rises towards the nucleus and falls from the nucleus (Jespersen 1904). In other words, sonority 'is simply the intrasyllabic counterpart of stress'.

Kiparsky's proposal contains an important insight, but there are two problems. First, the syllables Kiparsky assumes are too big. If the CVX theory is correct, no language has syllables larger than CVX. Second, the metrical structure is ill formed, because it contains adjacent strong beats, or 'stress clash', which violate a fundamental property of rhythm, which is the alternation between strong and weak beats (apparent counter-examples, such as *sardine* and *alpine*, need not involve stress clash either, if we adopt moraic feet).

The CVX theory can solve both problems in Kiparsky's analysis, yet keep his insight that syllable structure reflects metrical structure. Let us assume that the simplest rhythm is the alternation between S and W beats, or ...SWSW..., where there is no 'clash', which is SS, or 'lapse', which is WW. In addition, let us assume that each syllable has only one peak. Now consider the structures in (28), where V is a strong beat and C a weak one.

(28)	String	Rhythm	Analysis
	*CCV	WWS	bad rhythm: lapse of WW
	*VCC	SWW	bad rhythm: lapse of WW
	*VCV	SWS	good rhythm but bad syllable: two peaks
	CVC	WSW	good rhythm and good syllable
	VC	SW	good rhythm and good syllable
	CV	WS	good rhythm and good syllable

The analysis predicts that CCV and VCC are not good syllables (unless CC can form a complex sound), nor is VCV, but CVC, VC, and CV are.

The metrical analysis I just offered is only a preliminary one. A full analysis may require both moraic feet and syllabic feet in the same language (Duanmu et al. 2005). For example, a heavy syllable is a moraic foot, and two syllables can make syllabic foot. For lack of space, such issues cannot be covered here.

12 *Summary and Implications*

There is no doubt that many languages have CVX syllables (CVC or CVV). What I have proposed is that CVX is also the upper limit on syllable size. While the proposal may seem radical, it is essentially a descriptive generalization: an overwhelming percentage of word-medial syllables are limited to CVX and extra consonants at word edges are mostly attributable to the morphology of a language. In particular, a word has the schematic structure C_mCSCC_m, where C_m is one or more affix or affix-like consonants, C is a consonant supported by a potential V from an affix, and S is one or more syllables whose maximal size is CVX. Exceptions to the generalization are rare, regardless of how they are accounted for.

If the CVX theory is correct, there are some interesting implications. First, while some linguists believe that the notion of the syllable is central to phonological analysis (e.g. Ladefoged 2001), other linguists doubt whether the syllable is a primary phonological entity (e.g. Chomsky and Halle 1968, Gimson 1970, Lamontagne 1993, Steriade 1999, Blevins 2004, and many participants at the 2007 CUNY Syllable Conference). For example, while Blevins (2004, 232) believes syllables to be 'important constructs in phonological systems', she also believes that syllables can be derived from phonotactic patterns at word edges. If the maximal syllable size is CVX, it is a real phonological entity, not always derivable from word-edge patterns, and the best term for it seems to be the syllable.

On the other hand, if the CVX limit can be derived from metrical structure, as I have suggested, there is a more fundamental aspect of language to be investigated, which is the nature of rhythm. Indeed, the manifestation of rhythm is not limited to language alone.

The CVX theory also has implications for the analysis of language variation. In generative phonology, the standard way to account for language variation is to use 'parameters' (Chomsky 1981). For example, parameters for stress patterns have been proposed by Halle and Vergnaud (1987) and Hayes (1995). Likewise, Blevins (1995) proposes six parameters for the maximal syllable size, rephrased in (29), along with the values (or 'settings') for English. Similar parameters have been proposed before by Clements and Keyser (1983, 28–30).

(29) Binary parameters for the maximal syllable size (Blevins 1995, 219)

Parameters	English settings
Can the onset contain two sounds?	Yes
Can the nucleus contain two sounds?	Yes
Is the coda allowed?	Yes
Can the coda contain two sounds?	Yes
Can extra C occur initially?	No (Yes)
Can extra C occur finally?	Yes

If all parameters are set to 'yes', a syllable can be CCVVCC in non-edge positions and CCCVVCCC in monosyllabic words. In fact, Clements and Keyser (1983, 32) assume that C and V can each repeat at least three times, so that a maximal possible syllable is at least CCCVVVCCC.

Like previous analyses, the CVX theory recognizes cross-linguistic variations in the maximal size of a monosyllabic word. However, unlike previous analysis, which attributes the variations to syllable parameters, the CVX theory attributes the variations to morphology, which must be recognized independently. In addition, the CVX theory recognizes the fact that complex sounds can result from gestural overlap. If we exclude such factors, the maximal syllable is found to be CVX, much smaller than has been proposed before, such as CCCVCCC (Cairns 1988), CCCCVCCC (Hooper 1976, 229), or CCCVVVCCC (Clements and Keyser 1983, 32).

When one looks at the world's languages, it is easy to get the impression that there is a wide range of patterns. People have often wondered about the question: How different can human languages be and what are the limits of variation? With regard to syllables, I have proposed that there is no variation in the maximal size. The range of possible syllables is therefore far smaller than has been conceived before. In other words, in at least some parts of language there is no structural variation, despite apparent diversity at first sight.

124   SAN DUANMU

References

Abercrombie, David. 1967. *Elements of general phonetics*. Edinburgh: Edinburgh University Press.

Alcantara, Jonathan Brett. 1998. *The Architecture of the English Lexicon*. PhD diss., Cornell University.

Archangeli, Diana. 1988. Aspects of underspecification theory. *Phonology* 5: 183–207.

Baayen, R. Harald, Richard Piepenbrock and Leon Gulikers. 1995. *The CELEX Lexical Database (Release 2) [CD-ROM]*. Philadelphia, PA: Linguistic Data Consortium, University of Pennsylvania.

Bagemihl, Bruce. 1991. Syllable structure in Bella Coola. *Linguistic Inquiry* 22: 589–646.

Bailey, Charles-James Nice. 1978. Gradience in English syllabification and a revised concept of unmarked syllabification. Distributed by the Indiana University Linguistics Club, Bloomington.

Bates, Dawn and Barry Carlson. 1992. Simple syllables in Spokane Salish. *Linguistic Inquiry* 23: 653–659.

Bethin, Christina Y. 1992. *Polish syllables: the role of prosody in phonology and morphology*. Columbus: Slavica Publishers.

Blevins, Juliette. 1995. The syllable in phonological theory. In *The handbook of phonological theory*, edited by John Goldsmith, 206–244. Cambridge, MA: Blackwell.

——. 2004. *Evolutionary phonology: The emergence of sound patterns*. Cambridge: Cambridge University Press.

Borowsky, Toni. 1986. Topics in the lexical phonology of English. PhD diss., University of Massachusetts, Amherst.

——. 1989. Structure preservation and the syllable coda in English. *Natural Language and Linguistic Theory* 7: 145–166.

Browman, Catherine P. and Louis Goldstein. 1989. Articulatory gestures as phonological units. *Phonology* 6: 201–251.

Burzio, Luigi. 1994. *Principles of English stress*. Cambridge, UK: Cambridge University Press.

Burzio, Luigi. 1996. Surface constraints versus underlying representation. In *Current trends in phonology: models and methods*, vol. 1, edited by Jacques Durand and Bernard Laks, 123–141. Salford: European Studies Research Institute, University of Salford Publications.

Butskhrikidze, Marika. 2002. The consonant phonotactics of Georgian. PhD diss., Universiteit Leiden. [Distributed by Netherlands Graduate School of Linguistics, Utrecht.]

Cairns, Charles. 1988. Phonotactics, markedness and lexical representation. *Phonology* 5: 209–236.

Chao, Yuen-Ren. 1934. The non-uniqueness of phonemic solutions of phonetic systems. *Bulletin of the Institute of History and Philology, Academia Sinica*. 4: 363–397.

Chomsky, Noam. 1981. *Lectures on government and binding*. Dordrecht: Foris.

Chomsky, Noam and Morris Halle. 1968. *The Sound Pattern of English*. New York: Harper and Row.

Clements, George N. 1999. Affricates as noncontoured stops. In *Proceedings of LP'98: Item Order in Language and Speech (Columbus, the Ohio State University, September 15–20, 1998)*, Vol. I, edited by Osamu Fujimura, Brian D Joseph, and Bohumil Palek, 271–299. Prague: Karolinum Press (Charles University in Prague).

Clements, George N. and Samuel J. Keyser. 1983. *CV phonology: A generative theory of the syllable*. Cambridge, MA: MIT Press.

Cohn, Abigail C. 1993. Nasalisation in English: phonology or phonetics. *Phonology* 10: 43–81.

Davis, Stuart. 1988. *Topics in syllable geometry*. New York: Garland Press.
Dell, François and Mohamed Elmedlaoui. 2002. *Syllables in Tashlhiyt Berber and in Moroccan Arabic*. Dordrecht: Kluwer.
Duanmu, San. 1990. A formal study of syllable, tone, stress and domain in Chinese languages. PhD diss., MIT.
——. 1994. Against contour tone units. *Linguistic Inquiry* 25: 555–608.
——. 2009. *Syllable structure: The limits of variation*. Oxford: Oxford University Press.
Duanmu, San, Hyo-Young Kim, and Nathan Stiennon. 2005. Stress and syllable structure in English: approaches to phonological variations. *Taiwan Journal of Linguistics* 3: 45–77.
Frisch, Stefan A., Nathan R. Large and David B. Pisoni. 2000. Perception of word-likeness: Effects of segment probability and length on the processing of nonwords. *Journal of Memory and Language* 42: 481–496.
Fudge, Erik. 1969. Syllables. *Journal of Linguistics* 5: 253–87.
Fujimura, Osama. 1979. An analysis of English syllables as cores and affixes. *Zeitschrift für Phonetik, Sprachwissenschaft und Kommunikationsforschung* 32: 471–476.
Giegerich, Heinz. 1985. *Metrical phonology and phonological structure: German and English*. Cambridge: Cambridge University Press.
——. 1989. Syllable structure and lexical derivation in German. Distributed by Bloomington, Indiana: Indiana Linguistic Club.
——. 1992. *English phonology*. Cambridge: Cambridge University Press.
Gimson, Alfred C. 1970. *An introduction to the pronunciation of English*, 2nd edition. New York: St. Martin's Press.
Goldsmith, John. 1990. *Autosegmental and metrical phonology*. Cambridge, MA: Basil Blackwell.
Gouskova, Maria. 2004 Relational hierarchies in optimality theory: The case of syllable contact. *Phonology* 21: 201–50.
Gussmann, Edmund. 2002. *Phonology: analysis and theory*. Cambridge: Cambridge University Press.
Hall, Tracy Alan. 2001. The distribution of superheavy syllables in Modern English. *Folia Linguistica* 35: 399–442.
——. 2002. Against extrasyllabic consonants in German and English. *Phonology* 19: 33–75.
Halle, Morris. 2003. Phonological features. In *International encyclopedia of linguistics*, 2nd ed., edited by William J. Frawley. Oxford: Oxford University Press.
Halle, Morris and Jean-Roger Vergnaud. 1987. *An essay on stress*. Cambridge, MA: MIT Press.
Hammond, Michael. 1999. *The phonology of English: a prosodic Optimality Theoretic approach*. Oxford: Oxford University Press.
Harris, John. 1994. *English sound structure*. Oxford, UK: Blackwell.
——. 2006. The phonology of being understood: further arguments against sonority. *Lingua* 116: 1483–1494.
Harris, John and Edmund Gussmann. 1998. Final codas: why the west was wrong. In *Structure and interpretation in phonology: studies in phonology*, edited by Eugeniusz Cyran, 139–162. Lublin: Folia.
Haugen, Einar. 1956a. Syllabification in Kutenai. *International Journal of American Linguistics* 22: 196–201.
——. 1956b. The syllable in linguistic description. In *For Roman Jakobson* edited by Morris Halle, Horace Lunt, Hugh MacLean, and Cornelis van Schooneveld, 213–221. The Hague: Mouton.
Hayes, Bruce. 1982. Extrametricality and English stress. *Linguistic Inquiry* 13: 227–276.
——. 1995. *Metrical stress theory: Principles and case studies*. Chicago: University of Chicago Press.

Herbert, Robert K. 1975. Reanalyzing prenasalized consonants. *Studies in African Linguistics* 6: 105–123.

——. 1986. *Language universals, markedness theory, and natural phonetic processes.* Berlin: Mouton de Gruyter.

Hoard, James E. 1971. Aspiration, tenseness, and syllabification in English. *Language* 47: 133–140.

Hooper, Joan Bybee. 1976. *An introduction to natural generative phonology.* New York: Academic Press.

Huang, Parker Po-fei. 1970. *Cantonese dictionary: Cantonese-English, English-Cantonese.* Yale University Press, New Heaven and London.

Jespersen, Otto. 1904. *Lehrbuch der Phonetik.* Leipzig & Berlin: Teubner.

Jones, Daniel. 1950. *The pronunciation of English*, 3rd edition. Cambridge, England: Cambridge University Press.

Kager, René. 1992. Shapes of the generalized trochee. *Proceedings of The West Coast Conference On Formal Linguistics* 11: 298–312.

Kahn, Daniel. 1976. Syllable-based generalizations in English phonology. PhD diss., MIT.

Keating, Patricia. 1988. Underspecification in phonetics. *Phonology* 5: 275–292.

Kenstowicz, Michael. 1994. *Phonology in Generative Grammar.* Oxford: Blackwell.

Kiparsky, Paul. 1979. Metrical structure assignment is cyclic. *Linguistic Inquiry* 10: 421–441.

——. 1981. Remarks on the metrical structure of the syllable. In *Phonologica 1980*, edited by Wolfgang V. Dressler, Oskar E. Pfeiffer and John E. Rennison, 245–256. Innsbruck: Institute für Sprachwissenschaft der Universität Innsbruck.

Kumar, Aman. 2005. Aspects of Hindi Syllable Structure. PhD diss., University of Michigan, Ann Arbor.

Ladefoged, Peter. 2001. *Vowels and consonants: an introduction to the sounds of languages.* Malden, MA: Blackwell.

Ladefoged, Peter and Morris Halle. 1988. Some major features of the International Phonetic Alphabet. *Language* 64: 577–582.

Ladefoged, Peter and Ian Maddieson. 1996. *The sounds of the world's languages.* Cambridge, MA: Blackwell.

Lamontagne, Gregory. 1993. Syllabification and consonant cooccurrence conditions. PhD diss., University of Massachusetts, Amherst.

Leben, William. 1971. On the segmental nature of tone in Thai. *Quarterly Progress Report No. 101*: 221–224. Research Laboratory of Electronics, Massachusetts Institute of Technology.

Liberman, Mark and Alan Prince. 1977. On stress and linguistic rhythm. *Linguistic Inquiry* 8: 249–336.

Lin, Xiangrong. 1993. *Jiarongyu yanjiu [Studies on the Jiarong (rGyalrong) language].* Chengdu: Sichuan Minzu Chubanshe.

Lombardi, Linda. 1990. The nonlinear organization of the affricate. *Natural Language and Linguistic Theory* 8: 374–425.

Lowenstamm, Jean. 1996. CV as the only syllable type. In *Current trends in phonology, models and methods* edited by Jacques Durand and Bernard Laks, 419–443. Salford: European Studies Research Institute, University of Salford Publications.

Malécot, André. 1960. Vowel nasality as a distinctive feature in American English. *Language* 36: 222–229.

McCarthy, John. 1979. On stress and syllabification. *Linguistic Inquiry* 10: 443–465.

Olaszy, Gábor. 2007. Consonant clusters in Hungarian speech: Spoken word database for the presentation of acoustic structure and coarticulation in consonant clusters. http://fonetika.nytud.hu/cccc/adatbazisrol_en.html

Pierrehumbert, Janet. 1994. Syllable structure and word structure: a study of triconsonantal clusters in English. In *Papers in Laboratory Phonology III: Phonological structure and phonetic form*, edited by Patricia A. Keating, 168–188. Cambridge: Cambridge University Press.

Pike, Kenneth L. 1947. On the phonemic status of English diphthongs. *Language* 23: 151–159.

Sagey, Elizabeth. 1986. The representation of features and relations in nonlinear phonology. PhD diss., MIT.

Scheer, Tobias. 2004. *A lateral theory of phonology: what is CVCV, and why should it be*? Berlin: Mouton de Gruyter.

Selkirk, Elisabeth. 1982. The syllable. In *The structure of phonological representations*, part 2, edited by Harry van der Hulst and Norval Smith, 337–383. Dordrecht: Foris.

Steriade, Donca. 1982. Greek prosodies and the nature of syllabification. PhD diss., MIT.

——. 1987. Redundant values. *Chicago Linguistic Society* 23, 2: 339–362.

——. 1989. Affricates are Stops. Presented at Conference on Features and Underspecification Theories, October 7–9, MIT.

——. 1999. Alternatives to syllable-based accounts of consonantal phonotactics. In *Proceedings of LP '98: Item order in language and speech*, vol. 1, edited by Osamu Fujimura, Brian D. Joseph and Bohumil Palek, 205–245. Prague: Charles University in Prague—The Karolinum Press.

Vennemann, Theo. 1988. *Preference laws for syllable structure and the explanation of sound change*. Berlin and New York: Mouton de Gruyter.

Wang, Jenny Zhijie. 1999. Vowel Length in Cantonese. Presented at the 11th North American Conference on Chinese Linguistics, Harvard University.

Wells, John Christopher. 1990. Syllabification and allophony. In *Studies in the pronunciation of English, A commemorative volume in honour of A.C. Gimson* edited by Susan Ramsaran, 76–86. London and New York: Routledge.

Zec, Draga. 1994. *Sonority constraints on prosodic structure*. New York: Garland.

CHAPTER FIVE

THE SYLLABLE AS DELIMITATION OF THE BASE
FOR REDUPLICATION

Jason D. Haugen

1   Introduction:
The Syllable in Morphology, Reduplicative and Otherwise

The purpose of this chapter is to demonstrate that access to the prosodic category of the *syllable* is crucial for certain morphological processes in some languages. Specifically, this chapter shows that the syllable can serve as a delimitation on the base for copying in reduplication. This, coupled with other morphologically based evidence, indicates that the syllable must be a legitimate constituent in phonology, and one that must be accessible by the morphology.

Some recent work dealing with issues at the interface of phonology and morphology has made the claim that reference to syllable boundaries is possible in certain morphological constructions. Feng (2003, 2006), for example, proposes to capture the isolating nature of Chinese morphology by proposing a constraint, Align[σ], which forces syllables to align to morpheme boundaries and vice versa. Feng introduces Align[σ] as a cover constraint for the following alignment constraints operating in Chinese:

(1)   Align(Morpheme, Left; Syllable, Left)
      Align(Morpheme, Right, Syllable, Right)
      Align(Syllable, Left; Morpheme, Left)
      Align(Syllable, Right; Morpheme, Right)

Crucial reference to the syllable has also been made in various recent works on reduplication-specific morphology. For example, Hicks Kennard (2004) utilizes Suzuki's (1998) Generalized Obligatory Contour Principle (*X...X, which stipulates that a sequence of X's is prohibited) and Yip's (1998) *Repeat to the level of the syllable, in order to provide a unified analysis of four divergent reduplication patterns in the Tawala (Oceanic) durative. The two most relevant of these

patterns for the present discussion are illustrated in (2).[1] (The reduplicant appears in italics throughout this chapter).

(2) Two patterns of Tawala durative reduplication (Hicks Kennard 2004,
    304)

    a. ge.le.ta   'arrive' → *ge.le*.ge.le.ta   'be arriving'   *ge.ge.le.ta
    b. be.i.ha   'search' → *bi*.be.i.ha   'be searching'   *be.be.i.ha/
                                               **be.i*.be.i.ha

The typical pattern of reduplication for Tawala verb stems with a CV.CV-
initial sequence is a full copy of the first foot of the stem, as in (2a).
$CV_1.V_2$- initial stems (as in 2b), however, do not allow for the copying of both vowels contained in the stem's first foot. Hicks Kennard
explains this fact by proposing a highly ranked ONSET constraint that
prohibits onsetless syllables in the reduplicant; thus, **be.i*.be.i.ha. As
illustrated in (2b), however, an odd fact about the pattern that does
emerge in such cases is that it is the non-contiguous *second* vowel that
actually gets copied, rather than the first vowel; thus, *bi*.be.i.ha rather
than *be.be.i.ha. Hicks Kennard proposes a highly ranked constraint
*REPEAT, which is applied to level of the syllable, so that candidates
which copy the second vowel are preferred to those which would copy
the first vowel and in so doing would create the disallowed sequence
of two identical syllables.

    Another area within the domain of reduplicative morphology where
crucial reference to the syllable might be made is in syllable-based 'templatic back-copying' effects, such as is seen in Guarijío (Uto-Aztecan).
Miller (1996) presents data for what he calls 'abbreviated reduplication,'
a pattern of verbal reduplication which indicates inceptive aspect and
involves the reduplication of a light (CV) syllable and the simultaneous
truncation of all segments which do not appear in the first syllable of
the base. This truncation ostensibly occurs in order to match the 'base'
with the reduplicated syllable.

(3) Guarijío 'Abbreviated' Reduplication (Miller 1996, Caballero 2006)

    a. to.ní   'to boil'   →   *to*-tó   'to start boiling'
    b. mu.hí.ba 'to throw'   →   *mu*-mú   'to start throwing'

---

[1] The other two patterns involve a VC- prefixal reduplicant (e.g. a.pu 'bake' > *a*.pa.
pu 'be baking') and 'moraic epenthesis' (e.g. to.to.go 'sick' > to.*o*.to.go 'be sick'). See
Hicks Kennard's (2004) paper for her OT account which captures all four patterns
under a single constraint ranking.

Caballero (2006) points out that such data conform to the 'templatic back-copy' pattern, wherein the constraint ranking that has MAX-BR and a reduplicative template (e.g. RED=σ$_μ$) outranking MAX-IO predicts truncation in the base in order for the base to match the reduplicative template. Such a pattern has often been presumed not to exist, and this problem is referred to in the Optimality Theoretic literature as the 'Kager-Hamilton problem' (McCarthy and Prince 1999a).[2] The Kager-Hamilton problem has played a large role in many OT theorists abandoning reduplicative templates in favor of the Generalized Template Theory of McCarthy and Prince (1999b).[3] Although Caballero (2006) shows that a templatic back-copying analysis is possible for the Guarijío abbreviated reduplication data, she prefers an analysis within Morphological Doubling Theory (MDT) (Inkelas and Zoll 2005; IZ) wherein both the base and the reduplicant, which in MDT are conceived of as being unrelated 'daughters' in a kind of compounding construction with identical root inputs, are associated with the same co-phonology. This co-phonology (here, 'X') requires truncation of the verb stem in both daughters of the compound construction in order to match the equivalent of a light syllable template.

(4) MDT Analysis of Guarijío Abbreviated Reduplication (cf. Caballero 2006: 286 [14])

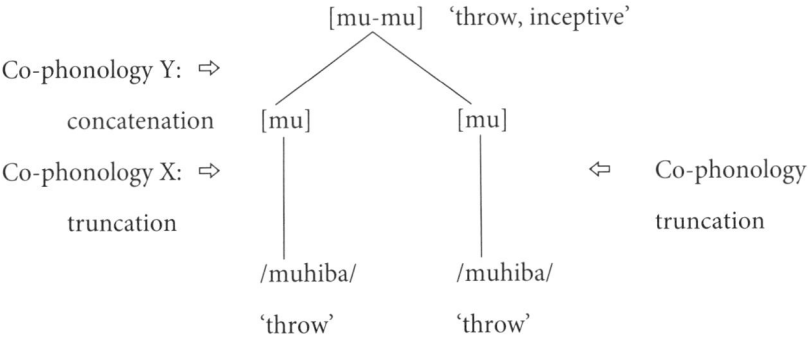

(MDT will be discussed in more detail below in section 6).

---

[2] Similar examples can also be found in English affective slang, such as *po-po* < *police (officer)* and *cray-cray* < *crazy*.

[3] Gouskova (2007) presents another case of an apparent "templatic back-copy" effect in Tonkawa (Coahuiltecan), where long vowels in verb stems regularly shorten to match the short vowels of their counterparts in reduplicants. However, Gouskova uses the RED=σ$_μ$ "template" only as a cover constraint for other reduplicant-specific lexically-indexed markedness constraints, thus deriving a reduplicative light syllable without actually referring to the notion of "light syllable" as the definition of the reduplicant.

Although different analyses of such data might be available, the crucial insight that any theory of reduplication (or morphology more generally) must grapple with is the identical syllabic form of the two daughters (or the reduplicant and its base) in these examples. In sum, Feng, Hicks Kennard, and Caballero all crucially utilize the notion of *syllable* in their morphological analyses. Other cases involving morphological reference to syllable boundaries will be detailed below.

The thesis of the present chapter is that the syllable can serve as a delimitation on the base for reduplicative copying—i.e. that the prosodic demarcation of a syllable boundary can inform what may or may not be copied from a given stem when the process of reduplication applies to that stem. Interestingly, in at least one language, Hiaki (Yaqui), this delimitation seems to be made on the underlying representation, rather than the actual surface form, of the stem. As a result, the demarcation of the first syllable of the stem as the delimitation of the base for reduplication in such cases is opaque in the output.

This chapter is organized as follows. Section 2 discusses the notion of delimiting a subset of a given stem as the base for reduplication, and then section 3 will discuss such base-delimitation in the context of the typologically unusual pattern of 'syllable copy' reduplication. Although different analyses of the syllable copy pattern are possible, not all of which would rely on the delimitation of the syllable as the base for reduplication, section 4 presents definitive example of the syllable serving as the base for reduplication. Section 5 outlines the aforementioned opacity in base-assignment from Hiaki, and section 6 briefly reviews the concept of base delimitation in theoretical approaches that do not utilize 'phonological copying'. Section 7 concludes.

2   *Base Delimitation in Reduplication*

For the exposition of most of this chapter I will be assuming a phonological copying approach to reduplication, wherein the phonological material of some morphological stem (the *base*) is repeated to express the exponence of a separate morpheme (the *reduplicant*). Variations on this general approach are by far the most common ways to analyze reduplication in contemporary phonology and morphology, although of course there are different theories about how this phonological copying occurs. There are also, however, alternative views on reduplication which do not involve a phonological copying approach (e.g. the theories of Raimy 2000 and IZ), but a discussion of the implications of the following data for such theories will be delayed until section 6.

Although little has actually been explicitly claimed about the nature of the base as a morphological entity, the standard consensus in phonological copying theories seems to have been that in the default case *the base* is the entire stem to which a reduplicative morpheme is affixed.[4] There are cases, however, where some subset of a given stem seems to be all that is available for reduplicative copying. I will refer to the demarcation of any subset of a stem as being available for reduplicative copying as *base delimitation*.

The notion that the base for reduplicative copying can be delimited is not new. A well-known candidate for such delimitation is found in Yidinʸ (Pama-Nyungan), where reduplicants appear as copies of the first foot of the stem. Whereas most theories posit that the burden of form requirements are placed on the reduplicant (e.g. through a CV skeleton or prosodic template, as in Marantz 1982 and older versions of Prosodic Morphology: McCarthy and Prince 1986, 1993), Yidinʸ reduplicants show form variation based on the output shape of the base.

(5) Yidinʸ (Pama-Nyungan) Reduplication (McCarthy and Prince 1986)

    a. kin.tal.pa → *kin.tal*-kin.tal.pa **kin.ta*-kin.tal.pa [kin.tal].pa
    b. mu.la.ri → *mu.la*-mu.la.ri **mu.lar*-mu.lar.i [mu.la].ri

When the second syllable of the base contains a coda consonant it is copied (as in 5a), therefore it must be the case that codas are allowed to occur in this position in the reduplicant, and, in fact, they are actually required to occur in such cases (thus, *kin.ta-kin.tal.pa). However, when the second syllable of the stem does not contain a coda, the onset of the third syllable is not allowed to copy from the coda position of the base (cf. 5b). One possible explanation for the ungrammaticality of examples like *mu.lar-mu.la.ri is that the third syllable is simply beyond the scope of reduplicative copying. The delimitation of the first foot of the stem as the base is indicated with square brackets in the final column of (5) above.

Shaw (2005) has recently formally encoded the delimitation of the reduplicative base in her re-definition of the standard Anchor

---

[4] See Haugen (2009) for a recent review and critique of different definitions of "the base".

constraints, which are required in Correspondence Theory to allow
faithfulness constraints to assess identity between the reduplicant and
its base.[5] Shaw proposes her refinement as an improvement over an
earlier assumed definition of the base, the Adjacent String Hypothesis,
which proposed that the base is defined as 'an adjacent string in the
input' (Urbanczyk 1999, 395, referencing McCarthy and Prince 1993)
(p. 161). In Shaw's critique, "[w]hereas the Adjacent String Hypothesis
places no restrictions on the size or grammatical coherence of an 'adjacent string' Base, the Constituent Base Hypothesis [CBH] significantly
delimits the range of potential Bases to a narrow, finite set of independently motivated categories" (p. 197). The finite set of categories that
Shaw proposes as possible constituents that may serve as a base for
reduplication include both morphological and prosodic constituents,
as outlined in (6).

(6) The Constituent Base Hypothesis: Definition of the Base (Shaw 2005,
    167 [6])

   The Base in a Reduplicant-Base correspondence relation is a constituent, i.e.
   a. MCat: Word, Stem, Root
   b. PCat: Prosodic Word, Foot, Syllable, Nucleus, Mora
   c. PHead: HeadFoot, ó = FootHead, Nuc = σHead, Headμ
   d. CanonicalCat: Canonical Root = [CVC]
                         Canonical Stem = [CVCV]

Shaw gives examples of base delimitation with a morphological constituent, Base=Root, in Nisga'a (Tsimshianic), Nɬeʔkepmxcin (Salishan)
(in the distributive), and Lillooet (Salishan) (in the distributive), as well
as prosodic constituents: Base=HeadFoot, in Nɬeʔkepmxcin (in the
diminutive) and Lillooet (in the diminutive), and Base=ProsodicStem
in Nuxalk (Salishan).

---

   [5] Shaw's proposal is formally encoded in the following way:
(i) ANCHOR$_{R-B}$ L/R (Redup; MCat/PCat)
       The left/right peripheral element of a Redup[licant] corresponds to the left/right
       peripheral element of a constituent in the Base-Output. (Shaw 2005, 172)
Opposite-edge anchoring (and therefore mirror-image reduplication and other non-
attested anchoring patterns) is ruled out by a more general ANCHOR constraint:
(ii) ANCHOR$_{I-O, O-O}$ Edge (Cat1, Cat2) =def
       ∀ Cat1 ∃ Cat2 such that Edge of Cat1 and Edge of Cat2 coincide, where Cat1,
       Cat2 ∈ PCat ∪ GCat, Edge ∈ {Right, Left}. (Shaw 2005, 172)

This chapter will further support Shaw's CBH by showing that one of the prosodic constituents predicted to be able to serve as a base for reduplication, i.e. the syllable, in fact does so in certain languages.

3   *Syllable Copy Reduplication*

It was mentioned above that most theorists have placed the burden of output form requirements upon the reduplicant itself, e.g. through a fixed CV skeleton affix in Marantz (1982), or through a prosodic template in Prosodic Morphology (McCarthy and Prince 1986) and early Optimality Theory (McCarthy and Prince 1993). Such a view results in certain predictions about what kinds of reduplicative patterns ought to be expected in the world's languages.

One such prediction, first pointed out by Moravcsik (1978) and which I will subsequently refer to as *Moravcsik's Generalization*, is a proscription on so-called 'syllable copy' reduplication, where the shape of the reduplicant would depend upon the syllable structure of its base. The Yidin[y] case cited above is one possible example frequently cited in the literature, although it involves two syllables (cf. Marantz 1982, 453–456) (or a foot, in the later Prosodic Morphology frameworks). Such a pattern is often assumed to be rare (at a minimum), but in some cases is explicitly claimed to be impossible when applied to the level of a single syllable. McCarthy and Prince (1998) explain such a proscription against single syllable copying in the following way:

> On the face of it, the idea that reduplication involves affixing a template may seem surprising, since a natural, naïve expectation is that reduplication involves an operation like 'copy the first syllable,' as illustrated in [7]:
>
> [7] 'Copy first syllable,' hypothetically
>
> | | | |
> |---|---|---|
> | ta.ka | → | *ta*-ta.ka |
> | tra.pa | → | *tra*-tra.pa |
> | tak.pa | → | *tak*-tak.pa |
>
> Moravcsik (1978) and Marantz (1982) observe that syllable copying, in this sense, does not occur. Rather, reduplication always specifies a *templatic target* which is affixed to the base, and is satisfied by copying elements of the base. (p. 286, emphasis in original)

Note that Moravcsik's Generalization, based on her early typological survey of the reduplication patterns found in a large but limited sample of the world's languages, can be taken in one of two potentially differentiable ways: (i) as an empirical claim about the attested patterns of reduplication, and (ii) as a theoretical claim about the possible mechanisms involved in reduplicative morphology. The empirical claim involving single syllables is counter-exemplified in at least two languages: Hiaki (Uto-Aztecan) and Yapese (Oceanic). The second claim, involving some kind of procedure of 'syllable copying,' is possible in, but perhaps not actually required by, some phonological copying theories. Regardless of one's theoretical perspective, though, the empirical facts suggest that all theories must be able to account for the 'syllable copy' pattern in some way.

Hiaki (also known as Yaqui or Yoeme) is a Southern Uto-Aztecan language indigenous to Northwestern Mexico and also spoken in Southern Arizona. Hiaki has several distinct patterns of reduplication, and there is a lack of consistent mapping between different forms of reduplication and the various functions that reduplication serves in this language (for discussion see Escalante 1985; Demers, Escalante and Jelinek 1999; Harley and Amarillas 2003, Harley and Florez Leyva 2009; Haugen 2003). These forms include a CVCV- pattern of reduplication (in most but not all words of at least three syllables) (e.g. he.chi.te 'scratch' > *he.chi*-he.chi.te 'always scratching'); geminating heavy syllable reduplication which copies the first consonant and vowel of the stem and then geminates the first consonant onset of the stem into the coda of the reduplicant (e.g. noo.ka 'sing' > *non*-no.ka 'gossip'); morphological gemination (or 'mora affixation,' or 'morphological mora augmentation'), which triggers gemination (or vowel lengthening) internal to the stem, between the first and second syllable (e.g. ma.ve.ta 'receive' > maʋ.ve.ta 'receive habitually'). The fourth and final type, which is the type relevant to the present discussion, involves simple syllabic reduplication. Which reduplication patterns apply to which stem is not always predictable from the phonological make-up of the stem, so must be somehow lexically stipulated (Haugen 2003). This can be seen in the following data of trisyllabic near minimal pairs which reduplicate in one of three unpredictable ways.

(7) Some near minimal pairs for the Hiaki habitual (Molina et al. 1999)

a. ʔí.vak.ta	→	*ʔi.* ʔi.vak.ta	'hug someone'
b. kí.nak.te	→	*ki.na.*ki.nak.te	'squint'
c. má.ve.ta	→	maʋ.ve.ta	'receive'

The most common (and probably the default) pattern of reduplication in Hiaki is light syllable reduplication, which generally exhibits the unexpected syllable copy effect: if the first syllable of the stem is CV, then the reduplicant is CV (as in 8a); if the first syllable is CVC, then the reduplicant is CVC (as in 8b).

(8) 'Syllable Copy' Reduplication in Hiaki (Uto-Aztecan) (Haugen 2003)

    a. CV.CV-initial stems

i. vu.sa	*vu*.vu.sa	*vus.vu.sa	'awaken'
ii. chi.ke	*chi*.chi.ke	*chik.chi.ke	'comb one's hair'
iii. he.wi.te	*he*.he.wi.te	*hew.he.wi.te	'agree'
iv. ko.ʔa.rek	*ko*.ko.ʔa.rek	*koʔ.ko.ʔa.rek	'wear a skirt'

    b. CVC.CV-initial stems

i. vam.se	*vam*.vam.se	*va.vamse	'hurry'
ii. chep.ta	*chep*.chep.ta	*che.chep.ta	'jump over'
iii. chuk.ta	*chuk*.chuk.ta	*chu.chuk.ta	'cut with a knife or saw'
iv. bʷalkote	*bʷal*.bʷal.ko.te	*bʷa.bʷal.ko.te	'soften, smooth'

It is important to note that Hiaki is not the only language for which such a syllable copy pattern is attested. Ballantyne (1999) has reported the same kind of pattern in the completely unrelated Oceanic language Yapese.

(9) 'Syllable Copy' Reduplication in Yapese (Oceanic) (Ballantyne 1999)

    a. CV- initial stems

i. tsu.ŋuːr	*tsu*.tsu.ŋuːr	*tsuŋ.tsu.ŋuːr
'to slap'	'to slap hard'	
ii. ðɪ.ʔaβ	*ðɪ*.ðɪ.ʔaβ	*ðɪʔ.ðɪ.ʔaβ
'to cut'	'to slice'	

    b. CVC- initial stems

i. teːj	*teːj*.teːj	*te-/teː.tej
'to stare'	'to stare repeatedly'	
ii. suɣ.ʔaːl	*suɣ*.suɣ.ʔaːl	*su.suɣ.ʔaːl
'to be slow'	'to be very slow'	

A Moravcsik- or Marantz-style CV skeleton approach to reduplication cannot straightforwardly account for such a pattern. Those theories would affix a fixed skeletal template and then associate the segments of the stem to it. The stem-based variability of reduplicative forms is not captured by either a CV or CVC prefix, as shown in (10) and (11), respectively.

(10) CV prefix

    a. *vu*-vu.sa

    b. *va*-vam.se   (?*vam*-vam.se)

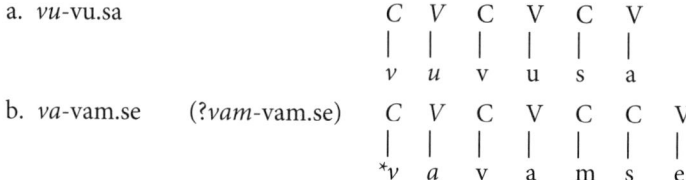

(11) CVC prefix

    a. *vus*-vu.sa   (?*vu*-vu.sa)

    b. *vam*-vam.se

Of course, the actual attested pattern is the one in (12).

(12) CV and CVC prefixing

    a. *vu*-vu.sa   (*vus-vu.sa)

    b. *vam*-vam.se   (*va-vam.se)

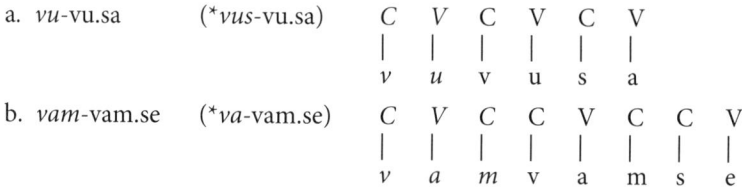

The stem-based variation would have to be completely stipulated under the above approach.

    The Prosodic Morphology approach of McCarthy and Prince (1986) correctly recognizes syllable structure, and could straightforwardly allow for the fact that what is being copied seems to be a prosodic constituent, not just a random string of consonants and vowels.

(13) a. vu.sa   → |*vu*|– vu.sa

    b. vam.se   → |*vam*|– vam.se

(14) a.

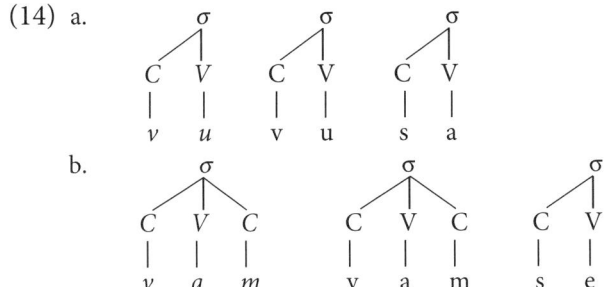

b.

(See Marantz 1982: 453–6 for a similar, yet tentative, analysis of the disyllabic reduplication pattern of Yidinʸ).

There are multiple possible ways to account for this particular pattern of reduplication. One would be simply to stipulate in some way that the base is limited to the first syllable. In a framework like Correspondence Theory (McCarthy and Prince 1995) this could be done by constraints, either through generalized alignment (e.g. an ALIGN constraint requiring alignment of the right edge of the base to the right edge of a syllable; à la Haugen, Hicks Kennard and Kennedy 2002), or through anchoring (e.g. an ANCHOR constraint requiring that the base anchor to the right edge of a syllable; à la Shaw 2005). Such constraints would require that the edge of the base be coterminous with the edge of a syllable; requiring that the base be limited to the *first* syllable might have to be accomplished through some other kind of size restriction. Haugen (2005) suggests that such base minimization could be accomplished through Hendricks' (1999) mechanism of *compression*, where competition for left-edge alignment between prefixal reduplicants and their following bases favors the minimal expression of the reduplicants.

Tableaux illustrating the workings of a constraint-based delimitation of the base as the first syllable of the stem (σ_1), represented informally as a cover constraint BASE = σ_1, are shown in (15) and (16); output segments included in the base are enclosed in brackets.

(15)

/ RED1 + vusa /	BASE = σ_1	DEP_BR	MAX_BR
a. *vu* [vu.sa]	*!		sa
b. ☞ *vu* [vu].sa			
c. *vus* [vu].sa		s!	
d. *vu.sa* [vu].sa		s!a	
e. *vu.sa* [vu.sa]	*!		
f. *vu* [vu.s]a	*!		s

(16)

/ RED1 + vamse /	BASE = σ_1	DEP$_{BR}$	MAX$_{BR}$
a. *vam*[vam.se]	*!		se
b. *va* [vam].se			m!
c. ☞ *vam*[vam].se			
d. *vam.se*[vam.se]	*!		
e. *vam.se*[vam].se		s!e	

Candidates which include in the base more material than actually occurs in the first syllable are ruled out by BASE = σ_1 (cf. 15a, e, f; 16a, d). Candidates that have reduplicants with segments not included in the base but appearing in the reduplicant would be eliminated by DEP$_{BR}$ (cf. 15c, d; 16e). Candidates that incompletely copy from the base would be cast off by MAX$_{BR}$ (cf. 16b). This last result will be problematic in some cases, however, since there are some examples of incomplete syllable copying in Hiaki, as we will see shortly.

Acknowledging that explicitly defining the base in such a way might be somewhat controversial, a second approach to the syllable-copy pattern could simply invoke positional faithfulness to rule out candidates with onsets of the second syllable of the base serving as codas in the reduplicant. Such a constraint is suggested by McCarthy and Prince (1993), as in (17).

(17) STRUC-ROLE$_{BR}$: The structural role of segments in the reduplicant are identical to the structural roles of segments in the base (McCarthy and Prince 1993).

Following Demers et al.'s (1999) contention that coda consonants are non-moraic in Hiaki, a ranking of a light syllable template (RED1=σ_μ) over STRUC-ROLE$_{BR}$ and both of those constraints over MAX$_{BR}$ would yield the correct output patterns.

(18) RED1=σ_μ >> STRUC-ROLE$_{BR}$ >> MAX$_{BR}$

/ RED1 + vusa /	RED1=σ_μ	STRUC-ROLE$_{BR}$	MAX$_{BR}$
a ☞ *vu* vu.sa			sa
b. *vus* vu.sa		*!	a
c. *vu.sa* vu.sa	*!		

(19) RED1=σ$_\mu$ >> STRUC-ROLE$_{BR}$ >> MAX$_{BR}$

/ RED1 + vamse /	RED1=σ$_\mu$	STRUC-ROLE$_{BR}$	MAX$_{BR}$
a. *va* vam.se			mse!
b. ☞ *vam* vam.se			se
c. *vam.se* vam.se	*!		

However, there are certainly cases of violations of STRUC-ROLE in Hiaki reduplication, e.g. the cases of gemination of the stem onset into coda position of heavy syllable reduplicants in what Demers et al. (1999) call 'secondary reduplication' and Haugen (2003) calls 'marked heavy syllable reduplication'. Whereas simple syllable reduplication typically indicates habitual action, this secondary, gemination-inducing pattern typically indicates 'iterative' action or some idiosyncratic meaning (although see Harley and Florez Leyva 2009 for a more detailed discussion of the semantics of Hiaki reduplication).

(20) Hiaki marked heavy syllable reduplication (RED2) (Molina et al. 1999)

a.	bwii.ka	'sing'	*bwib*.bwi.ka
b.	tee.ka	'lay it across'	*tet*.te.ka
c.	va.hu.me	'swim'	*vav*.va.hu.me
d.	ye.na	'smoke (tobacco)'	*yey*.ye.na
e.	ʔom.te	'get angry'	ʔoʔ.ʔom.te

This secondary pattern often occurs on the same roots that allow syllabic reduplication, and indicates some contrasting semantic function (e.g. noo.ka 'speak' > *no*-no.ka 'talk all the time' vs. *non*-no.ka 'gossip').

In addition, the analysis of the base being limited to σ$_1$ of the stem is supported by variable reduplication patterns that appear in dialectal and/or idiolectal variants of Hiaki, wherein incomplete reduplication of the first syllable is attested, but copying from the second syllable is not (at least in single syllable reduplication).

(21) Dialectal and/or Idiolectal Variation in Hiaki Syllable Reduplication (Haugen 2003)

Stem	Reduplicated Form in Sonora Hiaki	Reduplicated Form in Arizona Hiaki	Gloss
a. hak.ta	*hak*.hak.ta	*hak*.hak.ta	'inhale'
b. huk.te	*huk*.huk.te	*hu*.huk.te	'choke on liquids'
c. bʷak.ta	*bʷa*.bʷak.ta	*bʷak*.bʷak.ta	'take out of'

That is, reduplicated words following the syllabic reduplication pattern can sometimes omit a coda consonant from a CVC-initial stem (as in 21b for Arizona Hiaki and 21c for Sonora Hiaki), but they *never* allow a coda consonant in CV-initial stems (e.g. *vus-vu.sa). That is, in single syllable reduplication copying only takes place from σ_1, and never σ_2.

The foregoing discussion on 'syllable copy' reduplication has been focused on a single scenario where base delimitation is a plausible explanation for the extant reduplication pattern, but alternative accounts of such data are also possible. We now turn to a much more clear-cut case of a base being delimited to the first syllable of the stem.

4 $B_{ASE}=\sigma_1$

Hagberg (1993) presents a straightforward case of differential base assignment in a single language, Mayo, which happens to be the Uto-Aztecan language most closely related to Hiaki. Mayo has two classes of words which are differentiated on the basis of where primary accent (pitch accent or stress) occurs: on the first syllable of the word or on the second. Hagberg refers to these two classes as 'accented' and 'unaccented,' respectively. Mayo also has two patterns of reduplication, which for younger speakers appear in free variation to serve the same semantic function, namely indicating habitual action.

Light syllable reduplicants in these two classes appear as a copy of the first CV of the stem, and are thus indistinguishable. Heavy syllable reduplicants, on the other hand, appear differently according to which word class is involved. Words of both classes that have a CVC first syllable in the stem reduplicate a copy of that CVC syllable, thus the reduplicants are indistinguishable between the two classes for this situation as well.[6] With CV- initial stems, however, the mechanism of reduplication for the heavy syllable reduplicant varies, as illustrated in the third columns of (22) and (23) below.[7]

---

[6] With respect to the moraicity of coda consonants, then, Mayo is different than Yaqui.

[7] Note that in words of both classes the accent falls on the same place within the word, i.e. on σ_1 or σ_2, with or without reduplication. That is, for example, in verbs of the accented class the accent falls on the first syllable. When 'accented' verbs are reduplicated the reduplicant becomes the first syllable, so the accent then falls on the reduplicant. More on this point will be discussed below.

(22) Mayo accented words: Gemination at Red-Base juncture (Hagberg 1993)

Stem	RED1=σ_μ	RED2=$\sigma_{\mu\mu}$	Unattested	Gloss
a. yú.ke	*yú*.yu.ke	*yúy*.yu.ke	**yúk*.yu.ke	'rain'
b. wóm.te	*wó*.wom.te	*wóm*.wom.te	**wów*.wom.te	'be frightened'
c. nók.wa	*nó*.nok.wa	*nók*.nok.wa	**nón*.nok.wa	'known language'
d. nó.ka	*nó*.no.ka	*nón*.no.ka	**nók*.no.ka	'know a language'

(23) Mayo unaccented words: Copy from second syllable of stem (Hagberg 1993)

Stem	RED1=σ_μ	RED2=$\sigma_{\mu\mu}$	Unattested	Gloss
a. bwa.ná	*bwa*.bwá.na	*bwan*.bwá.na	**bwab*.bwa.na	'cry'
b. bwi.ká	*bwi*.bwí.ka	*bwik*.bwí.ka	**bwib*.bwi.ka	'sing'
c. ʔom.té	*ʔo*.ʔóm.te	*ʔom*.ʔóm.te	**ʔoʔ*.ʔom.te	'hate'
d. no.ká	*no*.nó.ka	*nok*.nó.ka	**non*.no.ka	'speak'

The contrast is most clearly seen in the (d) examples, which illustrate heavy syllable reduplication with the minimal pair *nó.ka* 'know a language' and *no.ká* 'speak'; these roots vary only according to word class assignment (and hence, where the primary accent falls). Because the unaccented form *no.ká* copies from the second syllable to yield the expected heavy syllable reduplicant *nok-*, while *nó.ka* only copies from the first syllable (and thus triggers gemination of the onset of the first syllable of the base to realize the second mora of the heavy syllable), these two classes of reduplication thus have different bases available for reduplication. The base for the unaccented class is the entire stem (as presupposed in most phonological copying theories of reduplication), whereas the base for the accented class is limited to the first syllable of the stem (i.e. σ_1) only.

Haugen (2004) proposes that there is an opacity in the assignment of the base in these two classes: i.e. the base for reduplication is demarcated at the right edge of the stressed/accented syllable in the unreduplicated form. (24) shows how this can be accounted for quite straightforwardly in a derivational analysis which assigns stress (24a), aligns the base to the right edge of the stressed syllable (24b), reduplicates (copies) a heavy syllable within that base (24c), and then re-assigns stress to the correct syllable (via a rule of stress-maintenance) (24d).

(24) A Derivational Account of the Mayo reduplication patterns (Haugen 2004)

    a. Assign stress:[8]
       no.ka$_A$ →   nó.ka
       no.ka$_U$ →   no.ká
    b. Align Base to the right edge of the stressed syllable
       nó.ka   →   [nó].ka
       no.ká   →   [no.ká]
    c. Copy: Reduplicate a heavy syllable
       <u>nó</u>.ka   →   *non.*[nó].ka
       <u>no.ká</u>   →   *nok.*[no.ká]
    d. Stress-Maintenance: Ensure that the accent appears in the correct position within the prosodic word (i.e. Re-Apply Rule A).
       non.<u>nó</u>.ka → *nón* . [no].ka
       nok.<u>no.ká</u> → *nok* . [nó.ka]

See Haugen (2004) for a constraint-based, non-derivational account of these patterns which utilizes separate alignment constraints for the assignment of the base and for the accent. (The gemination at the juncture of the reduplicant and its base can be derived via a relatively low ranking constraint prohibiting gemination as compared to constraints mitigating against other ways of creating a heavy syllable, e.g. a long vowel, cf. *LONG-V; or an epenthetic segment, cf. DEP$_{IO}$).

The important point here is the need for the morphology to recognize the syllable boundaries of the stem form in order to derive the correct reduplicant for the accented class. One way to account for this pattern is to allow a theory to define the base by constraint, as is suggested in Shaw's (2005) Constituent Base Hypothesis.

An alternative account, based on analyses proposed by Gouskova (2007) and others, might posit a lexically-indexed markedness constraint (e.g. STRUC-ROLE) that would apply to words in the accented class only. However, lexically-indexed markedness constraints were originally proposed and are typically designed to account for arbitrarily-assigned lexical stipulations as to which stems fall into which classes. The use of such a constraint here would completely miss the phonological regularity of the pattern, as well as the opaque nature of the base assignment as depicted in (24). The generalization to be accounted for

---

[8] The subscripts 'A' and 'U' indicate the lexical assignment of roots to the 'accented' and 'unaccented' classes, respectively. The minimal pair at hand shows that this assignment must be lexical and cannot be based solely on phonological or morphological information alone.

is that heavy syllable reduplicants only copy from σ_1 of the stem within the accented class, a class defined solely on the basis of where accent falls within the word (i.e. σ_1).

Before proceeding observe that the limitation on copying only within σ_1 seems to be quite common among the Uto-Aztecan languages (see Haugen 2005, 2008 for discussion and illustration), and a variety of strategies to create a heavy syllable without copying from σ_2 of the stem are employed by various languages.[9] These include, within Uto-Aztecan: reduplicant-base junctural gemination, which is by far the most common pattern and is also found, in addition to the examples from Hiaki and the accented class of Mayo above, in at least the Tepiman and Numic branches of Uto-Aztecan; long vowels (as in Nahuatl and the 'marked plurals' of Tohono O'odham); and through the epenthesis of an unmarked consonant (typically a laryngeal: /ʔ/ or /h/), as in Guarijío, Nahuatl, and Mono. Expanding our view to a cross-linguistic vista beyond Uto-Aztecan, other ways that languages create heavy syllable reduplicants without copying from σ_2 include nasal substitution (as in Pohnpeian, cf. Kennedy 2003), or the appearance of a pre-specified consonantal segment in the coda position (as in Turkish, cf. Wedel 1999).

5   *Opacity in Base Assignment*

It was just argued that the assignment of the base in the Mayo accented word class constitutes an example of opacity: the base is aligned to the right edge of the accented (i.e. the first) syllable in the unreduplicated form. This demarcation is obscured in the output form because the accent actually falls on (i.e. shifts to) the reduplicant when reduplication applies. In order to account for such a base delimitation the grammar must somehow recognize the syllable boundaries of the stem.

A similar situation also occurs in Hiaki, which we saw above must also involve the morphology recognizing syllable boundaries in order to correctly generate reduplicants in the "syllable copy" pattern: i.e. second syllable onsets within the stem may not serve as codas for the reduplicant. An intriguing extension of this generalization is that it appears to be the syllable structure of the stem *in the underlying representation* that is of relevance to phonological copying. That is, the

---

[9] The copying from σ_2 that we see in the Mayo unaccented class thus seems to be relatively rare in Uto-Aztecan; see Haugen (2008) for further discussion and examples.

delimitation of the base to σ_1 seems to apply to the underlying form of the stem rather than the surface form.

This distinction can be demonstrated by observing how reduplication operates in cases where a reduplicated verb stem also appears with suffixes which lead to stem-final vowel deletion. In such cases this vowel deletion can result in a word-medial consonant cluster, as shown in (25).[10]

(25) Hiaki Verb Stem + Final Vowel-Deleting Suffix

noo.ka 'speak'   +   -tai.te 'inceptive'   >   nok.tai.te 'starting to speak'

Given what has been said above about 'syllable copy' reduplication in Hiaki, we should expect a complex verb stem like *nok.tai.te* to allow the entire σ_1 of the surface verb stem (i.e. *nok-*) to copy, but this is not the case: the reduplicant only copies from the first syllable of the *underlying*, non-affixed stem (i.e. *no-*).

(26) Reduplication of Hiaki Verb Stem + Final Vowel-Deleting Suffix

nok.tai.te   +   Reduplication   >   *no*-nok.tai.te 'starting to speak (habitually)'
                                     **no*k-nok.tai.te

This raises an interesting issue for surface-based phonological theories such as Base-Reduplicant Correspondence (McCarthy and Prince 1995), as the delimitation of the base as σ_1 in such cases seems to precede the vowel-deletion and consonant cluster-formation triggered by suffixation, thus resulting in another case of opacity in base assignment. This opacity is illustrated in (27).

(27) noo.ka   ⇨   [noo]ka   ⇨   [no]ka + -tai.te   ⇨...
        | | |
        UR   Assign Base   Add Suffix
                                             (+ Shorten First V)[11]

      ...⇨   [no]k.tai.te   ⇨   *no*-[no]k.tai.te
                  | |
               Delete Stem-Final V   Copy Base

---

[10] Only a few verbal suffixes take the basic free form of the verb without causing such final vowel deletion; the suffixes which do not cause shortening of the stem seem to be limited to -k 'perfective'; -n 'past continuative'; -ka 'past participle'; and -o 'if/ when' (Dedrick and Casad 1999: 259ff). The shortening of the first vowel is also a regular occurrence with any affixation for verb stems like noo.ka 'speak'; see Demers et al. (1999) for discussion.
[11] See footnote 10.

It is crucial to recognize here that the limitation on copying from σ_1 is strictly phonological—the root form of the verb is at least composed of *nok-* (if it is not the full verb stem *no(o)ka*). Thus, no appeal to underlying morphological structure can generate the correct reduplicant. This phonological restriction on base assignment is predicted to be possible by Shaw's CBH but not by Inkelas and Zoll's MDT, which limits (their theoretical equivalent of) base delimitation to morphological constituents. We will now consider MDT and another alternative approach to phonological copying theories, that proposed by Raimy (2000), to see how the phonological nature of delimiting the base to σ_1 of the stem poses a problem for such theories.

6 Base Delimitation in Approaches to Reduplication without Phonological Copying

Thus far we have been assuming a traditional notion of reduplication that proposes an operation of phonological copying, or, equivalently, 'correspondence' between a 'reduplicant' morpheme and its corresponding 'base' stem. Of course, alternatives to this view have been proposed. This section will briefly address two such theories, those of Raimy (2000) and Inkelas and Zoll (2005), and will point out the implications that the above discussion has for each.

Raimy (2000) proposes a linear precedence model of reduplication within Precedence Based Phonology (PBP), wherein reduplication derives from the introduction of a "jump link", i.e. a re-adjustment rule triggered by a (typically) null affix, into the phonological representation of a stem. This jump link is just an additional 'arrow' added into the linear ordering of the segments of the stem; such ordering is usually taken for granted but it is explicitly encoded into the representation in PBP. Following this jump link prior to final linearization results in the reduplication construction: i.e. the repetition of some of the segments of the stem, as illustrated in (28).

(28) a. Hiaki Verb Stem with Linear Precedence Specified (cf. Raimy 2000)
$$\# \rightarrow v \rightarrow u \rightarrow s \rightarrow a \rightarrow \%$$
b. Introduction of a Jump Link
$$\# \rightarrow v \rightarrow u \rightarrow s \rightarrow a \rightarrow \%$$
c. The Result After Linearization
v u v u s a

In the version of PBP presented in Raimy (2000), the rules introducing and placing such jump links do not refer to syllable structure, but
instead refer to the linear order of segments. These rules generally
involve stipulation (e.g. "the first vowel precedes the segment which
precedes the first vowel"—see Raimy 2000: 113 for a formalization of
this rule). If such rules could not recognize prosodic structure then
there would be no way for PBP to naturally account for the patterns of
reduplication surveyed above, which depend crucially upon recognizing syllable boundaries within the stem to derive the right reduplicant.
As configured in Raimy (2000), the PBP rules that would be required
to derive the correct patterns in the *vu*-vu.sa / *vam*-vam.se alternation
would completely miss the generalization that it is the syllable boundary which lets the speaker know how much of the stem is available
for copying. This is, of course, the same problem faced by the CV
skeleton theory outlined in (12) above. (See Haugen 2008: 60–66, for
further discussion of this approach to reduplication, and an alternative approach within the same morphological framework that Raimy
employs—Distributed Morphology, Halle and Marantz 1993; Harley
and Noyer 1999; etc.).[12]

IZ propose a novel approach to reduplicative morphology called
Morphological Doubling Theory (MDT), which abandons the phonological copying perspective in favor of considering reduplication to be
a kind of compounding construction. For IZ the identity between the
'reduplicant' and its 'base' is not phonological but rather semantic. In
a certain sense IZ propose that reduplication is in fact the compounding of a root or stem with a semantically equivalent root or stem which
happens to have the same root as its input; in another sense, then,
a 'reduplicant' is not at all a 'copy' of some other 'base' stem but is
rather a kind of *Doppelgänger*. In this view reduplication is placed on
a par with morphologically similar juxtaposition constructions, such
as synonym, near-synonym, and antonym constructions.

---

[12] It is important to note that versions of PBP described in Raimy (2009) and elsewhere make reference to syllable structure, including syllable boundaries. For example, Cairns and Raimy (2008) present PBP analyses that indicate that languages may
vary with respect to whether rules refer to syllable structure or not. Their analysis of
perfective reduplication in Attic Greek, for example, requires the identification of, and
an internal structure for, syllabic onsets.

Each daughter in the reduplication construction is associated with its own co-phonology (one of which often leads to the truncation of one of the daughters, a situation which has heretofore been considered to be 'partial reduplication'), as is the mother node (i.e. the construction as a whole). IZ's schematic model of reduplication is presented in (29).

(29) A Schematic of the Reduplication Construction in MDT (IZ, 19)

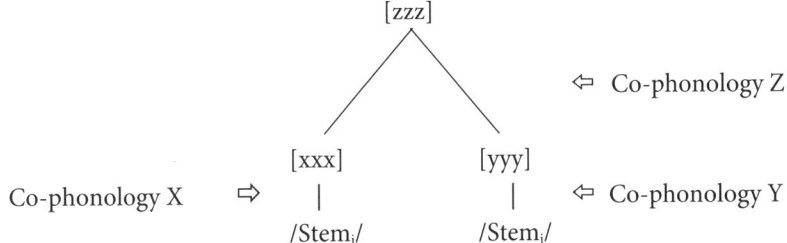

Like Shaw (2005), IZ recognize that different morphological constituents can serve as bases for reduplication, e.g. in the situation when a morphological subset of a stem is delimited as the base, in the terminology employed above. Unlike Shaw, however, IZ specifically rule out prosodic constituents serving as potential delimited bases, an exclusion which is encoded in IZ's *thesis of morphological targets* (cf. 30).

(30) The Thesis of Morphological Targets (IZ, 25)

> A reduplication construction calls for morphological constituents (affix, root, stem or word), not phonological constituents (mora, syllable, or foot).

The data presented above clearly contradict a strict interpretation of this thesis. However, IZ would be able to account for the patterns that we have been discussing if they amend their theory to allow for the syllable boundaries of the stem to be marked in the input and then demarcated for truncation.

   In the traditional phonological copying account of the patterns presented above, the prosody of the stem (specifically, the boundary of σ_1) is what determines the shape of the reduplicant. In MDT the two

stems have no phonological relationship whatsoever, so there is no
way for the phonological material forming [xxx] in (29) to identify the
syllabic boundaries of the phonological material in [yyy]. However, the
identical root input into both [xxx] and [yyy] ('/stem$_i$/') can surface differently if Co-Phonology X differs from Co-Phonology Y. Although
in 'full copy' reduplication the co-phonologies of both stems are presumably the same,[13] for cases of partial reduplication, IZ claim, one
of the stems (i.e. that of the 'reduplicant') has a special co-phonology
which requires truncation. In their analyses this truncation typically
involves a template-like size constraint, such as OUTPUT=$\sigma_{\mu\mu}$, as in IZ's
analysis of Sanskrit reduplication examples like krand > *kan*-i-krand
but not **ka*-i-krand (2005, 76–77), or OUTPUT=CV (or, equivalently,
OUTPUT=σ_μ) as in Caballero's (2006) analysis of abbreviated reduplication in Guarijío (cf. 4 above).

The postulation of such output templates, however, would be the
equivalent of, and result in the same missed analysis as, the templates proposed in (10)–(12) above. And, as with the lexically-indexed
markedness constraint approach to the Mayo accented word class,
lexical stipulations for co-phonologies requiring σ_μ (CV) or $\sigma_{\mu\mu}$ (CVC)
output templates would completely ignore the phonological regularity
of the emerging reduplication patterns.

To somewhat reify the metaphorical graphic presentation of MDT
vs. phonological copying approaches to reduplication, the analysis that
has been proposed above to be required for σ_1 base delimitation is that
shown in (31).

(31) σ1 Base-Delimitation in the Phonological Copying Approach

    [xx]   [[yy].yy]

In MDT there is no 'horizontal' relationship between the two output stems [xx] and [[yy].yy]. However, the 'syllable copy' and other

---

[13] Cases where both stems truncate to match the same template, i.e. the 'templatic back-copy' effect, could also involve an identical co-phonology for both daughter
stems; refer back to our discussion of Caballero's (2006) analysis of Guarijío in (4)
above.

BASE=σ_1 patterns could be derived by encoding the syllable structure directly into the input. An MDT alternative to (31) would be (32).

(32) The $\sigma 1$ Base-Delimitation Effect in MDT

$$\text{Co-Phonology X} \quad \Rightarrow \quad \begin{array}{c} [yy(y)] \\ | \\ [yy(y).yy]_i \end{array} \quad \begin{array}{c} [yy(y).yy] \\ | \\ [yy(y).yy]_i \end{array} \quad \Leftarrow \quad \text{Co-Phonology Y}$$

The two different outputs (truncated [yy(y)] vs. unaltered [yy(y).yy]) would have to depend on the two different co-phonologies applying to the identical compounded underlying stems, i.e. [yy(y).y]$_i$ and its *Doppelgänger*. If Co-Phonology X could contain a constraint like (33) in order to yield the truncation of everything in the input that is not contained within σ_1, then the effect would be accounted for.

(33) OUTPUT=σ_1: delete everything in the stem beyond the boundary of the first syllable.

Such a move would somewhat dilute the strong version of the Thesis of Morphological Targets, but only in so far as the targeting of phonological targets in a reduplication construction would involve such targeting only within the "*Doppelgänger* stem". That is, IZ could maintain the thesis of MDT that the output of the "reduplicant" stem (e.g. [yy(y)] in 32) is completely independent of the "base stem" (e.g. [yy(y).yy] in 32), even though certain morphological or phonological processes do in fact target a prosodic subset of that (or, in fact, the other) stem. In such a case a phonological target would be regarded as possible, given the caveat that the phonological target is intrinsic to the stem itself, and is not otherwise reliant on one stem 'seeing' the prosodic structure of the other stem (as must be the case in the phonological copying representation in 31).

To conclude, given the *Doppelgänger* nature of stems in reduplicative constructions as proposed by IZ, the equivalent of prosodic base delimitation should be a possibility, if such stems are marked for prosody in the input. On the other hand, the *Doppelgänger* status of the reduplicant in MDT also renders any kind of claim of dependency on the prosodic structure of the 'base' (in phonological copying theories) to be effectually impossible: IZ can always fall back on the theoretical claim that the input to the two different stems (X or Y) is prosodically identical. For this reason, prosodic base delimitation can probably not be regarded as a fatal flaw as far as the empirical coverage of this theory goes, but a conceptual issue regarding non-testability remains.[14]

7   Conclusion

In conclusion, this chapter has attempted to support Shaw's (2005) Constituent Base Hypothesis by showing how the prosodic constituent of the syllable may serve as a domain to be targeted for reduplication: i.e. that the syllable may serve as a delimitation on the base for reduplicative copying. Relevant empirical data from 'syllable copy' reduplication in Hiaki and Yapese, as well as $\text{BASE}=\sigma_1$ reduplication in the accented word class of Mayo, has been presented in support of this contention. This chapter has discussed the implications of these data for a variety of different theoretical approaches to reduplication, and concludes that any adequate account of these patterns must in some way recognize the boundary between the first and second syllable of the stem. This chapter has also shown how such base delimitation can form an opacity, if base-assignment precedes other processes which obscure the environment for the delimitation of the base, e.g. in stress-shift (as in Mayo) or word-medial consonant cluster formation resulting from affixation (reduplicative or otherwise, as in Hiaki). If the preceding is a successful argument, then the syllable itself must be a legitimate prosodic unit, and crucially, one which must be accessible by the morphology.

---

[14] There are other additional conceptual issues which might necessitate a critical view in regard to MDT. For example, MDT relies on ubiquitous synonymy constructions and near-ubiquitous (and in most cases otherwise reduplication-specific) truncation constructions in the world's languages. Further, IZ do not manage to empirically support their potentially plausible linkage of reduplication constructions to morphological synonymy constructions by showing that the latter are as susceptible to the truncation that is well known to be so typical of the former.

References

Ballantyne, Keira. 1999. Reduplication in Yapese: A case of syllable copying. In *Proceedings of AFLA VI: The Sixth meeting of the Austronesian Formal Linguistics Association*, edited by Carolyn Smallwood and Catherine Kitto, 17–24. Toronto: University of Toronto Department of Linguistics: Toronto Working Papers in Linguistics.
Caballero, Gabriela. 2006. "Templatic backcopying" in Guarijío abbreviated reduplication. *Morphology* 16: 273–289.
Cairns, Charles and Eric Raimy. 2008. Raimy rules in Spokane and elsewhere. Unpublished Ms., City University of New York and University of Wisconsin-Madison.
Dedrick, John M. and Eugene H. Casad. 1999. *Sonora Yaqui Language Structures*. Tucson: University of Arizona Press.
Demers, Richard, Fernando Escalante, and Eloise Jelinek. 1999. Prominence in Yaqui words. *International Journal of American Linguistics* 65: 40–55.
Escalante, Fernando. 1985. A preliminary view of the structure of Yaqui. MA thesis, University of Arizona.
Feng, Guanjun Bella. 2003. Syllable-size morpheme restriction in shaping reduplication. Presented at the 8th Southwest Workshop on Optimality Theory (SWOT 8). Tucson, AZ: University of Arizona.
——. 2006. Morpheme recognition in prosodic morphology. Ph.D. diss., University of Southern California.
Gouskova, Maria. 2007. The reduplicative template in Tonkawa. *Phonology* 24: 367–396.
Hagberg, Lawrence. 1993. An Autosegmental Theory of Stress. PhD diss., University of Arizona.
Halle, Morris and Alex Marantz. 1993. Distributed Morphology and the pieces of inflection. In *The View from Building 20: Essays in Linguistics in Honor of Sylvain Bromberger*, edited by Kenneth Hale and Samuel J. Keyser, 53–109. Cambridge, MA: MIT Press.
Harley, Heidi and Maria Amarillas. 2003. Reduplication multiplication in Yaqui: Meaning X form. In *Studies in Uto-Aztecan*, edited by Luis M. Barragan and Jason D. Haugen, 105–139. Cambridge, MA: MITWPL.
Harley, Heidi and Maria Florez Leyva. 2009. Form and meaning in Hiaki (Yaqui) verbal reduplication. *International Journal of American Linguistics* 75: 233–272.
Harley, Heidi and Rolf Noyer. 1999. Distributed Morphology. *Glot International* 4: 3–9.
Haugen, Jason D. 2003. Allomorphy in Yaqui reduplication. In *Studies in Uto-Aztecan*, edited by Luis M. Barragan and Jason D. Haugen, 75–103. Cambridge, MA: MIT Working Papers on Endangered and Less Familiar Languages #5.
——. 2004. An opacity problem in Mayo reduplication. *Kansas Working Papers in Linguistics* 27: 139–156.
——. 2005. Reduplicative allomorphy and language prehistory in Uto-Aztecan. In *Studies on Reduplication*, edited by Bernard Hurch, 315–349. Berlin: Mouton de Gruyter.
——. 2008. *Morphology at the Interfaces: Reduplication and Noun Incorporation in Uto-Aztecan*. Amsterdam: John Benjamins Publishing Company.
——. 2009. What is the base for reduplication? *Linguistic Inquiry* 40: 505–514.
Haugen, Jason D., Catherine Hicks Kennard and Robert Kennedy. 2002. The Basis for Bases: Assigning Reduplicative Bases via Alignment Constraints. Presented at the 76th Annual Linguistic Society of America Meeting, San Francisco, CA.
Hendricks, Sean Q. 1999. Reduplication without Template Constraints: A Study in Bare Consonant Reduplication. PhD diss., University of Arizona.
Hicks Kennard, Catherine. 2004. Copy but don't repeat: The conflict of dissimilation and reduplication in the Tawala durative. *Phonology* 21: 303–323.

Inkelas, Sharon and Cheryl Zoll. 2005. *Reduplication: Doubling in Morphology*. Cambridge: Cambridge University Press.

Kennedy, Robert. 2003. Confluence in Phonology: Evidence from Micronesian. PhD diss., University of Arizona.

Marantz, Alec. 1982. Re reduplication. *Linguistic Inquiry* 13: 435–482.

McCarthy, John and Alan Prince. 1986. Prosodic morphology. Unpublished Ms., University of Massachusetts-Amherst and Rutgers University.

——. 1993. Prosodic Morphology I: Constraint interaction and satisfaction. Unpublished Ms., University of Massachusetts-Amherst and Rutgers University.

——. 1995. Faithfulness and reduplicative identity. In *University of Massachusetts Occasional Papers in Linguistics* 18: 249–384. Amherst, MA: Graduate Linguistics Student Association.

——. 1998. Prosodic Morphology. In *The Handbook of Morphology*, edited by Andrew Spencer and Arnold Zwicky, 283–305. Oxford: Blackwell Publishers.

——. 1999a. Faithfulness and identity in Prosodic Morphology. In *The Prosody-Morphology Interface*, edited by Rene Kager, Harry van der Hulst and Wim Zonnefeld, 218–309. Cambridge: Cambridge University Press.

——. 1999b. Generalized Alignment. Rutgers Optimality Archive [Rutgers Optimality Archive #7, http://roa.rutgers.edu].

Miller, Wick R. 1996. *Guarijío: Gramática, Textos y Vocabulario*. México, D.F.: UNAM.

Molina, Felipe S., Herminia Valenzuela and David Leedom Shaul. 1999. *Hippocrene Standard Dictionary: Yoeme-English English-Yoeme, with a Comprehensive Grammar of Yoeme Language*. New York: Hippocrene Books.

Moravcsik, Edith. 1978. Reduplicative constructions. In *Universals of Human Language vol. 3: Word Structure*, edited by Joseph H. Greenberg, 297–334. Stanford, CA: Stanford University Press.

Raimy, Eric. 2000. *The Phonology and Morphology of Reduplication*. Berlin: Mouton de Gruyter.

——. 2009. Deriving reduplicative templates in a modular fashion. In *Contemporary Views on Architecture and Representations in Phonology*, edited by Eric Raimy and Charles Cairns, 383–404. Cambridge, MA.: MIT Press.

Shaw, Patricia A. 2005. Non-adjacency in reduplication. In *Studies on Reduplication*, edited by Bernard Hurch, 161–210. Berlin: Mouton de Gruyter.

Suzuki, Keiichiro. 1998. A Typological Investigation of Dissimilation. PhD diss., University of Arizona.

Urbanczyk, Suzanne. 1999. Double reduplications in parallel. In *The Prosody-Morphology Interface*, edited by Rene Kager, Harry van der Hulst, and Wim Zonnefeld, 390–428. Cambridge: Cambridge University Press.

Wedel, Andrew. 1999. Turkish emphatic reduplication. Phonology at Santa Cruz, Linguistics Research Center, UC Santa Cruz. http://escholarship.org/uc/item/6sm3953w

Yip, Moira. 1998. Identity avoidance in phonology and morphology. In *Morphology and its relation to Phonology and Syntax*, edited by Steven G. Lapointe, Diane K. Brentari and Patrick M. Farrell, 216–246. Stanford: CSLI.

CHAPTER SIX

GEMINATES: HEAVY OR LONG?

Catherine O. Ringen and Robert M. Vago

1   *Introduction*

Two separate views have been advocated for the representation of underlying monomorphemic ("true") geminate consonants. Under the *syllabic weight* analysis of what might be called classical moraic theory (Hyman 1985, McCarthy and Prince 2001, Hock 1986, Hayes 1989, Morén 2001, among others) geminates are inherently heavy: they are represented with a single segmental node which is associated with a mora unit. Within the context of phonological representations, the geminate property is a function of double prosodic association. Length, then, is encoded in terms of weight. Under the *segmental length* analysis, suggested in most detail by Selkirk (1990), geminates are inherently long: they have double nodes on what we will refer to as the *timing tier*, without inherent moraic affiliation. On this view, phonological length is interpreted directly off the timing tier, in terms of two nodes sharing one segmental specification.[1]

The contrasting representations of underlying geminates and geminates occurring in intervocalic syllabified positions are shown in (1):[2]

---

[1] When we refer to the length of geminates, we are primarily interested in phonological representation rather than phonetic implementation. For some discussion on the relationship between the two domains, see Broselow et al. (1997), Ham (2001), Gordon (2002, 2004, 2005, 2006), and Shaw (2006), among others.

[2] Representational models that have been proposed in the literature may refer to a skeletal tier and/or a root tier, exclude an explicit weight (mora) tier, or include more specific syllabic constituent units (such as onset, nucleus, coda). These issues are beyond the scope of our discussion; see in particular Tranel (1991), Pulleyblank (1994), Broselow (1995), Curtis (2003), and Gordon (2004) for detailed overviews. Also excluded from the domain of our focus are cases of moraic inconsistency or mismatches (cf. Crowhurst 1991, Steriade 1991, Hyman 1992, Broselow 1995, Hayes 1995, and Gordon 2004, 2006, among others) and phonetically motivated syllable weight (see, among others, Zec 1994, Broselow, et al. 1997, Gordon 2002, 2004, 2006, Kraehenmann 2001, 2003, and Kavitskaya 2002).

(1) a. The syllabic weight analysis of geminates

        Underlying   *Intervocalic*

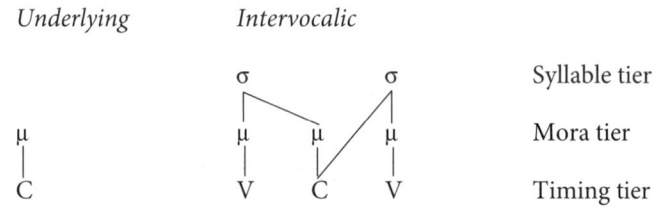

    b. The segmental length analysis of geminates

        Underlying   *Intervocalic*

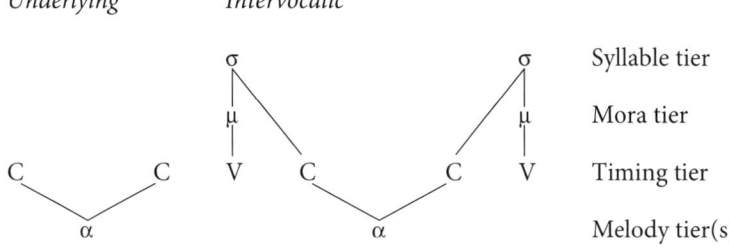

Throughout this work, the timing tier symbols C, CC, V, and VV represent single consonants, consonant clusters, short vowels, and long vowels, respectively. We will also use the symbol G to refer to geminates.

Subsequent to the initial proposals of the two opposing views of the representation of length, discussions have focused on individual language studies, the majority of which adopt the syllabic weight treatment (with variations in representational detail; see fn. 2). Our purpose here is to bring together arguments against the inherent weight analysis and motivate the double slot representation as the only universal property of underived geminates.[3] It is not our goal to present an exhaustive list of geminate behavior in support of our claims; rather, the evidence adduced below is meant to be representative.

The syllabic weight analysis of geminates involves two crucial representational claims: (a) geminates are inherently heavy, and (b) geminates have single specification on the timing tier. The evidence reported in this chapter suggests that both claims are false: not all geminates are mora bearing and geminates have bipositional specification.[4] The arguments

---

[3] Derived geminates, which do not necessarily have the same properties as basic, underlying geminates, will not be treated here.

[4] Research advocating the bipositional representation of geminates is split on the issue of inherent weight: see for instance Curtis (2003) pro, Hume, et al. (1997) and Baker (2008) con.

below indicate that underlying geminate structure contains double units on the timing tier and no inherent prosodic properties. Geminates can become heavy in this view, in case consonants in the coda, or less frequently, in the onset, in general are heavy in a particular language.[5]

In section 2 we bring forth problematical cases for the syllabic weight position from the point of view of the patterning of geminates in terms of weight. In section 2.1 we look at weightless (light) geminates in coda position, in section 2.2 in onset position. In section 3 we examine the patterning of geminates from the point of view of length. In section 3.1 we motivate bipositional, doubly linked geminate structure, and in section 3.2 we discuss cases where geminates pattern together with consonant clusters. In section 4 we summarize our findings and our position on the representation of geminates.

2   Weightless Geminates

2.1   Light Geminates in Coda Position

If geminates have inherent weight, then syllables closed by the first half of a geminate should count as heavy, or bimoraic, since the vocalic nucleus and the geminate coda each contribute to syllable weight. However, this does not appear to be always the case, as claimed for a variety of languages by Lahiri and Koreman (1988), Selkirk (1990), Tranel (1991), Blevins (1991), and Baker (2008). We will take up two cases here.

2.1.1   Selkup Stress
Consider the facts in Selkup, a West Siberian language, where stress falls on the rightmost heavy syllable (or else on the initial syllable). Halle and Clements (1983) cite the following examples:

(2) Selkup Stress

    a. Stress rightmost heavy syllable: [qumo:qlılí:] 'your two friends'
    b. Medial CVC syllables are light: [ámɨrna] 'eats'
    c. Medial CVG syllables are light: [ú:cɨkkak] 'I am working'

The token in (2a) contains two long vowels (heavy syllables); as seen, it is the rightmost heavy syllable that bears stress. (2b) shows that CVC

---

[5] The phonological weight of consonants, including that of geminates, can sometimes be traced to historical developments; see Blevins (2004).

syllables count as light: they are not stressed. Now if geminates are inherently mora bearing, then a syllable closed by the first half of a geminate will be heavy and should therefore attract stress. But this prediction is not borne out, as seen in (2c), where the rightmost heavy syllable is the initial one containing the long vowel, and not the penultimate one, containing the geminate (G).

Ever since the original data presented in Halle and Clements (1983), the weight analysis of CVG syllables in Selkup has remained controversial (for discussion, see Tranel 1991, Davis 2003, and Curtis 2003). The problem is that the data contain only one example where a syllable closed by a geminate (CVG) is not followed by a long vowel (VV). This form is given in (2c); as seen, CVG is preceded by a long vowel. It is further observed that the initial VV syllable attracts stress over the medial CVG syllable. The facts leave room for the weight analysis of geminates, whereby both VV and CVG syllables are heavy, augmented by the hypothesis that stress targets (rightmost) VV heavy syllables preferentially over CVG heavy syllables (see Davis 2003). The length analysis of geminates, on the other hand, explains the facts by claiming that CVG syllables are light and that stress falls on (rightmost) heavy (VV) syllables.[6]

Words of the shape CVCVGV(C), i.e. those containing a CVG medial syllable flanked by short vowels, provide the critical empirical testing ground for the claims of the two opposing theories. On the uncontroversial assumption that stress targets heavy syllables over light ones, the weight analysis predicts stress to fall on the putatively heavy CVG syllable, while the length analysis predicts default stress on the initial light syllable (in the absence of heavy syllables).

The Taz dialect of Selkup, among other dialects, provides the missing information. In Taz Selkup (Helimski 1998) stress falls on the initial syllable, unless, as expected from the discussion above, a long vowel occurs in a non-initial syllable (or a morphologically defined heavy suffix is added). Consider the following examples (Helimski, p.c.):

(3) Taz Selkup Stress

    a. Stress rightmost heavy syllable: [ɛssíːqo] 'to happen (already)'
                                     [čeːlóːqün] 'in the day'
    b. Medial CVC syllables are light: [qápürümpütül] 'which became fat'

---

[6] Under both views, CVC syllables are uncontroversially light and stress defaults to the initial vowel in words that do not contain a long vowel.

c. Medial CVG syllables are light: [páčütta] 'he cuts down (a tree)'
   [ésükka] '(it) happens (occasionally)'

(3b) establishes that the medial CVC syllable is light, as shown by the fact that it does not attract stress. (3c) leads to the same conclusion about medial CVG syllables.[7] Light CVG syllables falsify the prediction of the weight analysis of geminates: on this account, CVG is bimoraic (due to the inherent mora of G) and hence should attract stress.[8]

2.1.2 *Ngalakgan Stress*

A particularly revealing instantiation of coda geminates that have light weight is found in the Northern Australian language of Ngalakgan, as described by Baker (2008).[9] The general stress pattern of trisyllabic roots is as follows: stress falls on the medial syllable if it is heavy (closed by the first member of a heterorganic consonant cluster), otherwise, i.e. if the medial syllable is light, on the initial syllable. Contrast (4a) with (4b) and (4c):

(4) Ngalakgan trisyllabic stress

   a. Heavy CVC medial syllables: medial stress
      [luŋúrwa] 'vine sp.'
      [moɲɔ́cpɔr] 'mud cod'
      [burɔ́ʈci] 'water python'
   b. Light CV medial syllables: initial stress
      [mónaŋa] 'European'
      [wálama] 'face'
      [wáɖiya] 'multiparous woman'
   c. Light CVG medial syllables: initial stress
      [jábatta] 'freshwater tortoise sp.'
      [gámakkʊn] 'properly'
      [mɔ́ɭɔppɔɭ] 'shovelhead catfish'

If geminates are inherently heavy, then CVG medial syllables (those closed by the first half of a geminate) are expected to attract stress. As seen in (4c), that is not the case, however.

---

[7] The geminates in (3c) are suffix internal (Helimski, p.c.), hence monomorphemic (underived).

[8] See our comment in section 4 on possible modifications to the syllabic weight theory of geminates to accommodate light geminates.

[9] See also Hayes (1995) for several cases of light geminates with respect to stress.

2.2   *Light Geminates in Onset Position*

It has been acknowledged, starting with early studies of moraic phenomena, notably Hyman (1985), that syllable initial consonants do not, in general, contribute to phonological weight. In this light, how do we interpret the claim of the weight analysis of geminates that they are inherently mora-bearing? Clearly, it is not possible to maintain the position that initial geminates are disallowed on theoretical grounds, that is, to claim that initial geminates are illicit because geminates are moraic but initial consonants are not. The fact is, geminates do occur in onset position (see in particular Muller 2001 and Curtis 2003),[10] and in some cases initial geminates can clearly be shown to be moraic (Davis 1999, Topintzi 2008).[11] But in other cases initial geminates have been argued to lack weight. These would seem to falsify the basic claim of the theory that assigns inherent weight to geminates. We now turn to a brief discussion of two such cases.

2.2.1   *Leti Initial Geminates*

In the Austronesian language of Leti, as argued by Hume et al. (1997), words must be minimally bimoraic. If onset geminates are mora bearing, one way to satisfy the word minimality constraint is to have words consisting of an initial geminate followed by a short vowel. But in point of fact, no such words are countenanced.

Stress assignment is another case in point. Word initial heavy syllables attract stress, as do penultimate syllables: contrast for example *má:nʷorʸóri* 'crow,' where the initial long vowel is stressed, with *matrúna* 'master of the house,' where the initial short vowel is not. Crucially, initial geminates do not combine with short vowels to create heavy syllables, as the weight analysis would have it. Thus, in *ppunárta*, 'nest's egg,' the initial syllable lacks stress. The conclusion reached by Hume et al. (1997) is that initial geminates in Leti are not mora bearing.[12]

---

[10] Singleton onsets can also be mora bearing; see McCarthy and Prince (1990), Bagemihl (1991), Lin (1997), and Muller (2001), among others.

[11] Davis (1999) adopts Hayes's (1989) suggestion that the mora of the initial geminate should be treated in extrasyllabic terms, while Topintzi (2008) proposes fully syllabified moraic onsets.

[12] See however Curtis (2003), according to whom the evidence for or against the moraic affiliation of Leti initial geminates is inconclusive.

2.2.2 *Thurgovian Swiss Initial Geminates*

Thurgovian Swiss is another language in which initial geminates behave as non-moraic. Consider the data in (5) (Muller 2001; Krae-henmann 2003).

(5) Thurgovian Swiss roots

Root shape	Base	Plural	Singular
a. CVC	/has/ 'hare'	has-e	ha:s
b. CVCC	/purk/ 'castle'	purk-e	purk
c. CVG	/aff/ 'monkey'	aff-e	aff
d. GVC	/ttak/ 'day'	ttak-e	tta:k

Kraehenmann's (2003) analysis is as follows. Thurgovian Swiss words are subject to a bimoraic word minimality constraint, weight-by-position, and word final extrametricality. The underlying representation of a root is suggested by non-final contexts, such as the plural in (5). The root base undergoes modifications in the singular, where it occurs in word final position. In (5a) the root final C is extrametrical, bringing the root in violation of the bimoraic word minimality constraint; lengthening the root vowel resolves the issue.[13] In (5b), where the root ends in a consonant cluster, root vowel lengthening is obviated by the moraic (via weight-by-position) post-vocalic C. Final geminates are also moraic, as seen in (5c) by the fact that the root vowel does not undergo lengthening.[14] Interestingly, initial geminates are not moraic, as seen clearly in (5d). Here, the final root C is extrametrical, as in (5a). The fact that the root vowel lengthens is explained on the view that initial geminates do not contribute to weight. If they did, root vowel lengthening would be curious.

---

[13] Polysyllabic roots do not undergo vowel lengthening: e.g. *Boke* 'arch,' *Pomfrit* 'French fries' (Kraehenmann 2001: 122). This underscores the position that long vowels in monosyllabic roots of the shape in (5a) are due to word minimality, rather than, say, final lengthening (ignoring word final extrametrical C).

[14] Note, *in passim*, that extrametricality on a word final geminate analyzed in terms of a single root node would violate word minimality, predicting, incorrectly, vowel lengthening.

3   Long Geminates

In section 2 we have considered issues for the underlying analysis of geminates from the perspective of weight sensitive processes. In this section we turn to issues of a segmental nature. We provide evidence that geminates have bipositional linked structures (section 3.1) and that they pattern together with consonant clusters, further strengthening the claim for double slot representations (section 3.2).

3.1   Double Linked Geminates

The Ngalakgan stress data presented in section 2.1.2 above can be accounted for in a straightforward manner if codas closed by geminates are assumed to be light. Then trisyllabic words have penultimate (medial) stress on heavy syllables, i.e. CVC, antepenultimate (initial) stress if the penultimate syllable is light, i.e. either CV or CG. In point of fact, medial syllables of the shape CVN, where N is a nasal which is homorganic to a following stop, are also light, as evidenced by the fact that they do not attract stress either. Note the following examples (Baker (2008):

(6) Ngalakgan Light CVN medial syllables
     [ŋɔ́lɔŋgɔ] 'eucalyptus sp.'
     [jáganda] 'female plains kangaroo'
     [ŋúruɳɖʊc] 'emu'

In sum, there are three types of possible CVC medial syllables in Ngalakgan trisyllabic words, and they pattern as follows: (a) syllables closed by a consonant which is followed by a heterorganic consonant are heavy (4a); (b) syllables closed by a geminate (4c) are light; (c) syllables closed by a nasal which is followed by a homorganic consonant (6) are light. The common behavior of geminates and homorganic nasals as opposed to heterorganic consonant clusters follows if geminates and homorganic nasals have linked place nodes:[15]

(7) a. Heterorganic CC (heavy)

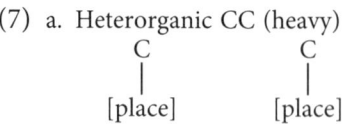

---

[15] On Baker's (2008) view, bigestural clusters are heavy, monogestural clusters are light with respect to stress placement in trisyllabic words.

b. G (light)   Homorganic NC (light)

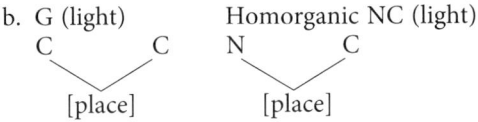

As far as representation is concerned, the affinity between geminates and homorganic NC clusters can be expressed nicely on the double CC, but not the single C analysis of geminates.

3.2 The Cluster Patterning of Geminates

Segmental processes provide a critical domain for the proper representation of geminates. To see this, consider the respective claims of the two theories of geminate representation as laid out in (8).

(8) Timing tier representations

$$
\begin{array}{lcccccc}
 & & C & CC & & G & \\
 & & & & & | & \\
 & & & & & \mu & \\
\text{Weight analysis:} & & C & C & C & C & \\
 & & & & & & \\
\text{Length analysis:} & & C & C & C & C \quad\diagdown\quad C \\
 & & & | & | & \quad\diagup & \\
 & & & \alpha & \beta & \alpha & \\
\end{array}
$$

Under the weight analysis, geminates are expected to be grouped together with single consonants, since both single and geminate consonants have a single unit representation on the timing tier, as opposed to consonant clusters, which have two (or more) units. On the other hand, the segmental length analysis makes geminates natural candidates to pattern together with consonant clusters, as Selkirk (1990) first pointed out: both have bipositional representations on the timing tier.

   Phonological processes that look to the timing tier for applicability are appropriate testing tools to evaluate the opposing predictions of the two theories of geminates. The conclusion in this regard is one sided: the empirical evidence overwhelmingly supports the claims of the segmental length theory. We will look at a few cases next.

3.2.1 Leti Geminate Patterning
Leti, as analyzed by Hume et al. (1997), provides a battery of support for the bipositional nature of geminates, as illustrated in (9).

(9) Leti G and CC patterns

    a. Underlying G and CC occur only word initially:
    ppuna 'nest'   pninu 'fool'
    mmanan 'food   mninivu 'soft'

    b. Word final VC metathesis:
- applies before CC: /kunis/ 'key' + /vnutan/ 'iron' → [kunsivnutan] 'iron key'
- applies before G: /ukar/ 'finger' + /ppalu/ 'bachelor' → [ukrappalu] 'index finger'
- blocked before single C: /mɛsar/ 'teacher' + /lavan/ 'big' → [mɛsarlavan] (*[mɛsralavan]) 'professor'

    c. Word final /a/ deletion:
- applies before single C: /samɛla/ 'mouse' + /nura/ 'coconut tree' → [samɛlnura] 'tricolored squirrel'
- blocked before G: /samɛla/ 'mouse' + /ttɛnan/ 'spine' → [samɛlattɛnan] (*[samɛlttɛnan]) 'mouse's spine'
- blocked before CC: /samɛla/ 'mouse' + /tpunan/ 'throat' → [samɛlatpunan] (*[samɛltpunan]) 'mouse's throat'

    d. Secondary articulation induced by word final /i/:
- realized on initial single C: /kkani/ 'plate' + /tani/ 'soil' → [kkantʸani] 'earthenware plate'
- blocked on initial G: /sivi/ 'chicken' + /ttɛi/ 'female' → [sivittɛi] (*[sivttʸɛi]) 'hen'
- blocked on initial CC: /ai/ 'wood' + /vlakar/ 'crossed' → [aivlakar] (*[avʸlakar]) 'cross'

The first piece of evidence that Leti geminates pattern with consonant clusters is obtained from distributional data: underlying geminates and consonant clusters both occur only in word initial position; cf. (9a). Second, when words are combined to form phrases, word final VC sequences are metathesized if the next word begins with either a consonant cluster or a geminate, but not if the next word begins with a single consonant; cf. (9b). Third, as seen in (9c), a word final low vowel is deleted if the next word begins with a single consonant, but is retained if the next word begins with either a geminate or a consonant cluster. And fourth, a word final front high vowel induces palatalization on the initial single consonant of the next word, but secondary articulation is blocked if the next word begins either with a geminate of a consonant cluster, as evident in the examples cited in (9d).

3.2.2 Hungarian Epenthesis

In Hungarian, as analyzed by Vago (1992; 2007; 2008), a *CC[+coronal] constraint motivates the insertion of a low vowel after verbal stems, as seen in (10).[16]

(10) Hungarian epenthesis before suffix initial coronals

    a. No epenthesis after C- or V-final stems:

	'3sg'	'2sg'	'Infin.'
'receive'	[kɒp]	[kɒp-s]	[kɒp-ni]
'grow'	[nö:]	[nö:-s]	[nö:-ni]

    b. Epenthesis after CC-final stems:

	'3sg'	'2sg'	'Infin.'
'bless'	[a:ld]	[a:ld-ɒs]	[a:ld-ɒni]
'pour'	[önt]	[önt-ɛs]	[önt-ɛni]

    c. Epenthesis after G-final stems:

	'3sg'	'2sg'	'Infin.'
'hear'	[hɒll]	[hɒll-ɒs]	[hɒll-ɒni]
'depend'	[függ]	[függ-ɛs]	[függ-ɛni]

The forms in (10a) establish that epenthesis does not apply following verbal stems that end in either a single consonant or a vowel; (10b) shows that stem final clusters trigger epenthesis.[17] Taken together, the following generalization suggests itself: epenthesis is triggered by two stem final C slots on the timing tier. The two theories of geminate representation make different predictions with respect to epenthesis after verbal stems ending in a geminate. If geminates have a single C node, they are not expected to trigger epenthesis; on the other hand, if geminates have double CC nodes, they are expected to behave like consonant clusters and induce epenthesis. In point of fact, it is the claim of the segmental length theory that is substantiated, as shown in (10c).

An alternative interpretation of the facts is that the "epenthesizing" suffixes have two allomorphs (one with an initial V and one without) and verbs are subcategorized as to which allomorphs they select (cf. Siptár and Törkenczy 2000; Curtis 2003). However, this analysis based on allomorphy misses the generalization that the choice of allomorphs is entirely correlated with the final segment(s) of the verbal stems. It

---

[16] Some stems allow vowel epenthesis optionally, others not at all. See Vago (1980, 1992, 2007, 2008) for discussion.

[17] The inserted vowel shows the effects of the well-known palatal vowel harmony process of Hungarian.

also renders fortuitous the fact that only those suffixes have allomorphic variants that begin with a coronal consonant.

There are other possible ways to account for the Hungarian facts in (10), but that is irrelevant to the main point: under any analysis, suffixes like those in (10) are vowel initial if and only if the preceding verbal stem ends in either CC or G. Crucially, this patterning is consistent with the claims of the segmental length analysis of geminates (CC), but not with the claims of the syllabic weight analysis (C).

3.2.3 Cypriot Greek Nasal Deletion

In Cypriot Greek the definite articles *ton* (masculine) and *tin* (feminine) lose their final nasal consonant if the next word begins either with a consonant cluster or geminate, motivated by a *CCC constraint.[18] The facts are as in (11) (Muller 2001).

(11) Cypriot Greek definite article allomorphy

    a. Final nasal stays before V or C
       ton ápparon 'the horse'
       ton tíxon 'the wall'
    b. Final nasal deletes before CC
       ti psačín 'the poison'
       to flókkon 'the mop'
    c. Final nasal deletes before G
       to pparán 'the money'
       to ttaván 'the stew'

As seen, the final nasal of the article is kept before a vowel or a single consonant (11a), but is deleted before consonant clusters (11b) and geminates (11c). If geminates have single C node representations, their patterning with consonant clusters rather than single consonants is not explained. In contrast, the double CC analysis of geminates predicts the facts correctly.

4 Conclusion

We postulate an invariant, universal structure for geminates, one that contains double units on the timing tier and no inherent prosodic properties:

---

[18] CCC clusters where the second C is a stop and the third C is a liquid are permitted; see Muller (2001).

(12) The segmental length analysis: universal representation of G

Geminates are free to occur in all positions, and are free to exhibit the full extent of possibilities with respect to prosodic patterning, more specifically, weight. Indeed, either one or both parts of geminates are found syllable initially as well as syllable finally, in both weight-bearing and weightless flavors. Weightless geminates, which we will call *light geminates*, are found in onset position in languages such as Leti (section 2.2.1) and Thurgovian Swiss (section 2.2.2), and in coda position in languages such as Selkup (section 2.1.1) and Ngalakgan (section 2.1.2). Geminates that are weight bearing, which we will call *heavy geminates*, occur in onset position in languages such as Trukese (Davis 1999), Pattani Malay, and Marshallese (Topintzi 2008), and in coda position in a host of languages (Kenstowicz 1994). We assume that heavy geminates in coda position come about as a result of Weight by Position (Hayes 1989) and that this analysis is extended to heavy geminates in onset position.

Proponents of the syllabic weight theory of geminates have, of course, been aware of the fact that geminates are not weight bearing in some languages. The typical move has been to claim that weightless geminates are not real geminates, but rather "fake" geminates (doubled consonants). On this view, "true" geminates are represented in terms of a single mora bearing C slot, while "fake" geminates are represented in terms of weightless double C slots, which either have two sets of feature specifications corresponding to each C slot (Davis 2003) or share the same features (Topintzi 2008). These approaches constitute a serious theoretical weakening in that they forgo a single, universal representation of morpheme internal long, i.e. geminate consonants.

With respect to quantity sensitive processes, all descriptions of single C geminates known to us are reanalyzable into CC representations; we are not aware of any compelling argument to the effect that some geminate structure must contain a single C node and not a double CC node; some facts are not compatible with the single C node hypothesis (see section 3). Therefore the full range of evidence supports the strong position that geminates are uniformly long.[19]

---

[19] This chapter is not claiming that geminates and consonant clusters necessarily pattern together with respect to phonological processes or phonotactic restrictions.→

References

Bagemihl, Bruce. 1991. Syllable structure in Bella Coola. *Linguistic Inquiry* 22: 589–646.

Baker, Brett J. 2008. *Word structure in Ngalakgan*. Palo Alto, CA: Stanford University Center for the Study of Language and Information.

Blevins, Juliette. 1991. Evidence for the independent representation of length and weight. Unpublished Ms., Stanford University.

——. 2004. *Evolutionary phonology: The emergence of sound patterns*. Cambridge: Cambridge University Press.

Broselow, Ellen. 1995. Skeletal positions and moras. In *The handbook of phonological theory*, edited by John Goldsmith, 175–205. Cambridge, MA: Blackwell.

Broselow, Ellen, Su-I Chen and Marie Huffman. 1997. Syllable weight: Convergence of phonology and phonetics. *Phonology* 14: 47–82.

Crowhurst, Megan. 1991. Demorification in Tübatulabal: Evidence from initial reduplication and stress. *Proceedings of the North East Linguistic Society* 21: 49–63.

Curtis, Emily Kathryn Jean. 2003. Geminate weight: Case studies and formal models. PhD diss., University of Washington.

Davis, Stuart. 1999. On the representation of initial geminates. *Phonology* 16: 93–104.

——. 2003. The controversy over geminates and syllable weight. In *The syllable in optimality theory*, edited by Caroline Féry and Ruben van de Vijver, 77–98. Cambridge: Cambridge University Press.

Gordon, Matthew. 2002. A phonetically-driven account of syllable weight. *Language* 78: 51–80.

——. 2004. Syllable weight. In *Phonetically based phonology*, edited by Bruce Hayes, Robert Kirchner, and Donca Steriade, 277–312. Cambridge: Cambridge University Press.

——. 2005. A perceptually-driven account of onset-sensitive stress. *Natural Language and Linguistic Theory* 23: 595–653.

——. 2006. *Syllable weight: Phonetics, phonology, and typology*. New York and London: Routledge.

Halle, Morris and George N. Clements. 1983. *Problem book in phonology*. Cambridge, MA: MIT Press.

Ham, William. 2001. *Phonetic and phonological aspects of geminate timing*. New York and London: Routledge.

Hayes, Bruce. 1989. Compensatory lengthening in moraic phonology. *Linguistic Inquiry* 20: 253–306.

——. 1995. *Metrical stress theory: Principles and case studies*. Chicago: University of Chicago Press.

Helimski, Eugene. 1998. Selkup. In *The Uralic Languages*, edited by Daniel Abondolo, 548–579. London and New York: Routledge.

Hock, Hans. 1986. Compensatory lengthening: In defense of the concept 'mora.' *Folia Linguistica* 20: 431–460.

Hume, Elizabeth, Jennifer Muller and Aone van Engelenhoven. 1997. Non-moraic geminates in Leti. *Phonology* 14: 371–402.

Hyman, Larry M. 1985. *A theory of phonological weight*. Dordrecht: Foris.

The approach reported here allows for variation: geminates and clusters are distinguishable from each other in structural terms (branching vs. non-branching feature organization at some level of the hierarchy). The point is that when the patterning is similar, the single C representation of geminates is wanting.

——. 1992. Moraic mismatches in Bantu. *Phonology* 9: 255–266.
Kavitskaya, Darya. 2002. *Compensatory lengthening: Phonetics, phonology, diachrony.* London: Routledge.
Kenstowicz, Michael. 1994. *Phonology in Generative Grammar.* Oxford: Blackwell.
Kraehenmann, Astrid. 2001. Swiss German stops: Geminates all over the world. *Phonology* 18: 109–145.
——. 2003. *Quantity and prosodic asymmetries in Alemannic: Synchronic and diachronic perspectives.* Berlin: Mouton de Gruyter.
Lahiri, Aditi and Jacques Koreman. 1988. Syllable weight and quantity in Dutch. *Proceedings of the West Coast Conference on Formal Linguistics* 7: 217–228.
Lin, Yen-Hwei. 1997. Syllabic and moraic structures in Piro. *Phonology* 14: 403–436.
McCarthy, John and Alan Prince. 1990. Foot and word in prosodic morphology: The Arabic broken plural. *Natural Language and Linguistic Theory* 8: 209–283.
——. 2001. Prosodic Morphology: Constraint interaction and satisfaction. [Rutgers Optimality Archive #482, http://roa.rutgers.edu]
Morén, Bruce. 2001. *Distinctiveness, coercion and sonority: A unified theory of weight.* New York and London: Routledge.
Muller, Jennifer S. 2001. The phonology and phonetics of word-initial geminates. PhD diss., Ohio State University.
Pulleyblank, Douglas. 1994. Underlying mora structure. *Linguistic Inquiry* 25: 344–353.
Selkirk, Elisabeth. 1990. A two root theory of length. *University of Massachusetts Occasional Papers in Linguistics* 14: 123–171.
Shaw, Jason. 2006. Deriving initial geminate moraicity from temporal coordination. Unpublished Ms., New York University.
Siptár, Péter and Miklós Törkenczy. 2000. *The phonology of Hungarian.* Oxford: Oxford University Press.
Steriade, Donca. 1991. Moras and other slots. *Proceedings of the Formal Linguistics Society of Midamerica* 1: 254–280.
Topintzi, Nina. 2008. On the existence of moraic onset geminates. *Natural Language and Linguistic Theory* 26: 147–184.
Tranel, Bernard. 1991. CVC light syllables, geminates and moraic theory. *Phonology* 8: 291–302.
Vago, Robert M. 1980. *The Sound Pattern of Hungarian.* Washington, DC: Georgetown University Press.
——. 1992. The root analysis of geminates in the moraic phonology of Hungarian. In *Approaches to Hungarian, vol. 4: The Structure of Hungarian*, edited by István Kenesei and Csaba Pléh, 177–194. Szeged: JATE.
——. 2007. On the analysis of lowering in Hungarian. Presentation at the 8th International Conference on the Structure of Hungarian, CUNY Graduate Center and New York University.
——. 2008. On the phonology of Hungarian inflections. Presented at the Research Institute for Linguistics of the Hungarian Academy of Sciences, Budapest, Hungary.
Zec, Draga. 1994. *Sonority constraints on prosodic structure.* New York: Garland.

THE SYLLABLE IN PERFORMANCE: SONG AND METRICS

CHAPTER SEVEN

SINGING IN TASHLHIYT BERBER, A LANGUAGE THAT ALLOWS VOWEL-LESS SYLLABLES

François Dell

1 Introduction

A song is a composite object with two components, a linguistic object, the 'text', and a musical object, the 'melody'. The two objects have structures that are independent of one another, and each can be realized in the absence of the other. An essential feature of singing is that the text and the melody are produced simultaneously by the same machinery, i.e. the mind and the vocal apparatus of the same person. An interesting question is what happens when the text and the melody make conflicting demands on that machinery, as in the case of singing in a tone language. This article deals with singing in Tashlhiyt, a language in which some syllables are entirely made up of voiceless consonants. What happens to the musical pitches associated with such syllables?

This work is part of a larger endeavor, the search for a theory that would account for text-to-tune alignment in the world's singing traditions. Our discussion of text setting in Tashlhiyt has at least three implications that are of general interest. One is that text-to-tune alignment may make crucial use of properties of the speech stream that do not play any role in the phonology of the language nor in the composition of metrical verse. Another is that text/melody mappings must be represented at two different levels of abstraction. The third implication is that the representations for text-to-tune alignment in singing differ from those of autosegmental phonology in at least one important respect: they only allow one-to-one correspondences. This difference is related to the fact that musical melodies have an intrinsic temporal structure, whereas sequences of tones do not.

2   *Some Basic Assumptions About Text-To-Tune Alignment*

We first present some basic assumptions about text-to-tune alignment in singing. (1) below shows the melody of the French children's song *J'ai lié ma botte*, and (2) shows the text of three stanzas, Berthier (1979, 149). The boxed letters will be explained later.

(1)

(2) a. Au bois voisin l'y a des v⟦i⟧olett⟦e⟧s, de l'aubépine et de l'églantier.
        In the woods nearby there are violets, hawthorn and eglantine.

   b. J'en cueillis tant, j'en avais plein ma hott⟦e⟧. Pour les porter j'ai dû les lier.
       I gathered lots of them, so that my basket was full. To carry them I had to tie them up.

   c. En revenant j'ai rencontré un princ⟦e⟧. Avec mes fleurs je l'ai salué.
       On my way back I met a prince. With my flowers I greeted him.

This song has a strophic form. In songs with a strophic form, the same melody is repeated over and over and each repetition is combined with a different portion of the text. Strophic songs are useful for understanding text-to-tune alignment in singing. They are a natural experiment in which the text varies while the melody is held invariable, or nearly so.

The melody is a sequence of notes and the text is a sequence of syllables. The two sequences are mapped onto one another. The syllables in each of the three chunks of text in (2) are associated with the notes in (1). The result is shown in (3)–(4) below, where the score in (1) has been broken into two halves to fit between the margins of the printed page. (The dashed line in (1) indicates the breaking point.) The capital letters above the notes of (4) have been added as an aid for readers who are not familiar with musical notation.

(3)

a.	au	bois	voi	sin	l'y	a	des	vi	o	let	tes
b.	j'en	cueil	lis	tant	j'en	a	vais	plein	ma	hot	te
c.	en	re	ve	nant	j'ai ren	con	tré	un		prin	ce

Musical scores like (1) are conventional ways of representing melodies in the Western musical tradition, but when one wants to understand the structure of melodies and their relation to texts in singing, representations like (5) below are more insightful.

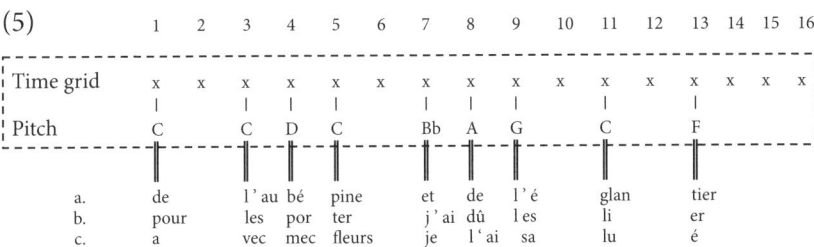

(5) represents the same three settings as those displayed in (4). The representation of the melody is that part of the diagram which is enclosed in the dashed box. Two kinds of information are necessary in order to characterize a given melody: one must specify a certain sequence of pitches and one must specify the time intervals that separate the attack points of the successive pitch events. For the purposes of this paper, the only difference between (4) and (5) that matters has to do with how durations are represented. In (5) pitches are symbolized by capital letters and durations are represented in terms of a time grid. A time grid is a sequence of positions which represent points evenly spaced in time. Every pitch in the melody is linked to a grid position that represents the point in time when that pitch begins, i.e. its attack point. The time grid in (5) is a sequence of sixteen positions, which are numbered for ease of reference. As grid positions are evenly spaced in time, durations are measured by counting grid positions. We see for instance that the duration between the attack of Bb and the attack of the preceding C is twice the duration between the attack of that same

Bb and that of the following A.[1] In what follows the terms 'note' and 'pitch event' are used interchangeably to refer to a pitch together with its associated grid position. In (5), grid positions 1, 3 and 5 are the loci of three different pitch events with the same pitch C.

We now turn to the correspondence between the melody and the text, which is represented by double bars in (5). Each syllable is linked to a note. As a consequence of being linked to a note, every syllable is linked to a grid position. This point bears emphasizing. In the view of textsetting that we are advocating, the melody and the text do not play symmetrical roles as far as timing is concerned. The timing of the speech flow is melody-driven, meaning that the relationship between the text and the time grid is mediated by the melody. Because it is mapped onto the melody, the text has a time structure which is in part dictated by that of the melody. The melody provides a rigid temporal frame to which the text must adapt. In French and in Tashlhiyt this adaptation is effected primarily by stretching the vowels. In our view the basic conditions that govern textsetting in these two languages are the following:

(6) Basic conditions on text-to-tune alignment:

    a. Every syllable must be associated with one and only one note.
    b. Two syllables may not be associated with the same note.

These conditions prohibit many-one correspondences between the two sequences, an important difference from autosegmental representations in phonology, which allow correspondences between the tonal tier and the segmental tier that are not one-one. Lack of space prevents us from justifying (6) here. Let us just point out one implication that will be relevant when we discuss textsetting in Tashlhiyt.

In (1) the melody is comprised of 20 notes and in (2) each stanza can be parsed as a sequence of 20 syllables, and so in (3)–(4) each syllable carries just one note, but this is not always the case; a syllable

---

[1] Our time grids are simplified versions of the objects commonly known as metrical grids, for a detailed presentation of which see Lerdahl and Jackendoff (1983). Metrical grids are multi-tiered representations in which each grid position has two attributes, a location in time and a metrical strength. As metrical strength does not play any role in this paper, we restrict our attention to timing, which can be represented on a single tier. For discussions of textsetting that make use of full-blown metrical grids, see e.g. Halle and Lerdahl (1993), Hayes and Kaun (1996), Dell and Halle (2009).

may carry several notes in succession. For instance, if at the end of (2a) the phrase *de l'églantier* (4 syllables) is replaced by *des roses* (3 syllables), the changed text can still be set to the melody so as to abide by the conventions of traditional French singing. This is shown in (7), which depicts only the second half of the modified stanza (cf. (4a)).

(7)

In (7) the first syllable of *roses* is drawn over two notes. The change from pitch G to pitch C occurs approximately at the halfway point in the production of the vowel [o]. If we use a time grid instead of a conventional musical score to represent the facts of (7), we get (8), in which the C pitch is not linked to *ro-*:

(8)

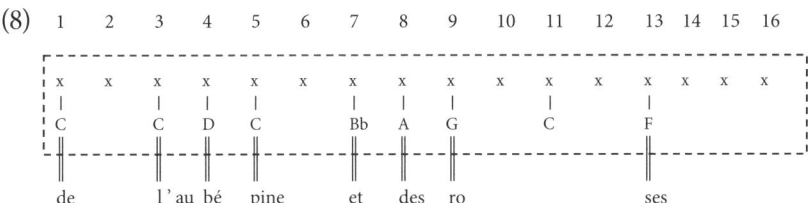

Note that although (6) requires every syllable to be linked to a note, it does not require the converse, and so (6) is not contravened by the C pitch at position 11, that does not have an associated syllable. In (8) the syllable *ro-* serves as a carrier for two pitch events in succession: the note G associated with *ro-*, and the unassociated note C that follows it. There is no need to draw an association line between C and *ro-*, for the fact that the final portion of the vowel [o] serves as a carrier for the note C is already implicit in (8). To see why this is so, consider how representations like (8) are implemented phonetically.

We stated earlier that when a pitch is linked to a grid position, that position represents the inception of the pitch event. This implies that in the implementation of the melody in (8), the pitch change from G to C must occur at position 11, regardless of where position 11 happens to be located in relation to the vowels and consonants in the text. We assume furthermore that when a syllable and a note are linked, the beginning of the syllable's nucleus is simultaneous with the note's attack (Sundberg and Bauer-Huppmann 2007). In (8), if the attack of the note F coincides with the beginning of the vowel in the syllable -*ses*, the preceding note C can only be realized on the vowel of *ro*-.[2]

Configurations in which successive notes are carried by the same syllable are called melismas. In (8) the syllable *ro*- is said to be melismatic. Melismas occur when a melody has more notes than there are syllables in the associated text. In such circumstances, some notes must be left unassociated in order to ensure that text-to-tune alignment is to meet condition (6a).

Melismas have only a limited freedom of occurrence, but in general their distribution is not predictable, and consequently their location in a song must be memorized. A case in point is the fifth line in every stanza of the *Marseillaise*, in which the melody is made up of nine notes while the text has only eight syllables. Consider for instance the first stanza, where the text of the fifth line is *L'étendard sanglant est levé* '(Tyranny's) blood-soaked standard has been raised'. (9a) and (9a') below are alternate settings for this line. ((9b, b') will become relevant later.)

(9)

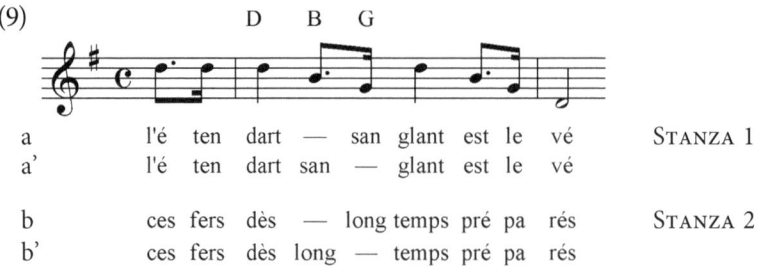

	l'é	ten	dart	—	san	glant	est	le	vé	
a	l'é	ten	dart	—	san	glant	est	le	vé	STANZA 1
a'	l'é	ten	dart	san	—	glant	est	le	vé	
b	ces	fers	dès	—	long	temps	pré	pa	rés	STANZA 2
b'	ces	fers	dès	long	—	temps	pré	pa	rés	

Settings (9a) and (9a') are both well attested. The choice between them is not a matter of free variation. Some speakers are used to one setting, others to the other. To memorize a song, then, it is not enough to memorize the melody and the text independently of one another; the location of melismas must also be memorized. Diagrams like (5) and (8) represent the knowledge that a person has when one says that that person knows a song. These representations are of a rather

---

[2] An additional assumption is that it is vocalic segments that undergo most of the durational adjustments involved in text-to-tune alignment (Scotto di Carlo 2007): in (8) the initial consonant of -*ses* cannot be stretched so as to take up the time interval between positions 11 and 13, and so it is the vowel of *ro*- that must be drawn out.

abstract nature and we call them 'underlying' to set them apart from less abstract ones that reflect the correspondences between texts and melodies that are observed in actual song performances. As we shall see in our discussion of Tashlhiyt, there are cases where an underlying melisma does not have a melisma as its surface reflex, and others in which a melisma occurs in the surface at a point where none is present in the underlying representation.

A notable feature of traditional singing in French and in Tashlhiyt is that melismas recur at the same place in every stanza. Returning to our example from the first stanza of the *Marseillaise,* the corresponding line in the second stanza, also a sequence of eight syllables, is *Ces fers dès longtemps préparés* 'These long-prepared fetters.' Someone who sings the line in the first stanza with a D-B melisma on the third syllable will do the same with this line (cf. (9a, b)), whereas someone who sings the line in the first stanza as in (9a') will sing this line as in (9b'), with a B-G melisma on *long-*. The level of representation at which this parallelism across stanzas is enforced is the underlying level.[3] At the surface level, the parallelism is sometimes perturbed locally, as we shall see below.

3   Syllables and Meter in Tashlhiyt Berber

This discussion of text-to-tune alignment in Tashlhiyt draws heavily on work done in collaboration with Mohamed Elmedlaoui, currently at the Institut Universitaire de la Recherche Scientifique in Rabat, see especially Dell and Elmedlaoui (2002, 2008), henceforth DE. Tashlhiyt, henceforth TB, is a Berber language of Western Morocco spoken by around five million people. TB speakers have their own distinctive musical tradition, which differs from that of the other Berber languages and from that of Moroccan Arabic. Due to the deep changes that Moroccan society is undergoing, TB singing is in a phase of rapid evolution, and we will be concerned here only with the traditional singing style, what TB speakers call *amarg aqqdim* 'old poetry'. *Amarg aqqdim* is still very much alive in the countryside. Up till very recently, in TB-speaking villages everyone was fluent in it. There is no explicit teaching of the conventions which regulate the structure of TB verse or its relation to music. Children simply

---

[3] The uniform distribution of melismas across stanzas is a consequence of 'positional parallelism', on which see Dell and Halle (2009).

acquire these conventions by listening to songs and singing along with others. TB has no instituted writing system. Most composers of TB verse are illiterate in any language.[4]

(10) below is a list of the simplex phonemes of TB. Except for /a/, /i/ and /u/, every phoneme in the table has a geminate counterpart not listed there.[5]

(10) The phonemes of Tashlhiyt Berber

		t	tˤ				k	kʷ	q	qʷ	
	b	d	dˤ				g	gʷ			
f	s	sˤ	š	šˤ				x	xʷ	ħ	
			ž	žˤ				ʁ	ʁʷ	ʕ	ɦ
m	n	nˤ									
w	l	lˤ	r	rˤ	y						

u		i		a

TB allows long consonant clusters, but syllable structure is rather simple. As a result, some syllables contain only consonants, with even voiceless stops acting as syllable nuclei. Here I follow the analysis of TB syllabification in verse that is given in DE (2002), where readers can find detailed references to other work on TB phonology. That analysis is summarized in (11).

(11) THE CENTRAL TENETS OF SYLLABIFICATION IN TB VERSE.
      A and B are inviolable; they take precedence over C when they conflict with it.

      A Syllables must satisfy the syllable template in (12a) below, where O, R, N and C respectively stand for Onset, Rhyme, Nucleus and Coda. Except for /a/, which can only be a nucleus, any simplex segment can be an onset, a nucleus or a coda. Only geminates can act as complex codas.

---

   [4] On music and poetry in TB-speaking areas, see e.g. Schuyler (1979a,b), Lortat-Jacob (1980), Rovsing Olsen (1997), DE (2008). Our data on performance in songs come from commercial recordings on tape cassettes by professional artists. DE (2008) contains a CD with audio recordings of nine songs discussed in the text. These record-ings are divided into line-size portions labeled for easy reference to the line-by-line parses in the text.
   [5] 'š', 'ž' and 'x' respectively stand for IPA 'ʃ', 'ʒ' and 'χ'.

B Except at the beginning of lines, syllables must have an onset (no
  hiatus allowed).

C Sonority peaks are syllable nuclei.

(12b) and (12c) are given by way of exemplification. A geminate is
represented as a single bundle of distinctive features associated with
two skeletal positions, which are symbolized there as '•', to keep them
apart from grid positions, symbolized as 'x'. (While grid positions are
part of the make-up of melodies, skeletal positions belong to phonological representations.) Note the boxed syllables, whose nuclei are
voiceless obstruents, /t/ in (12b) and /s/ in (12c).

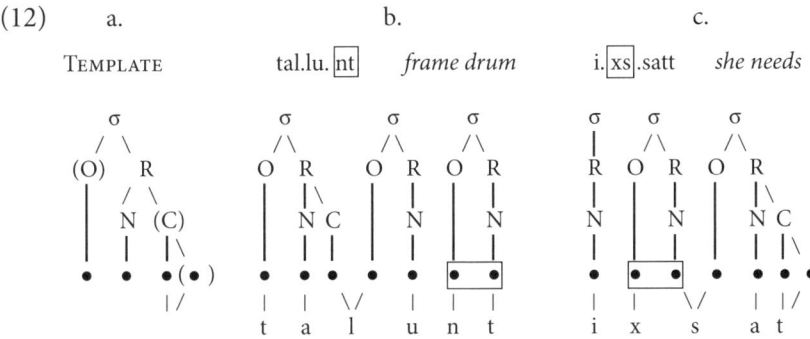

(13) below shows how the phoneme sequence of a line of verse is
divided into syllables according to the analysis summarized in (11).[6]

(13) iqqand akk asiʁ, nsbr issaʕtnk nzzritnt
    iq qan dak ka si ʁn sb ris saʕ tn knzz ri tn <t
    I must take you (as you are), accept this episode with you and live
    through it.

The lyrics of TB songs have a metrical structure. TB songs have a
strophic form and in most songs all the lines are built on the same
meter. The basic principles of TB versification were discovered by Hassan Jouad, see Jouad (1983, 1995). TB meters are based on a distinction between heavy (H) and light (L) syllables. When two lines follow
the same meter, they have the same number of syllables, with H and
L syllables arranged in the same order. In (14) the upper half of the

---

[6] Line 30 in Song 7 in DE (2008). The angled bracket indicates a line-final segment
that is extrasyllabic; see DE (2008) on line-final extrasyllabicity.

table displays the syllabic parses of five lines in a song whose meter requires that every line have 13 syllables, with the 2nd, the 9th and the 11th syllables H and all the other syllables L.[7]

(14)	1	2	3	4	5	6	7	8	9	10	11	12	13	
	L	H	L	L	L	L	L	L	H	L	H	L	L	<
1a	a	daʁ	su	lu	ri	ri	na	ra	ʁitt	mu	nad	wa	ya	<d
2a	i-	qan	da-	ka	si	ʁn	sb	ri-	saʕ	tn	knzz	ri	tn	<t
3a	n	šrk	di	wn	ma	du	ra-	tu	nar	ki	ʁngg	za	ka	<l
4a	i	ninn	si	kn	ga-	sa	ħt	ky	yin	tr	mit	gi	tn	<ʁ
5a	ha-	nur	da	sg	ga	su	la	si	nad	la-	ħlx	ba	rn	<k
1b	a	daʁ	su	lu	ri	ri	na	ra	ʁitt	mu	nadə	wa	ya	<d
2b	i-	qan	da-	ka	si	ʁnə səb	ri-	saʕ	tnə	kənzzə	ri	tn	<t
3b	nə šrək	di	wnə	ma	du	ra-	tu	nar	ki	ʁnəggə	za	ka	<l
4b	i	ninn	si	knə	ga-	sa	ħət kəy	yin	trə	mitə	gi	tnə	<ʁ
5b	ha-	nur	da	səg	ga	su	la	si	nad	la-	ħləxə	ba	rnə	<k

In TB verse syllabic weight is assigned as follows: syllables without a coda are L and syllables with a coda are H, except that when a coda is the first half of a geminate the syllable where it occurs can count as either L or H. In (14) and hereafter such 'ambiguous' codas are represented by hyphens.[8]

The mastery of verse forms like that in (14) is not limited to a small group of people with special training. In the countryside all TB speakers have an intuitive grasp of these meters. We are now ready to discuss how melodies and texts are put together in TB songs.

4   Schwa as a Carrier for Pitch

In addition to the underlying vowels /a, i, u/, TB has a vowel-like sound that we call schwa. The status of schwa in the phonology of TB is discussed at length in our earlier work, where it is argued that schwas are nothing more than transitions between adjacent consonants.[9] TB schwas do not play any role in the phonology of the language (e.g. in syllable structure) nor in versification. In text-to-tune alignment,

---

[7] Lines 36, 30, 26, 28 and 16 in Song 7 in DE (2008). The lower half of the table will be explained below.

[8] The parse in row 2a is that in (13) rewritten so as to follow this convention.

[9] See Hall (2006) on other languages with 'intrusive vowels'.

however, schwas acts as carriers for pitch, exactly like *bona fide* vowels, as we shall now see.

The transcriptions in the lower half of (14) indicate how the five lines in the upper half actually sound in a recording of the song. Syllables with schwas are boxed for the sake of conspicuousness. Even in singing, schwa does not occur in all syllables with consonantal nuclei (see syllable 13 in row 2b in (14)), but its distribution is the following in those syllables where it does occur:

(15) Schwa is always adjacent to the nucleus. (a) If the nucleus belongs to a geminate, schwa precedes it. Otherwise, (b) schwa precedes the nucleus if it is an obstruent, and (c) schwa follows it if it is a sonorant.

(15) does not cover the schwas which are in italics in column 11 in (14); these represent a special case that will be discussed below.[10] Otherwise the schwas in the lower half of (14) all obey (15), except for syllable 11 in line 2b, which contradicts (15c). (15c) is only a first approximation; see DE (2008) for details.

To illustrate the role of schwa in singing, let us consider (16) below, which shows how the first two lines in (14) are set to music. Line 1 is aligned above the score, and line 2 is aligned under it. The center of interest is actually line 2; line 1, in which all the nuclei are vowels, is given only to provide a baseline.

(16)-2a shows the underlying correspondence between syllables and pitch events, and (16)-2b shows how this correspondence is implemented phonetically. Let us list the syllables with consonantal nuclei

---

[10] See (17) and the text around it.

(nuclei are in italics): /ʁn/ (6), /sb/ (7), /tn/ (10), /knzz/ (11), /tn/ (13).
In the last syllable, which is not realized with a schwa, the nuclear consonant /n/ serves as a carrier for the associated C pitch. The four other
syllables are pronounced with schwas and it is those schwas, rather
than the nuclear consonants, that serve as carriers for pitch. Take for
instance syllable 6, which must bear the pitch sequence E-D. In line 1,
the articulation of vowels and consonants in the text is timed so that
the attack of E is heard to coincide with the beginning of the nucleus
/i/. In line 2, on the other hand, where the nucleus of syllable 6 is /n/,
the melisma is not realized on that nucleus but on the following schwa,
whose articulation is maintained as long as required by the combined
durations of notes E and D. The principle which governs text-to-tune
alignment at the phonetic level seems to be the following: when a syllable is linked to a note, the note must begin at the same point as that
portion of the syllabic rhyme which is highest on the sonority scale.
The same principle holds trivially for French, where it is always the
nucleus which has the highest sonority within a syllabic rhyme.

   Schwa occurs in a wider range of contexts in singing than in everyday speech. We have for instance encountered occurrences of schwa
between two voiceless consonants,[11] a context where schwa never seems
to occur in everyday speech.[12] Other occurrences of a kind found only
in singing are those after syllable 11 in (16), which serve as carriers
for a note that does not have any associated syllable at the underlying
level. Like syllable 6, syllable 11 in (16) is underlyingly melismatic,
meaning that at the underlying level it is followed by an unlinked note,
and one would expect it to be melismatic on the surface as well, as is
the case for syllable 6. No melisma is heard on syllable 11, however.
What happens instead is depicted in (17) below, which represents the
situation in (16)-1. In (17), the left-hand side depicts the underlying
correspondence between the melody and the text, and the right-hand
diagram shows how the correspondence is implemented phonetically.

---

[11] Syllable 7 in (14)-4b is a case in point.
[12] On syllables that are phonetically voiceless, see our previous work and also Ridouane (2003, 2008).

(17)

	1	2	3			1	2	3
grid	x	x	x			x	x	x
	|	|	|	⇨		|	|	|
pitch	D	A	C			D	A	C
	|		|			|	|	|
	nad		wa			nad	ə	wa

At the underlying level, the note D associated with /nad/ is followed by a note A which does not have any syllable linked to it. One would expect the vowel in /nad/ to take up most of the time interval between positions 1 and 3 so as to serve as a carrier for notes D and A in succession: the portion of [a] between positions 1 and 2 would be sung to pitch D, and the portion between positions 2 and 3 would be sung to pitch A. Instead, the coda of /nad/ is released into a schwa that begins at position 2 and serves as a carrier for the A pitch. A schwa is heard after syllable 11 in every line of the song; these schwas are underlined in row 11 of (14). What is special about them is that they occur only in environments that meet certain requirements on metrical structure and on the associated melody: the preceding syllable must be an H linked to a note immediately followed by a note not associated with any syllable; see DE (2008) for more details.

At this point it is instructive to compare TB schwas with the para-phonological vowels that occur in French singing. I adopt the term 'paraphonology' from Kiparsky (1977) to designate phonological patterns that arise from conventions specific to poetry. French singing allows pronunciations that are not licit in the colloquial language. Take for instance *violettes* in (2a). In conversational Parisian French this word's only licit pronunciation is [vjɔlɛt], which is bisyllabic, but as sung in (3a) it is pronounced quadrisyllabic: [vi.jɔ.lɛ.tə]. The word has in addition two trisyllabic pronunciations that are licit in singing but not in the colloquial language, [vi.jɔ.lɛt] and [vjɔ.lɛ.tə]. *Violettes* illustrates the two main paraphonological phenomena that occur in French singing: the blocking of prevocalic gliding and the occurrence of schwas unacceptable in other styles of delivery.[13] In (2) paraphono-logical vowels are enclosed in boxes.

---

[13] The paraphonology of singing is not the same as that of classical French poetry. For a summary of the facts about schwa in French singing, see Dell (1989).

There is an important difference between paraphonological vowels in French singing and schwa in TB: TB schwa is metrically irrelevant. It is absent from the representations which are inputs to syllabification and to the computation of syllabic weight; see e.g. the representations in the upper half of (14). Its only relevance is to text-to-tune alignment below the syllable level. This is in marked contrast with French, where paraphonology provides alternative syllable counts not available in everyday speech, as the following example illustrates.

Let us return to the word *violettes* in (2a). Instead of singing it as [vi.jɔ.lɛ.tə] as in (3a), if one sings it as [vjɔ.lɛ.tə], the utterance to be mapped onto the melody in (3) has one syllable less, and consequently one note must be left without an associated syllable. One felicitous setting is depicted below in (18a') with the setting (3a) reproduced as (18a) for the sake of comparison.

(18)

		C	C	D	C	Bb	A	G	C	Bb	A	F
a	a	au	bois voi	sin	l'y	a		des	vi	o	let	tes
a'	a	au	bois voi	sin	l'y	—	a	des	vio		let	tes

In (18a'), to compensate for the gap due to the monosyllabic pronunciation of *vio-*, the words *a* and *des* move over to the right, which leaves the note A unassociated, and so the syllable *l'y* is prolonged so as to serve as a carrier for it, in addition to the preceding note Bb. In the case of TB, an analogue of this example would be one in which the suppression of a schwa would necessitate a change in the mapping of two syllables before that schwa. TB has indeed paraphonological processes which provide alternate syllable counts for an expression, but none of these involves schwa.[14]

TB is not the only language on record in which textsetting makes use of phonetic material that is not metrically relevant. Khmer inserts nasal consonants to serve as pitch carriers, but these consonants do not play any role in versification. (see Jacob 1966).

---

[14] /a/ or /wa/ may be inserted at certain line-internal syntactic breaks to round off the meter (DE 2008, 63), and certain morphemes have poetic variants.

5   *Derived melismas*

In all the examples discussed up to this point, syllables with consonantal nuclei can serve as carriers for pitch because glottal vibration
is involved in their production: pitch is realized on a schwa adjacent
to the nucleus, or if there is no schwa, pitch is realized on the nucleus
itself, a sonorant, as in syllable 13 in (16)-2b. Let us now consider
syllables whose rhymes are produced without glottal vibrations, i.e.
syllables in which the nucleus is a voiceless consonant and there is no
abutting schwa. This situation is dealt with in two ways in TB singing.
One way is simply not to sing the note associated with the syllable
in question. The unrealized note is presumably reconstructed by the
listeners' minds.[15] The other way is what we call 'rightward shift': the
note is realized on the preceding syllable, which becomes melismatic.
Rightward shift is illustrated in line b in (19) below; there is no shift
in line a, which is given for the sake of comparison.[16]

(19)

(19) shows how syllables and notes are aligned at the underlying level.
The nucleus of syllable 6 in line b is a voiceless stop and there is no
schwa adjacent to it. The arrow is meant to suggest what is actually
heard in the recording: syllable 6 is shifted to the right and its associated note G# is realized on the preceding syllable. Our analysis of the
situation is that rightward shift is an epiphenomenon of delinking.
This analysis is diagrammed in (20) below, where line a is again given
for the sake of comparison:

---

[15]   See DE (2008) for details.

[16]   Lines a and b in (19) are the respective parses of lines 9 and 2 in Song 2 in DE
(2008). In (19b) the onset of syllable 6 is an underlying /ʁ/ devoiced under the influence of the following consonant. That consonant is in fact /kʷ/, but the right super-
script 'w' that represents rounding is omitted for typographic convenience.

(20)

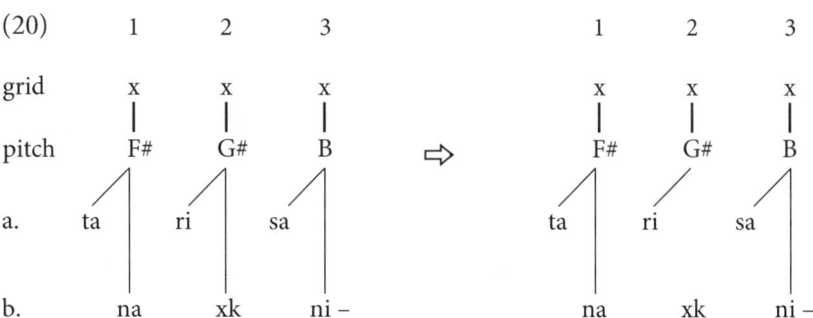

In (20), the left-hand side depicts the mapping between the text and
the melody at the underlying level and the right-hand side depicts it
at the surface level. The left and right diagrams are identical for line
a. For line b, on the other hand, the syllable /xk/, which is linked to
G# in the underlying representation, is no longer linked in the surface representation. As a consequence of this delinking, the surface
representation of text-to-tune alignment does not make any demands
of its own on how the time interval between grid positions 1 and 3
is to be divided up between the segments in the sequence /axkn/, i.e.
in the portion of the speech stream that extends from the beginning
of [a] in /na/ to the beginning of [i] in /ni-/. Since consonants can be
prolonged only to a limited extent and voiceless segments cannot bear
pitch anyway, the vowel [a] takes up most of the time interval and the
attack of G# occurs during the production of [a], whence an F#-G#
melisma on /na/.

It is important to understand that rightward shift concerns only the
relative timing of a syllable and its associated note; the temporal structure of the melody remains unaffected. At the surface level, the attack
of G# is located at midpoint in the time interval between the attack of
F# and that of B, and this holds for line b as well as for line a or any
other line sung to the tune in (19).

In the TB songs we have examined there are numerous cases where
a syllable is shifted in time and its associated note is realized on an
adjacent syllable. In none of these instances does the shifted syllable
contain a full vowel or a schwa. We take this as evidence that rightward
shift aims at keeping the melody invariable regardless of the phonetic
material mapped onto it, i.e. that rightward shift seeks to ensure that
every note is phonetically realized and that it begins at its appointed
position on the time grid.

Another remarkable property of the shift is that it is always to the right. Our explanation for this fact is that rightward shift is the smallest change needed to keep the melody invariable. Shifting the syllable to the left would also achieve this aim, but only at an additional cost. Returning to example (20), let us see what would happen if /xk/ were shifted to the left so that its associated note was realized on the following syllable. Such a leftward shift is depicted below in (21).

(21)

	1	2	3			1	2	3
grid	x	x	x			x	x	x
	|	|	|	⇨		|	|	|
pitch	F#	G#	B			F#	G#	B
	|	|	|			|	|	
	na	xk	ni –			na xk	ni –	

In the output of (21) the syllable /ni-/ bears a melisma G#-B whose first note is the G# underlyingly associated with /xk/. The melody is identical on both sides of the arrow, but whereas the only change involved in the rightward shift in (20) is the delinking of /xk/, the leftward shift in (21) requires in addition that /ni-/ be delinked from B and reassociated with G#.

We noted earlier that the representations we are using for text-to-tune alignment differ from those of autosegmental phonology in that they do not allow many-one associations. In particular, we hold that linking a syllable with several notes is not the appropriate manner of representing melismas; see condition (6a). Rightward shift provides us with one piece of evidence in favor of this claim. (22) below shows how rightward shift and leftward shift would be characterized using standard autosegmental representations. (The delinking of /xk/ from G#, which occurs both in right- and leftward shift, is not represented.)

(22) /xk/ shifts...   to the right (20)   to the left (21)

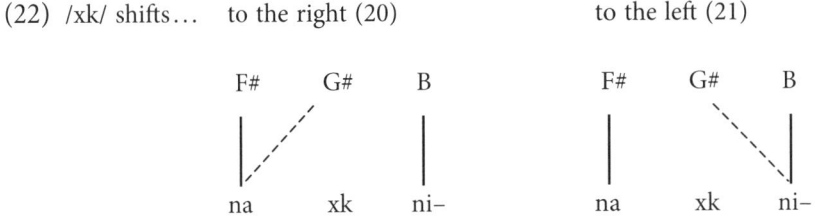

In standard autosegmental terms, the two shifts are mirror images of one another and there does not seem to be any reason why one should be preferred over the other. The picture given by (22) is deceptive, of course, in that it leaves out the time grid, i.e. it glosses over a fundamental difference between singing and the phonology of tone, which is that musical melodies have an intrinsic temporal structure whereas sequences of tones do not. If one is to look for a phonological analogue to rightward shift, it is compensatory lengthening that should come to mind, rather than the formation of contour tones.

Rightward shift also occurs in Japanese, where it affects obstruent moras.[17] In Japanese singing the basic linguistic units involved in text-to-tune alignment are moras rather than syllables. Based on the discussions in Vance (1987, 67–70) and in Hayes (2008), and also on our examination of 25 songs in Anonymous (1967), we can state with confidence that to fit the facts of Japanese, our basic condition (6a) must be reworded by replacing 'syllable' with 'mora'.[18] The second mora of a Japanese syllable can be a short vowel, the final part of a long vowel, a nasal consonant or the first half of a geminate obstruent, the second half being the onset of the next syllable. The obstruent moras of Japanese present text-to-tune alignment with a challenge that is analogous to that of nuclear obstruents not flanked by a schwa in TB.

To illustrate, let us consider two homologous lines from *See kurabe* ('Comparing heights'), a well-known children's song. The text of these lines is given in (23). Each line is a sequence of twelve moras which is in a one-one correspondence with a twelve note melody, as shown in (24).[19]

(23) a. tendeni senobi siteitemo
      b. hakatte kureta seeno take

---

[17] The phenomenon is briefly noted in Vance (1987, 67).

[18] It is not clear at this point whether condition (6b) must be changed in a similar manner. In any case syllables seem to play a role in Japanese textsetting, in addition to moras. Hayes (2008) notes that in the setting of bimoraic syllables there is a strong tendency for the position of the first mora to be metrically stronger than that of the second mora.

[19] See Anonymous (1967, 116–117). The meaning of line a is 'Although they all stand on tiptoe to make themselves taller'; that of line b is 'The height that he measured (for me)'. A recording of this song can be heard on the internet at the end of the file *http://masaring.blogzine.jp/music/dohyohunno.mp3*.

(24)

| a. | te n de ni | se no bi | si te i | te | mo |
| b. | ha ka t | te | ku re ta | se e no | ta | ke |

Like /de/ in line a, the second mora of /kat/ in line b is linked to the third pitch event (A), but whereas in line a the vowel of /de/ serves as a carrier for A, in line b it is the preceding [a] that bears that pitch. The underlying alignment in line b and its surface realization are depicted below in (25).

(25)

	1	2	3	4		1	2	3	4
grid	x	x	x	x		x	x	x	x
pitch	B	A		A	$\Rightarrow$	B	A		A
	ka	t		te		ka	t		te

Given that in /kat/ the second mora is underlyingly linked to a pitch event at position 2, the closure of the geminate /tt/ would be expected to begin at position 2, which would require that closure to take up the whole time interval between positions 2 and 4. What happens instead is that the /t/ mora delinks from A and the preceding [a] is prolonged to serve as a carrier for the note A. [a] is sung to pitch B over the first third of its duration, and to pitch A over the rest.

Melismas due to obstruent moras are always borne by the preceding mora, i.e. like that of syllable shift in TB, the direction of mora shift in Japanese is always to the right. For someone not looking beyond the facts of Japanese, rightward shift looks at first blush like evidence pointing to the relevance of syllables in Japanese singing. For Japanese, a plausible explanation of the direction of the shift could be that shifting the obstruent to the right, rather than to the left, allows the associated note to stay within the confines of the same syllable: in the input of (25), for instance, B and the following A are both linked to moras that belong to the same syllable /kat/, and in the output they are both borne by the same syllable, as they are both realized on the same vowel. However, if Japanese mora shift and TB syllable shift are the same phenomenon, as we think they are, the explanation for the direction of Japanese mora shift is the same as that proposed earlier for the direction of TB syllable shift, which has nothing to do with tautosyllabicity.

6 Concluding Remarks

In the preceding discussion, text-to-tune alignment is represented at two levels of abstraction. In the underlying representations the objects that are put into correspondence are *structural units* in their respective domains: notes in the melody, syllables (TB, French) or moras (Japanese) in the text. In the surface representations, on the other hand, text-to-tune alignment is a correspondence between *points* in the melody and *points* in the speech stream. The points in the melody are the attacks of notes. Note attacks are linked to the left edges of portions of the speech stream best suited to bear pitch: full vowels or schwas when they are available, and sonorant consonants otherwise.[20] Rightward shift in TB and in Japanese is evidence in favor of this framework, which does not allow many-to-one associations, unlike autosegmental representations in phonology.[21]

We began this paper by bringing up situations of phonetic conflict between the melody and the text. Note that such conflicts are not a logical necessity. They only arise because the textual entities that are associated with musical notes at the underlying level are authentic linguistic units (syllables, moras), and in some languages not all such units are suitable for carrying pitch. One can conceive of alternative textsetting conventions which would make conflicts impossible altogether. Imagine for instance that in condition (6), 'syllable' is replaced by 'pitch span', a pitch span being defined as a maximal sequence of adjacent voiced sonorants. Presumably, singing idioms that abide by this modified version of (6) do not exist, and the reason why is that pitch spans as defined above do not play a role in the phonology of any language.

---

[20] See Gordon (2001) for some discussion of the fact that certain segment types are better suited than others to carry pitch.

[21] The data discussed in this paper are drawn from three singing idioms that are very much alike. It remains to be seen how this framework can accommodate singing idioms of a rather different type, such as free rhythm singing in TB (see DE 2008) or the idioms used for chanting Psalms in Latin and in English that are discussed in an autosegmental framework in Chen (1983, 1984).

References

Anonymous. 1977. *Nihon dōyō meika 110 kyokushū; 110 Famous Japanese Children's Songs*. Tokyo: ZEN-ON Music Co.

Berthier, Jean-Edel. 1979. *Mille chants. Anthologie du chant populaire*, tome 3. Paris: Presses de l'Ile-de-France.

Chen, Matthew. 1983. Toward a Grammar of Singing: Tune-Text Association in Gregorian Chant. *Music Perception* 1: 84–122.

——. 1984. The interfacing of language and music. *Language and Communication* 4: 159–194.

Dell, François. 1989. Concordances rythmiques entre la musique et les paroles dans le chant. In *Le souci des apparences* edited by Marc Dominicy, 121–36. Brussels: Éditions de l'Université de Bruxelles.

Dell, François and Mohamed Elmedlaoui. 2002. *Syllables in Tashlhiyt Berber and in Moroccan Arabic*. Dordrecht: Kluwer.

——. 2008. *Poetic Meter and Musical Form in Tashlhiyt Berber Songs*. (Enclosed audio CD) Cologne: Rüdiger Köppe Verlag.

Dell, François and John Halle. 2009. Comparing musical textsetting in French and in English songs. In *Towards a Typology of Poetic Forms* edited by Jean-Louis Aroui and Andy Arleo, 63–78. Amsterdam: Benjamins.

Gordon, Matthew. 2001. A typology of contour tone restrictions. *Studies in Language* 25: 423–462.

Hall, Nancy. 2006. Cross-linguistic patterns of vowel intrusion. *Phonology* 23: 387–429.

Halle, John and Fred Lerdahl. 1993. A generative textsetting model. *Current Musicology* 55: 3–23.

Hayes, Bruce. 2008. Two Japanese Children's Songs. Revised version of ASUCLA Lecture Notes, Winter 1995. Los Angeles: UCLA.

Hayes, Bruce, and Abigail Kaun. 1996. The role of phonological phrasing in sung and chanted verse. *Linguistic Review* 13: 243-303.

Jacob, Judith. 1966. Some features of Khmer versification. In *In Memory of J. R Firth* edited by Charles E. Bazell, 227–241. London: Longman.

Jouad, Hassan. 1983. *Les éléments de la versification en berbère marocain tamazight et tachelhit*. Doctorat de Troisième Cycle, Université Paris 3.

Jouad, Hassan. 1995. *Le calcul inconscient de l'improvisation*. Paris and Louvain: Peeters.

Kiparsky, Paul. 1977. The rhythmic structure of English verse. *Linguistic Inquiry* 8: 189–247.

Lerdahl, Fred and Ray Jackendoff. 1983. *A Generative Theory of Tonal Music*. Cambridge, Mass.: MIT Press.

Lortat-Jacob, Bernard. 1980. *Musique et fêtes au Haut-Atlas*. Paris: Mouton et École des Hautes Études en Sciences Sociales.

Ridouane, Rachid. 2003. *Suites de consonnes en berbère: phonétique et phonologie*. PhD diss., Université Paris 3.

——. 2008. Syllables without vowels: phonetic and phonological evidence from Tashlhiyt Berber. *Phonology* 25: 321–359.

Rovsing Olsen, Miriam. 1997. *Chants et danses de l'Atlas*. Arles: Cité de la Musique / Actes Sud.

Schuyler, Philip D. 1979a. *A Repertory of Ideas: the Music of the Rways, Berber Professional Musicians from Southwestern Morocco*. PhD diss., University of Washington.

——. 1979b. Rways and Ahwash: Opposing tendencies in Moroccan Berber music and society. *The World of Music* 21: 65–80.

Scotto di Carlo, Nicole. 2007. Speech-rate and tempo effects on the organization of spoken and sung syllables. Paper for the *16th International Congress of Phonetic Sciences*. http://aune.lpl.univ-aix.fr/lpl/personnel/scotto/scottopub.htm

Sundberg, Johan and Julia Bauer-Huppmann. 2007. When does a sung tone start? *Journal of Voice* 21: 285–293.

Vance, Timothy J. 1987. *An Introduction to Japanese Phonology*. Albany: SUNY Press.

THE SYLLABLE IN PERFORMANCE:
SPEECH PRODUCTION AND ARTICULATION

THE ROLE OF THE SYLLABLE IN SPEECH PRODUCTION IN AMERICAN ENGLISH: A FRESH CONSIDERATION OF THE EVIDENCE

Stefanie Shattuck-Hufnagel

1 *Introduction*

The syllable has been irresistibly attractive to both theorists and experimentalists addressing the problem of what kinds of representational units play a role in speech production processing, i.e. for models of both the planning of a spoken utterance and the execution of that plan. For example, Stetson (1951) proposed the syllable as the unit of respiratory production; Dell et al. (1999) proposed it as the unit of position similarity constraints on segmental error interactions; and Browman and Goldstein (1988) proposed it as the unit of articulatory cohesion. Building on these earlier claims, Levelt et al. (1999) proposed the syllable as the unit of phonetic selection during speech production planning for languages like Dutch and English. In their model, prosodic-word-sized elements such as *escort us* undergo syllabification, e.g. into [e]+[skor]+[tus], and the speaker can then retrieve the required syllable-sized articulatory plans for the syllables in that prosodic word (PWd) from the pre-computed articulatory syllabary. In this chapter we critically examine a range of traditional arguments often cited in support of the syllable as a unit of speech production (or even as 'the' unit). We argue that much of this evidence is equivocal, and can be interpreted in terms of other types of constituents. Further, we argue that a broader view of the production process, that hypothesizes a number of processing representations that make use of different sizes of constituents for different purposes, may provide a more appropriate model.

This chapter focuses on the possible role of the syllable in the production of English; a number of lines of evidence in the literature suggest that speakers of different languages do not necessarily share the same processing representations for perception, and it is certainly possible that the same claim can be made for production. In fact, there appears to be a significant difference in speaker intuitions about syllable boundaries in languages as closely related as English and Dutch (see chapter 9, this volume). As a result, we do not seek to generalize the arguments and hypotheses expressed here beyond English. In section 2 we review evidence that is traditionally cited in support of the syllable as a representational constituent, raising a number of caveats for the interpretation of these lines of evidence. In section 3 we provide a more detailed look at one particular kind of evidence, i.e. systematic regularities in sublexical speech errors, that is often cited as the basis for syllable-based planning models. In section 4 we consider a new line of evidence based on syllable frequency effects; in section 5 we summarize an alternative model to these syllable-based approaches; and we conclude in section 6 with a number of lessons to be learned from a careful re-evaluation of arguments for the role of the syllable in speech production.

2   Traditional Evidence Invoked in Support of the Syllable as a Representation Unit in Speech Production

Not only does the syllable seem intuitively obvious to many observers; there are also many lines of more quantifiable evidence that seem to support the view that speakers represent words and utterances in terms of their syllables. As a result, the syllable plays a preferential role in many models of the speech production process. In this section we examine some of these different lines of evidence carefully, to determine whether they a) actually require the postulation of syllabic representations; b) are merely consistent with such representations (but also with other structural constituents); or c) are in fact more consistent with a different set of representational constituents.

2.1   Observation 1: Speakers can Count Syllables

As speakers of English, we feel that we know about the syllables of a spoken utterance; we know which syllables the utterance contains, what order they come in, how many of them there are and where in time they occur. For example, we can tap to the rhythm of an utterance, whether regular or irregular, and that rhythm seems to be based on the pattern of occurrence of strong and weak syllables. Note, however, that this skill requires only that we know how many syllable nuclei an utterance contains, not that we represent each syllable as a separate unit. In fact, for speakers of American English it is often difficult to be certain where the boundary between two syllables is. For example, in words like *tipple* or *puppy*, the status of the intervocalic /p/ between the strong and the weak syllable is unclear (Kiparsky 1979).

Another line of evidence is that many speakers, with some encouragement, can successfully imitate an utterance using reiterant speech, i.e. replacing each syllable of the utterance with a given syllable, as when *Take a potato to Susie and Sasha* becomes *Ma ma mamama ma Mama ma Mama*. But there are many utterances, at least in American English, in which the number of syllables is unclear. For example, when speakers are asked to produce sentences like *One male lion ran more than a mile* in reiterant speech, they often are uncertain whether to imitate words like *lion* and *mile* with one syllable or two. (One speaker in such an experiment complained that he needed a way to produce 'one and a half syllables' in order to deal with these words.)

To conclude the discussion of the counting evidence: although as speakers or listeners we may be able to count the number of syllables in an utterance, this skill may not require the representation of syllables as individual structural constituents, but only a knowledge of the number and location of vowels (or of sonorant consonants that function similarly). Moreover, speakers of American English are not always sure how many syllables there are in an utterance, or, critically, where their boundaries are.

2.2   Observation 2: Syllables Seem Clear and Separable in an Acoustic Waveform Display

Another observation that seems at first to support the syllable as a separately represented unit in speech planning is the fact that syllables seem to be identifiable in a visual representation of a spoken utterance, such as a wave form or a spectrogram, in the form of higher-amplitude vocalic regions separated by lower-amplitude consonantal ones. Although this is true for many utterances, particularly strings of CV syllables with sonorant consonants (Figure 1) where the abrupt acoustic landmarks correspond to C-V and V-C boundaries (Stevens 2002), it can be less clear for other utterances, particularly those including clusters of consonants (Figure 2).

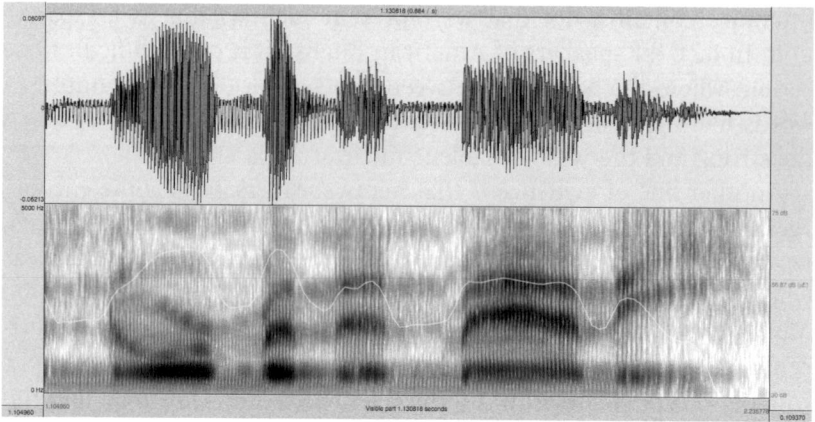

Figure 1   Norman and Manny

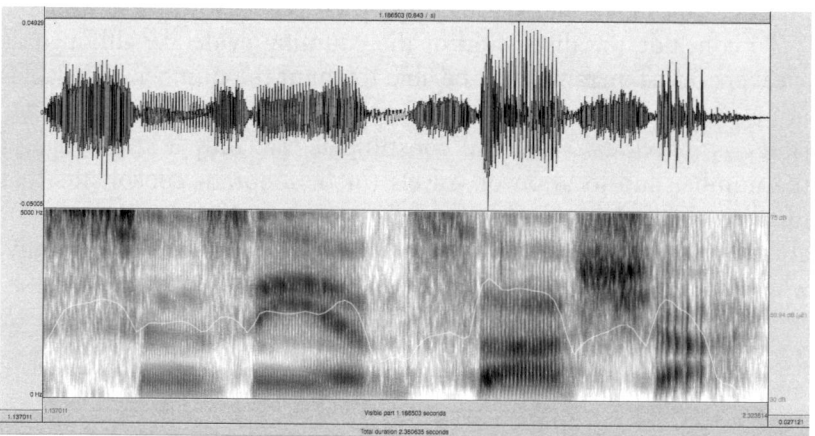

Figure 2   Susie and Sasha

Moreover, it is not clear from the sheer alternation between high-amplitude vocalic regions and lower-amplitude regions of consonantal narrowing or closure which vowels the consonants might affiliate with to form a syllable. As noted earlier, this affiliation problem is particularly challenging for a consonant that occurs between a strong preceding vowel and a weaker following vowel or syllabic nucleus, as in *butter, city* or *topple*. Intuitions about how to syllabify such words can differ substantially among native speakers of American English; for some, strong-weak bisyllabic words like *movies* have a clear syllabification into e.g. *mo-* and *–vies* because the first vowel is tense and so can occur in syllable-final position, but for others the affiliation of the medial consonant is ambiguous even for words of this type. Finally, some 'syllables' in the speech stream lack an observable acoustically voiced region corresponding to a syllable nucleus, as when the word *to* is produced as an aspirated /t/, or *it's* is produced as /s/, as in 'S *time t' go*. The fact that the speech stream is not necessarily made up of phonetic syllables with clearly defined nuclei and boundaries means that the intuitive evidence for syllables from acoustic displays is not as compelling as it might appear at first glance. However, it may be that syllables correspond to processing units at the level of phonological (as opposed to acoustic-phonetic) representations, or it may be that the division of the speech stream into syllables is more reliably accomplished in the articulatory domain (see below for further discussion).

2.3   *Observation 3: There is Evidence for Syllable-related Activity in the Respiratory Muscles*

Researchers such as Stetson (1951) and Ladefoged and Loeb (2002) have reported a pattern of muscle activity associated with each syllable in an utterance. However, careful consideration of their data suggests that these peaks in respiratory muscle activity are associated not with each syllable of an utterance, but with the prominent syllables, e.g. those with lexical stress or perhaps even those with pitch accents. If that is generally the case, this pattern of activity is more consistent with marking the head of a higher-level constituent, such as a foot, that groups a strong syllable with the following weaker syllables. It would be of interest to explore this question in languages other than Engish, where it has been suggested that the syllable plays a stronger role in speech and language processing, for example, Cutler et al. note that:

> Speech segmentation procedures may differ in speakers of different languages. Earlier work based on French speakers listening to French words suggested that the syllable functions as a segmentation unit in speech processing. However, while French has relatively regular and clearly bounded syllables, other languages, such as English, do not. No trace of syllabifying segmentation was found in English listeners listening to English words, French words, or nonsense words. French listeners, however, showed evidence of syllabification even when they were listening to English words. We conclude that alternative segmentation routines are available to the human language processor. In some cases speech

segmentation may involve the operation of more than one procedure. (Cutler et al 1986, 385)

Thus for languages such as French, which show a pronounced effect of syllable-based segmentation in perception, it would be of interest to see respiratory muscle data for production. But at the moment the evidence for a burst of respiratory muscle activity associated with each syllable in an utterance is not fully persuasive, at least for English. Although peaks in respiratory muscle activity have been recorded in concert with prominent syllables, it is far from clear that these data support the hypothesis of syllable-by-syllable patterns of pulse-like activity. Moreover, Slifka (2000) describes physiological measures of subglottal pressure which indicate a relatively flat (slightly declining) value for this parameter throughout the working phase of a spoken utterance, without large peaks even at the accented syllables.

2.4   *Observation 4: Speakers can Manipulate Syllable-sized Constituents*

Many investigators have pointed out the existence of spontaneously arising language games in which syllables or structural subunits of syllables are moved or changed in some systematic way. This manipulability has been taken as evidence for the independent representation of these constituents. For example, language games often involve the systematic movement or replacement of onset consonants, as in Pig Latin (or *ig-Pay atin-Lay*). People sometimes amuse themselves by constructing entire narratives in which the consonant onsets of adjacent words are exchanged, as in *Back and the Jeanstalk* (for *Jack and the Beanstalk*). However, these systems often involve the onset of each word, rather than of each syllable in the utterance; to the extent that this is true, these manipulations support the word or morpheme, rather than the syllable, as a representational unit to which speakers have access in production planning. Similarly, other common language game patterns involve manipulation of another subconstituent, the rhyme, as in Op (*c-op-an y-op-u sp-op-eak op-Op?*) or Ubbie-Dubbie (*G-ub-ive m-ub-e m-ub-y t-ub-ooth br-ub-ush*). Interestingly, however, it appears that producing fluent utterances using this system is much easier if the syllables of the utterance to be transformed are also monosyllabic words: the interested reader can compare the effort involved in transforming a four-syllable word like *institution* with that for a four-monosyllable sequence like *You can be there*. This again raises the possibility that speakers are representing and manipulating structural elements of words, e.g. word onset consonant clusters or 'word rhymes', rather than of syllables per se. This possibility finds further support in the fact that games involving the manipulation of entire syllables of the target words are rare in English, if they exist at all. (There are games that involve the insertion of whole syllables, such as the addition of buh to transform e.g. Can you say this? into *Can-buh you-buh say-buh this-buh?*, but this manipulation can be considered the creation of a strong-weak foot.) As we will see below, evidence from spontaneous speech errors is similarly ambiguous as to whether it supports the syllable and its substructures, or something more like the word and its substructures; this ambiguity arises in part because so many of the words in most English utterances are monosyllables (Shattuck-Hufnagel and Veilleux 2000).

Another kind of manipulation skill that is often used to support the role of the syllable in speech processing involves experimental manipulation tasks, in which for example speakers are asked to blend two words together, such as *black* and *green*. When speakers are instructed to break the words at the onset-rhyme boundary and re-blend the fragments to give e.g. *bleen* or *grack*, they find it considerably easier than if the words to be blended must be broken at some other location, such as after the first consonant, giving e.g. *breen* or *glack* (Treiman 1983). That is, performance on these tasks is better if the manipulation units line up with the syllabic subunits of onset and rhyme. However, when the target words are monosyllables, the results can equally well be taken as support for word-based structural constituents such as word onset and 'the rest of the word' which are also indicated by some aspects of speech error patterns.

For American English, then, the evidence from manipulation skills is strongest for subconstituents, not for whole syllables, and in many cases it is possible that the units that speakers find to be the most manipulable are subconstituents of words, not of syllables.

2.5   *Observation 5: Syllables Play a Role in the Phonological and Phonetic Systematicities of the Grammar*

It has often been noted that English (along with other languages) does not allow the occurrence of certain sound segments or combinations of segments in certain locations, and these positional prohibitions are often stated in terms of syllable structure (Kahn 1976). For example,

/tl/ is not a permissible syllable onset in English, nor is /ng/. Moreover, regularities in the phonetic implementation of phonemic contrasts are often positionally expressed, as in 'final /ptk/ may be glottalized, i.e. produced with a vocal-fold configuration which causes irregular pitch periods or even a stop-like silence with a glottal release'. Various investigators have held differing views, however, on the nature of the unit that best captures these positional constraints. For example, is the ban on /tl/ in onsets best stated in terms of syllable onsets, or in terms of word onsets and position with respect to segmental and metrical context (such as before lexically-stressed vowels)? Pierrehumbert (1994) has suggested that constraints on word-medial consonant clusters are not fully predicted simply by combinations of constraints on syllable codas and onsets, as would be expected if syllabic units are simply combined to make words. In a related line of argument, Steriade (1999) proposes that, while syllable structure is an undoubted aspect of phonology, syllable structure may be inferred from word-based phonotactic constraints when it is required, and may thus be less clearly represented than other aspects of structure. Blevins (2003) has raised related concerns about the necessity of syllable structure in phonology, as has Samuels (2008).

One line of linguistic argument sometimes invoked to support the syllable is positional allophony: a given phonemic segment or feature bundle like the voiceless alveolar stop /t/ is typically produced with different articulatory configureations and different sets of acoustic cues in different contexts, and these contexts are often described in terms of syllable structure (see Chapter 12 in this volume). However, if it is possible to specify these contexts in terms of a) position in the word or morpheme (e.g. word-final for the glottalized voiceless stop in *can't*), and/or b) immediately adjacent segmental context (e.g. a preceding fricative for the non-aspirated realization of /p/ in words like *spin*) or stress context (e.g. a strong-weak sequence for the unaspirated and often flap-like /ptk/ in words like *guppy, putter* and *pukka*), then much of the force of the allophonic argument for the significance of syllable structure in speech processing is diminished. Consider, for example, one of the apparently strongest arguments for syllable position rather than word or stress position as the environment for glottalization of voiceless final stops: words like *butler, subtler, Hitler, battling, Cartwright, jitney*, where it appears that syllable-final /t/ is glottalized. But in many such examples, the context can be described in terms of a high-sonority following segment like a nasal or a liquid. Similarly, a pre-nasal /k/ in words like *technical*, where it is followed by a nasal, can be glottalized in some dialects. If counterexamples like the proper names *Butkus* and *Atkins* prove to be special cases, and if all lexical-word examples involve glottalization only before sonorant consonants, it may be possible to unite this phenomenon with the observation that voiceless stops can be glottalized in words like *Clinton, mountain* and *Newton* when they are produced so that the following segment is a nasal that plays the structural role of a vowel. That is, the generalization would be that glottalization of /ptk/ occurs in the context of a following sonorant consonant, rather than that it occurs in syllable-final position.

To summarize the evidence from phonological and phonetic constraints that refer to structural contexts, the significant question is which phenomena for which the syllable is often invoked as an explanation really require the syllable. Just because we *can* describe a phenomenon in terms of syllable position, doesn't mean that we must or even should; we need to take another look, and explore other possible accounts, weighing the overall bulk of the evidence before accepting the syllable as the constituent of choice.

2.6   *Observation 6: Articulatory Cohesion is Stronger within Syllables than between Syllables*

Articulatory phonologists suggest that the articulatory cohesion (i.e. mutually consistent timing of articulatory gestures) is stronger within a syllable, and within syllabic subconstituents, than for sequences that cross syllable boundaries (Browman and Goldstein 1992, 1995). However, these observations have been made primarily for the onsets and vowels of strong syllables, which can also be viewed as the heads of feet, and have not yet been carried out for foot-internal -CVC structures where the vowel is weak. Until those data are available, we cannot rule out the possibility that for speakers of English this cohesion difference highlights the strong link between a foot onset and its vocalic nucleus, rather than between a syllable onset and its nucleus. Interestingly, arguments from articulatory cohesion favor a syllabic subconstituent made up of the onset + vocalic nucleus, because articulatory evidence shows that the gestures for these two elements begin at about the same time, with more variable timing relations for the coda gestures. Although the CV in CVC words and syllables does not emerge as an error unit in the MIT Speech Error Corpus (henceforth

MITSEC), where the VC is a more common unit, Laubstein (1986) reports CV as more common than VC in her corpus of errors in Canadian English. A confounding factor in the interpretation of these data in all corpora is the fact that many onset interaction errors occur in the context of identical following vowels (e.g. *pay the player* → *play the payer*), making it difficult to be certain what the size of the error unit is in many cases. However, if the CV were a common error unit, we would expect to see errors like *cut the rope* → *rote the cup, and we do not find this error pattern in error corpora such as the MIT Speech Error Corpus (MITSEC; see below). Thus, while the articulatory data suggest the onset CV- as a cohesive unit, there is little support for this constituent as a multi-segment error unit, at least in some error corpora, and both kinds of data fail to resolve the ambiguity between the word and the syllable as the larger unit of representation of which these constituents form a part.

To summarize, the evidence for close articulatory timing cohesion between gestures for an onset C and its following V is strong. However, this evidence does not explicitly require strings of syllables as independently represented constituents in the planning process, and may be best interpreted as support for differential grouping of motor sequences in the motor stages of production planning.

2.7   Observation 7: Syllable Frequency Effects Suggest that Speakers Store Information about Individual Syllables

A number of studies have recently suggested that speakers store information about how frequently some syllables occur in their speech, because this information influences their speaking behavior. Evidence includes differences in degree of variability between high-and low-frequency syllables (Benner et al. 2007) and differences in the degree to which shared onset syllables in a set of target words prime the spoken output of those words (Cholin et al. 2004 and Cholin, Chapter 9, this volume). We return to this question in section 4 below, but we point out here that, as noted in Chapter 9, these results are consistent with a role for the syllable somewhat late in the word-form encoding process.

2.8   Observation 8: Syllable Frames Prime Production

Sevald et al. (1995) have shown a priming effect for abstract monosyllabic templates in production, i.e. strings of syllables with the same

CV structure can be produced more rapidly and more accurately than strings with different CV structure. However, this result is equally compatible with a word-based structural frame. Future research on this question will be useful, to determine whether the templates that the speaker forms are word- or syllable-based.

2.9 *Summary of Traditional Evidence for the Syllable*

As the preceding discussion has illustrated, a number of lines of evidence have traditionally been cited in support of the hypothesis that speakers have access to representations of syllables as discrete individual entities during speech production planning. However, each of these lines of evidence has some ambiguity, leading to some caveats re their interpretation. Despite these caveats, the syllable has proved to be irresistibly tempting as a unit of representation in models of the complex process of speech production and speech production planning. One line of evidence that has seemed particularly compelling for those who seek to model the representations that speakers generate during the production planning process comes from speech error patterns. In the next section we examine this evidence in some detail, to determine whether it provides the kind of strong support for the representation of syllables in speech processing that is often claimed for it.

3   *Speech Error Evidence that Bears on the Role of the Syllable in Speech Production Processing*

Ever since Fromkin (1971) focused attention on speech errors as a source of evidence for the mental processes involved in speaking, and pointed out that these patterns provide information about the role of grammars, grammatical structures and grammatical constituents in speech production processing, analysts have been scanning the distributional facts about error corpora for evidence that the syllable plays a role in the representations that speakers generate during production. These arguments take several forms: a) claims that syllables and syllabic substructures undergo a serial ordering process during production planning, suggesting that they are independently represented structures; b) claims that interaction errors between individual segments generally involve pairs of segments that occupy similar positions in their respective syllables (onsets with onsets, codas with codas, etc.), leading to proposals that syllabic frames provide the organizing principle for the serial ordering process of smaller elements such as individual segments; c) claims that hypothesizing stored syllable-sized motor programs that are retrieved during the process of production planning provides the best account of patterns of phonetic variation. We will examine the evidence for each of these possibilities in turn.

3.1   Claim 1: Syllables and Syllabic Subconstituents undergo a Serial Ordering Process

Speech error evidence suggests that phonological planning includes a serial ordering process for sublexical elements (Lashley 1967, Fromkin 1971, Shattuck-Hufnagel 1979, 1983, among others). It may seem counterintuitive that the sounds of a word must undergo a serial ordering process, since their order of occurrence must be specified in the lexicon, in order to distinguish among different words that share the same set of segments, such as *act*, *tack*, and *cat*. However, error patterns clearly show, (1), that misorderings do occur, i.e. a variety of different sublexical element types can become misordered, and these patterns have been interpreted as evidence for a serial ordering process in production planning (examples drawn from the MITSEC).

(1) Features: *tomato* → *ponato*
     Segments: *your car towed* → *your tar cowed*
     Morpheme subcomponents: *back and forth* → *borth and fack*
     Morphemes: *installing telephones* → *intelephoning stalls*

One can then ask whether syllables and their subconstituents, such as onsets, rhymes, nuclei and codas, provide the best description of the units that undergo serial ordering (as evidenced by mis-ordering errors). To address this question, investigators have examined evidence from large corpora of errors collected by listening to ambient speech, including the MITSEC and the UCLA Speech Error Corpus for American English, as well as a number of error corpora collected in German, Spanish, Turkish etc. Interestingly, for large corpora of errors in American English, there is almost no unambiguous evidence for syllable-sized error units. For example, almost all error units that could be regarded as syllables can also be viewed as monosyllabic words. While this might be in part because a large proportion of words in samples of continuous speech in this language are monosyllabic, it is striking that individual syllables in polysyllabic words do not habitually serve as units in interaction errors like exchanges, anticipatory additions or shifts. Thus, errors like *packed my trunks* → *trunked my packs* may be just as easily accounted for as an exchange of word- or morpheme-sized units, rather than as an exchange of syllables, particularly in light of a) the documented occurrence of exchanges that involve interactions between a monosyllabic and a polysyllabic morpheme (as in *intelephoning stalls*), which are clearly better described at the morphemic level, and b) the lack of exchanges that involve an individual syllable of a polysyllabic morphemes (e.g. **installephoning tells*). In other words, although the high proportion of interactions between monosyllabic words <u>could</u> be interpreted as evidence for the representation of syllable-sized planning units that undergo a serial ordering process, this interpretation is at best ambiguous, and there is reason to believe it provides evidence for the word or morpheme as a planning unit instead.

Not only is the evidence for syllable-sized error units ambiguous, there is similarly little unambiguous evidence for interaction errors among syllabic subcomponents, such as onsets, rhymes, nuclei or codas. It is true that a high proportion of sublexical error units <u>can</u> be described in terms of syllable subcomponents, as in (2).

(2) Onset: *speak fast* → *feak spast* (but see also onset-fragments as in *sprit blain*)
     Nucleus: *milk burning* → *murk bilning*
     Coda: *sit down* → *sin dowt*

By far the largest proportion of such interaction errors involve onsets, and these onsets may be the initial subconstituents of other constituent structures, such as lexical words, PWds or metrical feet, due to the highly nested nature of language structures.

This ambiguity as to the nature of the position similarity or position preference for sublexical speech errors is only one aspect of the plethora of descriptions that is possible for most error tokens. As a result, ambiguity is pervasive in error classification data. Not only is the positional status of the error units often uncertain there is also often indeterminancy in the type of error, as well as in the relationship between the error and its possible source. It is important to recognize the extent of this ambiguity, in order to prevent misinterpretation based on selection of one particular description among many possible formulations that might be appropriate for specifying constraints and patterns in the error data. This observation led to a comprehensive effort in our laboratory toward labeling the ambiguities in the extensive set of errors in the MITSEC. As a result of this effort, each entry in this collection of 10,000+ errors has been categorized as in (3).

(3) MITSEC Categorizations

   a. the error unit involved (e.g. distinctive feature, segment, string, syllable, morph, word, phrase…);
   b. the type of error (exchange, substitution, addition, omission, blend…);
   c. for errors that suggest an interaction between two elements in the planned utterance, the direction of influence from the source to the target (anticipatory, perseveratory, both (i.e. exchange) or neither (i.e. no apparent source));
   d. the position of each error element in its larger constituent, etc.

Critically, for each of these dimensions, an error is coded for ambiguity as to its categorization, and a major goal of the enterprise was to explicitly document each of the ways in which an error is ambiguous. The reason for this extensive effort was to emphasize the pervasive nature of ambiguity, because unrecognized ambiguity in error patterns can lead to unwarranted assumptions in production planning models.

An illustrative example of this rampant ambiguity is found in the error: *He placed the highly paid players alone* → *He placed the highly [pled] players alone*. Possible categorizations of this error include those listed in (4).

(4) Whole word substitution: (*paid* → *played*)
   Anticipatory morpheme substitution from *players*: (*pay* → *play*)
   Perseveratory phoneme string substitution from *placed*: ([pe] → [ple])
   Anticipatory onset substitution from *players*: ([p] → [pl])
   Perseveratory onset substitution from *placed*: ([p] → [pl])
   Anticipatory segment addition from *players*: ([(no seg)] → [l])
   Anticipatory segment addition from *alone*: ([(no seg)] → [l])
   Perseveratory segment addition from *placed*: [(no seg)] → [l])

Explicitly marking all of these possible descriptions of the error is important, because without this explicit categorization, it is easy to ignore alternative possibilities. As a result, it is easy to mistakenly lump such errors in with a particular type of unambiguous error, with the result that the description of the distribution among error types is skewed in ways that lead to unfounded assumptions about what the production mechanism must be able to account for. One example is the often-made suggestion that anticipatory errors are more common than perseverations. This interpretation of the error data has inspired models in which strongly-activated elements which belong later in an utterance can sometimes reach activation threshold too early, resulting in anticipatory substitutions and additions. The apparent asymmetry in favor of anticipatory over perseveratory errors in the corpus arises largely from the inclusion of what we categorize as *incomplete errors* (Shattuck-Hufnagel 1987). To understand the significance of this inclusion, we compared the position preference for three kinds of errors in the MITSEC.

(5) MITSEC error types

   a. Complete exchanges: e.g. *shop talk* → *top shalk*
   b. Complete anticipations: e.g. *shop talk* → *top talk*
   c. Incomplete interactions: e.g. *shop talk* → *top—shop talk*

In contrast to earlier treatments of error corpora, in this study the incomplete interactions were labeled as ambiguous as to error type, rather than as anticipations; because they were interrupted before completion, it is not certain whether they would have been completed as anticipations (*top talk*) or as exchanges (*top shalk*). This ambiguity might seem at first to be of little consequence. However, separating ambiguous incomplete errors from complete anticipations permitted further analysis of the word position in which the three types of errors occur preferentially. As a result, it is possible to calculate that anticipatory and perseveratory errors occur at approximately the same rate in the MITSEC. That is, we found the following preference rates for word-onset position among the three error types (looking at consonant interaction errors only).

(6) Error rates

   a. Exchanges = 70–80% in word-onset Cs (consistent with Fromkin 1971)
   b. Complete anticipations = 40–50% word-onset C's

The difference between exchanges and complete anticipations in the degree of preference for word-onset locations suggests that these two types of errors are not governed by the same set of constraints, and may even arise at different stages in the production planning process. But it also provides a way of estimating the proportion of incomplete errors that were actually interrupted anticipations. This proportion turns out to be intermediate between the high proportion for complete exchanges and the lower proportion for complete anticipations. In fact, if the proportion of incomplete interactions that arose as anticipations is estimated based on the preference for word-onset position in complete anticipations, the proportion of anticipatory errors is no greater than the proportion of perseverations (e.g. *shop shalk*, in this context).

The importance of this observation is that it changes the constraints that error patterns impose on production planning models: i.e., it raises questions about whether planning models must generate a disproportionate number of anticipations, and instead strengthens the case for models in which a serial ordering mechanism selects among a set of elements destined for a particular type of structural location, so that malfunctions of various types result in approximately equal proportions of anticipations and perseverations.

It should also be noted that the predominance of consonant errors in word-onset positions that we observe in American English is not universal; in particular, it has been reported that for Spanish errors, the preference is for consonants in syllable onsets regardless of the position of the syllable in the word (del Viso et al. 1991), perhaps because there are many more CV (as opposed to CVC) syllables in Spanish than in English. This observation underscores the importance of carrying out cross-language comparisons of error data, and of avoiding the assumption that speakers of all languages use a single common set of structural representations in planning utterances. Similar caveats have been proposed for cross-language variation in the syllable as a representational unit during perceptual processing, as noted above.

In sum, careful annotation of the ambiguity of the structural position shared by two units that interact in an error provides at least some hedge against the temptation to favor one of the potential structural frameworks (such as the syllable), by making sure that all of the possibilities are acknowledged. The annotated MITSEC emphasizes this point, by requiring the explicit marking of ambiguity in the description of the error unit, the error type, the error source and the position of the target and source in their higher-level structures.

To summarize the evidence for syllable-based error units more generally, although many of the errors in the MITSEC and other error databases drawn from American English speech can be described in terms of the movement or change in constituents which are syllable-sized or correspond to sub-syllabic constituents like onset and rhyme, these units can also be described as subunits of other constituents, such as the word or the metrical foot. Thus they provide only ambiguous evidence for the syllable and its structural sub-constituents as independently-represented elements that undergo serial ordering.

3.2   Claim 2: Syllables Provide a Planning Framework for the Serial Ordering of Sublexical Units During Production Planning

Even if syllables and their subcomponents do not undergo serial ordering, might these structures nevertheless form the planning framework for the sublexical serial ordering process? Speech error evidence might help to answer this question. For example, interaction errors between sublexical elements might obey a syllable position similarity constraint, so that a pair of phonemic segments that are being serially ordered into their respective syllable onset positions would be more likely to interact in an error than two segments that were destined for an onset and coda position respectively. In a model informed by such a syllable-based position similarity constraint, the speaker generates a planning frame that corresponds to syllable structure, and associates the segments of each lexical item with the onsets, nuclei and codas in that planning frame. In contrast, Shattuck-Hufnagel (1992) presents arguments against the syllable, and in support of the word or morpheme as the representational unit that best describes the position similarity constraint on segmental interactions in sound-level speech errors.

Do sublexical interaction errors reliably involve pairs of sound segments in analogous syllable positions? It is often observed that interactions between pairs of sublexical components in an utterance, as in an exchange or anticipatory substitution, generally involve two elements that are in parallel positions in their respective syllables, and this observation has been embodied in production planning models with syllable-based planning frames (Dell 1988). But if the similarity constraint is better stated in terms of a different constituent, such as the word or the stress foot, then we might postulate that the planning frame is built on this structure instead of the syllable. Note that if the planning frames are syllable-based, their slots are somewhat flexibly defined, sometimes treating the rhyme as a unit and sometimes the nucleus and coda separately, and sometimes treating the onset as a unit and sometimes its individual phonemes separately. However, this is a problem for any postulated unit for the planning framework, whether it is the syllable, the word or the foot.

There are certainly many sublexical errors that involve two segments in onset position (such as *speak fast* → *feak spast*), or two vowels that form syllabic nuclei (e.g. *come back* → *cam buck*), or (more rarely) two codas (e.g. *blot up* → *blop utt*), but almost no errors that involve an interaction between an onset and a coda (e.g. *big can* → *nig cab*). Interestingly, the few cases in the MITSEC that do involve an onset-coda interaction occur within a single word, e.g. *fish* → *shif*. While the observation that interacting segments generally share syllable position is true, it is not the only possible way of describing the position similarity constraint. For example, as noted above, in most cases the syllable onsets that interact in an error are also word onsets as well as foot onsets, and the codas are also word-final consonants. Moreover, there are a few errors in which two interacting onset consonants are word onsets but not foot onsets (e.g. *math review* → *rath meview*) and a few others in which a sequence which looks very much like 'the rest of the word minus the onset' seems to serve as the error unit (e.g. *Howard and Claire* → *Haire and Cloward*), further implicating the word or morpheme as the planning frame that is the source of constraints on both the size and positional similarity of sublexical interaction error units. Keeping this possibility in mind is important, because the assumption that the syllable is the appropriate constituent for stating the position similarity constraint has quite naturally led to the postulation of a syllable-based frame for production planning.

As this discussion makes clear, if we could determine whether word or (stressed) syllable was the appropriate unit for stating the position similarity constraint, it would be useful for constraining models. An experiment comparing the predictions of these two hypotheses was reported in Shattuck-Hufnagel (1992), based on elicited errors using 20 quadruples of tongue twister stimuli such as those in (7).

(7) Tongue twisters

    a. *parade fad foot parole* (p/f occur in same word position but not in same stress syllable/foot position)

    b. *repair fad foot repaid* (p/f in same stress syllable/foot position but not same word position)

    c. *parrot fad foot peril* (p/f in same word and stress syllable/foot positions)

    d. *ripple fad foot rapid* (p/f in different word and stress syllable/foot positions)

This design allowed comparison of the effects of word-position similarity vs. syllable-position similarity on the rate of interaction errors between pairs of segments, such as /p/ and /f/, which have a high rate of error interaction in the MITSEC. Results might have told us the domain of the position-similarity constraint on interaction errors, and indeed there was some tendency for the error rate to be higher when the two target segments only occurred in lexical-word-onset position (*parade fad foot parole*) than when they only occurred in the same stressed-syllable-onset position (*repeat fad foot repaid*). Unfortunately, this difference did not reach significance (possibly because of the great variation in error rates across the 20 speakers in the experiment), so we are left with the hypothesis that both position factors operate similarly. However, there were almost no interaction errors between two segments when they shared neither word-onset nor stressed-syllable-onset position (*ripple fad foot rapid*), supporting the view that the ambisyllabic position of a consonant removes it from the pool of easily-confusable onset target segments.

    To sum up the implications of error data for syllable-based planning frameworks: Unambiguous evidence for the independent representation of whole-syllable constituents is non-existent; evidence for the independent representation of syllabic subconstituents in production planning is equivocal, i.e. much of it can be interpreted in other ways. Similarly equivocal is the evidence for syllable structure as a factor governing sublexical interaction errors, via a position similarity constraint on interacting elements imposed by a presumed planning frame.

    A final note about the value of transcriptional error corpora, i.e. collections of errors recorded by listeners, is that statistical distribution patterns in sublexical error corpora collected by ear are best regarded as sources of hypotheses about production planning representations to be tested experimentally. This caveat is important for several reasons. First, as Pouplier and Goldstein (2005) have shown, under somewhat extreme articulatory conditions (i.e. repeated utterance of tongue-twister-like sequences) it is possible to elicit misarticulations which are not easily perceivable by a listener, and such misarticulations may also occur under the less challenging conditions of spontaneous speech. Second, in addition to missing some perceptually undetectable misarticulations, listeners may be subject to additional filtering mechanisms by which an errorful production is distorted by a perceptual system that is focused on extracting the meaning of the speaker's communicative act. Such distortions may cause an utterance to seem well-formed, even if it contains an error that might be perceptible under conditions of careful or repeated listening. This does not mean that error corpora collected by listening are not useful; only that distribution patterns in such corpora must be interpreted with care, and are mainly useful as a source of hypotheses about speech production processing that can be tested experimentally.

3.3   Claim 3: Syllables are the Units of Stored Motor Programs

The hypothesis that syllables are the units of stored motor programs is embedded in a thoroughly-worked-out model of production planning described in Levelt, Roelofs and Meyer (1999); see Chapter 9 in this volume for further discussion. This hypothesis incorporates proposals by Browman and Goldstein (1988) based on a theory of articulatory organization (see also Crompton 1982). On this view, syllabification occurs during the phonetic encoding portion of the production planning process; after the retrieval of unsyllabified word form specifications from the lexicon (phonological encoding), the syntactically structured string of lexical words for the planned utterance is formed into PWds, the syllable structure is formulated for each PWd, and the stored motor programs for these newly-formulated syllables are then retrieved. The motivation for syllabifying within the PWd (rather than storing syllabifications with the word form in the lexicon) is to allow for apparent resyllabification within this constituent. For example, Levelt et al. note that the syllabification of a word like *deciding* in British English is *de.ci.ding*, with the lexical-word-final /d/ of *decide* resyllabified into the onset position of the vowel-initial syllable of the following inflection *-ing*, and for a phrase like *escort us* it is *es.cor.tus*, with the lexical-word-final /t/ of *escort* resyllabified into the onset of the following pronoun *us*.

This view of resyllabification across lexical word/morpheme boundaries is shared by other Dutch investigators (e.g. Booij 1985), and supported by the observation from British English that the /t/ in *escort us* is produced with a noisy release, seeming to indicate an onset allophone.

However, two lines of argument might give us pause before accepting this interpretation. The first is that in at least some dialects of British English, the word-final /t/ of *escort* is produced with a noisy release in many (if not all) contexts, including in utterance-final position where presumably no resyllabification takes place. As a result, the observation of a noisy release in *escort us* may not be good evidence for resyllabification, making the assumption that syllables are formed within PWds before retrieval of their motor programs less compelling. This is a situation that cries out for closer acoustic analysis of the release of final /t/ in various contexts in utterances of British English, as well as of the release of a word-medial /t/ before an unstressed vowel (which might be more directly analogous to the *us* in *escort us*).

The second line of argument that might give us pause is the small but growing amount of evidence that such re-syllabification does not take place across lexical boundaries in American English. For example, Shattuck-Hufnagel (2007) reports evidence for a constituent boundary at *us* in phrases like *edit us*, but no such evidence for a boundary at *-ing* in *editing*. On the other hand, Shattuck-Hufnagel and Turk (2009) find evidence for polysyllabic shortening of [beik] in phrases like *bake us apples*, compared to *bake apples*, at least for some speakers, suggesting that *bake us* may have been grouped into a prosodic constituent for the purposes of timing adjustment. Clearly, further work is needed to determine the degree to which phonetic syllables reflect the re-syllabification of lexico-phonological structure in production.

The preceding suggests that the arguments for resyllabification across lexical boundaries require further evaluation, particularly for American English. Moreover, without this support, the arguments for phonetic encoding of one PWd at a time are weak, because there are phonological interactions between PWds (Keating and Shattuck-Hufnagel 2002), such as a) stress shift/early pitch accent in response to stress clash between PWds, and b) sublexical interaction errors, which typically occur between PWds. However, it is still possible that precompiled motor programs for syllable-sized units are stored in some form and retrieved once an appropriate representation has been generated, whatever the nature of that representation. Before returning to this question in section 5 below, we present a summary of an alternative model of speech production planning in which the entire hierarchy of prosodic constituents plays a role in word form encoding.

4   An Alternative Model of Production Planning: Higher-Level Prosodic Constituents First

The Levelt et al. model could be described as a 'Prosody Last' approach, in which the prosody of the utterance is built from the bottom up, starting with the PWd, and phrase-level prosody is subsequently computed on the string of already-syllabified PWds. An alternative to this 'Prosody Last' model can be described in conceptual terms as a 'Prosody First' model, in which the prosodic framework of the utterance (or perhaps of each phrase of the utterance) is built from the top down (Keating and Shattuck-Hufnagel 2002). In this approach, the speaker begins with an utterance- or phrase-level frame, which is expanded into a more-detailed prosodic description at each level of processing. This view adopts the insight from Levelt et al. that all of the information about a word that is stored in the lexicon need not be retrieved in a single step. Instead, different kinds of lexical information can be retrieved as needed for each processing step, including a) the number of syllables (or possibly feet) in each word, b) its metrical pattern, and c) the segments themselves. One advantage of such a model is that the prosodic shape of an entire phrase or utterance is available in some form, to influence the process of phonological/phonetic encoding as it unfolds. This is consistent with a number of related observations such as those in (8).

(8) Prosody First Model

    a. Phrasal structure influences early accent patterns, in the sense that for late-main-stress words like *Mississippi* or *institution*, a pitch accent occurs on the earlier secondary stress syllable if it is the first pitch accent in an intonational phrase, but on the later main-stress syllable if it is the last or nuclear pitch accent (Bolinger 1958, Shattuck-Hufnagel et al. 1995);

    b. phrase-level pitch accent patterns influence segmental error patterns (Croot et al., 2010), suggesting that pitch accents are already assigned when these errors occur;

    c. phrase-sized constituents appear to be the domain of sublexical interaction errors (Keating and Shattuck-Hufnagel 2002).

These and other observations are consistent with the idea that some representation of the overall prosody of at least a phrase (although not necessarily all of the details of the prosodic structure) is in place, at the point when the phonological/phonetic coding of its words occurs.

Although Levelt et al.'s arguments for phonological/phonetic encoding one PWd at a time, and building higher-level prosody on that structure, are not entirely persuasive, their arguments for the retrieval of stored syllable-sized motor plans are promising. This proposal is also consistent with more recent experimental evidence for effects of syllable frequency on certain late aspects of speech production planning behavior, and with a line of experiments that have been carried out by Cholin and her colleagues (Chapter 9 in this volume). In the next section we briefly review the evidence for syllable frequency effects, and its implications for the role of the syllable in speech planning representations.

5   Implications of Syllable Frequency Effects

Although the evidence for syllabic units as independently-represented constituents that undergo serial ordering is not entirely compelling, and the evidence for syllable-based planning frames is equivocal, there is some evidence for syllable frequency effects, particularly for languages other than English (e.g. Carreiras and Perea 2002 for Spanish). In the next chapter in this volume, Cholin points out that syllable frequency effects provide good evidence for syllable-sized representations (see also Cholin, Schiller and Levelt 2004); otherwise, it is difficult to see how information about syllable frequency could be stored and retrieved. She notes that syllable frequency effects in priming studies suggest that these constituents play a role late in the planning process, i.e. during the stage called phonetic encoding in Levelt et al.'s model. Moreover, the interaction with metrical structure in Cholin's studies of pseudo-word production in English suggests that these speakers may rely more on a larger planning unit, such as the trochaic foot, than on the syllable.

Aside from these studies, other methods have also been used to investigate syllable frequency effects. For example, Benner et al. (2007) report that high-frequency syllables show significantly more co-articulation effects and greater variability than low-frequency syllables in a reading task in German, as well as in spontaneous speech. They interpret this as evidence that high-frequency syllables are stored as pre-compiled constituents; on their view, selection among these stored units provides an extra route to phonetic/motor encoding for high-frequency syllables, while low-frequency syllables can only be phonetically encoded by building them from their component segments.

The implications of this evidence for syllable frequency effects must be considered carefully for speakers of American English, in light of the 'blurry' nature of the syllable boundaries reported by these speakers. One way of interpreting this 'weaker, blurry' boundary is that the constituent in question for speakers of American English is the foot, rather than the syllable; on this view, weaker partial priming might be expected because the processing unit, the foot, is not fully primed by the onset syllable.

Note also that a pure syllable-frequency-based account of differential phonetic behavior will not be adequate to account for differences based on the structural characteristics of the context in which the syllable occurs. Such differences are found, for example, in the observation that the syllable *for* is often produced with strikingly different phonetic shapes depending on whether it occurs in the word *for* vs. the word *four*, etc. Additional evidence is found in Berkenfield's (2001) study of differential reduction patterns for *that* in its instantiations as a demonstrative pronoun, demonstrative adjective, relative clause marker and complementizer. If speakers retrieved precompiled articulatory programs for syllables without regard for these morphosyntactic (and very probably prosodic) differences, these systematic differences in pronunciation would not be possible.

6   Conclusion: Syllables in Production Processing: What have we Learned?

The preceding examination of some of the available evidence regarding the role of syllabic representations in speech production planning for American English has highlighted the fact that apparent support for an active role for syllables and syllable structure should be evaluated with care. We need to ask questions like those in (9).

(9) Questions for Syllables in Production

    a. Do apparent 'syllable position effects' in interaction errors actually require syllables, or could these position constraints be accounted for by other kinds of structures?

    b. Does evidence for syllabic subconstituents as representational units necessarily mean that syllables themselves are represented, or could these units be subconstituents of other kinds of structures?

We have observed that there may be alternative accounts for what looks at first like convincing evidence for syllable structure, in the sense that this evidence may be equally well or better viewed as effects of phonological context, or of word or foot structure. However, there is evidence from a widening variety of methods, including production priming and brain imaging, for effects of syllable frequency, and such effects argue for the existence of a stored set of precompiled abstract syllable-sized constituents for high-frequency syllables in a number of languages. Significant differences in the nature of these frequency effects across languages, however, highlight the necessity of proceeding carefully in attempts to generalize from results for one language to more general claims about the representations developed by human speakers when they talk.

Perhaps the most important lesson to be learned from this review of evidence relating to the role of syllables in speech production planning is the need to ask the right questions. We need to consider which aspect of the syllable are supported by which kinds of evidence, i.e. when in the production process is a particular representation active, and what specific role does it play? Also, observational data must lead to hypotheses about different candidate sublexical constituents, which make contrasting predictions about the expected results of critical experiments. We must also consider whether the role played by the syllable and its sub-constituents is different for speakers of different languages. In short, the nature of the role played by syllabic structure in speech production planning will only be clarified by substantial further study.

References

Benner, Uta, Ines Flechsig, Grzegorz Dogil and Bernd Moebius. 2007. Coarticulatory resistance in a mental syllabary. In *Proceedings of the 16th International Congress of Phonetic Sciences*, http://www.icphs2007.de/.

Berkenfield, Catie. 2001. The role of frequency in the realization of English 'that'. In *Frequency and the Emergence of Linguistic Structure*, edited by Joan Bybee and Paul Hopper, 281–308. Amsterdam: John Benjamins.

Blevins, Juliette. 2003. The independent nature of phonotactic constraints: an alternative to syllable-based approaches. In *The syllable in optimality theory*, edited by Caroline Féry and Ruben van de Vijver, 375–403. Cambridge: Cambridge University Press.

Bolinger, Dwight. 1958. A theory of pitch accent in English. *Word* 14: 109–149.

Booij, Gert. 1985. Coordination reduction in complex words: a case for prosodic phonology. In *Advances in nonlinear phonology*, edited by Harry van der Hulst and Norval Smith, 143–160. Dordrecht: Foris.

Browman, Catherine P. and Louis Goldstein. 1988. Some notes on syllable structure in articulatory phonology. *Phonetica* 45: 140–155.

——. 1992. Articulatory Phonology: An Overview. *Phonetica* 49: 155–180.

——. 1995. Gestural syllable position effects in American English. In *Producing speech: Contemporary issues*, edited by F. Bell-Berti and L. Raphael, 19–33. NY: American Institute of Physics.

Carreiras, Manuel and Manuel Perea. 2002. Masked priming effects with syllabic neighbors in the lexical decision task. *Journal of Experimental Psychology: Human Perception and Performance* 28: 1228–1242.

Cholin, Joana, Niels O. Schiller and Willem J. M. Levelt. 2004. The preparation of syllables in speech production. *Journal of Memory and Language* 50: 47–61.

Crompton, Andrew. 1982. Syllables and Segments in Speech Production. In *Slips of the Tongue and Language Production*, edited by Anne Cutler, 109–162. Berlin: Mouton Publishers.

Croot, Karen, Au Claudia and Amy Harper. 2010. Prosodic structure and tongue twister errors. In *Laboratory Phonology 10*, edited by Cécile Fougeron, Barbara Kühnert, Mariapaola D'Imperio and Nathalie Vallée. New York: Mouton de Gruyter Mouton.

Cutler, Anne, Jacques Mehler, Dennis Norris and Juan Segui. 1986. The syllable's differing role in the segmentation of French and English. *Journal of Memory and Language* 25: 385–400.

del Viso, Susana, José Igoa and José E. Garcia-Albea. 1991 On the autonomy of phonological encoding: Evidence from slips of the tongue in Spanish. *Journal of Psychological Research* 20: 161–185.

Dell, Gary S. 1988. The retrieval of phonological forms in production: Tests of predictions from a connectionist model. *Journal of Memory and Language* 27: 124–142.

Dell, Gary S., Franklin Chang and Zenzi M. Griffin 1999. Connectionist models of language production: lexical access and grammatical encoding. *Cognitive Science* 23: 517–542.

Fromkin, Victoria. 1971. The non-anomalous nature of anomalous utterances. *Language.* 47: 27–52.

Kahn, Daniel. 1976. Syllable-based generalizations in English phonology. PhD diss., MIT.

Keating, Patricia and Stefanie Shattuck-Hufnagel. 2002. A prosodic view of word form encoding. *UCLA Working Papers in Phonetics* 101: 112–156.

Kiparsky, Paul. 1979. Metrical structure assignment is cyclic. *Linguistic Inquiry* 10: 421–441.

Ladefoged, Peter and G. Loeb. 2002. Preliminary experiments on respiratory activity in speech. Unpublished Ms., http://www.linguistics.ucla.edu/people/ladefoge/.

Lashley, Karl. 1967. The problem of serial order in behavior. In. *Cerebral mechanisms in behavior*, edited by Lloyd A. Jeffress, 112–167. New York: Wiley.

Laubstein, Ann. 1987. Syllable structure: the speech error evidence. *Canadian Journal of Linguistics* 32: 339–363.

Levelt, Willem J. M., Ardi Roelofs and Antje Meyer. 1999. A theory of lexical access in speech production. *Behavioral and Brain Sciences* 22: 1–38.

Pierrehumbert, Janet. 1994. Syllable structure and word structure: a study of triconsonantal clusters in English. In *Papers in Laboratory Phonology III: Phonological structure and phonetic form*, edited by Patricia A. Keating, 168–188. Cambridge: Cambridge University Press.

Pouplier, Marianne and Louis Goldstein. 2005. Asymmetries in the perception of speech production errors. *Journal of Phonetics* 33: 47–75

Samuels, Bridget. 2008. A string theory of syllables. Presented at the CUNY Phonology Forum Conference on the Syllable. http://www.cunyphonologyforum.net/syllconf.php.

Sevald, Christine A., Gary S. Dell and Jennifer S. Cole. 1995. Syllable structure in speech production: Are syllables chunks or schemas? *Journal of Memory and Language* 34: 807–820.

Shattuck-Hufnagel, Stefanie. 1979. Speech errors as evidence for a serial ordering mechanism in sentence production. In *Sentence Processing: Psycholinguistic studies presented to Merrill Garrett*, edited by William E. Cooper and Edward C. T. Walker. Hillsdale, 295–342. N.J.: Lawrence Erlbaum.

——. 1983. Sublexical units and suprasegmental structure in speech production planning. In *The production of speech*, edited by Peter MacNeilage. New York: Springer.

——. 1987. The role of word onset consonants in speech production planning: New evidence from speech error patterns. In *Motor and sensory processing in language*, edited by Eric Keller & Myrna Gopnik, 17–51. Hilllsdale, NJ: Erlbaum.

——. 1992. The role of word structure in segmental serial ordering. *Cognition* 42: 213–59.

——. 2006. Prosody first or prosody last? Evidence from the phonetics of word-final /t/ in American English. In *Papers in Laboratory Phonology 8: Varieties of Phonological Competence*, edited by Louis Goldstein, D. H. Whalen and Catherine Best, 445–472. Cambridge: Cambridge University Press.

——. 2007

Shattuck-Hufnagel, Stefanie, Mari Ostendorf and K. Ross. 1995. Pitch accent placement within lexical items in American English. *Journal of Phonetics* 22: 357–388.

Shattuck-Hufnagel, Stefanie and Alice Turk. 2009. An experimental investigation of Abercrombian feet in American English. Presented at the CUNY Phonology Forum Conference on the Foot. http://www.cunyphonologyforum.net/footconf.php.

Shattuck-Hufnagel, Stefanie and Nanette Veilleux. 2000. The Phonological Characteristics of Monosyllabic Function Words in English. In *Sixth International Conference on Spoken Language Processing (ICSLP 2000)*. http://www.isca-speech.org/archive/icslp_2000.

Slifka, Janet. 2000. Respiratory constraints on speech production at prosodic boundaries. PhD diss., MIT.

Steriade, Donca. 1999. Alternatives to syllable-based accounts of consonantal phonotactics. In *Proceedings of LP '98: Item order in language and speech*, vol. 1, edited by Osamu Fujimura, Brian D. Joseph and Bohumil Palek, 205–245. Prague: Charles University in Prague—The Karolinum Press.

Stetson, Raymond Herbert. 1928, 1951. *Motor Phonetics: A study of speech movements in action*. (2nd edition, 1951), Amsterdam: North Holland Publishing Company.

Stevens, Kenneth. 2002. Toward a model for lexical access based on acoustic land-marks and distinctive features. *Journal of the Acoustical Society of America* 111: 1872–1891.

Treiman, Rebecca. 1983. The structure of spoken syllables: Evidence from novel word games. *Cognition* 15: 49–74.

CHAPTER NINE

DO SYLLABLES EXIST?
PSYCHOLINGUISTIC EVIDENCE FOR THE RETRIEVAL OF SYLLABIC UNITS IN SPEECH PRODUCTION

Joana Cholin

1 *Introduction*

Do syllables exist? Do syllables represent functionally relevant units in the course of speech production planning? Are syllables parts of the word forms that are stored in long term memory? Do syllables exist independently of the word forms, as separately stored units that are accessed during late stages in word form encoding? At what levels do syllables come into play, i.e. what is the psycholinguistic evidence for syllables as phonological and /or as phonetic units? Do syllables constitute applicable articulation units? How can we envision the interplay and coordination of syllabic units on different encoding levels?

This chapter aims to find answers to these questions by a) reviewing theories of word production and their different assumptions regarding the involvement of syllables at different encoding levels during speech planning and b) by contrasting psycholinguistic evidence for and against these different assumptions.

The focus within the presentation of psycholinguistic evidence will lie on the presentation of syllable-frequency effects in different languages. Because only stored units are expected to exhibit frequency effects, effects of *syllable* frequency provide strong evidence for the assumption that syllables are (separately) stored units. In particular, a series of experiments will be presented that investigates the effects of syllable frequency in mono- and disyllabic Dutch and English pseudo-words. The comparison of the results for disyllabic pseudo-words in Dutch (a language with relatively clear syllable boundaries) and English (a language with less clear syllable boundaries) will give insight into the temporal coordination of adjacent syllables.

1.1 *Theories of Word Production and the Involvement of Syllables*

Theories of word production generally agree that syllabic units are
involved in speech production planning (e.g. Dell 1986, 1988, Levelt,
Roelofs and Meyer 1999, Shattuck-Hufnagel 1979, 1983 but see Shattuck-Hufnagel, chapter 8, this volume), however, there are contrasting assumptions regarding at what level(s) syllables come into play.
While some researchers (Dell 1986, 1988, Shattuck-Hufnagel 1979,
1983) assume that syllables are an inherent part of the lexicalized word
forms, others (e.g. Cholin, Schiller and Levelt 2004, Levelt, Roelofs and
Meyer 1999, Schiller and Costa 2006) argue that syllables (as abstract
phonological units) emerge during context-dependent online syllabification processes and are separately stored and retrieved as phonetic
syllable programs (Cholin, Levelt and Schiller 2006, Cholin and Levelt
2009, Crompton 1981, Laganaro and Alario 2006, Levelt and Wheeldon 1994).

Current theories of word production start with the activation (Dell
1986) or the selection (Levelt, Roelofs and Meyer 1999) of a semantic-
syntactic representation, the so-called lemma which, in turn, activates
its corresponding word form. The different theories make different
assumptions with respect to the quality of the word form, or rather
with respect to the kinds of information that are released upon retrieval
of the word form. Dell (1986, 1988) assumes that the word's phonological code is syllabified. In his theory, word form retrieval makes two
kinds of information accessible: a) phonological syllabic units (bundles
of segments) and b) syllabic frames or word-shape headers, that specify the consonant-vowel (hereafter CV-) structure of the syllable and
syllable-internal positions such as onset, nucleus, and coda (for similar assumptions see MacNeilage 1998, Shattuck-Hufnagel 1979, 1983).
The frames or word-shape headers serve as placeholders in which the
segmental content will be filled in during the process of segment-to-
frame-association.

On the other hand, Levelt, Roelofs and Meyer (1999) assume that
the phonological code of a word form merely consists of an ordered
set of phonological segments. Crucially, at the stage of phonological
encoding, phonological segments are not yet assigned to syllabic positions. Unlike the Dell model, which assumes that the metrical structure
is an inherent feature of the retrieved word-shapes, the Levelt, Roelofs
and Meyer theory assumes that the stress pattern for a given word is
only stored in case of a non-default stress pattern. For monosyllabic

words and for all other polysyllabic words with a default stress pattern (in Dutch and English, it is the first syllable that carries stress), it is not stored but computed online depending on the context in which the word appears (see also Schiller, Fikkert and Levelt 2004). During online syllabification, retrieved segments are incrementally combined to form successive syllables, starting from the left edge of a word and proceeding incrementally rightwards. The incremental composition of syllables follows both universal syllabification constraints (such as maximization of onsets and sonority gradations) and language-specific phonotactic rules. The output of phonological encoding is a phonological word, specified for its metrical, syllabic, and segmental properties.

1.1.1 *Phonetic Encoding and Access to the Mental Syllabary*

During the next production step, phonetic encoding, the previously generated abstract phonological syllables will be converted into phonetic syllables. According to the Levelt, Roelofs, and Meyer theory, this conversion can be done by translating the single segments of a syllable one by one, which is referred to as the *online-assembly of segments* or by accessing pre-assembled syllables that are stored in a mental syllabary (Crompton 1981, Levelt and Wheeldon 1994). Retrieving precompiled syllables (or corresponding abstract motor programs) should be less effortful than the online-computation of syllables and, as already pointed out, sensitive to effects of syllable frequency.

Accessing stored representations in the syllabary involves the activation of potential syllable programs, followed by the selection of one (or more in the case of multi-syllabic words) program that matches the output of phonological encoding (Roelofs 1997a, b). A stored syllable within the syllabary becomes active as soon as a part of it (e.g. its onset) has been generated during phonological encoding. Thus, not only the eventual target-syllable but also syllable programs that only partially match the output of phonological encoding become active as well.

Thus, there is always an activation of multiple syllables within the syllabary, a) because of the activation of all stored syllables that exhibit segmental overlap with the addressing phonological syllable and b) because the activation of syllables triggered by the second and potential subsequent syllables of a phonological word might occur before the selection of the first syllable is completed. Within the WEAVER++ computer simulation of the mental syllabary theory (Roelofs 1997a, b)

verification links between the phonetic syllables in the syllabary and
the phonological syllables generated one level above verify the successful selection of the target syllable upon a match of all corresponding
segments.

The retrieved motor programs are still abstract, i.e. their execution is
highly context-dependent (due to allophonic variation, coarticulation
and, as a result of this, assimilation). The actual details of the movements in realizing the gestures, such as lip protrusion and jaw lowering, are within the domain of the articulatory system (e.g. Goldstein
and Fowler 2003). The articulatory network, a coordinative motor system that includes feedback mechanisms (Goldstein and Fowler 2003,
Saltzman 1986, Saltzman and Kelso 1981), transforms these articulatory plans into overt speech.

1.2   Empirical Evidence for Syllables in Speech Production Research

In the following, evidence for and against the involvement of syllables
during speech planning will be reviewed. While some tasks clearly
suggest that syllables constitute functionally relevant production units,
they remain rather neutral with respect to the relevant planning level;
other tasks provide evidence to pinpoint the level at which syllables
come into play.

1.2.1   Speech Errors and Meta-Linguistic Tasks

Speech errors, in particular segmental exchange errors, have often been
argued to provide evidence for a syllabic organization of the mental
lexicon: phonological speech errors that involve segmental exchanges
generally obey syllable internal positions, respecting the *syllable position
constraint* (Berg 1988, MacKay 1970, Meyer 1992, Nooteboom 1969,
Shattuck-Hufnagel 1979, 1983, Stemberger 1982, Vousden, Brown
and Harley 2000). This constraint specifies that onsets exchange with
onsets, as in "*sp*ictly *str*eaking" (Garrett 1982), or "*h*eft *l*emisphere"
(Fromkin 1973), nuclei with nuclei, as in "cl*ea*p p*i*k" (Fromkin 1971),
and codas with codas. The vast majority of segmental errors, though,
are those that take place in onset position and, as argued by Shattuck-
Hufnagel (this volume, see also Shattuck-Hufnagel 1987, 1992 and
Meyer 1992, for a critical review), involve word or morpheme onsets,
and thus may reflect a general onset constraint rather than a syllable
onset constraint. However, the analysis of a large speech error corpus
(Vousden, Brown and Harley 2000) indicate that segmental errors are

more likely to occur in syllable onset position than in syllable final position and, more importantly, that the syllable onset effect cannot be accounted for by a word onset effect.

Furthermore, evidence stemming from meta-linguistic tasks may also suggest that syllables play a role during speech planning. For example, in a series of syllable reversal experiments, Schiller, Meyer and Levelt (1997) asked Dutch participants to produce the syllables of auditorily presented disyllables in reversed order (e.g. /tʉs—kɑk/ after hearing /kɑk.tʉs/[1]). Specifically, they investigated how Dutch speakers syllabify items comprising intervocalic consonants following short (/kɑk.tʉs/) and long (/kaː.mər/) vowels and schwa (/rə.bɛl/). Results showed that participants could easily reverse the syllables by applying a rather small set of phonological rules. Treiman and Danis (1988) (see also Treiman 1983, 1984) reported similar effects in English syllable reversal studies. These findings suggest that speakers encode syllables at some level during speech planning. As Schiller and colleagues (Schiller, Meyer and Levelt 1997) argue, the fact that participants' choices to syllabify words vary (within a given set of rules) may suggest the existence of an online-syllabification mechanism as opposed to a retrieval of precompiled, stored phonological syllables. However, other (cognitive as well as linguistic) strategies might help to perform the syllable reversal task and hence the interpretation at what level this syllabification takes place has to remain tentative (see Bagemihl 1995, for a review and also Shattuck-Hufnagel, this volume).

Taken together, the findings from speech errors and meta-linguistic tasks suggest the involvement of syllabic units at some point during speech planning but they are agnostic with regard to the level at which syllables come into play. The next sections will review evidence from chronometric data in an attempt to locate the levels on which syllables play a role.

1.3 *Syllable-Congruency Studies*

Many researchers have tried to identify syllables as functional production units by presenting syllable-congruent primes prior to a to-be-produced target syllable, e.g. *po###* as a prime for *po*.lo or *pol###* as a prime for *pol*.ka. Under the assumption that syllables constitute

---

[1] Periods indicate syllable boundaries.

functionally relevant units during speech planning it was predicted that syllable-congruent primes would speed up production relative to a syllable incongruent prime, e.g. *po###* as a prime for *pol*.ka or *pol###* as a prime for *po*.lo. However, after some positive evidence in French (Ferrand, Segui and Grainger 1996) and English (Ferrand, Segui and Humphreys 1997), many studies in different languages could not replicate the initial syllable-congruency effect (Dutch: Baumann 1995, Schiller 1997, 1998; English: Schiller 1999, 2000, Schiller and Costa 2006; French: Brand, Rey and Peereman 2003; Evinck 1997; Spanish: Schiller, Costa and Colomé 2002). What was consistently found was a *segmental length* effect (see Schiller 2004), i.e. the more segments that were shared between the prime and the target, the more efficient the prime was, irrespective of the syllable congruency. Even under optimized conditions (i.e. longer and unmasked prime presentation), no syllable-congruency could be demonstrated for production (Schiller and Costa 2006).

The finding of a segmental length effect is surprising under an account that assumes syllabified word forms (e.g. Dell 1986, 1988). Under this scenario, one would have expected that a syllable-congruent prime would be more effective than a syllable-incongruent prime. The production model by Levelt and colleagues (1999) offers an explanation that might account for the absence of the syllable-congruency effects: the syllabic prime (CV or CVC) that is never overtly articulated taps into the level where word forms are retrieved from memory. Recall that, according to their model (Levelt, Roelofs and Meyer 1999), the word form does not contain syllabic information. Rather, it only specifies an ordered string of segments. Consequently, the more segments that are pre-activated by the prime, the more efficient this prime is, leading to the segmental length effect, regardless of the syllabic congruency.

However, there are also findings that support the assumption that the word forms retrieved from memory contain more than just the segmental string (Costa and Sebastián-Gallés 1998, Ferrand and Segui 1998, Sevald, Dell and Cole 1995). These studies show that speakers benefit from a shared abstract syllable structure (i.e. the CV structure) in the absence of a segmental overlap. These findings support accounts that assume that word forms activate two kinds of information, the segments and a syllabic frame into which the segments will be inserted during *segment-to-frame-association* (e.g. Dell 1986, 1988). In contrast, Roelofs and Meyer (1998), on the other hand, failed to find facilitatory effects for a shared CV structure when the segmental content was not also shared. Hence, support for the storage of an abstract syllabic frame is mixed.

If phonological syllables were indeed stored, one would have expected a syllable congruency effect and not the consistently reported segmental length effect (e.g. Schiller and Costa 2006). Another argument against storing pre-syllabified structure is the observation that syllable boundaries change depending on context. For example, while the word 'demand' is syllabified as *de.mand* in isolation, the structure changes in some contexts, such as *de.man.ded*. Likewise, 'both are' will be resyllabified as *bo.thar*. Levelt and colleagues argued that resyllabifying words in connected speech, which involves breaking apart the stored syllables and then rebuilding new syllables, would be too processing intensive (e.g. Levelt, Roelofs and Meyer 1999). A statistical analysis by Schiller et al (1996) showed that in Dutch connected speech, every sixth word is resyllabified, i.e. differs from its canonical syllable structure, to match its new environment (see also Baumann 1995).

It should be noted though that for other, non-European languages that have a smaller inventory of syllables and in which no resyllabification occurs, the storage of phonological syllables might be different. For example, Mandarin Chinese has (not counting tone) a syllable inventory of 400 different syllables whereas languages such as Dutch and English have more than 12,000 different syllables. Moreover, syllables in Mandarin Chinese are not resyllabified in connected speech. Here, it might be the case that the syllable structure is in fact stored within the word form that is retrieved from the mental lexicon. Indeed, Chen, Chen and Dell (2002) showed clear syllable priming effects in Mandarin Chinese. Differences in the number of syllables within a language and the demands of resyllabification may explain why a significant syllable priming effect could be found in Mandarin Chinese but not in Indo-European languages (see O'Seaghdha, Chen and Chen 2010).

1.4 *Implicit Priming Studies*

In the search for the syllable, another paradigm had been chosen that is known to be sensitive to the late processes in word form encoding (e.g. Meyer 1990, 1991). The *implicit priming paradigm*, or *form preparation paradigm*, makes use of the fact that implicit knowledge of certain aspects of an action accelerates the execution of this action (Rosenbaum, Inhoff and Gordon 1984). In this paradigm, participants

learn sets of prompt-response pairs in which the responses are either
phonologically related to one another (e.g. *lo.tus, lo.ner, lo.cal*) or phonologically unrelated (e.g. *lo.tus, ti.mer, ba.sil*). The overlap between
the responses within one set (i.e. the homogeneous set) functions as an
implicit prime and allows faster and less error prone responses compared to sets consisting of unrelated items (i.e. the heterogeneous set).
Speakers can prepare an utterance more successfully when segmental
(and syllabic structures) are shared between members of the response
set (Cholin, Schiller and Levelt 2004, Janssen, Roelofs and Levelt 2004,
Meyer 1990, 1991, Roelofs and Meyer 1998).

In the original studies (Meyer 1990, 1991), participants learned
sets of semantically related prompt response pairs in Dutch. In the
homogeneous sets, the phonological overlap of responses ranged from
the first segment (*suiker, sofa, sable, sinas, serie*) to an overlap of up
to the first three segments (*komijn, komiek, komeet*). Heterogeneous
sets were created by regrouping the prompt response pairs into new
sets that lacked any shared phonological property among responses.
The time between the onset of the prompt (the implicit prime) and
the speech onset, i.e. the voice onset latency, was measured. The prediction was that speakers prepare for the segments that are shared
between the items within the homogeneous response sets in advance,
i.e. before the prompt appears on the computer screen. Faster voice
onset latencies for the homogeneous sets compared to heterogeneous
sets can be interpreted as the expected *preparation* effect.

Meyer (1990, 1991) reported such an effect only when the response
words in the homogeneous sets shared one or more word-initial segments; no effect was found for shared word-*final* segments, indicating
that phonological encoding is a serial process that proceeds from the
beginning to the end of a lexical item. Furthermore and more importantly, the preparation effect was found to increase with the number
of shared segments, regardless of the segments' syllabic affiliation. In
other words, analogous to the reported syllable priming studies, it
seems that the number of shared segments leads to an increased effect
size and not the syllabic congruency. However, in her 1991 study,
Meyer reported equivalent preparation effects for sets with open initial
syllables (CV) that share only two initial segments and sets with closed
syllables (CVC) that shared three initial segments. Against the background of the segmental length effect, this result is surprising because
a larger preparation effect would be predicted for the CVC sets since

Table 1   Examples for a constant and a variable set within the
odd-man-out version of the implicit priming paradigm

Constant sets	Variable sets
spui.en, CCVV [to drain]	*spoe*.len, CCVV [to rinse]
spui.de, CCVV [drained]	***spoel***.de, CCVVC [rinsed]
spui.er, CCVV [person who drains]	*spoe*.ler, CCVV [person who rinses]
spui.end, CCVV [draining]	*spoe*.lend, CCVV [rinsing]

they share one segment more. This finding suggests the possibility of syllabic effects that are independent of segmental length.

Cholin, Schiller, and Levelt (2004) used an odd-man out variant of the implicit priming paradigm (Janssen, Roelofs and Levelt 2002) to investigate whether speakers would not only benefit from implicit knowledge about overlapping segments but also from a shared syllable structure. Similar to the design in the classic implicit priming paradigm, in the modified version, participants learn sets of responses in which the members share the initial segments and the CV structure of the first syllable (the so-called *constant* sets) or only the initial segments but not the CV structure of the first syllable (the so-called *variable* sets), see Table 1 for examples of both sets.

The one item with the deviant syllable structure serves as the odd-man-out in the variable sets (see the shaded cell in Table 1). The underlying hypothesis of this study was that, under the assumption that the syllable is a relevant unit in speech production, speakers not only need knowledge about the initial segments but also information about the current syllabic structure in order to successfully prepare for an utterance. If knowledge about the syllable structure is necessary for advanced planning, a larger preparation effect is expected for constant sets, since speakers can plan the entire first syllable even before the prompt is presented. In contrast, in variable sets, speakers can only prepare the segmental content but not for the first syllable since information about the current syllable structure is not given prior to prompt presentation. Crucially, the odd-man-out with the deviant syllable structure is expected to spoil the preparation effect for the entire set, i.e. even when the odd-man-out items are removed from the analysis of reaction times, the preparation effect for the remaining responses in the variable sets should (also) be reduced (see Cholin, Schiller and Levelt 2004 for the details of the statistical analyses).

Two experiments were designed with constant items that had initial syllables with a CVV structure (Exp. 1, the structure of the first syllables of the odd-man-out items was CVVC) or CCVV (Exp. 2, the structure of the first syllables of the odd-man-out items was CCVVC).

The results of the two studies confirmed the predictions: significantly larger preparation effects for constant than for variable sets were found. Control studies showed that variable sets also yielded a preparation effect in comparison to a baseline condition where no phonological property was shared between members in a response set. Thus, responses in variable sets can also be prepared for, although to a lesser extent; this graded preparation effect for variable sets suggests that preparation based on shared segments alone is less efficient than preparation based on segmental and syllabic structure. Against the background of the absence of a syllable-congruency effect, the larger preparation effect for constant sets can be interpreted as evidence for the emergence of syllables during online syllabification.

The question of whether or not preparation of first syllables in constant sets includes access to the mental syllabary was the subject of another study and will be further discussed in the remainder of this chapter (see section 2.1.2). In the following, a series of experiments will be presented that investigate syllable-frequency effects. Frequency effects provide strong evidence for stored units since only holistically represented units are expected to exhibit frequency effects. Studies investigating effects of word frequency found that high-frequency words are reliably produced faster than low-frequency words. These findings were interpreted as reflecting faster retrieval times for high-frequency words (e.g. Jescheniak and Levelt 1994, Oldfield and Wingfield 1965). Hence, effects of syllable frequency would provide strong evidence for the notion of a mental syllabary that stores entire syllables. The investigation of syllable-frequency effects therefore seems to be a promising endeavor in the search for evidence for stored syllabic units.

2   Syllable Frequency Experiments

Levelt and Wheeldon (1994) started the search for stored syllabic units by means of syllable-frequency effects in speech production. They investigated naming latencies for Dutch words consisting of high-versus low-frequency syllables while controlling for word-frequency.

Their finding of a significant syllable-frequency effect seemed to support the notion of the mental syllabary, where syllables are stored separately from words. However, in an attempt to replicate these findings, Levelt and Meyer (reported in Hendriks and McQueen 1996) ran an experiment in which a large number of possible confounding factors were controlled for and did not find a syllable or a phoneme frequency effect. But although the Levelt and Wheeldon study had some drawbacks, it gave a clear outline of the mental syllabary and made clear prediction about retrieval procedures of syllables from the syllabary. One of those predictions was that an effect for second syllables in disyllabic words was expected but not for first syllables because "the bulk of the syllable-frequency effect is due to the word-final syllable" (Levelt and Wheeldon 1994, 260). This argument assumes that speakers start articulation only if all syllables belonging to one (phonological) word are ready to be executed. Their finding of a significant syllable-frequency effect for the second syllable was interpreted in favor of this assumption and, more generally, for the notion of a mental syllabary.

Cholin, Levelt and Schiller (2006) and Cholin, Dell and Levelt (in press) used a symbol-position association learning task and contrasted the production of high- and low-frequency syllables in mono- and disyllabic pseudo-words in Dutch and English. Dutch and English are interesting candidates for the investigation of syllable-frequency effects: both languages belong to Germanic (stress-timed) languages that have a stress-based rhythm and might be less prone to use syllables as their primary segmentation units (Vroomen and de Gelder 1994) compared to Romance languages that use syllables as their primary rhythmic units (Abercrombie 1967, for psycholinguistic evidence see Cutler 1997, Cutler, Mehler, Norris and Segui 1986, for a critical, cross-linguistic review see Cutler, McQueen, Norris and Somejuan 2001). Furthermore, the comparison of Dutch and English is interesting because Dutch has relatively transparent syllable boundaries, whereas English has relatively fuzzy syllable boundaries; thus, it might be even more difficult to identify (separate) syllable units in English than in Dutch. Whereas Zwitserlood, Schriefers, Lahiri and van Donselaar (1993) found evidence that Dutch speakers use syllables as segmentation units, to date, there is no such effect in English (Cutler, Mehler, Norris and Segui 1986, 1992) though it seems clear that the syllable plays a role in the phonology of English (e.g. Hooper 1972, Selkirk 1992) and a number of studies actually suggest that syllable units are accessible to subjects' intuitions in meta-linguistic games (Derwing 1992, Treiman 1983, 1984, Treiman and Danis 1988).

The material that was used to investigate effects of syllable frequency on production latencies in English and Dutch was selected following the exact same procedures aiming for a maximal comparability between the two languages, as will be described in the next section.

2.1 *Syllable-Frequency Effect in Mono-Syllabic Pseudo-Words in Dutch and English*

Syllable frequency counts were obtained from the computer database CELEX (CEntre for LEXical Information; Baayen, Piepenbrock and Gulikers 1995) which has a Dutch lexicon based on 42 million word tokens, and an English lexicon based on 17.9 million word tokens. Syllable frequency was counted for phonetic syllables in both languages.[2] The phonetic script differentiates the reduced vowel schwa from full vowel forms, giving approximately 12,000 individual syllable types per language.

For the Dutch syllable frequency experiments, the experimental high- and low-frequency items should differ only in their syllable frequency. Therefore, it was crucial to construct an experimental item set that was controlled for number of phonemes, phoneme frequency, CV structure and bigram/biphone frequency and transitional probabilities. To control for all of these factors, only CVC syllables that allowed for specific combinations were considered. Quartets of four CVC-syllables, two of high- and two of low-frequency, were selected sharing the same nucleus (e.g. /ʏ/), two different onsets (e.g. /b/ and /l/), and two different offset (e.g. /r/ and /x/). The two syllables sharing the same onset were of different frequencies (high vs. low) such as /bʏr/ (high-frequency) and /bʏx/ (low-frequency). The same holds for the two syllables sharing the same offset, such as /lʏx/ (high-frequency) and /lʏr/ (low-frequency). The English material was constructed in the exact same way (the onset, e.g. /zɪ/ appeared once in a high-frequency syllable /zɪz/ as well as in a low-frequency syllable /zɪn/. The rhyme of those syllable /ɪz/ and /ɪn/, respectively, appeared in a high- and in a low-frequency syllable: /gɪn/ (high-frequency) and

---

[2] The phonetic syllable corpus was derived from a morphological corpus that included inflections and derivations such as *ro.ses* and *pro.tect.ted.*

Table 2   Example for experimental quartets consisting of two high- and
            two low-frequency syllables in Dutch and in English

| Dutch | | English | |
high-frequency	low-frequency	high-frequency	low-frequency
bʏr	bʏx	zɪz	zɪn
lʏx	lʏr	gɪn	gɪz

/gɪz/ (low-frequency), see Table 2 for a depiction of a syllabic quartet
in Dutch and in English.

By this specific grouping of four syllables into one quartet, potential
confounds were carefully controlled for. In total, eight of those syllabic quartets were constructed for each language to serve as the basic
material set.

Two syllables from two different syllable quartets were paired to
form one experimental pair. Only items of the same frequency, i.e.
either high- or low-frequency items, were combined to build one item
pair. Care was taken that there was no segmental overlap within the
frequency-homogeneous pairs (which implied that only items from different quartets could build a pair). The pairing of two syllables resulted
in 16 different pairs, that is, 8 high- and 8 low-frequency pairs. Identical onsets were always presented in analogous high- and low-frequency
pairs (e.g. high-frequency: *fæk—nɪʃ*; low-frequency: *fæl—nɪd*).

A symbol-position association learning task was used to contrast the
production latencies for high- and low-frequency syllables. The participants' task was to respond as fast as possible to one of two visually
presented production cues that had previously been associated with
the respective target-syllables (or disyllables) of one pair. The experiment consisted of alternating learning, practice and test phases. In
learning phases, participants were presented with a symbol on one
of two potential positions (the left or right position on a computer
screen) and were simultaneously presented with the to-be-associated
word via headphones (Acoustic versions of the syllables were spoken
by a female native speaker of Dutch and (American) English, respectively). There was no difference in duration between high-frequency
and low-frequency items (*ts* < 1)). In practice phases, participants
had to demonstrate that they knew which target was associated with
which screen side by pressing the spatially corresponding button on
a response box after they heard the corresponding sound file. In the
test phase, the same symbol was shown on one of the two positions

Table 3   Mean voice onset latencies and difference scores (in ms) for high-
and low-frequency monosyllabic pseudo-words in Dutch and English

Frequency	Dutch M	English M
High	436	464
Low	445	469
Difference scores	−9**	−5*

Note: significance is indicated by superscripts * = $p < .05$; ** = $p < .01$

on the screen to prompt the previously associated target utterance.
The auditory presentation of the target in the practice phase ensured
that potential confounds stemming from orthographic factors could
be excluded (for further details on the design and the procedure, see
Cholin, Schiller and Levelt 2006).

The experiments with monosyllabic pseudo-words showed significant syllable-frequency effects for Dutch and English. High-frequency
syllables are produced faster than low-frequency syllables in both languages. As potential confounds were carefully controlled for, those
effects can be interpreted as small but significant syllable-frequency
effects, see Table 3 for means and difference scores.

As already pointed out, syllable-frequency effects are expected to
be found only for stored units. Thus, these results clearly support the
notion of a mental syllabary. The rather small effects are in line with
other small but reliable syllable-frequency effects reported independently (12–19 ms, Levelt and Wheeldon 1994; Spanish: 10–14 ms, Carreiras and Perea 2004).

In English, Croot and Rastle (2004) also investigated effects of syllable frequency in a series of experiments. They compared naming latencies, durational length, and spectral measurements of coarticulation
for high-frequency syllables and novel syllables. The results revealed
a difference of 5 ms in naming latencies in the predicted direction
which did not reach statistical significance. Also, the analysis of the
spectral correlates of coarticulation showed stronger coarticulatory
effects for high-frequency syllables than for novel syllables. Croot and
Rastle (with regard to the Dutch results by Cholin, Levelt and Schiller 2006) hypothesize that the lack of a significant syllable-frequency
effect in their study might be due to a lack of power. While in the studies of Cholin and colleagues (Cholin, Levelt and Schiller 2006, Cholin,
Dell and Levelt in press) eight repetitions per syllable were collected,

only one production per syllable was measured in the other study (see Croot and Rastle 2004 for a discussion of the different materials and paradigms).

Taken together, the syllable-frequency effects in Dutch as well as in English suggest that syllables, independent of the transparency of the syllables in a given language, are stored as entire units.

2.1.2   *Where Can the Mental Syllabary be Located?*
Two recent studies that specifically asked where syllable-frequency effects can be located, found evidence for the assumption that syllable-frequency effects are independent of word frequency and suggest that syllables are retrieved at a post-lexical encoding level (Cholin and Levelt 2009, Laganaro and Alario 2006). Using an implicit priming technique, Cholin and Levelt (2009) compared high- and low-frequency syllable productions contrasting homogeneous blocks consisting of items with the same initial syllable with heterogeneous blocks consisting of words with different initial syllables. If advanced preparation proceeds beyond phonological planning, thus, including the retrieval of stored syllables, the preparation effect (i.e. the time difference between the heterogeneous and the homogeneous blocks) should differ for high- and low-frequency syllable items. Results showed that the preparation allowed by homogeneous blocks led to a greater facilitation for low-frequency than for high frequency syllables. It thus seems that speakers, if provided with all relevant information, can proceed with their production preparation of the first syllable through all stages of word form encoding, including syllabary access. Contrary to the priming effects reviewed above, the effects obtained in the implicit priming paradigm are considered to be also sensitive to phonetic manipulations. In the light of the failure to find any syllabic effects with the standard priming paradigm, the obtained preparation effect for syllables can be located at a post-lexical phonetic level.

Laganaro and Alario (2006) come to a similar conclusion. They found a syllable-frequency effect in a delayed naming task only when the delay was filled with an articulatory suppression task that prevented speakers from preparing the target utterances. They proposed to locate the syllable-frequency effect at the level of phonetic encoding, arguing that the interfering task disrupts phonetic but not phonological encoding. Taken together, both of these studies seem to suggest that the mental syllabary is located at a post-lexical phonetic level.

2.2   Syllable-Frequency Effects in Multi-Syllabic Utterances

In a series of subsequent experiments, it was tested whether syllables as part of disyllabic words will be sensitive to frequency effects. To this end, Cholin and colleagues (Cholin, Levelt and Schiller 2006, Cholin, Dell and Levelt in press) investigated high- and low-frequency syllables as first and second syllables in disyllabic pseudo-words in Dutch and English. This examination might reveal insights into the temporal coordination of how adjacent syllables are retrieved and integrated into multi-syllabic utterances. As already mentioned, Levelt and Wheeldon (1994) made specific predictions concerning potential frequency effects of the first versus the second syllable. They tested Dutch disyllabic pseudo-words and found that the second syllables were sensitive to frequency manipulations and argued that this result reflects an underlying principle, namely that "[...] the speaker cannot or will not begin to articulate the word before its phonetic encoding is complete." (Levelt and Wheeldon 1994, 254). In other words, even if the first syllable's motor program has been retrieved before phonetic encoding of the second syllable has been completed, articulation will wait until both syllabic programs of the disyllabic target word are available in the output buffer to be executed as a whole. As a consequence, a potential frequency effect of the first syllable will not become apparent.

However, several studies have shown that speakers in fact start articulation with the first available syllable and do not necessarily wait until all syllables of a multisyllabic word are ready to be executed (e.g. Bachoud-Lévi, Dupoux, Cohen and Mehler 1998, Carreiras and Perea 2004, Meyer, Roelofs and Levelt 2003, Schriefers and Teruel 1999). Thus, in the next experiments, syllable-frequency effects in disyllabic pseudo-words were investigated to shed light onto the question whether the first and/or the second syllable would be sensitive to frequency effects.

3   Disyllabic Dutch and English Pseudo-Words with the Frequency-Manipulation on the First and the second Syllable

Disyllabic Dutch and English pseudo-words were used to investigate effects of syllable frequency. The same CVC-syllables from the mono-syllabic pseudo-word experiment described above were used to construct disyllabic pseudo-words by combining them with eight high-frequency CV-syllables that formed either the first or the second syllables, respectively (e.g. /gɪn.rə/ versus /rə.gɪn/). One high-frequency syllable was always assigned to all four members of one quartet in order to guarantee the comparability between the high- and low-frequency members of each quartet (see Table 4 for examples). The eight high-frequency syllables (e.g. /rə/) that were used to construct the first and second syllables in the disyllabic pseudo-words were among the first percentile of the most high-frequency Dutch and English syllables. These very high-frequency syllables are most likely to be stored within the syllabary and their retrieval should therefore be fast and least error-prone. Moreover, by always appending the same CV syllable to all four members of one quartet, the transition from the first to the second syllable within the disyllabic pseudo-words is controlled for; that is the frequency of the bigrams/biphones is the same for high- and low-frequency syllables within one quartet, within and across both experiments.

All of the resulting pseudo-words were phonotactically possible strings of Dutch or English, respectively, but none of those words constituted existing Dutch or English words. See Table 4 for an example of the materials.

The disyllabic pseudo-words were recorded with stress on the manipulated syllable. It has been suggested that articulatory routines for stressed and unstressed syllables are independently represented in the repository (Crompton 1981, Levelt 1989). Thus, in order to keep the basic syllable material between the experiments as consistent as possible, it was opted to always have the main stress on the manipulated

Table 4   Examples for disyllabic Dutch and English pseudo-words with the frequency-manipulation on the first syllable and the second syllable

language	Dutch				English			
frequency	high	low	high	low	high	low	high	low
disyllabic pseudo-words with high- and low-frequency first syllables	bʏr.ko	bʏx.ko	lʏx.ko	lʏr.ko	gɪn.rə	gɪz.rə	zɪz.rə	zɪn.rə
disyllabic pseudo-words with high- and low-frequency second syllables	ko.bʏr	ko.bʏx	ko.lʏx	ko.lʏr	rə.gɪn	rə.gɪz	rə.zɪz	rə.zɪn

Table 5   Mean voice onset latencies and difference scores (in ms) for disyllabic pseudo-words with the frequency-manipulation on the first and the second syllable in Dutch and English

| Frequency | Dutch | | English | |
	first syllables manipulated M	second syllables manipulated M	first syllables manipulated M	second syllables manipulated M
High	417	435	465	500
Low	427	435	475	514
Difference scores	−10**	0	−10**	−14**

Note: significance is indicated by superscripts * = $p < .05$; ** = $p < .01$

syllable. The inter-experimental comparability (within as well as between the languages) should thereby be guaranteed.

The results for disyllabic Dutch and English pseudo-words with frequency-manipulated first syllables again showed significant effects in both languages: disyllabic pseudo-words with high-frequency *first* syllables were on average produced 10 ms faster than targets with low-frequency syllables. Thus, these experiments replicate the results of the experiments with monosyllabic pseudo-words and also provide support for the notion of a mental syllabary. By looking at the experiments with Dutch and English disyllabic pseudo-words having the frequency-manipulation on the *second* syllable, an interesting difference between the two languages becomes evident: whereas there was no syllable-frequency effect for Dutch, there was a significant syllable-frequency effect for the English experiment, see Table 5 for means and difference scores.

Let us first consider the Dutch results. The finding of significant syllable-frequency effects for disyllabic Dutch pseudo-words with high- and low-frequency *first* syllables speaks against the prediction that speakers use a fixed planning scope, i.e. that speakers wait with articulation initiation until all phonetically encoded syllables belonging to one (phonological) word are collected. Under consideration of the null result with Dutch disyllabic pseudo-words with frequency-manipulated *second* syllables, Cholin, Levelt and Schiller (2006) concluded, quite to the contrary, that speakers are in fact flexible to start articulation of the first syllable while the second syllable of the disyllabic word is still under construction. Since a significant syllable-frequency effect for Dutch mono-syllabic pseudo-words and disyllabic pseudo-words with high- and low-frequency first syllables was found, it seems rather unlikely that the difference between our data (i.e. a null-effect for the second syllable) and that of Levelt and Wheeldon (1994) (a significant effect for the second syllable) could be attributed to a difference in the material set. In Levelt and Wheeldon's experiments, participants had to learn and reproduce four existing Dutch words within one set, whereas participants in the Cholin et al. experiments had to memorize only pairs of two items. Even though it might be easier to learn existing words, the higher number of words also leads to an increased memory load which might be reflected in the much slower overall speed (i.e. more than 200 ms longer reaction times in the 4-item context). The higher speed in the two-item set design might have led participants to generally apply a faster response criterion. Several studies suggest that participants can adopt different time criteria for when to respond, contingent on task difficulty and speed (Lupker, Brown and Colombo 1997, Monsell et al 1992, Taylor and Lupker 2001). The fact that the two-item sets consisted of pseudo-words, whereas the four-item sets consisted of existing words might have added to this effect in the following way: Speakers may be more likely to collect all syllables of an *existing* word before articulation initiation because they prefer to articulate the single constituents of a word as a whole, i.e. apply a larger planning scope. This might be less important for the constituents of a pseudo-word in which "belonging-together" is considered less important. Hence, in pseudo-words, constituents might be more likely to be broken up and articulated separately. This assumption is supported by findings for Spanish pseudo-words that showed an effect for first but not for the second syllables in disyllabic targets (Carreiras and Perea 2004).

However, there are also studies using *existing words* that suggest that speakers can start articulation before all of the word's components are phonetically encoded (Bachoud-Lévi et al. 1998, Meyer, Roelofs and Levelt 2003, Schriefers and Teruel 1999, see also Meyer et al 2007). These findings speaks against the assumption that speakers generally "wait" with articulation until all components of a polysyllabic word are phonetically encoded, as proposed by Levelt and Wheeldon (1994). It should be noted though that Levelt and Wheeldon never explicitly tested frequency-manipulated first syllables. Their finding of a second syllable-frequency effect does not rule out a potential effect for the first syllable of a disyllabic word. Under a serial account of speech planning, the frequency of both syllables could have an impact on production times. Beyond that, the moment in time when articulation is initiated seems to not only depend on the availability of the first encoded production unit, but also on the corresponding planning scope.

Before returning to the discussion of the coordination of planning scopes and the initiation of articulation, let us first consider the English results: why was there a significant syllable-frequency effect for English second syllables that was not observed for Dutch second syllables? On the basis of the significant effects for monosyllabic pseudo-words and for first syllables in disyllabic pseudo-words in both languages, it was concluded that syllables are stored articulation units, regardless of the transparency of the language's syllables. Syllabic transparency, however, may have an influence on the coordination of incremental planning and articulatory units. Cholin, Dell and Levelt (in press) interpreted the divergent results for second syllables in this light: the presence of an effect in English and the absence of this effect in Dutch might indicate that English operates with a larger planning scope for articulation than Dutch. It was hypothesized that Dutch uses syllables as a minimal planning scope, whereas English might use a slightly larger unit for its planning scope for articulation: *metrical feet*. But before it was concluded that these differences were in fact language-specific and not due to differences between the Dutch and the English material set, a possible confound needed to be addressed. By comparing the material sets that were used for the Dutch and English experiments with frequency-manipulated second syllables, a consistent difference between the *first* syllables that were used in the two material sets was found that might have been responsible for the different results. In Dutch, only open CV syllables served as first syllables, such as /koː.bʏr/; whereas in English, all CV syllables ended in schwa, such as /rə.gɪn/. Recall that the (auditorily presented) pseudo-words were always stressed on the manipulated syllable: that is, the disyllabic targets with high- and low-frequency second syllables were presented as iambic words (as in /koː.ˈbʏr/ and /rə.ˈgɪn/) and thus comply with the non-default stress pattern in Dutch and English (Dutch and English are languages with a predominant trochaic stress pattern, see Booij, 1995; Trommelen and Zonneveld, 1989; Hammond, 1999; Hayes, 1982). The fact that all targets were pseudo-words that, therefore, cannot rely on any stored (irregular) stress pattern, might have led speakers to fall back on the default stress pattern. If speakers in fact applied a trochaic stress pattern, the Dutch speakers were more likely to find the right base to do so: as already pointed out, the Dutch first syllables consisted of open CV syllables (e.g. /koː/ in /ˈkoː.bʏr/) that receive a long pronunciation and were more likely to attract stress. As such, the speech planning system might have regarded the stressed syllables as sufficient 'chunks' for articulation themselves and hence initiated articulation as soon as this first syllables was phonetically encoded. This might have been different for the English pseudo-words: here, all of the first syllables ended in schwa (e.g. /rə./ in /rə.ˈgɪn/); schwa mostly occurs in unstressed syllables and schwa is often reduced and deleted. Thus, even though English speakers might also tend to fall back on a trochaic stress pattern in producing the disyllabic pseudo-words, the English first syllables are highly unlikely to receive stress.

On the contrary, the schwa syllables might have been even more reduced and hence attached to the second syllables, thereby unlikely to constitute separate units for articulation. In other words, participants in the English experiments might have opted to actually comply with the presented iambic pattern and executed the first syllables (e.g. rə.) only after the corresponding second syllable was also available for articulation. In this scenario, the frequency of the second syllable should (also) influence production times and not only the first syllable, as was argued in the explanation of the Dutch results.

Of course, this reasoning is speculative, but it cannot be excluded that the difference described between the Dutch and the English material set led to the divergent results. To test this hypothesis, a further experiment with English disyllabic pseudo-words bearing the frequency manipulation on the second syllable was carried out. In this experiment, first syllables were chosen that were more comparable to the former Dutch syllables: open syllables with diphthongs and long vowels see Table 6.

Following the same procedure as in the previous experiments, the same CV (CVV, respectively) syllables were combined with each member of one quartet to guarantee the comparability between all four items and to control for the transitions between first and second

Table 6   Examples for disyllabic English pseudo-words with the frequency-manipulation on the second syllable

high-frequency	low-frequency	high-frequency	low-frequency
rɔɪ.gɪn	rɔɪ.gɪz	rɔɪ.zɪz	rɔɪ.zɪn
kɑː.nɪʃ	kɑː.nɪd	kɑː.pɪd	kɑː.pɪʃ

syllables within quartets. Long vowels and diphthongs occupy two slots in the syllable structure (e.g. Clements and Keyser 1983) as do vowels in open syllables in Dutch (Booij 1995). The pseudo-words in the current experiment were again presented with stress on the manipulated, second syllable. The English pseudo-words are maximally comparable to the Dutch pseudo-words (with open first CV syllables and stress on the second syllable). It was tested whether the English participants would now opt to start articulation as soon as the first syllable was available, or whether execution of the first syllables was still delayed until the second syllable was also available for articulation, in which case syllable-frequency effects are expected.

The results point towards this latter scenario: Disyllabic pseudo-words with high-frequency second syllables were produced significantly faster compared to pseudo-words with low-frequency second syllables, see Table 7.

These findings might indicate that English speakers in fact use a larger planning scope for articulation than Dutch speakers: while it was speculated that the material set for the first study, with the frequency-manipulation on the second syllable, possibly did not provide the right base for a planning scope of syllabic size, the material set of the second experiment with the same manipulation was "optimized" in the sense that the first syllables with diphthongs and long vowels are stressable units (as the first syllables in Dutch) and therefore might have been better candidates to serve as syllabic planning units. Nevertheless, English speakers seemingly opted to start articulation only after both consecutive syllables were available because the second syllable did influence production times.

It can thus be further speculated that the syllabic transparency of a given language is yet another factor that determines the planning

Table 7   Mean voice onset latencies and difference score (in ms) for English disyllabic pseudo-words with the frequency-manipulation on the second syllable

Frequency	M
High	432
Low	438
Difference score	−6*

Note: significance is indicated by superscripts * = $p < .05$; ** = $p < .01$

scope for articulation. It cannot be excluded that there are circumstances under which English speakers would start articulation upon availability of the first syllable and Dutch speakers would opt to collect subsequent syllables before articulation is initiated. But, with regard to English, even under experimental conditions that explicitly instructed participants to set a maximally speeded response criterion with pseudo-words where linguistic integrity makes no demands, and thus, the premise for "decide on" minimal planning units of syllabic size seems optimal, participants chose to initiate articulation only after the two consecutive syllables of a disyllabic pseudo-word were both phonetically encoded. This finding might allow for the conclusion that English speakers in fact use a larger planning scope for articulation, namely, as Cholin, Dell and Levelt (in press) proposed, *feet* instead of *syllables*. In other words, in English, speakers are likely to start articulation on the basis of the first available foot rather than on the first syllable. Clearly, further research has to investigate whether different languages in fact use different (default) planning scopes for articulation and how different speaking contexts may constrain the scope of planning.

Taken together, the syllable-frequency effects observed in mono- and disyllabic Dutch and English pseudo-words strongly support the notion of the mental syllabary. These findings are in line with effects of syllable frequency in other languages (see above). The comparison of effects in Dutch and English (see Table 8 for a summary of the results) suggests on the one hand that there are stored abstract motor units for syllables in both languages, and on the other hand, that Dutch

Table 8   Summary of the syllable-frequency effects in mono- and disyllabic pseudo-words in Dutch and English

Manipulation	Dutch	English	Dutch	English	Dutch	English	English
	mono syllabic		disyllabic first		disyllabic second		
Frequency	M	M	M	M	M	M	M
High	436	464	417	465	435	500	432
Low	445	469	427	475	435	514	438
Diff. scores	−9**	−5*	−10**	−10**	0	−14**	−6*

Note: significance is indicated by superscripts * = $p < .05$; ** = $p < .01$

and English might be different with respect to the size of the planning scope as a result of differences in stress patterns and in the transparency of syllable boundaries.

4   *Conclusion*

In this chapter, it is argued for the existence of syllables as functionally relevant units in speech production, primarily on the basis of psycholinguistic reaction-time data. The available evidence strongly points towards the conclusion that syllables play a role during later stages of word form encoding and, most likely, in the form of separately stored phonetic units. The findings from a series of priming studies showed that only shared initial segments but not syllables could be pre-activated by congruent versus incongruent syllable primes. Only with very specific manipulations could the emergence of syllables be traced with a version of the implicit priming paradigm. It was therefore argued that phonological syllables are computed from scratch during online syllabification. In a subsequent step, the phonetic syllabic counterparts are accessed in a mental syllabary that contains abstract phonetic syllables or motor programs that facilitate the last planning stages between phonological encoding and articulation. Evidence for the assumption of stored precompiled phonetic syllables or abstract motor programs stem from a number of studies investigating syllable-frequency effects. High-frequency syllables were found to be produced faster than low-frequency syllables. It was discussed that Romance languages might be more prone to have syllables as their primary rhythmic units compared to Germanic languages which have a stress-based rhythm. However, as is evident from the reported syllable-frequency effects in Dutch and English, it seems that syllables are separately stored phonetic units also in both of these languages. Stress pattern and syllabic transparency, as argued, might have an influence on the scope of planning.

References

Abercrombie, David. 1967. *Elements of general phonetics*. Edinburgh: Edinburgh University Press.

Baayen, R. Harald, Richard Piepenbrock and Leon Gulikers. 1995. *The CELEX Lexical Database (Release 2) [CD-ROM]*. Philadelphia, PA: Linguistic Data Consortium, University of Pennsylvania.

Bachoud-Lévi, A.-C., E. Dupoux, L. Cohen and J. Mehler. 1998. Where is the length effect? A cross-linguistic study of speech production. *Journal of Memory and Language* 39: 331–346.

Bagemihl, Bruce. 1995. Language games and related areas. In *The handbook of phonological theory*, edited by John Goldsmith, 697–712. Cambridge, MA: Blackwell.

Baumann, M. 1995. The production of syllables in connected speech. PhD. diss., Nijmegen University.

Berg, Thomas. 1988. *Die Abbildung des Sprachproduktionsprozesses in einem Aktivationsflußmodell. Untersuchungen an englischen und deutschen Versprechern* [The representation of the speech production process in a spreading activation model: Studies of German and English speech errors]. Tübingen: Niemeyer.

Booij, Gert. 1995. *The phonology of Dutch*. Oxford: Clarendon Press.

Brand, Muriele, Arnaud Rey and Ronald Peereman. 2003. Where is the syllable priming effect in visual word recognition? *Journal of Memory and Language* 48: 435–443.

Carreiras, Manuel and Manuel Perea. 2004. Naming pseudowords in Spanish: Effects of syllable frequency in production. *Brain and Language* 90: 393–400.

Chen, Jenn-Yeu, Train-Min Chen and Gary S. Dell. 2002. Word form encoding in Mandarin Chinese as assessed by the implicit priming paradigm. *Journal of Memory and Language* 46: 751–781.

Cholin, Joana, Gary S. Dell and Willem J. M. Levelt. In press. Planning and articulation in incremental word production: Syllable-frequency effects in English. *Journal of Experimental Psychology: Learning, Memory and Cognition*.

Cholin, Joana and Willem J. M. Levelt. 2009. Effects of syllable preparation and syllable frequency in speech production: Further evidence for the retrieval of stored syllables at a post-lexical level. *Language and Cognitive Processes* 24: 662–684.

Cholin, Joana, Willem J. M. Levelt and Niels O. Schiller. 2006. Effects of syllable frequency in speech production. *Cognition* 99: 205–235.

Cholin, Joana, Niels O. Schiller and Willem J.M. Levelt. 2004. The preparation of syllables in speech production. *Journal of Memory and Language* 50: 47–61.

Clements, George N. and Samuel J. Keyser. 1983. *CV phonology: A generative theory of the syllable*. Cambridge, MA: MIT Press.

Costa, Albert and Nuria Sebastián-Gallés. 1998. Abstract phonological structure in language production: Evidence from Spanish. *Journal of Experimental Psychology: Learning, Memory and Cognition* 24: 886–903.

Crompton, Andrew. 1981. Syllables and segments in speech production. *Linguistics* 19: 663–716.

Croot, Karen and Kathleen Rastle. 2004. Is there a syllabary containing stored articulatory plans for speech production in English? *Proceedings of the 10th Australian International Conference on Speech Science and Technology*, Macquarie University, Sydney.

Cutler, Anne. 1997. The syllable's role in the segmentation of stress languages. *Language and Cognitive Processes* 12: 839–845.

Cutler, Anne, James McQueen, Dennis Norris and A. Somejuan. 2001. The roll of the silly ball. In *Language, Brain and Cognitive Development: Essays in honor of Jacques Mehler*, edited by Emmanuel Dupoux, 181–194. Cambridge, MA: MIT Press.

Cutler, Anne, Jacques Mehler, Dennis Norris and Juan Segui. 1986. The syllable's differing role in the segmentation of French and English. *Journal of Memory and Language* 25: 385–400.
——. 1992. Limits on bilinguism. *Cognitive Psychology* 24: 381–410.
Dell, Gary S. 1986. A spreading-activation theory of retrieval in sentence production. *Psychological Review*, 93, 283–321.
——. 1988. The retrieval of phonological forms in production: Tests of predictions from a connectionist model. *Journal of Memory and Language* 27: 124–142.
Derwing, Bruce. 1992. A 'pause-break' task for eliciting syllable boundary judgments from literate and illiterate speakers: preliminary results for five diverse languages. *Language and Speech* 35: 219–235.
Evinck, S. 1997. Production de la parole en français: Investigation des unités impliquées dans l'encodage phonologique des mots [Speech production in French: Investigation of the units implied during the phonological encoding of words]. PhD. diss., Bruxelles University.
Ferrand, Ludovic and Juan Segui. 1998. The syllable's role in speech production: Are syllables chunks, schemas, or both? *Psychonomic Bulletin & Review* 5: 253–258.
Ferrand, Ludovic, Juan Segui and Jonathan Grainger. 1996. Masked priming of word and picture naming: The role of syllable units. *Journal of Memory and Language* 35: 708–723.
Ferrand, Ludovic, Juan Segui and Glyn W. Humphreys. 1997. The syllable's role in word naming. *Memory and Cognition* 25: 458–470.
Fromkin, Victoria. 1971. The non-anomalous nature of anomalous utterances. *Language.* 47: 27–52.
Fromkin, Victoria, ed. 1973. *Speech errors as linguistic evidence.* The Hague: Mouton.
Garrett, Merrill F. 1982. Production of speech: Observations from normal and pathological language use. In *Normality and pathology in cognitive functions*, edited by Andrew W. Ellis, 19–76. London. Academic Press.
Goldstein, Louis and C. A. Fowler. 2003. Articulatory phonology: A phonology for public language use. In *Phonetics and Phonology in Language Comprehension and Production: Differences and Similarities* edited by Niels O. Schiller and Antje S. Meyer, 159–207. Berlin: Mouton de Gruyter.
Hammond, Michael. 1999. *The phonology of English: a prosodic Optimality Theoretic approach.* Oxford: Oxford University Press.
Hayes, Bruce. 1982. Extrametricality and English stress. *Linguistic Inquiry* 13: 227–276.
Hendriks, H. and James McQueen, eds. 1996. *Annual Report 1995.* Max Planck Institute for Psycholinguistics, Nijmegen, The Netherlands.
Hooper, Joan Bybee. 1972. The syllable in phonological theory. *Language* 48: 525–540.
Janssen, Dirk P., Ardi Roelofs and Willem J. M. Levelt. 2002. Inflectional frames in language production. *Language and Cognitive Processes* 17: 209–236.
——. 2004. Stem complexity and inflectional encoding in language production. *Journal of Psycholinguistic Research* 33: 365–381.
Jescheniak, Jörg D. and Willem J. M. Levelt. 1994. Word frequency effects in speech production: Retrieval of syntactic information and of phonological form. *Journal of Experimental Psychology: Learning, Memory, and Cognition* 20: 824–843.
Laganaro, Marina and F-Xavier Alario. 2006. On the locus of the syllable frequency effect in language production. *Journal of Memory and Language* 55: 178–196.
Levelt, Willem J. M. 1989. *Speaking: From intention to articulation.* Cambridge, MA: MIT Press.
Levelt, Willem J. M., Ardi Roelofs and Antje Meyer. 1999. A theory of lexical access in speech production. *Behavioral and Brain Sciences* 22: 1–38.

Levelt, Willem J. M. and Linda Wheeldon. 1994. Do speakers have access to a mental syllabary? *Cognition* 50: 239–269.

Lupker, Stephen J., Patrick Brown and Lucia Colombo. 1997. Strategic control in a naming task: Changing routes or changing deadlines. *Journal of Experimental Psychology: Learning, Memory and Cognition* 23: 570–590.

MacKay, Donald G. 1970. Spoonerisms: The structure of errors in the serial order of speech. *Neuropsychologia* 8: 323–350.

MacNeilage, Peter F. 1998. The frame/content theory of evolution of speech production. *Behavioral and Brain Sciences* 21: 499–546.

Meyer, Antje S. 1990. The time course of phonological encoding in language production: The encoding of successive syllables of a word. *Journal of Memory and Language* 29: 524–545.

——. 1991. The time course of phonological encoding in language production: Phonological encoding inside a syllable. *Journal of Memory and Language* 30: 69–89.

——. 1992. Investigation of phonological encoding through speech error analyses: Achievements, limitations, and alternatives. *Cognition* 42: 181–211.

Meyer, Antje S., Eva Belke, Christine Häcker and Linda Mortensen. 2007. Use of word length information in utterance planning. *Journal of Memory and Language* 57: 210–231.

Meyer, Antje, Ardi Roelofs and Willem J. M. Levelt. Word length effects in object naming: The role of a response criterion. *Journal of Memory and Language* 48: 131–147.

Monsell, Stephen, Karalyn E. Patterson, Andrew Graham, Claire H. Hughes and Robert Milroy. 1992. Lexical and sublexical translation of spelling to sound: Strategic anticipation of lexical status. *Journal of Experimental Psychology: Learning, Memory and Cognition* 18: 452–467.

Nooteboom, Sieb. 1969. The tongue slips into pattern. In *Nomen: Leyden studies in linguistics and phonetics*, edited by A. G. Sciarone, A. J. von Essen and A. A. van Raad, 114–132. The Hague: Mouton.

Oldfield, R. C. and A. Wingfield. 1965. Response latencies in naming objects. *Quarterly Journal of Experimental Psychology* 17: 273–281.

O'Seaghdha, Padraig G., Jen-Yeu Chen and Train-Min Chen. 2010. Proximate units in word production: Phonological encoding begins with syllables in Mandarin Chinese but with segments in English. *Cognition* 115: 282–302.

Roelofs, Ardi. 1997a. Syllabification in speech production: Evaluation of WEAVER. *Language and Cognitive Processes* 12: 657–693.

——. 1997b. The WEAVER model of word form encoding in speech production. *Cognition* 64: 249–284.

Roelofs, Ardi and Antje S. Meyer. 1998. Metrical structure in planning the production of spoken words. *Journal of Experimental Psychology: Learning, Memory and Cognition* 24: 922–939.

Rosenbaum, David A., Albrecht W. Inhoff and Andrew W. Gordon. 1984. Choosing between movement sequences: A hierarchical editor model. *Journal of Experimental Psychology: General* 113: 372–393.

Saltzman, Elliot. 1986. Task dynamic coordination of the speech articulators: A preliminary model. In *Generation and Modulation of Action Patterns*, edited by Herbert Heuer and Christoph Fromm, 129–144. New York: Springer.

Saltzman, Elliot and J. A. Kelso. 1987. Skilled actions: A task-dynamic approach. *Psychological Review* 94: 84–106.

Schiller, Niels O. 1997. The role of the syllable in speech production. Evidence from lexical statistics, metalinguistics, masked priming, and electromagnetic midsagittal articulography. PhD diss., Nijmegen University (MPI series; 2).

——. 1998. The effect of visually masked primes on the naming latencies of words and pictures. *Journal of Memory and Language* 39: 484–507.

———. 1999. Masked syllable priming of English nouns. *Brain and Language* 68: 300–305.

———. 2000. Single word production in English: The role of subsyllabic units during speech production. *Journal of Experimental Psychology: Learning, Memory and Cognition* 26: 512–528.

———. 2004. The onset effect in word naming. *Journal of Memory and Language* 50: 477–490.

Schiller, Niels O. and Albert Costa. 2006. Activation of segments, not syllables, during phonological encoding in speech production. *The Mental Lexicon* 1: 231–250.

Schiller, Niels O., Albert Costa and Angels Colomé. 2002. Phonological encoding of single words: In search of the lost syllable. In *Papers in Laboratory Phonology 7*, edited by Carlos Gussenhoven and Natasha Warner, 35–59. Berlin: Mouton de Gruyter.

Schiller, Niels O., Paula Fikkert and Clara C. Levelt. 2004. Stress priming in picture naming: An SOA study. *Brain and Language* 90: 231–240.

Schiller, Niels O., Antje S. Meyer and Willem J. M. Levelt. 1997. The syllabic structure of spoken words: Evidence form the syllabification of intervocalic consonants. *Language and Speech* 40: 103–140.

Schiller, Niels O., Antje S. Meyer, R. Harald Baayen and Willem J. M. Levelt. 1996. A Comparison of Lexeme and Speech Syllables in Dutch. *Journal of Quantitative Linguistics* 3: 8–28.

Schriefers, Herbert and Encarna Teruel. 1999. Phonological facilitation in the production of two-word utterances. *European Journal of Cognitive Psychology* 11: 17–50.

Selkirk, Elisabeth. 1982. The syllable. In *The structure of phonological representations*, part 2, edited by Harry van der Hulst and Norval Smith, 337–383. Dordrecht: Foris.

Sevald, Christine A., Gary S. Dell and Jennifer S. Cole. 1995. Syllable structure in speech production: Are syllables chunks or schemas? *Journal of Memory and Language* 34: 807–820.

Shattuck-Hufnagel, Stefanie. 1979. Speech errors as evidence for a serial ordering mechanism in sentence production. In *Sentence Processing: Psycholinguistic studies presented to Merrill Garrett*, edited by William E. Cooper and Edward C. T. Walker. Hillsdale, 295–342. N.J.: Lawrence Erlbaum.

———. 1983. Sublexical units and suprasegmental structure in speech production planning. In *The production of speech*, edited by Peter MacNeilage. New York: Springer.

———. 1987. The role of word onset consonants in speech production planning: New evidence from speech error patterns. In *Motor and sensory processing in language*, edited by Eric Keller & Myrna Gopnik, 17–51. Hilllsdale, NJ: Erlbaum.

———. 1992. The role of word structure in segmental serial ordering. *Cognition* 42: 213–59.

Stemberger, Joseph. 1982. The nature of segments in the lexicon: Evidence from speech errors. *Lingua* 56: 235–259.

Taylor, Tamsen E. and Stephen J. Lupker. 2001. Sequential effects in naming: A time-criterion account. *Journal of Experimental Psychology: Learning, Memory and Cognition* 27: 117–138.

Treiman, Rebecca. 1983. The structure of spoken syllables: Evidence from novel word games. *Cognition* 15: 49–74.

———. 1984. On the status of final consonant clusters in English syllables. *Journal of Verbal Learning and Verbal Behavior* 23: 343–356.

Treiman, Rebecca and Catalina Danis. 1988. Syllabification of intervocalic consonants. *Journal of Memory and Language* 27: 87–104.

Trommelen, Mieke and Wim Zonneveld. 1989. *Klemtoon en metrische fonologie* [Stress and metrical phonology]. Muiderberg: Coutinho.

Vousden, Janet, Gordon D. A. Brown and Trevor A. Harley. 2000. Oscillator-based control of the serial ordering of phonology in speech production. *Cognitive Psychology* 41: 101–175.
Vroomen, Jean and Beatrice de Gelder. 1994. Speech segmentation in Dutch: no role for the syllable. In *Third International Conference on Spoken Language Processing (ICSLP 94).* http://www.isca-speech.org/archive/icslp_1994
Zwitserlood, Pienie, Herbert Schriefers, Aditi Lahiri and Wilma van Donselaar. 1993. The role of syllables in the perception of spoken Dutch. *Journal of Experimental Psychology: Learning, Memory and Cognition* 19: 260–271.

CHAPTER TEN

PHONOLOGICAL ENCODING IN HEALTHY AGING: ELECTROPHYSIOLOGICAL EVIDENCE

Yael Neumann, Loraine K. Obler, Hilary Gomes and Valerie Shafer

Research on language production in older adults with unimpaired cognitive abilities suggests that the naming problems associated with advanced age arise in, or just before, the phonological stage. Various theories as to why there are lexical access difficulties have been proposed. The Transmission Deficit Hypothesis (TDH; Burke et al. 1991, James and Burke 2000, MacKay and Burke 1990) is one well-supported theory explaining that breakdowns, particularly with age, are due to a failure in the transmission of available semantic/syntactic information to the phonological system (Abrams, White and Eitel 2003, Burke et al. 1991, Cross and Burke 2004, Heine, Ober and Shenaut 1999, James and Burke 2000, Rastle and Burke 1996, White and Abrams 2002). The TDH proposes that older people are especially prone to word-retrieval problems due to weakening of lexical-phonological connections in memory.

But why are features at the phonological level more vulnerable to retrieval breakdowns than semantic/syntactic features at the conceptual/lexical level? The reasoning is that the phonological level generally has fewer inter-connections (e.g., one phoneme represents one sound), whereas the lexical-semantic system has multiple inter-connections (e.g., many words/concepts linked to a given word) (James and Burke 2000, MacKay and Abrams 1996). Aging weakens the links in the system, in particular, affecting the least innervated links. Factors such as word frequency or recency of use presumably influence the strength of phonological connections within a word and thus retrieval of those elements. Therefore, the lower the frequency of a word and the less recently it has been used, the weaker the connections to its phonological shape and the greater the difficulties in retrieving it.

The purpose of this chapter is to provide a neurolinguistic basis for understanding phonological encoding breakdowns in speech production in older persons using evidence from an electrophysiological study of substages of phonological encoding in healthy aging (Neumann 2007).

Levelt and colleagues (1999) have constructed a model of spoken word recognition that provides the theoretical framework for this research (see also Dell and O'Seaghdha 1992). In this model there are two encoding stages in lexical retrieval. During the first stage, people conceptualize the word they want to say, which activates the semantic and syntactic description of the lexical item referred to as the lemma. During the second stage of encoding, the target lemma is phonologically encoded into a lexeme, which is an abstract representation of the phonological specifications of the lexical item.

There are various substages of phonological encoding according to this model. For example, when encoding the lemma "dresses", first the segmental and metrical frame is created. This involves retrieval of morphemic and phonological codes, such that individual phonemes or 'segments' (e.g. /d/ /r/ /ɛ/ /s/ /ə/ /z/) are ordered and spelled out. As well, the metrical structure or 'frame' of the target word is created which includes the number of syllables and location of stress (e.g. /drɛsəz/ has two syllables and initial syllable stress). The segments are inserted into the lexeme's frame to construct a phonological word frame (e.g. /drɛ́/ /səz/, initial syllable stress). This is known as 'segment-to-frame association'. The final substage is retrieval of the syllabic gestural codes from the mental syllabary, an abstract store of highly-practiced phonetic syllables. These phonetic codes are understood and accomplished by the articulatory apparatus, resulting in articulation, i.e. overt speech.

It is only within the past decade that researchers have begun to use the dynamic measure of real-time activation of event-related potentials (ERPs) and other imaging techniques to detect the temporal encoding of distinct types of word information in speech production (see Indefrey and Levelt 2004 for a meta-analytic review of imaging literature on word production). Most studies have used evoked cortical responses such as the lateralized readiness potential (LRP) and/ or N200 to assess the points in time when different types of lexical information are retrieved for speech production.

The standard task employed is picture-naming, as it is assumed that this task requires the speaker to activate the complete process, both selection and encoding of a specific concept for word-retrieval (Glaser 1992). The LRP indexes response preparation (for example, getting ready to press a button to make a language-related judgment). It is obtained over the motor cortex contralateral to the response hand. The N200 indexes response inhibition (for example, withholding a button-press response for a similar task). It is seen as a large negative peak occurring between 100–300 ms over frontocentral scalp sites (e.g. Gemba and Sasaki 1989, Thorpe, Fize and Marlot 1996).

Van Turennout, Hagoort and Brown (1997) were forerunners in applying the Go/Nogo paradigm with ERP methodology, to test predictions of speech production models. A two-choice Go/Nogo classification task was used to elicit the LRP. In this paradigm, participants were asked to categorize picture names along a semantic-conceptual domain (animate vs. inanimate) and a phonological domain (final phonemes /n/ vs. /r/). The electrophysiological component of interest was the LRP which is detected before or even in the absence of an overt button-press response but only when enough information is available for a decision to be made. This motor-related brain activity is assumed to reflect an upper limit on the moment in time when a Go (press the button) or Nogo (do not press the button) decision, based on either phonological or semantic information, must be available.

Findings of van Turennout, Hagoort and Brown (1997) revealed that the time course of semantic encoding preceded that of phonological encoding (word-final segment information). Furthermore, as part of the same study, in order to uncover the time course for full phonological encoding, they devised another Go/Nogo experiment, with a focus on retrieval of semantic information and word-initial phonological information. Results demonstrated that semantic information was retrieved approximately 40 ms prior to initial-word-position phonological information and approximately 120 ms prior to final-phoneme encoding. When comparing the length of time for the Nogo LRP in word initial vs. word final phoneme conditions, it takes about 80 ms longer to encode word-final than word-initial form for words with an average of 4.5 phonemes.

Van Turennout, Hagoort and Brown (1998) found a similar pattern in LRP responses when they replaced the semantic task with a syntactic task. In this study their focus was on the time course from syntactic encoding (grammatical gender decision: common vs. neuter gender of Dutch nouns) to phonological encoding (initial /b/ vs. /s/; initial /k/ vs. /v/). Findings revealed that the encoding of syntactic information (which started at 370 ms) preceded initial phonological encoding (which started at 410 ms) by 40 ms. Thus, after lemma selection, it takes approximately 40 ms to begin construction of the initial word form in an implicit naming task.

Another group of researchers (Schmitt, Munte and Kutas 2000) replicated the findings of van Turennout, Hagoort and Brown (1997) by using the N200 ERP component, in addition to the previously used LRP, to investigate the time course of semantic (object vs. animal) and phonological encoding (initial phoneme: vowel vs. consonant). Results for both the N200 and LRP corroborated findings from van Turennout, Hagoort and Brown's (1997) study demonstrating that both components reveal that semantic encoding precedes phonological encoding during a picture naming task.

ERP studies thus far have focused on the timing and the order of conceptual, semantic, syntactic and phonological encoding stages. However, there is little research concerning encoding within the substages of the general phonological stage. The exceptions are a series of studies by Schiller and colleagues. Two studies, which we will focus on in this paper, are a study investigating the encoding of 'metrical spellout' (Schiller, Bles and Jansma 2003) and one investigating lexical stress encoding (Schiller 2006).

The Schiller, Bles and Jansma (2003) study explored the time course of 'metrical spellout' (retrieval of stress information and syllabification) using an implicit Go/Nogo naming task with the N200. The decision regarding place of word stress required participants to choose whether the picture name had initial or final stress. The syllabification decision, reflecting the process of placing phonological segments into their correct syllabic frames, required participants to judge whether the first consonant after the vowel was part of the first syllable (e.g. puLpit) or second syllable (e.g. caNoe).

Two early N200 effects reflected speech production components at 250–350 ms and 300–350 ms time intervals, and one late effect was claimed to reflect internal self-monitoring at 400–800 ms. The first early effect for the metric task revealed an unexpected 'reverse N200' such that the Nogo wave was more positive than the Go wave. The syllable task revealed a 'classic N200' with the Nogo wave more negative than the Go wave. The second early effect showed the opposite pattern, namely the metric task demonstrated the 'classic N200' and the syllable task the 'reverse N200'. The authors speculated that the positive N200 might be related to an overlap with the P300 which reflects task difficulty. However, this explanation of the polarity switch and particularly of the positive N200 needs clearer support.

The peak latencies for the metrical and syllable tasks for the first early effect were 255 ms and 269 ms (classical N200), respectively. The second early effect had peak latencies of 335 ms (classical N200) and 329 ms, for the metric and syllable tasks respectively. Thus overall both metric and syllable tasks showed N200 effects during the time window of 250–350 ms, especially at frontal sites. As the time window for these phonological effects occurs within the time frame for phonological encoding as reported by Indefrey and Levelt (2000), namely between 275–400 ms, these early effects support the conclusion that they reflect phonological encoding processes for speech production.

The late effect, however, occurred at a much later time (between 400–800 ms) than that reported by Indefrey and Levelt (2004) and thus cannot be explained as reflecting phonological production processing. Thus, the authors suggested that this late ERP component reflects internal self-monitoring that occurs before a response is made. This is based on a proposal by Wheeldon and Levelt (1995) that phonological information is available to the speaker only after the full phonological word, placed in an articulatory buffer, is monitored for stress and syllable information. This monitoring process is what Schiller, Bles and Jansma (2003) propose is reflected in the identified late effect.

Overall, findings from Schiller, Bles and Jansma revealed that there was little difference in peak latency, i.e. availability of metrical and syllabic information, thus supporting the theory of parallel processing for encoding these phonological substages. Additionally, the finding of a positive N200 effect and a late effect suggests that processing beyond retrieval of the component information itself is occurring and might be related to task performance and/or self-monitoring.

In another study, Schiller (2006) investigated the time course of lexical stress encoding in picture naming. Go/Nogo decisions were made regarding position of stress in bi-syllabic words. Results revealed faster RT and N200 latency to initial vs. final stress decisions. These findings support the view that metrical retrieval occurs in an incremental fashion.

Thus overall, these studies of Schiller and colleagues indicate that metrical encoding of stress and syllabification occurs in parallel fashion and incrementally. This precise detailing of phonological encoding is a valuable strategy for researchers interested in further testing predictions of speech production models.

The Neumann (2007) study aimed at providing refined temporal information regarding the first two phonological substages, segment and syllable retrieval, which are most implicated in lexical access problems. Thus, one question addressed was: *What is the time course for encoding of segmental versus syllabic information? Do these substages proceed in parallel or serial fashion?*

Additionally, previous research on speech production has focused solely on the younger adult, not the older adult, population, yet lexical retrieval has been demonstrated to be quite problematic in aging (Albert, Heller and Milberg 1988, Ardila and Rosselli 1989, Barresi, Nicholas and Connor 2000, Burke et al. 1991, Goulet, Ska and Kahn 1994, MacKay et al. 2002, Ramsay et al. 1999). The Neumann (2007) study investigated how aging influences phonological substages in the word-retrieval process. Hence, the second question addressed was: *How do younger vs. older individuals compare in retrieval of phonological information, namely, segmental and syllabic information?*

The study used event-related potentials (ERPs), specifically, N200, in an implicit naming Go/Nogo paradigm to investigate the timing of substage phonological information. The motivation for this study arose from research investigating tip-of-the-tongue (TOT) states in the non-clinical population (Burke et al. 1991) and from the aphasia literature exploring lexical access problems in the clinical post-stroke population (Dell et al. 1997, Wambaugh, Linebaugh and Doyle 2001). Results from the typical healthy younger and older adult population in Neumann (2007) tested Levelt et al.'s model of phonological substages in naming, indicating how these substages manifest differently at different points across the adult lifespan. As well, they established baseline norms of phonological encoding for word-retrieval in both groups.

The experiment focused on the phonological substages of segmental and syllabic information, as this information is often difficult to fully recall during naming problems associated with advancing age, indicating that access problems are likely to occur at these substages (Brown and McNeill 1966, Brown 1991). Additionally, the task was designed to require access of final, rather than initial, segment information as the TOT phenomenon generally allows access to the initial sounds of a word, but not the final sounds.

The study included 16 healthy younger ($M = 28.3$ years, range 23–40, 7 males) and 16 healthy older ($M = 73.3$ years, range 68–80, 5 males) monolingual adults who were matched for level of education. Exclusion from the study was based on having a history of neurological or psychiatric illness, history of speech-language or learning deficits, less than high-school level of education and knowledge of a second language prior to puberty.

Picture stimuli (digitized bitmap files) were compiled from the colored version of standardized pictures from Snodgrass and Vanderwart (1980). A set of 12 pictures was used for the practice testing performed before each phonological task (10 practice items/task). Experimental stimuli consisted of a different set of 28 pictures. Picture names were classified as follows: seven final /n/ one-syllable words, seven final /n/ two-syllable words, seven final /r/ one-syllable words, and seven final /r/ two-syllable words. Each picture was repeated ten times (once per block) within a given task (segment and syllable) yielding a total of 280 trials per task (140 Go and 140 Nogo responses). Words were repeated to minimize opportunities for naming error in order a) to investigate normal lexical retrieval and b) to decrease the occurrence of error-related ERP negativities (Falkenstein et al. 1995).

Each of the ten blocks of 28 items was pseudo-randomized such that no more than three Go or three Nogo responses occurred consecutively. As well, pictures from the same semantic group (e.g. foods, body parts, animals) were separated by at least two non-semantically related items in order to minimize any semantic priming advantage in retrieval of picture names within the same category.

The 28 picture names were of moderate frequency with an average word frequency of 37 per million (range: 6 to 148 per million, SD=33) (Francis and Kucera 1982) and mean number of phonemes of 3.6 (range: 1 to 6 phonemes, SD=1.2). For the segment task, the pictures were divided into Go vs. Nogo categories based on final phoneme (/n/ or /r/) (see Neumann 2007 for more detailed information and complete lists of practice and experimental stimuli). Pictures were input into an E-prime program for output onto a computer screen.

Each participant performed two phonological tasks. In task 1, participants were instructed to make a segment decision (is the final sound /n/ or /r/) about a picture name, which was the same type of choice used in the van Turennout, Hagoort and Brown (1997) study. Two instruction sets were created and participants were randomly assigned to receive either one of these instructions. Namely, half of the participants were asked to "Go" (i.e. press the button) if the name ended with a /n/ sound and "Nogo" (i.e. don't press the button) if the name ended with a /r/ sound, while the other half of the participants received opposite instructions.

In task 2, participants were instructed to make a syllable-length judgment. Again two instruction sets were created and participants within each age group were randomly assigned to receive either one of these instructions. Half of the participants were asked to "Go" if the name had one-syllable and "Nogo" if the name had two-syllables, while the other half of the participants received opposite instructions.

Participants were fitted with a 65 channel Geodesic Sensor net and then seated in a comfortable chair in a 9'×10' ft electrically shielded booth in front of a computer screen. Test stimuli were presented on the screen and behavioral responses were collected using E-prime software and a Serial Response Box. A trial began with a fixation point (+) in the middle of the computer screen for 0.75 seconds, followed after an additional 0.75 seconds by a picture. The picture was displayed for 1.5 seconds. The inter-trial interval (ITI) was 0.75 seconds, followed by the fixation point again to indicate an upcoming new trial.

The EEG was collected with a bandpass of 0.1 to 41.3 Hz and at a sampling rate of 250 Hz. After recording, the continuous EEG was processed off-line and segmented into epochs with an analysis time of 1500 ms post-stimulus and 100 ms pre-stimulus baseline. ERPs were time-locked to the appearance of the picture. The 100 ms pre-stimulus period included the end of the appearance of the fixation point and the blank screen. Epochs were baseline corrected and then artifact decontamination procedures were employed. Trials with artifact (e.g., eye movements) were discarded and the remaining trials averaged for each category. ERP averages were calculated for both tasks and referenced to the average-reference. The averaged response to the Go stimuli was then subtracted from that of the Nogo stimuli to derive difference waveforms.

The ERP waveforms to the Go and Nogo trials were compared at a midline frontal site (near the hairline) between 200 and 600 ms. The N200 response is seen as greater negativity in this time interval for the Nogo compared to the Go trials. In this experiment the N200 effect was called the N2d (Nogo minus Go waves).

Behavioral findings revealed group differences both in reaction time (RT) and in the type of errors produced. The older group was significantly slower than the younger group on both phonological tasks ($F (1, 60) = 18.718$, $p = < .001$; by 96 ms on the segment task and 106 ms on the syllable task; see Table 1 for means and SDs), as so often happens on cognitive and language tasks with advancing age (e.g. Ardila and Roselli 1989, Falkenstein, Yordanova and Kolev 2006).

Table 1   Mean reaction time (standard deviation) in milliseconds on the
Segment and Syllable tasks

Group	Segment Reaction Time (RT)	Syllable RT
Younger	663 (81)	665 (110)
Older	759 (90)	771 (90)

In terms of errors, the older group had significantly more omission errors (mean = 4.9, SD = 5.3) as compared to the younger group (mean = 1.7, SD = 2.2), (F (1, 60) = 12.182, p = .001), and particularly on the syllable task (F (1, 60) = 3.789, p = .056). However, both groups had comparable commission errors on both tasks. It should be noted, though, that overall, as we expected, both younger and older groups performed with high accuracy on both the segmental and syllabic phonological tasks.

Electrophysiological data revealed a significant N2d in the younger group between 301–450 ms on the segment task, and between 351–450 ms on the syllable task, while in the older group, a significant N2d was found between 401–500 on the segment task, and between 451–500 on the syllable task (Time by Group interaction: F (3, 90) = 6.105, p = .005) (see Figure 1). Thus overall, a between group difference was found on both tasks as the N2d began approximately 100 ms later in the older as compared to the younger group (see Table 2).

Additionally, direct comparisons of tasks for each group showed a significantly later onset of the N2d for the syllable task compared to the segment task for the older group (Task by Time interaction [F (3, 45) = 4.297, p = < .001, η2 = 0.223], but no significant difference in N2d onset for the younger group. Thus, only the older group demonstrated a significant within-group difference in access of segment vs. syllable information, showing earlier access to segmental information.

Latencies for visual evoked potential (VEP) components that reveal stages of early visual encoding of the pictures at the cortical level revealed no differences in the timing of access to the visual information in this study. Thus, the age-related differences in accessing phonological information are not due to visual processing delays.

We concluded that findings from our study support the TDH (Burke et al. 1991, James and Burke 2000) that older adults have greater difficulty than younger adults in phonological retrieval during naming. Results suggest that although both segmental and syllabic retrieval are implicated, the syllabic level may be more affected than the segmental

A) Segment Task:

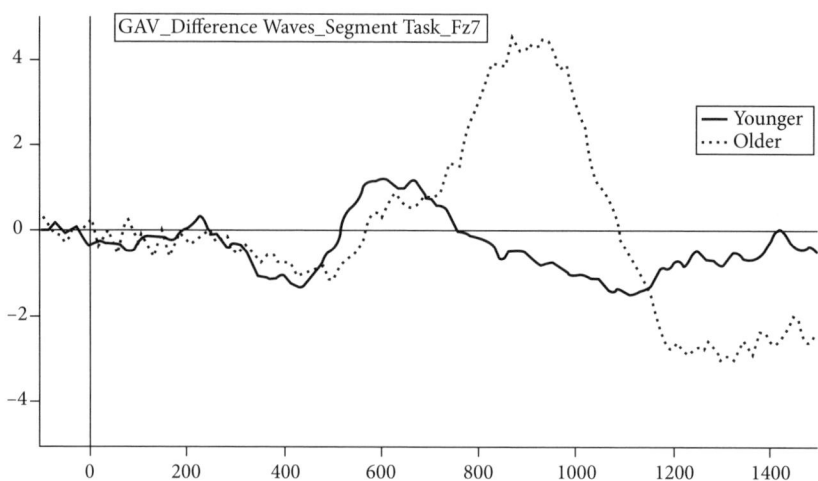

B) Syllable Task

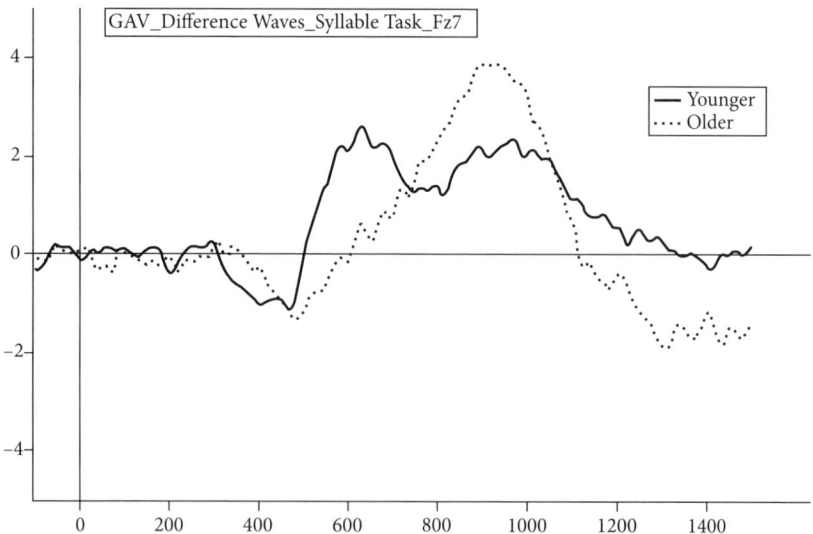

Figure 1   Group comparison of (GAV) N2d waves at frontocentral site
Fz7 on the A) Segment and B) Syllable tasks. Results revealed that older,
as compared to younger, participants had a later N2d peak (negative peak
between 251–600 ms) on both phonological tasks.
x-axis=time (ms); y-axis=amplitude (μV)

Table 2   N2d latency (milliseconds) on the Segment and Syllable tasks for
the two groups

Group	Segment latency	Syllable latency
Younger	301–450	351–450
Older	401–500	451–500

level (F (3, 45) = 4.297, p = .020, η2 = .223). Findings clearly showed later access of syllabic compared to segmental information for the older group, but no significant difference in timing for these two sub-stages for the younger group. Delays in accessing syllabic information found in the older group would explain the increase of word-finding difficulties with age, as greater difficulty in accessing syllabic information halts the process of retrieving the corresponding phonetic syllabic codes from the mental syllabary, which is a necessary precursor to activate speech production (Levelt and Wheeldon 1994). However, since the separate analyses for the two tasks suggest earlier access of segmental than syllabic information for the younger group as well as the older group, replication of these findings will be necessary.

The phonological encoding results from our study further provide insight into the time course of phonological encoding during the normal process of lexical retrieval for speech production. Previous research has proposed that segmental and metrical retrieval occur in parallel fashion incrementally (Levelt, Roelofs and Meyer 1999, Roelofs and Meyer 1998). Additionally, evidence from Schiller, Bles and Jansma (2003) suggests that metrical retrieval, specifically, stress and syllabic information, proceeds in parallel. Data from the younger group in our study appears to support the finding of parallel encoding within phonological encoding, as the very small and non-significant difference in access of segmental and syllabic information suggests that they are independent from each other and roughly parallel.

Data from the older group, however, suggests that retrieval of segmental information precedes that of syllabic information by roughly 100 ms. This does not necessarily indicate that as we age the processes are no longer "parallel" in the sense of being independent, of course. It seems unlikely that the output of the segmental process feeds into the input of the syllabic process, given the findings with the younger group. If there is no additional reason, there is no reason to believe phonological encoding is substantially different for older compared to younger adults. An alternative would be that aging affects access generally. Our findings, however, do suggest that aging affected access to syllabic information more adversely than to segmental information, as seen as an even greater delay.

In conclusion, results of this study indicated later access to segmental and syllabic information on phonological tasks in the older, compared to younger, adults. Furthermore, retrieval of syllabic information was delayed even more than segmental information for the older compared to younger adults. This change in phonological encoding with age is consistent with the TDH.

VEP findings revealed comparable latencies both between and within groups. Thus, the data suggests that phonological encoding delays in the older group, as reflected in later N2d, were not due to early visual encoding delays, but rather to stage-specific phonological encoding deficits, as predicted by the TDH.

Furthermore, N2d results support the parallel view of encoding for the two phonological substages of segment and syllable information in the younger adults. We suspect that encoding of segment and syllable information is probably also parallel in the older adults, although the data showed that syllabic access is affected more by aging than segmental access. This study, however, only provides a relative estimate for when information becomes available in segmental versus syllabic tasks that indirectly tap the word retrieval process. That is, these two tasks are metalinguistic in nature in that they required participants to report (using a button press) the presence of a segment in terms of a sound or syllable-length in terms of a number. Thus, there is an unknown time delay from the point of retrieving the phonological information and checking it to answer the metalinguistic task. A different type of task, e.g. priming with explicit picture naming, will be necessary to more precisely determine the timing of retrieval of phonological information.

The TDH also argues that word retrieval problems are due to weakening of connections at the phonological level. Our analysis does not directly address whether there is evidence from the ERP data of such weakening. ERPs do have the potential to address this question because they reflect firing of populations of neurons involved in information encoding. Different methods of analyses that focus on components other than the N2d and that examine individual trials, e.g. correct vs. incorrect trials, will be necessary to evaluate this aspect of the TDH.

Future studies should investigate the effects of phonological practice in improving word retrieval in aging. Crucially, a study of word-initial phoneme encoding should be carried out, since there is indication that word-initial information can be useful in prompting lexical access (Brown and McNeill 1966, Brown 1991). At the same time, it will also be important to determine to what extent repetition priming facilitated word retrieval in this study, as the pictures used were shown multiple times. A future experiment should consider using different pictures for each experimental block to reduce the influence of a priming advantage. Findings will probably reveal greater delays with age than those evidenced in the Neumann (2007) study.

References

Abrams, Lise, Katherine K. White and Stacy L. Eitel. 2003. Isolating phonological components that increase tip-of-the-tongue resolution. *Memory and Cognition* 31: 1153–1162.
Albert, Marilyn, Hope Heller and William Milberg. 1988. Changes in naming ability with age. *Psychology and Aging* 3: 173–178.
Ardila, Alfredo and Monica Rosselli. 1989. Neuropsychological characteristics of normal aging. *Developmental Neuropsychology* 5: 307–320.
Barresi, Barbara A., Marjorie Nicholas, Lisa T. Connor, Lorain K. Obler and Martin L. Albert. 2000. Semantic degradation and lexical access in age-related naming failures. *Aging, Neuropsychology and Cognition* 7: 169–178.
Brown, Alan S. 1991. A review of the tip-of-the-tongue experience. *Psychological Bulletin* 109: 204–223.
Brown, Roger and David McNeill. 1966. The "tip of the tongue" phenomenon. *Journal of Verbal Learning Behavior* 5: 325–337.
Burke, Deborah M., Donald G. MacKay, Joanna S. Worthley and Elizabeth Wade. 1991. On the tip of the tongue: What causes word-finding failures in young and older adults? *Journal of Memory and Language* 30: 542–579.
Cross, Emily S. and Deborah M. Burke. 2004. Do alternative names block young and older adults' retrieval of proper names? *Brain and Language* 89: 174–181.
Dell, Gary S. and Padraig G. O'Seaghdha. 1992. Stages of lexical access in language production. *Cognition* 42: 287–314.
Dell, Gary S., Myrna F. Schwartz, Nadine Martin, Eleanor M. Saffran and Deborah A. Gagnon. 1997. Lexical access in aphasic and nonaphasic speakers. *Psychological Review* 104: 801–838.
Falkenstein, Michael, N. A. Koshlykova, V. N. Kiroj, Jörg Hoormann and Joachim Hohnsbein. 1995. Later ERP components in visual and auditory Go/Nogo tasks. *Electroencephalography and Clinical Neurophysiology* 96: 36–43.
Falkenstein, Michael, Juliana Yordanova and Vasil Kolev. 2006. Effects of aging on slowing of motor-response generation. *International Journal of Psychophysiology* 59: 22–29.
Francis, W. Nelson and Henry Kucera. 1982. *Frequency analysis of English usage: Lexicon and grammar*. Boston: Houghton Mifflin Company.
Gemba, Hisae and Kazuo Sasaki. 1989. Potential related to no-go reaction of go/no-go hand movement task with color discrimination in human. *Neuroscience Letters* 101: 263–268.
Glaser, Wilhelm R. 1992. Picture naming. *Cognition* 42: 61–105.
Goulet, Pierre, Bernadette Ska and Helen J. Kahn. 1994. Is there a decline in picture naming with advancing age? *Journal of Speech and Hearing Research* 37: 629–644.
Heine, Marilyn K., Beth A. Ober and Gregory K. Shenaut. 1999. Naturally occurring and experimentally induced tip-of-the-tongue experiences in three adult age groups. *Psychology and Aging* 14: 445–457.
Indefrey, Peter and Willem J. M. Levelt. 2004. The spatial and temporal signatures of word production components. *Cognition* 92: 101–144.
James, Lori E. and Deborah M. Burke. 2000. Phonological priming effects on word-retrieval and tip-of-the-tongue experiences in young and older adults. *Journal of Experimental Psychology: Learning, Memory, and Cognition* 26: 1378–1391.
Levelt, Willem J. M., Ardi Roelofs and Antje Meyer. 1999. A theory of lexical access in speech production. *Behavioral and Brain Sciences* 22: 1–38.
Levelt, Willem J. M. and Linda Wheeldon. 1994. Do speakers have access to a mental syllabary? *Cognition* 50: 239–269.

MacKay, Donald G. and Lise Abrams. 1996. Language, memory and aging: Distributed deficits and the structure of new versus old connections. In *Handbook of the psychology of aging, Fourth Edition*, edited by James E. Birren and Klaus Warner Schaie, 251–265. San Diego: Academic Press.

MacKay, Donald G. and Deborah M. Burke. 1990. Cognition and aging: A theory of new learning and the use of old connections. In *Aging and cognition: Knowledge, organization and utilization*, edited by Thomas M. Hess, 213–263. Oxford, England: North-Holland.

MacKay, Anna J., Lisa Tabor Connor, Martin L. Albert and Loraine K. Obler. 2002. Noun and verb retrieval in healthy aging. *Journal of the International Neuropsychological Society* 8: 764–770.

Neumann, Yael. 2007. An electrophysiological investigation of the effects of age on the time course of segmental and syllabic encoding during implicit picture naming in healthy younger and older adults. PhD diss., City University of New York.

Ramsay, Christine, Marjorie Nicholas, Rhonda Au, Loraine K. Obler and Martin L. 1999. Verb naming in normal aging. *Applied Neuropsychology* 6: 57–67.

Rastle, Kathleen G. and Deborah M. Burke. 1996. Priming the tip of the tongue: Effects of prior processing on word retrieval in young and older adults. *Journal of Memory and Language* 35: 585–605.

Roelofs, Ardi and Antje S. Meyer. 1998. Metrical structure in planning the production of spoken words. *Journal of Experimental Psychology: Learning, Memory and Cognition* 24: 922–939.

Schiller, Niels O. 2006. Lexical stress encoding in single word production estimated by event-related brain potentials. *Brain Research* 1112: 201–212.

Schiller, Niels O., Mart Bles and Bernadette M. Jansma. 2003. Tracking the time course of phonological encoding in speech production: An event-related brain potential study. *Cognitive Brain Research* 17: 819–831.

Schmitt, Bernadette M., Thomas F. Munte and Marta Kutas. 2000. Electrophysiological estimates of the time course of semantic and phonological encoding during implicit picture naming. *Psychophysiology* 37: 473–484.

Snodgrass, Joan G. and Mary Vanderwart. 1980. A standardized set of 260 pictures. *Journal of experimental psychology: Human learning and memory* 6: 174–215.

Thorpe, Simon, Denis Fize and Catherine Marlot. 1996. Speed of processing in the human visual system. *Nature* 381: 520–522.

Turennout, Miranda van, Peter Hagoort and Colin M. Brown. 1997. Electrophysiological evidence on the time course of semantic and phonological processes in speech production. *Journal of Experimental Psychology: Learning, Memory, and Cognition* 23: 787–806.

——. 1998. Brain activity during speaking: From syntax to phonology in 40 milliseconds. *Science* 280: 572–574.

Wambaugh, Julie L., Craig W. Linebaugh, Patrick J. Doyle, Aida L. Martinez, Michelene Kalinyak-Fliszar and Kristie A. Spencer. (2001). Effects of two cueing treatments on lexical retrieval in aphasic speakers with different levels of deficit. *Aphasiology* 15: 933–950.

Wheeldon, Linda and Willem J. M. Levelt. 1995. Monitoring the time course of phonological encoding. *Journal of Memory and Language* 34: 311–334.

White, Katherine K. and Lise Abrams. 2002. Does priming specific syllables during tip-of-the-tongue states facilitate word retrieval in older adults? *Psychology and Aging* 17: 226–235.

THE SYLLABLE IN PERFORMANCE:
SPEECH PERCEPTION AND EXPERIMENTAL MANIPULATION

THE IMPACT OF EXPERIMENTAL TASKS ON SYLLABIFICATION JUDGMENTS: A CASE STUDY OF RUSSIAN

Marie-Hélène Côté and Viktor Kharlamov

1 *Introduction*

Different types of evidence are used to define the syllable and predict the location of its boundaries and/or the syllabic affiliation of segments. Phonologists primarily consider evidence gathered from the analysis of segmental and suprasegmental processes and more or less abstract principles such as sonority sequencing and constituent binarity. At the same time, a lot of research has been devoted to complementing these indirect arguments with more direct evidence for syllable structure. Phoneticians have looked for articulatory and/or acoustic/perceptual correlates of the syllable and more psycholinguistically oriented work has developed an array of experimental procedures designed to tap into speakers' judgments on the location of syllable boundaries or the syllabic position of specific segments. Relatively little attention has been paid, however, to how the choice of the experimental task affects the results. Are data obtained with different procedures directly comparable? Are all tasks equally valid for the purpose of identifying syllable boundaries and structure?

The majority of syllabification studies utilize a single procedure or do not discuss the comparability of the results obtained with different tasks. Those that do address this issue generally note that results vary depending on the task the participants were asked to perform. However, since the prevailing assumption is that different procedures should exhibit the same syllabification tendencies, the observed differences are commonly interpreted as artifactual consequences of the tasks and are not elaborated upon. Thus, it remains to be explored to what extent different task-specific factors are likely to interfere with syllabification and obscure the results and how different syllabification protocols vary with respect to their relative sensitivity to the factors that have been shown to influence syllabification judgments, such as the level and profile of sonority of the consonants, the phonotactic constraints operating at word edges, morphological structure, the position of stress, and vowel length and quality.

In order to assess the global comparability of syllabification judgments obtained with different experimental procedures, we investigated the syllabification of intervocalic consonants and clusters in Russian, a language that has received little attention in the experimental literature on syllabification. We tested the same set of stimuli using five different syllabification tasks. The tasks varied along various dimensions, which allowed us to assess the impact of a number of task-specific factors on syllabification judgments. Correlatory analyses show that fewer than half of the possible combinations of two tasks yield positively correlated results. More specifically, those tasks that involve the production of only part of the input form appear to be subject to more interfering factors than the tasks that require participants to consider the entire form. The results of the present study further reveal that some of the factors traditionally argued to affect syllabification in Russian (e.g., stress placement) may not necessarily play any statistically significant role and that the significance of frequency-based factors is not uniform among the five experimental procedures.

2   Background

As a point of departure, let us briefly review the different tasks that have been used in experimental studies of syllabification, with the English form *demon* as an illustration. Note that in most cases the word 'syllable' is not used in the instructions given to the participants.[1]

2.1   Tasks

2.1.1   Pause Insertion
Participants produce test items with the insertion of a short pause between syllables; e.g. 'demon' ⇒ 'de...mon' (Fallows 1981, Schiller

---

[1] The list of tasks presented here is not exhaustive. For instance, Ali et al. (this volume) use a different type of experiment, in which participants are presented with audio-visually incongruent stimuli, e.g. an audio stimulus [map] aligned with a visual stimulus [mat]. This is often perceived as [mak], a process known as audio-visual fusion. The rate of fusion for a given consonant may be a possible indicator of its syllabic affiliation, as fusion appears to be more frequent with coda than with onset consonants. See also Mattys and Melhorn's (2005) syllable migration technique.

et al. 1997, Gillis and Sandra 1998, Barry et al. 1999, Zamuner and Ohala 1999, Ishikawa 2002, McCrary 2004, Goslin and Floccia 2007). The pause insertion task has a perceptual variant, the so-called *pause-break task*, in which participants choose which of several alternative divisions of a word sounds the most natural. The words are presented auditorily with a short pause between syllables; e.g. a) 'de…mon' ~ b) 'dem…on' ⇒ a (Derwing 1992). Both the production and perception variants of this procedure also have written versions. In the *written slash/space-insertion task*, participants indicate where the syllable boundary lies in written words by inserting a slash or writing the word with a space; e.g. 'demon' ⇒ 'de/mon' (McCrary 2004, Redford and Randall 2005). The pause-break task can be administered as a *written/online questionnaire*, i.e. participants choose one of the syllabification options given on a sheet of paper/computer screen; e.g. a) 'de/mon' ~ b) 'dem/on' ~ c) 'dem/mon' ⇒ a (Treiman and Danis 1988, Treiman and Zukowski 1990, Treiman et al. 1992, Eddington et al. 2008).

2.1.2   *Syllable Reversal/Permutation*
Participants produce test items by reversing the order of the syllables; e.g. 'demon' ⇒ 'mon-de' (Treiman and Danis 1988, Treiman 1992, Schiller et al. 1997, Barry et al. 1999, Berg and Niemi 2000, Berg 2001, Content et al. 2001, Cebrian 2002, Bertinetto et al. 2007). Syllable reversal yields a higher rate of errors than any other task and it is often avoided for this reason, especially with children.

2.1.3   *Syllable Reduplication*
Participants produce test items while reduplicating one of the syllables; e.g. 'demon' ⇒ 'dedemon' (first-syllable reduplication) or 'demon' ⇒ 'demonmon' (second-syllable reduplication) (Fallows 1981, Treiman and Zukowski 1990, Treiman 1992, Bertinetto et al. 1994, 2007, Berg and Niemi 2000, Berg 2001).

2.1.4   *Syllable Repetition*
Participants produce only one syllable of the test item; e.g. 'demon' ⇒ 'de' (first-syllable repetition) or 'demon' ⇒ 'mon' (second-syllable repetition) (Fallows 1981, Treiman et al. 1992, Goslin and Frauenfelder 2000, Content et al. 2001, Cebrian 2002, Goslin 2002, Treiman et al. 2002).

2.1.5 *Syllable Substitution*
Participants produce test items by replacing one of the syllables with a specified sequence ([vu] in Bertinetto et al. 1994); e.g. 'demon' ⇒ 'vumon' or 'devu'.

2.1.6 *Fragment Insertion*
Participants produce test items, or only part of them, and insert additional material before or between the syllables; e.g. 'demon' ⇒ 'I say de and then mon' or 'I say de' or 'I say mon' (Content et al. 2001).

2.2 *Factors*

The experimental tasks presented above vary along various dimensions; four differentiating factors will be briefly discussed here, which may result in different tasks yielding different syllabification judgments even with identical stimuli.

2.2.1 *Ambisyllabicity*
An important difference between these tasks is the extent to which they may generate ambisyllabic responses. For example, syllable reversal often yields responses like 'mon-dem', in which the [m] appears to be part of both syllables. Such an option is not possible in the written slash-insertion task, and it is marginal in pause-insertion. This is related to the issue of contingency discussed in Goslin and Frauenfelder (2000, 421). When participants are asked to choose between different options, the ambisyllabic one may or may not be offered. Whether the availability of ambisyllabicity is an advantage or a disadvantage of a task depends in part on the specific hypotheses that are being tested, on one's conception of syllable representation (whether ambisyllabicity is considered a valid concept), and on how ambisyllabic responses should be interpreted (as an indication of ambisyllabicity *per se* or, more indirectly, as an expression of some other kind of variability in syllabification). The experiment described in section 3 uses only tasks that almost completely eliminate the ambisyllabic option, which has the advantage of maximizing the comparability of the results.

2.2.2 *Written vs. Oral Tasks*
Written tasks may be more sensitive to spelling and/or hyphenation rules explicitly taught in school, but spelling has also been shown to influence the results of oral production tasks (Treiman and Danis 1988,

Content et al. 2001, see Goslin and Floccia 2007 for a recent summary of the role of literacy in syllabification). It remains unclear, however, to what extent nonce forms, which have no established orthographic representations, are sensitive to the distinction between oral and written procedures. McCrary (2004) used a combination of real and nonce forms in pause-insertion and slash-insertion tasks and found no significant difference between the results of both tasks.

2.2.3   *Medial vs. Edge Segments*

The tasks described above are designed to investigate the syllabification of intervocalic consonants and clusters. In some tasks, such as syllable reduplication, the relevant consonants appear in medial position (as they do in the stimulus item); in other tasks they end up in initial or final position (e.g. syllable permutation or repetition). The tasks leading to consonants appearing at an edge are expected to be more sensitive to phonotactic constraints operating at word edges, which may result in a possible underestimation of syllabification patterns in which onsets or codas do not correspond to attested word-initial or final sequences.

Let us consider an input such as [matla] 'mattress' presented to a speaker of French, a language in which [tl] is not attested word-initially. The issue is whether [tl] may still be analyzed as a complex onset, which would be suggested by the following possible outputs to different syllabification tasks listed in (1).

(1) Outputs of syllabification tasks suggesting the syllabification [ma.tla]

a.	syllable reversal	[tla-ma]
b.	second-syllable repetition	[tla]
c.	pause insertion	[ma...tla]
d.	second-syllable reduplication	[matla-tla]
e.	first-syllable repetition	[ma]
f.	first-syllable reduplication	[ma-matla]

Since [tl] is not a possible word-initial sequence, outputs such as [tla-ma] and [tla] are expected to be avoided more than the others, in particular [ma] or [ma-matla]. The output of pause insertion [ma...tla] constitutes an intermediate case, where the sequence [tl] is neither clearly internal nor clearly at an edge. As a consequence, second-syllable repetition and syllable permutation are likely to underestimate the wellformedness of [tl] as an (internal) complex onset.

2.2.4   Complete vs. Partial Production

Some production tasks require the participants to produce or consider the entire stimulus (e.g. pause insertion, syllable reversal), whereas others involve only one of the syllables (e.g., syllable reduplication or repetition). This distinction is associated with at least two possible effects. First, single-syllable repetition may be sensitive to word-minimality effects which play no role in complete repetitions. Content et al. (2001) and Cebrian (2002) found that first-syllable repetition of CVCV(C) stimuli yielded substantially more CVC responses than syllable reversal. No explanation has been offered for this tendency, but it is plausible to think that it follows from a constraint on the optimal size of words, which should contain at least two moras (a heavy syllable or more than one syllable).

Second, partial production tasks may be subject to another kind of minimality effect, whereby participants simply repeat the smallest possible sequence. Bertinetto et al. (1994, 2007) found clear effects of this sort in Italian and Polish: their participants showed a tendency to repeat a minimal CV sequence in both first- and second-syllable reduplication of input items CVCCV, rather than CVC for first syllables or CCV for second syllables. When comparing the results of the syllable reduplication and syllable reversal tasks in Polish, Bertinetto et al. (2007) also observed that CVCCV stimuli (e.g. gopli) yielded systematically more CV answers in first-syllable reduplication (go-gopli) than the corresponding CCV-CV answers in syllable reversal (pli-go), and systematically more CV answers in second syllable reduplication (gopli-li) than the corresponding CV-CVC answers in syllable reversal (li-gop).

Exactly the same effect can be seen in Berg and Niemi's (2000) comparison between syllable reversal and reduplication in German, although the authors provide a different interpretation. German participants often reduplicate a form like [jansta] as [ja-jansta], from which Berg and Niemi conclude that [nst] is a possible onset. This complex onset, however, does not surface in syllable reversal, since [jansta] never yields [nsta-ja]. This is interpreted as stemming from a phonotactic constraint banning [nst] sequences word-initially. In other words, syllable reduplication brings out an onset maximization strategy that is prevented from emerging in the reversal task because of independent word-initial phonotactic constraints. An alternative interpretation is that [ja-jansta] answers illustrate a tendency toward minimal reduplication that is irrelevant in reversal.[2]

This parsimony effect raises the issue of the status of the repeated part in syllable repetition or reduplication. It has been assumed that the repeated part corresponds to a syllable in the input form. Thus a CVCCV word that surfaces as CV-CVCCV in a first-syllable reduplication task or as CV in a first-syllable repetition task is taken to indicate a CV.CCV segmentation of the stimulus item. However, even if the reduplicant or the repeated syllable is a syllable-size constituent, there is no evidence that this constituent necessarily corresponds to a syllable in the input. CV-reduplication is in fact very common cross-linguistically. In other words, [ja-jansta] forms do not necessarily follow from the syllabification [ja.nsta].

3   Experiment

The following experiment compares the syllabification judgments obtained with five tasks in order to evaluate the degree of correlation between the results and the extent to which they are affected by task-dependent factors.

(2) Experimental tasks

   a. Pause insertion
   b. First-syllable repetition
   c. Second-syllable repetition
   d. Slash insertion
   e. Evaluation questionnaire

We will look in particular at some of the effects described in the previous section: written vs. oral tasks (sect. 2.2.2), word-edge phonotactic constraints (sect. 2.2.3), word minimality and parsimony in repetition

---

[2] Finnish participants, unlike German ones, only rarely produced forms like [ja-jansta], which Berg and Niemi (2000) explain by the absence of an onset maximization strategy in Finnish (due to the low frequency of word-initial clusters in this language). Another interpretation is that since Finnish has fixed initial stress, participants reduplicate at least CVC in initial position to ensure the heaviness of the stressed syllable. See Anttila (1997) for another illustration of the role of this weight constraint in Finnish.

(2.2.4). We will also consider the significance of usage frequency as a possible explanatory factor in each task.

Task (2e) contrasts with the more familiar ones in (2a–d) in that it involves a gradient evaluation of different syllabification options rather than an absolute choice. This task was designed to more directly observe the relative wellformedness of alternative patterns.

3.1 *Stimuli*

The same set of stimuli was used in all five tasks. To avoid possible lexical effects (orthography and/or stored syllabic representations), only nonce words were used. The stimuli were always bisyllabic and resembled Russian nominal word forms. Two structural types were used: CVCVC and CVCCVC (e.g., /gúzun/, /páksul/). The CVCVC stimuli were added as filler items and the intervocalic consonant varied at random among non-palatalized stops, fricatives and sonorants. Twenty clusters of two consonants were used in the CVCCVC stimuli: /bm/, /bn/, /gz/, /kn/, /ks/, /kt/, /mb/, /nb/, /pn/, /ps/, /pt/, /sk/, /sm/, /sn/, /sp/, /st/, /tm/, /tn/, /vs/, and /vz/. The initial and final consonants were chosen such that none of the possible syllabification patterns could result in any part of the stimulus being identical to an existing Russian nominal word form. The tokens were presented in Cyrillic. Half of the items had initial stress and the remaining tokens carried final stress; the location of stress was indicated with an accent mark above the stressed vowel. The stressed vowel was /a/, /u/ or /o/; the unstressed vowel was either /a/ or /u/. Other Russian vowels were not used in order to control for any possible effects related to palatalization and/ or vowel reduction. The list of stimuli is given in the appendix.

In tasks (2a), (2d) and (2e), the participants were presented with 50 tokens of the CVCVC type and 120 tokens of the CVCCVC type (6 tokens per consonant cluster). Due to timing considerations, the participants saw only half of the tokens in tasks (2b) and (2c), for a total of 60 CVCCVC items (3 tokens per consonant cluster) and 25 CVCVC items per task. For participants who performed tasks (2b) and (2c), the full set of stimulus items was divided randomly between the two tasks and the same item never appeared in both.

3.2   *Participants*

Participant recruitment and testing took place in Perm, Russia. Twenty participants performed tasks (2a), (2b), and (2c) (the same participants in all three tasks; the order of tasks was randomized). 56 and 49 speakers took part in tasks (2d) and (2e), respectively (24 participated in both tasks). All participants either originated from or were long-term residents of the Perm district and represented the same dialectal variety. The speakers were mostly monolingual and had limited exposure to languages other than Russian. A number of participants were raised in bilingual families (Russian and Komi, Tatar, or Udmurt), but were no longer using the non-Russian language actively in their daily lives and did not consider themselves to be fluent in that language. All speakers were recruited at a university campus (none majored in linguistics). The participants were male and female aged 18 to 33 years (with a mean age of 20).

3.3   *Procedure*

The first three tasks involved an oral response; tasks (2d) and (2e) generated written responses. To minimize the impact of any pre-existing knowledge of syllabification patterns or rules, the term 'part' rather than 'syllable' was used throughout the experiments. The participants were told explicitly that there were no correct or incorrect answers and the exact goal of the study was not revealed to them.

3.3.1   *Task (2a): Pause Insertion*

The participants were tested individually in a university laboratory. The stimuli were presented on a computer screen one token at a time using the DMDX presentation software (Forster and Forster 2003). Each token remained in the center of the screen for 1 second and was followed by two consecutive prompts (asterisk symbols of different colors) that were separated from each other by a delay of 1 second. The speakers were instructed to a) read the whole word as soon as it appeared on the screen, b) pronounce the first part of the word when the first prompt appeared, and c) pronounce the second part when the second prompt appeared. The participants were asked to divide the tokens such that the outcome sounded 'natural' to them. The experimental session started with 5 trial items. Only feedback related to the timing of responses was provided. During the main session, oral responses were recorded using a Marantz recorder and transcribed offline. The participants could not see the experimenter (the second author). They took a short break in the middle of the experimental session.

3.3.2   Tasks (2b) and (2c): First and Second Syllable Repetition
The testing procedure was the same as in task (2a) with one exception: after the token disappeared from the computer screen, the participants saw a single prompt and were instructed to repeat only the *first* or the *second* part of the word.

3.3.3   Task (2d): Slash Insertion
The participants were tested in small groups at a university campus. The speakers were seated separately from each other and instructed to work independently. Each participant received a typed list of words (from a number of randomized versions) and was asked to divide every token into two parts such that the resultant pattern sounded 'natural' to the speaker and to insert a written slash at the boundary. The participants did not receive any feedback regarding their performance.

3.3.4   Task (2e): Evaluation Questionnaire
The overall procedure was similar to task (2d), but this time the speakers received typed questionnaires with two syllabification patterns per token. For the CVCVC stimuli, the patterns were a) CV-CVC and b) CVC-VC. For the items containing an intervocalic consonant cluster (i.e. CVCCVC), the two options were a) CV-CCVC and b) CVC-CVC. The participants were asked to evaluate the 'naturalness' of each syllabification option on a scale from 1 (completely unnatural) to 5 (very natural).

3.4   Results

Even though the word 'syllable' was never used during the testing procedure, none of the responses included a single consonant separated from the rest of the segments and/or two vowels in the same syllable, indicating that the participants divided the words into syllable-sized constituents. As can be seen in Table 1 and Table 2 below, in tasks (2a) through (2d) participants showed a very strong preference for CV-CVC and CVC-CVC responses. At least 70% of the tokens with a single intervocalic consonant and 90% of the tokens containing a consonant cluster fell into these categories. Table 1 below also demonstrates that, for the CVCVC items, the participants gave substantially more CVC responses (CVC-VC syllabification) when performing

Table 1   CVCVC Filler Items: Percentages of Responses

Task	CV-CVC	CVC-VC
Pause insertion	88.1	11.9
1st-syllable repetition	72.8	27.2
2nd-syllable repetition	88.4	11.6
Slash insertion	82.8	17.2

Table 2   CVCCVC Items: Percentage of Responses

Task	CV-CCVC	CVC-CVC	CVCC-VC
Pause insertion	4.0	95.8	0.2
1st-syllable repetition	1.8	97.7	0.5
2nd-syllable repetition	0.3	98.1	1.6
Slash insertion	6.4	91.5	2.1

first-syllable repetition than any other task. The preference for CV-CVC answers was much stronger in the other three tasks, especially so in the case of pause insertion and second-syllable repetition.

Differences in response types across the four experimental tasks were also present in the CVCCVC items. As can be seen in Table 2, the participants preferred to generate CVC sequences in all four tasks. However, for the first-syllable repetition procedure, the second most common response involved producing CV sequences, whereas in second-syllable repetition, the participants repeated VC sequences (suggesting an initial CVCC syllable) more often than CCVC sequences (suggesting an initial CV syllable). In the case of pause insertion and slash insertion, the second most common choice was to place the boundary after the first vowel: CV-CCVC.

Figure 1 below shows the mean number of segments in the first syllable for each of the 20 consonant clusters tested in tasks (2a) through (2d). In Figure 1, lower values denote more CV-CCVC responses for a particular cluster and task and higher values correspond to more CVCC-VC responses. Clusters that were consistently split in half in a given task (i.e., CVC-CVC) received the score of 3.0.

Higher evaluation scores for the same response types were also found in task (2e). For the CVCVC items, the CV-CVC pattern received a mean score of 3.67 compared to a score of 2.51 for the CVC-VC pattern and a two-tailed paired t-test confirmed the statistical significance of the differences in evaluation scores at the 0.05 alpha level ($t(48) = 6.43$, $p < 0.001$). For CVCCVC items, the CVC-CVC pattern

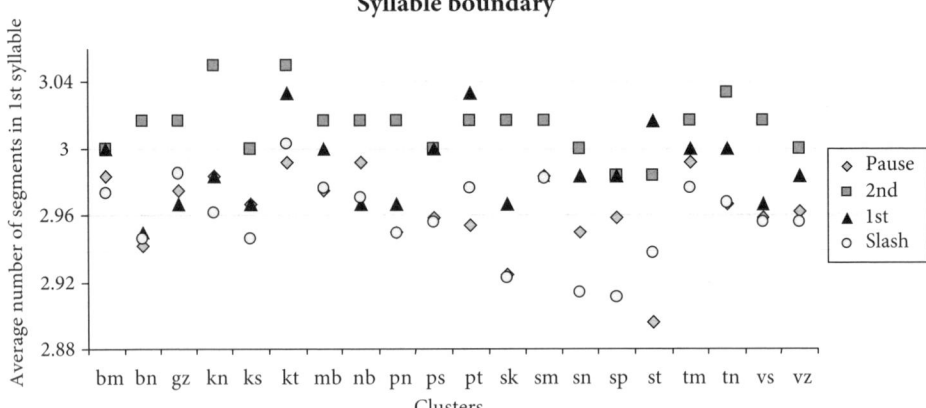

Figure 1   CVCCVC Items: Mean Number of Segments in the First Syllable,
Tasks (2a)–(2d)

also scored significantly higher than CV-CCVC (3.76 vs. 2.69, respectively; $t(48) = 8.51$, $p < 0.001$). To analyze the results of task (2e), differences in the mean evaluation scores of the two syllabification patterns were calculated by subtracting the mean score of the CV-CCVC pattern from the mean score of the CVC-CVC pattern for each of the 20 consonant clusters. In Figure 2, higher difference scores correspond to a stronger preference for the CVC-CVC pattern (e.g., /nb/) and lower values denote a higher acceptance of CV-CCVC (e.g., /vz/).

It should be noted that ambisyllabic responses were extremely rare in all five tasks ($n < 5$). This avoidance of ambisyllabicity is not unexpected given the controlled timing between the pronunciation of the two parts of the stimulus in task (2a), repetition of a single syllable in tasks (2b) and (2c), absence of any mention of using multiple slashes in the instructions to task (2d), as well as the absence of ambisyllabic options in task (2e).

To address the overall comparability of the results obtained with different tasks, correlatory analyses were performed on the averaged CVCCVC data. As can be seen in Table 3 below, the results of the five experimental procedures did not always correlate at a statistically significant level. For pause insertion, significant positive correlations were observed with second-syllable repetition, slash insertion, and the evaluation questionnaire. The results of the first-syllable repetition task did not correlate with those of any other task at a significant level. For second-syllable repetition, significant positive correlations were pres-

Syllabification evaluation: difference scores

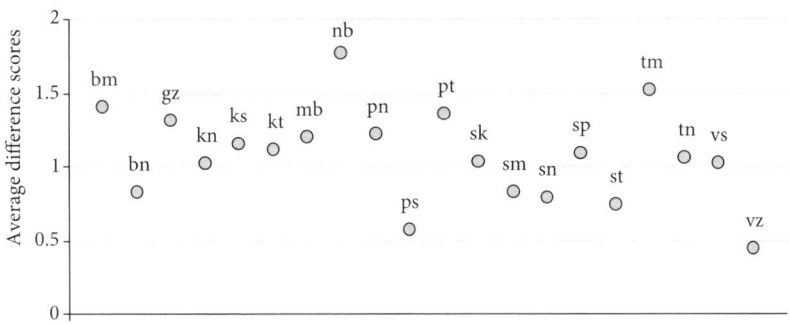

Figure 2   CVCCVC Items: Difference Scores, Task (2e)

ent with pause insertion and slash insertion only. The slash insertion task showed significant positive correlations with pause insertion and second-syllable repetition. The results of the evaluation questionnaire correlated at a statistically significant level only with the results of the pause insertion task. For the slash insertion and evaluation question- naire tasks, no significant differences were found between the subjects who participated in both procedures and those who took part in a single task.

Beyond the global comparability of the results of different experi- mental procedures, it is useful to see whether all tasks are equally sen- sitive to specific factors known to influence syllabification judgments. Stress placement (initial vs. final) is one such factor, but it did not show a statistically significant effect in any of the five experiments. This result should be interpreted with caution, however, since some participants had problems following stress indications: they often did not stress the expected vowel and tended to stress the second vowel, even in words bearing an accent on the first. It turns out that those participants were not comfortable with the practice of indicating stress with an accent on the relevant vowel, even if it is used in school. The type of stressed vowel (/a u o/) was also tested, without any statisti- cally significant effect. Factors such as the sonority or nature of the consonants could not be tested since the stimuli were not controlled accordingly; however, it was possible to study the potential impact of consonant cluster frequency. The CVCCVC data averaged by conso- nant cluster were subjected to a series of stepwise regression analyses. Three predictor variables were introduced: a) word-initial frequency, b) word-final frequency and c) total frequency of the C_1C_2 biphone

Table 3   CVCCVC Items: Correlation between the Results of Any Two Tasks

Task		Pause insertion	2nd-syllable repetition	1st-syllable repetition	Evaluation questionnaire
Slash insertion	Pearson Cor.	.665**	.595**	.394	.376
	Sig. (2-tailed)	.001	.006	.085	.102
Pause insertion	Pearson Cor.		.499*	.062	.483*
	Sig. (2-tailed)		.025	.796	.031
2nd-syllable	Pearson Cor.			.109	.250
repetition	Sig. (2-tailed)			.647	.289
1st-syllable	Pearson Cor.				.015
repetition	Sig. (2-tailed)				.951

** Correlation is significant at the 0.01 level (2-tailed); * Correlation is significant at the 0.05 level (2-tailed).

sequence. The measurements were calculated on the basis of frequency values reported in Sharoff (2008).

The results of the regression analyses revealed that, for the pause insertion task, the total frequency of the biphone sequence significantly predicted the placement of syllable boundaries and explained a substantial proportion of variance in the data (β = (-).76; R^2 = .578; $F_{1,19}$ = 24.68; $p < .001$). For first-syllable repetition, the word-final frequency of the C_1C_2 sequence was the only frequency-based factor identified in the regression. The factor was only marginally significant at best and the resultant model could explain only a small proportion of variance in the data (β = .381; R^2 = .145; $F_{1,19}$ = 3.05; p = .098). For the slash insertion task, the most significant model identified by the regression analysis accounted for almost 50% of variance in the syllabification scores (R^2 = .495; $F_{2,18}$ = 8.34; p = .003), with two variables emerging as significant: word-final frequency (β = 1.5; p = .003) and total frequency (β = (-)1.78; p = .001). Word-initial frequency was not significant for any task and none of the frequency factors was significant for either the second-syllable repetition or the evaluation questionnaire. The results of the regression analyses are summarized in Table 4 below.

Table 4   CVCCVC Items: Role of Cluster Frequency

Task	Significant factor(s)
Pause insertion	Total frequency (p<.001)
1st-syllable repetition	Word-final frequency (p=.098)
2nd-syllable repetition	—
Slash insertion	Word-final frequency (p=.003) & Total frequency (p=.001)
Evaluation questionnaire	—

4   Discussion

4.1   Comparison with the Literature on Russian Syllabification

The issue of syllabification of intervocalic consonants in Russian has been addressed in a number of works. However, the majority of publications are prescriptive in nature and describe the so-called full (formal) style (e.g. Vinogradov et al. 1953, Scherba 1983, Avanesov and Sidorov 1945, Wade 1994, Kasatkin 2001). Only a few studies are based on actual production data (e.g. Bondarko 1977, 1998, Kalnyn and Maslennikova 1985). Table 5 below summarizes the predictions of several works for the 20 consonant clusters as well as the CVCVC filler items used in the current study. As can be seen, predictions vary for consonant clusters, and factors such as stress placement, sonority sequencing and dialectal variation are thought to play a role. Single intervocalic consonants are claimed to be syllabified as onsets.

The results of the present study do not always correspond to the syllabification patterns reported in the literature. The works shown in Table 5 did not predict the relatively common CVC-VC pattern for the CVCVC items, even after stressed vowels. In addition, the strong preference for the CVC-CVC response for all clusters contradicts the majority of predictions (Avanesov and Sidorov 1945, Bondarko 1977, 1998, Kasatkin 2001, Scherba 1983, Vinogradov et al. 1953, Wade 1994) but is in line with descriptions of the Northern Russian dialect (Kalnyn and Maslennikova 1985). Stress placement is given as a guiding factor in syllabification (Vinogradov et al. 1953, Scherba 1983), but it did not appear to play a role in the experimental results (as noted above, however, this conclusion should be revisited).

Table 5   Literature on Russian Syllabification

Publications	VCV	VCCV
Vinogradov et al. (1953), Scherba (1983)	V-CV	V_1C-CV_2 if V_1 is stressed; V_1-CCV_2 if V_1 is not stressed
Avanesov and Sidorov (1945), Wade (1994), Kasatkin (2001)	V-CV	Vm-CV, Vn-CV; V-CCV for all other clusters
Bondarko (1977, 1998)	V-CV	V-CCV
Kalnyn and Maslennikova (1985)	n/a	VC-CV for speakers of the Northern dialect; V-CCV for speakers of the Southern dialect (Vm-CV, Vn-CV are also possible)

4.2   Comparability of the Results Obtained with Different Procedures

Overall, the results of the five experimental tasks often fail to correlate: only four of the ten pairs of tasks yield results that are comparable at a significant level for the CVCCVC items. This brings into question the common (tacit) assumption that different procedures are equivalent when it comes to investigating syllabification preferences. However, some tasks appear to generate more similar results than others. First-syllable repetition yields judgments that are most clearly different from those of the other tasks, for both CVCCVC (the results of first-syllable repetition do not correlate with those of any other task) and CVCVC items (higher proportion of CVC answers for the first syllable). Second, a distinction possibly emerges between the tasks requiring participants to produce or consider the entire word (pause insertion, slash insertion and questionnaire) and the two single-syllable repetition tasks. A better correlation appears to hold among the 'complete' tasks than between them and the partial ones or between the two repetition tasks. The results of pause insertion are correlated with those of both slash insertion and the questionnaire, and the questionnaire is positively correlated only with pause insertion.

The strong positive correlation for CVCCVC items between pause and slash insertion, which are the oral/written counterparts of each other, suggests that the written-oral distinction may not be so important after all, at least for nonce words. This is in line with the results of McCrary (2004), who found no distinction between the results of pause and slash insertion.

The results of first-syllable repetition display the word-minimality effect mentioned in section 2.2.4. For CVCVC items, this task yields substantially more CVC responses for the first syllable than the other tasks. This presumably follows from a word-size constraint favoring (lexical) words that are sufficiently heavy. The same tendency emerges in Content et al. (2001) and Cebrian (2002). This minimality effect is more difficult to detect in CVCCVC items, given that CVC is by far the preferred option in all tasks anyway. The smaller proportion of CV-CCVC responses in first-syllable repetition than in pause or slash insertion could, however, also result from the same minimality constraint.

Second-syllable repetition reveals a possible effect of parsimony (sect 2.2.4) and/or edge constraints (sect 2.2.3). It is the only task in which VC responses are more common than CCVC ones. This may plausibly be interpreted in terms of the tendency to repeat the shortest possible sequence, as noted in Bertinetto et al. (2007). An alternative interpretation involves edge effects: CCVC is more strongly avoided in second-syllable repetition because many of the CC intervocalic sequences are unattested word-initially (see Steriade 1999 for a word-based account of syllabification); however, more experimental data would be necessary to distinguish the two explanations. Notice that for first-syllable repetition, the two minimality effects conflict in the CVCVC items: parsimony favors CV while word minimality favors CVC. In this case it appears that word minimality overrides the conflicting parsimony effect.

Regarding the impact of cluster frequency on syllabification judgments, it is surprising that word-initial frequency did not come out as significant in any task. Standard accounts of syllabification consider that the possibility of two consonants being syllabified together in a complex onset crucially depends on whether this sequence is attested word-initially. One could have expected, therefore, a positive correlation between word-initial frequency and the frequency of the CV-CCVC answers. While this is not the case, total frequency and even word-final frequency appear significant for some of the tasks. This may suggest a more general interpretation to the role of frequency in syllabification: the more frequently two consonants appear together, in any position in the word, the more they tend to syllabify together, without a necessary correspondence between position in the syllable and position in the word. However, since the main goal of testing frequency-based predictor variables was not to account for variability in the syllabification data but rather to investigate whether the same statistical factors would be identified as significant for all five datasets regardless of the limited correlations between the results of different tasks, the present study was not designed specifically to explore the role of usage frequency in syllabification and the present findings would need to be verified independently with well-controlled stimuli items before making any explicit claims on the role of usage frequency in syllabification.

The evaluation questionnaire generates at least one interesting result that other tasks cannot reveal. While participants prefer the CV-CVC and CVC-CVC options, which get higher scores, their evaluation of the alternative patterns CVC-VC and CV-CCVC remains relatively positive (Table 2). Given that the CVC-CVC pattern is chosen 91.5 and 95.8% of the time in the tasks that require evaluation of a complete stimulus, one could have predicted a sharper contrast between a positive evaluation for CVC-CVC and a clearly negative one for CV-CCVC. This is not the case. It remains unclear how exactly this result should be interpreted. One option to be explored involves a more gradient notion of syllabification: consonants are associated with each of their adjacent segments to a relative degree, in contrast to the standard view based on strict constituency. Content et al. (2001) have moved in that direction to some extent by abandoning the concept of syllable boundaries; their results rather support the view that the location of syllable onsets and offsets involve distinct processes.

5   Conclusions

The main conclusion of this chapter is that syllabification data collected using different procedures may not be directly comparable. Experimental tasks cannot be expected to be equally sensitive to the factors affecting syllabification judgments. In some cases, increased sensitivity to a given factor can be predicted from the nature of the task, such as word-minimality effects in single-syllable responses or phonotactic constraints at word edges when the consonants appear in initial or final position. Other factors are less predictable, for example the different reactions to cluster frequency.

Generally, partial tasks such as syllable reduplication and repetition appear to be subject to various minimality and edge effects that other tasks are immune from or less sensitive to. In addition, there is no evidence that the repeated or reduplicated portion of the stimulus item directly indicates the syllabification of the intervocalic consonants in the complete form. This suggests that tasks involving a single syllable may be less appropriate than complete ones when investigating the syllabification of medial consonants. This suggestion runs contra Goslin and Frauenfelder (2000), who propose that the optimal task is single-syllable repetition, with first- and second-syllable repetition being performed in separate blocks, but it is consistent with the opinion of Goslin and Floccia (2007, 345), who chose the pause insertion task because of its "simplicity and efficacy" and its higher segmentation consistency.

Whatever conclusion may be drawn about the appropriateness of different tasks for the study of the syllable, it still leaves open the issue of the relationship between syllabification judgments and the syllabic structure considered relevant in phonology. Radically opposing views on this question can be entertained, with a variety of intermediate positions. At one end, the phonological syllable can be seen as a purely abstract constituent, upon which experimental results have little bearing. At the other end, syllabification may be considered as a metalinguistic procedure which results from a complex interplay of phonetic, phonological and morphological factors, including segmental regularities. Phonological processes would then operate independently from syllabification and syllable wellformedness. Thus, more research is needed to not only confirm the tendencies found in the present study or to uncover other important differences between various experimental procedures, but also to determine the exact implications of the availability of speakers' judgments for the formal concept of the syllable used in phonological theory.

References

Anttila, Arto. 1997. Deriving variation from grammar. In *Variation, change and phonological theory*, edited by Frans Hinskens, Roeland van Hout and Leo Wetzels, 35–68. Amsterdam: John Benjamins.

Avanesov, Ruben I. and Vladimir N. Sidorov. 1945. *Ocherk grammatiki russkogo literaturnogo jazyka.* Moscow.

Barry, William, Cordula Klein and Stephanie Köser. 1999. Speech production evidence for ambisyllabicity in German. *Phonus* 4: 87–102.

Berg, Thomas. 2001. An experimental study of syllabification in Icelandic. *Nordic Journal of Linguistics* 24: 71–106.

Berg, Thomas and Jussi Niemi. 2000. Syllabification in Finnish and German: Onset filling vs. onset maximization. *Journal of Phonetics* 28: 187–216.

Bertinetto, Pier Marco, Marco Caboara, Livio Gaeta, and Maddalena Agonigi. 1994. Syllabic division and intersegmental cohesion in Italian. In *Phonologica 1992: Proceedings of the 7th international phonology meeting*, edited by Wolfgang U. Dressler, Martin Prinzhorn and John R. Rennison, 19–33. Torino: Rosenberg & Sellier.

Bertinetto, Pier Marco, Sylwia Scheuer, Katarzyna Dziubalska-Kolaczyk, and Maddalena Agonigi. 2007. Intersegmental cohesion and syllable division in Polish. In *Proceedings of the 16th International Congress of Phonetic Sciences*, http://www.icphs2007.de/

Bondarko, Liya V. 1977. *Zvukovoj stroj sovremennogo russkogo jazyka.* Moscow: Prosveshenie.

Bondarko, Liya V. 1998. *Fonetika sovremennogo russkogo jazyka.* St. Petersburg.

Cebrian, Juli. 2002. Phonetic similarity, syllabification and phonotactic constraints in the acquisition of a second language contrast. PhD diss., University of Toronto.

Content, Alain, Ruth K. Kearns and Uli H. Frauenfelder. 2001. Boundaries versus onsets in syllabic segmentation. *Journal of Memory and Language* 45: 177–199.

Derwing, Bruce. 1992. A 'pause-break' task for eliciting syllable boundary judgments from literate and illiterate speakers: preliminary results for five diverse languages. *Language and Speech* 35: 219–235.

Eddington, David, Rebecca Treiman, Dirk Elzinga, and Mark Davies. 2008. The syllabification of American English: Evidence from a large-scale experiment. Presented at the CUNY Phonology Forum Conference on the Syllable. http://www.cunyphonologyforum.net/syllconf.php

Fallows, Deborah. 1981. Experimental evidence for English syllabification and syllable structure. *Journal of Linguistics* 17: 309–318.

Forster, Kenneth I. and Jonathan C. Forster. 2003. DMDX: A windows display program with millisecond accuracy. *Behavior Research Methods, Instruments, and Computers* 35: 116–124.

Gillis, Steven and Dominiek Sandra. 1998. Children's and adults' syllabification: The influence of spelling. In *Perspectives on language acquisition*, edited by Ayhan Aksu-Koç, Eser Erguvanli-Taylan, A. Sumru Özsoy and Aylin Kuntay, 336–354. Istanbul: Bogazici University Press.

Goslin, Jeremy. 2002. Theoretical and human syllabification. PhD diss., University of Sheffield.

Goslin, Jeremy and Caroline Floccia. 2007. Comparing French syllabification in pre-literate children and adults. *Applied Psycholinguistics* 28: 341–367.

Goslin, Jeremy and Uli H. Frauenfelder. 2000. A comparison of theoretical and human syllabification. *Language and Speech* 44: 409–436.

Ishikawa, Keiichi. 2002. Syllabification of intervocalic consonants by English and Japanese speakers. *Language and Speech* 45: 355–385.

Kalnyn, Ljudmila E. and Ljudmila I. Maslennikova. 1985. *Opyt izuchenija sloga v slavjanskih jazykah.* Moscow.

Kasatkin, Leonid L., ed. 2001. *Russkij jazyk.* Moscow: Academia.

Mattys, Sven L., and James F. Melhorn. 2005. How do syllables contribute to the perception of spoken English? Insight from the migration paradigm. *Language and Speech* 48: 223–253.

McCrary, Kristie M. 2004. Reassessing the role of the syllable in Italian phonology: An experimental study of consonant cluster syllabification, definite article allomorphy and segment duration. PhD diss., University of California, Los Angeles.

Redford, Melissa A. and Patrick Randall. 2005. The role of juncture cues and phonological knowledge in English syllabification judgments. *Journal of Phonetics* 33: 27–46.

Scherba, Lev V. 1983. *Teorija russkogo pisma.* Leningrad.

Schiller, Niels O., Antje S. Meyer and Willem J. M. Levelt. 1997. The syllabic structure of spoken words: Evidence form the syllabification of intervocalic consonants. *Language and Speech* 40: 103–140.

Sharoff, Serge. 2008. The frequency dictionary of Russian. Online corpus. http://www.comp.leeds.ac.uk/ssharoff/frqlist/frqlist-en.html

Steriade, Donca. 1999. Alternatives to syllable-based accounts of consonantal phonotactics. In *Proceedings of LP '98: Item order in language and speech*, vol. 1, edited by Osamu Fujimura, Brian D. Joseph and Bohumil Palek, 205–245. Prague: Charles University in Prague—The Karolinum Press.

Treiman, Rebecca. 1992. Experimental studies of English syllabification. In *Phonologica 1988*, edited by Wolfgang U. Dressler, Hans C. Luschützky, Oskar E. Pfeiffer and John R. Rennison, 273–281. Cambridge: Cambridge University Press.

Treiman, Rebbeca, Judith A. Bowey and Derrick Bourassa. 2002. Segmentation of spoken words into syllables by English-speaking children. *Journal of Experimental Child Psychology* 83: 213–238.

Treiman, Rebecca and Catalina Danis. 1988. Syllabification of intervocalic consonants. *Journal of Memory and Language* 27: 87–104.

Treiman, Rebecca, Jennifer Gross and Annemarie Cwikiel-Glavin. 1992. The syllabification of /s/ clusters in English. *Journal of Phonetics* 20: 383–402.

Treiman, Rebecca and Andrea Zukowski. 1990. Toward an understanding of English syllabification. *Journal of Memory and Language* 29: 66–85.

Vinogradov, Viktor V., Evgenija S. Istrina and Stepan G. Barkhudarov, eds. 1953. *Grammatika russkogo jazyka. Vol. 1. Fonetika i morfologija.* Moscow: Academy of Science of the USSR.

Wade, Terence. 1994. *A comprehensive Russian grammar.* Oxford: Blackwell.

Zamuner, Tania S. and Diane K. Ohala. 1999. Preliterate children's syllabification of intervocalic consonants. In *BUCLD 23 proceedings*, edited by Annabel Greenhill, Heather Littlefield and Cheryl Tano, 753–763. Somerville: Cascadilla Press.

Appendix: Test Items
CVCCVC ITEMS

ва́бнук	зо́ктан	но́птул	та́бмуг	бавзо́т	канбо́п	наксу́л	сабма́р
ва́кнар	зо́спул	ну́псал	та́псар	вапто́с	катну́г	нукто́л	савза́к
ва́ктап	зо́тмур	ну́птум	та́снук	вубна́т	кугза́р	нумбо́з	сакну́м
ва́нбул	зу́ктул	ну́смар	то́взул	гапту́л	куспу́м	нупна́т	сакту́м
во́кнуп	зу́стах	па́взук	то́всап	гаску́т	кутмо́н	нуспо́м	сапно́л
во́снур	ка́мбап	па́гзан	то́гзул	гуксо́п	лабно́к	пакна́т	тасна́п
ву́бмар	ка́птар	па́ксул	ту́бнак	дабму́н	лагзу́н	патна́к	тукно́м
ву́тмас	ка́тнап	па́тмун	ту́нбат	дукта́р	ласму́б	пувса́р	туста́г
до́бмар	ку́всаб	по́скуз	ту́скап	жавсу́л	луска́м	пусмо́н	хакса́г
ду́кнап	ло́нбул	ра́всун	фо́бнар	жасма́р	лусну́м	равзу́н	хаско́п
ду́ксул	ло́стап	ро́пнак	фо́псун	жасно́л	мабну́т	рагзо́м	шамбу́д
ду́тнур	лу́взан	су́гзак	ха́спур	жасто́х	мапну́р	рамба́п	шаспа́г
жа́скап	лу́мбат	хо́смар	ха́стум	жасту́н	мапса́г	рапсу́н	шатму́р
жа́сман	лу́спак	хо́тнус	хо́ксар	занбу́т	мувсо́п	ратма́с	шупсо́д
за́пнар	му́пнаг	шу́снар	хо́мбуг	кабмо́с	мунба́г	рутно́л	шупта́н

CVCVC ITEMS

ба́ган	зо́дун	мо́сун	ру́пак	бужа́г	гану́д	лану́т	таву́р
бо́наж	зо́фат	но́маг	са́рун	бупа́т	дуза́х	нузо́м	туго́б
ву́кап	ко́ган	по́нук	са́шур	ваду́з	жудо́б	пуго́з	фазу́л
гу́зун	ку́нар	пу́наз	фа́дус	вако́х	зуна́р	раво́б	хабу́л
гу́рах	ла́бут	ро́нап	фу́лаг	вапу́л	када́п	сабо́д	хапа́г
ду́зан	ма́сур	ро́нут	ха́лус	вула́р	лагу́с	сула́х	шуду́к
жа́зук				вуло́с			

CHAPTER TWELVE

SYLLABLES IN SPEECH PROCESSING: EVIDENCE FROM PERCEPTUAL EPENTHESIS

Andries W. Coetzee

1 Syllables in Speech Production and Processing

Much of phonological theory assumes that speech is both discrete and hierarchical. The speech stream can be divided into discrete units (segments/sounds), and these units are hierarchically organized into larger chunks such as syllables, feet, prosodic words, etc. (Nespor and Vogel 1986, Selkrik 1978, 1986, etc.). Phonological rules are often formalized in terms of these higher order groupings of sounds. This approach presents many problems to phonological theory. Not only is it difficult to define these higher order categories accurately, but it is probably even harder to find evidence of their reality.

Speech is transferred between speaker and listener as continuously varying air pressure fluctuations. The structure of the pressure fluctuation is sometimes such that discontinuities can be detected easily—for instance at the transition between a plosive and a vowel. This lends some support to the idea that speech is discrete—the speech stream can be divided into discrete chunks based on its physical properties. However, the boundaries between segments are not always demarcated clearly in the physical speech stream, as anyone who has ever tried to find the boundary between a vowel and glide on a spectrogram or waveform can attest. The fact that it is not always possible to find correlates to concepts like segments in the physical world has lead some to doubt the existence of discrete segments (Port and Leary 2005).

Just as difficult as finding physical evidence for the division of the speech stream into discrete segments, is finding physical evidence for the grouping of these segments into larger prosodically defined units such as feet, syllables, etc. Although there are temporal and intonational properties of the speech stream that have been shown to correlate with the boundaries of some of these larger prosodic units (Beckman and Edwards 1990, Byrd and Saltzman 2003, Coetzee and Wissing 2007, Selkirk 1981, 2001, Sugahara 2005, Turk and Shattuck-Hufnagel 2000, etc.), this correlation is not very strong, as is clear from chapter 8 of this Handbook. The observed variation in these temporal and intonational measures is often large, and the differences between different prosodic units are often very small (McQueen 1998, 21).

Given the difficulty of finding consistent physical correlates for these higher prosodic units, a question that needs answering is whether (all of) these units are real. If physical evidence of these units is lacking, is there evidence that language users parse the speech stream in terms of these units? If a positive answer can be given to this question, then it can be concluded that some of these prosodic units are at least psychologically real—that is, even if they do not exist in the physical properties of the speech stream, the mind of the language user imposes these structures onto the speech stream in the process of planning speech production and perceiving speech. These structures may then have mental reality even if they lack physical reality.

This chapter discusses evidence that listeners do parse the speech stream into higher order prosodic groupings during the process of speech perception. Specifically, it shows that listeners are sensitive to syllabically defined allophonic distributions. In English, aspirated voiceless stops appear only in syllable initial position. When presented with an acoustic signal such as [spʰika] with an unambiguous aspirated [pʰ], listeners impose a percept on this stimulus where [pʰ] appears in syllable initial position. This leaves the [s] prosodically stranded—there is no vowel in the actual acoustic stimulus to which the [s] can affiliate. The evidence presented below shows that the listeners "perceive" a vowel between the [s] and [pʰ] in this kind of situation, i.e. they perceive [səpʰika]. The [ə] that forms part of the percept is not present in the physical stimulus, and is therefore imposed onto the percept by the perceptual system of the listener. This is evidence that the perceptual system does impose higher order structure onto the speech stream, and that this part of the speech processing process is even robust enough to result in percepts for which there is no physical evidence.

Before getting into the details of the current study, we briefly review some existing evidence for the mental reality of such higher order prosodic structures in both production and perception. It is not the goal of this section to review the extensive literature about this, but rather to discuss just a few examples of the evidence that language users do use syllables both in production and perception. Similar evidence for other prosodic constituents also exists (Clifton et al. 2006, Schafer et al. 2000, Wightman et al. 1992, etc.).

1.1 *Evidence for Syllables in Speech Production*

As we saw in Chapter 8, one of the arguments for the use of syllables in speech production comes from studies of speech errors. In a classic paper, Fromkin (1971, 38–40) shows that naturally occurring speech errors point to the syllable as a planning unit for speech production. Exchange errors nearly always respect the syllabic affiliation of the segments involved. Onsets exchange with onsets ('carp-si-hord' for 'harp-si-chord') and rhymes with rhymes ('hunk of jeap' for 'heap of junk'). Very rarely observed are errors where the onset of one syllable exchanges with the coda of another syllable. Fromkin claims that her corpus of errors contains only one such example ('whip-ser' for 'whis-per'). This suggests that the exchanges are not mere segment exchanges, but exchanges of segments in the same syllabic position, implying that the segments must be parsed into syllables at the point in the production planning when the exchange occurs. Similarly, Fromkin notes that speech errors that omit complete syllables ('tre-men-ly' for 'tre-men-dous-ly') are rather common, while errors that omit a segment span that includes parts of two syllables are virtually non-existent ('tre-men-dy' for 'tre-men-dous-ly').

Speech production models, such as those of Levelt (2001), also often contain a stage where the phonological information is encoded into syllables. Levelt and his colleagues have conducted several experiments over the past two plus decades that show evidence for this syllabic stage of speech planning. Cholin et al. (2004) present a recent example. These authors presented Dutch speakers visually with groups of four morphologically related words. There were two kinds of such groups: 'constant', where the first syllable of each word was always the same, and 'variable', where the initial syllable in one word was different. In both conditions, however, all four words had the same segmental make-up up to the affixes. The difference between the two lists is thus purely in terms of the syllable structure of one member. Examples are given in (1).

(1)   *Constant*   *Variable*
     Meaning   'lead'   'smoke'
     Infinitive   [leɪ.dən]   *leiden*   [roː.kən]   *roken*
     Gerund   [leɪ.dənt] *leidend*   [roː.kənt] *rokend*
     Noun   [leɪ.dər]   *leider*   [roː.kər]   *roker*
     Past   [leɪ.də]   *leidde*   [roːk.tə]   *rookte*

Participants had to read each list out loud as accurately and fast as possible. Cholin et al. found the response latency to be significantly greater in the variable than the constant condition. They interpret this as evidence that the participants perform speech planning in terms of syllables. In the constant condition, only one initial syllable has to be planned while two have to be planned in the variable condition, accounting for the longer latency in the latter condition.

1.2   *Evidence for Syllables in Speech Perception*

There is just as large a body of evidence that syllables play a role in speech perception, and this section discusses only a few examples from the recent literature. Mattys and Melhorn (2005) conducted a dichotic listening experiment in which they presented participants simultaneously with two different disyllabic auditory stimuli in the left and right ear, respectively. Neither of the two stimuli were actual English words. However, exchanging corresponding parts of the left and right stimuli did create a word. In one condition, the parts that need to be exchanged to form a word corresponded to full syllables. For example, participants could be presented with [kir.fɪn] in the left ear and [dɔl.mæl] in the right ear, where exchanging the initial syllables results in the real word 'dolphin'. In another condition, the parts that need to be exchanged consisted only of the nucleus of a syllable. Participants could be presented with [dil.fɪn] in the left and [kɔr.mæl] in the right ear. Exchanging the vowel of the first syllables now creates the word 'dolphin'. In this experiment, participants would first hear a production of the actual word [dɔl.fɪn] played simultaneously in both ears. After that, they would hear one of the two dichotic stimuli described just above. Their task was to decide whether the second presentation contained the word they just heard. Mattys and Melhorn found that participants were significantly more likely to detect the word in the dichotic stimulus when full syllables have to be exchanged than when only syllabic nuclei have to be exchanged—i.e. more *yes* responses in [kir.fɪn]~[dɔl.mæl] than in [dil.fɪn]~[kɔr.mæl]. They interpret this as evidence that the acoustic signal from each ear is mapped onto a syllable sized representation before perceptual blending of the two stimuli happens. The blending is then performed by manipulating these syllable sized chunks, with the result that units smaller than a syllable are less accessible to the blending operation.

Another recent study that points to a role for the syllable in speech processing is the perceptual epenthesis study reported by Kabak and Idsardi (2007)—see also Berent et al. (2007), Dupoux et al. (1999, 2001) and Lennertz and Berent (2007). This study is of particular interest, because the experiments reported below also investigate the phenomenon of perceptual epenthesis. Kabak and Idsardi tested the perception by Korean listeners of consonant sequences that are disallowed in Korean. They used two kinds of disallowed sequences. The first kind violates restrictions on the syllable structure of Korean. Korean allows only a small set of consonants in coda position—e.g. [k] is a possible coda while [tʃ] is not. The token [pʰaktʰa] is hence a possible Korean word, while [pʰatʃtʰa] is not. The second kind of disallowed sequence violates not restrictions on syllable structure, but rather restrictions on consonants that are allowed to follow each other. Although Korean allows [k] in coda position, it does not tolerate a sequence of an oral consonant followed by a nasal consonant. Like [pʰatʃtʰa], [pʰakma] is hence also not a possible word. However, the reason for the impossibility of these two tokens is quite different. [pʰatʃtʰa] is impossible because it has a disallowed coda [tʃ]. On the other hand, in [pʰakma], no single consonant appears in a syllabic position where it is not allowed. This form is impossible because of the oral plus nasal sequence.

Dupoux et al. (1999, 2001) demonstrated that Japanese listeners perform perceptual epenthesis when presented with stimuli that contain disallowed consonantal sequences—i.e. they perceive a vowel between the two disallowed consonants even if there is no actual vowel present. When presented with an acoustic stimulus like [ebzo], Japanese listeners perceive [ebuzo], since the sequence [bz] is disallowed in Japanese. Based on this, Kabak and Idsardi hypothesized that Korean listeners should do the same when presented with disallowed forms like [pʰatʃtʰa] and [pʰakma]. They performed a discrimination experiment where participants were presented with pairs of tokens, and required to judge whether the two members in a pair were identical or not. The crucial pairs consisted of one of the disallowed forms, and a corresponding form with a vowel intervening between the two consonants—i.e. [pʰakma]~[pʰakʊma] and [pʰatʃtʰa]~[pʰatʃɪtʰa]. If Korean listeners perform perceptual epenthesis, they should not be able to distinguish the members of these pairs. Kabak and Idsardi found significantly better discrimination on pairs like [pʰakma]~[pʰakʊma] than on pairs like [pʰatʃtʰa]~[pʰatʃɪtʰa]. Perceptual epenthesis was therefore significantly more likely to happen when a token was ill-formed for syllable structure reasons than if it was ill-formed for reasons of consonant sequencing. Kabak and Idsardi conclude that this gives evidence that the acoustic signal is processed in syllable-sized chunks during perception.

2 The Use of Allophonic Distributions to Determine Syllable Structure

This chapter follows in the footsteps of earlier research on perceptual epenthesis by showing that listeners perceive illusory vowels in order to arrive at a final percept that is syllabically well-formed. However, we will deviate from this research tradition in two ways. First, earlier research used acoustic stimuli that are phonemically ill-formed. As discussed in Chapter 15 of this Handbook, Berent et al. (2007) presented English listeners with stimuli like [lbɪf, bdɪf, bnɪf], and found that these listeners perceive the stimuli with an intrusive vowel—i.e. as [ləbɪf, bədɪf, bənɪf]. A stimulus like [lbɪf] cannot be brought into agreement with English phonotactic grammar simply by mapping [l] onto some other allophone of /l/, [b] onto some other allophone of /b/, or even by a combination of these two options. No allophone of /l/ can appear in word-initial position followed by any other consonant in English. These earlier studies therefore do not answer the question of at which level of perceptual abstraction the acoustic stimulus is parsed into syllables (but see Lennertz and Berent 2007). Is each of the individual segments first mapped onto its corresponding phoneme, and then these phonemic percepts are syllabically parsed—i.e. allophonic variation is factored out before syllabic parsing? Or is the syllabic parse performed on a percept that still contains allophonic information?

In order to address the questions posed in the preceding paragraph, the studies reported below used stimuli that are allophonically ill-formed but phonemically well-formed. Specifically, they used stimuli like [spʰika]. In English, the aspirated allophone [pʰ] of the phoneme /p/ is not allowed in onset position after an [s]. But another allophone of /p/ is allowed in this position, namely [p]. If listeners first map the segments in an acoustic signal onto phonemes and then parse the phonemes into syllables, then [spʰika] would have been transformed to /spika/ by the point that the syllabic parse is performed. The percept /spika/ can be parsed into well-formed English syllables. On the other hand, if the syllabic parse is performed on a percept that still contains allophonic information, then [spʰika] has to be syllabified, and no well-formed syllabification of such a representation is possible. If listeners perform perceptual epenthesis when presented with a token like [spʰika], it would be evidence that syllabification happens before allophonic information is abstracted away.

The second way in which this study differs from previous studies is on a methodological detail. In order to show that the vowels perceived by listeners are actually because of perceptual epenthesis and not just an artifact of some unforeseen acoustic property of the stimulus, it is necessary to have some control condition. In earlier studies, the control was always provided by listeners from a different language in which the stimuli were well-formed. Kabak and Idsardi (2007) use English listeners, since English allows both [k] and [tʃ] in coda position. They showed that English listeners do not perceive an epenthetic vowel in stimuli like [pʰatʃtʰa]. The fact that the Korean listeners in their experiment do perceive such a vowel therefore cannot originate in the acoustic properties of their stimuli, but must arise during grammar mediated perceptual processing. Dupoux et al. (1999) similarly use French listeners as control (since stimuli like [ebzo] are well-formed in French), and Berent et al. (2007) use Russian controls (since [bd, lb, bn] are possible onset clusters in Russian). The study reported here used the exact same listeners both in the perceptual epenthesis condition and in the control condition. This is possible because the stimuli were ill-formed in English simply because of the context in which they appear. The exact same stimuli are well-formed in a different acoustic context—that is, no well-formed syllabic parse of [spʰika] is possible, but splicing [la-] onto this exact same stimulus gives [laspʰika] for which a well-formed syllabic parse is possible. If English listeners perceive a vowel between [s] and [pʰ] in [spʰika] but not in [laspʰika], then we can conclude that the vowel percept in [spʰika] does not originate in some unforeseen acoustic properties of the [s] and [pʰ]. This methodological difference between the study reported here and earlier studies is important for two reasons. First, it is logistically easier in that listeners of only one language need to be recruited. Secondly, by using the same listeners in both the experimental and the control conditions the effect of perceptual epenthesis can be tested within individuals rather than across different listeners with different native languages.

Aspirated stops are observed only in absolute syllable initial position in all dialects of English. It is not the case that all voiceless stops in syllable initial position are aspirated—in American English, inter-vocalic /t/ is often flapped in the onset of an unstressed syllable, and in some British dialects such /t/'s are often glottalized. But what is true is that all aspirated stops appear in syllable initial position. If listeners pay attention to allophonic details such as aspiration, and if they use this allophonic information when they parse the acoustic signal into syllables, then they should insert a syllable boundary before every aspirated stop in the syllabic parse imposed on the stimulus.

The design of the experiments reported below rests on the assumption that perceptual processing consists of at least two stages. During the first stage of *acoustic encoding* a faithful acoustic copy of the percept is created. No higher order prosodic structure, such as syllable structure, is present in the acoustic representation formed during this stage, implying that the illusory epenthetic vowels are also still absent at this stage of processing. In the second stage, *phonological interpretation*, the listener parses the acoustic representation into higher order prosodic units, and tests these structures for well-formedness against the grammar of his/her language. If the prosodic parse of the acoustic representation is well-formed, the final linguistic percept is equal to this parse. However, if the prosodic parse of the acoustic representation is ill-formed, the perceptual system performs an extra step in which the representation is altered in some fashion so that it is brought into agreement with the requirements of the grammar of the listener. This is the step during which, for instance, perceptual epenthesis occurs. The listener then settles on a linguistic percept that differs from the original acoustic representation created. This model is represented in Figure 1. See Kingston (2005) and Poeppel et al. (2008) for support of such a multi stage model.

Some of the implications of this model are tested in experiments discussed in the rest of this chapter. Specifically: a) in this model, prosodic parsing is performed on the acoustic representation—i.e. before allophonic information is abstracted away. Allophonic information will therefore influence the prosodic structure imposed on the stimulus, so that a token like [spʰika] will receive a different prosodic parse from a token like [spika]. b) If a well-formed prosodic parse exists that is faithful to the actual acoustic properties of the stimulus, then this is the percept on which the listener will settle—[spika] will be perceived as [spi.ka]. On the other hand, if no such a parse exists, the acoustic representation will be altered in some way to create a representation

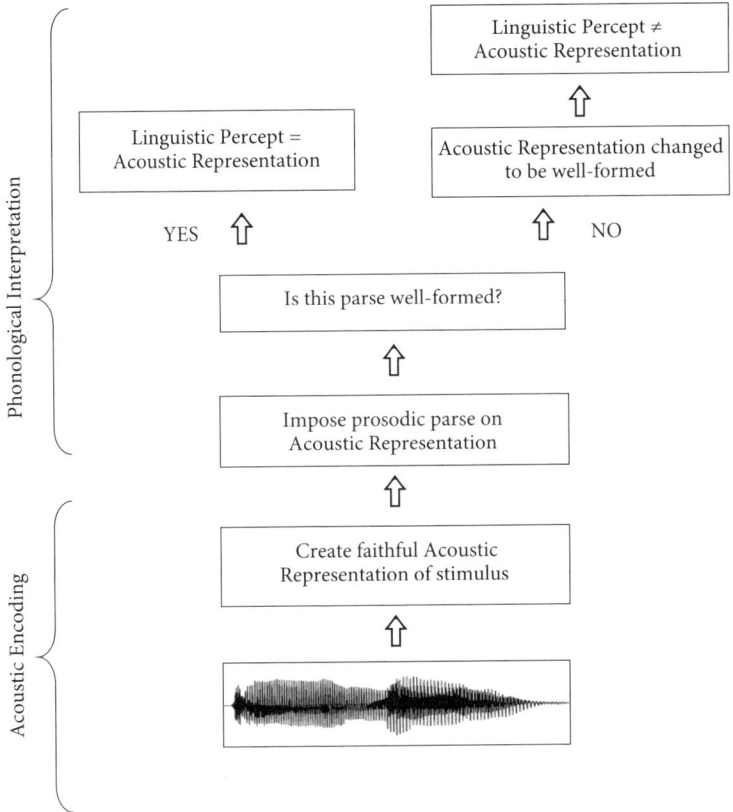

Figure 1   Stages in Perceptual Processing

that can be parsed into a well-formed prosodic structure—[spʰika] will be perceived [sə.pʰi.ka]. c) Since the perception of a stimulus like [spʰika] involves an extra processing step, listeners should be slower in arriving at a perceptual decision to this kind of stimulus. d) During the early stages of processing (acoustic encoding) stimuli like [səpʰika] and [spʰika] will be represented differently, and this difference will only disappear in later processing stages (phonological interpretation). In the next three sections, we discuss three perception experiments designed to test these hypotheses.

3   Experiment 1: Same or Different?

In this experiment, participants are presented with pairs of stimuli, and their task is to decide whether the members of a pair are the same or a different "word". This task taps into the later stages of perceptual processing. Not only do listeners have to listen to at least the first member of a stimulus pair in full, but the task requires of participants to treat the stimuli as "words", hence increasing the likelihood that participants will rely on grammatical processing of the stimulus. The expectation is hence that the participants' responses will reflect the output of phonological processing in the model represented in Figure 1. If the hypotheses stated above are correct, participants should have difficulty distinguishing the members of pairs such as [səpʰika]~[spʰika]. Because no well-formed syllabic parse exists for the second member of this pair, participants are expected to perform perceptual epenthesis on this stimulus and therefore to perceive the stimulus as [səpʰika]— i.e. identical to the other member of the pair. On the other hand, when presented with a pair of stimuli that are identical to [səpʰika]~[spʰika] except that each member is preceded by [la-], participants should more easily distinguish the members of the pair. Well-formed syllabic parses are possible both for [lasəpʰika] and for [laspʰika], and the participants should therefore arrive at different perceptual decisions for the members of such a pair.

3.1 Methods

Participants
Fifteen undergraduate students from the University of Michigan participated in this experiment. They were all native speakers of American English, reporting no hearing or speaking deficits. Participants were paid for their participation.

Token selection and stimuli creation
The stimuli used in this experiment were all based on the non-words in (2). All of these non-words have the structure [CV.sə.Cʰv́.CV] where [Cʰ] is one of the voiceless aspirated stops of English, and [v́] is a stressed vowel. We recorded a native, phonetically trained, female speaker of American English reading each of these tokens ten times. From the ten recordings, we selected one to use in the creation of the stimuli. The token was chosen to ensure that all of the sounds, and specifically the [ə], were clearly articulated. All of the tokens were then equalized in intensity using the *Scale intensity*...function in *Praat* (Boersma and Weenink).

(2)   *Labial*   *Coronal*   *Dorsal*
       vɛsəpʰímu   masəpʰáli   kusətʰíla   lusətʰápi   basəkʰífa   fisəkʰána
       lasəpʰíka   visəpʰáno   fasətʰímo   misətʰáku   masəkʰílu   pisəkʰámi

The processing of [lusətʰápi] discussed here is an example, but each of the other tokens was processed in exactly the same way. All acoustic manipulation was done in *Praat*. From [lusətʰápi], we created two additional stimuli by splicing out first only the [ə], and then both the [ə] and the aspiration associated with [tʰ]. From each of these three stimuli (the original [lusətʰápi] and the two created by splicing out [ə] and [ʰ]), we then created yet another stimulus by splicing off the initial [lu]. This gave the six stimuli shown in (3).

(3)   *[s] word-medial*   *[s] initial*
       [ə] and [ʰ] present   lusətʰápi   sətʰápi
       [ə] spliced out   lustʰápi   stʰápi
       [ə] and [ʰ] both spliced out   lustápi   stápi

These six stimuli were used to create stimuli pairs. Four 'identical' pairs were created by matching up each of the four stimuli with [ʰ] with itself. Four 'different' pairs were created by matching a stimulus with both [ə] and [ʰ] with stimuli from which [ə], and both [ə] and [ʰ] have been deleted. Two different instantiations of each of the different pairs were created—with the stimuli appearing in each of the two possible orders. Stimuli in a pair were separated from each other by 500 ms of silence. These stimuli pairs were presented to participants in a same/different task. Given the hypotheses set out in the previous section, the expected responses to the different pairs are given in (4)—only one of the two orders between the stimuli is given, but the same response is expected for both orders. When the stop in Token 2 is unaspirated, [s]-initial and [s]-medial pairs are expected to be equally discriminable. Legal syllable parses faithful to the acoustic percept are possible for all four stimuli in these pairs, and it is expected that the listener will arrive at percepts that are acoustically identical to the stimuli. However, when Token 2 is aspirated, it is expected that the [s]-medial pair will be more discriminable than the [s]-initial pair. There is no legal syllabic parse of [stʰápi], and the listener is expected to perform perceptual epenthesis, and hence to arrive at the percept [sətʰápi] for this token, identical to the expected percept for Token 1.

(4) Expected responses to different pairs

Token 2 [+asp]?	Position of [s]	Token 1	Token 2	Expected response	Reason
No	Medial	lusətʰápi	lustápi	Different	Legal syllabic parse possible for both tokens.
	Initial	sətʰápi	stápi	Different	Legal syllabic parse possible for both tokens.
Yes	Medial	lusətʰápi	lustʰápi	Different	Legal syllabic parse possible for both tokens.
	Initial	sətʰápi	stʰápi	Same	No legal parse for Token 2 possible, perceptual epenthesis expected.

Procedure

Stimuli presentation and response collection were controlled with the *SuperLab* software package. Participants were run in groups of up to three. Data collection was done in a sound attenuated room. Participants were seated in front of individual laptop computers, each with a response button box attached. Stimuli were presented via headphones, and responses were collected via the button boxes. In each experimental block, each of the 12 pairs (4 identical, 4 different in two orders) was presented once. Since stimuli pairs were created from all 12 tokens in (2), each block contained 144 stimuli pairs. Before a stimulus pair was presented, a visual cue was presented in the middle of the computer screen. A token pair was then presented, and participants indicated their choice by pushing one of two buttons marked as "same" and "different". Participants were instructed to respond as quickly and accurately as possible. The block was presented four times, with participants allowed a self paced break between repetitions. Stimuli pairs were differently randomized for each participant in each repetition. Before the first block, participants were given 10 practice trials on stimuli pairs created in the same manner as described above, but from tokens not used in the actual data collection part. Participants received no feedback during the experiment.

3.2 *Results and Discussion*

The response patterns were transformed to d'-scores as in Signal Detection Theory (MacMillan and Creelman 2005) before they were statistically analyzed. Higher d'-scores correspond to higher discriminability. The d'-scores were submitted to 2 × 2 ANOVA's, both by participants and by items, with factors aspiration (both members aspirated, one member unaspirated) and [s]-position (word-initial, word-medial). Both main effects were found to be significant: aspiration (by participant $F(1, 14) = 139.0$, $p < .001$; by item $F(1, 11) = 575.9$, $p < .001$), and [s]-position (by participant $F(1, 14) = 15.7$, $p < .002$; by item $F(1, 11) = 73.4$, $p < .001$). Also the interaction between the factors was significant (by participant $F(1, 14) = 12.0$, $p < .005$; by item $F(1, 11) = 12.8$, $p < .005$). The average by participant d'-scores are represented graphically in Figure 2.

The first thing to note is that the discrimination is better for the pairs where one of the tokens in the pair does not contain aspiration. This is a direct result of the actual size of the physical acoustic difference between the members of a pair. Discrimination is better when the

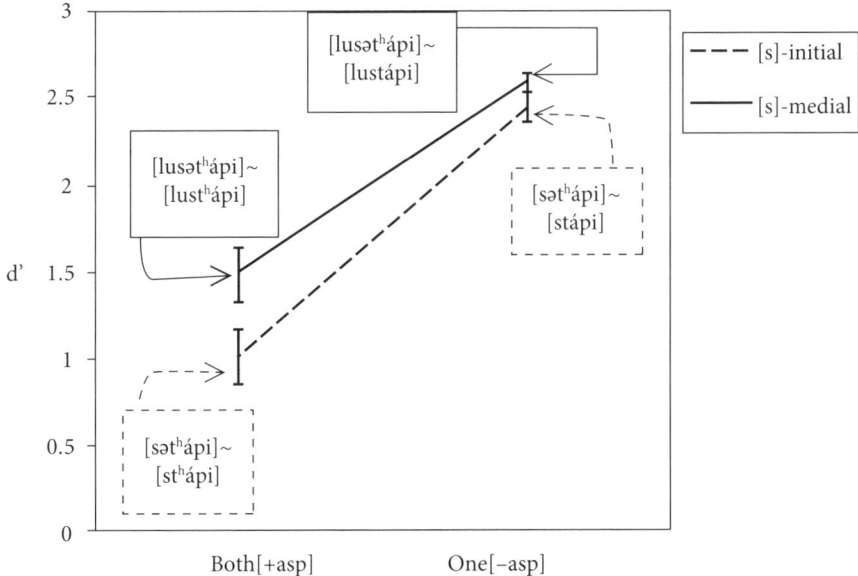

Figure 2   Mean d'-scores by Participant for Experiment 1. Error bars show 95% confidence intervals

members differ both in terms of aspiration and the presence/absence of a schwa, than if they differ only in terms of the presence/absence of a schwa. Discrimination is also better for the pairs where [s] appeared in word-medial position than the pairs where [s] appeared in word-initial position. However, as indicated by the significant interaction between factors, and as is also clear from Figure 2, this difference comes primarily from the pairs where both tokens contain an aspirated stop. The d'-scores for [s]-initial and [s]-medial pairs with one unaspirated pair member do not differ significantly from each other, as indicated by the overlapping confidence intervals. On the other hand, d'-scores for pairs where both pair members are aspirated do differ significantly. Specifically, discrimination is significantly better for pairs like [lusətʰápi]~[lustʰápi] than for pairs like [sətʰápi]~[stʰápi]. Put differently, having aspiration on both pair members is more detrimental to discriminability in the [s]-initial condition than in the [s]-medial condition.

It is important to remember that the actual size of the acoustic difference between [lusətʰápi] and [lustʰápi], and between [sətʰápi] and [stʰápi] is exactly the same. In fact, since all these stimuli were created from the same token, these two pairs are acoustically identical except for the presence/absence of the initial syllable [lu-]. The difference in discriminability between these two pairs therefore cannot originate in the acoustic differences between pair members. The perceptual systems of the participants in this experiment are more likely to map [sətʰápi] and [stʰápi], than [lusətʰápi] and [lustʰápi], onto the same percept. We interpret this as evidence that the participants in this experiment tended to perceive the acoustic stimulus [stʰápi] with an intrusive schwa between the [s] and [tʰ].

We interpret the results of this experiment as evidence that listeners parse acoustic percepts into prosodic structure, and that these parses are evaluated against the grammar of the listener. However, there is another possible explanation for these results that should be considered. It is true that in the mental lexicon of an English listener, the sequence [#sətʰ...] has higher probability than the sequence [#stʰ...]. In fact, [#stʰ...] probably has zero probability. It is hence also possible that the effect observed in this experiment follows from such frequency statistics calculated over the lexicon rather than from prosodic parsing and grammatical evaluation. Listeners could posit several perceptual hypotheses that are partially consistent with the acoustic stimulus, and then settle on the percept that has a higher statistical likelihood (Connine et al. 1993, Newman et al. 1997). When presented with a stimulus like [stʰápi], the listener could therefore posit both [stʰápi] and [sətʰápi] as perceptual hypotheses and consult his/her mental lexicon to determine the probability of each of these percepts. Since the probability of [stʰ...] is lower than that of [sətʰ...], the listener then settles on [sətʰápi].

There are reasons to doubt this interpretation of the results. In all of the previous studies that investigated the phenomenon of perceptual epenthesis, it has been shown that the results do not originate from such frequency statistics (Berent et al. 2007, Dupoux et al. 2001, Kabak and Idsardi 2007). However, to test this frequency based explanation more explicitly, we conducted a control experiment. We calculated the frequency of the sequences [#sək, #səp, #sət] and [#sik, #sip, #sit] in CELEX (Baayen et al. 1995). The log transformed frequencies are given in (5).

(5) Log transformed CELEX frequencies

	#sVk	#sVp	#sVt
V = [ə]	2.03	4.22	2.15
V = [i]	3.49	1.81	1.70

The frequencies with the two vowels have the following relative ordering for each of the three places of articulation: (#sik > #sək), but (#səp > #sip) and (#sət > #sit). Under the frequency based account, the prediction is hence that for a stimulus like [skʰ...] a percept with an intrusive [i] will be more likely than a percept with an intrusive [ə]. However, for [spʰ...] and [stʰ...], a percept with an intrusive [ə] should be more likely. To test this, we ran a second experiment that was identical to the one described just above with one exception: the recordings from which the stimuli were created had the structure [CV.si.Cʰv́.CV] rather than [CV.sə.Cʰv́.CV]. In order to make the two sets of stimuli as comparable as possible, tokens for the control experiment were selected such that the durations of [i] and [ə] did not differ significantly (two-tailed $t(22) = 1.52$, $p = .14$). Stimuli creation, and experimental design and procedure were exactly the same as for Experiment 1. Thirteen native speakers of American English participated in the control experiment. By comparing the response patterns between these experiments, the predictions of the frequency based account can be tested. The expected differences in the response patterns between the experiments under the frequency based account are given in (6).

(6) Expected response patterns under the frequency based account

Token pair		Expected epenthetic vowel percept	Expected discriminability
sVkʰámi	skʰámi	[i] (#sik > #sək)	Better when V = [ə]
sVpʰáno	spʰáno	[ə] (#səp > #sip)	Better when V = [i]
sVtʰáki	stʰáki	[ə] (#sət > #sit)	Better when V = [i]

The d'-scores for the crucial pairs in the two experiments are represented in (7). The d'-scores were higher in the control experiment (when the vowel was [i]) than in Experiment 1 (when the vowel was [ə]) for token pairs at all three places of articulation. This goes against the predictions of the frequency based account given in (6). The fact that discriminability is lower when V = [ə], shows that an intrusive vowel percept is most likely to be [ə], irrespective of the frequency of the sequences involved. Given that epenthetic vowels in English production are also more [ə]-like (Davidson 2006, 2007), this is what is expected if this intrusive vowel percept is the result of the grammar of the listeners rather than an influence of frequency statistics calculated over the lexicon.

(7) Comparison between the results of Experiment 1 and the control experiment

Token pair		d'-score	
		V = [ə]	V = [i]
sVkʰámi	skʰámi	1.25	1.82
sVpʰáno	spʰáno	0.61	1.54
sVtʰáki	stʰáki	1.14	1.84

Having shown that a frequency based account is unlikely, there still remains an alternative explanation for the effect that also assumes that the effect has its origins in the syllable structure grammar of English. All that the discrimination experiment shows is that participants were less successful at discriminating pairs like [sətʰápi]~[stʰápi]. However, based only on the results of this experiment, we do not know whether this is because they perceive [stʰápi] with an intrusive schwa, or whether they perform perceptual deletion on [sətʰápi] and perceive this stimulus without the schwa. Experiment 2 was designed to differentiate between these two explanations. In this experiment, participants were presented with tokens such as [sətʰápi] and [stʰápi] with the task of counting the number of syllables in each token. If they perform perceptual epenthesis, they should count three syllables in [stʰápi]. On the other hand, if they perform perceptual deletion, they should count two syllables in [sətʰápi].

4   Experiment 2: Syllable Count

Berent et al. (2007) use a syllable count task to investigate the phenomenon of perceptual epenthesis. This task has two advantages over the discrimination task. First, as explained in the previous paragraph, it is better at diagnosing what the perceptual system does—perceptual epenthesis or perceptual deletion? Secondly, in a syllable count task, participants hear only one token before they have to respond. The time that elapses between stimulus presentation and response is hence considerably shorter, so that the syllable count task gives better insight into the time course of the processing involved in the perception of these stimuli. However, the syllable count task still taps into the later phonological interpretation stages of speech processing. Participants are asked to count "syllables" which implies that prosodic structure must be present by the time that they respond. The nature of the task also requires of participants to listen to the whole stimulus before a response can begin, thereby also slowing down the response and increasing the likelihood that the response will be given only after phonological interpretation has taken place.

4.1   Methods

Participants
Twelve undergraduate students from the University of Michigan participated in this experiment. All participants were native speakers of American English with no known speech or hearing deficits. There was no overlap in participants between Experiment 1 and 2. Participants were paid for their participation.

Token selection and stimuli creation
The stimuli used in this experiment were created from the 12 non-words in (8). These tokens have the form [CV.sə.Cʰv́C] where [Cʰ] is one of the voiceless aspirated stops of English, and [v́] is a stressed

vowel. The same female speaker as in Experiment 1 was recorded reading these non-words ten times. We again selected one repetition of
each token to use for stimuli creation. As in Experiment 1, the token
was selected so that all of the sounds in the token were clearly articulated, and these selected tokens were equalized for intensity in *Praat*.

(8)   *Labial*   *Coronal*   *Dorsal*
    vɛsəpʰím   masəpʰál   kusətʰíf   lusətʰám   basəkʰíp   fisəkʰán
    lasəpʰíf   visəpʰáf   fasətʰík   misətʰál   masəkʰíf   pisəkʰáf

Each of these 12 non-words was processed in the same way to create
stimuli. We discuss the processing of [fisəkʰán] here as an example.
From [fisəkʰán], we created two additional stimuli by splicing out first
only the schwa (i.e. [fiskʰán]), and then both schwa and the aspiration
associated with [kʰ] (i.e. [fiskán]). One additional stimulus was created
from each of these three stimuli by also deleting the initial [fi-] (i.e.
[səkʰán], [skʰán], and [skán]). The other 11 non-words were processed
in the same way, creating six stimuli from each. These stimuli were
presented to participants in a syllable count task. Based on the hypotheses set out at the end of section 2, the expected response pattern for
this experiment is given in (9).

(9) Expected responses in Experiment 2

Example	[s]-position	Schwa?	[+asp]?	Actual syllable count	Expected response
fisəkʰán	Medial	Yes	Yes	3	3
fiskʰán		No	Yes	2	2
fiskán		No	No	2	2
səkʰán	Initial	Yes	Yes	2	2
skʰán		No	Yes	1	2
skán		No	No	1	1

The response is expected to agree with the actual syllable count for all
but one of the six token types. Well-formed syllable parses exist for
all of the stimuli except for [skʰán]. In agreement with the hypothesis
that the perceptual system settles on a final percept that is identical
to the acoustic input if a well-formed prosodic parse of the acoustic
input exists, the expectation is hence that participants will accurately

perceive the number of syllables for all but [sk^{h}án]. For [sk^{h}án], the aspirated [k^h] has to be parsed into syllable onset position, leaving the word-initial [s] stranded. The perceptual system is then expected to perform perceptual epenthesis to supply [s] with a syllabic nucleus.

Procedure

Stimuli presentation and response collection were performed exactly as for Experiment 1. Six stimuli were created from each of the 12 non-words in (8), for a total of 72 stimuli. To these stimuli, 60 fillers were added. The fillers were created from non-words of the form [CV.C$_1$ə.C$_2$v́C], where [C$_2$] is a sonorant consonant, and [C$_1$C$_2$-] is a possible syllable onset in English. From the non-word [lusəmát], for instance, were created the fillers [lusəmát], [lusmát], [səmát], and [smát]. All test stimuli were presented 8 times each, and fillers 4 times each. Stimuli presentation was differently randomized for each participant. Participants were allowed a self-paced break halfway through the experiment. Before a stimulus was presented, a visual cue was presented in the middle of the computer screen. The stimulus was then presented, and participants indicated their responses by pressing one of three buttons on a response box marked as [1], [2] and [3], respectively. The response time was recorded from the onset of each stimulus up to the point where the participant registered a response. Participants received no feedback during the experiment. Before the experiment began, participants did 10 practice trials, randomly selected from the fillers. Participants were instructed to respond as accurately and quickly as possible.

4.2   Results and Discussion

Responses were coded as 'correct' or 'error' in terms of the actual syllable count of each token, as given in (9). The average response pattern per participant is represented in Figure 3. The percent correct responses on each stimulus type was subjected to a one sample *t*-test to determine whether it was significantly above chance. The results of these *t*-tests are given in (10). Except for the [sk^{h}án]-type stimuli, the responses were indeed significantly above chance both by participants and by items. For the [sk^{h}án]-type stimuli, neither the participants nor the items analysis returned a significant result. In fact, the average percent correct responses was actually below chance for these stimuli.

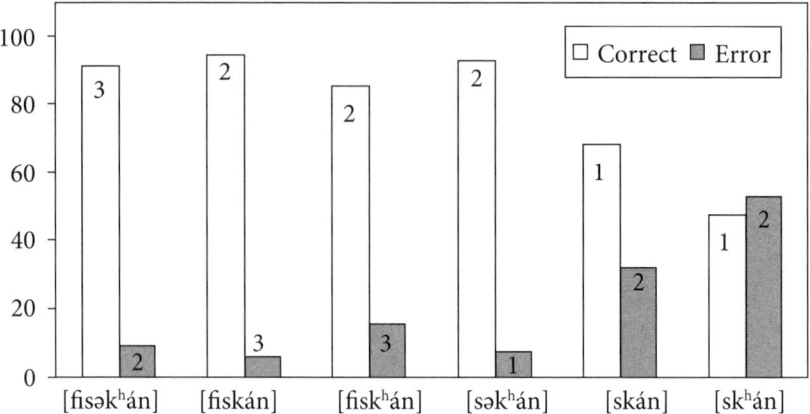

Figure 3   Mean syllable counts for Experiment 2 by participant for each token type. Numbers written in or on top of the bars indicate the response represented by the bar. Each category on the x-axis represents all stimuli of that type.

(10) Results of *t*-tests for Experiment 2

Stimulus type	Participant analysis		Item analysis	
	$t(11)$	p	$t(11)$	p
[fisəkʰán]	12.3	< 0.001	36.0	< 0.001
[fiskán]	21.5	< 0.001	88.0	< 0.001
[fiskʰán]	12.2	< 0.001	6.1	< 0.001
[səkʰán]	30.7	< 0.001	45.9	< 0.001
[skán]	2.0	< 0.04	9.2	< 0.001
[skʰán]	−0.3	0.78	−0.9	0.37

The most informative comparison here is between [fiskʰán] and [skʰán]. These stimuli are acoustically identical except for the presence/absence of the initial [fi-]. Since participants were very accurate in their responses to [fiskʰán]-type stimuli, the extra syllable percept to [skʰán]-type stimuli cannot come from some unforeseen acoustic property of these stimuli. In the [s]-initial condition, participants perceive an extra vowel between [s] and [kʰ], but in the [s]-medial condition they do not perceive such a vowel between the exact same [s] and [kʰ]. This vowel percept therefore originates in the perceptual system and not in the acoustic properties of the stimulus. This result also answers the one question that was left open at the end of Experiment 1. The results of Experiment 1 showed that participants cannot accurately discriminate stimuli such as [sətʰápi] and [stʰápi]. What was not clear was whether this is because they incorrectly perceive [sətʰápi] as [stʰápi], or whether they incorrectly perceive [stʰápi] as [sətʰápi]. The fact that the participants in Experiment 2 perceived [skʰán] with an intrusive vowel, indicates that it is [stʰápi] that was misperceived in Experiment 1.

The response times for Experiment 2 were also statistically analyzed. For each participant, the response times were first standardized. Response times for [s]-initial and [s]-medial stimuli were separately standardized, since the [s]-medial stimuli were all slightly longer because of the extra initial [CV-]. After the response times where thus transformed, all responses that were more than two standard deviations from the mean were excluded. This led to the exclusion of just over 4% of all responses.

The response times on the [fisəkʰán]- and [fiskʰán]-type stimuli, and the [səkʰán]- and [skʰán]-type stimuli were compared, using one-tailed paired-sample t-tests. [fisəkʰán] contains an extra [ə] that is absent from [fiskʰán]. Since response time was measured from the onset of a stimulus, the extra [ə] therefore contributes a little to the response time measured for [fisəkʰán], and similarly for the extra [ə] in [səkʰán]. If only the actual duration of a stimulus determines the response time, then the response times to [fisəkʰán] and [səkʰán] should on average be longer than those to [fiskʰán] and [skʰán]. The analyses for [s]-medial tokens like [fisəkʰán] and [fiskʰán] returned non-significant results both by items ($t(11) < .01$, $p = .50$) and by participants ($t(11) = 0.29$, $p = .39$). The response times to these two types of tokens therefore did not differ significantly. However, the results for the [s]-initial tokens like [səkʰán] and [skʰán] were quite different. They were highly significant by items ($t(11) = 8.3$, $p < .001$) and tended toward significance by participants ($t(11) = 1.6$, $p = .07$). These results are represented graphically in Figure 4. Inspection of this figure shows that the response time for [fisəkʰán] and [fiskʰán] is about equal, as is expected from the results of the t-tests reported just above. The response time for [səkʰán] is also shorter than that for [fisəkʰán] and [fiskʰán], which is again expected since [səkʰán] is physically shorter, lacking the initial [fi-]. However, the response time for [skʰán]-type stimuli is longer than that for [fisəkʰán]- and [fiskʰán]-type stimuli. This is true in spite of the fact that the [skʰán]-type stimuli are in reality the shortest of the four stimuli types compared in this figure.

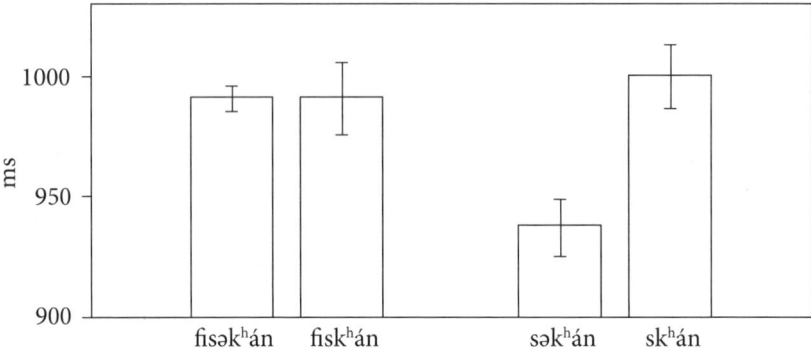

Figure 4   Mean response times by item for [fisəkʰán]-, [fiskʰán]-, [səkʰán]-, and [skʰán]-type stimuli. Error bars show 95% confidence intervals.

Most importantly, the response time for [skʰán]-type stimuli is significantly longer than that for [səkʰán]-type stimuli, in spite of the fact that the [səkʰán]-type stimuli are actually longer. The longer response time for [skʰán]-type stimuli therefore does not originate in the acoustic properties of these stimuli, but rather in the processing time dedicated to these stimuli. In the processing model represented above in Figure 1, stimuli like [skʰán] are subject to an extra stage of processing. The perceptual system first creates an acoustic representation of the stimulus, and then imposes a prosodic parse on this representation. This prosodic parse is then measured against the demands of the grammar, and if it is found to be well-formed a perceptual decision is taken. However, no well-formed prosodic parse of [skʰán] is possible. At this stage, the perceptual system therefore has to change the mental representation of the stimulus (via perceptual epenthesis) and re-parse the stimulus prosodically. This additional step takes up additional processing time, resulting in slower response times for stimuli like these.

5   Experiment 3: Begins on...

The results of Experiments 1 and 2 show that listeners represent stimuli like [stʰapi]~[sətʰapi] and [səkʰan]~[skʰan] the same during late stages of perceptual processing, in agreement with the processing model represented in Figure 1. However, these results do not give evidence for the earlier stage of acoustic encoding proposed in Figure 1, where the members of these pairs are hypothesized to have different mental representations. Although the results of Experiments 1 and 2 are hence consistent with the model represented in Figure 1, they are also consistent with other processing models. Another possibility is that the percept [səkʰán] is activated for both [skʰán] and [səkʰán] stimuli right from the earliest stages of processing, but that activation of this percept reaches the critical decision level sooner for an input stimulus that is actually identical to this percept. Such an interpretation would be consistent with a perceptual processing model that does not contain an initial stage of phonetic encoding that is informed only by the actual acoustic input stimulus. If this were correct, then both [skʰán] and [səkʰán] will be mentally represented as [səkʰán] from the earliest stages of processing. There should then be no stage of processing where the perceptual system can discriminate these stimuli consistently. On the other hand, if there is an initial stage of phonetic encoding, as represented in Figure 1, where the mental representations of [skʰán] and [səkʰán] stimuli differ, then there must be a stage of processing where the perceptual system can discriminate these two types of stimuli.

The experimental tasks used in Experiments 1 and 2 by their very nature tap into the later stages of perceptual processing and therefore cannot give evidence about the earlier stages of processing. Experiment 3 is designed to address this issue. In this experiment, participants are presented with the same stimuli as in Experiment 2. However, rather than counting syllables, participants are instructed to decide whether a stimulus begins on, for instance, [sk…] or [sək…]. This task does not require prosodic parsing, nor does it require of participants to listen to the full token before responding. Participants can thus respond faster so that their responses may reflect earlier stages of processing.

5.1 *Methods*

Participants
Eleven undergraduate students from the University of Michigan participated in this experiment. All participants were native speakers of American English with no known speech or hearing deficits. There was no overlap between participants in this and earlier experiments. Participants were paid for their participation.

Token selection and stimuli
The exact same stimuli as in Experiment 2 were used in Experiment 3.

Procedure

As with Experiments 1 and 2, stimulus presentation and response collection were controlled with *Superlab*. Presentation of each token was preceded by a visual cue on the computer monitor of two options represented in English orthography. The two options always corresponded to a percept with and without a schwa, with schwa represented with the letter *e*. For [s]-initial tokens, the options therefore consisted of *s* or *se* followed by one of {*p, t, k*}. For example, a token like [skʰán] would be preceded by the visual cue "sk…OR sek…". For [s]-medial tokens, the visual cue consisted of an orthographic representation of the initial syllable, followed by *s* or *se* and one of {*p, t, k*}. For example, [fisəkʰán] would be preceded by "feesek…OR feesk…". In the first syllable of these [s]-medial tokens, [i] was always represented by the letters *ee*, [u] by *oo*, [ɛ] by *e*, and [a] by *a*. The order between the cue with the schwa and without the schwa was balanced by token type. Participants were instructed to read the visual cue before the auditory token was presented, and to decide on which sound sequence the auditory stimulus begins by pushing either the leftmost or the rightmost button on the response box. Response times were recorded from the onset of the auditory stimulus to the moment that a participant pushed a button on the response box. In order to increase the likelihood that participants' responses will be based on earlier stages of processing, they were encouraged to respond as quickly as possible, even before the full token has played if that was possible. Each token was included once per experimental block, for 72 total tokens. The block was presented 4 times, with participants allowed a short self paced break between blocks. Tokens were differently randomized for each participant and each block. Before the experimental trials began, participants received 20 practice trials, randomly selected from the experimental trials. A different selection was made for each participant. Participants received no feedback.

5.2   *Results and Discussion*

In order to determine whether the different design succeeded in eliciting faster responses, and hence responses based on earlier stages of processing, the response times of Experiment 3 were analyzed. The response times were first standardized, exactly as in Experiment 2, and responses more than 2 standard deviations from the mean for each participant were excluded, resulting in the exclusion of just under 4%

of all responses. As a rough measure of success, the response times to different tokens in Experiment 2 (μ = 999 ms) and Experiment 3 (μ = 930 ms) were compared using a one-tailed, paired sample t-test, returning a highly significant difference ($t(71)$ = 3.76, p < .001). On average, response times in Experiment 3 were therefore shorter than in Experiment 2. However, the more important comparison is the response time to [sk^{h}án] type tokens between the two experiments. The goal of Experiment 3 is to elicit responses for these tokens at an earlier stage of processing, and we therefore need the response time to these tokens to be faster in Experiment 3 than Experiment 2. The response times on these tokens for the two experiments are represented in Figure 5. These response were also compared using one-tailed, two sample t-tests. These tests returned significant results both by items ($t(22)$ = 5.8, p < 0.001) and by participants ($t(21)$ = 2.0, p < 0.03). We conclude that the difference in task in Experiment 3 has therefore resulted in speeding up the responses of the participants.

Responses were coded as 'correct' or 'error' in terms of the actual acoustic properties of each token. The average response pattern per participant is represented in Figure 6. The percent correct responses on each stimulus type was subjected to a one sample t-test to determine whether it was significantly above chance. The results of these t-tests are given in (11).

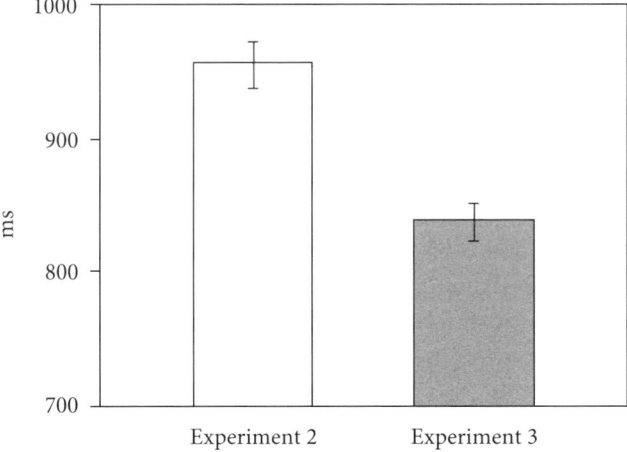

Figure 5   Average response time by item to [sk^{h}án] type stimuli in Experiments 2 and 3. Error bars show 95% confidence intervals.

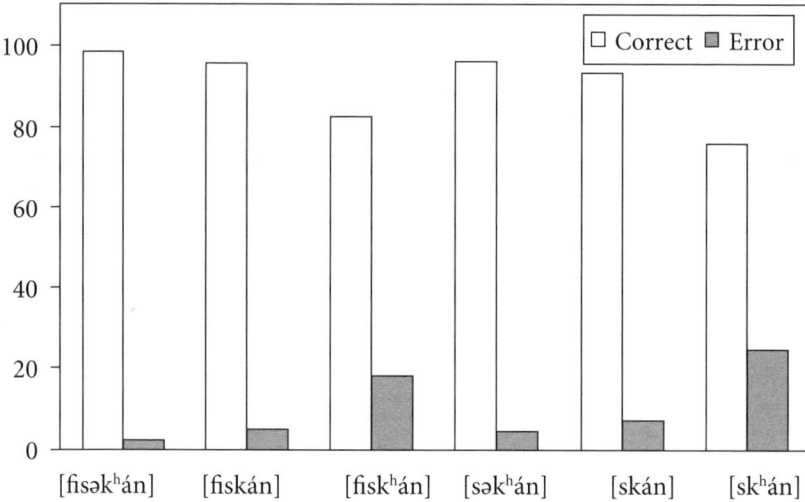

Figure 6   Mean percent correct for Experiment 3 by participant for each
token type

(11) Results of *t*-tests for Experiment 3

Stimulus type	Participant analysis		Item analysis	
	t(10)	*p*	*t*(11)	*p*
[fisək^hán]	76.5	< 0.001	94.9	< 0.001
[fiskán]	33.9	< 0.001	54.1	< 0.001
[fisk^hán]	8.3	< 0.001	5.9	< 0.001
[sək^hán]	45.3	< 0.001	52.2	< 0.001
[skán]	21.0	< 0.001	25.8	< 0.001
[sk^hán]	5.4	< 0.001	7.2	< 0.001

The percent correct response was significantly above chance for all token types. Most importantly, the response pattern to [sk^hán] token types in Experiment 3 is different from those in Experiment 2. In Experiment 2, participants were about equally as likely to perceive these tokens as [sək^hán] (with two syllables) or as [sk^hán] (with only one syllable). However, in Experiment 3, participants overwhelmingly perceive these stimuli as starting on [sk...], and therefore distinguish these stimuli from [sək^hán] type stimuli. Participants differentiate [sk^han] and [sək^han] at the faster response rates of Experiment 3 but they confuse [sk^han] with [sək^han] at slower response rates in Experiment 2. We interpret this as evidence that though [skʰan] and [səkʰan] receive the same mental representation at later stages of processing, there is, in accordance with the model in Figure 1, an earlier stage of phonetic encoding where these types of tokens have separate representations.

6   General Discussion

6.1   Mismatch between Stimulus and Percept as Evidence about Grammar

The human perceptual system does not function like a photocopier. It does not merely translate the input signal into a faithful mental representation. It rather takes the input signal and transforms it into a percept that bears resemblance to the input signal, but that also differs from it in lawful ways. This is true of all aspects of human perception—visual (Gordon 2004), olfactory (Wilson and Stevenson 2006), tactile (Schiff and Foulke 1982), auditory (Warren 2008), etc. One of the central goals of cognitive psychology is to discover the laws that dictate the ways in which the percept can deviate from the actual input. Part of the deviation is just the result of the physiological properties of the different organs involved in perception. But physiology does not explain all of perception. There are also operational or processing laws that influence the way in which the stimulus is processed once it has been translated by the primary perceptual organs into some kind of mental representation. One of the processing related factors that influence the auditory perception of speech is the grammar of the listener. Over the past several decades, a large body of evidence has been amassed showing that the exact same acoustic speech stimulus can be perceived very differently by speakers of different languages. Under the assumption that there are no major differences in the physiology of the auditory perception organs between speakers of different languages, such differences must have their origin somewhere in the processing that happens in the mind after the auditory speech stimulus has been translated into a mental representation. In order to understand the human perceptual system and the cognitive processes that support perception, it is therefore necessary to understand which aspects of grammar can influence speech perception, and how these aspects influence speech perception.

In the same way that the study of speech perception is important for our general understanding of human cognition, it is also important for our understanding of the grammatical competence of the language user. Studying the mismatches between acoustic speech stimuli and the percepts that listeners form, can give us insight into the structure of grammar. In this chapter, we have seen how such a mismatch can provide evidence that speech is parsed into higher order prosodic structure. The percept at which listeners arrive for the exact same acoustic stimulus depends partially on the position that the stimulus occupies in higher order prosodic structure. Specifically, an acoustic stimulus that corresponds to the phone sequence [st^h] is perceived as such when it appears in a context where a syllable boundary can be lawfully inserted between the [s] and [t^h]—i.e. in a context such as [lu__ápi]. But this same acoustic stimulus is perceived as [sət^h] when it appears in a context where this syllable parse is not possible—i.e. in a context such as [__ápi].

In English, aspirated stops are only tolerated in absolute syllable initial position. This presents a possible solution for the mismatch between the acoustic stimulus [st^h] and the percept [sət^h] in the [__ápi] context. The listener accurately perceives the aspiration in the acoustic stimulus. The aspiration is taken as the cue for the start of a new syllable, and the first three phones of the [st^{h}ápi] stimulus are hence prosodically parsed as [s.t^{h}á...]. This leaves the word-initial [s] stranded without a syllabic nucleus with which it can affiliate, and causes the perceptual system to perceive an illusory schwa between the [s] and [t^h]. In the [lu__ápi] context, this is not necessary. As before, the aspiration is taken as a cue to start a new syllable, resulting in a prosodic parse [lus.t^{h}a...]. Since the [s] is now preceded by a vowel with which it can affiliate, this sequence is well-formed, and there is no need for an illusory vowel. Somewhere during the processing of the speech stimulus, higher order prosodic structure is therefore imposed on the stimulus. Even though it is impossible to detect a syllable boundary between [s] and [t^h] in the acoustics of the stimulus, the way in which this stimulus is processed gives evidence for the reality of such a prosodic boundary.

It is important to note what the repair is that is imposed on the stimulus. When faced with a prosodically ill-formed representation such as [s.t^{h}a...], there are several ways in which it could be changed to become well-formed. The aspiration can be perceptually deleted, so that the percept can be parsed syllabically as [stá...]. Alternatively, the initial [s] can be perceptually deleted, giving the well-formed parse [tʰá...]. Another conceivable perceptual repair is to perceptually insert a vowel before [s], as in [əs.tʰá...]. All of these would result in prosodically well-formed percepts. However, the English listeners in the experiments reported above preferred a different repair—perceptually inserting a vowel between the [s] and [tʰ]. A question that this chapter does not address is whether the specific perceptual repair used to remedy such prosodically ill-formed stimuli is determined by the grammar of the listeners (i.e. it is language specific), or whether the same repair will be observed irrespective of the language of the listeners. Further research would be required to answer this question—though see Fleischhacker (2001) for an exploration of the idea that the perceptual repair is selected that is acoustically most similar to the actual acoustic stimulus.

6.2 *The Time Course of Perceptual Epenthesis*

Behavioral data, such as those reported in this paper, are rather course-grained in their time resolution, and therefore not optimal for probing into the time course of mental processing where very small time differences can be at play. Even so, behavioral data can reveal much about processing. The model represented in Figure 1 makes two very specific predictions with regard to the time course of processing, and the experiments presented above provide evidence for both of these predictions.

First, the model predicts that there will be an additional processing step involved in tokens that are prosodically ill-formed, and hence that such tokens will take longer to process. The results of Experiment 2 are in agreement with this prediction. Although [stʰáp]-type stimuli are physically of shorter duration than [sətʰáp]-type stimuli, participants are slower at responding to [stʰáp]-type stimuli. During acoustic encoding, faithful acoustic representations of both of these token are made. In the next step of processing, prosodic parses are imposed on these acoustic representations, and these parses are compared against the grammar for well-formedness. Since a well-formed prosodic parse of [sətʰáp] is possible, namely [sə.tʰáp], no additional processing is required for this token. On the other hand, no well-formed parse of [stʰáp] exists—both [stʰáp] and [s.tʰáp] are not in agreement with English phonological grammar. An additional processing step is hence required to bring this token type into agreement with the phonology of English, resulting in slower processing.

However, although the longer processing time associated with [stʰáp]-type stimuli are consistent with the extra processing step of the model represented in Figure 1, it does not actually confirm the existence of such an extra processing step. It is also possible that multiple perceptual hypotheses are entertained from the earliest stages of perceptual processing, so that the percept [sətʰáp] is activated for both [stʰáp] and [sətʰáp] stimuli even during early auditory processing, but that activation of this percept reaches the critical decision level sooner for an input stimulus that is actually identical to this percept. Such an interpretation would be consistent with a perceptual processing model that does not contain an initial stage of phonetic encoding that is informed only by the actual acoustic input stimulus. However, the results of Experiment 3 give evidence for the existence of such an early acoustic encoding stage in speech processing. In this experiment, participants responded faster to and clearly differentiated [stʰáp] and [sətʰáp] type stimuli.

Even the task in Experiment 3 is still behavioral in nature, and therefore not ideally suited to tap into the earliest stages of auditory processing. Non-behavioral methods that directly measure real time brain response to stimulus presentation, such as ERP (event related potentials) studies, are better suited to studying early stages and the fine-grained time course of processing (Praamstra et al. 1994, Praamstra and Stegeman 1993). In ERP studies, two stimuli are presented with a short inter stimulus interval, and brain activity is measured during the presentation of the second stimulus. Some of the stimuli pairs presented are identical, while others differ from each other. By comparing brain activity between the "same" and "different" conditions, it can be determined whether these two conditions are processed differently by the brain.

Wagner and Schafer (2008) conducted such an ERP study with stimuli very similar to those used in the experiments discussed in this chapter. The stimuli in their "same" condition contained pairs like [ptaki]~[ptaki]/[pətaki]~[pətaki], and the stimuli in their "different" conditions pairs like [ptaki]~[pətaki]/[pətaki]~[ptaki]. The participants in their study performed a same/different task similar to that used in Experiment 1 above. They found that English listeners could not consistently identify [ptaki]~[pətaki] pairs as "different", giving more evidence of perceptual epenthesis. The crucial difference between their experiment and Experiment 1 is that they collected ERP data while their participants were performing the same/different task. They found evidence for early differences in brain activity between same and different pairs, around 500 ms after the onset of the second pair member. But this difference disappears at later processing stages, somewhere around the 1000 ms mark. They interpret this as evidence for a separate early stage of processing, consistent with the phonetic encoding stage proposed in Figure 1 above. The behavioral same/different response happens later than the 1000 ms time point, and is therefore based on the later processing stages where the [ptaki] and [pətaki] are no longer distinguished.

Dehaene-Lambertz et al. (2000) perform a similar study with Japanese listeners, investigating the results of Dupoux et al. (1999, 2001) further. Dupoux et al. showed that Japanese listeners cannot discriminate tokens like [ebzo] and [ebuzo] consistently because of perceptual epenthesis in [ebzo]. The ERP results of Dehaene-Lambertz et al., however, are in conflict with those of Wagner and Schafer described just above. They did not find evidence for consistent differences in the brain activity of Japanese listeners between the "same" ([ebzo]~[ebzo], [ebuzo]~[ebuzo]) and "different" ([ebzo]~[ebuzo], [ebuzo]~[ebzo]) conditions, not even during the earliest stages of processing. They conclude that their results "suggest that the impact of phonotactics takes place early in speech processing and support models of speech perception, which postulate that the input signal is directly parsed into native language phonological format" (Dehaene-Lambertz et al. 2000, 635). Their results thus speak against the initial stage of phonetic encoding proposed in Figure 1.

Given these conflicting results, it cannot be decided definitively at current whether there is indeed a separate level of phonetic encoding—however see Kingston (2005) and Poeppel et al. (2008) for more arguments for such a level. More research, and specifically more ERP type investigations of similar phenomena, is necessary.

References

Baayen, R. Harald, Richard Piepenbrock and Leon Gulikers L. Gulikers. 1995. *The CELEX Lexical Database (Release 2) [CD-ROM]*. Philadelphia, PA: Linguistic Data Consortium, University of Pennsylvania.

Beckman, Mary E. and Jan Edwards. 1990. Lengthenings and shortenings and the nature of prosodic constituency. In *Papers in Laboratory Phonology I: Between the Grammar and the Physics of Speech*, edited by John Kingston and Mary E. Beckman, 152–178. Cambridge: Cambridge University Press.

Berent, Iris and Tracy Lennertz. 2007. What we know about what we have never heard: Beyond phonetics. Reply to Peperkamp. *Cognition* 104: 638–643.

Berent, Iris, Donca Steriade, Tracy Lennertz and Vered Vaknin. 2007. What we know about what we have never heard: Evidence from perceptual illusions. *Cognition* 104: 591–630.

Boersma, Paul and David Weenink. no date. Praat: Doing phonetics by computer. http://www.praat.org

Byrd, Dani and Elliot Saltzman. 2003. The elastic phrase: modeling the dynamics of boundary-adjacent lengthening. *Journal of Phonetics* 31: 149–180.

Cholin, Joana, Niels O. Schiller and Willem J. M. Levelt. 2004. The preparation of syllables in speech production. *Journal of Memory and Language* 50: 47–61.

Clifton, Charles, Katy Carlson and Lyn Frazier. 2006. Tracking the what and why of speakers' choices: Prosodic boundaries and the length of constituents. *Psychonomic Bulletin and Review* 13: 854–861.

Coetzee, Andries W. and Daan Wissing. 2007. Global and local durational properties in three varieties of South African English. *The Linguistic Review* 24: 263–289.

Connine, Cynthia M., Debra Titone and Jian Wang. 1993. Auditory word recognition: extrinsic and intrinsic effects of word frequency. *Journal of Experimental Psychology: Learning, Memory, and Cognition.* 19: 81–94.

Davidson, Lisa. 2006. Phonology, phonetics, or frequency: Influences on the production of non-native sequences. *Journal of Phonetics* 34: 104–137.

——. 2007. The relationship between the perception of non-native phonotactics and loanword adaptation. *Phonology* 24: 261–286.

Dehaene-Lambertz, Ghislaine, Emmanuel Dupoux and Ariel Gout. 2000. Electrophysiological correlates of phonological processing: a cross-linguistic study. *Journal of Cognitive Neuroscience* 12: 635–647.

Dupoux, Emmanuel, Kazuhiko Kakehi, Yuki Hirose, Christophe Pallier and Jacques Mehler. 1999. Epenthetic vowels in Japanese: A perceptual illusion? *Journal of Experimental Psychology: Human Perception and Performance* 25: 1568–1578.

Dupoux, Emmanuel, Christophe Pallier, Kazuhiko Kakehi and Jacques Mehler. 2001. New evidence for prelexical phonological processing in word recognition. *Language and Cognitive Processes* 5: 491–505.

Fleischhacker, Heidi. 2001. Cluster-dependent epenthesis asymmetries. In *UCLA Working Papers in Linguistics 7, Papers in Phonology 5*, 71–116. Los Angeles: UCLA Linguistics Department.

Fromkin, Victoria. 1971. The non-anomalous nature of anomalous utterances. *Language* 47: 27–52.

Gordon, Ian E. 2004. *Theories of Visual Perception*. New York, NY: Psychology Press.

Kabak, Bariş and William J. Idsardi. 2007. Perceptual distortions in the adaptation of English consonant clusters: Syllable structure or consonantal contact constraints? *Language and Speech* 50: 23–52.

Kingston, John. 2005. Ears to categories: New arguments for autonomy. In *Prosodies: With Special Reference to Iberian Languages*, edited by Sonia Frota, Marina Vigario and Maria João Freitas, 177–222. New York: Mouton de Gruyter.

Lennertz, Tracy and Iris Berent. 2007. Markedness constraints on the perception of s/z-initial onset clusters. Presented at the Workshop on Variation, Gradience and Frequency in Phonology, Stanford University. http://www.stanford.edu/dept/linguistics/linguist/nsf-workshop/Lennertz&Berent_Poster.pdf.

Levelt, Willem J. M. 2001. Spoken word production: A theory of lexical access. *Proceedings of the National Academy of Sciences of the United States of America.* 98: 13464–13471.

MacMillan, Neil A. and C. Douglas Creelman. 2005. *Detection Theory: A User's Guide.* Mahwah, NJ: Lawrence Erlbaum.

Mattys, Sven L., and James F. Melhorn. 2005. How do syllables contribute to the perception of spoken English? Insight from the migration paradigm. *Language and Speech* 48: 223–253.

McQueen, James M. 1998. Segmentation of continuous speech using phonotactics. *Journal of Memory and Language* 39: 21–46.

Nespor, Marina and Irene Vogel. 1986. *Prosodic Phonology.* Dordrecht: Foris.

Newman, Rochelle S., James R. Sawusch and Paul A. Luce. 1997. Lexical neighborhood effects in phonetic processing. *Journal of Experimental Psychology: Human Perception and Performance* 23: 873–889.

Poeppel, David, William J. Idsardi and Virginie van Wassenhove. 2008. Speech perception at the interface of neurobiology and linguistics. *Philosophical Transactions of the Royal Society B* 363: 1071–1086.

Port, Robert F. and Adam P. Leary. 2005. Against formal phonology. *Language* 81: 927–964.

Praamstra, Peter, Antje S. Meyer and Willem J. M. Levelt. 1994. Neurophysiological manifestations of phonological processing: Latency variation of a negative ERP component timelocked to phonological mismatch. *Journal of Cognitive Neuroscience* 6: 204–219.

Praamstra, Peter and Dick F. Stegeman. 1993. Phonological effects on the auditory N400 event-related brain potential. *Cognitive Brain Research* 1: 73–86.

Schafer, Amy, Katy Carlson, Charles Clifton and Lyn Frazier. 2000. Focus and the interpretation of pitch accent: Disambiguating embedded questions. *Language and Speech* 43: 75–105.

Schiff, William and Emerson Foulke, eds. 1982. *Tactual Perception: A Sourcebook.* Cambridge: Cambridge University Press.

Selkirk, Elizabeth. 1978. On prosodic structure and its relation to syntactic structure. In *Nordic Prosody II*, edited by Thorstein Fretheim, 111–140. Trondheim: Tapir.

——. 1981. On the nature of phonological representation. In *The Cognitive Representation of Speech*, edited by Terry Myers, John Laver and John Mathieson Anderson, 379–388. Amsterdam: North Holland.

——. 1986. On derived domains in sentence phonology. *Phonology Yearbook* 3: 371–405.

——. 2001. On the phonologically driven non-realization of function words. *Berkeley Linguistics Society* 27: 257–270.

Sugahara, Mariko. 2005. Post-FOCUS prosodic boundaries in Tokyo Japanese: Asymmetric behavior of an F0 cue and domain-final lengthening. *Studia Linguistica* 59: 144–173.

Turk, Alice E. and Stefanie Shattuck-Hufnagel. 2000. Word-boundary-related duration patterns in English. *Journal of Phonetics.* 28: 397–440.

Wagner, Monica Palmieri and Valerie Shafer. 2008. Phonotactic influences on the perception of consonant clusters by English and Polish listeners. Presented at the CUNY Phonology Forum Conference on the Syllable. http://www.cunyphonologyforum.net/syllconf.php.

Warren, Richard M. 2008. *Auditory Perception: An Analysis and Synthesis.* Cambridge: Cambridge University Press.

Wightman, Colin W., Stefanie Shattuck-Hufnagel, Mari Ostendorf and Patti J. Price. 1992. Segmental durations in the vicinity of prosodic phrase boundaries. *Journal of the Acoustical Society of America* 91: 1707–1717.

Wilson, Donald A. and Richard J. Stevenson. 2006. *Learning to Smell: Olfactory Perception from Neurobiology to Behavior*. Baltimore, MD: Johns Hopkins University Press.

CHAPTER THIRTEEN

ANGLOPHONE PERCEPTIONS OF ARABIC SYLLABLE STRUCTURE

Azra Ali, Michael Ingleby and David Peebles

In this chapter, we use a novel empirical method based on incongruent audiovisual speech data to highlight the mediating role that syllabic structure plays in speech perception. To emphasize the internalization of the syllable, we describe experiments probing the differences between Arabophones and Anglophones in the mental models mediating perception. The two groups respond differently to English and Arabic incongruent speech stimuli, and we argue that the contrasting behavior reflects a basic difference in the internal syllabic structure engaged during perception.

Many studies have shown that a syllable has a hierarchical structure with two main constituents: the consonantal onset and the vocalic rhyme. The theoretical consensus is divided between preferences for an onset-rhyme structure, and for inclinations to use an intermediate mora bearing notions of weight and duration (see, e.g., Ewen and van der Hulst 2001, for a general view; and for uses of moraic structure as a representation of field data on dialect variation Watson 2002 and Kiparsky 2002 and chapter 2, this volume). Most psycholinguistic experiments to test the cognitive reality of the syllable and its constituents in the mental models of humans have taken the onset-rhyme pathway in their analysis of laboratory results. Earliest experiments have involved word games using word-stimuli with concealed parts. The simplest games used monosyllabic words C(C)VC(C) (Treiman 1983, 1985). In most of Treiman's work, participants were asked to coin a new word from given pairs of words. The participants created new words by splitting given words at perceived inner boundaries, usually located between onset and rhyme positions. They took either the onset of the first word with the rhyme of the second, or the onset of the second and the rhyme of the first. These studies concluded that participants make onset-rhyme partitioning more often than by chance—suggesting the empirical reality of an onset-rhyme boundary in the cognitive word model of participants. Priming experiments in which an auditory prime stimulus precedes a visual presentation of a target word are also indicative of the reality of this constituent boundary. Experiments with visual prime preceding audio target, and either target or prime masked, yield results in the form of decision-times for target perception. The decision times are sensitive to the location of the mask, and change most notably as the mask location is moved to cross a constituent boundary. Such psycholinguistic experiments are designed on the supposition that perception of the priming stimulus and the separate perception of the target stimulus are mediated by the same structural model of lexical items, even when one is auditory and the other is visual—textual or pictorial (Segui and Ferrand 2002). It is possible that this identity of structure maybe false, and therefore empirical probes that engage only one kind of perceptual processing are especially valuable. We have sought for such a probe, targeting the natural processing that humans use to understand speech when watching audiovisual presentations—for example, 'head-shots' in a news broadcast or documentary program.

Our selected probe uses the McGurk effect which is a response to dubbed recordings of natural speech in which the audio and visual channels differ phonetically at a key segment, but remain temporally aligned. The classic McGurk-MacDonald experiment (MacDonald and McGurk 1978, McGurk and MacDonald 1976) focused on audiovisual fusion in onset of CV syllables, as represented by the notation (1) below. The rule represents the outcome of presenting an audiovisual incongruent speech stimulus with labial place of articulation [ba] in the Audio channel (A) and velar gesture [ga] in the Visual channel (V), to a group of participants who reported a fusion (F) percept [da] in 64% of the cases, 9% reported audio syllable [ba] and 27% reported the visual channel [ga] of the stimulus. With different voiceless plosive stimulus as in (2), 50% of the participants reported fusion percept [ta] and 50% of the participants reported the audio syllable [pa] (MacDonald and McGurk 1978: 255).

(1) $_A(ba \parallel ga)_V \rightarrow (da)_{F\ 0.64}$, $(ba)_{A\ 0.09}$, $(ga)_{V\ 0.27}$

(2) $_A(pa \parallel ka)_V \rightarrow (ta)_{F\ 0.50}$, $(pa)_{A\ .50}$

There is a long history of using incongruent speech in experiments. Something similar to the McGurk effect also occurs in purely audio contexts when there is incongruence between signals presented to left and right ears of participants. Cutting (1975) noted phonological fusion when using dichotically incongruent audio stimuli, in which the left-ear (L) and right-ear (R) signal differed at a single segment. Dichotic fusion patterns are shared by adults and children in all stages of linguistic development, and can also be represented symbolically as in the following examples (3) to (4).

(3) $_L$(leɪ || peɪ)$_R$ → (pleɪ)$_{AF}$, (lpeɪ)$_{AF}$, (leɪ)$_L$, (peɪ)$_R$

(4) $_L$(tæs || tæk)$_R$ → (tæsk)$_{AF}$, (tæks)$_{AF}$, (tæs)$_L$, (tæk)$_R$

In (3), the phonologically licit percept 'play' respects the phonotactic constraints of English branching onsets, and was reported even when the temporal alignment favored the phonologically illicit 'lpay'. In (4), however, there are two fusion responses reported by English participants, (tæsk)$_{AF}$ and (tæks)$_{AF}$ and these both have branching codas that are equally licit in English phonotactics.

More recent laboratory work on dichotic incongruence has focused more on so-called migration than on fusion. The classic experiments (Kolinsky and Morais 1993, Mattys and Melhorn 2005) also relate to the notion of an internalized syllabic structure mediating speech perception. The stimulus tends to evoke an illusory percept M, made up of contiguous groups of segments from R and L channels that migrate unchanged into the percept as in (5) (Mattys and Melhorn).

(5) $_L$(dɒlmal || kɛːrfɪn)$_R$ → (dɒlfɪn)$_M$, (kɛːrmal)$_M$, (dɒlmal)$_L$

Rule (5) represents participants reporting migration percept [dɒlfɪn] and [kɛːrmal], and some participants opting for the left-channel signal [dɒlmal] and the right-channel signal [kɛːrfɪn]. With dichotically-presented polysyllables, the recombinative illusions with the highest rates occur as migrations of units that are close correlatives of the syllables of traditional linguistic analysis (rather than segments or other units). Such experiments provide confirmatory evidence for the role of syllable in lexical access.

Our use of the illusions elicited in McGurk fusion is analogous to such migration studies, and probes several organizational features of the mental lexicon: empirical correlates of syllabic onsets and codas, the cohesion of morphological affixes, etc. In section 2, we outline evidence that the different fusion rates (frequency of fusion responses) represented in these rules are typical of a tendency for higher rates when the incongruent segment is in the syllabic coda, lower rates at onsets. Furthermore, they show empirically that syllable structure is indeed part of speakers' mental phonological representation. In sections 3 and 4, we illustrate this by showing how fusion rate trends differ systematically between participant groups of Arabic and English mother tongue when they are given the same stimuli.

Although early research on McGurk fusion with CV syllables was psychophysical in orientation, observation of group response to incongruent data in natural language context provides a direct route to the lexical access mechanisms in human cognition. It is relatively free of metalinguistic factors that might influence word-games with masked and primed stimuli. In addition, it can be given a high degree of ecological validity by placing incongruent stimuli randomly amongst congruent audiovisual stimuli, thus ensuring that participants process incongruent speech using the same mental apparatus that is engaged by congruent speech. In this way one can probe rather directly the internal mediation of speech cognition by structural organization of the mental lexicon. Such directness is important when investigating constituent structure as perceived by different groups.

1   *McGurk Fusion and the Mental Lexicon*

McGurk fusion studies have been accumulating in many laboratories for more than thirty years. The illusion is persistent even when participants are told that the soundtrack does not match the visual lip movements of the speaker. It survives size reduction of the video image, and it is also robust against acoustic noise (Tiippana et al. 2000, and others) and against visual noise (Fixmer and Hawkins 1998). In fact, precise temporal alignment of the audio and visual channel is not needed for experiencing McGurk fusion (van Wassenhove et al. 2007). Fusion responses still occurred even with temporal asynchronies from −30 ms to +170 ms.

McGurk fusion phenomena are also known to survive embedding in many natural languages, occurring amongst speakers of different mother tongues: French (Colin et al. 1998), Dutch (de Gelder et al. 1995), Finnish (Sams et al. 1998), and Chinese (de Gelder et al. 1995). More recent studies have used the McGurk effect to probe the lexical knowledge and semantic processing in Finnish (Sams et al. 1998), in German (Windmann 2004) and in English language (Brancazio 2004; Barutchu et al. 2008). Sams et al. focused on McGurk fusion in real or nonce words which were presented either in isolation or in a three word phrase context. Windmann used a semantic priming approach, where the isolated incongruent audiovisual stimuli were either semantically coherent or incoherent with a textually-presented prime. Her results showed greater fusion rates for semantically related primes than for semantically unrelated primes. Both Sams and Windmann studies show that lexical effects influence but do not over-ride McGurk fusion.

If fusion is truly a predominantly phonological process, then the fusion found in responses to incongruent consonant segment should also occur in incongruent vowel segments too. This is indeed the case, as shown in studies with Swedish and English vowels (Öhrström and Traunmüller 2004; Ali and Ingleby 2002). In these studies, an incongruent vowel segment was embedded in real words and nonsense CVC syllables which evoked fusion at similar rates to those found in consonant fusion.

2   *Probing Syllable Structure*

With appropriate statistical analysis, experiments on the McGurk effect have been successful in probing syllabic structure. The probe was a set of word stimuli in which an audiovisually incongruent segment was in either an onset site, or a vowel nucleus, or a coda site. The key experimental finding was that the site of the incongruent segment significantly affects the phonological fusion rate. This fact allows one to infer, from fusion rate comparisons, whether a given segment is part of, say, an onset, or of some other syllabic constituent. In this section, we briefly detail some of our earlier work using the McGurk effect to probe syllabic structure in English words, then in sections 3 and 4 we detail a feasibility study working with incongruent segments embedded in Arabic words.

In our earliest fusion studies (Ali and Ingleby 2004), stimuli were restricted to simple monosyllabic words of CVC type. An incongruent consonant segment was embedded either in the onset or in the coda site. In order to generate a stimuli set, word-triples are required; for example, a word in the audio channel, a word in the visual channel, and the expected fusion, that differs only at a single place segment, as illustrated in typical segmental incongruence and qualitative fusion results in (6) and (7).

(6) $_A$(beɪt || geɪt)$_V$ → (deɪt)$_F$, (beɪt)$_A$,...   {onset}

(7) $_A$(flæp || flæk)$_V$ → (flæt)$_F$, (flæp)$_A$,...   {coda}

Our simple, monosyllabic, word-triple stimuli are listed in Appendix 1. The experimental method and procedure was the essentially same as that used in the bilingual study of sections 3.2 to 3.4, except the words were English and all participants were Anglophones. From the small sample of stimuli tested, quantitatively, fusion rates were greater for consonantal codas than onset consonants (60% and 48% respectively, statistically significant). Our observed fusion rate contrasts were obtained from sequences including congruent audiovisual stimuli—for assurance of ecological validity and of the effects of signal-quality perception inaccuracy. Although we did not control for equal number of voiced and voiceless word-triples, for future work, we have managed to generate a much larger word-triple list with equal number of voiced and voiceless plosives.

In later monolingual experiments, we explored the onset-coda contrast in branching constituents, placing the incongruent segment either in the first or second branch of an onset, or in the coda position, as illustrated by cases (8) to (11).

(8) $_A$(breɪz || greɪz)$_V$ → (dreɪz)$_F$, (breɪz)$_A$,...   {onset: Cr}

(9) $_A$(speəz || skeəz)$_V$ → (steəz)$_F$, (skeəz)$_A$,...   {onset: sC}

(10) $_A$(kɒbz || kɒgz)$_V$ → (kɒdz)$_F$, (kɒbz)$_A$,...   {coda: Cs}

(11) $_A$(kɔːrp[1] || kɔːrk[1])$_V$ → (kɔːrt)$_F$, (kɔːrp)$_A$,...   {coda: cC}

Our stimuli with branching constituents are also listed in Appendix 1. Again, the experimental method was the same as in the previous CVC experiment. Some researchers might argue that the stimuli in case (9) are questionable, that they are not branching onsets because word initial [s]+stop clusters violate the Sonority Sequencing Principle (SSP; Clements, 1990). The SSP states that the segments of a syllable are arranged in a way that their sonority increases, from the beginning of

---

[1] Articulated rhotically by a Scottish speaker, to avoid problems with /r/ amongst English speakers.

the syllable onset to the nuclear peak, and decreases afterwards to the end of the syllable. Therefore, SSP governs the permissible sequences of consonants within syllables. The permissible ordering follows the so called Giegerich scale (Giegerich 1995). Kaye (1992), and Pan and Snyder (2004) have taken the view that SSP-violating word-initial sC clusters are structurally different from other branching onsets. Kaye proposes that word initial sC is binary, with [s] extrasyllabic, and has attempted to support this with evidence/examples from Italian, Portuguese, Ancient Greek, and English. Our motivation for keeping the sC as nominal branching constituents was to see whether or not the fusion rates are the same as onset Cr as in case (8). There are some similar concerns about [s] and [z] in the second branch of a branching coda. The concern relates to the polymorphic nature of English plurals, with or without voicing of [s] to form [z] via voicing harmony. Perhaps these segments might be considered extra-syllabic or otherwise exceptional on SSP grounds.

Our measurements, however, showed that incongruity sited in the first branch of an onset (Cr) influenced fusion much as in the second branch (sC): C-fusion rates for onset Cr and sC were 27.0% and 27.3% respectively, not significantly different. Also, as in the onset case, the effect of the plural markers in the first branch of coda constituent (Cs) was much the same as for second branch constituent (cC): C-fusion rates were 40.1% and 40.9% respectively. The results confirm a significant main effect in fusion rates between branches of coda and branches of onsets, but no significant effect within branches of onsets or within branches of codas.

2.1 *Perceptual Place Cues in Onset and Coda*

There might be some concerns about plosive fusion perception in the coda position, because plosives, (especially phonemes [p] and [t]), are generally hard to distinguish on the basis of their burst spectrum. Usually, formant transitions in syllable onsets are more reliable cues to consonant place of articulation (POA) than coda transitions (Liberman et al. 1967; Wright 2004). Wright (2001) tested intelligibility rate of consonants in onsets and in codas in presence of variable acoustic signal-to-noise. Misperceptions of consonant POA were made by participants, but mainly in noisy conditions, and POA misperceptions were more frequent for consonants in the coda position than in the onset position. Thus, it is important to check whether the alveolar fusions perceived in coda by many of our participants were genuine and were not a confusion of place contrasts (between [p] and [t] and between [b] and [d]), more frequent in coda than onset consonants.

We argue that the alveolar fusion reported by the participants in our studies were genuine perceptions rather than matters of confusion. Our argument is based on four points. Firstly, our experiments were not presented in presence of noise at the levels used by Wright to elicit confusion (our audio signals were presented binaurally over headphones rather than through speakers). Secondly, with congruent audiovisual stimuli which were embedded as controls amongst incongruent stimuli, our participants achieved 100% accuracy for place recognition. Thirdly, our participants were operating audiovisually with visible lip gestures supporting place perception. And fourthly, Clement and Carney (1999) showed that with incongruent audiovisual speech stimuli, the visual signal is favoured more when the audio signal is degraded. This is consonant with the findings of Sumby and Pollack (1954)—that the accuracy rate in presence of noise is greater for audiovisual speech stimuli than for audio only modality—and the findings of Inverson, Bernstein and Auer (1998)—that in visual mode only and in audiovisual modality visual, POA cues are clearly distinguishable. The subject of visual POA cues has been related to external lip-shapes corresponding to labial, alveolar and velar mouth gestures. Shapes have been sketched (Harris and Lindsey 1995) and proffered as the visual cues of phonological elements of speech. They classify these visual cues as a wide mouth opening for element A, a rectangular, tight lip-shape for element I and a rounding of lips for element U (Harris and Lindsey 1995). Via such cues, the different elements can be detected both in combination and in isolation within phonetic segments. A phonological framework, whose subsegmental primitives are, to an extent, both audible and visible, is ideal for modeling audiovisual speech phenomena such as McGurk fusion as illustrated in Ingleby and Ali (2003).

3   Codaless Languages and Arabaphone Perception of Arabic Syllable Structure

In a language without codas, the quantitative distinction between fusion rates in codas and onsets obviously cannot persist. The case of Arabic is especially interesting. The Arabic tradition of Sybawaih, on which the (phonetic) Arabic alphabet is founded, uses CV units only, symbolised orthographically by a consonant bearing a vowel diacritic.

This is also visible in the Quranic script, where consonants are clearly marked with vowel diacritics and where there are no vowels, a *sukuun*, a circle diacritic denoting silence, is marked above the consonants. The Western tradition of classical scholars, treating Arabic like Latin and Greek, postulated that there are CVC, CVVC, CVCC syllables, and assigned to consonant segments a notional 'coda' or 'onset' label. Yet others have maintained that Arabic words are built on one type of syllable: CV (Guerssel and Lowenstamm, 1996). The CV view is developed at a level of phonological abstraction above what is customary when dealing with the phonetics/phonology interface, but newer findings closer to the interface are emerging.

The most interesting findings were made by Baothman and Ingleby (2002), confirming empirically in a large corpus of spoken Saudi Arabic, that, unsurprisingly, it has no branching onsets but more significantly that sukuun has a complex articulatory presence. They found evidence in recordings and spectrograms that, far from being merely an orthographic device, a phonologically active correlative of *sukuun* is present within consonantal clusters such as [bʒ]. Its presence is revealed in the durations of clusters, which are longer by a short-vowel interval than the sum of the consonant durations when they are not clustered. In addition, the 'phonological sukuun' triggers the phonological processes of consonant devoicing and vowel epenthesis. For example, in the final cluster of Arabic بَحْر ([baħr] = 'sea') a schwa vowel [ə] can be heard and also detected as vowel material in spectrograms. This articulatory evidence indicates that *sukuun* is a cognitive reality for Modern Standard Arabic (MSA) speakers. In section 5, we discuss this further.

We suggest that if the mental lexicon of Arabophones has no codas, as in Sybawaihan tradition and in the work of Baothman and Ingleby, then there should be no statistical difference in fusion rates measured for onsets and 'notional codas' (consonants labeled as codas in the Western tradition). The issue can be tested via the perceptions of native speakers using Arabic word stimuli with an incongruent phonetic segment that would be a notional 'coda' in the Western tradition, but an onset in the Sybawaih view. Consonants in word-medial (e.g., C_2, Figure 1) position of English words can be either codas (as in 'habit', 'hacker', 'haddock', 'halo') or onsets (as in 'habituate', 'hallo', 'harangue'). The onset cases are less frequent and only occur when the second syllabic nucleus carries the primary stress. Thus, Anglophones will tend by habituation to perceive word-medial consonants in nonce

$C_1 V C_2 V C_3$

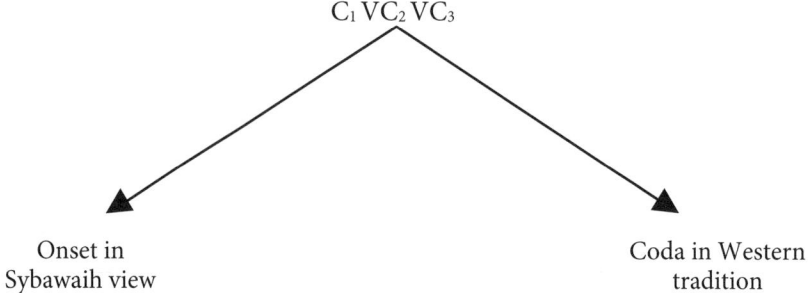

Onset in
Sybawaih view

Coda in Western
tradition

Figure 1   Possible syllabification

words or Arabic words as codas. The Arabic examples that we have
used have in some cases second nuclei that are long vowels (/habaa/
etc.). An Anglophone reading these will mispronounce and place primary stress on the second nucleus, making the preceding consonant
onset-like. Our participants, however, were not given this opportunity because they received the words audiovisually from an Arabic
speaker placing stress on the first short nucleus for morphological
reasons.

Thus, in our feasibility study, we have two predictions:

1. In Sybawaih view, we predict that Arabophones should show similar fusion rates in all 3 consonantal positions, thus, indicating a no
   onset-coda distinction.
2. In Western tradition, we predict that Anglophones should show
   differences in fusion rates: greater fusion in C_2 and C_3 than in C_1,
   so C_2 is likely to behave as notional coda than as an onset.

3.1   *Phonological Context of Arabic Consonants*

Arabic has many distinct dialects, but there is a *koiné dialektikos* used
by many educated native speakers in business, media and education.
It is close to the classical Arabic whose elocutionary form finds expression in the *tajweed* of Quranic scholars, and is usually referred to as
Modern Standard Arabic (MSA). Our speaker data is taken from users
of this MSA. The speakers do not share mother-dialect with all of the
participants in our perception experiments, but speakers and participants share a set of phonological segment contrasts even though they
do not realize them phonetically in the same way. For example, users
of MSA articulate the orthographic 'qaaf' as voiceless uvular [q] while

in Yemen, for example, a voiced velar [g] is common. The place of articulation contrasts used in our English stimuli are lacking in MSA, which has:

- no voiceless labial [p] except word-finally as output of a devoicing process, ruling out [p]-[k] incongruent pairs;
- no voiced velar [g], ruling out [b]-[g] incongruence pairs;
- two velar places, a front velar [k] and a back velar or purely uvular [q] from the letter 'qaaf';
- pharyngeal (or emphatic) place contrasts that complicate the pairing of incongruous segments—whereas [b] has no pharyngeal variant, [d] and [t] have both alveolar forms د and ت, and pharyngeal forms ض and ط, representable in IPA as [dˤ] and [tˤ] respectively.

In addition to these place and manner complications, there are contextual issues different from those of English. All Arabic consonants can be geminated, and this complicates the simple classification of consonants as onset or coda. One needs to experiment with geminates as well as singleton consonantal, but that is for later studies.

3.2 *Participants and Experimental Design*

Ten participants took part in the experiment, with an age range between 24 to 31 years, all university graduates familiar with MSA. Their mother tongue was Arabic in the dialects of Jordan, Kuwait, Oman or Israel/Palestine. The participants did not have any specialized knowledge of linguistics or psychology and were from computing and business disciplines.

A small lexicon of Arabic words with appropriate place contrasts are shown in examples (12) to (14). A full list of Arabic word-triples is detailed in Appendix 1. To avoid problems with the [k]–[q] contrast, we favoured words with [q] whenever possible. In the interest of assuring ecological validity, a sample of congruent stimuli was also included in the experiment, and all words were real meaningful words. The stimuli were constructed from the speech of a male speaker (from Morocco) and a female speaker (from Syria), both native Arabic speakers accustomed to MSA, with postgraduate education and age in the range 20–40 years.

(12) ₐ(balla || qalla)ᵥ → (dalla)ꜰ ,....   {C-initial}

ₐ(بلَّ || قلَّ)ᵥ → (دلَّ)ꜰ ,....

(13) $_A$(ḥabaa ‖ ḥaqaa)$_V$ → (ḥadaa)$_F$,....　　　　　{C-medial}

$_A$(حَىَ ‖ حَقىَ)$_V$ → (حَداَ)$_F$,....

(14) $_A$(nahab ‖ nahaq)$_V$ → (nahad)$_F$,....　　　　　{C-final}

$_A$(نَهَبْ ‖ نَهَقْ)$_V$ → (نَهَدْ)$_F$,....

3.3 Creating incongruent stimuli

Video recordings were done inside a quiet laboratory using a standard 8 mm digital Sony Camcorder with a built-in microphone for audio. The speakers uttered each word twice, to enable best selection from the two in terms of audibility and visibility. The speakers produced the words with clear voice to prevent effects of coarticulation of the sort that might affect place perception. The video recording was spliced into individual word recordings. These splices were stored in a standard *.avi file format with a frame size 640 × 512 pixel and 25 frames per second.

For the creation of incongruent stimuli, standard editing software (Adobe Premier 5.5) was used. Recordings differing in one phonetic segment were paired: for example [baal] (video 1) with [qaal] (video 2). The audio channel from video 1 was imported into video 2 and aligned with the audio and visual channel of video 2. The experimenter made fine judgments of proper alignment manually, after previewing the video clip. After alignment, the audio of [qaal] (video 2) channel was erased. The resultant video was thus [baal] in the audio channel aligned with visual lip movements saying [qaal]. All the stimuli (congruent and incongruent audiovisual stimuli) were stored in a standard *.avi file format using the 640 × 512 pixel frame size at 25 frames per second.

3.4 Instruction Sheet, Response Form, and Procedure

The participants were provided with report forms on which to record 'what they thought the speaker was saying' when receiving an experimental stimulus. The forms listed options corresponding to the words in audio and video channels, the expected fusion response, two random words and finally, a space to write in any word not explicit in the list. The experiment was carried out in a controlled laboratory with minimal background noise. Participants sat about half a meter from the 17" monitor screen and used headphones connected to the computer to listen to the audio. Using headphones maximized the audio signal rather than presenting the audio signal via speakers which can be degraded when it reaches the participant's ear. Participants were simply asked to wear the headphones provided, watch the video and decide what the speakers were saying. There was no time limit set and participants were not given any feedback.

3.5   *Results*

Firstly, the data for congruent stimuli were analyzed, revealing that 94% of the participants accurately perceived what the speaker was saying, eliminating poor vision or hearing as a factor influencing results. Secondly, group averages for fusion responses to incongruent stimuli were compiled, which revealed that fusion rates were similar in all three consonantal positions. Since only a small set of Arabic stimuli were tested, we used exploratory categorical statistical analysis only, which showed no main effect of consonantal site (χ^2 = 4.083, *df* = 2, *p* = .130). Since C-medial and C-final consonants are 'notional codas,' fusion rates for onsets vs. notional codas were, 61% and 69% respectively. Statistically again showing no significant main effect of consonantal site (χ^2 = .722, *df* = 1, *p* = .395).

Given that lexical access to Arabic words by Arabophones is performed without onset-coda distinctions, the question of why such distinctions are made by Western scholars arises. Perhaps the teaching of 'classical Arabic' by Western scholars, who use notions of syllable with onset and rhyme from their own and classical languages, is a cultural imposition. To explore the suggestion further, with the idea that it may originate in the cognition of Westerners, we put Arabic stimuli as nonce words to a group of Anglophone participants with no knowledge of Arabic.

4   *Anglophone Perception of Arabic Syllable Structure*

The aim of giving Arabic stimuli to Anglophones was to investigate whether or not, from internalized lexical access models learned from their English mother tongue, they imposed onset-coda distinctions on segments embedded in unfamiliar Arabic speech.

4.1   *Stimuli, Response Form and Procedure*

We put the same Arabic stimuli from our Arabophone experiment to Anglophones. We gave participants an open choice when reporting their percepts. The response forms consisted of words which were trans-literated from Arabic into an English equivalent, for example, أَرَابٌ [ʔaraab] was transliterated into English as <aaraab> so that our participants unfamiliar with IPA could respond. Our transcriptions ignored the distinction between the glottal stop, hamza (ء) and the glottal fricative, ayn (ع), rendering both by the textual apostrophe used for English dialect words like ['appen] and [da'abase]. The forms included options corresponding to the words in audio and video channels, the expected fusion response, two random words and a space to write in any word not explicit in the list. The rest of the procedure was exactly the same as Arabophone experiment (Section 3.4).

Eleven participants, 4 females and 7 males, took part in the experiment. All were native British English speakers, with an age range between 21 to 47 years. They had no specialized linguistic or psychology training, nor any knowledge of the Arabic language, nor any experience of visiting any Arab country.

4.1   *Results*

Firstly, the data for congruent stimuli were analyzed, revealing participants with no knowledge of Arabic are capable of reporting correctly to the congruent stimuli. In fact 93% (compared to 94% for Arabophones) of Anglophone participants accurately perceived what the speaker was saying, eliminating poor vision or hearing as a factor influencing results. Secondly, fusion rates were greater in C-medial and C-final than in C-initial position. Statistically, there was a significant main effect for consonantal site ($\chi^2 = 19.898$, $df = 2$, $p < .000$). Fusion rates for onsets vs. notional codas were, 38% and 72% respectively. Statistically, again showing a main effect for consonantal site ($\chi^2 = 15.063$, $df = 1$, $p < .000$). In summary, glancing at Table 1, the fusion rates for Anglophone participants for English and Arabic stimuli were very similar for onsets (40% and 39% respectively), but only slightly different for codas (65% and 73% respectively). Our feasibility study appears to show that Anglophones treat Arabic syllable structure similar to their native language, thus showing an onset-coda distinction.

In later experiments, we put the same Arabic stimuli to Anglophones who had been learning Arabic for at least 3 years on a part-time basis. The results are summarized in Table 1, and we discuss this in section 5.

Table 1. Average fusion rates at coda and onset sites

Stimuli and Participants	Onsets	Codas
1. English stimuli*—Anglophone participants	40%	65%
2. Arabic stimuli—Arabophone participants	61%	69%
3. Arabic stimuli—Anglophone participants	39%	73%
4. Arabic stimuli—Anglophones learning Arabic	63%	68%

* average fusion rates based on monosyllabic and polysyllabic words.

Of course, within the limitations of small-scale experimentation these results may or may not be replicable in a wider sample. Power analysis using G*Power (Faul et al. 2007) suggests that they are replicable: the effect of size at 0.19 turns out to be not a major factor in the results.

5   Discussion

The primary purpose of this chapter was to show that McGurk fusion can be used as a tool for probing internalized syllable percepts in the mental lexicon and determining their structure in two exemplar languages. This was achieved by measuring the variation of fusion rate with the context in which an incongruent consonant speech segment is embedded. Our studies from English and Arabic define a basis for empirical measurement of the syllable context; in particular it allows codas and onsets of syllables to be distinguished empirically.

There are different vulnerabilities to fusion in English; codas are more prone to fusion than onsets and are statistically significant and are robust in monosyllabic words (non-branching and branching constituents). This robustness means that fusion patterns can be used to test hypotheses about whether or not a language has the same onset-nucleus-coda patterns as English, a phonologically interesting question, given that theorists sometimes claim that certain languages are made up entirely of codaless syllables.

Although no-coda languages are known, Arabic syllabic structure is sometimes contested. The nature of the contest is summarized in Section 3: an historical Eastern CV tradition at the heart of standard orthography, versus an external Western scholarly tradition inspired by the syllabification of Latin and Greek. In more recent times, Baothman and Ingleby (2002) have developed a CV model of Arabic speech patterns using element phonology and a codeless constituent structure. It represents all the known coarticulation processes of Arabic and leads to a stress-prediction algorithm that is much simpler than those based on the syllabification of the Western classical tradition. More recent studies have shown vowel epentheses between consonant clusters in Lebanese and Palestinian Arabic (Gouskova and Hall 2007) and in Moroccan Arabic (Ali et al. 2008) that fit a CV model of phonological process. This tilts the contest to favor the Eastern tradition.

In this chapter, we used incongruent stimuli to open up the contest to experimental test. The test was to seek the segments that show too much fusion at all consonantal sites to be onsets: if the search fails, then there are no codas in the sample tested, which should be chosen to be representative of the language under test. In the first experiment (Arabic stimuli put to Arabophones), incongruent consonant segment was at either an onset or a 'coda' position (word-medial or word-final). When we put these stimuli to our Arabophones, results showed that there were no significant differences in fusion rates between onsets and 'codas'. This adds to the growing evidence that Arabic is a CV language, where syllables are coda-less not only at the underlying level, but also at the surface level, and also at the perception level. Of course the no onset-coda difference of fusion rates is also compatible with a VC phonology, but the absence of word-initial vowels in classical Arabic and several (but not all) modern dialects pushes the balance strongly towards CV. The counterbalancing cases have been reviewed by Kiparsky (2003) from the point of view of moraic theory, but they could also be thought of as the output of phonological processes favored by a dialect group, the processes operating on an underlying onset-rhyme CV structure. In the second experiment, we put the same Arabic stimuli to Anglophones with no knowledge of Arabic. These are nonce words to Anglophones and they showed an onset-coda distinction. They showed a similar perceptual pattern to our English syllable studies—higher fusion rates for 'codas' than for onsets. This indicates that in the mental models of Anglophones codas do exist and they are clearly distinguished from onsets. Thus, we have shown empirically that syllable structure is indeed part of speakers' mental phonological representation: Anglophones show an onset-coda distinction, whilst Arabophones do not.

It is possible that the results can be interpreted differently, considering that lexical access and speech processing in Arabic may be root based. The root consonants are not adjacent to one another in all words that share a root, e.g., root *k-t-b* 'write' is shared by the verb form '*kataba*' ='he wrote' and derivatives like '*yaktab*'= 'he is writing'. In other words, roots are abstract and discontinuous morphemes, stored in the lexicon with no syllable structure. They are given a syllable structure when they are associated with prosodic templates to form words. But, in English, morphemes are stored with their syllable structure and this can be seen as the difference between Semitic languages and Indo-European languages. To some extent this was demonstrated, for example, by Idrissi et al. (2008) with an aphasic bilingual Arabic-French speaking adult that Arabic consonantal roots are abstract morphemic units rather than surface phonetic units. However, we believe that once at the phonological component, the word pattern follows a CV structure, with no distinction between onset and coda. The experimental work presented in this chapter supports this.

In our most recent experiment, we put the same Arabic stimuli to Anglophones who had been learning Arabic for at least 3 years on a part-time basis. Surprisingly, the structure of Arabic in their mental representation shifted towards a CV pattern; showing a no onset-coda distinction (see Table 1, point 4).

In this chapter, Arabic words were used; these were real words for speakers of Arabic, but nonce words for the English speakers with no knowledge of Arabic. In contrast, for future study, we aim to use nonce Arabic words that would be put to Arabophones; our hypothesis is that Arabic speakers will still show a similar pattern to their own language, a no onset-coda distinction.

Finally, we would like to emphasize that experimental and phonetic analysis on Arabic roots and syllable structure has been very limited to date. Only few experimental studies have probed the mental lexicon (Idrissi et al. 2008, Prunet et al. 2000, Boudelaa and Marslen-Wilson 2004, and our own studies presented in this chapter). Few phonetic studies have begun to show phonologically active *sukuun* and vowel epentheses in consonant clusters (Baothman and Ingleby 2002, Guskova and Hall 2007, Ali et al. 2008). Recently, Rosenhouse (2007, 131) stated, "what can be hoped for the future is to further develop phonetic/phonological studies in order to learn more about the system of the Arabic language". We would like to add that experimental work is also essential because it can probe rather directly the internal mediation of speech cognition by structural organization of the mental lexicon.

6 Conclusion

In this chapter, we have shown from the statistics of response to incongruent speech stimuli that internalized syllables do exist. We have further shown that internalized English syllables have a structure in which the coda and onsets are distinct. An abiding pattern in all the context-embeddings that we have investigated in this chapter is that fusion rate patterns and the structural features inferred from them remain significantly different for English and Arabic. In English, codas and onsets embedded in monosyllabic words, are two distinct entities whilst there is only a single consonantal entity in Arabic.

In the extended study, we continue to use the McGurk effect embedded in Arabic words, with an aim of generating a large corpus of incongruent audiovisual stimuli. But we are also motivated by using the syllable migration paradigm for probing Arabic consonantal roots as well as the syllabic structure. We have also begun to investigate contrasting fusion rate patterns for singleton and geminate Arabic consonants. The latter are phonemic in Arabic and very common, whereas in English, though textual gemination is a common orthographic feature, truly phonemic gemination is rarer. When attested, it is a product of collisions—morphological (e.g. 'unknown' and 'soulless'), or cross-word for example 'big game' or 'top post' or across phrase boundaries, for example, 'Jack, cutting in, said...' or 'Pop, posing a question, stood...' etc.

References

Ali, Azra N. and Michael Ingleby. 2002. Perception difficulties and errors in multi-modal speech: The case of vowels. In *Proceedings of the 9th Australian International Conference on Speech Science & Technology*, edited by C. Bow, 438–443. Canberra: Australian Speech Science and Technology Association (ASSTA).

——. 2004. Probing cognitive mental models of speech using the McGurk effect. In *The proceedings of the 4th International Conference on the Mental Lexicon*, 44.

Ali, Azra N., Mohamed Lahourchi and Michael Ingleby. 2008. Vowel epenthesis, acoustics and phonology patterns in Moroccan Arabic. In *Interspeech-2008*, 1178–1181. Causal Production: Australia.

Baothman, F. and Michael Ingleby. 2002. Representing coarticulation processes in Arabic speech. In *Perspectives on Arabic Linguistics XVI*, edited by Sami Boudelaa, 95–102. Current Issues in Linguistic Theory 266, Amsterdam: John Benjamin Publishing Co.

Barutchu, Ayla, Sheila G. Crewther, Patricia Kiely, Melanie Murphy and David P. Crewther. 2008. When /b/ill with /g/ill becomes /d/ill: Evidence for a lexical effect in audiovisual speech perception. *European Journal of Cognitive Psychology* 20: 1–11.

Boudelaa, Sami and William Marslen-Wilson. 2004. Abstract Morphemes and lexical representation: The CV-Skeleton in Arabic. *Cognition* 92: 271–303.

Brancazio, Lawrence. 2004. Lexical influences in audiovisual speech perception. *Journal of Experimental Psychology: Human Perception and Performance* 30: 445–463.

Clement, Bart and Arlene Carney. 1999. Audibility and visual biasing in speech perception. *Journal of Acoustical Society of America* 106: 2271.

Clements, George. N. 1990. The role of the sonority cycle in core syllabification. In *Papers in laboratory phonology 1: Between the grammar and physics of speech*, edited by John Kingston and Mary Beckman, 283–333. NY: Cambridge University Press.

Colin, Cecile, Monique Radeau and Paul Deltenre. 1998. Intermodal interactions in speech: a French study. In *Auditory-Visual Speech Processing (AVSP'98)*, edited by Denis Burnham, Jordi Robert-Ribes, and Eric Vatikiotis-Bateson, 55–60. Terrigal-Sydney, Australia. http://www.isca-speech.org/archive/avsp98/

Cutting, James E. 1975. Aspects of phonological fusion. *Journal of Experimental Psychology: Human Perception and Performance* 1: 105–120.

Ewen, Colin J. and Harry van der Hulst. 2001. *The phonological structure of words*, Cambridge: Cambridge University Press.

Faul, Franz, Edgar Erdfelder, Albert-Georg Lang and Axel Buchner. 2007. G*Power 3: A flexible statistical power analysis for the social, behavioral, and biomedical sciences. *Behavior Research Methods* 39: 175–191.

Fixmer, Eric and Sarah Hawkins. 1998. The influence of quality of information on the McGurk effect. InAVSP'98: *Proceedings of the International Conference on Auditory-Visual Speech Processing*, edited by Denis Burnham, Jordi Robert-Ribes and Eric Vatikiotis-Bateson, 27–32. Terrigal, Australia.

Gelder, Beatrice de, Paul Bertelson, Jean Vroomen and Hsuan Chin Chen. 1995. Interlanguage differences in the McGurk effect for Dutch and Cantonese listeners. In *Eurospeech-1995*, 1699–1702. http://www.isca-speech.org/archive/eurospeech_1995/

Giegerich, Heinz. 1992. *English phonology*. Cambridge: Cambridge University Press.

Gouskova, Maria and Nancy Hall. 2007. Levantine Arabic Epenthesis: Phonetics, Phonology and Learning. Presented at Variation, Gradience and Frequency in Phonology Workshop, Stanford University.

Guerssel, Mohand and Jean Lowenstamm. 1996. Ablaut in Classical Arabic measure I active verbal forms. In *Studies in Afroasiatic grammar*, edited by Jacqueline Lecarme, Jean Lowenstamm and Ur Shlonsky, 123–134. The Hague: Holland Academic Graphics.

Harris, John and Geoff Lindsey. 1995. The elements of phonological representation. In *Frontiers of phonology: atoms, structures, derivations*, edited by Jacques Durand and Francis Katamba, 34–79. Longman: Harlow, Essex.

Idrissi, Ali, Jean-François Prunet and Renée Béland. 2008. On the Mental Representation of Arabic Roots. *Linguistic Inquiry* 39: 221–25.

Ingleby, Michael and Azra N. Ali. 2003. Phonological Primes and McGurk Fusion. In *Proceedings of the 15th International Congress of Phonetic Sciences*, edited by Maria Solé, Daniel Recasens and J. Romero, 2609–2612. Barcelona: Futurgraphic.

Inverson, Paul, Lynne Bernstein and Edward T. Auer Jr. 1998. Modeling the interaction of phonemic intelligibility and lexical structure in audiovisual word recognition. *Speech Communication* 26: 45–63.

Kaye, Jonathan. 1992. Do you believe in magic? The story of s+C sequences. *SOAS Working Papers in Linguistics* 2: 293–313.

Kiparsky Paul. 2003. Syllables and Moras in Arabic. In *The syllable in optimality theory*, edited by Caroline Féry and Ruben van de Vijver, 147–182. Cambridge: Cambridge University Press.

Kolinsky, Regine and Jose Morais. 1993. Intermediate representations in spoken word recognition: a cross-linguistic study of word illusions. In *EUROSPEECH'93*, 731–734. http://www.isca-speech.org/archive/eurospeech_1993

Liberman, Alvin, Franklin Cooper, Donald Shankweiler and Michael Studdert-Kennedy. 1967. Perception of the speech code. *Psychological Review*. 74(6): 431–461.

MacDonald, John and Harry McGurk. 1978. Visual influences on speech perception processes. *Perception and Psychophysics* 24: 253–257.

Mattys, Sven L., and James F. Melhorn. 2005. How do syllables contribute to the perception of spoken English? Insight from the migration paradigm. *Language and Speech* 48: 223–253.

McGurk, Harry and John MacDonald. 1976. Hearing lips and seeing voices. *Nature* 264: 746–748.

Öhrström, Niklas and Hartmut Traunmüller. 2004. Audiovisual perception of Swedish vowels with and without conflicting cues. In *Proceedings, FONETIK 2004*, 40–43. Stockholm University.

Pan, Ning and William Snyder. 2004. Acquisition of /s/-initial clusters: A parametric approach. In *Proceedings of the 28th Boston University Conference on Language Development*, edited by Alenja Brugos, Linnea Micciulla and Christine E. Smith, 436–446. Somerville, MA: Cascadilla Press.

Prunet, Jean-François, Renée Beland and Ali Idrissi. 2000. The mental representation of Semitic words, *Linguistic Inquiry* 31: 609–648.

Rosenhouse, Judith. 2007. Arabic phonetics in the beginning of the third millennium. In *Proceedings of the16th International Congress of Phonetic Science*, 131–134. http://www.icphs2007.de/

Sams, Mikko, Petri Manninen, Veikko Surakka, Pia Helin and Riitta Kättö. 1998. McGurk effect in Finnish syllables, isolated words, and words in sentences: Effects of word meaning and sentence context. *Speech Communication* 26: 75–87.

Segui, Juan and Ludovic Ferrand. 2002. The role of syllabic units in speech perception and production. In *Phonetics, Phonology and Cognition*, edited by Jacques Durand and Bernard Laks, 151–167. Oxford: Oxford University Press.

Sumby, W. H. and Irwin Pollack. 1954. Visual contribution to speech intelligibility in noise. *Journal of the Acoustical Society of America* 26: 212–215.

Tiippana, Kaisa, Mikko Sams and Riikka Möttönen. 2002. The effect of sound intensity and noise level on audiovisual speech perception. Multisensory Research Conference, abstracts, 36.

Treiman, Rebecca. 1983. The structure of spoken syllables: Evidence from novel word games. *Cognition* 15: 49–74.

——. 1985. Onsets and rimes as units of spoken syllables: evidence from children. *Journal of Experimental Child Psychology* 39: 161–181.

van Wassenhove, Virginie, Ken Grant and David Poeppel. 2007. Temporal window of integration in bimodal speech. *Neuropsychologia* 45: 598–607.

Watson, Janet. 2002. *Phonology and morphology in Arabic*. Oxford: Oxford University Press.

Windmann, Sabine. 2004. Effects of sentence context and expectation on the McGurk illusion. *Journal of Memory and Language* 50: 212–230.

Wright, Richard. 2001. Perceptual cues in contrast maintenance. In *The role of speech perception in phonology*, edited by Elizabeth V. Hume and Keith Johnson, 251–277. London: Academic Press.

——. 2004. A review of perceptual cues and cue robustness. In *Phonetically based phonology*, edited by Bruce Hayes, Robert Kirchner and Donca Steriade, 34–57. Cambridge: Cambridge University Press.

Appendix 1

English word-triples (simple monosyllabic words)

onset	bait—gate—date	/beɪt/—/geɪt/—/deɪt/
	bain[1]—gain—dane[1]	/beɪn/—/geɪn/—/deɪn/
	bad—gad[2]—dad	/bæd/—/gæd/—/dæd/
	bold—gold—doled	/bəʊld/—/gəʊld/—/dəʊld/
	pat—cat—tat[3]	/pæt/—/kæt/—/tæt/
	pill—kill—till	/pɪl/—/kɪl/—/tɪl/
	pod—cod—tod	/pɒd/- /kɒd/—/tɒd/

[1] are names
[2] a form of a steel bar
[3] used in conjunction, for e.g. 'tit for tat'

coda	cheep—cheek—cheat	/tʃiːp/—/tʃiːk/—/tʃiːt/
	bap—back—bat	/bæp/—/bæk/—/bæt/
	kip—kick—kit	/kɪp/—/kɪk/—/kɪt/
	lop—lock—lot	/lɒp/—/lɒk/—/lɒt/
	flap—flack—flat	/flæp/—/flæk/—/flæt/
	map—mack—mat	/mæp/—/mæk/—/mæt/
	tap—tack—tat	/tæp/—/tæk/—/tæt/

English word-triples (branching monosyllabic words)

Onset

Cr	brill—grill—drill	/brɪl/—/grɪl/—/drɪl/
	brain—grain—drain	/breɪn/—/greɪn/—/dreɪn/
	brew—grew—drew	/bruː/—/gruː/—/druː/
	braze—graze—drays	/breɪz/—/greɪz/—/dreɪz/
	prude—crude—trued	/pruːd/—/kruːd/—/truːd/
	pride—cried—tried	/praɪd/—/kraɪd/—/traɪd/
	prays—craze—trays	/preɪz/—/kreɪz/—/treɪz/
	press—cress—tress	/pres/—/kres/—/tres/

sC	spares—scares—stares	/speəz/—/skeəz/—/steəz/
	spate—skate—state	/speɪt/—/skeɪt/—/steɪt/
	spill—skill—still	/spɪl/—/skɪl/—/stɪl/
	spore—score—store	/spɔː /—/skɔː/—/stɔː/
	spud—scud—stud	/spʌd/—/skʌd/—/stʌd/
	spar—scar—star	/spɑː/—/skɑː/—/stɑː/
	spear—skier—steer	/spɪə/—/skɪə/—/stɪə/
	spool—school—stool	/spuːl/—/skuːl/—/stuːl/

Coda

Cs	cobs—cogs—cods	/kɒbz/—/kɒgz/—/kɒdz/
	tabs—tags—tads	/tæbz/—/tægz/—/tædz/
	bubs—bugs—buds	/bʌbz/—/bʌgz/—/bʌdz/

	cops—cocks—cots	/kɔps/—/kɔks/—/kɔts/
	tips—ticks—tits	/tɪps/—/tɪks/—/tɪts/
	pups—pucks—puts	/pʌps/—/pʌks/—/pʌts/
	peps—pecks—pets	/peps/—/peks/—/pets/
	maps—macks—mats	/mæps/—/mæks/—/mæts/
cC	harp—hark—hart*	/hɑːrp/—/hɑːrk/—/hɑːrt/
	corp—cork—cork*	/kɔːrp/—/kɔːrk/—/kɔːrt/
	wisp—whisk—whist	/wɪsp/—/wɪsk/—/wɪst/

* articulated rhotically by a Scottish speaker

Arabic word-triples

C-initial	دَلَّ—قَلَّ—بَلَّ	/balla/—/qalla/—/dalla/
		'wet'—'few'—'show'
	دَالُ—قَالُ—بَالُ	/baal/—/qaal/—/daal/
		'urinate'—'say'—'rotate'

C-medial	رَدَعَ—رَقَعَ—رَبَعَ	/rabaʕa/—/raqaʕa/—/radaʕa/
		'gallop'—'patch'—'keep'
	حَدَا—حَكَى—حَبَا	/ħabaa/—/ħakaa/—/ħadaa/
		'creep'—'report'—'urge'
	عَدْلُ—عَقْلُ—عَبْلُ	/ʕablun/—/ʕaqlun/—/ʕadlun/
		'plump'—'mind'—'virtue'

C-final	نَهَدَ—نَهَقَ—نَهَبَ	/nahab/—/nahaq/—/nahad/
		'rob'—'donkey'—'injection'
	أَرَادُ—أَرَاقُ—أَرَابُ	/ʔaraab/—/ʔaraaq/—/ʔaraad/
		'curdle'—'pour'—'wanted'

CHAPTER FOURTEEN

THE ROLE OF SYLLABLE STRUCTURE:
THE CASE OF RUSSIAN-SPEAKING CHILDREN WITH SLI

Darya Kavitskaya and Maria Babyonyshev

1 *Introduction*

Specific Language Impairment (SLI) is a neurodevelopmental disorder that affects language acquisition, while nonverbal IQ is within a normal range, and no neurological, sensory or physical impairments directly affect the use of spoken language (Bishop 1997, Leonard 1998). SLI is a heterogeneous disorder with several different profiles of impairment possible that can be responsible for the low performance on the standardized verbal tests.[1]

There is a general agreement that phonology is frequently impaired in children affected by SLI, but the precise nature of the phonological deficit is not completely agreed upon. Two theories are most relevant for the study presented below. The first theory (Gathercole and Baddeley 1990, Conti-Ramsden 2003) holds that the underlying cause of SLI is impairment in phonological short-term memory as revealed by poor performance in pseudo-word repetition tasks. The second theory (van der Lely and Howard 1993, Marshall et al. 2002, 2003) argues against the directionality of causation assumed by Gathercole and Baddeley (1990), proposing that the underlying cause of SLI is a phonological deficit, which results in an impairment of phonological memory and therefore poor performance on pseudo-word repetition tasks.

As argued by Marshall et al. (2003), Roy and Chiat (2004), van der Lely (2004), van der Lely et al. (2004), the limitations on phonological memory alone cannot explain the whole range of the findings on pseudo-word repetition for children with SLI and Typically

---

[1] For example, van der Lely and colleagues have identified a separate class of SLI, called G-SLI, which is characterized by "a primary, domain-specific deficit in the computational grammatical system" (van der Lely 1994, 1998, Davies and van der Lely 2000, among many others).

Developing (TD) children. Various other factors, such as syllable structure, word-likeness, stress, and articulatory complexity, have been claimed to affect children's performance on the pseudo-word repetition task (see Roy and Chiat 2004 for an overview). One such claim, advanced by Marshall et al. (2003), holds that only the most unmarked syllable structure (Consonant-Vowel, henceforth, CV) is available to children with SLI. For example, non-words such as [dɛ.pə], consisting of two unmarked CV syllables, are predicted to be easier to represent and therefore repeat for children with SLI than [dɛmp], consisting of the same number of phones, but comprising one CVCC syllable which is more marked than a CV syllable.[2]

The study reported in this chapter tests the hypothesis of Marshall et al. (2003) regarding the role of syllable structure representation in SLI phonological impairment. We do not consider the question of the direction of causality in phonological deficit typical of children with SLI resolved and do not necessarily see our study as providing evidence which can be used to further this debate. However, the study does provide evidence against the most simplistic application of the theory that the cause of SLI is solely the impairment in phonological short-term memory measured by the number of phonemes in a word. The study shows that both phonological memory and syllable complexity play a role in determining children's ability to remember pseudo-words. We also explore whether syllable complexity crucially relies on sonority, a factor that has not been adequately considered in previous studies.

2   Syllable Structure and Markedness

The syllable plays a central role in phonological theory as a constituent that represents phonologically significant groupings of segments (Zec 2007, 162). However, even the existence of the syllable is not altogether uncontroversial, as is emphasized by most chapters of this volume. As the point of departure, the present study assumes one theory of syllable structure widely used in the current phonological literature (for summary, see Blevins 1995, Zec 2007). Under a model of syllable structure illustrated in Figure 1, onset and rhyme are constituents, and

---

[2] Another possible reason for the difficulty of the second word as opposed to the first one is the presence of a consonant cluster in the second word. In what follows, we will attempt to distinguish between these two explanations.

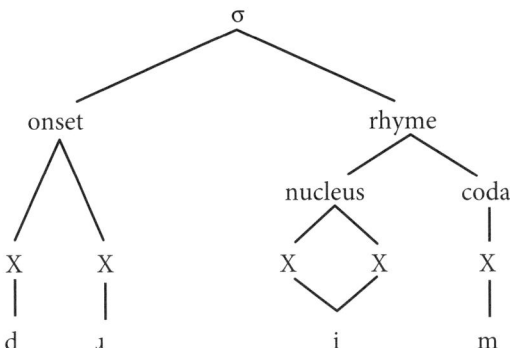

Figure 1   The syllabic structure of the English word *dream* (from Blevins 1995, 213)

rhyme can be further subdivided into nucleus and coda. The nucleus is also referred to as the syllable peak, and onset and coda as the syllable margins, see Figure 1.[3]

The notion of sonority is important in defining syllable structure. Intuitively, sonority is related to the overall acoustic energy of segments, however, the precise definition of sonority and the way it is incorporated into the grammar is still under debate (see Vennemann 1972, Selkirk 1984, Clements 1990, Zec 1995, de Lacy 2004, among others). The most uncontroversial sonority scale, where the classes of segments are listed in the order of increasing sonority, is in (1).

(1) Stops < Fricatives < Nasals < Liquids < Glides < Vowels

The segmental composition of onsets and codas exhibits striking regularities across the world's languages. These regularities have been stated in terms of the Sonority Sequencing Principle (Hooper 1976, Kiparsky 1979, Steriade 1982, Selkirk 1984, Clements 1990, Zec 1995, Blevins 1995, among others), provided in (2).

(2) Sonority Sequencing Principle (SSP)

Sonority increases towards the peak of the syllable and decreases towards its margins.

---

[3] While other representations of the syllable have been proposed in the literature (see Zec 2007 for an overview), the difference among them is not crucial to this study.

The sequencing of segments in Figure 1 exemplifies the SSP: in the syllable [dɹim], the initial consonant [d] is less sonorous than the following [ɹ], that is in turn less sonorous than the syllable peak [i], and the coda [m] is less sonorous than the syllable peak, thus showing an increase in sonority toward the peak and its decrease towards the margins.

While the SSP can be taken as a tendency, it is by no means exceptionless. For instance, English, which in general obeys the SSP, has some onsets of falling sonority, such as, for instance, /sp st sk/ and some codas of rising sonority such as /ps bz ks/, that violate the SSP. Russian is even more lenient with respect to the SSP, allowing such onset clusters as /lb lʲd rt mx/ and such coda clusters as /br tr blʲ/, even though these are much less frequent than the clusters that obey the SSP.[4]

As Rice (2007) remarks, phonologists have long noted that certain types of structures occur more frequently cross-linguistically and are acquired earlier in first language acquisition. These properties were taken to suggest that such structures are less *marked* than others, typologically less common and acquired later by children. For instance, CV syllables are taken to be less marked than CCV syllables and CVC syllables, since in the first case the syllable has a complex onset, more marked than a simple onset, and in the second case, the syllable is closed and thus more marked than an open one.

Recent literature contains criticisms of the notion of markedness on the grounds that its definition lacks precision and as a result is ambiguous. For example, Haspelmath (2006, 26) lists twelve possible uses of the term *markedness*, such as markedness as complexity (including specification for a phonological distinction, semantic markedness, formal markedness), markedness as difficulty (in phonetics, morphology, and as conceptual difficulty), markedness as abnormality (textual, situational, typological, distributional), etc.

Even though we agree in principle with Haspelmath's criticisms of the notion of markedness, we will continue using the term in the sense that has been traditionally used in the SLI literature. The usage in question corresponds to Haspelmath's subtype of markedness as abnormality, classified as "markedness as typological implication or

---

[4] On the basis of Sharoff's (2008) corpus consisting of 69,307 words, we estimate that only 1.06% of Russian consonant clusters show sonority violations.

cross-linguistic rarity" (Halpelmath 2006, 26). For instance, Russian has both /bl/ and /lb/ onsets, but since crosslinguistically /bl/ onset is widely attested and /lb/ is quite rare, in the typological sense of markedness the latter is more marked than the former. The notion of markedness in this sense is crucial in the formulation of the hypothesis advanced in Marshall et al. (2003), who claim that for children with SLI only an unmarked CV syllable template is available. In the current study, we test this hypothesis and offer a new analysis based on our results.

3   Specific Hypotheses

For the purposes of the current study, we manipulated two general factors: word length and syllable complexity. In the present context, word length is defined as the number of syllables in a word: monosyllabic, bisyllabic, and trisyllabic words were used in the experiment. There is general agreement in the literature that there is an impairment of phonological memory in children with SLI. Therefore, if Russian follows the general pattern, we expect TD children to be significantly better than children with SLI in this respect.[5]

The second factor manipulated in the experiment was syllable complexity. We used the following syllable templates: CV, CCV, CVC, CVCC, CCVC, CCVCC. As was mentioned earlier, Marshall et al. (2003, 516) advance the following hypothesis: "We propose an interpretation of the data whereby children with G-SLI have only unmarked parameter values available to them, meaning that they have just a CV template. There is no room on this template for additional consonants."

According to the model of syllable structure given in Marshall et al. (2003), Figure 2, only the first consonant in the syllable-initial cluster is regularly available to children with SLI presumably because only this

---

[5] Yet another possible factor that has been suggested in previous studies is stress. Given that stress in Russian is lexically determined so that there is no apparent regularity to its placement, we would predict that the location of stress does not affect the children's performance on the pseudo-word repetition task. Other studies show the effect of stress in languages where stress is more regular than in Russian (see Sahlén et al. 1999 for Swedish, Marshall et al. 2003 and van der Lely 2005 for English). We believe that there is no reason to expect that the role of stress is going to be any different for TD children than for SLI children, but testing it experimentally is the topic for a future study.

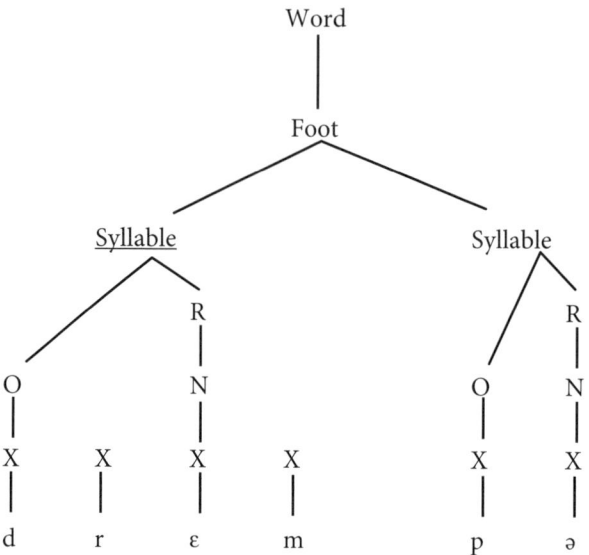

Figure 2   Representation of syllable complexity in the G-SLI child (From Marshall et al. (2002, 516))

consonant is structurally associated to the onset. Additional onset consonants and coda consonants are not associated to the higher structure and thus are not regularly available for storage and recall. This can be interpreted to mean that children with SLI have to remember more complex syllables as partially unstructured sequences of phonemes, which could result in making short term memory recall less efficient for them than for TD children.

In the current study we test the hypothesis with respect to onset cluster simplification as well as discuss our results with respect to coda cluster simplification. We think that it is plausible for TD children and children with SLI to have similar phonotactic constraints governing syllable structure. We predict that the pattern of difficulty of cluster repetition will be similar for TD and children with SLI. Whatever patterns we observe in TD children with respect to the SSP are expected to hold for children with SLI as well.

Given the preceding discussion, we expect complex onsets to be harder than simple onsets and complex codas to be harder than simple codas (or no codas) for both groups. However, languages vary with respect to their preference of complex onsets to complex codas, and vice versa. For example, Dakota allows complex onsets but bans complex codas, and Klamath allows complex codas but bans complex onsets (Zec 2007, 165). On the other hand, some languages allow both complex onsets and complex codas but are analyzed as preferring one to the other (e.g., an analysis of Bulgarian as preferring complex onsets to complex codas was proposed on the basis of the site of vowel epenthesis, Barnes 1997). The preference for complex onsets has been analyzed as an instance of onset maximization. The most general version of the onset maximization principle holds that VCV sequences are cross-linguistically syllabified as V.CV rather than VC.V. This version of the onset maximization principle is virtually exceptionless. An extension of the onset maximization principle is the syllabification of intervocalic clusters. For instance, VCCV sequences syllabify as V.CCV rather than VC.CV, thus maximizing the number of consonants in the onset. Kozhevnikov and Chistovich (1965) describe Russian as an onset-maximizing language, and Kodzasov (1990) also suggests that there is a version of onset maximization present in Russian. Coté and Kharlamov (Chapter 11, this handbook) show that the most likely syllabification of obstruent-obstruent clusters is heterosyllabic. Our results help to clarify this issue.

4   Methods

4.1   Participants

This study was conducted with monolingual Russian-speaking children. The experimental group subjects come from a village in Northern Russia in which the presence of language disorders is significantly higher than in the general population. This work is part of a larger study of familial Disorders of Spoken and Written Language (DSWL) in a geographically isolated population (Grigorenko et al. in progress). The probands were identified through a screening of all children (n = 33) of ages 4 to 11 and then matched with a group of TD children from the same sample. Each participant's parents agreed that their child could participate in this and related studies conducted at the same time under guidelines approved by the Yale University Human Subjects Research Review Committee and Northern State Medical University.

Nineteen monolingual Russian-speaking children aged 4;7–10;7 took part in the experiment. The subjects were classified based on three measures of general language ability developed for use in Russian with normal and impaired populations.

The first measure, called the Assessment of the Development of Russian Language (ORRIA) (Babyonyshev et al., unpublished ms.), was developed in conjunction with data collection on a larger sample from which a subsample was drawn. The ORRIA language assessment battery consists of seven subtests designed to evaluate the children's mastery of the major subcomponents of grammar. These tests addressed sentence structure, sentence repetition in context, expressive vocabulary, basic concepts, phonological awareness, word structure, and logical concepts. The test battery provides a measure of expressive and receptive knowledge in the areas of syntax, lexicon, morphology, and phonology, and allows for comparison of a given child's receptive and expressive linguistic abilities.

Two additional measures of language ability were calculated for all subjects: Mean Length of Utterance (MLU) and Syntactic Complexity (SC). In order to calculate MLU and SC, narrative samples were collected by asking children to tell a story on a basis of a picture book.[6] SC was defined as the number of complex structures in the narrative, e.g., relative clauses, embedded clauses, adjunct clauses, conjoined clauses, passive structures, and wh-questions, divided by the total number of words in that narrative for each child. It was previously shown that MLUs and SCs collected using the frog stories are an effective tool for diagnosing SLI (Reilly et al. 2004).

The scores on the MLU and SC were combined into a standard score on the same metric as the ORRIA. A cutoff for impaired status was established based on the percentile associated with two standard deviations below the mean for the TD group on *either* the ORRIA or the MLU/SC combined. Six of the subjects were classified as SLI (age range 4;7–10;7, mean age 8;0) and thirteen as TD (age range 4;10–10;6, mean age 8;5). Non-verbal IQs for children with SLI were ranged 66–98, mean IQ 80 and for TD children, the IQ range was 69–130, mean IQ 90.

---

[6] We used the frog stories, which are frequently utilized for this purpose. Note that the MLU was calculated in terms of words, rather than morphemes, as is customary for highly inflected languages, like Russian.

4.2   *Study Design*

This study was designed to test the hypothesis that marked syllable structures are unavailable to children with SLI and to explore the importance of phonotactics in general for these children. To achieve this goal, we manipulated syllable complexity with respect to the number of consonants in the syllable onset and coda and the total number of syllables in presented words. Taken together, these parameters allowed us to examine the effect of the general working memory load, the complexity of syllable structure, and the interaction of these factors. Additionally, we examined the effects of the SSP as evidenced by children omitting certain consonants in consonant clusters.

The experiment utilized a pseudo-word repetition task. In constructing pseudo-words, the following factors were manipulated: the number of syllables in a word (1 vs. 2 vs. 3) and syllable structure (CV, CCV, CVC, CVCC, CCVC, CCVCC).

Note that the syllable structure factor can be viewed as a combination of onset complexity (one-C onsets: CV, CVC, CVCC vs. two-C onsets: CCV, CCVC, CCVCC) and coda complexity (no coda: CV, CCV vs. one-C coda: CVC, CCVC vs. two-C coda: CVCC, CCVCC). The manipulated syllable in a word was stressed; all the unstressed syllables were of the CV form.[7]

The dependent variable was the number of correct repetitions of pseudo-words. An example of the relevant conditions for a one-syllable pseudo-word is in (3).

(3)   a. CV; 1syll   PA
       b. CVC; 1 syll   PAK
       c. CCV; 1 syll   PRA
       d. CVCC; 1syll   PASK
       e. CCVC; 1 syll   PRAK
       f. CCVCC; 1 syll   PRASK

The 144 pseudo-words were presented in a pseudo-random order to the subjects, who were asked to repeat the words exactly as they were

---

[7] Given the peculiarities of Russian syllabification, it is not always possible to determine the syllabic affiliation of consonants within clusters in intervocalic positions (see Kodzasov 1990). As was mentioned above, we made an assumption that intervocalic obstruent-obstruent clusters are heterosyllabic. We have also treated intervocalic obstruent-liquid clusters as onsets and intervocalic liquid-obstruent clusters as heterosyllabic sequences.

pronounced by the experimenter. Before the start of the experiment, the children were told that the words they would hear were not real, but made up, so they should not be surprised if they sound unfamiliar or strange. If a child failed to provide a response for five seconds, the experimenter repeated the word once. No other repetitions were allowed; the experimenter did not provide any corrections or other reactions, regardless of the child's performance.

The experiment was administered to the children individually, in a quiet room, by an experimenter who spoke the same dialect of Russian as the children. The experiment was recorded on a digital voice recorder (Olympus DSS Player 2002). The responses were phonetically transcribed by a linguistically trained native Russian listener. A second native Russian listener checked the reliability of the transcription in 20% of the data, and the discrepancy rate between the two judgments constituted less than 5%. In certain ambiguous cases the data were analyzed acoustically, through examining spectrograms and waveforms in Praat (Boersma and Weenink).

The data were coded as correct/incorrect responses based on the transcribed records. The following criteria were used for judging answers as incorrect: deletion of one segment or more, insertion of one segment or more, substitution of one segment for another, metathesis of segments, and the absence of an audible answer. In certain cases it was unclear whether the deletion of a segment was complete or partial. In the latter case, it would not be counted as deletion. Such questionable cases were decided on the basis of spectrogram examination. The answers were not judged as incorrect in the following cases: audible but noisy and thus not transcribable answer, substitution of [l] with [w] (a characteristics of Northern Russian dialects), and substitution of [r] with [w], which is a common characteristics of children's speech.

5   Results

A set of factorial analyses of variance was conducted in order to assess the difference in mean levels for the levels of the factors described above, as well as their interactions, on the number of correct repetitions. The analyses were conducted using standard statistical routines for the general linear model (Proc GLM) in SAS (2003). Omnibus tests for all of the models were significant ($p < .0001$). The findings for all main effects and interaction effects are reported individually below.

A three-way ANOVA ($2 \times 3 \times 6$) showed three significant main effects and two significant two-way interactions. A significant main effects of *group* on number of correct repetitions of pseudo-words ($F(1, 306)$ = 8.9, p < .01), of *syllable number* ($F(2, 306)$ = 126.2, p < .0001), and of *syllable structure* ($F(5, 306)$ = 17.4, p < .0001) were shown.

In addition, the analysis shows a significant interaction of *group* by *syllable number* ($F(2, 306)$ = 5.9, p < 0.01), illustrated in Figure 3.

There was also a significant *syllable number* by *syllable structure* interaction ($F(10, 306)$ = 5.53, p < .0001), shown in Figure 4.

However, the interaction of *group* by *syllable structure* was not significant ($F(5, 341)$ = 0.74, ns.). The three-way interaction of *group* by *syllable number* by *syllable structure* was also not significant ($F(10, 341)$ = 0.45, ns.).

Third, in a more fine-grained analysis of *syllable complexity*, this factor was further operationalized into two separate factors: *onset complexity* and *coda complexity*. Specifically, a three-way ANOVA ($3 \times 2 \times 2$) showed main effects of both *onset complexity* ($F(1, 306)$ = 8.8, p < .01) and *coda complexity* ($F(2, 306)$ = 38.6, p < .001). The main effect of *group* remained significant in this model, as anticipated ($F(1,306)$ = 8.9, p < .01).

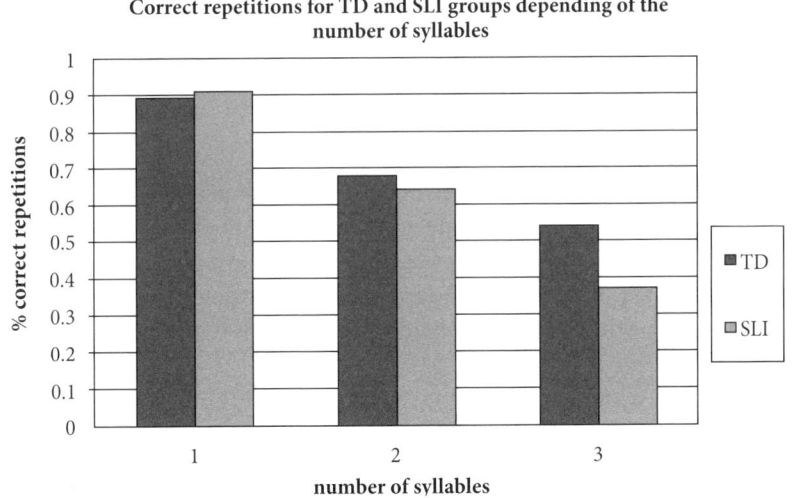

Figure 3   Group by syllable number

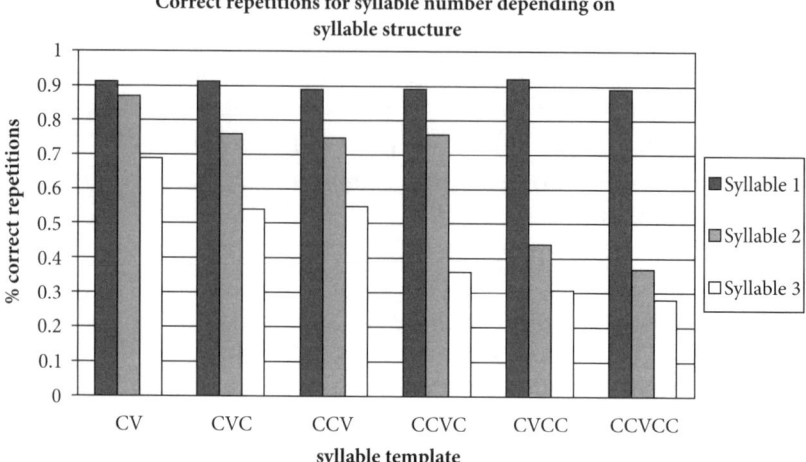

Figure 4   Syllable number by syllable structure

Two interactions of theoretical interest were evaluated: the *group* by *onset complexity* interaction was not significant (F(1, 306) = 0.72, ns.), and the *group* by *coda complexity* interaction was also not significant (F(2, 306) = 0.36, ns.). There were no other significant interactions in the analysis.

6   *Discussion*

6.1   *General results*

As predicted, the results show that the number of syllables in a word greatly affects the children's performance on the pseudo-word repetition task. Pseudo-words of one syllable are reproduced more accurately than pseudo-words of two syllables, and pseudo-words of two syllables are reproduced more accurately than pseudo-words of three syllables for both TD children and children with SLI. The interaction of *syllable number* by *group* (TD and SLI) is also significant, showing that children with SLI perform worse than TD children with respect to the task that varies syllable number. This result supports the hypothesis that working memory capacity is an extremely important factor in word storage and recall in Russian, as in other languages.

The second factor that affects the accuracy of the children's performance on the task is syllable structure. It is more difficult to represent and recall a word with complex syllables than with simple syllables.

There is also a significant interaction of *syllable number* and *syllable structure*, which means that it is more difficult to repeat more complex syllables in longer words. However, the interaction of *group* by *syllable structure* is not significant, demonstrating that children with SLI have the same access to the full inventory of syllable templates available in Russian that TD children have. Note that this result mirrors the findings of Marshall et al. (2003), which also did not show a significant interaction of group by syllable structure (cluster number in their terms).[8]

Additionally, our results show a main effect of both *onset complexity* and *coda complexity*. For onsets, syllables with one consonant in the onset are significantly easier than syllables with two-consonantal onsets. For codas, open syllables are significantly easier than syllables containing one consonant in the coda, which in turn are significantly easier than syllables with two consonants in the coda. There is no interaction of *onset complexity* by *group* nor *coda complexity* by *group*, which demonstrates once again that both TD children and children with SLI have access to the same phonotactics constraints.

6.2   *Cluster Simplification*

We also examined the types of errors made by children when repeating pseudo-words containing onset and coda consonant clusters. We looked at the words that contained two-consonantal clusters in word-initial and word-final position. The clusters were of falling, rising, and equal sonority for both onsets shown in (4) and codas shown in (5).

(4) Onsets

   a. Rising sonority: bl, dr
   b. Falling sonority: lg, rd
   c. Equal sonority: bd, kt

(5) Codas

   a. Falling sonority: rk, lp
   b. Rising sonority: tr, pl
   c. Equal sonority: kp, kt

---

[8] Regardless of this result, Marshall et al. (2003) develop a theory that SLI children have an impoverished syllable template compared to TD children.

We chose to examine these particular combinations of consonants because they represent relatively less marked structures (onsets of rising sonority and codas of falling sonority) and more marked structures (onsets of falling sonority and codas of rising sonority). Onset and coda clusters in which there is a sonority plateau are considered to be more marked than clusters in which sonority rises towards the nucleus and less marked than clusters in which sonority rises towards the margin. Table 1 summarizes consonant deletions in complex onsets and complex codas.

While there are too few data points for a meaningful statistical analysis to be performed, the data still exhibit certain patterns that can be informatively interpreted. First, in onset clusters there are zero cases out of 35 (0%) where both consonants are deleted, as opposed to 12 cases out of 131 (9%) in coda clusters where both consonants are deleted. This is not surprising given that a universally unmarked core syllable is CV, and thus the deletion of both consonants in the onset would lead to a less preferred onsetless syllable. On the other hand, the deletion of both consonants in the coda results in a preferred CV syllable.

Note that in onset clusters of either rising or falling sonority it is always the first consonant that deletes (Marshall et al. 2003, based on their chosen representation of syllable structure for children with SLI,

Table 1   The number of simplifications of complex onsets (syllable template CCV(C)(C)) and complex codas (syllable template (C)(C)VCC) (Note that O–obstruent, L–liquid, V–vowel)

Onset		OLV		O_1O_2V		LOV
Simplified as	LV	13 (100%)	O_1V	2 (18%)	OV	11 (100%)
	OV	0	O_2V	9 (82 %)	LV	0
	V	0	V	0	V	0
Total errors: 35	13		11		11	

Coda		VLO	VO_1O_2			VLO
Simplified as	VO	22 (51%)	VO_1	37 (59%)	VO	14 (56%)
	VL	17 (40%)	VO_2	25 (40 %)	VL	4 (16%)
	V	4 (9%)	V	1 (1%)	V	7 (28%)
Total errors: 131	43		63		25	

predicts the opposite). The pattern seems to be the following: the child builds a core CV syllable, choosing an onset consonant that is closest to the vowel, that is, in a cluster C_1C_2V the core syllable will be C_2V. The same pattern is observed in onset clusters of equal sonority, however, it is not exceptionless (the first obstruent is deleted 9 times out of 11 (82%), and the second obstruent is deleted 2 times out of 11 (18%)).

A different pattern emerges from the behavior of coda clusters. In codas of falling, rising, and equal sonority, the choice of the deleted consonant in the cluster appears to be random (in the codas of falling sonority the obstruent is deleted 22 times (51%) and the liquid is deleted 17 times (40%) out of 43, in the codas of rising sonority the obstruent is deleted 14 times (56%) and the liquid is deleted 4 times (16%) out of 25, and in the codas with a sonority plateau, the first obstruent is deleted 37 times (59%) and the second obstruent is deleted 25 times (40%) out of 63). A possible explanation for the pattern of errors observed is as follows: complex codas are marked and thus simplified to a simple coda. However, since the presence of a coda is not required by the core syllable template, the choice of consonant does not matter.

The data suggest that the more or less marked status of onset and coda clusters with respect to the SSP does not play a role in the patterns of cluster simplification. For example, more marked onset clusters of falling sonority are simplified as often as less marked onset clusters of rising sonority. It is likely that this pattern is due to the fact that Russian does not obey the SSP.

7   Conclusions

The study reported in this chapter has made several important points. First, it demonstrated that phonological memory affects children's ability to recall words. In most general terms, the results tell us that for both children with SLI and TD children it is always more difficult to represent and recall a longer word than a shorter word, as expected. Importantly, children with SLI have been shown to have more difficulty than TD children in remembering longer words. This result also supports the findings of the previous literature.

Second, this chapter demonstrates that structural complexity is an important factor that affects the recall of pseudo-words. We should note that the effect on processing complexity cannot be explained by limitations on working memory capacity alone, because the complexity is not determined by the number of phonemes in a word, but rather by the phonological organization of that word. Two metrics could be used in determining this notion of structural complexity: the organization of phonemes into syllables or the number of consonants in a consonant cluster. Importantly, we have shown that it is syllable structure that matters in the patterns of cluster simplification. These patterns cannot be explained by reference to the number of consonants in a cluster without taking syllable structure into consideration.

Third, the results described in this chapter indicate that syllable complexity becomes more detrimental in longer words, two- and especially three-syllable ones. This shows that the overall complexity of the task is determined by the combination of length and syllable complexity rather than by either of these factors alone.

Fourth, the hypothesis of Marshall et al. (2003) regarding the availability of only the CV syllable for children with SLI as opposed to the full range of syllable structures available to TD children finds no support in the data described in this chapter. It is indeed true that the most unmarked syllable structure is easier to represent and recall than any other. However, this chapter suggests that there is no qualitative difference between unmarked structure and all other structures. Rather, the results indicate that there is a continuum of complexity of syllable structure, with CV being the easiest and CCVCC being the hardest in our data. Moreover, this holds to the same degree for TD children and children with SLI. The fact that there is no interaction of *group* by *syllable complexity, group* by *onset complexity*, and *group* by *coda complexity* conclusively demonstrates that the accuracy of repetition for children with SLI is affected by the same factors as for TD children.

Fifth, the results reveal several suggestive patterns with respect to cluster simplification. Both TD children and children with SLI use the same strategy in simplification of onset clusters. Namely, they omit the first consonant in the cluster and build the core CV syllable by choosing the consonant adjacent to the vowel. In the simplification of coda clusters, the omitted consonant is chosen randomly. In addition, there are cases of omission of both consonants in the coda cluster, but never in the onset cluster. These facts also argue for the importance of the core CV syllable, as well as for the presence of onset maximization in Russian.

Our findings lend preliminary support to the view that the syllable is not epiphenomenal, but rather a crucial part of the grammar. To test this conclusion, a number of studies could be undertaken. First, an experiment could be designed to further investigate the influence of sonority in onset and coda clusters on pseudo-word repetition. In designing this experiment we would contrast clusters that are frequent in Russian with clusters that are not attested. In this way, we will be able to pull apart the effects of sonority and lexical frequency of clusters, thus making sure that the results of the current study were not confounded by the latter factor. Should we find any effects of sonority in a follow-up study, it could clarify the question whether children with SLI have access to the same inventory of phonological structures and regularities as TD children have. Another possible study would either lend further support to the view that syllable is an integral part of the grammar or refute it. An experiment similar to the current one would need to be carried out with typically developing adults and the results analyzed using two models: one which assumes internal syllable structure and the other which posits that the only relevant factor is the length of the consonantal string. We expect an argument for a better approach to emerge through the comparison of the predictive power of the two models. In general, whenever a certain model requires reference to the notion of a syllable to explain experimental results, it constitutes important evidence in support of an analysis under which syllable exists. We consider our study to be a step in this direction.

References

Babyonyshev, Maria, Lesley Hart, Jodi Reich, Julia Kuznetsova, Robyn Rissman, and Elena Grigorenko. No date. The Assessment of the Development of Russian Language (ORRIA). Unpublished Ms.

Barnes, Jonathan. 1997. Bulgarian liquid metathesis and syllabification in Optimality Theory. In *Formal Approaches to Slavic Linguistics: The Connecticut Meeting 1997*, edited by Željko Bošković, Steven Franks and William Snyder, 38–53. Ann Arbor: Michigan Slavic Publications.

Bishop, Dorothy V. M. 1997. *Uncommon understanding: Development and disorders of language comprehension in children.* Psychology Press Ltd.

Blevins, Juliette. 1995. The syllable in phonological theory. In *The handbook of phonological theory*, edited by John Goldsmith, 206–244. Cambridge, MA: Blackwell.

Boersma, Paul and David Weenink. no date. Praat: Doing phonetics by computer. http://www.praat.org

Clements, George. N. 1990. The role of the sonority cycle in core syllabification. In *Papers in laboratory phonology 1: Between the grammar and physics of speech*, edited by John Kingston and Mary Beckman, 283–333. NY: Cambridge University Press.

Conti-Ramsden, Gina. 2003. Processing and linguistic markers in young children with specific language impairment (SLI). *Journal of Speech, Language, and Hearing Research* 46: 1029–1037.

Davies, Lea and Heather van der Lely. 2000. The use of negative particles in children with grammatical SLI. Presented at the 24th Boston University Conference on Language Development. Boston: Mass, USA.

de Lacy, Paul. 2004. Markedness conflation in Optimality Theory. *Phonology* 21: 145–199.

Gathercole, Susan E. and Alan D. Baddeley. 1990. Phonological memory deficits in language disordered children: Is there a causal connection? *Journal of Memory and Language* 29: 336–360.

Grigorenko, Elena, Roman Koposov, Maria Babyonyshev, Lesley Hart, Igor' Pushkin, Jodi Reich and Anastasia Strelina. In Preparation. Cognitive and language profiles of members of a large extended pedigree with disorders of spoken and written language. Unpublished Ms.

Haspelmath, Martin. 2006. Against markedness (and what to replace it with). *Journal of Linguistics* 42: 25–70.

Hooper, Joan Bybee. 1976. *An introduction to natural generative phonology.* New York: Academic Press.

Kiparsky, Paul. 1979. Metrical structure assignment is cyclic. *Linguistic Inquiry* 10: 421–441.

Kodzasov, Sandro V. 1990. Slog. In *Lingvisticheskij Entsiklopedicheskij Slovar'*, edited by V. N. Iartsev, 470. Moskva: Sovetskaia Entsiklopediia.

Kozhevnikov, V. A. and Chistovich L. A. 1965. Speech, articulation, and perception. *NTIS, US Dept. of Commerce, JPRS-30543.*

Leonard, Laurence B. 1998. *Children with specific language impairment.* Cambridge, MA: MIT Press.

Marshall, Chloe, Susan Ebbels, John Harris and Heather van der Lely. 2002. Investigating the impact of prosodic complexity on the speech of children with Specific Language Impairment. *UCL Working Papers in Linguistics* 14: 43–68.

Marshall, Chloe, John Harris and Heather van der Lely. 2003. The nature of phonological representations in children with Grammatical-Specific Language Impairment (G-SLI). In *The University of Cambridge First Postgraduate Conference in Language Research*, edited by D. Hall, T. Markopoulos, A. Salamoura and S. Skoufaki, 511–517. Cambridge: Cambridge Institute of Language Research, University of Cambridge.

Reilly, Judy, Molly Losh, Ursula Bellugi and Beverly Wulfeck. 2004. "Frog, where are you?" Narratives in children with specific language impairment, early focal brain injury and Williams syndrome. *Brain and Language* 88: 229–247.

Rice, Keren. 2007. Markedness in phonology. In *The Cambridge handbook of phonology*, edited by Paul de Lacy, 79–98. Cambridge University Press.

Roy, Penny and Shula Chiat. 2004. A prosodically controlled word and nonword repetition task for 2- to 4-year-olds: evidence from typically developing children. *Journal of Speech, Language, and Hearing Research* 47: 223–234.

Sahlén, Birgitta, Christina Reuterskioeld-Wagner, Ulrika Netterlbladt and Karl Radeborg. 1999. Non-word repetition in children with language impairment–pitfalls and possibilities. *International Journal of Language and Communication Disorders* 34: 337–352.

SAS Institute. 2003. *SAS statistical software* (Version 9.1). [Computer Software].

Selkirk, E. 1984. On the major class features and syllable theory. In *Language sound structure: Studies in phonology presented to Morris Halle by his teacher and students*, edited by Mark Aronoff and Richrad T. Oerhle, 107–136. Cambridge, MA: MIT Press.

Sharoff, Serge. 2008. The frequency dictionary of Russian. Online corpus. http://www.comp.leeds.ac.uk/ssharoff/frqlist/frqlist-en.html

Steriade, Donca. 1982. Greek prosodies and the nature of syllabification. PhD diss., MIT.

van der Lely, Heather. 1994. Canonical linking rules: Forward vs. Reverse linking in normally developing and specifically language impaired children. *Cognition* 51: 29–72.

——. 1998. SLI in children: movement, economy and deficits in the computational syntactic system. *Language Acquisition* 72: 161–192.

——. 2004. Evidence for and implications of a domain-specific grammatical deficit. In *The genetics of language*, edited by Lyle Jenkins, 117–144. Oxford: Elsevier.

——. 2005. Domain-specific cognitive systems: Insight from Grammatical-specific language impairment. *Trends in Cognitive Sciences* 9: 53–59.

van der Lely, Heather and David Howard. 1993. Children with Specific Language Impairment: linguistic impairment or short-term memory deficit? *Journal of Speech and Hearing Research* 36: 1193–1207.

van der Lely, Heather, Stuart Rosen and Alan Adlard. 2004. Grammatical language impairment and the specificity of cognitive domains: relations between auditory and language abilities. *Cognition* 94: 167–183.

Vennemann, Theo. 1972. On the theory of syllabic phonology. *Linguistische Berichte* 18: 1–18.

Zec, Draga. 1995. Sonority constraints on syllable structure. *Phonology* 12: 85–129.

——. 2007. The syllable. In *The Cambridge handbook of phonology*, edited by Paul de Lacy, 161–194. New York: Cambridge University Press.

CHAPTER FIFTEEN

SYLLABLE MARKEDNESS AND MISPERCEPTION: IT'S A TWO-WAY STREET

Iris Berent, Tracy Lennertz and Paul Smolensky

1 *Introduction*

A key argument for the postulation of the syllable as a constituent is presented by universal phonological preferences that specifically target the syllable as their domain. For example, syllables like *blif* are universally preferred to *lbif*. Not only are *lbif*-type syllables less frequent across languages, but their presence in any given language implies the presence of syllables such as *blif* (Greenberg 1978, Berent et al. 2007). Several linguistic accounts attribute such typological regularities to universal markedness constraints that are active in the linguistic competence of all speakers (Prince and Smolensky 2004, Smolensky and Legendre 2006) and potentially shape linguistic performance as well (Davidson et al. 2006). On an alternative explanation, the cross-linguistic preference for *blif-* type syllables reflects only extra-linguistic factors governing the transmission of language over time. Unmarked syllables like *blif* are typologically frequent because they are easier to perceive and produce (Ohala 1992, Kawasaki-Fukumori 1992), and consequently, their transmission across speakers is more stable (Blevins 2004, 2006). On this view, the typology of syllables, while providing clues concerning language transmission, is irrelevant to the study of linguistic competence, in general, and the grammatical theory of syllable structure, in particular.

The disagreement between these two accounts centers on two key issues. The first concerns the ontological status of markedness restrictions: are markedness constraints mentally represented in the brains and minds of individual speakers, or are they mere psychologically irrelevant descriptions, relics of language change and its nonlinguistic determinants—historic facts, the statistical structure of linguistic experience and the properties of nonlinguistic mechanisms governing perception and articulation? If markedness did play a role in the grammar, then a second question arises. It is well known that the ease of perception and articulation of linguistic objects correlates with their grammatical well-formedness, and such correlation may well indicate causation. The debate concerns the direction of the causal link between performance and competence: are performance difficulties the cause of grammatical markedness or its consequence?

The research described in this chapter addresses both issues by examining the universal restrictions on the structure of onset clusters. We begin by showing that the typological preference for *blif*-type syllables is synchronically active and it extends even to syllables that are unattested in one's language: marked syllables are systematically misperceived relative to less marked syllables. We next describe two novel experiments demonstrating that the misperception of marked syllables reflects preferences that are internal to the faculty of language. Such preferences are not explained by the properties of the lexicon nor are they byproducts of domain-general mechanisms of perception and articulation. The results reported in this chapter suggest that universal markedness restrictions are synchronically active in the grammars of all speakers, and are causally linked to perceptibility. But contrary to the proposal of evolutionary phonology, perceptibility can be a consequence of grammatical markedness, not necessarily its cause.

2   *Sonority Restrictions on Onset Clusters*

Before we can experimentally examine speakers' grammatical preferences regarding onset structure, we must briefly discuss some of the formal accounts of such preferences and their empirical support. The typological preference for syllables such as *blif* over *lbif* has been attributed to universal restrictions on sonority (s)—an abstract phonological property that correlates with intensity (Clements 1990, Parker 2002, Wright 2004). The least sonorous consonants are obstruents ($s = 1$), followed by nasals ($s = 2$), liquids ($s = 3$) and glides ($s = 4$). Accordingly, the obstruent-liquid combination in *blif* manifests a sonority rise of two steps: the sonority difference, Δs, is 2. By contrast, *lbif* manifests a fall in sonority: a negative sonority difference $\Delta s = -2$. The specific preference for *blif* over *lbif* may thus reflect broad markedness restrictions that disfavor onsets with smaller sonority differences— disfavoring, for example, $\Delta s = -2$ to $\Delta s = 2$ (e.g. Clements 1990, Smolensky 2006).

Sonority sequencing restrictions have been invoked in explaining various grammatical phenomena (syllable structure: Vennemann 1972, Hooper 1976, Steriade 1982, Selkirk 1984, Prince and Smolensky 2004, Smolensky 2006; syllable contact: Gouskova 2001, 2004; stress assignment: de Lacy 2007; reduplication: Pinker and Birdsong 1979, Steriade 1982, 1988, Morelli 1999, Parker 2002 and repair: Hooper 1976). The sonority of consonants also correlates with their production accuracy in first- (Ohala 1999, Pater 2004, Barlow 2005) and second-language acquisition (Broselow and Finer 1991, Broselow et al. 1998, Broselow and Xu 2004), developmental phonological disorders (e.g. Gierut 1999, Barlow 2001), aphasia (e.g. Romani and Calabrese 1998, Stenneken et al. 2005), speech errors (Stemberger and Treiman 1986), word games (Treiman 1984, Treiman and Danis 1988, Fowler et al. 1993, Treiman et al. 2002) and reading tasks (Levitt et al. 1991, Alonzo and Taft 2002).

Although these results strongly suggest that speakers possess preferences regarding the sequencing of onset consonants, they leave open some questions regarding the scope of such restrictions and their nature. Most existing evidence for sonority preferences concern preferences for unmarked onsets that are attested in one's language. Such preferences could be due to the familiarity with these particular onsets, rather than a broad preference for any onset with a large sonority difference. Although there is evidence that speakers' preferences might extend to syllables that are unattested in their language (Pertz and Bever 1975, Broselow and Finer 1991, Moreton 2002, Zuraw 2007), the small number of items used in these studies makes it difficult to determine whether the observed preferences concern sonority difference or some other grammatical properties of the clusters (Eckman and Iverson 1993, Davidson 2000, 2006a, b, Davidson et al. 2006, Zuraw 2007). Even if it were unequivocally shown that people prefer onsets with larger sonority differences, questions would still remain regarding the source of this preference: whether it reflects grammatical markedness, or performance pressures that favor the perception and production of unmarked syllables over marked onsets.

The following research examines both questions. Section 3 shows that English speakers broadly favor unmarked onsets to marked ones even when all onsets are unattested in their language. Section 4 explores the source of those preferences.

3   Are Speakers Sensitive to the Markedness of Onsets that are Unattested in their Language?

If all universal markedness constraints are synchronically active, and if onsets with smaller sonority differences are universally more marked, then speakers should favor onsets with larger sonority differences to those with smaller differences. Crucially, such preferences should be present even if all onset types are unattested in one's language. A series of experiments (Berent et al. 2007) evaluated this prediction with English speakers. English systematically allows only onsets with a difference of at least 2 (s-initial onsets are systematic exceptions in English as well as other languages, for discussions, see Selkirk 1982, Wright 2004). Of interest is whether English speakers extend their preference to unattested onsets. To address this question, we compared three types of onsets with obstruent-sonorant combinations: onsets with small sonority rises (mostly obstruent-nasal sequences, e.g., bnif, $\Delta s = 1$), more marked onsets of level sonority (e.g., bdif, $\Delta s = 0$) and highly marked onsets of falling sonority (sonorant-obstruent combinations, e.g., lbif, $\Delta s = -2$).

Speakers' preferences were inferred from the effect of markedness on perception. Previous research has shown that people tend to misperceive marked onsets that are unattested in their language (Massaro and Cohen 1983, Hallé et al. 1998, Dupoux et al. 1999, 2001). For example, English speakers misperceive the unattested onset tla as tela—separating the illicit consonant sequence by a schwa (Pitt 1998). (Here and below, epenthetic schwa is orthographically written as 'e'.) These results suggest that marked onsets tend to be repaired epenthetically in perception. Of interest is whether the rate of epenthetic misperception depends on sonority difference. If speakers are sensitive to the markedness of onsets that are unattested in their language, and if marked onsets with smaller sonority differences trigger epenthetic repair at a greater rate, then as the markedness of monosyllables increases, people should be more likely to misperceive them as disyllabic.

To examine these predictions, we investigated the perception of onsets with small sonority rises, sonority plateaus and falls. These onsets were incorporated into monosyllabic words, matched for the structure of their rhyme (e.g., bnif, bdif, lbif), and compared to disyllabic items which differed from their monosyllabic counterparts only on the presence of a schwa between the two initial consonants (e.g., benif, bedif, lebif). All items were recorded naturally by a native speaker of Russian (a language in which all relevant types of onsets are attested).

The perception of these items was investigated using several tasks (for a full description of the results, see Berent et al. 2007). Here, we focus on findings from a syllable count task. In this task, participants are presented with a single auditory item and asked to determine whether it includes one syllable or two. If the onset-cluster markedness of monosyllabic items leads them to be misperceived epenthetically, then as the markedness of the monosyllabic item increases, people should be more likely to perceive it as disyllabic. The results (see Figure 1, solid lines) are consistent with this prediction. On most trials, participants considered unmarked onsets with rising sonority monosyllabic (62% of the responses), but they were reliably less likely to do so for onsets of level sonority (28% of the responses) and even less so for sonority falls (19% of the responses). In fact, monosyllabic items with sonority plateaus and falls were reliably misperceived as disyllabic. The misperception of such onsets by English speakers is not due to stimulus artifacts, as Russian speakers, tested with the same materials and procedure, perceived these items as monosyllabic (see Figure 1, dotted lines). These results suggest that the misperception of marked onsets reflects a preference triggered, in part, by linguistic experience.

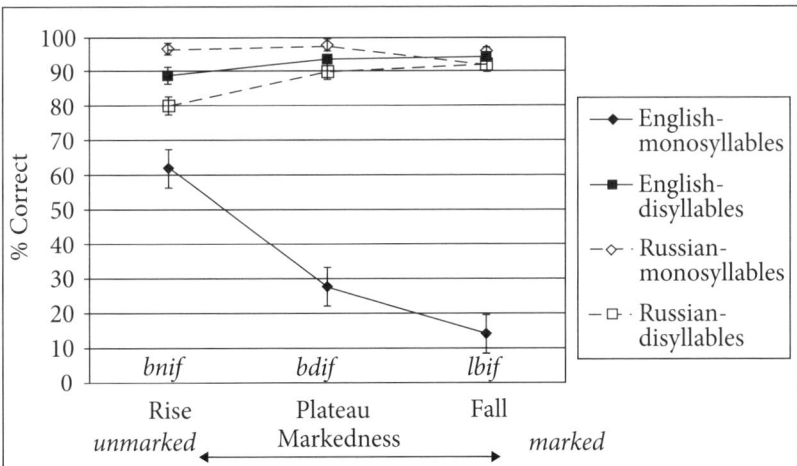

Figure 1   Mean response accuracy of English and Russian speakers as a function of the markedness of onsets and the number of syllables. Error bars represent confidence intervals constructed for the difference between the means. Data from Berent et al. (2007, Experiments 1–2)

Interestingly, however, the markedness of onset clusters also affected responses to their disyllabic counterparts. English speakers were more accurate responding to disyllabic items whose counterpart is marked (e.g., to *lebif*, counterpart of *lbif*) compared to those with an unmarked counterpart (e.g., to *benif*; a similar trend was also found with Russian participants). Additional analyses showed that the difficulties with *benif*-type items are not due to the phonetic length of the vowel. Instead, these difficulties appear to reflect a competition from the monosyllabic counterpart. Because participants in this task must make a forced choice as to whether the item has one syllable or two, their responses to disyllabic items are affected by the markedness of their monosyllabic counterparts: unmarked monosyllabic counterparts tempt participants to incorrectly choose the monosyllabic form, whereas disyllabic forms with marked counterparts are spared from such competition, and are consequently more likely to elicit correct disyllabic responses. Put differently, speakers' top-down grammatical dispreference shifts their interpretation of bottom-up phonetic evidence (Massaro and Cohen 1983). Specifically, the dispreference for sonority falls shifts the interpretation of the phonetic evidence for the schwa away from a monosyllabic response. Accordingly, a schwa is more likely to elicit a disyllabic response when it is flanked by a sonorant-obstruent compared to an obstruent-sonorant sequence.

These results suggest that people are sensitive to the markedness of onsets that are unattested in their language: onsets with small sonority differences tend to be misperceived, whereas their disyllabic counterparts tend to elicit more accurate responses.

4   Nature of Preferences and their Source

The performance of English speakers implies a preference for onsets with larger sonority differences. However, this result alone cannot determine the source of this preference. We first examine whether the observed preferences are due to grammatical restrictions or lexical analogies. Next, we investigate whether such preferences concern sonority difference, in general, or obstruent-sonorant combinations, in particular. The final section examines whether markedness is a cause or consequence of misperception.

4.1   *Lexical vs. Nonlexical Preferences*

One alternative explanation attributes the preference of large sonority differences not to an active grammatical component but to their analogical similarity to the English lexicon; some such mechanism would be required by a theory denying the psychological status of markedness constraints, placing the entire burden on the lexicon for carrying the residue of systematic language change. Although onsets such as *bn, bd,* and *lb* are all unattested in English, they nonetheless differ on their similarity to attested onsets. English onsets typically begin with an obstruent (as in *bn* and *bd*), rather than a sonorant (as in *lb*), and the second position of the onset is far more likely to include a sonorant (e.g., nasal) than by a stop. The *bn>bd>lb* preference could thus reflect the co-occurrence of such segments in the English lexicon, rather than their sonority difference.

Previous research evaluated and rejected this possibility by demonstrating that the preference for onsets with large sonority differences is inexplicable by various statistical properties of the English lexicon (phoneme probability, biphone probability, neighbor count and neighbor frequency, Berent et al. 2007; see also Albright 2007). Stronger evidence against the lexical account is presented by the replication of the English results with Korean speakers—whose language arguably lacks onset clusters altogether. These experiments (Berent et al. 2008) included the same materials and tasks used with English speakers, except for the addition of onsets with large sonority rises and their counterparts (e.g., *blif, belif*).

The results from the syllable count task (see Figure 2) closely match the findings observed with English speakers: as sonority difference decreased, monosyllabic items were perceived less accurately, whereas their disyllabic counterparts were more likely to elicit correct responses. Additional analyses suggested that the misperception of marked monosyllabic items is not likely to be due to proficiency with second languages, most notably English, nor is it due to various phonetic and phonological properties of Korean (the phonetic release of initial stop-consonants, their voicing, the distribution of [l] and [r] allophones, the experience with Korean words beginning with consonant-glide sequences, and the occurrence of CC sequences across Korean syllables). The finding that Korean speakers possess preferences regarding onset structure—preferences that mirror the

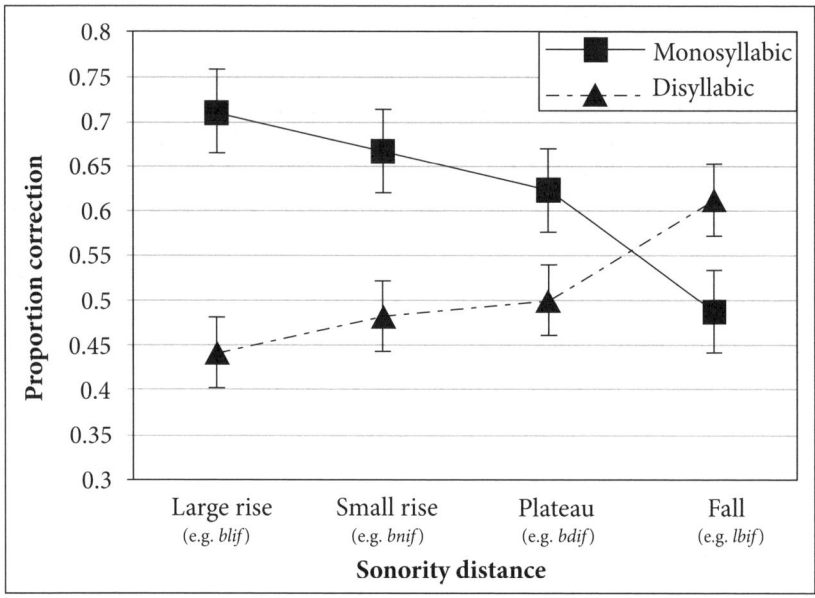

Figure 2   Mean response accuracy of Korean speakers as a function of the markedness of onsets and number of syllables. Solid line with squares is the monosyllabic condition while dotted line with triangles is the disyllabic condition. Error bars represent confidence intervals constructed for the difference between the means. Data from Berent et al. (2008, Experiment 1)

typological distribution of these onsets and converge with the preferences of English speakers—imply preferences that are broad and nonlexical in nature.

4.2   *The Scope of the Restrictions on Onset Structure: Sonority Difference or Obstruent-Sonorant Sequencing?*

Although English speakers' preference for onsets with large sonority difference is not based on the statistical properties of English words, it may not concern sonority difference specifically. Because the preference for large sonority differences were tested only with onsets comprising obstruent-sonorant combinations, it is impossible to determine whether it reflects a broad preference for a large sonority difference, in general, or a narrow preference for obstruent-sonorant sequences—sequences that also resemble the type of onsets attested in English.

To gauge the scope of these preferences, it is desirable to determine whether they are specific to comparisons involving obstruent-initial items. Here, we report two experiments that extend the investigation of sonority preferences to nasal-initial onsets. Our experiments compare two types of nasal-initial onsets. One onset type (e.g., *mlif*) manifested a sonority rise, a second type (e.g., *mdif*) manifested a fall in sonority. (Note that English has no nasal-liquid or nasal-obstruent onsets.) Each such onset was generated by a procedure of incremental splicing along the lines described in Dupoux et al. (1999).[1] We first had a native English speaker naturally produce the disyllabic counterparts (e.g., *melif* and *medif*), and selected pairs that were matched for length. We next continuously extracted the epenthetic vowel in five steady increments. This, in turn, yielded a continuum of six equal steps, ranging from the original disyllabic form to an onset cluster, in which the schwa was fully removed. Sonority rises and falls were each represented by three pairs of items, prepared in the same fashion.

These materials were presented to English speakers in an identity judgment task (AX). In each trial, participants were presented with two auditory stimuli and asked to quickly indicate whether they are identical. The experiment included an equal proportion of identity and nonidentity trials, which were further balanced for the number of marked and unmarked onsets, the phonetic length of the schwa, and order of presentation. Our interest concerns responses to nonidentity trials. Nonidentity trials paired each of the steps (the target) with one of the endpoints, which served as an anchor. In Experiment 1, the anchor corresponded to the disyllabic endpoint (step 6); in Experiment 2, we used the monosyllabic endpoint (step 1). This design systematically varied the phonetic distance between the anchor and the target (see Table 1), ranging from a distance of 1 (comparing either steps 6 and 5, in Experiment 1, or steps 1 and 2, in Experiment 2) to a distance of 5 (comparing steps 1 and 6).

Consider first the comparison of the target to the disyllabic anchor (in Experiment 1). Generally speaking, we expect the perceived distance

---

[1] For each member of the pair, we created a continuum of six stimuli by incrementally removing the schwa at the zero crossings. The excision of the medial vowel proceeded from the center of the schwa outwards, guided by the pitch period cycles. Stimulus one contained only the onset cluster, removing all pitch periods associated with the vowel and consonant transitions. Stimulus two contained one pitch period at each end of the schwa (a total of two pitch periods); each subsequent stimulus from 3 to 5 had two additional periods (one at each end); stimulus six was the original disyllabic form. Within each pair, the mean length of the schwa in stimulus 6 was 68ms for both rises and falls, and it contained an average of 13.5 pitch period cycles (range of 12–15 cycles).

Table 1   The structure of nonidentity trials in Experiments 1–2

	Experiment 1		Experiment 2	
Distance	Anchor	Target	Anchor	Target
1	6	5	1	2
2	6	4	1	3
3	6	3	1	4
4	6	2	1	5
5	6	1	1	6

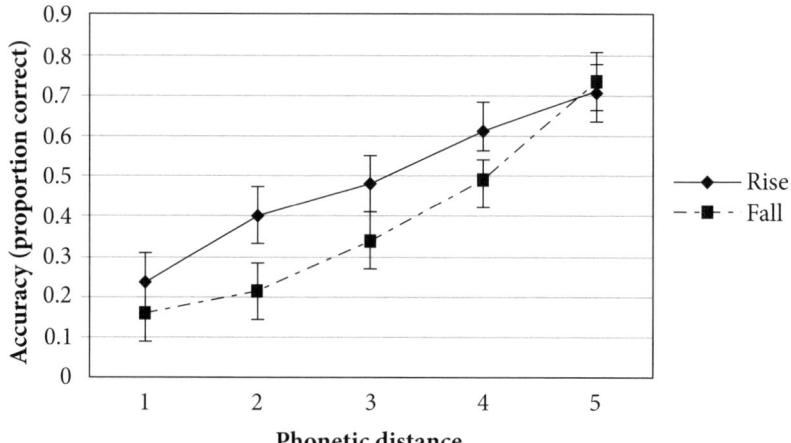

Figure 3   Mean response accuracy to sonority rises and falls in Experiment 1 as a function of phonetic distance. Error bars represent confidence intervals constructed for the difference between the means

between the target and anchor to increase with phonetic distance, resulting in better discrimination. Of interest is whether the perceived distance is also affected by the sonority profile of the onset. If people possess broad preferences concerning sonority difference, then the markedness of nasal-initial onsets of falling sonority should increase their epenthetic misperception compared to onsets of rising sonority. Thus, at any phonetic distance, perceptual distance should be smaller for sonority falls relative to rises, resulting in a reduction in response accuracy.

The results (of twelve English speakers, see Figure 3) are consistent with this prediction. As the distance between the two items increased, discrimination improved. However, discrimination was overall better with the less marked onsets of rising sonority compared to sonority falls. These conclusions are supported by a 2 (onset type: sonority rises vs. falls) × 5 (distance) ANOVA. The significant main effect of distance $F_{(4, 44)}=40.34$), MSE=.025, p<.0002) reflected an increase in identification accuracy with phonetic distance, and the marginally significant effect of onset type, $F_{(1, 44)}=3.78$, MSE=.078, p<.08, indicated that sonority rises produced higher accuracy than falls. However, the effect of onset type was modulated by phonetic distance, resulting in a significant interaction, $F_{(4, 44)}=3.10$, MSE=.013, p<.03. A series of tests for the simple main effect of onset type indicated that onsets of rising sonority produced reliably higher accuracy than sonority falls at distance 2, $F_{(1, 11)}=8.72$, MSE=.025, p<.02, and at distance 3, $F_{(1, 11)}=5.56$, MSE=.02, p<.04. No other effects were significant. This pattern suggests that the perceived distance between targets and anchors depends on both their phonetic distance and their sonority profile. Marked onsets tend to be misperceived epenthetically, and consequently, they produce lower accuracy than sonority rises. However, because phonetic distance improves accuracy, marked targets are protected at large phonetic distances (e.g., for distance 4–5). Another factor that might contribute to discrimination is the phonetic evidence for the schwa: targets with a substantial schwa might be protected from misperception. This factor might explain the lack of a sonority-difference effect at distance 1. Recall that distance 1 comprised of the disyllabic anchor and a nearly-disyllabic target of step 5. The strong phonetic evidence for the schwa might have protected *md*-type targets from misperception, rending their discrimination as good as their *ml*-type counterparts.

These results suggest that the perceptual advantage of onsets of rising sonority previously observed with obstruents generalizes to nasal-initial onsets. Markedness triggers the misperception of sonority falls, and consequently, it decreases their perceived distance from their counterpart items in a manner akin to the acoustic effect of phonetic distance.

4.3 *Markedness and Misperception: Chickens and Eggs*

Why are marked onsets misperceived? One possibility is that misperception reflects a phonological process (see Figure 4). Although we currently do not outline a formal model, our proposal attributes

a. Phonological account   b. Phonetic account

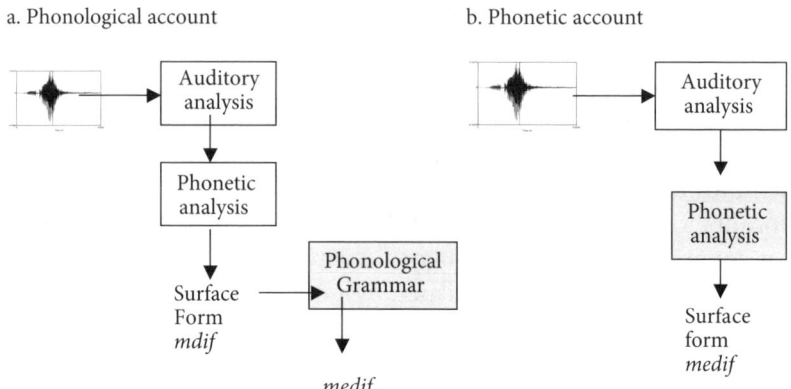

Figure 4   Phonetic vs. phonological explanations for the misperception of
unattested onsets

misperception to the ranking of the relevant markedness constraints
above faithfulness constraints, a state that prevents the faithful encoding of marked onsets. In this view, the misperception of marked onsets
does not necessarily affect the initial extraction of phonetic form from
the auditory input. In fact, this account is perfectly consistent with
the possibility that the initial phonetic encoding of marked onsets is
precise—as precise as that of unmarked onsets. Misperception occurs
at a subsequent grammatical process that actively alters the (faithful)
surface form to abide by markedness restrictions. Misperception is
thus a consequence of markedness.

On an alternative phonetic explanation, onsets like *mdif* are misperceived because their acoustic properties are similar to those of their
counterparts, *medif*, more so than for *mlif* vs. *melif*. Misperception
occurs at an initial stage of phonetic analysis due to a passive failure
to extract the phonetic form from the available acoustic information.
The phonetic fragility of sonority falls results in their instability during
language change and their infrequency in the typology. Markedness is
thus a consequence of misperception.

Although perceptibility failures might well constrain language
transmission and explain certain aspects of the typology (Blevins 2004,
2006) it is unclear that they can subsume the effects of grammatical
markedness. There are several cases in which phonological restrictions
can be dissociated from their functional motivations: some functionally motivated processes are unattested, whereas other attested processes are functionally unmotivated (see de Lacy 2006, de Lacy and

Kingston 2006). Here we present experimental evidence of such dissociations. We first review additional results with nasal-initial onsets, demonstrating that marked onsets are not invariably misperceived. In fact, when attention to phonetic detail is encouraged, people can represent marked onsets accurately—as accurately as they represent less marked onsets. We next show that the misperception of marked onsets and their aversion occurs even when people do not process auditory clusters. These findings will suggest that markedness is not solely a consequence of performance pressures but is potentially their cause.

4.3.1 *Marked Onsets are not Invariably Misperceived*

If the misperception of marked onsets were due to an inability to extract their phonetic form from the acoustic information, then one would expect marked onsets to be always misperceived relative to less marked onsets. In contrast, if misperception is an active phonological process that modifies the surface form, and if that surface form is accurate and accessible, then conditions encouraging its inspection should yield accurate performance with marked onsets.

One set of findings consistent with this prediction is presented by an experiment that follows up on the investigation of nasal onsets described in section 4.2. As in the previous experiment, participants engaged in an AX discrimination of a continuum of nasal-initial targets and a fixed anchor, but the fixed anchor was now set to the monosyllabic endpoint (step 1; see Table 1). Unlike the disyllabic anchors used in the previous experiment, the monosyllabic anchors are at risk of epenthetic misperception, as are the monosyllabic targets. But because anchors are frequently repeated (they are paired with every target in the nonidentity trials), people are more likely to store their surface phonetic form (other results indeed show that people store indexical phonetic information after a brief exposure, e.g., Goldinger 1998). Of interest is whether the surface phonetic form of such anchors is precise.

Given onsets of rising sonority, we expect the representation of both the target and anchor to be faithful, and consequently, monosyllabic targets (e.g., in step 2) should be difficult to discriminate from the anchor (step 1). Our interest concerns the perception of onsets of falling sonority. If epenthetic misperception is due to phonetic failure that occurs already at the initial stage of phonetic encoding, then the representation of marked targets and anchors should be effectively

identical (in both cases *mdif* → *medif*), and their discrimination should
be difficult. In contrast, if misperception is due to an active repair
of an accurate phonetic form, and if this form is accessible, then the
perceived distance between anchors and target of falling sonority will
increase: unlike the anchors, monosyllabic targets will undergo repair,
so their representation will differ from the faithful phonetic encoding
of the anchor. This account thus predicts a paradoxical reversal in the
effect of markedness on performance: marked onsets of falling sonority should produce higher accuracy compared to less marked onsets
with sonority rises.

The results (from twelve native English speakers, see Figure 5) agree
with this latter prediction. As in the previous experiment, response
accuracy increased with phonetic distance, but onsets of falling sonority now produced reliably higher accuracy relative to onsets of rising
sonority, especially when the phonetic distance was short. These conclusions were supported by a 2 (onset type: rises vs. falls) × 5 (distance)
ANOVA. The reliable main effect of phonetic distance, $F(4, 44)=20.04$,
MSE=.03. $p<.0002$, reflected an increase in performance accuracy with
phonetic distance, and the effect of onset type, $F(1, 11)=4.21$, MSE=.052

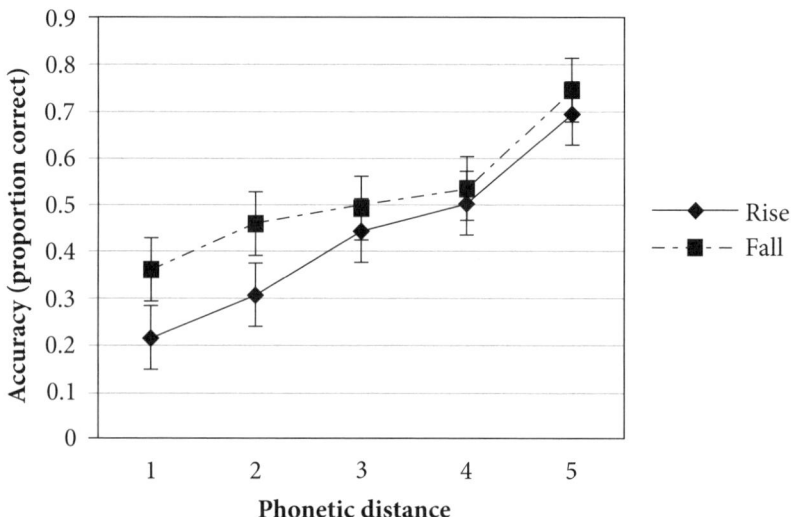

Figure 5   Mean response accuracy to sonority rises and falls in Experiment 2
as a function of phonetic distance. Error bars represent confidence intervals
constructed for the difference between the means

p<.07, suggested that sonority falls produced higher accuracy than rises. A test of the simple main effect of onset type showed that sonority falls yielded more accurate responses than rises at distance one, F(1, 11)=7.00, MSE=.018 p<.03, and marginally so at distance two, F(1, 11)=4.08, MSE=.035 p<.07. No other effects were significant.

The better discrimination of onsets of falling sonority suggests that the representation of the marked monosyllabic anchor was more faithful than the target. Had participants misperceived anchors of falling sonority, then their representation should have been identical to the (epenthesized) target, and the disadvantage of marked onsets (demonstrated in Experiment 1) should have persisted. The misperception of the marked anchor should have also increased its similarity to disyllabic targets (e.g., to step 6, in distance 5). Unlike these targets (protected from misperception by the strong phonetic cues for the schwa), the monosyllabic anchor would have been repaired, resulting in a paradoxical *decrease* in perceived distance as phonetic distance increases. But our results do not support either prediction. As phonetic distance increased, accuracy improved, suggesting an increase in perceived distance, and sonority falls produced higher accuracy than rises. These results suggest that the repetition of highly marked anchors of falling sonority allowed participants to extract a faithful phonetic representation, thereby increasing the perceived distance with (repaired) targets. Our findings demonstrate that onsets of falling sonority are not invariably misperceived.

Note that these results do not specifically demonstrate that the representation of marked onsets is as precise as that of unmarked onsets, but this interpretation is certainly consistent with these results, and it is directly supported by additional experiments examining the perception of obstruent-sonorant combinations (Berent et al. 2007, Experiments 5–6). These experiments gauged the representation of onset clusters with sonority plateaus and falls by examining their potential to elicit identity priming. Identity priming reflects the change (typically facilitation) in the identification of a target (e.g., *lbif*) when it is preceded by an identical prime (e.g., *lbif-lbif*) relative to a nonidentical control prime (e.g., *lebif-lbif*). We expect that if people misperceive the prime (e.g., *lbif* → *lebif*) then its potential to prime an identical target (e.g., *lbif*) should be diminished relative to a less marked prime (e.g., *bdif-bdif*), and the results indeed supported this conclusion. However, when participants were encouraged to attend to the phonetic properties of the prime (by manipulating the constitution of distractor trials), the ability of sonority falls to prime the target was restored, and did not differ from that of sonority rises. These results show that, not only can people represent onsets of falling sonority accurately, but that the representation of marked onsets is as precise as less marked onsets. These observations are inconsistent with the proposal that the misperception of marked onsets is due to an inability to encode their surface phonetic form.

4.3.2   *The Dispreference of Marked Onsets is not Limited to the Perception of Auditory Onsets*

The hypothesis that markedness reflects performance difficulties in perception and production assumes that such difficulties are the sole reason for the misperception of marked onsets. So far, we have argued against this possibility by showing that marked onsets are not necessarily harder to perceive from the acoustic input. These results, however, do not necessarily show that the misperception is due to the phonological grammar. A modified version of the phonetic account, depicted in Figure 4b might maintain that repair still occurs at the phonetic stage, rather than a phonological analysis. To explain people's ability to perceive marked onsets accurately under certain conditions, this modified account asserts that people also maintain a precise, lower-level representation of the input, which allows them to circumvent the effects of repair. Regardless of whether that precise representation of the input is phonetic (on the phonological account) or echoic (on the modified phonetic version), the results clearly show that people can accurately represent the surface form of marked onsets that they typically misclassify as disyllabic. Nonetheless, it might be interesting to dissociate these two explanations by examining the circumstances triggering repair. If the aversion to marked structures and their repair reflects difficulties in phonetic analysis, then they should occur only when participants experience difficulties in the extraction of phonetic form from the auditory signal. In contrast, the phonological account allows for the possibility that the effects of markedness and repair might persist even when no perceptual difficulties are expected. This latter prediction is supported by several demonstrations.

One line of evidence comes from cases in which aversion to marked onset clusters affects the processing of forms that do not in fact have clusters. Recall that English and Korean speakers both exhibit difficulties in the perception of the disyllabic counterparts of unmarked onsets. For example, *benif,* counterpart of *bnif,* produced significantly fewer disyllabic responses relative to *lebif* (counterpart of *lbif*). As discussed earlier, the better performance with *lebif* reflects a top-down bias against *lbif*. Because such aversion to marked onset clusters emerges even when people do not process these acoustic forms, it cannot be attributed to difficulties in extraction of the phonetic properties of marked onsets.

In fact, the difficulties in discriminating marked onsets and their epenthetic counterparts emerge even when acoustic processing is altogether eliminated—when the input is printed (Berent and Lennertz 2010). In these experiments, participants engage in an identity judgment (AX task) of two printed words, presented at an onset asynchrony of 2.5 seconds—an interval that promotes the coding of the items in phonological working memory. The materials and procedure are otherwise identical to the ones previously used with auditory clusters (Berent et al. 2007; the only other difference is the addition of accuracy feedback). The results show that participants take longer to distinguish marked onsets from their epenthetic counterparts (e.g., *lbif* vs. *lebif*) relative to unmarked onsets (e.g., *bnif* vs. *benif*) just as they do with auditory materials. Clearly, the misperception of marked onsets is not confined to auditory stimuli. These results suggest that misperception can be a symptom of markedness, not invariably its cause.

5   Conclusions

The research described in this chapter gauged the role of universal markedness preferences and their interaction with the perceptual system. To this end, we examined whether English speakers are sensitive to the sonority distance of onset cluster types that are unattested in their language. The results suggest that the perception of unattested onsets varies as a function of their markedness: unattested onsets with smaller sonority differences are systematically misperceived compared to unattested onsets with larger differences. These misperceptions are inexplicable by various non-grammatical sources. Specifically, the perceptual advantage of onsets with large sonority rises is unlikely due to lexical analogies, as the perceptual advantage of large rises remained after controlling for several statistical properties of English, it extended to nasal-initial onsets, and it obtained even among speakers of Korean despite the absence of onset clusters from their language. The misperception of marked onsets is also not due to an inability to encode their phonetic form. We showed that onsets of falling sonority can be encoded accurately when their phonetic form becomes more salient (through repeated presentations) or relevant to task demands. In fact, the dispreference for onsets with small sonority differences is observed even when people do not process their phonetic form at all—when they process their disyllabic counterparts, and with printed materials. These results suggest that the systematic misperception of onsets with small sonority differences is not due to a passive failure to encode their surface form, but rather to an active grammatical process that converts a faithful surface form to a less marked representation. These results further suggest that speakers possess markedness restrictions concerning the sonority difference of onsets that are unattested in their language, and that such restrictions shape the perception of marked onsets.

Our findings are consistent with the hypothesis that markedness restrictions are not mere relics of language change, language frequency and the properties of the mechanisms of perception and articulation. Rather, markedness restrictions are active in the brains of individual speakers. These conclusions do not preclude the role of performance factors in shaping markedness preferences—such factors, along with historical considerations might be necessary to explain why most typological generalizations are only statistical tendencies, rather than absolute statements (Berent 2009). Nonetheless, markedness is not invariably the consequence of misperception: it can also be its cause.

One question that is not directly addressed by our results concerns the precise domain of the restriction: whether the restrictions on the structure of words' onsets appeal to the left edges of syllables or words. Steriade (1999) suggests that the preference for forms such as *blif* reflects linear restrictions on consonant sequencing, motivated by knowledge concerning the perceptibility of consonant combinations at the word's edge. The preference for *blif* thus refers to knowledge about words, not syllables per se. Because our results invariably concern monosyllabic words, we cannot pinpoint the precise domain of the relevant knowledge. Nonetheless, our findings call into question the assertion that sequencing preferences invariably reflect knowledge of perceptibility. Specifically, the possibility that (mis)perception is shaped, in part, by markedness, suggests that the imperceptibility of certain linear sequences might, in fact, be the consequence of markedness, not necessarily its cause. The precise relationship between the grammar and perception awaits further research, but there is every reason to believe it is not unidirectional.

References

Albright, Adam. 2007. Is there a role for markedness biases in modeling well-formedness of onset-clusters? Presented at MIT Phonology Circle.

Alonzo, Angelo and Marcus Taft. 2002. Sonority constraints on onset-rhyme cohesion: evidence from native and bilingual Filipino readers of English. *Brain and language* 81: 368–383.

Barlow, Jessica. 2001. The structure of /s/-sequences: Evidence from a disordered system. *Journal of Child Language* 28: 291–324.

——. 2005. Sonority Effects in the Production of Consonant Clusters by Spanish-Speaking Children. In *Selected Proceedings of the 6th Conference on the Acquisition of Spanish and Portuguese as First and Second Languages*, edited by David Eddington, 1–14. Somerville, MA: Cascadilla Proceedings Project.

Berent, Iris. 2009. Unveiling phonological universals: A linguist who asks "why" is (inter alia) an experimental psychologist. *Behavioral and Brain Sciences* 32: 450–451.

Berent, Iris and Tracy Lennertz. 2010. Universal constraints on the sound structure of language: Phonological or acoustic. *Journal of Experimental Psychology: Human Perception and Performance* 36: 212–223.

Berent, Iris, Tracy Lennertz, Jongho Jun, Miguel Moreno and Paul Smolensky. 2008. Language universals in human brains. *Proceedings of the National Academy of Sciences* 105: 5321–5325.

Berent, Iris, Donca Steriade, Tracy Lennertz and Vered Vaknin. 2007. What we know about what we have never heard: Evidence from perceptual illusions. *Cognition* 104: 591–630.

Blevins, Juliette. 2004. *Evolutionary phonology: The emergence of sound patterns*. Cambridge: Cambridge University Press.

——. 2006. A theoretical synopsis of Evolutionary Phonology. *Theoretical linguistics* 32: 117–165.

Broselow, Ellen and Daniel Finer. 1991. Parameter setting in second language phonology and syntax. *Second Language Research* 7: 35–59.

Broselow, Ellen, Su-I Chen and Chilin Wang. 1998. The emergence of the unmarked in second language phonology. *Studies in second language acquisition* 20: 261–280.

Broselow, Ellen and Zheng Xu. 2004. Differential difficulty in the acquisition of second language phonology. *International Journal of English Studies* 4: 135–163.

Clements, George. N. 1990. The role of the sonority cycle in core syllabification. In *Papers in laboratory phonology 1: Between the grammar and physics of speech*, edited by John Kingston and Mary Beckman, 283–333. NY: Cambridge University Press.

Davidson, Lisa. 2000. Experimentally uncovering hidden strata in English phonology. In *Proceedings of the 22nd Annual Conference of the Cognitive Science Society*, edited by Lila Gleitman and Aravind Joshi, 1023. Mahwah, NJ: Lawrence Erlbaum Associates.

——. 2006a. Phonotactics and articulatory coordination interact in phonology: Evidence from nonnative production. *Cognitive Science* 30: 837–862.

——. 2006b. Schwa elision in fast speech: Segmental deletion or gestural overlap? *Phonetica* 63: 79–112.

Davidson, Lisa, Peter W. Jusczyk and Paul Smolensky. 2006. Optimality in language acquisition I: The initial and final states of the phonological grammar. In *The harmonic mind: From neural computation to Optimality-Theoretic grammar*, vol. 2, edited by Paul Smolensky and Géraldine Legendre, 233–278. Cambridge, MA: MIT press.

de Lacy, Paul. 2006. Transmissibility and the role of the phonological component. *Theoretical Linguistics* 32: 185–96.

——. 2007. The interaction of tone, sonority, and prosodic structure. In *The Cambridge handbook of phonology*, edited by Paul de Lacy, 281–307. Cambridge: Cambridge University Press.

de Lacy, Paul, and John Kingston. 2006. Synchronic explanation. Unpublished Ms., Rutgers University and the University of Massachusetts, Amherst.

Dupoux, Emmanuel, Christophe Pallier, Kazuhiko Kakehi and Jacques Mehler. 2001. New evidence for prelexical phonological processing in word recognition. *Language and Cognitive Processes* 5: 491–505.

Dupoux, Emmanuel, Kazuhiko Kakehi, Yuki Hirose, Christophe Pallier and Jacques Mehler. 1999. Epenthetic vowels in Japanese: A perceptual illusion? *Journal of Experimental Psychology: Human Perception and Performance* 25: 1568–1578.

Eckman, Fred, and Gregory Iverson. 1993. Sonority and markedness among onset clusters in the interlanguage of ESL learners. *Second Language Research* 9: 234–252.

Fowler, Carol, Rebecca Treiman and Jennifer Gross. 1993. The structure of English syllables and polysyllables. *Journal of Memory and Language* 32: 115–140.

Gierut, Judith A. 1999. Syllable onsets: Clusters and adjuncts in acquisition. *Journal of Speech, Language and Hearing Research* 42: 708–726.

Goldinger, Stephen. 1998. Echoes of echoes? An episodic theory of lexical access. *Psychological Review* 105: 251–279.

Gouskova, Maria. 2001. Falling sonority onsets, loanwords, and syllable contact. *Chicago Linguistics Society* 37: 175–186.

——. 2004 Relational hierarchies in optimality theory: The case of syllable contact. *Phonology* 21: 201–50.

Greenberg, Joseph. 1978. Some generalizations concerning initial and final consonant clusters. In *Universals of Human Language*, edited by Joseph H. Greenberg, Charles A. Ferguson and Edith A. Moravcsik, 243–279. Stanford, CA: Stanford University Press.

Hallé, Pierre, Juan Segui, Uli Frauenfelder and Christine Meunier. 1998. The processing of illegal consonant clusters: A case of perceptual assimilation? *Journal of Experimental Psychology: Human Perception and Performance* 24: 592–608.

Hooper, Joan Bybee. 1976. *An introduction to natural generative phonology*. New York: Academic Press.

Kawasaki-Fukumori, Haruko. 1992. An acoustical basis for universal phonotactic constraints. *Language and Speech* 35:73–86.

Levitt, Andrea, Alice Healy and David Fendrich. 1991. Syllable-internal structure and the sonority hierarchy: Differential evidence from lexical decision, naming, and reading. *Journal of Psycholinguistic Research* 20: 337–363.

Massaro, Dominic and Michael Cohen. 1983. Phonological constraints in speech perception. *Perception and Psychophysics* 34: 338–48.

Morelli, Frida. 1999. The Phonotactics and Phonology of Obstruent Clusters in Optimality Theory. PhD diss., University of Maryland.

Moreton, Elliott. 2002. Structural constraints in the perception of English stop-sonorant clusters. *Cognition* 84: 55–71.

Ohala, Diane. 1999. The influence of sonority on children's cluster reductions. *Journal of Communication Disorders* 32: 397–421.

Ohala, John. 1992. Alternatives to the Sonority Hierarchy for Explaining Sequential Constraints. *Chicago Linguistics Society* 26, 2: 319–338.

Parker, Steve. 2002. Quantifying the Sonority Hierarchy. PhD diss., University of Massachusetts, Amherst.

Pater, Joe. 2004. Bridging the gap between receptive and productive development with minimally violable constraints. In *Constraints in Phonological Acquisition*, edited by René Kager, Joe Pater and Wim Zonneveld, 219–244. New York: Cambridge University Press.

Pertz, Doris and Thomas Bever. 1975. Sensitivity to phonological universals in children and adolescents. *Language* 51: 149–62.

Pinker, Steven and David Birdsong. 1979. Speakers' sensitivity to rules of frozen word order. *Journal of Verbal Learning and Verbal Behavior* 18: 497–508.

Pitt, Mark. 1998. Phonological processes and the perception of phonotactically illegal consonant clusters. *Perception and Psychophysics* 60: 941–51.

Prince, Alan and Paul Smolensky. 2004. *Optimality theory: Constraint interaction in generative grammar*. Oxford: Blackwell Publishing.

Romani, Cristina, and Andrea Calabrese. 1998. Syllabic constraints on the phonological errors of an aphasic patient. *Brain and Language* 64: 83–121.

Selkirk, Elisabeth. 1982. The syllable. In *The structure of phonological representations*, part 2, edited by Harry van der Hulst and Norval Smith, 337–383. Dordrecht: Foris.

——. 1984. On the major class features and syllable theory. In *Language sound structure: Studies in phonology presented to Morris Halle by his teacher and students*, edited by Mark Aronoff and Richrad T. Oerhle, 107–136. Cambridge, MA: MIT Press.

Smolensky, Paul. 2006. Optimality in phonology II: Markedness, feature domains, and local constraint conjunction. In *The harmonic mind: From neural computation to optimality-theoretic grammar*, vol. 2, edited by Paul Smolensky and Géraldine Legendre, 27–160. Cambridge, MA: MIT Press.

Smolensky, Paul and Géraldine Legendre. 2006. *The harmonic mind: From neural computation to Optimality-Theoretic grammar*, vol 2. Cambridge: MIT Press.

Stemberger, Joseph and Rebecca Treiman. 1986. The internal structure of word-initial consonant clusters. *Journal of Memory and Language* 25: 163–180.

Stenneken, Prisca, Roelien Bastiaanse, Walter Huber and Arthur Jacobs. 2005. Syllable structure and sonority in language inventory and aphasic neologisms. *Brain and language* 95: 280–292.

Steriade, Donca. 1982. Greek prosodies and the nature of syllabification. PhD diss., MIT.

——. 1988. Reduplication and syllable transfer in Sanskrit and elsewhere. *Phonology* 5: 37–155.

——. 1999. Alternatives to syllable-based accounts of consonantal phonotactics. In *Proceedings of LP '98: Item order in language and speech*, vol. 1, edited by Osamu Fujimura, Brian D. Joseph and Bohumil Palek, 205–245. Prague: Charles University in Prague—The Karolinum Press.

Treiman, Rebecca. 1984. On the status of final consonant clusters in English syllables. *Journal of Verbal Learning and Verbal Behavior* 23: 343–356.

Treiman, Rebecca and Catalina Danis. 1988. Syllabification of intervocalic consonants. *Journal of Memory and Language* 27: 87–104.

Treiman, Rebbeca, Judith A. Bowey and Derrick Bourassa. 2002. Segmentation of spoken words into syllables by English-speaking children. *Journal of Experimental Child Psychology* 83: 213–238.

Vennemann, Theo. 1972. On the theory of syllabic phonology. *Linguistische Berichte* 18: 1–18.

Wright, Richard. 2004. A review of perceptual cues and cue robustness. In *Phonetically based phonology*, edited by Bruce Hayes, Robert Kirchner and Donca Steriade, 34–57. Cambridge: Cambridge University Press.

Zuraw, Kie. 2007. The role of phonetic knowledge in phonological patterning: Corpus and survey evidence from Tagalog infixation. *Language* 83: 277–316.

THE SYLLABLE IN PERFORMANCE:
ORTHOGRAPHY

CHAPTER SIXTEEN

SYLLABLES AND SYLLABARIES: WHAT WRITING SYSTEMS TELL US ABOUT SYLLABLE STRUCTURE

Amalia E. Gnanadesikan

1 Introduction

Though they have been largely ignored in modern linguistics, writing systems provide rich evidence for phonological structures. They are systems which analyze, encode, and transmit language, usually on a phonological basis. Though a number of them, such as the Roman alphabet as applied to English, are notoriously inexact, the fact that they are learnable and usable as ways to transmit language suggests that there is a relationship between what writing systems encode and the structures of language itself. And unlike any recent phonological theory, many writing systems have stood the test of time. Looking at writing systems for evidence of syllabic structures yields strong evidence for the linguistic reality of syllables, for a number of their properties (such as onset-coda asymmetry and the special status of /s/), and for their internal structure (moras, and onsets and rhymes).

1.1 Theoretical Preliminaries

According to Ray Jackendoff, "one crucial test of a theory of linguistic structure is whether it can be integrated into a theory of processing" (Jackendoff 1983, 5). The central claim of this chapter is that a writing system is by its nature a theory of processing: in writing, language is analyzed into discrete structures, encoded into signs, and then decoded into language again by the reader. The encoded structures must be ones that the reader and writer can access and manipulate. Therefore, the presence of a structure in a writing system is good evidence for the linguistic reality of that structure. Written evidence of syllables therefore constitutes evidence for their linguistic reality.

The linguistically naïve native speaker of a language employs unconsciously the manifold structures of the language. By contrast, becoming literate requires raising to some level of awareness (whether fully conscious or not) some subset of the language's structures (Mattingly 1972, Gombert 1992, Seymour 2006). Similarly, inventing a new writing system requires encoding for the first time the same kinds of structures. Some structures seem more available to the learner or inventor of a writing system than others. Specifically, syllables appear to be favored over phonemes. Explicit awareness of syllables developmentally precedes phonemic awareness across languages (Liberman et al. 1974, Goswami 2006). Not surprisingly, then, invented writing systems tend to be either syllabaries or logosyllabaries (combining syllabic writing with logographic—i.e. morphemic—writing), and not segmentally based alphabets (Daniels 1996). It is also the case that children learn to read more readily in syllabaries than in alphabets, whether in a syllabically simple language such as Japanese, the slightly more syllabically complex Korean (Taylor and Taylor 1995), or a syllabically varied language such as English (Gleitman and Rozin 1973).

The evidence from writing systems therefore suggests that syllables are if anything more linguistically real than segments, despite the fact that early generative phonology ignored them (see, for example, their absence in Chomsky and Halle 1968 and Chapter 1, this volume). Such an oversight can be attributed to an unconscious alphabetic bias in Western phonologists, conditioned by their script into perceiving the segment as the most important phonological unit.

1.2   The Theoretical Hurdle

The most obvious problem with the claim that syllabaries attest to the existence of syllables by encoding them is the fact that the strings which syllabaries encode are usually a poor match for the inventory of syllables in any given language. Syllabaries typically encode CV strings (with some V signs to start vowel-initial words), while many of the languages for which they are used contain more complex syllables. An extreme case of this mismatch is Linear B, a syllabary used in the Bronze Age for Mycenaean Greek (Chadwick 1987, Hooker 1980), shown below in (1). Linear B spellings are shown at top, followed by a transcription of those signs, followed by a segmental representation of the words (with segments left out in the Linear B spelling shown in parentheses), and finally the gloss. The actual Linear B signs are presented here in addition to the transcriptions to emphasize the fact that the Linear B signs—like syllabary signs generally—give no segmental information, a point that is lost in alphabetic transcription. In other words, the signs for *ka* and for *ko* have no internal similarity, and neither do *ka* and *ki*, despite the fact that each pair of syllables shares a segment.

(1) Linear B: written-spoken mismatch

⊕φ	ᗡᙏ	⋂ꞅꞔ
ka-ko	pe-ma	ti-ri-po
kʰa(l)ko(s)	(s)pe(r)ma	tripo(s)
'bronze'	'seed, grain'	'tripod'

As shown in the first two examples, some segments contained in the spoken words are left unrepresented in the written versions, while in the third example, a two-syllable word is represented with *three* written symbols. Thus there is a mismatch between the written signs and the spoken syllables both in content and in number.

The CV nature of most syllabaries has led some grammatologists (e.g. Rogers 2005, following Poser 1992) to consider syllabaries moraic rather than syllabic, as the signs contain only one mora each. By this view, writing systems traditionally termed 'syllabaries' would only inform us about constituents smaller than syllables. While moraic writing systems do exist, however (see section 2.4 below), many syllabaries cannot be reclassified as moraic, as they omit any representation of length in vowels or of gemination in consonants. I argue below that such syllabaries actually are syllabic, and that writing systems tell us a great deal about both the existence and the internal structure of syllables.

1.3   Scope of the Data

The writing systems considered in this chapter are among those surveyed in Daniels and Bright (1996); additional background information about many of them may be found in Gnanadesikan (2009). Pretheoretically, a writing system is a syllabary if it is a) *phonologically based* and b) does not (in at least some sizable portion of its signary) represent individual segments but rather some *string of segments*. In order not to bias the outcome, there are no restrictions placed on what sorts of strings of segments might occur. The question will then be what larger structures, if any, those strings of segments are collected into. If there are such larger structures, then considering the signs to be representing strings of segments is an inaccuracy brought on by an alphabetic perspective; the syllabary user would identify those larger structures (not the strings) as the objects encoded. However, the present definition will do as a way to identify candidate writing systems without prejudging what structures they actually represent.

Applying the definition, this chapter considers the syllabic portion of the Akkadian and Mayan writing systems, Linear B, Cypriot, Cherokee, the Japanese kana, Vai, Chinese Bopomofo, and Pahawh Hmong. Four of these—Cherokee, Vai, Pahawh Hmong and Bopomofo—are modern, all but the last of which having been invented by illiterate individuals who had heard of writing but had never been taught it. The Japanese kana date from medieval times, while Akkadian cuneiform, Mayan glyphs, Linear B and Cypriot are ancient.

A number of writing systems that have sometimes been called syllabaries are excluded by the above definition. First there are systems that have a strong morphological component, and are therefore more properly called logographic (or morphographic). Thus Chinese is not included, as its signs—though syllabically sized—encode morphological information (and so homophones are written differently).

Also left out are what might be called non-linear alphabets, i.e. writing systems that encode individual segments but group them together graphically in some way. In these scripts segmental signs do not simply follow each other linearly across the page as they do in 'Western' alphabets—i.e. the Greek-descended scripts—but individual segments are nevertheless specifically encoded. Thus this chapter does not include the *akṣara*-based scripts (also known as alphasyllabaries) of southern Asia and Ethiopia, in which vowel signs are appendages to consonants. Also excluded is Korean han'gŭl, which represents individual segments (and even certain individual features), but groups the segments into syllable-sized chunks. Cree 'syllabics' and related scripts of Canada are also omitted. Although these are usually called syllabaries, their CV signs are decomposable into shape, which gives consonant value, and orientation, which gives vowel quality (Nichols 1996). Thus, following Poser (2003), these scripts constitute alphabets.[1]

---

[1] This is not to say that such alphabets are of no interest to the study of syllables, merely that they are not of help in answering the question of which constituents a writing system will represent if it does not represent individual segments.

Finally, consonantal alphabets are not included here—Phoenician and its descendants (e.g. Aramaic, Hebrew, Syriac, and Arabic)—which write all the consonants in a word but usually omit all or some vowels. Although these have been considered syllabaries of a 'C + unspecified V' nature by Gelb (1963), the segmental identity of the consonants is clearly encoded.

2   Evidence for Syllables

The first question to consider is whether syllabaries actually encode a structural unit or whether they merely encode strings of segments, and if a structure, then is it really the syllable and not, say, the mora?

2.1   Strings or Syllables?

The most straightforward evidence for syllable representation comes from Mesopotamian cuneiform, an unusual writing system in many respects. As a development of the earlier proto-cuneiform script, it could claim to be the first writing system in the world, rivaled only by proto-Elamite and Egyptian hieroglyphs. Its use spanned over three millennia, from about 3300 BCE (as proto-cuneiform) to the last dated cuneiform tablet of 75 CE (Walker 1987). The full maturation of the script came only with its adaptation to the Semitic Akkadian language in the second half of the third millennium BCE.

The system was logosyllabic, meaning that its signs could have either phonological or morphological values. Looking only at the phonological signs, these included V, CV, CVC, and VC signs. This is an unusual list in that it includes C-final signs; most syllabaries omit them. The use of these signs was restricted, however, to syllables with codas, as shown in (2), which gives the Akkadian word on the left, followed by a transcription of the cuneiform spelling (Cooper 1996).

(2) Akkadian spelling

parāsu   pa-ra-su   'to decide'
              *par-as-u

As Cooper states it, "[w]ithin a word, a consonant-final sign cannot be followed by a vowel-initial sign" except at a morpheme boundary, or where the vowel-initial sign actually represents a glottal stop + vowel

(p. 48). In other words, a single sign never encoded segments from more than one syllable. Clearly, therefore, the signs were not simply encoding structureless strings of segments, but in fact syllables.

That these structures were syllables and not moras is emphasized by the omission of the vowel length (presumably moraic) from the transliteration in (2). Although syllables with a long vowel could have been spelled CV-V, in fact they rarely were except in the particular case when an "accented long final vowel" came about through contraction (Caplice and Snell 1988). In general, vowel length was left up to the reader to infer. A similar situation held for geminate consonants. Although geminates could be written—as CVC-CV—in fact they tended not to be, especially in older cuneiform (Ungnad and Matouš 1992). Thus the cuneiform writing system had very little regard for moras, but considerable regard for syllables.

2.2   Syllabic Membership

Most syllabaries, lacking C-final signs, are not as clear-cut as cuneiform in marking syllabic boundaries. Nevertheless, they find a number of ways to indicate syllabic membership. Even cuneiform did not always manage a one-to-one correspondence between signs and syllables, not having a sign for every CVC syllable. Closed syllables were often spelled with two signs, CV_i-V_iC, as in (3).

(3) More Akkadian spelling

   iprus   ip-ru-us   'he decided'

The repetition of the *u* did not indicate vowel length. Instead, it indicated that the two signs together formed a single syllable—that the two consonants were associated with the same vowel. It was, in a sense, a form of coindexation.

A similar system was employed in Mayan glyphs. The Mayan writing system was also a logosyllabary, used in Mesoamerica from perhaps the third century BCE (Saturno et al 2006) until after the Spanish Conquest in the 16th century CE. The phonological signs of Mayan were mostly CV, with plain V for vowel-initial words. In the spoken language, however, closed syllables occurred frequently; in fact, Mayan word roots tended to be CVC or CVCVC. This mismatch was resolved as in (4), in which tz represents the affricate [tˢ] in accordance with modern Mayan orthography (Coe and Van Stone 2005).

(4) Spelling Mayan codas

a. pakal   pa-ka-la   'shield'
   pitz   pi-tzi   'play ball'
   tzul   tzu-lu   'dog'
b. baak   ba-ki   'prisoner'
   muut   mu-ti   'bird, omen'
   ahk   a-ku   'turtle'

In (4a) the nuclear vowel is repeated, as in cuneiform, identifying both the onset and the coda with the nuclear vowel. However, here the vowel and the coda consonant appear out of linear order. The concept of a strict linear order of segments is a very alphabetic one, however; acoustically segmental order is less obvious (Liberman 1970), and users of the Mayan syllabary may not have considered it important.

In (4b) there is something special about the nucleus: it is long or aspirated. In such a case, the vowel written with the coda consonant would tend not to match the one written with the onset, although this pattern of vowel 'disharmony' was complicated and not entirely regular (Houston et al,1998). In these cases, both signs contained information about the same nucleus; thus both signs contributed to represent the same syllable.[2]

The Cypriot syllabary is another case where syllabic membership is indicated by the sharing of a vowel. This syllabary was used to write Greek on the island of Cyprus from the 8th (or possibly 11th) century BCE until Hellenistic times (Chadwick 1987). The script contained CV and V signs, with a few CCV signs for syllables beginning with *ks-*. The spelling rules invoked to fit Greek into this restricted inventory of signs were numerous, as shown in (5), with segments and clusters of interest underlined in the segmental representation at left (Woodard 1997).

(5) Cypriot spelling conventions

a. Geminates and long vowels simplified
   Apoll<u>ō</u>ni   a-po-lo-ni   'for Apollo'

---

[2] It could be argued that the signs in (4b) each represent one mora (assuming that coda consonants other than /h/ were nonmoraic), but as is clear from the examples in (4a), a second sign does not imply a second mora; so I do not accept that analysis here.

b. Word-final consonants (-s, -n, -r) usually spelled with epenthetic -e
   (but occasionally final -s and -n omitted)

ga<u>r</u>	ka-re[3]	'for'
kasignēto<u>s</u>	ka-si-ke-ne-to-se	'brothers,' acc.
mist^hō<u>n</u>	mi-si-to-ne	'of a fee'

c. Nasals omitted before stop or /s/

pa<u>n</u>ta	pa-ta	'all'
iō<u>n</u>si	i-o-si	'they should remain'

d. Word-initial clusters spelled with the following vowel

<u>St</u>asandrō	sa-ta-sa-to-ro	man's name, gen.

e. Otherwise, consonants in a cluster spelled with following vowel if the
   next C of level or rising sonority; with preceding vowel if next C of
   falling sonority

pa<u>tr</u>i	pa-ti-ri	'to the father'
me<u>mn</u>amenoi	me-ma-na-me-no-i	'having remembered'
a<u>rg</u>urō	a-ra-ku-ro	'of silver'
kate<u>st</u>ase	ka-te-se-ta-se	's/he placed'

Once again, moras are ignored, as shown in (5a), so the system is not moraic. But is it syllabic? Of interest here are conventions (5d) and (5e), where vowels are repeated to spell out consonant clusters. Much ink has been spilled (summarized in Woodard 1997) on debate as to whether the choice of vowel for a given consonant follows syllable-related or merely sonority-related rules. Woodard gives a number of reasons why the syllabification of the words, as indicated by classical meter, is not always as indicated by the vowels used in the spelling. In *memnamenoi*, for example, the syllable boundary would be between the m and the n, while the vowel choice of the syllabary suggests that the syllable boundary was between the e and the m. However, I believe it would be an error to miss the point that Cypriot spelling involved *combining consonants with vowels in a sonority-constrained manner*. This could almost be considered a definition of syllabification. In fact, the sonority hierarchy has been criticized (Ohala 1992, Harris 2006) for doing no valuable work in phonological theory except for describing syllabification constraints. It would be very unusual to have to invoke it here without also invoking syllables.

---

[3] Voicing and aspiration are not represented in the writing system.

The somewhat artificial sounding-out process of early scribal writing could easily have encouraged a certain amount of paralinguistic resyllabification, leading to slightly different syllable boundaries than are attested to metrically. Morpurgo Davies (1987) points out that the clusters that the Cypriot syllabary appears to accept as onsets are either those that can begin a word or have the same sonority profile as those that can begin a word.[4] In other words, they are clusters which can be forced into onset position. They also match well the clusters that later Classical Greek grammarians believed to be syllable onsets. This supports the idea of a paralinguistic resyllabification, as a slow sounding out of words would tend to make every syllable effectively word initial. Thus the Cypriot spelling does identify syllabic membership, modulo a slight resyllabification. Like Mayan, then, the Cypriot syllabary had a way to identify more than one consonant with a single vowel despite having to use two or more signs to encode the members of a single syllable

2.3   Onset-Coda Asymmetry and Extrasyllabicity of /s/

The Linear B syllabary, used on Crete and mainland Greece from about 1450 or earlier to about 1200 BCE (Hooker 1980), operated on similar orthographic principles as the Cypriot syllabary, but with omission of more consonants. Its signs were CV, V, and a few CCV. The traditional story (presented by Chadwick 1967 and Hooker 1980) is that onset consonants were written (except for /s/ before a stop), while coda consonants were not. Woodard (1997) again pursues a sonority analysis, stating the following rules: a) final consonants are omitted, b) a consonant is also omitted if it is followed by a consonant of lower sonority, and c) a consonant is written if it is followed by a consonant of equal or higher sonority (and will be written with the next vowel, if there is one). Examples of Linear B spelling (from Hooker 1980) are given in (6), with consonants of interest underlined in the segmental representation at left.

(6) Linear B spelling

| sperma | pe-ma | ▷𝕸 | 'seed, grain' |
| tripōs | ti-ri-po | 𝈅𝉀𝉆 | 'tripod' |

---

[4] Thanks to Ranjan Sen for drawing this work to my attention.

Phaistos	pa-i-to	𐀞𐀂𐀵	place name
anampukes	a-na-pu-ke	𐀀𐀙𐀢𐀐	'without headbands'
Amnisos	a-mi-ni-so	𐀀𐀖𐀛𐀰	place name
Knossos	ko-no-so	𐀒𐀜𐀰	place name
ksun	ku-su	𐀓𐀡	'together with'
potnia	po-ti-ni-a	𐀡𐀴𐀛𐀀	'lady'

Again, despite the apparent soundness of Woodard's claim that the associations here do not consistently match the syllabifications attested to elsewhere in ancient Greek, this is a case of *consonants being associated with vowels—or deleted—in a sonority-constrained manner.* This still looks suspiciously like syllabification. Consonants that associate forward are written, while those that associate backward (and /s/ before a stop) are not.[5] If, following Morpurgo Davies (1987), we allow for some paralinguistic resyllabification as in Cypriot, so that anything that can be forced into a word-initial onset is considered an onset, we return to the traditional analysis that onsets are written and codas (and /s/ before a stop) are not.

In Optimality Theoretic terms, this blatant preference for onsets over codas can be considered a case of positional faithfulness as described by Beckman (1999). The domain of analysis here is the correspondence between a word and its written representation, as opposed to between the input and output forms of a word or between a word and its reduplicant, as in analyses of purely spoken language. Onsets are associated with higher faithfulness constraints, so they must be faithfully represented; but codas are given no such privilege and are therefore deleted.[6]

Before leaving Linear B, there is also exceptional treatment of /s/ to consider. In a number of languages, including Greek (and English), /s/

---

[5] There are two possible exceptions: *wanaks* ('king') is written wa-na-ka, and *Aitʰiokʷs* (man's name) is written a₃-ti-jo-qo. However, note wa-na-ka-to and wa-na-ka-te (alongside wa-na-ke-te) for genitive *wanaktos* and dative *wanaktei* suggesting an alternative pronunciation or at least spelling exceptionality for this root. As Morpurgo Davies (1987) suggests, these forms may be the first signs of what later became the Cypriot spelling conventions.

[6] Following through on the idea of an OT correspondence between a language and its written representation, the fact that most syllabaries allow only the unmarked (C)V syllable shape in its signs can be considered a case of the emergence of the unmarked (as described by McCarthy and Prince 2004), occurring in the domain of the written representation (rather than, say, a reduplicant). As pointed out by Stephens and Justeson (1978), writing systems are highly sensitive to markedness.

is exceptional in that it can violate sonority constraints that otherwise hold on syllables. In Linear B such an /s/ was not represented, suggesting either that it was too marked for the unmarked domain of the written syllable, or that it was extrasyllabic (and thus, despite appearances, not able to be forced into an onset), or both.

The Cherokee syllabary gives further evidence for special treatment of /s/. This syllabary, first promulgated by it inventor, Sequoyah, in 1821, consists of signs for V, CV, and /s/ (Holmes and Smith 1976, Scancarelli 1996). The spoken Cherokee language, however, does have consonant clusters. These are represented in writing as in the examples (from Scancarelli 1996) shown in (7). The transliteration of the written symbols, given in the middle column, is in traditional Cherokee transliteration and uses voiced symbols for voiceless unaspirated segments and v for a nasalized schwa.

(7) Cherokee consonant clusters

a.	t^{h}aʔli	ta-li	ᏔᎵ	'two'
	suhti	su-di	ᏑᏗ	'fishhook'
b.	kałk^{w}o:ki	ga-li-quo-gi	ᎦᎵᏉᎩ	'seven'
	kt^{h}o:ʔa	gv-do-a	ᎬᏙᎠ	'it is hanging (of a long object)'
c.	sko:hi	s-go-hi	ᏍᎪᎯ	'ten'
d.	hijə̃wi:ja:s	hi-yv-wi-ya-s	ᎯᏴᏫᏯᏍ	'Are you an Indian?'

Like many syllabaries, written Cherokee ignores vowel length. Glottal stops and /h/ are not represented postvocalically (7a), but other consonants clusters are broken up with vowels (7b), using either a vowel from a morphologically related word, or a vowel of the writer's choice. The exception is /s/ (7c, d). The only non-syllabic character in the syllabary is Ꮝ, s. This character is used for /s/ both in onset clusters (7c) and in codas (7d). The Cherokee syllabary, like Linear B, acknowledges the exceptional status of /s/, but does so by giving it its own symbol rather than omitting it. Clearly /s/ has exceptional properties vis-à-vis syllabification; seeing it as extrasyllabic in certain positions may be appropriate.

2.4 *Moraic Structure*

Most syllabaries do not represent moras. Of the syllabaries considered so far, only Mayan represents vowel length; Cypriot, Linear B, Cherokee, and (usually) Mesopotamian cuneiform all ignore it.[7] Cypriot, Linear B, and (sometimes) cuneiform also ignore geminates, while Cypriot ignores word-internal coda nasals, Cherokee ignores coda /h/ and glottal stop, and Linear B ignores all coda consonants despite representing a quantity-sensitive language.

Nevertheless, some writing systems that are traditionally called syllabaries actually are moraic, adducing evidence for structures smaller than the syllable. The best-known examples are the two Japanese syllabaries, hiragana and katakana. These two scripts, dating from the ninth century CE, operate on the same principles. Both are used, along with kanji (Chinese logograms) in written Japanese today. The inventory of sign types in the two kana are V, CV, N (coda nasal), and Gem (first member of a geminate), as shown for hiragana in (8) (examples from Hadamitzky and Spahn 1981).

(8) Hiragana spelling

yūgata	yu-u-ga-ta	ゆうがた	'evening'
kirei	ki-re-i	きれい	'pretty'
jippun	ji-Gem-pu-N	じっぷん	'ten minutes'
tabun	ta-bu-N	たぶん	'probably'

As seen in (8), every mora gets a symbol in kana.

Similarly, in the Vai syllabary a word is written with as many symbols as it has moras. The Vai script was invented around 1834 by Mamoru Doalu Bukere, with the help of five friends (Koelle 1968 [1854]). The signs are of type V, CV, or N, where N stands for a nasal which can be either syllabic or syllable-final, and is usually pronounced [ŋ] (Singler 1996). Long vowels and diphthongs are written as two symbols, often with an 'epenthetic' glide onset on the second symbol, as in (9).

(9) Vai spelling (Singler 1996)

táá	ta-ha	'go'
kùú	ku-wu	'compound, home'
kéŋ	ke-ŋ	'house'

---

[7] Some alphabets ignore vowel length as well. Ancient Greek, for example, indicated length only in mid vowels, while Latin ignored it entirely.

In the examples of Vai and kana, therefore, we obtain information about structures smaller than, and presumably internal to, the syllable, as these encode moras.

2.5   Onset-Rhyme Structure

The onset-rhyme structure of the syllable is also attested to in the world's writing systems. Bopomofo is an auxiliary phonological script used in Taiwan to indicate pronunciation (information not well encoded by Chinese characters). Its use dates back to 1913. Unlike the pinyin system now used in mainland China, which is based on the Roman alphabet, Bopomofo is derived from Chinese characters. Signs are C_{onset}, V, VV, $V_{[-hi]}N$, and tone (Mair 1996). A syllable will be written as (initial)-(glide)-final-tone, where 'initial' is the consonantal onset, an on-glide is given the symbol of a high vowel, and the 'final' is the rhyme. If the vowel before a final nasal is high, the rhyme will be written as V+eN (the high vowel will then appear orthographically to be an on-glide), but other rhymes are not decomposed. In (10) are examples of (a) onset consonants, (b) single-vowel rhymes, (c) onglide-vowel shown as two symbols, and (d) complex rhymes encoded with one symbol apiece. In (e) is given the spelling of the word *hǎo*, 'good'.

(10) Bopomofo onsets and rhymes (Mair 1996)

a.	ㄅ	b	C_{onset}
	ㄏ	h	C_{onset}
b.	ㄨ	u	V
	ㄚ	a	V
c.	ㄨㄚ	ua	GV
d.	ㄠ	ao	VV
	ㄥ	eng	VN
	ㄢ	an	VN
e.	ㄏㄠˇ	h-ao-tone	'good'

The fact that most rhymes in Bopomofo are not decomposed into individual segments suggests that the rhyme is a structural unit that is relevant for Chinese.

A writing system that pays even more homage to the importance of the rhyme is the Pahawh Hmong script, originally created by Shong Lue Yang in 1959 and subsequently updated by him (Smalley et al.

1990). Signs for rhymes in Pahawh Hmong include signs of the types V, VV (both rising and falling diphthongs), and V_{mid}ŋ. A tone diacritic is written on the rhyme sign. A highly unusual aspect of this writing system is that although the writing in general proceeds left to right across the page, the rhyme of each syllable is written first (on the left), followed by the onset. Onsets may be simple—stops, fricatives, nasals, liquids, or glides—or they may be more complex—affricates, aspirated consonants, prenasalized stops or affricates, or a stop or prenasalized stop plus /l/. Each of these simple or complex onsets receives its own sign. There is also a sign for a zero onset, separate from the sign for a glottal stop onset, and also distinct from the default k- onset that is inferred if none is written.

Examples are in (11), where (a) gives complex onsets (with an -au rhyme inferred in the absence of a written rhyme), (b) gives complex rhymes (with a k- inferred in the absence of a written onset), and (c) gives an example of complete words (from Ratliff 1996).

(11) Hmong onsets and rhymes

a.	ᛗ	p^hl(au)		
	ᑘ	ml(au)		
	ᚦ̈	pl(au)		
	ᗡ̶	mp^hl(au)		
b.	ᚢ	(k)εŋ		
	ᑎ	(k)au		
	ᚼ	(k)ai		
	ᑌ	(k)ia		
c.	ʃɔ́ŋ lĩ̂	ɔ́ŋ-ʃ ĩ̂-l	ᚦᛁᚢ̃̈ ᛐᛚᚥ	Shong Lue (inventer of script)
	p^hâ hâu ^{h}mɔ́ŋ	â-p^h âu-h ɔ́ŋ-^{h}m	ᚣ̄ᚲ ᑎᛁᚱ ᚦᛆᛖ̈	Pahawh Hmong

While a number of the onsets in Hmong may be complex single segments rather than two segments (e.g. the prenasalized stops and affricates), those with stop-liquid combinations look like two-segment onsets represented with a single sign. Smalley et al (1990) consider these onsets to consist of a single complex segment, and the complex rhymes to be single complex vowels (diphthongs or nasalized vowels phonetically realized with a final ŋ), with the result that they consider the script to be alphabetic, i.e. segmental. This view accords with speaker's intuitions of the unity of the pre-vocalic material in each syllable. Ratliff (1996), on the other hand, terms the prevocalic signs 'onsets,' the others 'rhymes,' and the script as a whole 'demisyllabic.' While it is conceivable that Hmong uses sequences such as /pl/ as individual segments, it may also simply be that the onset is a particularly salient unit in Hmong. This would account both for the intuitions of native speakers and for Shong Lue Yang's decision to use single signs for complex onsets. The fact that there is a sign for an empty onset suggests that the script is operating at the level of structure (i.e. onset/rhyme) rather than segment. Furthermore, the arrangement of the script, with the rhyme of each syllable written first and the onset written afterwards, indicates that some level of syllabic organization is operating here even supposing an alphabetic analysis of the individual signs.

Pahawh Hmong and Bopomofo both pick out the rhyme as a constituent, while Pahawh Hmong seems to identify the onset as a constituent as well. These writing systems are unusual in the prominence they give to the rhyme (in the case of Pahawh Hmong the more unusual because the rhyme is written first). Such attention to rhyme is only practical because of the relatively small inventory of rhymes in the relevant languages, Chinese and Hmong. It is probably also related to the fact that these writing systems were both designed for tone languages, and the rhyme is the tone-bearing unit in these languages.

3   Conclusions and Speculations

Any writing system encodes only some subset of a language's phonological structures, generally unmarked ones (Stephens and Justeson 1978) or ones that are of particular importance to the language for which they are designed (as rhymes in Pahawh Hmong and Bopomofo). Most syllabaries encode only unmarked (C)V syllables in the shape of their individual signs; nevertheless they employ a number of ingenious methods to provide evidence of other syllable types and for the syllable as the basic unit in terms of which many of them operate.

Thus writing systems provide evidence for the psychological reality of syllables by way of their accessibility as units of encoding. They also provide evidence for some of their properties, namely onset over coda preference and exceptionality of /s/, and for the constituent structures of syllables, i.e. moras and onsets and rhymes. I am not claiming, however, that all these structures are relevant to all languages; indeed the special status of /s/ is one property that is clearly relevant only to some languages. Nevertheless, syllables come out as robustly supported by this study.

It is worth considering, therefore, why syllables have often been questioned or neglected in modern phonology. They are entirely absent from *The Sound Pattern of English* (Chomsky and Halle 1968), for example, and their existence is still a matter of active discussion in the present volume, over forty years later. Because a writing system encodes some structures and not others, and becoming literate involves becoming aware of specifically those encoded structures, a literate speaker is likely to have heightened awareness of the structures encoded by the writing system at hand. Thus Western phonologists, being alphabetically literate, begin with heightened awareness of segments and lower awareness of syllables, with consequences that play out in their theoretical work. It is worth trying to avoid such orthographic bias in the future.

In other work (Gnanadesikan 2009), I have explored a number of writing systems, many of which encode smaller phonological units than syllables. The *akṣara*-based scripts (or alphasyllabaries) distinguish between syllabic nuclei and margins, or roughly, vowels versus consonants. Alphabets in general pick the segment as the unit of representation. Some alphabets (most famously Korean han'gŭl) also encode phonological features. What I have not found in writing is any evidence for phonological units *larger* than the syllable: I have found no evidence of the foot. This may be related to the relatively slow rate of writing versus speaking: much metrical structure is lost at the slow speed of sounding out or of dictation. It may also suggest that there is a fundamental disjunction between syllables and smaller phonological structures on the one hand, and larger phonological structures on the other; for example, the former may be lexically encoded while the latter are not.

References

Beckman, Jill N. 1999. *Positional faithfulness: An optimality theoretic treatment of phonological asymmetries.* New York: Garland.

Caplice, Richard and Daniel Snell. 1988. *Introduction to Akkadian*, 3rd ed. Rome: Biblical Institute Press.

Chadwick, John. 1967. *The Decipherment of Linear B*, 2nd ed. Cambridge: Cambridge University Press.

———. 1987. *Linear B and Related Scripts.* London: British Museum.

Chomsky, Noam and Morris Halle. 1968. *The Sound Pattern of English.* New York: Harper and Row.

Coe, Michael and Mark Van Stone. 2005. *Reading the Maya Glyphs*, 2nd ed. London: Thames & Hudson.

Cooper, Jerrold. 1996. Sumerian and Akkadian. In *The World's Writing Systems*, edited by Peter Daniels and William Bright, 27–57. New York: Oxford University Press.

Daniels, Peter. 1996. The Invention of Writing. In *The World's Writing Systems*, edited by Daniels and William Bright, 579–586. New York: Oxford University Press.

Daniels, Peter and William Bright, eds. 1996. *The World's Writing Systems.* New York: Oxford University Press.

Gelb, Ignace. 1963. *A Study of Writing.* Rev. ed. Chicago: University of Chicago Press.

Gleitman, Lila and Paul Rozin. 1973. Teaching Reading by Use of a Syllabary. *Reading Research Quarterly* 8: 447–483.

Gnanadesikan, Amalia. 2009. *The Writing Revolution: Cuneiform to the Internet.* Malden, MA: Wiley-Blackwell.

Gombert, Jean. 1992. *Metalinguistic Development.* Chicago: University of Chicago Press.

Goswami, U. 2006. Orthography, Phonology, and Reading Development: A Cross-Linguistic Perspective. In *Handbook of Orthography and Literacy* edited by R. Malatesha Joshi and P. G. Aaron, 463–480. Mahwah, NJ: Lawrence Erlbaum.

Hadamitzky, Wolfgang and Mark Spahn. 1981. *Kanji and Kana: A Handbook and Dictionary of the Japanese Writing System.* Rutland, VT: Tuttle.

Harris, John. 2006. The phonology of being understood: further arguments against sonority. *Lingua* 116: 1483–1494.

Holmes, Ruth and Betty Smith. 1976. *Beginning Cherokee.* Norman, OK: University of Oklahoma Press.

Hooker, James T. 1980. *Linear B: An Introduction.* Bristol: Bristol Classical Press.

Houston, Stephen D., David Stuart and John Robertson. 1998. Disharmony in Maya Hieroglyphic Writing: Linguistic Change and Continuity in Classic Society. In *Anotomía de Una Civilización: Aproximaciones Interdisciplinarias*, edited by Andrés Ciudad-Ruiz et al, 275–296. Madrid: Sociedad Española de Estudios Mayas.

Jackendoff, Ray. 1983. *Semantics and Cognition.* Cambridge, MA: MIT Press.

Koelle, Sigismund. 1968 [1854]. *Outlines of a Grammar of the Vei Language, together with a Vei-English Vocabulary and an Account of the Discovery and Nature of the Vei Mode of Syllabic Writing.* London: Church Missionary House.

Liberman, Alvin. 1970. The Grammars of Speech and Language. *Cognitive Psychology* 1: 301–323.

Liberman, Isabelle, Donald Shankweiler, F. William Fischer and Bonnie. Carter. 1974. Explicit syllable and phoneme segmentation in the young child. *Journal of Experimental Child Psychology* 18: 201–212.

Mair, Victor. 1996. Modern Chinese Writing. In *The World's Writing Systems*, edited by Peter Daniels and William Bright, 200–208. New York: Oxford University Press.

Mattingly, Ignatius. 1972. Reading, the Linguistic Process, and Linguistic Awareness. In *Language by Ear and by Eye: The Relationships between Speech and Reading*, edited by James F. Kavanagh and Ignatius G. Mattingly, 131–148. Cambridge, MA: MIT Press.

McCarthy, John and Alan Prince. 2004. The Emergence of the Unmarked. In *Optimality Theory in Phonology: A Reader*, edited by John J. McCarthy, 483–494. Malden, MA: Blackwell.

Morpurgo Davies, Anna. 1987. Mycenaean and Greek Syllabification. In *Tractata Mycenaea: Proceedings of the Eighth International Colloquium on Mycenaean Studies, Held in Ohrid, 15–20 September 1985*, edited by Petar Hr. Ilievski and Ljiljana Crepajac, 91–104. Skopje: Macedonian Academy of Sciences and Arts.

Nichols, John. 1996. The Cree Syllabary. In *The World's Writing Systems*, edited by Peter Daniels and William Bright, 599–611. New York: Oxford University Press.

Ohala, John. 1992. Alternatives to the Sonority Hierarchy for Explaining Sequential Constraints. *Chicago Linguistics Society* 26, 2: 319–338.

Poser, William. 1992. The Structural Typology of Phonological Writing. Presented at the 66th Annual Meeting of the Linguistic Society of America, Philadelphia, PA.

——. 2003. Dʌlkʷahke: The First Carrier Writing System. Unpublished Ms. http://www.billposer.org/Papers/dulkwah.pdf

Ratliff, Martha. 1996. The Pahawh Hmong Script. In *The World's Writing Systems*, edited by Peter Daniels and William Bright, 619–624. New York: Oxford University Press.

Rogers, Henry. 2005. *Writing Systems: A Linguistic Approach*. Malden, MA: Blackwell.

Saturno, William, David Stuart and Boris Beltrán. 2006. Early Maya Writing at San Bartolo, Guatemala. *Science* 311: 1281–1283.

Scancarelli, Janine. 1996. Cherokee Writing. In *The World's Writing Systems*, edited by Peter Daniels and William Bright, 587–592. New York: Oxford University Press.

Seymour, Phillip. 2006. Theoretical Framework for Beginning Reading in Different Orthographies. In *Handbook of Orthography and Literacy*, edited by R. Malatesha Joshi and P. G. Aaron, 441–462. Mahwah, NJ: Lawrence Erlbaum.

Singler, John. 1996. Scripts of West Africa. In *The World's Writing Systems*, edited by Peter Daniels and William Bright, 593–598. New York: Oxford University Press.

Smalley, William, Chia Koua Vang and Gnia Yee Yang. 1990. *Mother of Writing: The Origin and Development of a Hmong Messianic Script*. Chicago: University of Chicago Press.

Stephens, Laurence and John Justeson. 1978. Reconstructing 'Minoan' Phonology: The Approach from Universals of Writing Systems. *Transactions of the American Philological Association* 108: 271–284.

Taylor, Insup and M. Martin Taylor. 1995. *Writing and Literacy in Chinese, Korean and Japanese*. Studies in Written Language and Literacy 3. Amsterdam: John Benjamins.

Ungnad, Arthur and Lubor Matouš. 1992. *Akkadian Grammar*. 5th ed. Atlanta, GA: Scholars Press.

Woodard, Roger D. 1997. *Greek Writing from Knossos to Homer: A Linguistic Interpretation of the Origin of the Greek Alphabet and the Continuity of Ancient Greek Literacy*. New York: Oxford University Press.

THE SYLLABLE IN PERFORMANCE:
DIACHRONY

DIACHRONIC PHONOTACTIC DEVELOPMENT IN LATIN: THE WORK OF SYLLABLE STRUCTURE OR LINEAR SEQUENCE?

Ranjan Sen

1 *Introduction*

There has been considerable debate in the phonological literature of the last few decades concerning the role played by the syllable in consonantal phonotactics. One party attributes the range of contrasts in each environment to positions within the syllable (the syllable-based approach; section 1.1); an opposing camp argues that linear segmental sequence, not syllable-internal position, determines phonotactics (the linear approach; section 1.2). Whereas the majority of previous studies have adopted a position in one or other camp with a solely synchronic focus,[1] this chapter evaluates the two approaches from a mainly diachronic perspective with reference to the development of Latin consonantal phonotactics, focusing upon assimilations. Our understanding of Proto-Indo-European (PIE) word-formation has long been sufficiently refined to furnish us with a rich array of securely reconstructed consonantal sequences in prehistoric Latin, whose outcome in the familiar classical language is much altered. As the two accounts make different predictions regarding the possible development of word-internal consonantal sequences, Latin presents a promising testing ground.

1.1 *The Syllable-Based Approach*

A syllable-based account of phonotactics can be found in early investigations into syllable-internal structure, which focused on the distribution of segments in different syllable constituents (Fudge 1969,

---

[1] Notable recent exceptions being the work of Blevins (2003, 2004).

Hockett 1947, Pike and Pike 1947).[2] The now much-refined syllable-based approach to phonotactics claims to explain assimilations and neutralisations at syllable boundaries. Three different strategies have emerged: positional licensing—the coda position has fewer licensing possibilities than the onset (Goldsmith 1990, 125); negative coda constraints—codas cannot contrast in certain features (Itô 1988, 1989); and positional faithfulness—onsets are more faithful to their underlying lexical forms than codas (Beckman 1999). All three have in common that codas exhibit fewer contrasts than onsets and therefore, all things being equal, regressive assimilation is preferred to progressive, as codas can assume the features of their ensuing onsets.

1.1.1 *Positional Licensing*

Developing the early idea that only a specific set of segments can appear in a given syllable position, the theory of positional licensing expands the notion of syllable position to any prosodic unit, and refers to features (or autosegments), not segments. This account is expounded by Goldsmith (1990, 123–127) and, with specific reference to voice neutralisation, by Lombardi (1995). Prosodic units license features; the syllable is a primary licenser, and the coda a secondary one, allowing only a subset of the possibilities available in the onset, which is directly licensed by the syllable. For example, it is common for the coda to be incapable of licensing place of articulation, resulting in the homorganicity of coda nasals and obstruents with the following onset, where place is licensed by the syllable (e.g. Lat. *eum.dem > eun.dem 'same (acc.)'),[3] or the realisation of the coda at a default place of articulation (e.g. Ancient Greek word-final nasals were realised as [n]).

---

[2] The earliest (Brosches 1765, Jespersen 1904, Saussure 1916, Sievers 1881, Whitney 1873) and most celebrated syllable-based governing principle for phonotactic organisation is undoubtedly the sonority sequencing generalisation/principle/constraint, which states that segments rise in sonority (perhaps maximally) from the start of the syllable to a peak, then fall (perhaps minimally) to the end of the syllable. Sonority is viewed as an inherent property of a segment. Given the ongoing debate surrounding its validity, it is perhaps advantageous that the present study requires no recourse to the principle as an explanatory tool. For further discussion and references, see Steriade (1982), Clements (1990), Zec (1995), and Ohala and Kawasaki-Fukumori (1997), among others.

[3] In this chapter, '*' indicates a reconstructed form, '>' a historical development (or 'is higher than' in the two hierarchies below), '.' a syllable boundary, '-' a morphological boundary, ⟨x⟩ orthographic x, and small capitals an inscriptional form. Attested forms are written in their received orthography, with the addition of the length mark ':' as appropriate.

1.1.2 Coda Constraints

Coda constraints are in effect a negative version of licensing: rather than positing prosodic units with licensing capabilities in accordance with their position in the prosodic hierarchy, codas are deemed specifically incapable of licensing certain features. One such formulation is Itô's Coda Condition (1988, 1989), prohibiting a place specification in coda consonants, but allowing doubly linked structures where the place feature is linked to a following onset as well as the coda (i.e. geminates and place-assimilated sequences).[4]

Under the coda constraint analysis, the labial place feature of the nasal in the coda of the first syllable of *eum.dem could not surface from the time when the condition prohibiting specified place in codas was introduced into the grammar. Instead, the coronal place feature of the following onset spread to the immediately preceding nasal, yielding *eundem*, with a doubly linked coronal place feature.

1.1.3 Positional Faithfulness

Under the positional faithfulness approach to phonotactics, the interaction of faithfulness and markedness constraints, which form an integral part of the Optimality Theoretic machinery (Prince and Smolensky 2004), can bequeath assimilated output forms to a language. Assimilation is the result of the existence of specific and general forms of the same constraint, where the former demands greater faithfulness in certain privileged positions, such as syllable onsets. Where a markedness constraint is ranked between specific and general versions of a faithfulness constraint, neutralisation of the relevant feature in unprivileged positions such as codas results.

It is argued (Beckman 1999, Lombardi 2001) that these constraints are well equipped to generate the correct typology of assimilation and neutralisation without recourse to the additional mechanisms of the licensing approach: word-internal regressive assimilation without word-final neutralisation can be derived simply through constraint ranking, whereas special word-final licensing possibilities would be required in a licensing approach (Lombardi 1999). However, note that the negative coda constraint is still invoked in some such analyses (Lombardi 2001).

---

[4] For further discussion regarding the form of coda constraints, see Blevins (1995, 227–229) and Lombardi (2001).

1.2   *The Linear Approach*

The linear approach claims that the features that can contrast in an environment are determined by linear segmental sequence alone, by means of the robustness of the perceptual cues for each feature in that environment. Its proponents (Blevins 1993, 2003, 2004, Rubach 1996, Steriade 1999a, b, 2001) claim that this approach is more descriptively adequate than syllable-based efforts, both language-internally and cross-linguistically, e.g. where languages with differing syllabifications of a sequence have identical phonotactic constraints. Furthermore, the dependence of the linear approach on the phonetic origins of consonantal sequences purportedly endows this account with greater explanatory force. This view has enjoyed considerable support in recent years.

Whereas the syllable-based approach, with contrasts determined by syllable position, is built upon purely phonological grounds, a key dimension to the linear approach is its reference to the phonetic basis of phonotactic constraints. As stated above, positions of contrast are those where perceptual cues for that contrast are most robust, whereas positions of neutralisation are those where the cues are least robust. Wright (2001, 2004, 36) defines a cue as "information in the acoustic signal that allows the listener to apprehend the existence of a phono-logical contrast." The portion of the signal in which this information is encoded can either correspond with the segment in which the feature resides (internal cues), or be found in neighbouring segments, cre-ated by coarticulation (external cues). Furthermore, Wright (2004, 52) defines robustness as "the redundancy of the cues minus the vulner-ability of those cues", meaning that "the more cues point to a contrast and the less susceptible to masking or loss those cues are the more likely the contrast is to survive." Finally, it should be noted that the relevant cues are different for each contrast, and different features are more reliably perceived in different environments.

1.3   *Selecting the Correct Analysis*

From the perspective of phonotactic development, the approaches make differing predictions with regard to the contrasts which survived in coda position in a given context, with more consistency demanded by the syllable-based approach. Where a sequence could have been syllabified in two different ways in Latin, e.g. intervocalic stop + liquid (VT.RV versus V.TRV), the syllable-based approach predicts that the sequence would have developed differently along the lines of those two syllabifications, whereas the linear approach predicts identical outcomes for the two linearly identical sequences. In theory, this sets out clear tracks for a course of investigation. In practice, the tracks themselves are barely visible where the Latin of the archaic period in question is concerned. How, for example, can one ascertain which consonant in a sequence was most robustly cued, or how stop + liquid sequences were syllabified at a time long before the existence of the helpful metrical evidence, or indeed whether there was any variation at all in the syllabification of a given sequence? This investigation therefore aims to decipher the phonetic and phonological circumstances the data betray, as well as to evaluate which approach accounts best for that data. Unless otherwise specified, the data regarding all the phenomena investigated in this chapter are drawn from the evidence reported in various handbooks dealing with Latin phonology (Allen 1973, 1978, Leumann 1977, Meiser 1998, Niedermann 1997, Sommer and Pfister 1977, Sihler 1995).

2   Voice Assimilation

We reconstruct Proto-Indo-European etymologies containing sequences of obstruents with different voice specifications, based upon our knowledge of PIE morphemes. In Latin, these sequences all showed a single voice specification, with regular regressive assimilation. Comparative evidence indicates that voice assimilation occurred in PIE, but must also have been operational at a much later date in several branches, and was certainly still occurring in formations within Latin (see *obtineo:* below), as a synchronic rule or constraint plausibly present in the grammar since PIE times.

(1) Stop + stop: *skri:b^h-tos > scri:ptus* 'written'

(2) Stop + fricative: *nu:b-sai > nu:psi:* 'I married'

(3) Fricative + stop: *is-dem > *izdem > i:dem* 'same'; contrast *kas-tos > castus* 'chaste'

The apparent failure of regressive voice assimilation in orthographically regular forms such as *obtineo:* 'I possess', *subtus* 'beneath' and *subti:lis* 'delicate' is in fact misleading, as the spelling ⟨pt⟩ was common in all periods and the evidence of the grammarians Quintilian (*Inst.* 1.7.7)[5] and Velius Longus (*G.L.* 7.62) both indicate the pronunciation [pt]. Orthographic ⟨bt⟩ reflects preservation or replacement by analogy of the prefixes, cf. *obdu:ro:* 'I persist', *subdolus* 'deceitful' (Niedermann 1997, 129), in spelling alone. Examples of inscriptional phonetic spellings are: *CIL* 1².7 OPSIDES = *obside:s* 'hostages' (3rd cent. B.C.), *CIL* 1².1570 OPTINVI = *obtinui:* 'I possessed', *CIL* 12.1783 OPTVLIT = *obtulit* 'he brought before', *CIL* 6.9797 SVPTILISSIMA = *subti:lissima* 'most delicate (fem.).'

Both the syllable-based and linear approaches are capable of accounting for the above data. The consonant which underwent assimilation in each case was in coda position, e.g. */skri:bʰ.tus/, */nu:b.sai/, but, from a linear perspective, it was also in preobstruent position, a context in which cues for the perception of voice contrasts in stops are often weak: failure to release stops (into a vowel or sonorant) removes cues to voicing in the release burst, aspiration noise (if present in the language) and VOT. The remaining cues to voicing (duration of the preceding vowel, closure duration and periodicity in the signal) are often weaker and no longer salient in the absence of the release cues (Wright 2004, 40–41). The linear explanation is weaker where the coda was a fricative, as the presence or absence of periodicity during frication noise is a strong cue to voicing (Cole and Cooper 1975). The absence of phonemic /z/ in Latin could explain the voicing of /s/ in robustly cued voiced contexts, as in (3) where the voiced stop C_2 was released. As there was no sibilant voice contrast, /s/ could become contextually voiced to provide further cues to the voicing of an adjacent consonant.

Regressive voice assimilation also took place in obstruent sequences forming complex codas or at any rate sequences which were not coda + onset. Thus, beside orthographically regular *ple:bs* 'people', we find inscriptional PLEPS (*CIL* 12.4333.12; 11 AD), and we also reconstruct the development **snig^{wh}-s > nix* 'snow', with an original labiovelar stop. Furthermore, we have grammarians' statements to support the voicelessness of the stop, at least in imperial times (e.g. Scaur. gram. *G.L.* 7.27.11ff.). The correct formulation for voice assimilation in Latin

---

[5] References and abbreviations regarding Latin authors and their works are as per Glare (1996).

Table 1   Assimilation in obstruent place and continuance

	C$_2$	Dorsal	Labial	Coronal
C$_1$				
Dorsal		*ekke > ecce 'look!'	(no secure native Latin examples)	lactis 'milk (gen.)'
+ fricative		(no dorsal fricative)	ecfero: (Plautus) 'I carry out'	*deiksai > di:xi: [di:ksi:] 'I said'
Labial		*obkaido: > occi:do: 'I knock down'	*obpeto: > oppeto: 'I encounter (prematurely)'	optimus 'best'
+ fricative		(no dorsal fricative)	opifici:na > *offici:na > offici:na 'workshop'	*nu:bsai > nu:psi: 'I married'
Coronal		*hodke > *hocce > hoc 'this (neut.)'	*quidpe > quippe 'for'	*pattos > *patstos > passus 'suffered'
+ fricative		(no dorsal fricative)	adfero: > affero: 'I deliver'	*quatsai > quassi: 'I shook'

▢ = apparent regressive assimilation in place and continuance[6]

must therefore be 'every part of an obstruent sequence came to agree in voice, regardless of syllabification', lending some weight to the linear approach over the syllable-based approach.

3   Place and Continuance

The Latin data relating to assimilations in obstruent place and continuance can be most insightfully represented in tabular form in Table 1.

Regressive place assimilation occurred regularly in C$_1$ regardless of its place when C$_2$ was a dorsal stop, and in coronal C$_1$ when C$_2$ was a labial obstruent. The contrast between all three major places survived before coronal stop C$_2$, although coronal stop + coronal stop yielded assibilated /ss/, probably via /tst/ (Niedermann 1997, 148). Sequences of a later origin with two coronal stops showed only regressive voice

---

[6] 'Apparent' due to the fact that the shading is somewhat speculative, intended purely to aid the extraction of a pattern from the data. There is no reason to shade any part of the dorsal + dorsal cell, and the homorganic stop + stop cells are shaded simply because of assimilation in the corresponding stop + fricative examples.

assimilation and no assibilation, thus *kedate > *kedte > cette 'give here! (pl.)'.

Unlike voice assimilation, place assimilation cannot be dated as far back as PIE, but was probably operational as far back as prehistoric Latin given the absence of unassimilated forms in the earliest attestations. Place assimilation was still operational after syncope in the 6th–5th cents. B.C. (Meiser 1998, 66–67), thus *sitikos (cf. sitis 'thirst') > *sitkos > siccus 'dry'.

How then do we correctly formulate the context for place assimilation? Observe that dorsal C_2 admitted no place contrast in C_1: place features were neutralised and the obstruent was assimilated in place to C_2. Slightly more permissive were labials, allowing dorsal C_1 to survive, but not recognising coronal C_1, which was assimilated to the labial place of C_2. Finally, the most permissive place in C_2 was coronal, allowing the survival of the contrast between labial and dorsal, as well as assibilated coronals. Alternatively, the formulation can be inverted by referring to C_1 rather than C_2: dorsals were the most resistant C_1, followed by labials, followed by coronals, the least identifiable before another consonant.[7]

Stop C_1 before fricative C_2 shows the same environment for regressive assimilation in continuance as for place:[8] there was no phonemic dorsal fricative, but before the labial fricative /f/, only a contrast between dorsal (Plautine ecfero:, but later effero:; see section 8 below)[9] and other places of articulation survived, with assimilation in continuance in labial C_1 (officina), and in both place and continuance in coronal C_1 (affero:). And the similarity with place assimilation continues when we look at coronal fricatives in C_2, which allowed both the manner and place of dorsal and labial C_1 to persist (di:xi:, nu:psi:), but which triggered neutralisation of manner in coronal C_1, realised as a fricative (*quat-sai > quassi: 'I shook').

The resulting pattern of shading in table 1 is neatly captured by reference to a hierarchy relating to place:

---

[7] Inherited labiovelar /k^w/ and /g^w/ behaved in precisely the same way as the dorsal stops preconsonantally (Niedermann 1997, 151), thus *eksting^{w}si: > exti:nxi: 'I extinguished', *ung^{w}tio: > u:nctio: 'anointing', *k^wok^{w}tos > coctus 'cooked'.

[8] Or alternatively, more thoroughgoing assimilation, as sequences homorganic in place assimilated in continuance, whereas we cannot tell whether place in C_1 of homorganic stop + stop sequences was neutralised or retained.

[9] Leumann (1977, 210) argues that the prefix ec- that appeared regularly only before roots beginning in /f/ developed from secondary *eks-, the inherited prefix analogically restored after the development *eks-fero: > effero: had occurred.

(4) The Place Hierarchy: dorsal > labial > coronal
    C_1 lower than or level with C_2 on the Place Hierarchy assimilated to C_2
    in place, and in continuance if a stop.[10]

This formulation is clearly in accord with the linear approach. Only by taking into account both the nature of a consonant and its environment (i.e. the interaction of C_1 and C_2) can the developments be correctly predicted. A syllable-based formulation would resemble 'coda stops came to be unspecified for coronal place regardless of the environment, and for labial place if followed by a labial or dorsal onset; coda obstruents were unspecified for continuance if unspecified for place' (see below regarding fricative C_1). The syllable-based approach is clearly unsatisfactory: there is no motivation for reference to syllable position; linear sequence is necessary and sufficient to capture the generalisation, as (4) demonstrates.

Furthermore, the syllable-based approach not only includes unnecessary information, it also undergenerates in the same way as we saw for voice assimilation: in word-final consonantal sequences, regressive assimilation in continuance still occurred despite the absence of a syllable boundary. The only fricative occurring word-finally was /s/, which being a coronal only triggered assimilation in another preceding coronal, thus */ts, ds/ > /ss/, an outcome sequence required for the correct scansion of early Latin verse (Plautus), but which simplified to /s/ in classical times, thus *miːlets > miːless > miːles 'soldier', *obseds > *obsess > obses 'hostage'. Contrast daps 'feast' and mox 'soon' for a preceding labial and dorsal respectively, surviving as stops.

Jun (2004, 63–64) formulates a hierarchy for resistance to assimilation according to the place of articulation of (unreleased) consonants which matches that in (4) above: dorsal > labial > coronal. He concludes, along the lines of Browman and Goldstein (1990), that the difference in coronal place and the others lies in the greater speed of tongue tip gestures, resulting in their being overlapped when in C_1 by tongue dorsum and lip gestures in C_2, whose beginnings are found in the VC transition. To explain the greater perceptibility of dorsals over labials, Jun cites the noticeable convergence of F2 and F3 in vowels adjacent to dorsals, based on the findings of Jakobson, Fant and Halle (1952) and Stevens (1989). Typological evidence bears out the predictions (Jun 2004, 67–68): if dorsals are targets of place assimilation,

---

[10] See section 4 regarding fricative and nasal C_1.

so are labials (e.g. Thai), but the reverse is not true, as labials can be targeted where dorsals are not (e.g. Korean, Inuktitut); if labials are targets, so are coronals (e.g. Hindi, Korean, Thai), but again the reverse is not true (e.g. Catalan, English, Lithuanian).

However, as the Latin data clearly illustrate, consideration of only the target consonant is insufficient, as we need to look at both target and trigger to achieve the formulation in (4) above. Jun (2004, 65) offers the same gestural explanation for the role of the trigger consonant (usually C_2) as for the target, noting the asymmetry between coronals and noncoronals as triggers in Latin stop assimilation. No further asymmetry between dorsals and labials as triggers in Latin is motivated, as we cannot tell whether dorsal C_1 retained its place or was assimilated before dorsal C_2.

4   Manner

A look at the manner of articulation of C_1 and C_2 further demonstrates that the interaction of the two consonants is paramount in place assimilation, and a consideration of any one of them in terms of syllable position is incapable of producing the right results. In table 1, we saw that fricative C_2 triggered place assimilation in stop C_1 wherever stop C_2 did as well, obeying the Place Hierarchy in both cases. However, the reverse is not true: fricative C_1 retained its place regularly before stops, and only assimilated before other fricatives, obeying the Place Hierarchy, thus *dis-facilis > difficilis 'difficult', with place assimilation in a coronal + labial fricative sequence, but dispo:no: 'I distribute', hospes 'guest', where /s/ survived before a labial, pri:scus 'ancient' where it survived before a dorsal, and castus 'pure' before another coronal. Therefore, fricatives were more resistant to place assimilation than stops.

Like stops, nasal C_1 assimilated in place to C_2 of any manner:

(5) Nasal + stop: *enprobos > improbus 'dishonest'; *tengo: > tingo: = [tiŋgo:] 'I dye'[11]

(6) Nasal + fricative: *komsol > co:nsul 'consul'

---

[11] See fn. 12 regarding the raising */e/ > /i/ before a dorsal nasal.

(7) Nasal + nasal: *enmaneo: > immineo: 'I overhang; threaten'

However, nasals were even less resistant to place assimilation than stops, as can be seen in the fact that place assimilation in a nasal + obstruent sequence was exceptionless, failing to obey the Place Hierarchy, thus *kemtom > centum 'hundred', showing assimilation of a labial to a following coronal. However, the Place Hierarchy was obeyed in nasal + nasal sequences, again showing that the interaction of the consonants was of the utmost importance, thus *enmaneo: > immineo: 'I overhang; threaten' with place assimilation in a coronal + labial sequence, but autumnus 'autumn', with no assimilation in a labial + coronal configuration.

This information can be captured by a hierarchy indicating the most to least resistant manners of articulation regarding place, as shown in (8).

(8) The Manner Hierarchy: fricative > stop > nasal.
    Fricative C_1 assimilated in place only before fricative C_2, in accordance with the Place Hierarchy. Stop C_1 assimilated in place before C_2 of any manner, in accordance with the Place Hierarchy. Nasal C_1 assimilated in place before C_2 of any manner, but only in accordance with the Place Hierarchy before nasal C_2, and without exception before obstruent C_2.

As with the Place Hierarchy, phonetic explanations for the Manner Hierarchy have appeared in prior phonological literature. Reporting the findings of studies by Kohler (1990), Hura, Lindblom and Diehl (1958) and Jun (1995), Steriade (2001, 223–224) concludes that perceptibility differences control the incidence of place assimilation (i.e. the linear approach), with nasals being the most confusable class, fricatives the least, and stops in the middle. Jun (2004, 61–63) discusses the proposed reason for this: in preconsonantal position, place in all consonants is cued by VC formant transitions, a relatively poor source compared to CV transitions. Whereas fricatives and approximants are enhanced by reliable internal cues to place, nasals are further handicapped by the characteristic nasalisation of the preceding vowel. The predicted hierarchy is borne out by language typology (Jun 2004, 66–67): continuants virtually never undergo place assimilation (although we have seen that this did occur in a constrained fashion in Latin), and if stops can be targeted for assimilation, so can nasals, but no language targets stops but not nasals.

Table 2   Assimilation in nasality and place

Nasal C$_2$ C$_1$	Labial	Coronal
Dorsal	*sekmentom > segmentum = [gm] 'piece'	*deknos > dignus = [ŋn] 'worthy'[12]
Labial	*supmos > summus 'highest'	*swepnos > somnus 'sleep'
Coronal	*kaidmentom > *kaimmentum > caementum 'rubble'	*atnos > annus 'year'

☐ = regressive nasal assimilation

■ = regressive nasal and place assimilation

These considerations provide a basis for the patterns we find in Latin and other languages. The Place and Manner Hierarchies have foundations in perceptibility and the pattern in Latin arises from their interaction.

5   Nasality

In this section, we look at assimilation in nasality in the sequence stop + nasal. Again, the evidence is most easily surveyed in tabular form (Table 2), recalling that there was no phonemic dorsal nasal.

The generalisation appears to be this: stop C$_1$ assimilated in nasality to nasal C$_2$, and also in place, in accordance with the Place Hierarchy. Regressive assimilation in nasality can be straightforwardly accounted for by considering the relevant articulatory gestures once again. The gesture of lowering the velum to articulate a nasal is relatively slow

---

[12] There are clear indications that ⟨g⟩ in ⟨gn⟩ sequences was a dorsal nasal: (1) the omission of ⟨n⟩ before ⟨g⟩ (⟨ng⟩ being the usual way of denoting a dorsal nasal) in *ignoːtus* 'unknown' < *en-gnoː-tos*, *cognaːtus* 'related by birth' < *kom-gnaː-tos*, suggest that ⟨g⟩ on its own represented [ŋ]; (2) inscriptional spellings such as sɪɴɴᴠ for *signum* and sɪɴɢɴɪꜰᴇʀ for *signifer* suggest a dorsal nasal; (3) the raising */e/ > /i/ occurred before ⟨gn⟩ just as before ⟨ng⟩ (= [ŋg]), thus *dek-nos > dignus* 'worthy', *leg-nom > lignum* 'wood', *teg-nom > tignum* 'timber' (note that this did not occur before ⟨gm⟩, providing evidence for the retention of the stop in that sequence).

compared to the articulation of major place features, which can result in a timing mismatch between the opening of the velic aperture and the intended start of the nasal consonant (Ladefoged and Maddieson 1996, 104–106). Such an effect is seen in the common nasalisation of vowels before nasals. Where a stop precedes, it can be realised partially or fully as a nasal if the velum lowers early; the paucity of cues for the stop manner could then result over time in the phonologisation of the nasalisation of the stop as a nasal.

There is an exception to nasal assimilation in Latin: the sequence dorsal + /m/ remained intact, with C_1 keeping its articulation as a stop (heterorganic in place with the nasal as would be expected per the Place Hierarchy), thus *sekmentom > segmentum = [gm] 'piece' (see fn. 12). There are consequences arising from this gap: the syllable-based approach could postulate that Latin coda stops came to be unspecified for nasality and therefore underwent nasal assimilation when followed by a specified nasal in an onset. However, a coda dorsal stop must be stipulated to have maintained its nonnasal specification before a labial nasal onset. This is quite clearly an unsatisfactory formulation.

A more parsimonious approach would do away with reference to syllable position, referring only to linear sequence. In investigating the occurrence of the gap in nasal assimilation, consideration of the robustness of the cues to the manner of articulation in different sequences provides a better starting-point. If regressive nasal assimilation results from the early lowering of the velum, while the preceding stop is being articulated, it follows that a slower stop articulation will have less of its articulation time overlapped by the opening of the velic aperture. As noncoronals, and arguably dorsals, have the slowest gestures, with long transitions (see section 3), it is unsurprising that dorsal stops escaped assimilation to the nasal. However, they did assimilate before /n/, the coronal nasal, and this can again be explained with reference to relative timing: the lowering of the velum could have occurred early before the slowly articulated labial nasal, but due to the time taken to articulate the labial place, the early opening of the velic aperture fell mainly within the time taken to articulate the nasal itself and not the preceding stop. Nasal assimilation in labial stop + labial nasal can be accounted for by the homorganicity in place: the articulators were already in position for labial place and therefore the early lowering of the velum could only encroach upon the labial stop gesture and not the time taken to form the place of articulation of the nasal, as it had already been formed.

a. Dorsal stop + Labial nasal   b. Dorsal stop + Coronal nasal

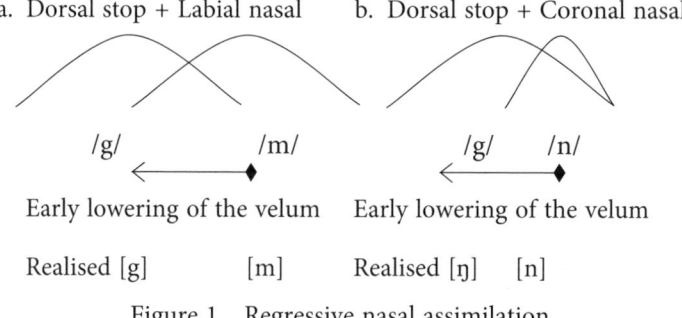

Figure 1   Regressive nasal assimilation

This rather complicated set of affairs can be neatly illustrated by diagrams (Figure 1), where the curved lines represent the articulatory gestures associated with formation of place of articulation, as in Jun (2004, 63, 65).

The articulators start moving towards the place of articulation of the nasal while the stop is still being articulated (the beginning of the second curve in each diagram). Coronals are rapidly articulated and therefore reach their target (the peak of the second curve) before labials. However, the velum also starts to lower to ensure the achievement of nasal manner by that target time (the curve peak), illustrated by the arrow pointing leftwards. In Latin, where the nasal was a slowly articulated labial (Figure 1a), the velic lowering encroached upon the dorsal only partially, allowing the accurate perception of a preceding dorsal stop. However, where the nasal was a rapidly articulated coronal (Figure 1b), the velic lowering encroached upon the dorsal stop sufficiently for a listener to perceive a dorsal nasal, resulting over time in its phonologisation as a nasal (which formulation maintains a perceptually driven analysis).

Traces of the effects of the long, slow transition between a dorsal stop and /m/ can perhaps be detected in the early Latin phenomenon of vocalic epenthesis in these sequences, thus Greek *drachmá:* 'coin' was borrowed into Latin with an alternative form *drac(h)uma*, containing an epenthetic vowel separating the sequence. Similarly, we find the native Latin word *tegmen* 'covering' with the alternative spellings *tegimen/tegumen*, resulting finally in regular *tegimen*. Contrast the mythological name *Procne:*, found in Latin in both this form, borrowed accurately from Greek with internal [kn], but also as *Progne:*, no doubt pronounced with [ŋn].

6   A Linear Hypothesis

The linear approach is more successful in accounting for the assimilations of voice, place, continuance and nasality than the syllable-based approach. (9) is an attempt to formulate this approach succinctly in phonological terms.

(9) Feature x, if poorly cued to a sufficient degree relative to an adjacent more robustly cued value of that feature, was assimilated to that value, where x is taken to range over [voice], [PLACE], [continuant] and [nasal].

Note the relativity of this formulation. It is not the case that a less robustly cued feature always assimilated to a more robustly cued value of that feature, which would have resulted in unconstrained assimilation of all features in all consonantal sequences. Therefore, the difference in the robustness of the two values of the feature is relevant. Only where a feature was poorly cued by a sufficient degree relative to that feature in an adjacent segment did assimilation occur.

Recall from section 1.2 that perceptual cues can be divided into internal and external cues. The most salient family of external cues we have witnessed resides in the release into a vowel; this affords a listener place, manner and voice cues in the stop release burst, place and manner cues in the CV formant transitions, and voice cues in aspiration noise and VOT (Wright 2004, 37–41). It is the absence of these often relatively robust cues in C_1 that resulted in the more robust cuing of C_2 over C_1 to trigger regressive, and not progressive, assimilation.

The Place Hierarchy is based mainly upon external VC transition cues in sequences of $V_1C_1C_2V_2$, with dorsal and labial C_2 being capable of affecting the transitions from V_1 to C_1 due to their long, slow gestures. Conversely, the Manner Hierarchy results mainly from internal cues (e.g. frication noise), although the position of stops above nasals on the hierarchy resides in the weak external cues to place in the nasalised vowels preceding nasal consonants.

7   Sonorant Voice Specification

7.1   A Puzzle

Recall from section 2 above that every member of an obstruent sequence came to agree in voice in Latin regardless of syllabification. Latin also inherited a series of sonorant consonants /r, l, m, n/, whose voice we could expect to be cued robustly by the periodicity in the signal during their articulation (an internal cue) and therefore be immune to voice assimilation when in C_1. Alternatively, the other robust manner cues for a sonorant (nasals: nasal murmur, nasal pole and zero, nasalisation of the previous vowel; liquids: relative gradualness of transitions, presence of formant structure throughout their peak of stricture), could render the vibration of the vocal folds by the speaker redundant in providing cues for the nature of the consonant, resulting in partial devoicing of the sonorant in voiceless environments, itself an external cue for the voice specification of an adjacent voiceless segment (Steriade 1999b).

Such considerations have led phonologists often to treat sonorants as redundantly voiced on the surface, or unspecified for voice in their underlying representation (Kiparsky 1995, 644–647), in languages where sonorants do not contrast for voice. If we can treat sonorants as lexically unspecified for voice in Latin, then perhaps it is possible to extend the range of the voice assimilation formulation to 'every part of a consonantal sequence, not just obstruents, came to agree in voice'. Such a formulation is in accord with the occurrence of a voice contrast in obstruent C_2 where C_1 was a sonorant:

(10) /r/ + stop: *verpa* 'penis' : *verba* 'words'

(11) /l/ + stop: *mulceo:* 'I soothe' : *mulgeo:* 'I milk'

(12) /m/ + stop: *computo:* 'I calculate' : *combu:ro:* 'I burn up'

(13) /n/ + stop: *pontus* 'sea' : *pondus* 'weight'

We could argue on this basis that sonorants were unspecified for voice preconsonantally: the cues to their manner were sufficiently robust for their identification, leaving contextual devoicing as a possibility in voiceless environments. This contextual devoicing could just as easily provide a robust cue for an obstruent C_1 when the sonorant was C_2, thus allowing a voice contrast to surface in the obstruent C_1, unlike in the obstruent sequences discussed in section 2, where C_1 could never contrast for voice. Note that C_1 was often a coda, lending further weight to the linear approach. And this is indeed the situation we find where C_2 was a liquid:

(14) Stop + /r/: *a:cri:* 'sharp (dat.)' : *agri:* 'field (gen.)'

(15) Stop + /l/: *planta* 'shoot' : *blanda* 'flattering (fem.)'

Liquids appear to have been unspecified for voice prevocalically as well as preconsonantally. However, the situation among nasals was different. The only sequence in which we can expect to detect voice assimilation, due to the failure of nasal assimilation, is dorsal + /m/ (see section 5). And here, nasal C_2 appears to have triggered voice assimilation in a formation which arose within Latin:

(16) (Dorsal) stop + /m/: **sekmentom* > *segmentum* 'piece'

This evidence suggests that /m/ came to be actively voiced prevocalically within the history of Latin, i.e. voice unspecified > [+voice]. Phonetically, this divergence among the sonorants can be attributed to the easier detection of cues to voicing of obstruents released into liquids than into nasals (Steriade 1999b).

The situation is confused further by the voicing of /s/ to [z] in archaic Latin postvocalically before any voiced consonant (with subsequent loss of [z] and compensatory lengthening of the preceding vowel), whether that consonant was a voiced obstruent (**nisdos* > **[nizdos]* > *ni:dus* 'nest'), a nasal, as expected given the evidence of (16) above, (*cosmis* > [kozmis] (cf. *CIL* 1².4 COSMIS) > *co:mis* 'friendly', **kasnos* > **[kaznos]* > *ca:nus* 'white(-haired)'), or even, unexpectedly, a liquid (**preslom* > **[prezlom]* > *pre:lum* 'wine-/oil-press'). Does this then indicate that /l/ was actively voiced prevocalically, contrary to (15) above?

And what of /r/? The sequence /sr/ did not survive into archaic Latin, having merged with Proto-Italic **[ðr]* or similar[13] and developed to /br/ at a prehistoric stage (Stuart-Smith 2004): **fu:nesris* > *fu:nebris* 'funereal'. The merger of /sr/ and a sequence of voiced fricative + /r/ is a strong indicator that the sibilant was voiced [z] at that prehistoric stage. In contrast, /sl/ seems to have survived into archaic Latin, whereas the Latin reflex of **[ðl]* (or similar) was /bl/ (PIE 'tool' suffix **-dʰlom* > Lat. *-blum*), in the same way as **[ðr]* > [br]. The divergence

---

[13] **[ð]* was the regular Proto-Italic reflex of PIE **/dʰ/*, merging with **[β]* from PIE **/bʰ/* in some contexts, e.g. before liquids.

of /s/ and *[ð] before /l/ suggests further that /s/ was not voiced in this context in prehistoric times. The conclusion that falls out of these patterns is that /r/ came to be actively voiced at this prehistoric stage, whereas /l/ only became actively voiced in archaic Latin.

Further evidence for the later phonological voicing of /l/, and furthermore /n/, comes from prehistoric consonantal epenthesis in /m/ + sonorant sequences. In /mr/, the epenthetic stop was voiced /b/: PIE *gʰeimrinos > *heimbrinos > hi:bernus 'wintry'. In contrast, the epenthetic stop in /ml/ and possibly /mn/ was voiceless /p/: *exemlom > exemplum 'example', autumnus > autumpnus 'autumn' (a variant form). Given the consistent appearance of /m/ in C_1 in these sequences, the different voicing of the epenthetic stop can only have been the result of the voicing of the sonorant C_2.

So far so good, but here we reach an impasse. If all the sonorants came to be actively voiced prevocalically by an early stage of the language, why do we find a voice contrast persisting into the classical language in obstruents before liquid C_2, as seen in (14) and (15) above? Surely the voiced sonorants would have triggered regressive voice assimilation in these sequences?

7.2   *The Return of the Syllable: TR Onsets*

This puzzle finds a solution in the very phonological entity that has enjoyed little success in this investigation thus far: the syllable. The difference between forms such as a:cri:, agri:, planta and blanda on the one hand, and *prezlom and *fu:nesris on the other is plausibly that the stop + liquid sequence (TR) was tautosyllabic in the former group, but heterosyllabic in the latter at the time when voice assimilation began to occur in these sequences (prehistoric for /r/; archaic for /l/). The regular tautosyllabic treatment of stop + liquid in the early dramatic verse of Plautus (3rd–2nd cents. B.C.) lends credence to the analysis of such words as a:cri: and capra 'she-goat' as having tautosyllabic TR in the immediately preceding archaic period. Evidence of their syllabification in archaic Latin from vowel reduction (6th–5th cents. B.C.) is unclear, but it appears that to some extent, syllable edges were aligned with transparent morpheme edges (see section 8), allowing us to interpret TR in these words as tautosyllabic.

We hypothesise then that a syllable-initial, simple onset sonorant came to be phonologically voiced in prehistoric/archaic Latin, whereas a sonorant which was not syllable-initial, but either a liquid in a com-

plex TR onset, or any sonorant in a syllable coda, remained unspecified for voice. The divergent voice specifications of liquids in simple
versus complex onsets can find a phonetic basis in the cross-linguistically common allophonic distribution of voiceless liquids, notably
/l/, in complex TR. Ladefoged and Maddieson (1996, 237) note that
"voiceless allophones of rhotics are quite common, especially in utterance-final position, and after voiceless stops," the second of which
could be either a simple onset or in complex TR. The behaviour they
report for laterals is more suggestive: /l/ has been well documented in
many languages to be subject not only to considerable coarticulatory
effect from adjacent voiceless consonants, especially preceding stops,
and adjacent vowels, but also to variation attributable to syllable and
morpheme position (Ladefoged and Maddieson 1996, 192 with references). Selkirk (1982, 359–360) and Gimson (2001, 201, 205) are more
explicit in reporting that in English, voiceless stop + /l/ is realised as
aspirated voiceless stop + voiceless [l̥] when a complex syllable onset,
but as unaspirated voiceless stop + voiced [l] when heterosyllabic, thus
incline [ɪn.kʰl̥ajn] versus *ink-line* [ɪŋk.lajn].[14] In Latin, the prominence
of the syllable-initial position possibly resulted in the speaker ensuring
that sonorants were articulated robustly in that position, maximising
the number and salience of cues to their character, whereas other positions did not demand such prominence and were therefore left with
unspecified voice.[15]

Support for this state of affairs at least in early Latin comes from the
rare instances where phonologically identical sequences were syllabified divergently. This is best witnessed in the noun **poplos* 'people' and
its adjectival derivative **poplikos* 'public' (Wachter 1987, 384–386): the
TR sequence in the former would be expected to have been tautosyllabic in archaic Latin, given the lack of a transparent morpheme
boundary, thus /po.plos/; and indeed we find that the classical Latin
outcome was *populus*, with vocalic epenthesis breaking up an earlier tautosyllabic onset sequence of /pl/ as expected. In the adjective
*poplikos, on the other hand, the TR sequence arguably came to be
treated as heterosyllabic, presumably on the basis of the association

---

[14] The variable pronunciations probably depend on other contextual factors to a
large degree, and are not simply due to syllabification.
[15] Note that all sonorants could have remained unspecified for voice in their underlying representation and only acquired positive voice specifications when they were
syllabified.

of the 'clear' allophone of /l/, found before /i/, with the syllable-initial
position,[16] thus /pop.li.kos/. This change in syllabification occurred at
a period after that in which syllable-initial sonorants became actively
voiced, leaving the new voiceless coda /p/ in a precarious position.
Therefore, despite its synchronic association with *poplos, the adjective developed into *poblikos, with regular regressive assimilation in
voice of sonorants to stops across a syllable boundary (cf. CIL 1².397
POBLICAI).[17] After breaking of the vowel in syllables closed by a labial
(*poublikos) and subsequent monophthongisation, we reach the classical Latin form puːblicus 'public'. For a similar divergence according
to syllabification, see the developments of vehiculum and neglegoː in
section 8 below.

We therefore must admit that syllable structure played a role in
archaic Latin phonotactics, and therefore an indirect role in assimilations: syllable structure determined which allophones of sonorants
surfaced, the syllable-initial actively voiced allophone triggering
regressive voice assimilation, which phenomenon can retain the linear formulation hypothesised in section 7.1 above: 'every member of a
consonantal sequence came to agree in voice.'

8   Morphological Pressures

To complete the picture regarding assimilations in the early history
of Latin, we must take into consideration the morphological pressures
giving greater prominence to roots than to affixes and requiring alignment of grammatical and prosodic constituents. In Latin, this is manifested in three ways.

First, we find more thoroughgoing regressive assimilation at prefix
+ verbal root contacts. For example, although we expect to find the
sequence /br/ to survive intact in Latin (e.g. eːbrius 'drunk') both across
a syllable boundary and as a complex onset, at a prefix + root bound-

---

[16] Consider in this context the metathesis witnessed in Lat. *plumoː > pulmoː 'lungs',
triggered by the association of the 'dark' allophone of /l/, found before /u/, with coda/
preconsonantal position (Blevins and Garrett 1998, 516–518).
[17] Note that this is not an unusual instance of neutralisation of an obstruent coda
to a voiced value, but rather regressive assimilation in voice, which could only occur
when C_1 was a coda before syllable-initial sonorant C_2 in Latin.

ary, it underwent total regressive assimilation to /rr/, thus *sub-rego: > surrigo: 'I rise'.

Second, there is generally more faithful retention of root shape in the verbal morphology of Latin than elsewhere, particularly at morpheme boundaries within the paradigm. Thus, beside expected *kemtom > centum 'hundred', with place assimilation in nasal C_1, we find *sumtos > su:mptus 'assumed', the past participle in *-to- in the paradigm of su:mo: 'I assume'. Consonantal epenthesis (see section 7.1) seems to have been the victorious repair strategy over place assimilation where the latter would break the uniformity of the paradigm.

Third, and possibly of greatest relevance in this study given the conclusions of section 7.2, morpheme boundaries which were transparent in archaic Latin were aligned with syllable boundaries (see Sen 2006 for discussion), which in turn resulted in the syllabification of some TR sequences as heterosyllabic. The consequent voiced sonorant in syllable-initial position could then trigger regressive voice assimilation across the morpheme boundary. Such an effect is seen in *nek-lego: (cf. nec 'and not' and lego: 'I choose') > neglego: (/neg.le.go:/) 'I neglect', versus vehiclum (/ve.hi.klum/) 'vehicle' (> class. Lat. vehiculum with regular vocalic epenthesis in originally tautosyllabic /kl/; see section 7.2).

9   Conclusions

This investigation evaluated two approaches claiming to account for assimilations, the syllable-based approach and the linear approach, from a diachronic perspective in relation to the early history of Latin. We found that assimilations were driven by linear segmental sequence alone, whereas syllable structure was relevant only in the assignment of allophones, a process which could in turn feed assimilations. A feature in a segment, if poorly cued to a sufficient degree relative to the value of that feature in an adjacent segment, was assimilated to that other value. Likely cues that we may identify for the language in this long-gone era, from a close reexamination of the data and typological evidence, included internal cues, such as frication noise or nasal murmur, as well as external cues, such as formant transitions in neighbouring vowels. The data allowed us independently to construct two hierarchies for the resistance to assimilation in place in Latin, based upon a combination of internal and external cues phonologized in the language: the Place Hierarchy (dorsal > labial > coronal) and the Manner Hierarchy (fricative > stop > nasal).

However, we found that although the syllable was irrelevant in correctly formulating the contexts for assimilations, syllable structure was still of phonotactic relevance through governing the distribution of the actively voiced allophones of sonorant consonants to syllable-initial position. These, but not the allophones unspecified for voice, could trigger voice assimilation, due to their resistance to contextual devoicing in a prominent position.

Finally, morphology could magnify the straightforward phonetic pressures involved in assimilations, resulting in either more thoroughgoing assimilation, such as the total assimilation found at prefix + verbal root boundaries, or greater resistance, demanding an alternative repair strategy, as at verbal root + paradigmatic suffix boundaries. Furthermore, morphology could influence phonotactics in a role two steps removed from assimilations via the alignment of morpheme boundaries with syllable boundaries and the resulting active voicing of sonorants.

In sum, between linear segmental sequence and morpheme structure constraints, the syllable only had a minor role to play in the development of Latin phonotactics.

References

Allen, W. Sidney. 1973. *Accent and rhythm: Prosodic features of Latin and Greek: A study in theory and reconstruction.* Cambridge studies in linguistics. Vol. 12. Cambridge: Cambridge University Press.

——. 1978. *Vox Latina: A guide to the pronunciation of classical Latin*, 2nd ed. Cambridge: Cambridge University Press.

Beckman, Jill N. 1999. *Positional faithfulness: An optimality theoretic treatment of phonological asymmetries.* New York: Garland.

Blevins, Juliette. 1993. Klamath laryngeal phonology. *International Journal of American Linguistics* 59: 237–279.

——. 1995. The syllable in phonological theory. In *The handbook of phonological theory*, edited by John Goldsmith, 206–244. Cambridge, MA: Blackwell.

——. 2003. The independent nature of phonotactic constraints: an alternative to syllable-based approaches. In *The syllable in optimality theory*, edited by Caroline Féry and Ruben van de Vijver, 375–403. Cambridge: Cambridge University Press.

——. 2004. *Evolutionary phonology: The emergence of sound patterns.* Cambridge: Cambridge University Press.

Blevins, Juliette and Andrew Garrett. 1998. The origins of consonant-vowel metathesis. *Language* 74: 508–556.

Brosches, Charles de. 1765. *Traité de la formation méchanique de langues, et de principes physiques de l'étymologie.* Paris: Chez Saillant, Vincent, Desaint.

Browman, Catherine P. and Louis Goldstein. 1990. Tiers in articulatory phonology, with some implications for casual speech. In *Papers in laboratory phonology 1: Between the grammar and physics of speech*, eds. John Kingston, Mary E. Beckman, 341–376. Cambridge: Cambridge University Press.

CIL =. 1862–. *Corpus Inscriptionum Latinarum.* Berlin: Preussische Akademie der Wissenschaften apud G. Reimerum.

Clements, George. N. 1990. The role of the sonority cycle in core syllabification. In *Papers in laboratory phonology 1: Between the grammar and physics of speech*, edited by John Kingston and Mary Beckman, 283–333. NY: Cambridge University Press.

Cole, Ronald A. and William E. Cooper. 1975. Perception of voicing in English affricates and fricatives. *The Journal of the Acoustical Society of America* 58: 1280–1287.

Fudge, Erik. 1969. Syllables. *Journal of Linguistics* 5: 253–87.

Gimson, Alfred C. 2001. *Gimson's pronunciation of English*, revised by Alan Cruttenden. 6th ed. London: Edward Arnold.

Glare, Peter G. W., ed. 1996. *Oxford Latin dictionary.* Oxford: Clarendon Press.

Goldsmith, John. 1990. *Autosegmental and metrical phonology.* Cambridge, MA: Basil Blackwell.

Hockett, Charles. 1947. Componential analysis of Sierra Popoluca. *International Journal of American Linguistics* 13: 258–267.

Hura, Susan L., Björn Lindblom and Randy L. Diehl. 1958. On the role of perception in shaping phonological assimilation rules. *Language and Speech* 35: 59–72.

Itô, Junko. 1988. *Syllable theory in prosodic phonology.* New York: Garland.

——. 1989. A prosodic theory of epenthesis. *Natural Language and Linguistic Theory* 7: 217–259.

Jakobson, Roman, C. Gunnar M. Fant and Morris Halle. 1952. *Preliminaries to speech analysis: The distinctive features and their correlates* [Technical Report 13]. Cambridge, Mass.: Acoustics Laboratory, Massachusetts Institute of Technology.

Jespersen, Otto. 1904. *Lehrbuch der Phonetik.* Leipzig & Berlin: Teubner.

Jun, Jongho. 1995. Perceptual and articulatory factors in place assimilation: An optimality theoretic approach. PhD diss., University of California, Los Angeles.

——. 2004. Place assimilation. In *Phonetically based phonology*, edited by Bruce Hayes, Robert M. Kirchner and Donca Steriade, 58–86. Cambridge: Cambridge University Press.

Kiparsky, Paul. 1995. The phonological basis of sound change. In *The handbook of phonological theory*, edited by John Goldsmith, 640–670. Cambridge, MA: Blackwell.

Kohler, Klaus. 1966. Is the syllable a phonological universal? *Journal of Linguistics* 2: 207–208.

Ladefoged, Peter and Ian Maddieson. 1996. *The sounds of the world's languages*. Cambridge, MA: Blackwell.

Leumann, Manu. 1977. *Lateinische Laut- und Formenlehre*. Munich: C. H. Beck.

Lombardi, Linda. 1995. Laryngeal neutralization and syllable wellformedness. *Natural Language and Linguistic Theory* 13: 39–74.

——. 1999. Positional faithfulness and voicing assimilation in optimality theory. *Natural Language and Linguistic Theory* 17: 267–302.

——. 2001. Why place and voice are different: Constraint-specific alternations in optimality theory. In *Segmental phonology in optimality theory: Constraints and representations*, edited by Linda Lombardi, 13–45. Cambridge: Cambridge University Press.

Meiser, Gerhard. 1998. *Historische Laut- und Formenlehre der lateinischen Sprache*. Darmstadt: Wissenschaftliche Buchgesellschaft.

Niedermann, Max. 1997. *Précis de phonétique historique du latin*. 5th ed. Paris: Klincksieck.

Ohala, John. and Haruko Kawasaki-Fukumori. 1997. Alternatives to the sonority hierarchy for explaining segmental sequential constraints. In *Language and its ecology: Essays in memory of Einar Haugen*, edited by Stig Eliasson and Ernst Håkon Jahr, 343–366. Berlin: Mouton de Gruyter.

Pike, Kenneth L. and Eunice Pike. 1947. Immediate constituents of Mazateco syllables. *International Journal of American Linguistics* 13: 78–91.

Prince, Alan and Paul Smolensky. 2004. *Optimality theory: Constraint interaction in generative grammar*. Oxford: Blackwell Publishing.

Rubach, Jerzy. 1996. Nonsyllabic analysis of voice assimilation in Polish. *Linguistic Inquiry* 27: 69–110.

Saussure, Ferdinand de. 1916. *Cours de linguistique générale*. Paris: Payot.

Selkirk, Elisabeth. 1982. The syllable. In *The structure of phonological representations*, part 2, edited by Harry van der Hulst and Norval Smith, 337–383. Dordrecht: Foris.

Sen, Ranjan. 2006. Vowel-weakening before *muta cum liquidā* sequences in Latin: A problem of syllabification? *Oxford University Working Papers in Linguistics, Philology and Phonetics* 11: 143–61. http://www.ling-phil.ox.ac.uk/download/OWP2006 .pdf.

Sievers, Eduard. 1881. *Grundzüge der Phonetik: Zur Einführung in das Studium der Lautlehre der indogermanischen Sprachen*. Bibliothek indogermanischer Grammatiken. 2nd ed. Vol. 1. Leipzig: Breitkopf und Härtel.

Sihler, Andrew L. 1995. *New comparative grammar of Greek and Latin*. New York; Oxford: Oxford University Press.

Sommer, Ferdinand and Raimund Pfister. 1977. *Handbuch der lateinischen Laut- und Formenlehre: Eine Einführung in das sprachwissenschaftliche Studium des Lateins*. 4th ed. Heidelberg: C. Winter.

Steriade, Donca. 1982. Greek prosodies and the nature of syllabification. PhD diss., MIT.

——. 1999a. Alternatives to syllable-based accounts of consonantal phonotactics. In *Proceedings of LP '98: Item order in language and speech*, vol. 1, edited by Osamu Fujimura, Brian D. Joseph and Bohumil Palek, 205–245. Prague: Charles University in Prague—The Karolinum Press.

——. 1999b. Phonetics in phonology: The case of laryngeal neutralization. *UCLA Working Papers in Linguistics* 2: 25–146.

——. 2001. Directional asymmetries in place assimilation: A perceptual account. In *The role of speech perception in phonology*, edited by Elizabeth V. Hume and Keith Johnson, 220–250. San Diego; London: Academic Press.

Stevens, Kenneth. 1989. On the quantal nature of speech. *Journal of Phonetics* 17: 3–45.

Stuart-Smith, Jane. 2004. *Phonetics and philology: Sound change in Italic*. Oxford: Oxford University Press.

Wachter, Rudolf. 1987. *Altlateinische Inschriften: Sprachliche und epigraphische Untersuchungen zu den Dokumenten bis etwa 150 v. chr.* Bern; New York: P. Lang.

Whitney, William Dwight. 1873. *Oriental and linguistic studies*. New York: Scribner, Armstrong and Company.

Wright, Richard. 2001. Perceptual cues in contrast maintenance. In *The role of speech perception in phonology*, edited by Elizabeth V. Hume and Keith Johnson, 251–277. London: Academic Press.

——. 2004. A review of perceptual cues and cue robustness. In *Phonetically based phonology*, edited by Bruce Hayes, Robert Kirchner and Donca Steriade, 34–57. Cambridge: Cambridge University Press.

Zec, Draga. 1995. Sonority constraints on syllable structure. *Phonology* 12: 85–129.

LIST OF CONTRIBUTORS

Azra Ali is a Lecturer at the University of Huddersfield. She received her Ph.D. from the University of Huddersfield in 2006. She is the co-author of the articles "Gradience in Morphological Binding: Evidence from Perception of Audiovisually Incongruent Speech" (Laboratory Phonology 2008) and "Experiments on Fine Phonetic Detail of Arabic Syllable Structure" (Laboratory Phonology 2008).

Maria Babyonyshev is an Assistant Professor at Yale University. She received her Ph.D. from the Massachusetts Institute of Technology in 1996. She is the author of the article "The Extended Projection Principle and the Genitive of Negation in Russian" (*Negation in Slavic*, Slavica Publishers) and co-author of "Discourse-based Movement Operations in Russian-speaking Children with SLI" (BUCLD 31).

Karen Baertsch is an Assistant Professor of Linguistics at Southern Illinois University-Carbondale. She earned her Ph.D. from Indiana University in 2002. She is the author of "Asymmetrical Glide Patterns in American English: The Resolution of CiV vs. CuV Sequences" (*Language Research*) and co-author of "Strength Relations between Consonants: A Syllable-based OT Approach" (*Strength Relations in Phonology*, Mouton de Gruyter).

Iris Berent is a Professor of Psychology at Northeastern University. She received her Ph.D. from the University of Pittsburgh in 1993. She is the author of the forthcoming *Phonological Mind* (Cambridge University Press).

Charles Cairns is Professor Emeritus of Linguistics at the Graduate Center and Queens College of the City University of New York. He received his Ph.D. from Columbia University in 1968. He is the co-editor of *Contemporary Views on Architecture and Representations in Phonology* (MIT Press).

Andries W. Coetzee is an Assistant Professor at the University of Michigan. He received his Ph.D. from the University of Massachusetts,

Amherst in 2004. He is the author of *Tiberian Hebrew Phonology: Focusing on Consonant Clusters* (Studia Semitica Nederlandia 38) and edited the special issue of the journal *Phonology* "Relations between Phonological Models and Experimental Data."

Joana Cholin is a Staff Scientist at the Basque Center on Cognition, Brain and Language (BCBL), Donostia, Spain. She earned her Ph.D. from the University of Nijmegen in 2004. She has co-authored the articles "SYLLABARIUM: An Online Application for Deriving Complete Statistics for Basque and Spanish Syllables" (*Behavior Research Methods*) and "Effects of Syllable Preparation and Syllable Frequency in Speech Production: Further Evidence for the Retrieval of Stored Syllables at a Post-lexical Level" (*Language and Cognitive Processes*).

Marie-Hélène Côté is Associate Professor and Chair of Linguistics at the University of Ottawa. She earned her Ph.D. from the Massachusetts Institute of Technology in 2000. She is the author of the articles "The Role of the Syllable in the Structure and Realization of Sound Systems" (*The Oxford Handbook of Laboratory Phonology*, Oxford University Press) and "French Liason" (*The Blackwell Companion to Phonology*, Wiley-Blackwell).

Stuart Davis is Professor and Chair of Linguistics at Indiana University. He received his Ph.D. from the University of Arizona in 1985. He is the author of the articles "Quantity" (*The Handbook of Phonological Theory, 2nd ed.*, John Benjamins) and "Geminates" (*The Blackwell Companion to Phonology*, Wiley-Blackwell).

François Dell is Directeur de Recherche (emeritus) at the CNRS (Paris). He received his Ph.D. from MIT in 1970. He has co-authored two books with Mohamed Elmedlaoui: *Syllables in Tashlhiyt Berber and in Moroccan Arabic* (Kluwer) and *Poetic Meter and Musical Form in Tashlhiyt Berber Songs* (Rüdiger Köppe Verlag).

San Duanmu is a Professor at the University of Michigan. He earned his Ph.D. from the Massachusetts Institute of Technology in 1990. He is the author of *Syllable Structure: The Limits of Variation* (Oxford University Press) and *The Phonology of Standard Chinese* (Oxford University Press).

Amalia E. Gnanadesikan is an associate research scientist at the University of Maryland. She earned her Ph.D. from the University of Massachusetts, Amherst in 1997. She is the author of *The Writing Revolution: Cuneiform to the Internet* (Wiley-Blackwell).

Hilary Gomes is an Associate Professor at the City College of New York. She received her Ph.D. from the Graduate Center of the City University of New York in 1994. She is the co-author of the papers "The Effects of Interstimulus Interval on the Nd Component: An Auditory Selective Attention Test of Perceptual Load Theory" (*Clinical Neurophysiology*) and "Development of Auditory Selective Attention: Event-related Potential Measures of Channel Selection and Target Detection" (*Psychophysiology*).

Jason D. Haugen is a Visiting Assistant Professor of Anthropology at Oberlin College. He received his Ph.D. from the University of Arizona in 2004. He is the author of *Morphology at the Interfaces: Reduplication and Noun-incorporation in Uto-Aztecan* (John Benjamins) and "Denominal Verbs in Uto-Aztecan" (*International Journal of American Linguistics*).

Michael Ingleby is a pattern recognition adviser in the Applied Criminology Centre, University of Huddersfield and 3M Innovation Center, Minneapolis. He received his Ph.D. from McMaster University in 1968. He is the co-author of the articles "Phonological Primes: Cues and Acoustic Signatures" (*Phonetics, Phonology and Cognition*, Oxford University Press) and "Representing Coarticulation Processes in Arabic Speech" (*Journal of Arabic Linguistics*).

Darya Kavitskaya is an Associate Professor at Yale University. She received her Ph.D. from the University of California-Berkeley in 2001. She is the author of *Crimean Tatar* (LINCOM Europa) and *Compensatory Lengthening: Phonetics, Phonology, Diachrony* (Routledge).

Viktor Kharlamov is a Ph.D. candidate at the University of Ottawa. He is the author of the article "Consonant Deletion in Russian" (*Formal Studies in Slavic Linguistics*) and co-authored "Decomposition into Multiple Morphemes During Lexical Access: A Masked Priming Study of Russian Nouns (*Language and Cognitive Processes*).

Paul Kiparsky is the Robert M. and Anne T. Bass Professor in the School of Humanities and Sciences at Stanford University. He received his Ph.D. from the Massachusetts Institute of Technology in 1965. He is the author of the articles "Reduplication in Stratal OT" (*Reality Exploration and Discovery: Pattern Interaction in Language & Life*, CSLI) and "Dvandvas, Blocking and the Associative: the Bumpy Ride from Phrase to Word" (*Language*).

Tracy Lennertz received her Ph.D. from Northeastern University in 2010. She is co-author of the articles "Listeners' Knowledge of Phonological Universals: Evidence from Nasal Clusters" (*Phonology*) and "Language Universals in Human Brains" (*Proceedings of the National Academy of Sciences*).

Yael Neumann is an Assistant Professor at Queens College, City University of New York. She received her Ph.D. from the City University of New York in 2007. She has co-authored the articles "Phonological vs. Sensory Contributions to Age Effects in Naming: An Electrophysiological Study" (*Aphasiology*) and "Neurolinguistic and Psycholinguistic Contributions to Understanding Healthy Aging and Dementia" (*Language and Communication Science*).

Loraine K. Obler is a Distinguished Professor at the City University of New York Graduate Center. She received her Ph.D. from the University of Michigan in 1975. She is the co-editor of *Clinical Communication Studies in Spanish Speakers: From Research to Clinical Practice* (Multilingual Matters) and co-author of *Language and the Brain* (Cambridge University Press).

David Peebles is a Senior Lecturer at the University of Huddersfield. He received his Ph.D. in Cognitive Science from the University of Birmingham in 1998. He is the author of "The Effect of Emergent Features on Judgments of Quantity in Configural and Separable Displays" (*Journal of Experimental Psychology: Applied*) and co-author of "Spaces or Scenes: Map-based Orientation in Urban Environments" (*Spatial Cognition and Computation*).

Eric Raimy is an Associate Professor at the University of Wisconsin-Madison. He received his Ph.D. from the University of Delaware in 1999. He is the author of *The Phonology and Morphology of Redupli-*

cation (Mouton de Gruyter) and co-edited *Contemporary Views on Architecture and Representations in Phonology* (MIT Press).

Catherine O. Ringen is a Professor at the University of Iowa. She received her Ph.D. from Indiana University in 1975. She is the co-author of the articles "German Fricatives: Coda Devoicing or Positional Faithfulness" (*Phonology*) and "Voicing and Aspiration in Swedish Stops" (*Journal of Phonetics*).

Ranjan Sen is a Research Associate at the University of Oxford. He received his doctorate (D.Phil.) from the University of Oxford in 2009. He is co-editor of *Topics in Comparative Philology and Historical Linguistics* (Oxford University Working Papers).

Valerie Shafer is an Associate Professor at the Graduate Center of the City University of New York. She received her Ph.D. from State University of New York, Buffalo in 1994. She is the author of "The Neurophysiology of Phonetics and Phonology" (*Cambridge Encyclopedia of the Language Sciences*, Cambridge University Press) and co-author of "Phonological vs. Sensory Contributions to Age Effects in Naming: An Electrophysiological Study" (*Aphasiology*).

Stefanie Shattuck-Hufnagel is a Principal Research Scientist at the Massachusetts Institute of Technology. She received her Ph.D. from the Massachusetts Institute of Technology in 1975. She is the author of "The Role of Word Structure in Segmental Serial Ordering" (*Cognition*) and the co-author of "Do Listeners Store in Memory a Speaker's Habitual Utterance-final Phonation Type?" (*Phonetica*).

Paul Smolensky is the Krieger-Eisenhower Professor of Cognitive Science at John Hopkins University. He received his Ph.D. from Indiana University in 1981. He is the co-author of *The Harmonic Mind, vol. 1 and 2* (MIT Press) and *Optimality Theory: Constraint Interaction in Generative Grammar* (Blackwell).

Robert M. Vago is Professor and Chair of the Department of Linguistics and Communication Disorders at Queens College, City University of New York. He received his Ph.D. from Harvard in 1974. He is the author of *The Sound Pattern of Hungarian* (Georgetown University Press) and the co-author of *English Grammar: Understanding the Basics* (Cambridge University Press).

INDEX OF AUTHORS

INDEX OF LANGUAGES

INDEX OF SUBJECTS